THE
AMERICAN
PAST

Part Two
A Survey of American History Since 1865

Second Edition

THE
AMERICAN
PAST

Part Two
A Survey of American History Since 1865

Second Edition

Joseph R. Conlin
California State University, Chico

Harcourt Brace Jovanovich, Publishers

San Diego   New York   Chicago   Austin
London   Sydney   Tokyo   Toronto

To J. R. C. and L. V. C.

A Note on the Paperbound Edition

This volume is part of a variant printing of *The American Past* in a two-volume paperbound format, which reproduces exactly the text of the one-volume version. A two-volume paperbound version is useful because it enables instructors to fit the text into the particular patterns of their teaching and scheduling. The first volume begins with the discovery of America and continues through Reconstruction. The second volume, repeating the chapter on Reconstruction (chapter 26, "Bringing the South Back In: The Reconstruction of the Union"), carries the historical account forward to the present day. This variant printing, then, is intended as a convenience to those instructors and students who have occasion to use either one part or the other of *The American Past*. The pagination and index of the one-volume version, as well as its illustrations, maps, and sidebars, are retained in the new printing. The difference between the one-volume and two-volume versions of the book is a difference only in form.

Preface to the Second Edition

When Harcourt Brace Jovanovich informed me that it was time to prepare a second edition of *The American Past*, I celebrated on two counts. First, the news meant that my notion of what a survey course textbook ought to be had won the approbation of enough of my colleagues to warrant keeping the book in print. Second, a new edition gave me the opportunity to make changes that, in some cases, seemed sorely in order after I had myself used the book for only one term. The list of changes grew as I heard from other historians throughout the country who had adopted *The American Past*.

Like the first edition, this book is designed to be a teacher's textbook. That is, beyond laying out the information and perspective that make up a fundamental knowledge of the history of the United States, I have tried to write a book that will help instructors arouse the minds of their students to the value of knowing the past.

The key to arousing students' interest, I think, is to remember during the writing of every page that students in American history survey courses are not professional historians already committed to the principle that the past is worth knowing. On the contrary, they are young men and women who are training for a multitude of different professions and, in many cases, "taking history" only because they are required to do so by state law or institutional requirement. The pleasures of knowing the past that come as second nature to those of us who have made history our life's work are not on students' minds when they walk warily into their first college or university class in American history. Many students—perhaps a majority of them—must be seduced to the proposition that knowledge of the past is not dead, dry, and useless, but vital to living our own lives fruitfully.

The heaviest end of this burden, of course, rests in the hands of the instructor at the head of the class. What a textbook author can contribute, in addition to a comprehensive rendering of the facts, is a narrative that is enjoyable to read.

I have sought to be comprehensive, dealing with social, cultural, intellectual, economic, political, constitutional, diplomatic, and military history. Comprehensiveness also means dealing with the neglected of history—minorities as well as majorities, common folk as well as individuals who shook the land, oppressed as well as privileged, workers as well as bosses, slaves as well as slave owners. I have, however, resisted compartmentalizing American history as if women, men, blacks, other minorities, and whites had nothing more in common than the fact that they occupied the same one-thousand-by-three-thousand-mile piece of real estate. A survey text should, I think, be a cohesive, smoothly flowing narrative that expresses the interactions of peoples and the continuity of history. To compartmentalize history is a trivial pursuit.

I have also elected not to digress into discussions of methodologies and historiographical debates. Again, the simple premise is that students in the survey course are not professional historians. To confront freshmen and sophomores majoring in everything from accounting to zoology with subtleties and introspections that belong in the professional journals is like teaching an appreciation of fine art by examining brush strokes and chisel marks. I have deliberately neglected methodologies and debates among historians in the interest of maintaining a lively, flowing narrative. Those students who are to become professional historians will move on to those facets quite on their own. If *The American Past* succeeds in seducing those students who go on to be accountants, business people, engineers, lawyers, nurses, and zoologists into reading history as an avocation, I shall account the book a success.

I have made a number of changes in the Second Edition. The chapter structure has been rearranged to balance the extent of treatment accorded the several periods into which American history is traditionally divided. I have incorporated the findings of historians that were published, or at least became current, during the past four years. There is a good deal of new information here. Indeed, although the Second Edition numbers two fewer chapters than the first, the text of the second is somewhat longer.

Many of the special features, the boxed inserts and the essays titled "How They Lived" and "Notable People," which accompany each chapter, are new. Deciding which features from the first edition "worked" and should be retained, and which were less successful in arousing student interest, was based on correspondence and discussion with instructors who have assigned *The American Past* in their courses.

Perhaps the author's greatest satisfaction in preparing a second edition is the opportunity, like the apocryphal surgeon's, to bury his mistakes. In the first edition, these mistakes took the forms of inadequate expression of an idea, resulting in distortion; slips-of-the-mind I cannot explain; and outright errors that can be commented upon only by remembering Samuel Johnson's confession when he was asked how he could possibly have defined a word in his dictionary as badly as he had done: "Ignorance, madame," he replied, "pure ignorance." I would be foolish to claim to have eliminated every gaffe from this edition, but the most egregious are gone.

Among those colleagues who graciously and gracefully pointed out errors or supplied useful comments to me were Charles W. Akers, Oakland University; Terry Alford, Northern Virginia Community College; Roy L. Askins, Missouri Western College; Edward Beechert, University of Hawaii, Manoa; David Beesley, Sierra College; Thelma Biddle, Virginia Commonwealth University; N. Terry Bullock, Muscatine Community College; Martin B. Cohen, George Mason University; Virginia Crane, University of Wisconsin, Oshkosh; Mike Crow, Orange Coast College; Frank Dawson, Pennsylvania State University, Fayette; Ronald L. DeLong, Western Washington University; Eugene Dermody, Cerritos College; Jose Espinosa, Rancho Santiago College; David Goldberg, Cleveland State University; John Hoeveler, University of Wisconsin, Milwaukee; Herbert T. Hoover, University of South Dakota; Everett L. Long, University of Wisconsin, Whitewater; Patricia Mulvey, Bluefield State College; Lorraine Murray, Oakton Community College; Clifford Norse, Radford University; Mario Perez, San Bernardo Valley College; Susan Schrepfer, Rutgers University; John H. Schroeder, University of Wisconsin, Madison; Paul Siff, Sacred Heart University; Pat Smith, Tulsa Junior College; Richard S. Sorrell, Brookdale Community College; George W. Spencer, Northern Illinois University; Leah Mercile Taylor, Wesleyan College; and Thomas R. Walther, Pittsburgh State University.

I owe a special debt to Bernard Sinsheimer of the University of Maryland's European Division, who read the first edition specifically for slips and awed both author and publisher with the breadth and depth of his erudition. I am likewise grateful to those colleagues who read the Second Edition in typescript and made valuable suggestions: Joseph Logsdon, University of New Orleans; Samuel T. McSeveney, Vanderbilt University; Thomas Wagstaff, California State University, Chico; C. H. Peterson, California State University, Chico; and Dale Steiner (who also prepared the test manual), California State University, Chico. Richard Mumford of Elizabethtown College prepared the imaginative and innovative Study Guide.

Drake Bush of Harcourt Brace Jovanovich, a friend as well as an editor, was patient with my crotchets. Manuscript editor Robert Watrous rode herd on my stylistic lapses and excesses. Designers Don Fujimoto and Jane Carey, production manager Lynn Edwards, production editor Debbie Hardin, and art editors Tricia Griffith and Avery Hallowell turned out a visually beautiful book.

J. R. C.

Contents

Contents

Maps

THE AMERICAN PAST

Part Two
A Survey of American History Since 1865

Second Edition

Bringing the South Back In

The Reconstruction of the Union

When the guns fell silent in 1865, the people of the South looked about them to see a society, an economy, and a land in tatters. Some southern cities, such as Vicksburg, Atlanta, Columbia, and Richmond, were flattened, eerie wastelands of charred timber, rubble, and free-standing chimneys. Few of the South's railroads could be operated for more than a few miles. Bridges were gone. River-borne commerce, the lifeblood of the states beyond the Appalachians, had dwindled to a trickle. Old commercial ties with Europe and the North had been snapped clean. All the South's banks were ruined.

Even the cultivation of the soil had been disrupted. The small farms of the men who had served in the ranks lay fallow by the thousands, many of them never to be claimed by their former owners. Great planters who had abandoned their fields to advancing Union armies discovered that weeds and scrub pine were more destructive conquerors. The people who had toiled in them, the former slaves, were often gone, looking elsewhere for a place to start new lives as free men and women.

Freedmen pose for a photographer in Richmond, Virginia, with the ruins of the city in the background (1865).

THE RECONSTRUCTION DEBATE

In view of the widespread desolation, the word *reconstruction* would seem to be an appropriate description of the twelve-year period following the Civil War. But the word does not refer to the literal rebuilding of the South, the laying of bricks, the spanning of streams, the reclaiming of the land.

Reconstruction refers to the political process by which the eleven rebel states were restored to a normal constitutional relationship with the twenty-five loyal states and their national government. It was the Union, that great abstraction over which so many had died, that was reconstructed.

Blood was shed during Reconstruction too, but little glory was won. Few political reputations—northern or southern, white or black, Republican or Democratic—emerged from the era without a stain. More than one historian has suggested that Abraham Lincoln comes down to us a heroic and sainted figure only because he did not survive the war. Indeed, the Reconstruction policy Lincoln proposed as early as 1863 was soundly repudiated by members of his own party. Lincoln anticipated the problems he did not live to face. He described as "a pernicious abstraction" the constitutional issue with which both sides in the bitter Reconstruction debate masked their true motives and goals.

Lincoln's Plan to Restore the Union

By the end of 1863, Union armies controlled large parts of the Confederacy, and ultimate victory was reasonable to assume. To provide for a rapid reconciliation of the sections, Lincoln declared on December 8, 1863, that as soon as 10 percent of the voters in any Confederate state took an oath of allegiance to the Union, the people of that state could organize a government and elect representatives to Congress. Moving quickly, Tennessee, Arkansas, and Louisiana complied.

Congress Checks the President

Congress refused to recognize the new governments, leaving the three states under the command of the

Prisoners from the Front, by Winslow Homer (1866). *As this painting depicts, Confederate soldiers were allowed to return home—to a shattered society and ruined economy.*

military. Motives for checking Lincoln's plan varied as marvelously as the cut of the chin whiskers that politicians were sporting, but two were repeatedly voiced. First, almost all Republican congressmen were alarmed by the broad expansion of presidential powers during the war. No president since Andrew Jackson (still a villain to those Republicans who had been Whigs) had assumed as much authority as Lincoln had—at the expense of Congress. Few congressmen wished to see this trend continue during peacetime, as Lincoln's plan for Reconstruction promised to do.

Second, Radical Republicans, abolitionists who had been at odds with Lincoln over his reluctance to move against slavery, objected that Lincoln's plan made no allowances whatsoever for the status of the freedmen, as the former slaves were called. They took the lead in framing the Wade-Davis bill of July 1864, which provided that only after 50 percent of the white male citizens of a state swore an oath of loyalty to the Union could the Reconstruction process begin. Then, the Wade-Davis bill insisted, Congress and not the president would decide when the process was complete.

Lincoln responded with a pocket veto and, over the following months—the last of his life—hinted that he was ready for compromise. He said he would be glad to accept any former rebel states which opted to re-enter the Union under the congressional plan and he let it be known he had no objection to giving the right to vote to blacks who were "very intelligent and those who have fought gallantly in our ranks." He urged the military governor of Louisiana to extend the suffrage to some blacks.

Stubborn Andy Johnson

Lincoln's lifelong assumption that blacks were inferior to whites and his determination to win back quickly the loyalty of southern whites prevented him from accepting black suffrage generally. However, he was willing to be flexible, which the man who succeeded him was not.

Like Lincoln, Andrew Johnson of Tennessee grew up in stultifying frontier poverty. Unlike Lincoln, who taught himself to read as a boy and was ambitious from the start, Johnson was illiterate as an adult, and working as a tailor when he swallowed his pride and asked a schoolteacher in Greenville, Tennessee, to teach him to read and write. She did, and later married him, encouraging Johnson to pursue a political career. Andrew Johnson had more political experience than Lincoln or, for that matter, most presidents. Johnson held elective office on every level, from town councilman to congressman to senator and, during the war, governor.

Obstinate, often vulgar, President Andrew Johnson was a self-taught student of the Constitution. Rigorous adherence to it, as he read it, and a reflexive distaste for the idea of black citizenship doomed his early friendly relationship with the Radical Republicans.

Experience, alas, is not the same thing as aptitude. Whereas Lincoln was an instinctive politician who was sensitive to the realities of what he could and could not accomplish, Johnson was unsubtle, insensitive, willful, and stubborn.

He narrowly escaped assassination in the plot that felled Lincoln, was ill when sworn in, bolted several glasses of brandy for strength, and took the oath of office drunk and thick-tongued. Johnson had the goodwill of the Radicals because he had several times called for the harsh punishment of high ranking Confederates. (He wanted to hang Jefferson Davis.) But he quickly lost Radical support when, like Lincoln, he insisted that he, the president, possessed the authority to decide when rebel states were reconstructed. Thus

POCKET VETO

Section 7 of Article I of the Constitution provides that if a president vetoes an act of Congress, he shall return the act to Congress within ten days "with his Objections." If he fails to do so, the act becomes law without his signature.

However, if Congress enacts a bill and then adjourns before ten days have passed, as was the case with the Wade-Davis bill, the president can veto it without explanation simply by failing to sign it, figuratively leaving it in his coat pocket. Thus, the pocket veto.

ensured the debate over what Lincoln had called "a pernicious abstraction."

Johnson: They Are Already States

Johnson based his case for presidential supervision on the assumption that the southern states had never left the Union because it was constitutionally impossible to do so: the Union was one and inviolable; it could not be dissolved. Johnson and the entire Republican party and most northern Democrats had held to that principle in 1861. He would stick by it in 1865.

There had indeed been a war and an entity known as the Confederate States of America. But individuals had fought the one and created the other; states had not. Punish the rebels, Johnson said—he approved several confiscations of rebel-owned lands—but not Virginia, Alabama, and the rest. They were still states in the *United* States of America. Seating their duly elected representatives in the Congress was a purely administrative matter. The president, the nation's chief administrator, would decide how and when to do it.

Logic Versus Horse Sense

There was nothing wrong with Johnson's logic; he was an excellent constitutionalist. The president's problem was his inability or refusal to see beyond constitutional tidiness to the world of human feelings, flesh, and blood—especially blood.

The fact was, virtually every senator and representative from the rebel states—Johnson was an exception—had left their seats in the winter and spring of 1861, and Congress and president had functioned as

Freedmen pose with their reading books in front of their log schoolhouse.

the Union through four years of war. More than half a million people had been killed and a majority of northerners blamed these deaths on arrogant, antagonistic, rich southern slaveowners who, when Johnson announced that he would adopt Lincoln's plan of Reconstruction (with some minor changes), began to assume the leadership in their states that they had always held.

Nor did Johnson's reputation as a man who wanted rebels punished seem to hold up. By the end of 1865 he pardoned 13,000 Confederate leaders, thus making them eligible to hold public office. In elections held in the fall under Johnson's plan, southern voters sent many of these rebels to Congress, including four Confederate generals, six members of Jefferson Davis's cabinet, and a senator from Georgia, former Confederate vice president, Alexander H. Stephens.

The Radicals: The Rebel States Have Forfeited Their Rights

To Johnson's argument, Thaddeus Stevens, Radical leader in the House of Representatives, replied that the former Confederate states had committed "state suicide" when they seceded. They were not states. Therefore, it was within the power of Congress to admit them. Senator Charles Sumner came to the same conclusion by arguing that the southern states were "conquered provinces" and therefore had the same status as the federal territories of the West.

These theories suited the mood of most northerners very well, but they were constitutionally indefensible. A rather obscure Republican, Samuel Shellabarger of Ohio, came up with the formula that appealed to angry, war-weary northerners and made constitutional sense: the rebel states had forfeited their rights as states. Congress's Joint Committee on Reconstruction found that "the States lately in rebellion were, at the close of the war, disorganized communities, without civil government, and without constitutions or other forms, by virtue of which political relations could legally exist between them and the federal government." Such a state of affairs meant that only Congress could decide when the eleven former Confederate states might once again function as members of the Union.

The Radicals

Congress refused to seat the senators and representatives who were sent to Washington under the Johnson plan. The leaders of the resistance were Radical Republicans, former abolitionists for the most part who, whatever constitutional arguments they put forward, were determined to crush the southern planter class they had hated for so long and, with varying degrees of idealism, wanted to help the black freedmen who had, for so long, been victimized and exploited by the slaveowners.

Some Radicals like Stevens and Sumner and Benjamin "Bluff Ben" Wade of Ohio believed in racial equality. George W. Julian of Indiana proposed to confiscate the land of the planters and divide it, in forty-acre farms, among the blacks; with economic independence they could guarantee their civil freedom and political rights. Other Radicals wanted to grant the freedmen citizenship, including the vote, for frankly political purposes. Black voters would provide the backbone for a Republican party in the South, which did not exist before the war.

The Radicals were a minority within the Republican party. However, they were able to win the cooperation of party moderates because of Johnson's repeated blunders and a series of events in the conquered South that persuaded a majority of northern voters that Lincolnian generosity would mean squandering the Union's military victory and making a mockery of the cause for which so many soldiers had died.

Idealistic women, mostly former abolitionists from New England, were the unsung heroes of the work done by the Freedmen's Bureau. These were school teachers in Norfolk, Virginia, in 1865.

THE CRITICAL YEAR

The reaction of most blacks to the news of their freedom was to test it by leaving the plantations and farms on which they had lived as slaves.

Many flocked to cities that they associated with free blacks. Others, after a period of wandering, gathered in ramshackle camps in the countryside, eagerly discussing the rumor that each household would soon be alloted "forty acres and a mule." Without a means of making a living in a stricken land, these congregations of people were potentially, and in some cases in fact, dens of hunger, disease, crime, and disorder.

The Freedmen's Bureau

In order to prevent chaos in conquered territory, Congress had created the Bureau of Refugees, Freedmen, and Abandoned Lands, popularly known as the Freedmen's Bureau. Administered by the army under the command of General O. O. Howard, the Bureau provided relief for the freedmen (and some whites) in the form of food, clothing, and shelter; attempted to find jobs for them; set up hospitals and schools run by idealistic black and white women from the northern states, sometimes at the risk of their lives; and otherwise tried to ease the transition from slavery to freedom. When the Freedmen's Bureau bill was first enacted, Congress had assumed that properly established state governments would be able to assume responsibility for these services within a year after the end of the hostilities. The Bureau was scheduled to expire in March 1866.

In February 1866, however, the process of Reconstruction was at a standstill. Congress had refused to recognize Johnson's state governments but had not created any to its own liking. The former Confederacy was, in effect, still under military occupation. So, Congress passed a bill extending the life of the Bureau.

Johnson vetoed it and, a month later, he vetoed another congressional act that granted citizenship to the freedmen. Once again, his constitutional reasoning was sound. The Constitution gave the states the power to rule on the terms of citizenship within their borders, and Johnson continued to insist that the state governments he had set up were legitimate.

He might have won his argument. Americans took their constitutional fine points seriously and Radical demands for black civil equality ran against the grain of white racism. However, the actions of the Johnson government toward blacks, and the apparent refusal of many southern whites to acknowledge their defeat in the war, nullified every point Johnson scored.

The Black Codes

Because blacks as slaves had been the backbone of the southern labor force, the southern legislatures natu-

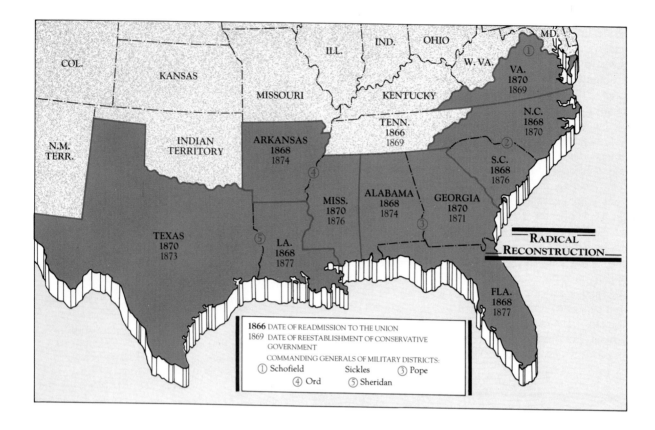

COL. · KANSAS · MISSOURI · ILL. · IND. · OHIO · W. VA. · MD.

VA. 1870 1869 ①

N.M. TERR. · INDIAN TERRITORY · ARKANSAS 1868 1874 · KENTUCKY · TENN. 1866 1869 · N.C. 1868 1870 ②

S.C. 1868 1876 ③

TEXAS 1870 1873 ⑤ · LA. 1868 1877 · MISS. 1870 1876 ④ · ALABAMA 1868 1874 · GEORGIA 1870 1871 ③

FLA. 1868 1877

RADICAL RECONSTRUCTION

1866 DATE OF READMISSION TO THE UNION
1869 DATE OF REESTABLISHMENT OF CONSERVATIVE GOVERNMENT
COMMANDING GENERALS OF MILITARY DISTRICTS:
① Schofield   Sickles   ③ Pope
④ Ord   ⑤ Sheridan

rally expected the blacks to continue to bring in the crops after the war. The freedmen wanted the work. Far from providing farms for them, however, the Johnsonian state governments did not even establish a system of employment that treated the blacks as free men and women. On the contrary, the black codes defined a form of second-class citizenship that looked to blacks and many whites like a step or two back into slavery.

In some states, blacks were permitted to work only as domestic servants or in agriculture, just what they had done as slaves. Other states made it illegal for blacks to live in towns and cities. In no state were blacks allowed to vote or to bear arms. In fact, few of the civil liberties listed in the Bill of Rights were accorded them.

Mississippi required freedmen to sign twelve-month labor contracts before January 10 of each year. Those who failed to do so could be arrested, and their labor sold to the highest bidder in a manner that (to say the least) was strongly reminiscent of the detested slave auction. Dependent children could be forced to work. Blacks who reneged on their contracts were not to be paid for the work that they already had performed.

The extremism of the black codes alienated many northerners who would gladly have accepted a milder form of second-class citizenship for the freedmen. (Only a few northern states allowed black people full civil equality.) Northerners were also disturbed when whites in Memphis, New Orleans, and smaller southern towns rioted, killing and injuring blacks, while the Johnson state governments sat passively by.

OLD THAD STEVENS

Few Radical Republicans were as sincerely committed to racial equality as Thaddeus Stevens of Pennsylvania. In his will he insisted on being buried in a black cemetery because blacks were banned from the one where he normally would have been interred.

Nevertheless, even Stevens came to terms with the racism of those northern whites who refused the vote to the blacks in their own states. In order to win their support for black suffrage in the South, Stevens argued that the situation was different in the South because blacks made up the majority of loyal Union men there. "I am for negro suffrage in every rebel state," he said. "If it be just, it should not be denied; if it be necessary, it should be adopted; if it be a punishment to traitors, they deserve it."

The Fourteenth Amendment

Perceiving the shift in mood, in June 1866, Radical and Moderate Republicans drew up a constitutional amendment on which to base congressional Reconstruction policy. The long and complex (and later controversial) Fourteenth Amendment banned from holding high federal or state office all high-ranking Confederates unless they were pardoned by Congress. This struck directly at many of the leaders of the Johnson governments in the South.

The amendment also guaranteed that all "citizens of the United States and of the State wherein they reside," in other words, blacks were to receive fully equal treatment under the laws of the states.

If ratified, the Fourteenth Amendment would preclude southern states from passing any more laws like the black codes. However, it also promised to cancel northern state laws that forbade blacks to vote, and in that aspect of the amendment Johnson saw an opportunity. Calculating that many northerners, particularly in the Midwest, would rather have Confederates in the government than grant full civil equality to blacks, Johnson decided to campaign against the Radicals on the amendment issue in the 1866 congressional election.

The Radical Triumph

The first step was the formal organization of a political party. Johnson, conservative Republican allies such as Secretary of State Seward and a few senators, and some Democrats therefore called a convention of the National Union party in Philadelphia. The message of the convention was sectional reconciliation; to symbolize it, the meeting was opened by a procession of northern and southern Johnson supporters in which couples made up of one southerner and one northerner marched arm in arm down the center aisle of the hall.

Unhappily for Johnson, the first couple on the floor was South Carolina governor James L. Orr, a huge, fleshy mountain of a man, and Massachusetts governor John A. Andrew, a little fellow with a way of looking intimidated. When Orr seemed to drag the mousy

---

DISCOURAGING REBELLION

Among other provisions of the Fourteenth Amendment, the former Confederate states were forbidden to repay "any debt or obligation incurred in aid of insurrection or rebellion against the United States." By stinging foreign and domestic individuals and banks that had lent money to the rebel states, the amendment was putting future supporters of rebellion on notice of the consequences of their actions.

Andrew down the length of the hall, Radical politicians and cartoonists had a field day. Johnson's National Union movement, they said, was dominated by rebels and preached in the North by cowardly stooges.

In the fall, Johnson sealed his doom. He toured the Midwest seeking support—he called it his "swing around the circle"—and from the start discredited himself. Johnson had learned his oratorical skills in the rough-and-tumble, stump-speaking tradition of eastern Tennessee. There, voters liked a red-hot debate between politicians who scorched each other and the hecklers that challenged them.

Midwesterners also liked that kind of ruckus, but not, it turned out, from their president. When Radical hecklers taunted Johnson and he responded gibe for gibe, Radicals shook their heads sadly that a man of so little dignity should be sitting in the seat of Washington and Lincoln. Drunk again, they supposed.

The result was a landslide. Most of Johnson's candidates were defeated. The Republican party, now led by the Radicals, controlled more than two-thirds of the seats in both houses of Congress, enough to override every veto that Johnson dared to make.

RECONSTRUCTION REALITIES AND MYTHS

The Republicans' Reconstruction program was adopted in a series of laws that were passed by the Fortieth Congress in 1867. These dissolved the southern state governments that had been organized under Johnson and partitioned the Confederacy into five military provinces, each commanded by a major general. The army would maintain order while voters were registered, blacks and those whites who were not specifically disenfranchised under the terms of the Fourteenth Amendment. The constitutional conventions that these voters elected were required to abolish slavery, give the vote to adult black males, and ratify the Thirteenth and Fourteenth Amendments. After examination of their work by Congress, the reconstructed states would be admitted to the Union, and their senators and representatives could take their seats in the Capitol. The Radicals assumed that at least some of these congressmen would be Republicans.

The Readmission of the Southern States

Tennessee complied immediately with these terms and was never really affected by the Radical experiment in remaking the South. Ironically, it was Andrew Johnson, as military governor during the war, who had laid the basis for a stable government in the Volunteer State.

In 1868, largely as a result of the black vote, six more states were readmitted. Alabama, Arkansas, Florida, Louisiana, North Carolina, and South Carolina sent Republican delegations, including some blacks, to Washington. In the remaining four states— Georgia, Mississippi, Texas, and Virginia—because some whites obstructed every attempt to set up a government in which blacks would participate, the military continued to govern until 1870.

In the meantime, with Congress more firmly under Radical control, Thaddeus Stevens, Charles Sumner, and other Radicals attempted to establish the supremacy of the legislative over the judicial and executive branches of the government. With the Supreme Court they were immediately successful. By threatening to reduce the size of the Court or even to try to abolish it, the Radicals intimidated the justices. Chief Justice Salmon P. Chase decided to ride out the difficult era by ignoring all cases that dealt with Reconstruction issues, just what the Radicals wanted.

As for the presidency, Congress took partial control of the army away from Johnson and then struck at his right to choose his own cabinet. The Tenure of Office Act forbade the president to remove any appointed official who had been confirmed by the Senate without first getting the Senate's approval of the dismissal.

The Impeachment of Andrew Johnson

Although Johnson had attempted to delay and obstruct congressional Reconstruction by urging southern whites not to cooperate, the strict constitutionalist in him had come to terms with the fact of the Radicals' control of the government. He had executed the duties assigned him under the Reconstruction acts. However, he decided to defy the Tenure of Office Act for the same constitutional reasons. To allow Congress to decide if and when a president could fire a member of his own cabinet was a clear infringement of the in-

A ticket of admission to the Senate gallery to witness the impeachment of Andrew Johnson.

dependence of the executive branch of the government. In February 1868, Johnson dismissed the single Radical in his cabinet, Secretary of War Edwin Stanton.

Strictly speaking, the Tenure of Office Act did not apply to Stanton's dismissal because he had been appointed by Lincoln, not by Johnson. Nevertheless, as the Constitution provided, the House of Representatives drew up articles of impeachment, passed them, and appointed a committee to serve as Johnson's prosecutors. The Senate acted as the jury in the trial, and the Chief Justice presided.

A President on Trial

All but two of the eleven articles of impeachment dealt with the Tenure of Office Act. As expected, Johnson's defenders in the Senate argued that it did not apply to the Stanton case, and, in any event, its constitutionality was highly dubious. The other two articles condemned Johnson for disrespect of Congress. These charges were undeniably true; Johnson had spared few bitter words in describing the Radicals who seemed to dominate both houses. But the president's defenders argued that sharp and vulgar language did not approach being the "high crimes and misdemeanors" that the Constitution stipulates as the reason for impeachment.

Removal of an impeached federal official requires a two-thirds majority of the Senate. In 1868, that meant 36 senators had to vote for conviction, no more than 18 for acquittal. The actual vote in Johnson's case was 35 to 19. He remained in office by a single vote.

Actually, it was not so close. About six Moderate Republican senators had agreed privately that if they were needed to acquit, they would vote for acquittal. They wanted to avoid going on record as favoring the president. Johnson had little support in the North, and they were practical politicians. However, they did not believe that the president should be removed from office simply because he was at odds with Congress. Moreover, if Johnson were removed from office, his successor would have been Ben Wade of Ohio, a Radical of such dubious deportment—he was a notorious foulmouth—that by comparison Johnson was a statesman. Finally, 1868 was an election year. Andy Johnson's days were numbered. The immensely popular Ulysses S. Grant would be the Republican nominee. Victory in November was a sure thing.

The Fifteenth Amendment

Grant easily defeated New York governor Horatio Seymour in the electoral college by a vote of 214 to 80. However, the popular vote was much closer, a hair's

This photograph of Ulysses S. Grant is a print from a restored glass plate negative.

quently, the Moderates in Congress supported Radicals in drafting a third "Civil War Amendment." The Fifteenth forbade states to deny the vote to any person on the basis of "race, color, or previous condition of servitude." Because Republican governments favorable to blacks still controlled most of the southern states, the amendment was easily ratified. The Radical Reconstruction program was complete.

Legends

By the end of the nineteenth century and increasingly after 1900, a legend of Reconstruction took form in American popular consciousness. Most white people came to believe that Reconstruction was a time of degradation and humiliation for white southerners. Soldiers bullied them, and they languished under the political domination of ignorant former slaves who were incapable of good citizenship, carpetbaggers (northerners who went south in order to exploit the tragedy of defeat), and scalawags (white southerners of low caste who cooperated with blacks and Yankees).

The "Black Reconstruction" governments, the legend continued, were hopelessly corrupt as well as unjust. The blacks, carpetbaggers, and scalawags looted the treasuries and demeaned the honor of the southern states. Only by heroic efforts did decent white people, through the Democratic party, *redeem* the southern states once they had retaken control of them. Some

breadth in some states. Nationwide, Grant won by 300,000 votes, and, some rudimentary arithmetic showed, he got 500,000 black votes in the southern states. Grant lost New York, the largest state, by a very thin margin. Had blacks been able to vote in New York (they were not), Grant would have carried the state easily. In Indiana, Grant won by a razor-thin margin. Had blacks been able to vote in that northern state (they were not), it would not have been close.

In other words, the future of the Republican party seemed to depend on the black man's right to vote in the northern as well as the southern states. Conse-

WAS JOHNSON IMPEACHED?

Andrew Johnson *was* impeached, the only American president to be so. *Impeachment* is not removal from office but the bringing of charges, the equivalent of indictment in a criminal trial. The official who is found guilty of the articles of impeachment is convicted and removed from office (and may be sent to prison or otherwise penalized if convicted in a subsequent criminal trial). Johnson was *not* convicted of the charges brought against him.

WHAT IF JOHNSON HAD BEEN CONVICTED?

What would it have meant for the structure of American government if Andrew Johnson had been removed from office for, in effect, disagreeing with Congress? It might have been a major step toward the parliamentary form of government that is practiced in most representative democracies. Whereas in the United States the executive branch of government is separate from the legislative branch, in parliamentary systems like that of Canada and Great Britain, the prime minister, the head of government, must be a member of Parliament and have the support of a majority of the members of Parliament. If the prime minister loses that support, he or she loses the office and Parliament elects a new prime minister or is dissolved, and new elections held. The American presidency would still have been constitutionally independent had Johnson been removed, but the precedent probably would have emboldened later Congresses to remove presidents of whose policies they disapproved. As it was, Johnson's acquittal and, in 1974, Richard Nixon's resignation before he was impeached, have helped to preserve the independence of the executive branch.

versions of the legend glamorized the role of secret terrorist organizations, such as the Ku Klux Klan, in redeeming the South.

The Kernel of Truth

As in most legends, there was a kernel of truth in this vision of Reconstruction. The Radical governments did spend freely. There was plenty of corruption in southern government; for example, the Republican governor of Louisiana, Henry C. Warmoth, banked $100,000 during a year when his salary was $8,000. In 1869, the state of Florida spent as much on its printing bill as had been spent on every function of state government in 1860.

Sometimes the theft was open and ludicrous. Former slaves in control of South Carolina's lower house voted a payment of $1,000 to one of their number who had lost that amount in a bet on a horse race. Self-serving carpetbaggers were numerous, as were vindictive scalawags and incompetent black officials.

The Legend in Perspective

Large governmental expenditures were unavoidable in the postwar South, however. Southern society was

This cartoon from the British magazine Puck *illustrates the view many southerners held of Reconstruction as ordered by Ulysses S. Grant and the Republicans. It was, the southerners believed, a harsh and heavy burden forced upon a weary but solid South.*

being built from scratch—an expensive proposition. It was the lot of the Radical state governments to provide social services—for whites as well as blacks—that had simply been ignored in the southern states before the Civil War. Statewide public school systems were not founded in the South until Reconstruction. Programs for the relief of the destitute and the handicapped were likewise nearly unknown before Republicans came to power.

Corrupt politicians are common in times of massive government spending, no matter who is in charge; shady deals were not unique to southern Republican governments during the 1860s and 1870s. The most flagrant theft from public treasuries during the period was the work of Democrats in New York, strong supporters of white southerners who wanted to reduce the blacks to peonage. In fact, the champion southern thieves of the era were not Radicals but antiblack white Democrats. After a Republican administration in Mississippi ran a clean, nearly corruption-free regime, the first post-Reconstruction treasurer of the state absconded with $415,000. This paled compared to the swag E. A. Burke, the first post-Reconstruction treasurer of Louisiana, took with him to Honduras in 1890—$1,777,000.

As for the carpetbaggers, many of them brought much-needed capital to the South. They were hot to make money, to be sure, but in the process of developing the South, not as mere exploiters. Many of the scalawags were by no means unlettered "poor white trash," as the legend had it, but southern Whigs who had disapproved of secession and who, after the war, drifted naturally, if briefly, into the Republican party that their northern fellow Whigs had joined.

Blacks in Government

The blacks who rose to high office in the Reconstruction governments were rarely ignorant former field hands, but well-educated, refined, even rather conservative men. Moreover, whatever the malfeasances of Reconstruction, the blacks could not be blamed; they never controlled the government of any southern state. For a short time, they were the majority in the legislatures of South Carolina (where blacks were the majority of the population) and precisely one-half of the legislature of Louisiana. Only two blacks served as United States senators, Blanche K. Bruce and Hiram Revels, both cultivated men from Mississippi. No black ever served as a governor, although Lieutenant Governor P. B. S. Pinchback of Louisiana briefly acted in that capacity when the white governor was out of the state. Whatever Reconstruction was, its color was not black.

Hiram Revels (left) and Blanche K. Bruce (right), both of Mississippi, were elected to the United States Congress during Reconstruction.

Redemption

The crime of Reconstruction in the eyes of most southern whites was that it allowed blacks the opportunity to participate in government. The experiment failed because black voters were denied an economic foundation on which to build their civil equality, and because northerners soon lost interest in the ideals of the Civil War.

Because they had no land, the blacks of the South were dependent on landowners for their sustenance. When southern landowners concluded that it was to their interest to eliminate the blacks from political life, they could do so by threatening unemployment.

Unprotected former slaves could not command the respect of poorer whites, who provided most of the members of terrorist organizations like the Ku Klux Klan, which was founded in 1866 by former slave trader and Confederate general Nathan Bedford Forrest. These nightriders, identities concealed within hoods, frightened, beat, and even murdered blacks who insisted on voting. Congress outlawed and, within a few years, effectively suppressed the Klan and similar organizations like the Knights of the White Camellia, but, in the meantime, many blacks had been terrorized into staying home on election day.

Congress was unable to counter the conviction of increasing numbers of white southerners that only through "white supremacy," the slogan of the southern Democratic parties, could the South be redeemed. In most southern states, where whites were the majority, an overwhelming white vote on this issue alone was enough to install legislators and governors who promptly found effective ways to disenfranchise the blacks.

In the North and West, each year that passed saw the deterioration of interest in the rights of southern blacks. At no time had more than a minority of northern whites truly believed blacks to be their equals. As an era of unprecedented economic expansion unfolded in the wake of the Civil War, and unprecedented scandals rocked the administration of Ulysses S. Grant, to whom the protection of black civil rights was entrusted, support for Reconstruction dwindled. Albion W. Tourgee, a white northerner who fought for black civil equality in North Carolina, wrote that trying to enforce the Fourteenth and Fifteenth Amendments without federal support was "a fool's errand."

THE GRANT ADMINISTRATION

Ulysses S. Grant was the youngest man to be president to his time, only 46 years of age when he took the oath of office in 1869. In some ways, his appearance remained as unimpressive as when reporters caught him whittling sticks on the battlefield. Stoop-shouldered and taciturn, Grant has a peculiar fright-

Before the Civil War, Nathan Bedford Forrest had been a slave trader, an occupation of low social status in the South. He distinguished himself in battle, however, and founded the Ku Klux Klan after the war.

ened look in his eye in most of the photographs of him, as though he knew that he had risen above his capabilities.

In fact, Grant hated the duties and power of the presidency. It was the perquisites of living in the White House that he fancied. He took with relish to eating caviar and *tournedos béarnaise* and sipping the best French wines and cognac. The earthy general whose uniform had looked like that of a slovenly sergeant developed a fondness for expensive, finely tailored clothing.

Indeed, the elegant broadcloth on his back was the emblem of Grant's failure as president. Money and fame had come too suddenly to a man who had spent his life struggling to survive. Both he and his wife were overwhelmed by the adulation heaped on him. When towns and counties took his name, and when cities made gifts of valuable property and even cash— $100,000 from New York alone—Grant accepted them with a few mumbled words of thanks. He never fully understood that political gift givers were actually paying in advance for future favors. Or, if he did understand, he saw nothing wrong in returning kindness with the resources at his disposal. Among the lesser of his errors, he gave federal jobs to any of his and his wife's relatives who asked and, a seedy lot, they were not bashful. Worse, Grant remained as loyal to them

as he had been loyal to junior officers in the army. In the military, backing up subordinates when they slip up is a virtue, essential to morale. Grant never quite learned that in politics backing up subordinates who steal is less than admirable.

Black Friday

Grant's friends, old and new, wasted no time in stealing. Unlucky in business himself, the president luxuriated in the flattery lavished on him by wealthy men. In 1869, two unscrupulous speculators, Jay Gould and Jim Fisk, made it a point to be seen in public with the president, schemed secretly with Grant's brother-in-law, Abel R. Corbin, and hatched a plot to corner the nation's gold supply.

That is, having won Corbin's assurance that he would keep Grant from selling government gold, Gould and Fisk bought up as much gold and gold futures (commitments to buy gold at a future date at a low price) as they could. Their apparent control of the gold market caused the price of the precious metal to soar. In September 1869, gold was bringing $162 an ounce. Gould's and Fisk's plan was to dump their holdings and score a killing.

Finally grasping that he was an accomplice, on Friday, September 24, Grant dumped $4 million in government gold on the market and the price collapsed. Gould and Fisk suffered very little. Jim Fisk simply refused to honor his commitments to buy at higher than the market price and hired thugs to threaten those who insisted. (High finance could be highly exercising during the Grant years.) But businessmen who needed gold to pay debts and wages were ruined by the hundreds, and thousands of workingmen lost their jobs. The luster of a great general's reputation was tarnished before he had been president for a year.

Other Scandals

During the construction of the Union Pacific Railway in the years following the Civil War, the directors of the U.P. set up a dummy corporation called the Crédit Mobilier. This company charged the U.P. some $5 million for work that actually cost about $3 million. The difference went into the pockets of Union Pacific executives. Because the U.P. was heavily subsidized by the federal government, and therefore under close scrutiny, key members of Congress were cut in on the deal. Among the beneficiaries was Schuyler Colfax, who was Grant's vice president. Speaker of the House James A. Garfield also accepted a stipend.

Three of Grant's appointees to the cabinet were involved in corruption. Carriers under contract to the Post Office Department paid kickbacks in return for

Grant's presidential campaign ribbon commemorated his march into Richmond, Virginia, during the Civil War.

exorbitant payments for their services. The Secretary of War, William W. Belknap, took bribes from companies that operated trading posts in Indian reservations under his authority. He and his subordinates shut their eyes while the companies defrauded the tribes of goods that they were due under the terms of federal treaties. Grant insisted that Belknap leave his post, but since Belknap was Grant's old crony, the president refused to punish him on behalf of cheated Indians.

Nor did Grant punish his Secretary of the Treasury, Benjamin Bristow, or his personal secretary, Orville E. Babcock, when he learned that they had sold excise stamps to whiskey distillers in St. Louis. Whenever the president came close to losing his patience (which was considerable), Roscoe Conkling or another stalwart reminded him of the importance of party loyalty. Better a few scoundrels escape than party morale be damaged and the Democrats take over.

The Liberal Republicans

Although the full odor of the Grant scandals was loosed only later, enough scent hung in the air in 1872 that a number of prominent Republicans broke openly with the president. Charles Sumner of Massachusetts, a senator since 1851 and chairman of the Senate Foreign Relations Committee, split with the president over Grant's determination to annex the island nation of Santo Domingo to the United States. Without Sumner's opposition to imperialism and a land-grab by cynical Republican profiteers, Grant would surely have succeeded.

Carl Schurz of Missouri and the British-born editor of *The Nation* magazine, E. L. Godkin, were appalled by the steamy atmosphere of corruption in Washington and the treatment of public office as a way of making a living rather than as performing a public service. Schurz and Godkin (but not Sumner) had also given up on Reconstruction, which, whatever his personal sentiments, Grant enforced. Although not necessarily convinced that blacks were inferior to whites, they had concluded that ensuring civil rights for blacks was not worth the instability of government in the South, nor the continued presence of troops in the southern states. Better to allow the white Redeemers to return to power.

The Election of 1872

This was also the position of the man whom the Liberal Republicans named to run for president in 1872, the editor of the New York *Tribune*, Horace Greeley. It was a terrible choice, for Greeley was a lifelong eccentric. Throughout his 61 years, Greeley had clambered aboard almost every reform and far-out

BLACKS IN CONGRESS

Better a white crook than a black crook; better a white grafter than a black of stature and probity. Such was the view of the "Redeemers," white Democrats who wrested control of southern state governments from the Republican party during Reconstruction. They depicted black officials as incompetent, corrupt, and uninterested in the welfare of the South as a whole. With most southern whites contemptuous of the recently freed slaves, it was an effective appeal. Other issues paled into near invisibility in what seemed the blinding urgency in asserting "white supremacy."

At low levels, many black officeholders were incompetent and self-serving. A few high in state administrations were venal grafters. That their Redeemer challengers were rarely better and often worse did not, however, lend a reflective bent to southern voting behavior. Rather, race was all.

While none of the blacks who sat in Congress in the wake of the Civil War may be said to have been statesmen of the first order, as a group they were as able and worthy a lot as the era's other "ethnic delegations" in the Capitol, any random selection of farmer-congressmen or businessmen-congressmen, any northern or western state delegation of either party, any random selection of 22 Redeemers.

Between 1869 and 1901, 20 blacks served in the House, two in the Senate. South Carolina, where blacks outnumbered whites, sent eight; North Carolina four; Alabama three; and Virginia, Georgia, Florida, Louisiana, and Mississippi one each. Both black senators, Hiram K. Revels and Blanche K. Bruce, represented Mississippi, where potential black voters also outnumbered whites.

Thirteen of the 22 had been slaves before the Civil War, the others were lifelong free blacks. Their educational attainment compared well with that of Congress as a whole. Ten of the black congressmen had gone to college, five had graduated. Six were lawyers (rather less than among all congressmen—nothing for which to apologize); three were preachers; four farmers. Most of the others were skilled artisans, by no means "the dregs of society" as the Redeemers ritually portrayed them.

Hiram Revels was a Methodist pastor. He was born in North Carolina in 1822 but, as a free black, prudently removed to Indiana and Ohio where, during the Civil War, he organized a black regiment. The end of the war found him in Natchez where a cultivated and conservative demeanor (and a willingness to defer to white Republicans) made him an attractive candidate for the Senate.

Blanche K. Bruce was born a slave in 1841, but he was well educated: his owner leased him to a printer. In 1861, he escaped from his apparently lackadaisical master and, in the wake of the Union troops, moved to Mississippi. His record in the Senate was conservative and quiet.

The most durable of the black congressmen was J. H. Rainey of South Carolina. He sat in Congress between 1869 and 1879, winning his last election in the year of the Hayes-Tilden debacle. In most of his district, blacks outnumbered whites by 6 to 1 and 8 to 1. He was retired in the election of 1878 only as a consequence of widespread economic reprisals against black voters and some little violence.

Rainey's parents had bought their freedom long before the Civil War but, in 1862, he was drafted to work on the fortifications in Charleston harbor, a condition that was tantamount to enslavement. However, Rainey escaped to the West Indies and worked his way to the North, returning to his home state early during Reconstruction.

Rainey was indeed vindictive toward the white South, exploiting racial hostilities as nastily as any Redeemer on the other side. Most of the black congressmen were, unsurprisingly, preoccupied with civil rights issues. No doubt, had South Carolina's blacks retained the franchise, Rainey would have exploited racial hostility as destructively as his opponents.

However, Rainey was by no means oblivious to other questions. By the end of the 1870's, he used his modest seniority to work for southern economic interests that transcended the color line. He defended the rights of Chinese in California on conservative "pro-business" Republican, as well as racial, grounds and attempted to improve relations with the black republic of Haiti.

George H. White was the last black to sit in Congress from a southern state before the passage of the Civil Rights Act of 1965. Born a slave in 1852, he attended Howard University in Washington (then a black institution), and practiced law in North Carolina.

In 1896, he won election to the House of Representatives by adding a number of white Populist votes to a black Republican bloc. At the time, some southern Populists, like Thomas Watson of Georgia, preached interracial political cooperation in an attempt to build a solid agrarian front to the "Bourbons" into which the Redeemers had been transformed. Unlike the northern Populists, who fastened on the Republican party as their chief enemy, southern Populists sometimes saw allies in black Republican voters. Their issues were agrarian: almost all southern blacks tilled the soil.

This put black politicians like White in an impossible situation. Preferment in the national Republican party required him to adhere to a line that, under President William McKinley, also elected in 1896, became conservative and imperialistic. White spoke out on behalf of a high tariff—albeit on the grounds that it favored the working man: "the ox that pulls the plow ought to have a chance to eat the fodder"—and favored the Spanish-American War.

Inevitably, his positions alienated those whites who had helped elect him. Moreover, southern Populism

438

A Currier and Ives print of the first black United States senator and black members of the House of Representatives in the 41st and 42nd Congresses. None were ignorant former fieldhands. Several were individuals of rare talent and accomplishment.

was undergoing a momentous transformation during the late 1890s. Shrewd Democratic party politicians like Benjamin "Pitchfork Ben" Tillman combined a populistic appeal to poor whites with an incendiary hatred of blacks.

Racial hatred was the staple of demagogues like Tillman (and, soon enough, Tom Watson in Georgia). However, they also hammered on the fact that southern blacks voted overwhelmingly Republican and that meant a "plutocratic" federal government.

Conservatives like White were easy targets and, in 1898, the North Carolina Populists switched sides, supporting the Democratic candidate and almost ousting White after only one term.

He knew his political future was doomed and compensated for "an organization man's" first term by speaking out loudly during his second about what was happening in the South (while most white Republicans merely shrugged). Only after 1898 did he fasten almost

exclusively on civil rights issues, describing himself as "the representative on this floor of 9,000,000 of the population of these United States."

By 1900, black voters in White's district had been reduced to a fragment. He did not even bother to stand for reelection and sure humiliation. Instead, in his farewell speech in 1901, he delivered his finest oration, an eloquent speech that served as the coda to Reconstruction's failure to integrate blacks into the American polity:

These parting words are in behalf of an outraged, heart-broken, bruised and bleeding, but God-fearing people, faithful, industrial, loyal people, rising people, full of potential force. The only apology that I have to make for the earnestness with which I have spoken is that I am pleading for the life, the liberty, the future happiness, and manhood suffrage for one-eighth of the entire population of the United States.

bandwagon that had rattled down the road, from abolitionism and women's rights at one end of the spectrum to vegetarianism, spiritualism (communicating with the dead), and phrenology (reading a person's character in the bumps on his or her head) at the other.

Even in his appearance, Greeley invited ridicule. He looked like a crackpot with his round, pink face exaggerated by close-set, beady eyes and a wispy fringe of white chin whiskers. He wore an ankle-length overcoat on the hottest days, and carried a brightly colored umbrella on the driest. Sharp-eyed Republican cartoonists like Thomas Nast had an easy time making fun of Greeley.

To make matters worse, Greeley needed the support of the Democrats to make a race of it against Grant, and he proposed to "clasp hands across the bloody chasm." This was asking too much of Republican party regulars. Voters who disapproved of Grant disapproved much more of southern Democrats.

Moreover, throughout his editorial career, Greeley had printed just about every printable vilification of the Democrats—particularly southerners—that the English language offered. The Democrats did give him their nomination. But southern whites found it difficult to support such a leader. A large black vote for Grant in seven southern states helped give the president a 286 to 66 victory in the electoral college.

THE TWILIGHT OF RECONSTRUCTION

The Liberals returned to the Republican party. For all their contempt for the unhappy Grant, upon whom the scandals piled during his second term, the Liberals found their flirtation with the Democrats humiliating. Among them, only Charles Sumner remained true to the cause of the southern blacks. His Civil Rights Act of 1875 (passed a year after his death) guaranteed equal accommodations for blacks in public facilities such as hotels and theaters and forbade the exclusion of blacks from juries. Congress quietly dropped another provision forbidding segregated schools.

The Act of 1875 was the last significant federal attempt to enforce equal rights for the races for 80 years. Not only had northerners lost interest in Civil War idealism, southern white Democrats had redeemed most of the former Confederacy. By the end of 1875, only three states remained Republican: South Carolina, Florida, and Louisiana.

The Disputed Election

The Democratic candidate in 1876, New York governor Samuel J. Tilden, called for the removal of troops from these three states, which would bring the white-supremacy Democrats to power. The Republican candidate, Governor Rutherford B. Hayes of Ohio, ran on a platform that guaranteed black rights in the South, but Hayes was known to be skeptical of black capabilities and a personal friend of a number of white southern politicians.

When the votes were counted, Hayes's opinions seemed to be beside the point. Tilden won a close popular vote, and he appeared to sweep the electoral college by a vote of 204 to 165. However, Tilden's margin of victory included the electoral votes of South Carolina, Florida, and Louisiana, where Republicans still controlled the state governments. After receiving telegrams from party leaders in New York, officials there declared that in reality Hayes had carried their states. According to these returns, Hayes had eked out a 185 to 184 electoral vote victory.

It was not that easy. When official returns reached Washington, there were two sets from each of the three disputed states—one set for Tilden, and one for Hayes. Because the Constitution did not provide for such an occurrence, a special commission was established to decide which set of returns was valid. Five members of each house of Congress and five members of the Supreme Court sat on this panel. Seven of them were Republicans; seven were Democrats; and one, David Davis of Illinois, a Supreme Court justice and once Abraham Lincoln's law partner, was known as an independent. Because no one was interested in determining the case on its merits, each commissioner fully intending to vote for his party's candidate, the burden of naming the next president of the United States fell on Davis's shoulders.

He did not like it. No matter how honestly he came to his decision, half the voters in the country would call for his scalp because he had voted down their candidate. Davis prevailed on friends in Illinois to get him off the hook by naming him to a Senate seat then vacant. He resigned from the Court and, therefore, the special commission. His replacement was a Republican, and the stage was set for the Republicans to "steal" the election.

The Compromise of 1877

The commission voted on strict party lines, eight to seven, to accept the Hayes returns from Louisiana, Florida, and South Carolina—thus giving Rutherford B. Hayes the presidency by a single electoral vote. Had that been all there was to it, there might have been further trouble. At a series of meetings, however, a group of prominent northern and southern politicians and businessmen came to an informal agreement that was satisfactory to the political leaders of both sections.

The "Compromise of 1877" involved several commitments, not all of them honored, for northern investment in the South. Also not honored was a vague agreement on the part of some conservative southerners to build a "lily-white" Republican party in the South based on economic and social views that they shared with northern conservatives.

As to the disputed election, Hayes would be permitted to move into the White House without resistance by either northern or southern Democrats. In return, he would withdraw the last troops from South Carolina, Florida, and Louisiana, thus allowing the Democratic party in these states to oust the Republicans and destroy the political power of the blacks.

Despite the proclamations before Inauguration Day that Democrats would fight if Tilden were not elected, there was no trouble. This was not because the men who hammered out the Compromise of 1877 were so very powerful. It merely reflected the growing disinterest of Americans in the issues of the Civil War and Reconstruction and their increasing preoccupation with the fabulous economic growth of the country. The southern blacks, of course, were the casualties of this watershed year, but since the price they paid was suppression, few whites heard their complaints and fewer were interested.

For Further Reading

Overviews and Classics

W. E. B. DuBois, *Black Reconstruction* (1935)

William A. Dunning, *Reconstruction: Political and Economic* (1907)

John Hope Franklin, *Reconstruction After the Civil War* (1961)

James McPherson, *Ordeal by Fire: The Civil War and Reconstruction* (1982)

John G. Randall and David Donald, *The Civil War and Reconstruction* (1969)

Albion W. Tourgee, *A Fool's Errand* (1880)

Valuable Special Studies

Herman Belz, *Reconstructing the Union* (1969)

Richard N. Current, *Three Carpetbag Governors* (1967)

Eric Foner, *Politics and Ideology in the Age of the Civil War* (1980)

Stanley Kitler, *Judicial Power and Reconstruction Politics* (1968)

Leon F. Liwack, *Been in the Storm So Long* (1979)

Eric McKitrick, *Andrew Johnson and Reconstruction* (1960)

Robert C. Morris, *Reading, 'Ritings, and Reconstruction: The Education of Freedmen in the South, 1861–1870* (1981)

Willie Lee Rose, *Rehearsal for Reconstruction* (1964)

Hans A. Trefousse, *The Radical Republicans* (1969)

A. W. Trelease, *KKK: The Ku Klux Klan Conspiracy and Southern Reconstruction* (1971)

C. Vann Woodward, *Reunion and Reaction: The Compromise of 1877 and the End of Reconstruction* (1951)

Biographies and Autobiographies

Fawn Brodie, *Thaddeus Stevens: Scourge of the South* (1959)

David Donald, *Charles Sumner and the Rights of Man* (1970)

Eric S. Lunde, *Horace Greeley* (1980)

William S. McFeeley, *Grant: A Biography* (1981)

Parties, Patronage, and Pork
Politics as Sport and Business

The presidents of the late nineteenth century do not inspire awe. Their portraits arranged side by side—Grant, Hayes, Garfield, Arthur, Cleveland, Harrison, Cleveland again—they resemble nothing so much as a line of mourners at a midwestern funeral. They were conscious of their dignity, to be sure, and grandly bewhiskered. They were competent to perform executive duties (except perhaps for Grant), devoted family men, sober-sided and drab (except for Chester A. Arthur), and unexciting across the board.

Their lack of charisma is one reason why twentieth-century Americans find them so uninteresting. In our age of instantaneous electronic media, it is the personable performer who has the edge in winning elections. Moreover, twentieth-century Americans have gotten used to vigorous chief executives who seize the initiative in domestic and foreign matters alike, while, from Grant through William McKinley, whose election in 1896 ended a political era, presidents believed Congress should take the lead. The president was to execute laws, steer the government, and, when necessary, apply a constitutional brake.

Finally, there is no doubt that what was most vital in late nineteenth-century America lay not in politics but in the fabulous growth of Ameri-

Political cartoonist Thomas Nast created the Republican elephant and the Democratic donkey, symbols that have been with the two parties for more than a century. The donkey cartoon here was drawn by Bernhard Gillam. The elephant was drawn by Nast in 1875 as an editorial comment on New York City's Tammany Hall.

can industry, the creation of big business, and the development of the great "Wild West" so central to American popular culture. The historian might easily be tempted to rush through the whole subject of politics with a few words—except for two striking facts.

First, politics was itself a business in the late nineteenth century, from White House down to city hall. Politics reflected the nation's preoccupation with getting ahead, with developing and organizing for material gain. Second, Americans loved the political game. In no other period of American history did a higher percentage of eligible voters actually exercise their right to vote. Despite the fact that their isolation made it difficult for many rural voters to get to the polls in wintry Novembers, and the fact that many blacks' constitutional right to vote was nullified in practice by fear of economic or violent reprisals, fully 80 percent of those who were eligible to vote in the 1870s, 1880s, and 1890s did vote. In the late twentieth century, by comparison, fewer than half the eligible voters turn out at a typical election.

HOW THE SYSTEM WORKED

Presidential elections brought out the most voters of all. In part this was because, nationally, the two major parties were so evenly matched. A man (and in a few states after 1890, a woman) found plenty of evidence that one vote really could make a difference. Between 1872, when Grant won reelection by a smashing 750,000 votes, and 1896, when William McKinley ushered in an era of Republican dominance with an 850,000 vote plurality, two presidential elections (1880 and 1884) were decided by fewer than 40,000 votes in a total of 9 to 10 million. In two elections (1876 and 1888), the winning candidates had fewer supporters than the losers: the winners collected their prize in the electoral college.

In 1892, the victorious Democrat, Grover Cleveland, scored a respectable popular majority. Even then his share of the vote cast was well under half of the total, 46.1 percent. In fact, the only presidential candidate of either party between 1872 and 1896 to win a majority of the popular vote was Samuel J. Tilden, who lost the "Stolen Election" of 1876. (Tilden won a larger share of the popular vote than any Democratic presidential candidate between 1832 and 1932!)

Solid South and Republican Respectability

The parties were not so well balanced by regional nor among distinct social groups. With the exception of Connecticut, which was evenly divided, New England voted heavily Republican. In the section where Federalism, Whiggery, and abolitionism had been strongest, distaste for the party of Jefferson, Jackson, and the old slaveowners prevented Democrats from winning more than occasional elections.

The upper and middle classes of the Northeast and Midwest were generally Republican. They thought of the G.O.P., or the "Grand Old Party," as a bastion of morality and respectability, another legacy of the Whigs to the Republican party. Ironically, most big cities, run by cynical if not corrupt political machines, also voted Republican. (The most important exception was Democratic New York, where corruption was worst of all.) Finally, those blacks who retained the right to vote were staunch Republicans. Although they got scant attention from the G.O.P. after 1877, it was still the party of Lincoln and emancipation.

The Democrats built their national vote upon the foundation of the "Solid South." Blacks and the white people of Appalachia who had opposed secession formed large Republican minorities in Virginia, North Carolina, and Tennessee. But not a single former slave state, Union or Confederate, including West Virginia, voted Republican in a presidential election during the late nineteenth century. The Democrats also invariably won New York City by appealing to immigrants, and they commanded a large majority of the immigrant and white ethnic vote elsewhere.

Swing States

As a result of these steady voting patterns, the outcome of national elections turned on the vote in a handful of "swing" states, particularly Illinois, Indiana, Ohio, and New York. In each of these states, with their large blocs of electoral votes, hard-core Republicans and Democrats were about equal in number; the decision was thus in the hands of independents who might swing either way depending on local issues, party organization, the personalities of the candidates, or a passing whim. Several presidential elections during the period were decided in New York State, where the result depended on how big a majority the New York City Democrats could turn in to counterbalance the Republican edge upstate.

Party leaders believed that the personal popularity of a candidate in the swing states could make the difference. Consequently, a disproportionate number of late nineteenth-century presidential and vice-presidential nominees came from Indiana, Ohio, and New York.

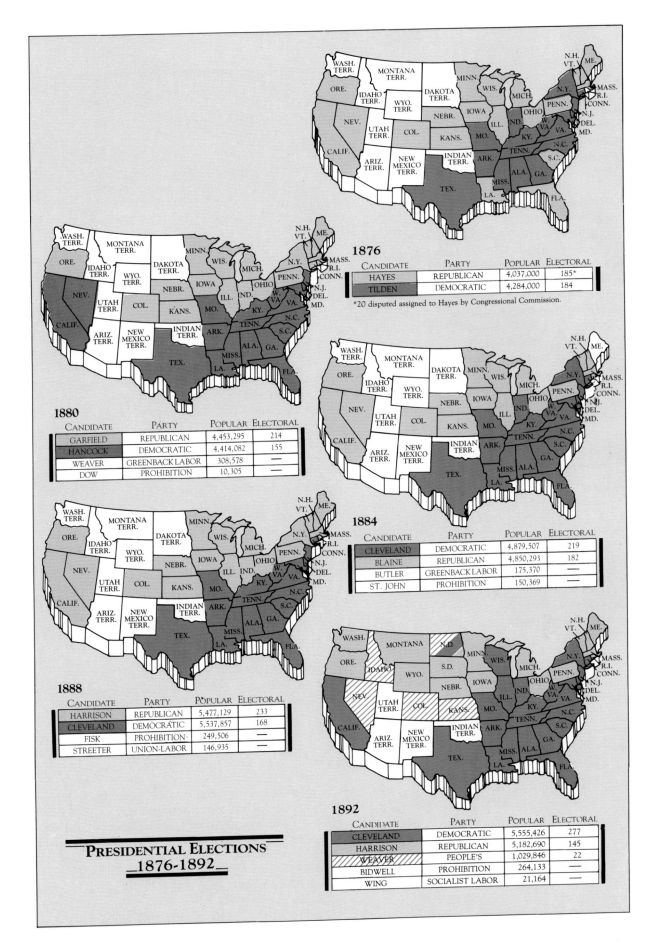

1876

Candidate	Party	Popular	Electoral
HAYES	REPUBLICAN	4,037,000	185*
TILDEN	DEMOCRATIC	4,284,000	184

*20 disputed assigned to Hayes by Congressional Commission.

1880

Candidate	Party	Popular	Electoral
GARFIELD	REPUBLICAN	4,453,295	214
HANCOCK	DEMOCRATIC	4,414,082	155
WEAVER	GREENBACK LABOR	308,578	—
DOW	PROHIBITION	10,305	—

1884

Candidate	Party	Popular	Electoral
CLEVELAND	DEMOCRATIC	4,879,507	219
BLAINE	REPUBLICAN	4,850,293	182
BUTLER	GREENBACK LABOR	175,370	—
ST. JOHN	PROHIBITION	150,369	—

1888

Candidate	Party	Popular	Electoral
HARRISON	REPUBLICAN	5,477,129	233
CLEVELAND	DEMOCRATIC	5,537,857	168
FISK	PROHIBITION	249,506	—
STREETER	UNION-LABOR	146,935	—

1892

Candidate	Party	Popular	Electoral
CLEVELAND	DEMOCRATIC	5,555,426	277
HARRISON	REPUBLICAN	5,182,690	145
WEAVER	PEOPLE'S	1,029,846	22
BIDWELL	PROHIBITION	264,133	—
WING	SOCIALIST LABOR	21,164	—

PRESIDENTIAL ELECTIONS
1876-1892

In the elections held between 1876 and 1892, the major parties filled twenty presidential and vice-presidential slots. Eighteen of the twenty (or 90 percent) were filled by men from the four key states. Eight were from New York, and five more from Indiana. Neither party was particularly interested in finding "the best man" for the job. They wanted to win an election. To do so they had to carry the swing states.

Bosses at Conventions

National conventions, which met every four years, played a much more important role in party politics than they do today. The difference was communications. Today, political leaders from every part of the country can discuss affairs with any other by picking up the phone or by hopping on a plane. In the late nineteenth century, congressmen saw one another in Washington on a regular basis. However, governors and state and city political bosses, who were often the real powers in party politics, did not.

When they did gather at their quadrennial meetings, they wheeled and dealed, bargained and traded, made and broke political careers. There was no army of

pushy television reporters around to shove a microphone in the midst of every group of politicians who gathered on the floor of the barnlike convention halls. Newspaper reporters could be kept away by strongarm bodyguards, often ex-boxers, when the discussion promised to be interesting.

Today, the primary system almost inevitably assures that a party's presidential candidate will be known long before the delegates answer the roll call at the conventions. In the late nineteenth century, nominations were more likely to be decided at the convention, perhaps on the floor, or just as likely by bosses in hotel corridors and suites over oysters, beefsteak, and free-flowing whiskey. Delegates, whose livelihood depended on party bosses, did as they were told.

In the Democratic party, the most important bosses were the head of New York's Tammany Hall, who reliably delivered that city's vote, and the Bourbon leaders of the Solid South. (They were named for their extreme conservatism, like that of the Bourbon kings of France—not after Kentucky's famous corn liquor.) In the Republican party, men like Boss Matthew Quay of Pennsylvania and Boss Thomas C. Platt of New York traded the support of their delegations for the promise of a prestigious cabinet post or a healthy share of the lucrative government offices and contracts that a victorious party had at its disposal.

The Patronage

The spoils system had come a long way since the days of Andrew Jackson and William Marcy. The United States was a big country. There was a lot of patronage—government jobs for the party faithfuls—to go around: 50,000 in Grant's time, 250,000 by the end of the century. Some government jobs involved real work. There was a postmaster in every town and hundreds of postal employees in the cities. Indian agents administered the government's treaty obligations to the tribes. In some federal bureaucracies like the Customs Service, there was enough paperwork to bury thousands of clerks wearing green visors and plastic cuffs to protect their white shirts from smudges of ink and graphite.

Campaign songs and songbooks were popular in the late nineteenth century, when election campaigns were fought with slogans and sentiments.

For Americans of the late nineteenth century, even the nursery was a fit place for presidential politics. This toy scale weighed the comparative merits of Democrat Grover Cleveland and Republican Benjamin Harrison.

Who got these jobs? For the most part, they were filled by supporters of the party in power. Political activists who worked to get the vote out were rewarded with government employment. In return, in election years their party assessed them a modest percentage of their income to finance the campaign. The result was politics for its own sake. The party scratched the jobholder's back; the jobholder reciprocated.

The higher ranking the party official, the more rewarding the job. Not only was corrupt income possible in some positions, but it was possible to grow quite rich legally in government service. The post of Collector of Customs in large ports was particularly lucrative. In addition to a handsome salary, the collector was paid a share of all import duties on goods reclaimed from smugglers who had been caught at their work. This curious incentive system made for a remarkably uncorrupt Customs Service; there was more to be made in catching violators than in taking bribes from them.

Thus, Collector of the Port of New York Chester A. Arthur earned an average $40,000 a year between 1871 and 1874, and in one big case he shared a bounty of $135,000 with two other officials. He was the best-paid government official in the country, earning more than even the president. And he was assessed a handsome sum for the privilege by the Republican party. On a rather more modest level, a handful of Southern blacks benefited from the patronage when the Republican party was in power. Some federal appointments in the South went to black people.

Pork

Other party supporters were rewarded with contracts for government work in "pork-barrel" bills. At the end of each congressional session, congressional coalitions pieced together bills to finance government construction projects in each member's district—a new post office here, a government pier there, the dredging of a river channel somewhere else. The idea was not so much to get needed work done, but to reward businessmen who supported the proper party.

Thus, the River and Harbor Bill of August 1886 provided for an expenditure of $15 million to begin over 100 new projects, although 58 government projects that had been started two years before remained unfinished.

Of course, there was not a job or contract for every voter. In order to turn out the vast numbers they did, the parties exploited the emotional politics of memory, the very rational politics of pensions, and ballyhoo that would have horrified Washington, Adams, Jefferson, and even William Henry Harrison.

The Politics of Memory

If most Republicans forgot the blacks, they remembered the Civil War. G.O.P. orators specialized in "waving the bloody shirt," reminding northern voters that Democrats had caused the Civil War. Lucius Fairchild, a Wisconsin politician who had lost an arm in battle, literally flailed the air with his empty sleeve during campaign speeches. With armless and legless veterans hobbling about every sizable town to remind voters of the bloodletting, it was an effective technique.

The Civil War loomed over the period. Between 1868 and 1901, every president but the Democrat Grover Cleveland had been an officer in the Union Army. When Cleveland, believing that sectional bitterness was fading, issued an order to return captured Confederate battle flags to their states for display at museums and war monuments, an angry protest in the North forced him to back down and contributed to his failure to win reelection the next year.

The man who defeated Cleveland in 1888, Benjamin Harrison, was still waving the bloody shirt after twenty years and not apologizing for it. "I would a thousand times rather march under the bloody shirt, stained with the lifeblood of a Union soldier," Harrison told voters, "than march under the black flag of treason or the white flag of cowardly compromise." Dwelling on the past could not possibly be constructive, but it won elections, even for the Democrats in the South.

They waved the Confederate Stars and Bars, reminding voters of the nobility of the lost cause and of the white supremacy that the Democratic Redeemers had salvaged from that cause and from the "Black Republicans."

Vote Yourself a Pension

In their pension policy, the Republicans converted the bloody shirt into dollars and cents. Soon after the war ended, Congress had provided for pensions to Union veterans who were disabled from wartime wounds and diseases. The law was strictly worded, excessively so. Many genuinely handicapped veterans did not qualify under its terms. Instead of changing the law, however, northern congressmen took to introducing *special* pension bills that provided monthly stipends for specifically named constituents who had persuaded them that their case was just.

By the 1880s, the procedure for awarding the special pension had become grossly abused. Congressmen took little interest in the truthfulness of the petitioner or the worthiness of his grievance. (One applicant for a pension had not served in the army because, he said, he had fallen off a horse on the way to enlist.) They simply introduced every bill that any constituent requested. When almost all Republicans and many northern Democrats had a few special pension bills in the hopper, the bills were rushed through collectively by voice vote. Instead of declining as old veterans died, the cost of the pension program actually climbed to $56 million in 1885 and $80 million in 1888. Pensions made up one of the largest line items in the federal budget, and a veterans' lobby, the Grand Army of the Republic (G.A.R.), came to serve effectively as a Republican political-action committee.

The G.A.R.

In 1888, Congress passed a new general pension bill that granted an income to every veteran who had served at least ninety days in the wartime army and was disabled for any reason whatsoever. An old soldier

In 1902, forty years after Antietam and Shiloh, members of the Grand Army of the Republic were still a staple of Memorial Day parades. They were almost always Republican voters.

who fell off a stepladder in 1888 was eligible under its terms.

President Cleveland vetoed the law and was sustained. The Republicans ran against him that year with the slogan "Vote Yourself a Pension" and won the election. The next year, the new president, Benjamin Harrison, signed an even more generous Dependent Pensions Act and appointed the head of the G.A.R., James "Corporal" Tanner, to distribute the loot. "God help the surplus," Tanner said, referring to the money in the Treasury. He meant it. By the end of Harrison's term, Tanner had increased the annual expenditure on pensions to $160 million. Local wits took wry notice of young women who married doddering old Billy Yanks who had a gleam in their eyes and a check in the mail.

Northern Democrats posed as the party of principle in the controversies over the bloody shirt and pensions. In the South, however, Democrats played the Civil War game in reverse. State governments provided benefits for Confederate veterans.

CIVIL WAR PENSIONS

Between 1890, when pensions for veterans of the Union Army and their dependents were paid practically for the asking, and 1905, when the practice was prohibited, it was by no means uncommon for very young ladies to marry very old veterans in order to collect widow's pensions after their bridegrooms died. As late as 1983, 41 Civil War widows were still receiving a monthly check of about $70 from the federal government.

PRESIDENTS AND PERSONALITIES

As a legacy of the Grant scandals, a presidential candidate's reputation for honesty was a popular campaign cry. In 1876, the Republicans turned to Rutherford B.

Hayes, and the Democrats to Samuel J. Tilden—in part because, as governors of Ohio and New York, respectively, they had never stolen a cent. When Hayes's supporters stole the election of 1876, the Democrats delighted in calling him "His Fraudulency" or "Rutherfraud" B. Hayes.

Hayes, Integrity, and Oblivion

In truth, Hayes was an honest man, amiable and obliging within the law. A Civil War hero who was twice seriously wounded, he was the first president who traveled for pleasure rather than on military or diplomatic missions. Perhaps most interesting about Hayes, who was president during a severe depression and widespread violence between workers and employers, he had serious reservations about the desirability of the capitalist system. His wife had very serious reservations about alcoholic beverages. She would not serve them at the White House, earning the by-no-means affectionate nickname, "Lemonade Lucy."

As president, Hayes pleased virtually no one but Lucy. Old Radical Republicans were ired by his abandonment of southern blacks (to which he was bound by the Compromise of 1877). Neither of the Republican party's two major factions, the "Stalwarts" (Grant supporters) or the "Half-Breeds" (critics of Grant) believed that Hayes allotted them less patronage than they deserved. There never was a question of renominating him; even Hayes yearned to hit the tourist road. Long before his term ended, two prominent Republicans announced their intention of succeeding him. One was James G. Blaine of Maine, leader of the Half-Breeds. The other was Ulysses S. Grant, out of office four years, just back from his own world tour, and nearly bankrupt. He needed the salary; he resented the fact that in becoming president earlier he had been obligated to give up his lifetime pay as a general. And the leader of the Stalwarts, an old Radical who despised Blaine, Roscoe Conkling of New York, persuaded Grant that it was his duty to run.

THE OLD SOLDIER

Rutherford B. Hayes was a posthumous child; his father died before he was born. Raised in an entirely feminine household, he took to soldiering in the Civil War with great enthusiasm, receiving two serious wounds leading his men into battle. Ironically for a man of mild and accommodating manners, he loved the military life. Throughout his life he attended every encampment ("convention") of the G.A.R. to which he was able to go.

Garfield: A Dark Horse

Neither Blaine nor Grant was able to win a majority of the delegates to the Republican convention. They were frustrated by the ambitions of several "favorite-son" candidates, men who came to Chicago backed only by their own states. The hope of the "favorite son" is that there will be a deadlock between the front runners, which would force the tired delegates to turn to them as compromise candidates.

Finally, after 34 ballots, the Blaine men recognized that the cause of their hero was lost. Instead of turning to one of the favorite sons whom they held responsible for their disappointment, they switched their votes to a man whose name was not even in nomination, James A. Garfield of Ohio. On the thirty-sixth ballot, he became the Republican candidate.

Garfield was a Half-Breed, a Blaine supporter, but he played on Roscoe Conkling's bottomless vanity by traveling to New York to seek the boss's blessing and to promise him a share of the patronage. Garfield went to the polls with a united party behind him.

The Democrats, having failed to win with an antiwar Democrat in 1868 (Seymour), a Republican

Looking like anything but "His Fraudulency," Rutherford B. Hayes was in fact a politician of scrupulous honesty.

maverick in 1872 (Greeley), and a reformer in 1876 (Tilden), tried their luck with their own Civil War general, Winfield Scott Hancock. An attractive if uninspiring man, he made the election extremely close. Garfield drew only 10,000 more votes than Hancock, just 48.3 percent of the total.

Another President Is Murdered

Garfield was a much more intelligent and substantial man than his opportunistic career would indicate. Whether or not he would have blossomed as president cannot be known for he spent his four short months as an active chief executive sorting out the claims of Republican party workers to government jobs. At one point he exclaimed in disgust to Blaine, his Secretary of State who wanted very badly to be president, that he could not understand why anyone pursued the post, considering all its trivial tawdry concerns.

Garfield tried to placate both wings of the party. But when he handed the choicest plum of all, the post of Collector of Customs of the port of New York, to a Blaine man, Roscoe Conkling openly broke with the president. He and his protégé in the state Republican machine, Thomas Platt, resigned their seats in the Senate. Their intention was to remind Garfield of their power in the New York Republican party by having the state legislature reelect them.

By the summer of 1881, it appeared that Conkling and Platt had lost their battle. The Garfield–Blaine Half-Breeds had succeeded in blocking their reelection. But the issue was finally resolved by two gunshots in a Washington train station. On July 2, 1881, Charles Guiteau, a ne'er-do-well preacher and bill collector who had worked for the Stalwarts but had not been rewarded with a government job, walked up to Garfield as he was about to depart on a holiday and shot him twice in the small of the back. After living in excruciating pain for eleven weeks, the second president to be murdered died on September 19.

James Garfield had served as president for only four months when he was shot and incapacitated.

"I am a Stalwart! Arthur is president!" Guiteau shouted when he fired the fatal shots. He meant that the new president was none other than Conkling's longtime ally, Vice President Chester A. Arthur. The deranged Guiteau expected Arthur to free him from prison and reward him for his patriotic act.

Once in office, however, Chet Arthur, recently the "prince of spoilsmen," proved to be an able and uncorrupt president who signed the first law to limit a party's use of government jobs for political purposes.

Civil-Service Reform

The Pendleton Act of 1883 established the Civil Service Commission, a three-man bureau that was empowered to draw up and administer examinations that applicants for some low-level government jobs were required to pass before they were hired. Once in these civil-service jobs, employees could not be fired simply because the political party to which they belonged lost the presidency.

At first, only 10 percent of 131,000 government workers were protected by civil service. But the Pendleton Act also empowered the president to add job classifications to the civil-service list at his discretion.

TURKEY

Roscoe Conkling was a physical-culture enthusiast. He exercised daily and was extremely proud of his exceptional physique. This provided his enemy, James G. Blaine, with an easy target when he described Conkling's "haughty disdain, his grandiloquent swell, his majestic, over-powering turkey-gobbler strut."

Ironically, because the presidency changed party hands every four years between 1880 and 1896, each incumbent's desire to protect his own appointees in their jobs—a violation of the *spirit* of civil-service reform—led by the end of the century to a fairly comprehensive civil-service system.

After the Democrat Grover Cleveland was elected in November 1884, but before he took office in March 1885, outgoing President Chester Arthur protected a number of Republican government employees by adding their jobs to the civil-service list. Cleveland did the same thing for Democratic government workers in 1888, Benjamin Harrison for Republicans in 1892, and Cleveland again for Democrats in 1896. By 1900, 40 percent of the federal government's 256,000 employees held civil-service positions. About 30 percent of government clerks were women, an unlikely proportion at a time when jobs were given out in order to win votes.

Another provision of the Pendleton Act was the abolition of the assessment system. That is, the parties were forbidden to insist that those of their members who held government positions "donate" a percentage of their salaries for political campaign chests each election year. Until the presidency of Benjamin Harrison

ORDINARY PEOPLE

Presidents were not so remote and sheltered from the people in the late nineteenth century, as Garfield's assassination shows. When he was shot, the president of the United States was waiting for a train on a public platform.

An incident that involved Rutherford B. Hayes after he left the White House illustrates the point more amusingly. While attending a G.A.R. encampment, Hayes was stopped by a policeman, who brusquely pulled him back to a park pathway, and gave him a finger-shaking lesson because he was walking on the grass. Likewise, President Grant, who never lost his love for fast horses, was written a ticket by a Washington officer for speeding.

(1889–93), the professional politicians were at a loss as to how to replace these revenues. Harrison's Postmaster General, John Wanamaker, came up with the solution. He levied "contributions" on big businessmen who had an interest, direct or ideological, in Republican victory at the polls. This method, with the Democrats finding their share of big business support, and later drawing from the treasuries of labor unions, remained the chief means of financing national political campaigns until the 1970s.

Honest Chet Arthur

Chester A. Arthur may have been president illegally. Enemies said he was not born in Fairfield, Vermont, as he claimed, but in a cabin a few miles north—in Canada. However that may have been, the urbane and elegant Arthur, resplendent in his furs and colorful waistcoats compared to the gray dour look of the Republicans around him, did a good job in the White House.

Arthur wanted a second term. He tried to mend fences with the Stalwarts by twice offering Roscoe

Chester A. Arthur, Collector of the Port of New York from 1871 to 1878, and later, James A. Garfield's successor as president.

Conkling (a superb lawyer) a seat on the Supreme Court. He tried to woo the Half-Breeds by deferring to Secretary of State James G. Blaine's judgment in foreign affairs. Blaine would have none of it and resigned from the cabinet. With Conkling's political career in eclipse, Blaine easily won the Republican nomination for the presidency, again at Chicago, in the summer of 1884.

1884: *Blaine Versus Cleveland*

Blaine expected to win the election as well. As usual, New York State seemed to be the key to victory, and Blaine believed that he would run more strongly there than most Republicans. Some old Liberal Republicans, now known as Mugwumps (an Algonkian word for "big chief," a reference to their self-righteous pomposity), had deserted the party, announcing that the Democratic candidate, Grover Cleveland, was the more honest man. But Blaine expected to make up this defection and more by winning the Irish vote, which usually did not go Republican. He was popular in the Irish-American community because, in an era when Republican leaders frequently disdained the Catholic Church, Blaine had Catholic relatives. Moreover, for reasons of his own, Blaine liked to "twist the lion's tail," taunt the British, the ancestral enemy in many unsmiling Irish eyes. Finally, news broke that seemed a bonus: it was revealed that while he was a lawyer in Buffalo, Grover Cleveland had fathered an illegitimate child. The stringent sexual code of the period seemed to dictate that such a libertine should not be president.

Cleveland nimbly neutralized the morality issue by publicly admitting the folly of his youth and explaining that he had tried to make amends by financially supporting the child. Indeed, the Democrats turned the scandal to their advantage when they argued that if Cleveland had been indiscreet in private life, he had an exemplary record in public office, whereas Blaine, who was admirable as a husband and family man, had engaged in several dubious stock deals as a congressman from Maine. Put Cleveland into public office where he shined, they said, and return Blaine to the private life that he richly adorned.

How Little Things Decide Great Elections

Just a few days before the election, disaster struck the Blaine campaign. The confident candidate made the mistake of dining lavishly with a group of millionaires in Delmonico's, the most regal restaurant in New York City. It was not a good idea when he wanted the votes of poor men. Before another group, he ignored the statement of a Presbyterian minister, Samuel Burchard, who denounced the Democrats as the party of

Grover Cleveland was the only Democratic president of the late nineteenth century, elected in 1884 and 1892. He was defeated in 1888.

"rum, romanism, and rebellion," that is, of the saloon, the Roman Catholic Church, and southern secession.

This was pretty ordinary stuff in Republican oratory of the period, but Blaine was not fighting the campaign with an ordinary strategy. He was wooing Irish-American votes, and the Irish were sensitive about their Catholic religion. When Democratic newspapers plastered the insult "romanism" across their front pages, Blaine rushed to express his sincere distaste for this kind of bigotry and to explain that had he heard Burchard's words, he would have called him on them. But the damage was done. The Irish voters trundled back into the Democratic column and blizzards upstate snowed many Republican voters in. New York State and the presidency went to Grover Cleveland.

In 1888, four years later, Cleveland was undone in his bid for reelection by a similarly trivial incident. A Republican newspaperman, pretending to be an Englishman who was a naturalized American citizen, wrote to the British ambassador in Washington asking which of the two candidates, Cleveland or Benjamin

Harrison of Indiana, would be the better president from the British point of view. Foolishly, the ambassador replied that Cleveland seemed to be better disposed toward British interests. The Republican press immediately labeled Cleveland the British candidate. Thousands of Irish Democrats in New York, who were reflexively hostile to anything or anyone the British favored, voted Republican and helped give that swing state to Harrison.

This sort of folderol, and the color and excitement of political rallies, seemed to make the difference in an era when the two parties were so evenly balanced. Unlike late twentieth-century Americans, who are flooded with entertainment from a dozen media and to whom elections are just one show among many, late nineteenth-century Americans enjoyed politics as a major diversion. They flocked to rallies in numbers almost unknown today in order to hear brass bands, swig lemonade or beer, and listen to speeches that were more show than statement of principle.

ISSUES

Principles and issues did play a part in late nineteenth-century politics. Within the Republican party, a shrinking minority of leaders tried to revive the party's commitment to protecting the welfare of southern blacks until as late as 1890. When President Grant tried to seize Santo Domingo in 1870, he was frustrated by the resistance of senators from his own party who were impelled by old antiexpansionist prejudices.

However, both episodes illustrate the fact that differences of principle and opinion were more likely to lie *within* the parties rather than to distinguish one from the other. The political party's business was to win power. Having cooperated in that effort, politicians lined up on issues with only casual or self-serving nods toward the organization to which they belonged.

Even the question of the tariff, the nearest thing to an issue that distinguished Republicans from Demo-

crats, found members of both parties on each side. The level at which import duties were set could inspire orators to sweating, thumping, prancing paroxysms of holy passion. But their position on the issue, low tariff or high protective tariff, depended on the place their constituents occupied in the economy, not on the party to which they belonged, an abstract principle, or even social class.

The Tariff

With the exception of the growers of a few crops that needed protection from foreign producers—like Louisiana's sugar cane planters—farmers inclined to favor a low tariff. Corn, wheat, cotton, and livestock were so cheaply produced in the United States that American farmers were able to undersell local growers of the same crops in large parts of Europe and Asia—if other countries did not levy taxes on American crops in response to high American duties on the goods that those countries shipped to the United States. Moreover, low duties on imported manufactured goods meant lower prices on the commodities that consumers of manufactured goods, such as farmers, had to buy.

The interest of agriculturalists in keeping import duties down meant that the Democratic party, with its powerful southern agrarian contingent, was generally the low-tariff party. However, Republican congressmen representing rural areas also voted for lower rates.

While industrialists, who wanted to protect their factories from foreign competition, were generally Republican and set the high-tariff tone of that party, equally rich and powerful railroad owners and bankers often supported lower duties. Some remained contentedly within the Republican party in the company of other wealthy capitalists; others—the grand financier August Belmont, for example—were Democrats. As far as bankers like Belmont were concerned, the more goods being shunted about the country the better, no matter whether they were foreign or domestic in origin. Railroaders had an added incentive to support a low tariff. They were huge consumers of steel for rails, which was one of the commodities that received the most protection.

In the late nineteenth century, high-tariff interests had their way. After bobbing up and down from a low of 40 percent (by no means a "low" tariff) to a high of 47 percent, rates were increased to 50 percent in the McKinley Tariff of 1890. That is, on the average, an imported item was slapped with a tax that was equivalent to half of its value.

When a depression followed quickly on the act, Grover Cleveland and the Democrats campaigned against the McKinley rates and won the election of 1892. But the tariff that Congress prepared, the Wilson-Gorman bill, lowered duties by only 10.1 percent—to a level of 39.1 percent of the value of imports. This rate was good enough for Cleveland's supporters in commerce and finance, but too high for the farmers who had voted for him. The president's rather wishy-washy way out of his quandary encapsulates the fact that tough issues were intra-party problems, not questions that divided the two parties. Cleveland did not sign the Wilson-Gorman bill; he did not veto it; he let it become law by ignoring it. When the head of a party divided on an issue, the president had to play to both sides.

Money

The issue that would, in the 1890s, shatter the political equilibrium of the 1870s and 1880s was money. The question was: what should be the basis of the circulating currency in America's rapidly expanding economy? Should it be gold and paper money redeemable in that metal from the bank that issued the note? Or should the supply of money be monitored and regulated by the government in such a way as to adjust to changing economic needs?

The controversy had its roots in the Civil War. In 1862, in order to help finance the war effort, the Union government authorized the printing of about $450 million in paper money that was *not* redeemable in gold. The greenbacks, so called because they were printed in green ink instead of gold on the obverse, were accepted at face value by the federal government. That is, their value in payment of taxes or other obligations was established in the law.

As long as the war went badly and the government's word was of dubious value, individuals involved in private transactions insisted on discounting the greenbacks, redeeming them in gold at something less than face value. Even after the war was won, bankers remained suspicious of any paper money that was not redeemable in gold. The Secretaries of the Treasury,

who shared the conservative views of the bankers, determined to retire the greenbacks. When the notes flowed into the Treasury in payment of taxes, they were destroyed and were not replaced by new bills.

The result was deflation: a decline in the amount of money in circulation and, therefore, an increase in the value of gold and of paper money that was redeemable in gold. Prices dipped; so did wages. It took less to buy a sack of flour or a side of bacon than it had when the greenbacks had flowed in profusion. That meant that the farmer who grew the wheat and slopped the hogs received less for his efforts.

Farmers, who were usually in debt, were hit hardest by deflation. They had borrowed heavily to increase their acreage and to purchase machinery when the greenbacks had been abundant and prices therefore high. After the Treasury began to retire the greenbacks, the farmers found themselves obligated to repay these loans in money that was more valuable and more difficult to get. For example, a $1,000 mortgage taken out on a farm during the 1860s represented 1,200 bushels of grain. By the 1880s, when a farmer might still be paying off his debt, $1,000 represented 2,300 bushels.

The Greenback Labor Party

Protesting the retirement of the greenbacks as a policy that enriched banker-creditors at the expense of producer-debtors, farmers formed the Greenback Labor party in 1876. In an effort to convince industrial wage-workers that their interests also lay in an abundant money supply, the party chose as its presidential candidate Peter Cooper, New York philanthropist and an exemplary, popular employer.

Cooper made a poor showing, but in the congressional race of 1878, the Greenbackers elected a dozen congressmen, and some Republicans and Democrats rushed to back their inflationary policy. However, President Hayes's monetary policy was as conservative as Grant's had been, and in 1879, retirement of the greenbacks proceeded apace. In 1880, the Greenback Labor ticket, led by a Civil War general from Iowa, James B. Weaver, won 309,000 votes, denying Garfield a popular majority but, once again, failing to affect policy.

In 1884, Benjamin J. Butler led the Greenbackers one more time, but received only one-third of the votes that Weaver had won in 1880. The demand to inflate the currency was not dead. Indeed, within a decade the structure of American politics was turned upside down and inside out because of it. But the greenbacks were gone. Just as, after all the fuss and fury had died down, industrialists had their way on the tariff, banking interests got the money policy they wanted. When political parties are not built around principles and issues, the best organized interest groups within the parties usually prevail.

POLITICS IN THE CITIES

By 1896, silver had replaced the greenbacks as the talisman of those Americans who wanted to inflate the nation's money supply. Both the Republican and Democratic parties were shaken by a fierce debate in which gold and silver became sacred symbols (see p. 566–67). The political atmosphere was religious, evangelical, even fanatical. "Gold bugs" and "free silverites" both believed they were engaged in a holy war against the other in which there could be no compromise, no quarter. The political equilibrium of the 1870s and 1880s were shattered, not to mention the minor role issues had played in distinguishing the parties.

The Democratic party convention of 1896 was the most tumultuous since the party of Jefferson and Jackson destroyed itself at Charleston in 1860. Richard Croker, the leader of New York City's Democrats, was bewildered by the fury in which the members of his party were running about, arguing, shaking their fists. He listened to an agitated gold versus silver debate and impatiently shook his head. He could not understand what the fuss was about. As far as he was concerned, gold and silver were both money, and he was all for both kinds.

The Political Machine

Urban politics in the late nineteenth century resembled national politics in some ways. Issues were of secondary importance. What counted first was winning elections. The big city political party existed, like a business, for the benefit of those who "owned" it. The technique of election victory, therefore, was the profession of the political leader. His skill and willingness

"WHO STOLE THE PEOPLE'S MONEY?" — DO TELL . N.Y.TIMES.   'TWAS HIM.

Everyone blames everyone else for the looting of New York City's treasury. William Marcy "Boss" Tweed is at left. Notice the Irish stereotypes at right.

to work for "the company," and his productivity in delivering votes, determined how high he rose in an organization as finely tuned as any corporation.

The chairman of the board of the urban political company was "the boss." He was by no means necessarily the mayor, who was often a respectable "front man." The boss coordinated the complex activities of the machine. Voters had to be aroused by the same sort of emotional appeals and hoopla that sustained national political campaigns. The machine was expected to provide small material incentives to more demanding citizens comparable to the G.O.P.'s pensions program. The party activists who worked to get the voters out to the polls (the company's "employees"), and kept them happy between elections, were "paid" with patronage and pork courtesy of the city treasury. Control of the municipal treasury was the purpose of politics, not the service of principles or the implementation of a program.

"You are always working for your pocket, are you not?" an investigator into government corruption asked Richard Croker, thinking to embarrass him. Croker snapped back, "All the time, the same as you." On another occasion, he told the writer, Lincoln Steffens, "Politics is business, and reporting—journalism, doctoring—all professions, arts, sports—everything is business." Candor as blunt as the prow of a ferryboat was one quality that distinguished municipal politicians from national politicians in the late nineteenth century. Another was that the control of cities that many political machines exercised was so nearly absolute that profiteering in government sometimes took the form of blatant thievery.

The Profit Column

The political machine in power controlled law enforcement. In return for regular cash payments, politicians winked at the operations of illegal businesses: unlicensed saloons, gambling houses, opium dens, brothels, even strong-arm gangs. "Bathhouse" John Coughlan and "Hinkey-Dink" Kenna, Chicago's "Gray Wolves," openly collected tribute from the kings and queens of Chicago vice at an annual ball.

The political machine in power peddled influence to anyone willing to make a purchase. Although he was no lawyer, William Marcy Tweed of New York, the first of the great city bosses, was on Cornelius Vanderbilt's payroll as a "legal adviser." What the Commodore was hiring was the rulings of judges who belonged to Tweed's organization. In San Francisco after the turn of the century, Boss Abe Ruef would hold office hours on designated nights at an elegant French restaurant; purchasers of influence filed in be-

---

THE ONLY WAY

A. Oakey Hall, mayor of New York under the Tweed Ring, explained why a machine was necessary: "This population is too hopelessly split up into races and factions to govern it under universal suffrage, except by the bribery of patronage, or corruption."

---

tween appetizer and entrée, entrée and roast, and made their bargains.

Kickbacks and Sandbagging

The rapid growth of cities in the late nineteenth century provided rich opportunities for kickbacks on contracts awarded by city governments. In New York, Central Park was a gold mine of padded contracts. The most notorious swindle of all was the New York County Courthouse, a $600,000 building that cost taxpayers $13 million to erect. Plasterers, carpenters, plumbers, and others who worked on the building had standing orders to bill the city two and three and more times what they actually needed to make a reasonable profit and kick back half the padding to Tammany Hall, the "men's club" that controlled the Democratic party in New York. For example, forty chairs and three tables cost the city $179,000. The most intriguing item was "Brooms, etc.," which cost $41,190.95.

Then it was possible to do business directly with the city at exorbitant prices. Boss Tweed was part owner of the stationery and printing companies that supplied and serviced the New York City government at ridiculous prices—$5 for each bottle of ink, for example.

Another technique for getting rich in public office was called "sandbagging." It worked particularly well in dealing with traction companies, the streetcar lines that needed city permission to lay tracks on public streets. It goes without saying that it took bribes to get such contracts in machine-run cities. Moreover, the most corrupt aldermen, such as Coughlan and

---

ABOVE THE ISSUES

The classic instance of a big-city machine politician avoiding issues occurred at a Fourth of July picnic. New York City boss Charles F. Murphy refused to sing "The Star-Spangled Banner" along with the crowd. When a reporter asked Murphy's aide for an explanation, the aide replied, "He didn't want to commit himself."

Kenna in Chicago, would grant a line the rights to lay tracks on only a few blocks at a time; thus the Chicago "Traction King," Charles T. Yerkes, would be back for a further franchise at an additional cost.

Another variety of sandbagging involved threatening an existing trolley line with competition on a nearby parallel street. Rather than have their traffic decline by half, traction companies coughed up the money to prevent new construction.

Political Patronage City Style

It was not necessary to break the law in order to profit from public office. A well-established member of a political machine could expect to be on the city payroll for jobs that did not really exist. In one district of New York City where there were four water pumps for fighting fires, the city paid the salaries of twenty pump inspectors. Probably, none of them ever looked at the pumps. Their purpose was to keep the political machine in power at taxpayer expense.

It was possible to hold several meaningless city jobs simultaneously. Cornelius Corson, who kept his ward safe for the New York Democratic party from an office in his saloon, was on the books as a court clerk at $10,000 a year, as chief of the Board of Elections at $5,000 a year, and as an employee of four other municipal agencies at $2,500 a year per job. Another ward boss, Michael Norton, held city jobs that paid him $50,000 a year.

This was a munificent income in the late nineteenth century, but the bosses at the top of the machine did much better. Altogether, the Tweed Ring, which controlled New York City for only a few years after the Civil War, looted the city treasury of as much as $200 million. (Nobody really knew for sure.) Tweed went to jail, but his chief henchman, Controller "Slippery" Dick Connolly, fled abroad with several million.

Richard Croker, head of Tammany Hall at the end of the century, retired to Ireland a millionaire. Timothy "Big Tim" Sullivan also rose from extreme poverty to riches as well as adulation; when he died as the result of a streetcar accident, 25,000 people attended his funeral.

Staying in Business

Big Tim's sendoff illustrates that despite their generally obvious profiteering, machine politicians stayed in office. Although few of them were above stuffing ballot boxes or marching gangs of "repeaters" from one polling place to the next, they won most elections fairly; the majority of city voters freely chose them over candidates who pledged to govern honestly.

The machines acted as very personalized social services among a hard-pressed people. During the bitter winter of 1870, Boss Tweed spent $50,000 on coal that was dumped by the dozens of tons at street corners in the poorest parts of the city. Tim Sullivan gave away 5,000 turkeys every Christmas. It was the duty of every block captain to report when someone died, was born, was making a First Holy Communion in the Catholic Church, or was celebrating a Bar Mitzvah in the Jewish synagogue. The sensible ward boss had a gift delivered.

Ward bosses brought light into dismal lives by throwing parties. In 1871, Mike Norton treated his constituents to 100 kegs of beer, 50 cases of champagne, 20 gallons of brandy, 10 gallons of gin, 200 gallons of chowder, 50 gallons of turtle soup, 36 hams, 4,000 pounds of corned beef, and 5,000 cigars.

Boss Richard Croker of New York's Tammany Hall made enough money in politics to own thoroughbred Irish racehorses. Here he poses with his trainer.

NICKNAMES

The Irish-Americans were resourceful (and cruel) makers of nicknames. Tammany Boss Timothy Sullivan liked "Big Tim" but he had another name that hearkened back to his modest beginnings. People called him "Dry Dollar" Sullivan because, as a young man, he had awakened drunk behind a saloon, found a federal tax stamp on a beer barrel, and was found trying to dry it out. He thought it was a dollar bill.

HOW THEY SPOKE, HOW THEY LISTENED

George Washington was no orator. Other delegates to both the Continental Congress and the Constitutional Convention are almost apologetic in their strident assertions that his contributions lay in other realms. Contemporaries compared him to Cincinattus. No one ever mentioned Cicero.

John Adams was a passionate courtroom lawyer, but his platform manner was fussy and irritable.

Thomas Jefferson's conversation sparkled like his prose. However, Jefferson suffered from a lisp and was painfully sensitive to his impediment. He hated to speak before a crowd. He mumbled his famous first inaugural address so incoherently that many people in the small chamber understood nothing until they had a chance to read it in print.

James Madison cut an even weaker figure on a podium. Small in stature, crinkled of face by the time he became president in 1809, Madison was also a hypochondriac, constantly complaining of aches, pains, and imminent collapse.

He did not have to beg off speaking to Congress. Washington had set the precedent of delivering presidential messages in writing. Not until 1913, when Woodrow Wilson, confident of his presence after a lifetime in the lecture-hall, strode into the Capital, would a president actually address a "State of the Union" speech to Congress.

The fact is, mastery of oratory was not the road to the White House. The two finest orators of the antebellum period, Henry Clay and Daniel Webster—both Whigs—never became president. Inferior, long-winded speeches delivered out of doors in extreme weather killed the two Whigs who did, William Henry Harrison and Zachary Taylor. (Harrison's was a suicide; he gave the longest and perhaps the most pompous inaugural address in presidential history during a frigid March storm; he died of pneumonia a month later.)

If Americans did not demand a silver tongue in their chief executives, the paintings of George Caleb Bingham, the perennial success of histrionic revivalist preachers, Ralph Waldo Emerson's long and lucrative career as a lecturer, and the inscription of "Rhetoric" and "Declamation" in every college curriculum remind us that Americans did love to hear others hold forth in public.

In the late nineteenth century they liked their political oratory "spread-eagle." Memorial Day, Confederate Day, the Fourth of July—all were occasions in city and country alike of long, gymnastic disquisitions on American heroism, sacrifice, and greatness.

The orator who did not run on for hours was not doing his job. (Lincoln's Gettysburg Address was faulted for its brevity.) The orator who did not work up a sweat flailing the air, shaking his fist, and beating his breast was a cold fish. (Armless Republican Lucius P. Fairchild had a technique by which he could release the empty sleeve of his coat—he had lost an arm in the Civil War—at climactic moments in damning Democrats; socialist Eugene V. Debs would fall to his knees in his revolutionary maledictions.) The orator who did not lace his speeches with allusions from the Bible, the classics, modern literature, the Declaration of Independence, was accounted superficial.

Americans of the late nineteenth century also wanted to be told, over and over, the stories of Concord Bridge, Cowpens, New Orleans, Vicksburg, Grant Before Richmond. They would even sit still to hear a politician explain—perhaps slyly, perhaps without shame—why his own august behind would honor the chair of Washington, Jefferson, Jackson, Lincoln.

And yet, with the possible exception of Benjamin Harrison, none of the presidents of the late nineteenth century were very good at pleading for themselves or some other grand old cause. In 1896, when the Republicans were faced with an opponent who could mesmerize an audience, William Jennings Bryan, party leader Mark Hanna instructed his candidate, William McKinley, to stay at home in Canton, Ohio. The Republicans contrasted McKinley's dignity with the unseemly behavior of his rival, rushing about the country *chasing* the presidency.

Nevertheless, Mark Hanna also made sure that a corps of Republican tub-thumpers followed Bryan wherever he went! He understood American ambivalence in the matter of oratory. Americans loved a rip-roaring speech—but as entertainment; they wanted their presidents dignified. The lesson had been taught at the beginning of the era, in 1866, by President Andrew Johnson. Johnson was trained in the Tennessee hills school of oratory, as entertaining a method as there was. He returned heckler's vulgarity with vulgarity, insult with insult. "Giving 'em hell" had brought him a long way.

During a presidential speaking tour in 1866, however, when he fought a running battle with Radical Republican hecklers, his opponents shook their heads, sadly and loudly, at his lack of dignity. Some privately stated that Johnson's greatest asset as a politician, his mastery of bumptious stump-speaking, had as much to do with his destruction as a president as his policies.

The Verdict of the People, *detail of a painting by George Caleb Bingham.*

Ward bosses fixed up minor (and sometimes major) scrapes with the law. In control of the municipal government, the machines had jobs at their disposal, not only the phoney high-paying sinecures that the bosses carved up among themselves, but jobs that required real work and that unemployed men and women were grateful to have. Boss James McManes of Philadelphia had more than 5,000 positions at his disposal; the New York machine controlled four times that number. When the votes of these people were added to those of their grateful relatives and friends, the machine had a very nice political base with which to fight an election.

The Failure of the Goo-Goos

Not everyone brimmed with gratitude. The property-owning middle classes, which paid the bills with their taxes, periodically raised campaigns for Good Government—the bosses called them "Goo-Goos"—and sometimes won elections. The Tweed Ring's fall led to the election of a reform organization, and in 1894, even the powerful Richard Croker was displaced. Chicago's "Gray Wolves" were thrown out of city hall, and a major wave of indignation swept Abe Ruef and Mayor Eugene Schmitz out of power in San Francisco in 1906. But until the turn of the century, reform governments were generally short lived. The machines came back.

One political weakness of the Goo-Goos was that they did not offer an alternative to the informal social services that the machine provided. They believed instead that honest government was synonymous with very inexpensive government. Faced with their great material problems and inclined from their European backgrounds to think of government as an institution that one used or was used by, the immigrants preferred the machines.

Indeed, Goo-Goos often combined their attacks on political corruption with attacks on the new ethnic groups, not a ploy that was calculated to win many friends among recent immigrants. In the persons of the successful machine politicians, however, the ethnics could take a vicarious pleasure in seeing at least some Irishmen, Jews, Italians, Poles, or blacks making good in an otherwise inhospitable society.

Erin Go Bragh

"The natural function of the Irishman," said a wit of the period, "is to administer the affairs of the American city." In fact, a few bosses had other lineages: Cox of Cincinnati and Crump of Memphis were WASPs; Tweed was of Scottish descent; Ruef was Jewish; and Schmitz was German. But a list of nineteenth-century

---

VOTE EARLY, VOTE OFTEN

Because voter-registration methods were quite lax in the nineteenth century, it was not difficult to march a group of men from one precinct house to the next, voting them in each one. When Tim Sullivan was a low-level worker in the New York machine, he used this system with his "repeaters"—unemployed men who voted "early and often" for the price of a day's wages or a day's drinking money:

When you've voted 'em with their whiskers on, you take 'em to a barber shop and scrape off the chin fringe. Then you vote 'em again with the side lilacs and a mustache. Then to a barber again, off comes the sides and you vote 'em the third time with the mustache. If that ain't enough and the box can stand a few more ballots, clean off the mustache and vote 'em plain face.

---

machine politicians reads like a lineup of marchers in a St. Patrick's Day parade: Richard Connolly, "Honest" John Kelley, Richard Croker, George Plunkitt, Charles Murphy, and Tim Sullivan of New York; James McManes (unlike the others, a Republican) of Philadelphia; Christopher Magee and William Finn of Pittsburgh; Martin Lomasney of Boston.

The Irish were so successful in politics in part because they were the first of the large ethnic groups in the cities, and in part because they had been highly political in their homeland as a consequence of rule by Great Britain. Moreover, the Irish placed a high premium on eloquent oratory, which led naturally to politics, and, most important of all, the Irish spoke the English language, a headstart in the race to succeed over the other major immigrant groups of the late nineteenth century.

Ethnic Brokers

The primacy of the Irish did not mean that the New Immigrants were shut out of politics. On the contrary, the political machine lacked ethnic prejudice. If a

---

CITIZENSHIP

The New York machine naturalized newly arrived immigrants almost as soon as they stepped off the boat. The record day was October 14, 1868, when a Tweed judge swore in 2,109 new citizens, 3 a minute. One James Goff attested to the "good moral character" of 669 applicants. Two days later, Goff was arrested for having stolen a gold watch and two diamond rings.

---

ward became Italian and an Italian ward boss delivered the votes, he was welcomed into the organization and granted a share of the spoils commensurate with his contribution on election day. In many cities, while the police forces retained an Irish complexion, sanitation departments and fire departments often were highly Italian. After the turn of the century, it became the unwritten law among New York Democrats that nominations for the three top elective offices in the city (mayor, president of the city council, and controller) be divided among New York's three largest ethnic groups—Irish, Italians, and Jews. Later, with the arrival of Puerto Ricans and of blacks from the South, certain public offices were assigned to their leaders—for example, president of the borough of Manhattan to a black and political leadership of the borough of the Bronx to a Puerto Rican. Other cities worked out similar arrangements.

For Further Reading

Overviews and Classics

Vincent P. DeSantis, *The Shaping of Modern America, 1877–1916* (1973)

Matthew Josephson, *The Politicos, 1865–1896* (1938)

H. Wayne Morgan, *From Hayes to McKinley: National Party Politics, 1877–1896* (1969)

Valuable Special Studies

A. B. Callow, Jr., *The Tweed Ring* (1966)

Justus T. Doenecke, *The Presidencies of James A. Garfield and Chester A. Arthur* (1981)

J. R. Hollingsworth, *The Whirligig of Politics: The Democracy of Cleveland and Bryan* (1963)

Ari Hoogenboom, *Outlawing the Spoils: A History of the Civil Service Reform Movement, 1865–1883* (1961)

Morton Keller, *Affairs of State: Public Life in Late 19th Century America* (1977)

Paul Kleppner, *The Third Electoral System, 1852–1892* (1979)

J. Morgan Kousser, *The Shaping of Southern Politics* (1974)

Seymour Mandelbaum, *Boss Tweed's New York* (1965)

R. O. Marcus, *Grand Old Party: Political Structure in the Gilded Age, 1880–1896* (1971)

Samuel T. McSeveney, *The Politics of Depression: Political Behavior in the Northeast, 1893–1896* (1972)

Horace L. Merrill, *Bourbon Democracy of the Middle West* (1953)

Walter T. K. Nugent, *Money and American Society, 1865–1880* (1968)

D. J. Rothman, *Politics and Power: The United States Senate, 1869–1901* (1966)

John G. Sproat, *The Best Men: Liberal Reformers in the Gilded Age* (1968)

Tom E. Terrill, *The Tariff, Politics, and American Foreign Policy, 1874–1901* (1973)

Robert H. Wiebe, *The Search for Order* (1967)

Biographies and Autobiographies

Harry Barnard, *Rutherford B. Hayes and His America* (1954)

R. G. Caldwell, *Gentleman Boss: The Life of Chester A. Arthur* (1975)

D. B. Chidsey, *The Gentleman from New York: A Life of Roscoe Conkling* (1935)

David S. Muzzey, *James G. Blaine: A Political Idol of Other Days* (1934)

Allan Nevins, *Grover Cleveland: A Study in Courage* (1932)

Allan Peskin, *Garfield: A Biography* (1978)

28

Big Industry and Big Business

Economic Development in the Late Nineteenth Century

In 1876, the American people celebrated their nation's centennial. It was a hundred years since the Founding Fathers had pledged their lives, their fortunes, and their sacred honor to the causes of liberty and independence. The party was held in Philadelphia, where the Declaration was written and signed. The Centennial Exposition was a splendid show. Sprawling over the hills of Fairmount Park, housed in more than two hundred structures, it dazzled 10 million visitors with its displays of American history, ways of life, and products.

The emphasis was on the products and the processes for making them. The center of the fair was not the Declaration of Independence, but Machinery Hall, a building that covered twenty acres and housed the latest inventions and technological improvements: from typewriters and the telephone through new kinds of looms and lathes for factories to a variety of agricultural machines.

Towering above all the pulleys and belts, five times the height of a man, and weighing 8,500

Andrew Carnegie's steel plant at Homestead, Pennsylvania, was the largest in the world.

tons, was the largest steam engine ever built, the giant Corliss. Hissing, rumbling, chugging, and gleaming in enamel, nickel plate, brass, and copper, the monster powered every other machine in the building. It was the heart of the exposition. It was to the giant Corliss that President Ulysses S. Grant came in order to open the fair. When he threw the switch that set Machinery Hall in motion, he wordlessly proclaimed that Americans were not just free and independent, but they were hitching their future to machines that made and moved things more quickly, more cheaply, and in far greater quantities than, just a few years earlier, the most visionary inventor could have imagined.

The Corliss steam engine was the centerpiece of the Centennial Exposition of 1876. No larger steam engine was ever built.

A COUNTRY MADE FOR INDUSTRY

Between 1865 and 1900, the population of the United States more than doubled, from fewer than 36 million to 76 million people. The wealth of the American people grew even more rapidly than population. At the end of the Civil War, the annual production of goods was valued at $2 billion. It increased more than six times in 35 years, to $13 billion in 1900.

Even in 1860, the United States had been the fourth largest industrial nation in the world with more than 100,000 factories capitalized at $1 billion. But before the Civil War there was no doubt that the United States was primarily a farmer's country. More than 70 percent of the population lived on farms or in small farm towns. In 1860, scarcely more than 1 million people worked in industrial jobs. Because many of them were women and children who did not vote, factory workers were an insignificant political force, scarcely more important to policymakers than were blacks or Indians.

By 1876, this was rapidly changing. Only the next year, railroads proved to be so important to the country that a strike by railway workers shook the nation to its foundations. By 1900, $10 billion was invested in American factories, and 5 million people worked in industrial jobs. During the first years of the 1890s, the industrial production of the United States surpassed that of Great Britain to put the United States in first place in the world.

Riches in Capital and Labor

Viewed from the late twentieth century, this success story seems to have been as predestined as John Winthrop's soul. All the ingredients of industrial transformation were heaped upon the United States in an abundance that no other country has enjoyed. In contrast to the plight of undeveloped countries today, Americans were rich in capital and able to welcome money from abroad without losing control of their own destinies. Once the Union victory in the Civil War assured foreign investors that American government was stable and friendly to commercial and industrial interests, the pounds, guilders, and francs poured in. By 1900, over $3.4 billion in foreign wealth, the bulk of it from England, fueled the American economy. Thanks to investors from abroad, Americans had to divert only 11 to 14 percent of their national income into industrial growth, compared with 20 percent in Great Britain half a century earlier and in the Soviet Union some decades later. As a result, the experience of industrialization was far less painful in the New World than in the Old. Americans had to suffer less on behalf of the future.

America was also blessed in both the size and character of its labor force. The fecund and adaptable farm population provided a pool of literate and mechanically inclined people to fill the skilled jobs the new industry created. Unlike peasants of Asia and Europe, who were attached to an ancestral plot of ground and suspicious of unfamiliar ways, American farmers had always been quick to move on at opportunity's call. In the late nineteenth century, not only did the opportunity of the new industry beckon seductively, the labor-saving farm machinery that factories sent back to the farm made it possible for farm families actually to increase production of crops while their sons and daughters packed themselves off to the city.

During these same years, Europe's population underwent a spurt of growth with which the European economy could not keep pace. Cheap American food products undersold crops grown at home, helping to displace European peasants. They emigrated to the United States by the hundreds of thousands each year, filling the low-paying, unskilled jobs that native-born Americans found beneath them. At every level in the process of industrialization, the United States was provided a plenitude of clever hands and strong backs.

A Land of Plenty

No country has been so blessed with such varied and abundant natural resources as the United States: rich agricultural land producing cheap food; seemingly inexhaustible forests supplying lumber; deposits of gold, silver, semiprecious metals, and dross such as phosphates and gravel. Most important of all in the industrial age were huge stores of coal, iron, and petroleum.

The gray-green mountains of Pennsylvania, West Virginia, and Kentucky seemed to be made of coal, the indispensable fuel of the age of steam. In the Marquette range of Michigan was a mountain of iron ore 150 feet high. The Mesabi range of Minnesota, just west of the birdlike beak of Lake Superior, was opened in the 1890s to yield iron ore richer and in greater quantity than any other iron mining region in the world.

The United States had a huge, ready-made market for mass-produced goods in its constantly growing population. And with the growth of industry (and the political influence of the industrial capitalist class), government in the United States proved quick to respond to the needs of manufacturers.

"American Ingenuity"

So were inventors. "As the Greek sculpted, as the Venetian painted," wrote an English visitor to the Centennial Exposition, "the American mechanizes." Actually, the new invention that turned the most heads at the great fair, the telephone, was the brainchild of a Scot who came to the United States via Canada, Alexander Graham Bell. Millions of people

picked up the odd looking devices he had set up and, alternately amused and amazed, chatted with companions elsewhere in the room. Young men at the fair dropped a hint of what was to come by "ringing up" young ladies standing across from them, respectably striking up conversations that would have been unacceptable face to face without proper introductions.

It was probably true that only in the United States could Bell have parleyed his idea into the gigantic enterprise it became, the American Telephone and Telegraph Company. As a writer in the *Saturday Evening Post* at the end of the century put it,

the United States is the only country in the world in which inventors form a distinct profession. . . . With us, inventors have grown into a large class. Laboratories . . . have sprung up almost everywhere, and today there is no great manufacturing concern that has not in its employ one or more men of whom nothing is expected except the bringing out of improvements in machinery and methods.

The Telephone

Bell was a teacher of the deaf who, while perfecting a mechanical hearing aid, realized that if he linked two of the devices by wire, he could transmit voice over

New inventions such as the phonograph were sold through another new invention—the mail-order catalog.

Young women quickly monopolized the profession of telephone operator when Bell's companies found "boys" to be impudent and impolite.

distance. Unable to interest the communications giant Western Union in his telephone, he set up a pilot company in New York and the telephone seized on the American imagination. Rutherford B. Hayes put a telephone in the White House in 1878. By 1880, only four years after they first heard of the thing, 50,000 Americans were paying monthly fees to hear it jangle on their walls. By 1890, there were 800,000 phones in the United States; by 1900, 1.5 million. People in the tiniest hamlets knew all about "exchanges," "party lines," and bored, nasal-voiced "operators."

Many systems were useful only locally. But as early as 1892, the eastern and midwestern cities were connected by a long-distance network, and rambunctious little western desert communities noted in their directories that "you can now talk to San Francisco with ease from our downtown office." By making it possible to communicate two ways with no delay, the telephone was indispensable to business and, important to some entrepreneurs, it left no written records of dubious transactions.

The All-American Wizard of Menlo Park

An even more celebrated inventor than Bell was Thomas Alva Edison. Written off by his boyhood teachers as a dunce, Edison was, in fact, befuddled throughout life by people who pursued knowledge for

its own sake. He was the ultimate, practical American tinkerer who looked for a need—an opportunity to make money from it—and went to work. Despite an obnoxious personality, Edison became a folk hero because he approached invention in a no-nonsense all-American way. He said that genius was 1 percent inspiration and 99 percent perspiration. He took pride in his work, not his thoughts. With a large corps of assistants sweating away in his research and development laboratory in Menlo Park, New Jersey, he took out more than a thousand patents between 1876 and 1900.

Electric Light

Most of these patents were for improvements in existing processes. (He perfected a transmitter for Bell.) However, a few of Edison's inventions were seedbeds for wholly new industries: the storage battery, the motion-picture projector, and the phonograph. The most important of his inventions was the incandescent light bulb, a means of converting electricity into stable, controllable light.

Edison solved the theoretical principle of the electric bulb—the 1 percent inspiration—almost immediately. Within a vacuum in a translucent glass ball an electrically charged filament or thread should burn (that is, glow) indefinitely. The perspiration part was discovering the fiber that would do the job. In 1879, after testing 6,000 materials, Edison came up with one that burned for 40 hours, enough to make it practical. Before he patented the incandescent light bulb early the next year, Edison improved the filament enough to make it work for 170 hours.

The financier, J. P. Morgan, who loathed the telephone, was fascinated by Edison's invention. His house and bank were among the first structures illuminated by Edison. Morgan realized that many people disliked gas, the principal source of nighttime light. Although clean enough (unlike kerosene), gas could be dangerous. Hundreds of fires were caused when, in a moment of ignorance, forgetfulness, or drunkenness, people blew out the flame instead of turning off the gas. Hotel managers nervously plastered the walls of rooms with reminders that the lights were gas.

The incandescent bulb succeeded as dramatically as the telephone. From a modest start in New York in 1882 with about 80 customers, Edison's invention spread so quickly that by 1900, more than 3,000 towns and cities were electrically illuminated. Within a few more years, the gaslight disappeared, and the kerosene lantern survived only on farms and in the poorer sections of the cities.

No single electric company dominated the industry, as American Telephone and Telegraph controlled Bell's patents. Nevertheless, like the railroads, the great regional companies were loosely associated by

Inventor Thomas A. Edison at work in his laboratory.

CLOUDED CRYSTAL BALLS

The fabulous success of Americans in exploiting technology can obscure the fact that technological pioneers often faced massive resistance in selling their inventions, and often themselves failed to understand the potential of what they had done.

This has been vividly true in the communications field. Thus, in 1845, the Postmaster General rejected an opportunity to purchase the patent for the telegraph for $100,000 because "under any rate of postage that could be adopted, its revenues could [not] be made equal to its expenditures." Within a generation, a private telegraph company, Western Union, was one of the most profitable giants of American business. In 1876, Western Union's president, William Orton, turned down an opportunity to buy Alexander Graham Bell's telephone, saying "What use could this company make of an electrical toy?"

In 1907, a businessman told radio pioneer, Lee De Forest that "all the radio . . . apparatus that the country will ever need" could be put in a single room. In 1985 there were 500 million radio receivers in the United States. If they were spread out evenly throughout the country, no person, even in the wilderness of Alaska, would be more than 233 feet from the chatter of a disc jockey.

In 1926, De Forest himself said of television that while it was theoretically and technically workable, "commercially and financially I consider it an impossibility, a development of which we need waste little time dreaming." As for the phonograph, its inventor Thomas Edison said it was "not of any commercial value." Today—every day in the United States— Americans buy 50,000 TV sets (and throw out 20,000 old ones). The record industry manufactures 574,000 record albums daily, 342,000 "singles," and imports another 66,000 disks.

interlocking directorates and the influence of the investment banks. Edison, a worse businessman than scholar, saw most of his profit go to backers like Morgan. He ended his working life as an employee of mammoth General Electric, the corporate issue of his inventive genius.

The Problem of Bigness

George Westinghouse became a millionaire from his invention of the air brake for railroad trains. By equipping every car in a train with brakes, operated from a central point by pneumatic pressure, Westinghouse solved the problem of stopping long strings of railroad cars. Not only did his air brake save thousands of lives, but it led to bigger profits for railroads by making longer trains possible.

Well established, Westinghouse turned his inventive genius to electricity and capitalized on Edison's stubborn resistance to alternating current. Direct current served very well over small areas. (It is still the common kind of power in Europe.) But direct current could not be transmitted over long distances. By perfecting a means to transmit AC, Westinghouse leapt ahead of his competitor by fully utilizing massive natural sources of power at isolated places such as Niagara Falls.

Like Bell, Westinghouse's invention confronted the single impediment Americans faced in their drive toward massive industrial development. The very vastness of the country was an impediment as well as a blessing. The United States spanned a continent that was dissected by rivers, mountains, and deserts into regions as large as the other industrial nations of the time. If geography had had the last word, the United States would have remained a patchwork of distinct manufacturing regions in which small factories produced goods largely for the people of the vicinity alone. Indeed, this is a fair description of manufacturing in the United States through the period of the Civil War.

THE RAILROAD IGNITES A REVOLUTION

The steam railroad conquered America's awesome geography. With its funnel-shape smokestack, piercing whistle, and tracks that could go almost anywhere—"two streaks of rust and a right of way"—the steam-powered locomotive made it possible for Pittsburgh steelmakers to bring together the coal of Scranton and the iron of Michigan as if both minerals were found just across the county line. Thanks to the railroad, the great flour mills of Minneapolis could scoop up the cheap spring wheat of the distant Northwest, grind it into flour, and put their trademarked sacks into every cupboard in the country.

Because so many western railroads found their way into Chicago, the Windy City quickly eclipsed river-based (and river-bound) Cincinnati as "hog butcher to the world" and the nation's dresser of beef. Livestock fattened on rangeland a thousand miles away rolled bawling into Chicago in rickety railroad cars and then rolled out—packed in cans, barrels, and refrigerator cars—to the east coast and from there around the world.

Early Chaos

By 1865, the United States was already the world's premier railway country with about 35,000 miles of track. With a few exceptions, however, individual lines were short, serving only the hinterlands of the

Chicago's proximity to major railroads helped make it the beef capital of the United States.

cities in which they terminated. In the former Confederacy, there were 400 railroad companies with an average track length of only 40 miles each. It was possible to ship a cargo between St. Louis and Atlanta by any of 20 routes. Competing for the business in cutthroat rate wars, not a single southern line was financially secure.

Few lines actually linked up with one another. Goods to be shipped over long distances, and therefore on several lines, had to be unloaded (hand labor added to costs), carted across terminal towns by horse and wagon (another bottleneck), and reloaded onto another train. No two of the six railroads that ran into Richmond shared a depot. Before the Civil War, Chicago and New York were linked by rail on the map, but a cargo going the entire distance had to be unloaded and reloaded six times.

Early railroaders actually encouraged inefficiency in order to discourage takeovers by companies interested in consolidation. They deliberately built in odd gauges (the distance between rails) so that only their own locomotives and rolling stock could run on their tracks. As little as two feet in mountainous areas, the distance between rails ran to five feet in the South. Until 1880, the important Erie Railroad clung to a monstrous six-foot gauge. The Illinois Central, third largest railroad, employed two different gauges.

Lack of coordination among railroads presented shippers and passengers with another headache. Each railway company scheduled its trains according to the official time in its headquarters city and local time varied even in cities just a few miles apart. When it was noon in Washington, D.C., it was 12:24 P.M. in Baltimore, 70 miles away. The Washington passenger who tried to catch a 12:00 Baltimore and Ohio train in Washington might discover that his watch was right but he was nearly half an hour too late to make the trip that day. In the train station in Buffalo, which served the New York Central and the Michigan Southern, three clocks were necessary: one for each railroad, and one for local time, which was different yet. In the Pittsburgh station there were six clocks.

The Consolidators

The advantages of long, integrated railway systems were too great for this chaos to endure indefinitely. Motivated by greed, but also by a desire to bring technological and economic order to transportation, J. Edgar Thomson of the Pennsylvania Railroad, and others like him, secretly purchased stock in small lines until he had control of them, drove other competitors out of business in ruthless rate wars, and built the "Pennsy" ever westward from New York, Philadelphia, and Pittsburgh (which the Pennsy practically owned) to Chicago and connections with lines that ran to the Pacific. All along the main line, feeders tapped the surrounding country.

Thomson was all business, a no-nonsense efficiency expert with little celebrity outside railroad circles. The founder of New York Central, the Pennsylvania's chief

rival in the Northeast, was the more colorful Cornelius Vanderbilt, who began his working life as a ferryman in New York City's crowded harbor. It was a rough business, no place for a milquetoast. Driven to destroy his competitors, the Commodore, as Vanderbilt styled himself (dressing in a mock naval uniform), fired the cannon that sank more than one competitor's harbor barge and negotiated many a contract with a stout club.

Vanderbilt gave up brawling as his shipping empire and responsibilities grew, but he was as tough and unscrupulous behind a broad oak desk as he had been at the tiller of a ferry. Once, when a reporter suggested that he had broken the law in a conflict with a rival, Vanderbilt snapped back gruffly, "What do I care about the law. Hain't I got the power?"

He had, and he used it masterfully to crush competition. By the time of the Civil War, Vanderbilt had a near-monopoly of New York harbor commerce. He even controlled the business that hauled New York City's monumental daily production of horse manure to farms in Staten Island. Vanderbilt's waterborne transportation empire led him naturally into moving the commerce of America's greatest city overland, too.

The Commodore was never quite respectable. His rough-and-tumble origins resonated in his wharf-rat language. The mention of his name caused ladies and gentlemen of genteel New York society to shudder—for a while. Because he said out loud what other businessmen did quietly—that ethics and social responsibility did not always make good business—he was an easy target for moralists. Vanderbilt could not have cared less. Like many of the great capitalists of the

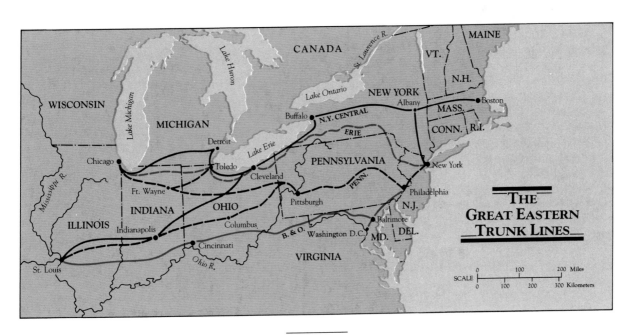

era, he regarded his fortune—$100 million when he died—as adequate justification for what he did.

The Pirates of the Rails

Compared to another breed of early railroader, the careers of men like Thomson and Vanderbilt can be justified very easily. In addition to making millions for themselves, Thomson and Vanderbilt built transportation systems of inestimable social value. The Pennsy was famous for safe roadbeds in an age of frequent, horrendous railroad accidents. The New York Central pioneered the use of steel rails and was equipped with the life-saving Westinghouse air brake while other lines halted (or did not halt) their trains mechanically. The Commodore's son and heir, William Vanderbilt, was best known for saying "The public be damned!" but he also played a major part in standardizing the American gauge at the present 4 feet, 8½ inches.

In contrast, some early railroaders simply took, making their fortunes by destroying what others had built.

The most famous of them were the unlikely trio that owned the Erie Railroad and succeeded in the even more unlikely, bilking Cornelius Vanderbilt.

Daniel Drew was a pious Methodist. He knew much of the Bible by heart, but put a very liberal interpretation on the verse in Exodus that said "Thou shalt not steal."

James Fisk, only 33 years old in 1867, was another sort altogether. No Bible for Jubilee Jim; he was a stout, jolly extrovert who fancied gaudy clothes and jewelry, tossed silver dollars at street urchins, and caroused openly in New York's gaslit restaurants and cabarets with showgirls from the vaudeville stage who were then considered little better than prostitutes. (One of them, Josie Mansfield, was his undoing; in 1872, Fisk was murdered by another one of her suitors.)

Jay Gould was a man of the shadows. When Drew went to church and Fisk slapped on cologne, Gould slipped home to his respectable Victorian family. Furtive in appearance as in fact, tight fisted, and close

THE GREAT RACE FOR THE WESTERN STAKES 1870

"Commodore" Cornelius Vanderbilt races James Fisk for control of the Erie R. R. in this 1870 cartoon. Newspaper readers followed the financial struggle as avidly as a fictional serial.

mouthed, Gould was probably the brains of the Erie Ring. Certainly he lasted the longest, becoming almost respectable and marrying a daughter to a European nobleman. But when it came to making money, Gould was at one with his partners in the Erie Gang: consequences of their piracy were beside the point.

The Erie War

In control of the Erie Railroad, the three men knew that Vanderbilt wanted their property and was secretly making large purchases of Erie stock. In order to separate him from as much of his fortune as possible, they watered Erie's stock; that is, they marketed shares in the dilapidated railroad far in excess of the Erie's real assets, from $24 million to $78 million in a few years when virtually nothing was done to improve the line. As Vanderbilt bought, they pocketed the money that should have gone into expanding the Erie's potential earning power.

The Commodore eventually went to the judges, whom he regularly bribed, to indict the trio. Forewarned, Drew, Fisk, and Gould escaped to New Jersey, where *they* owned the judges. (It was said in the streets that they rowed across the Hudson River in a boat filled with bank notes.)

A settlement was pieced together. In the meantime, the Erie amassed the worst accident record among world railroads and the company was devastated as a business. The Erie did not pay a dividend to its stockholders until the 1940s. For 70 years, what profits there were went to make up for the thievery of three men over six years. It would be a challenge to name Drew's, Fisk's, and Gould's contributions to American economic development.

THE TRANSCONTINENTAL LINES

In the Northeast and South, the creation of railroad systems meant consolidating short lines that already existed. This movement peaked during the 1880s, when the names of 540 independent railway companies disappeared from the business registers. In the West, railroad lines were extensive, integrated transportation systems from the start. Beyond the Mississippi, creating railroad systems was a matter of construction from scratch.

Public Finance

The great transcontinental railroads were built and owned by private companies but (with one exception: James J. Hill's Great Northern) financed by the public. The sparsity of population between the Mississippi Valley and the western states of California and Oregon

WATERING STOCK

Daniel Drew was notorious for watering the stock in companies he owned. A popular story about him had it that he had started young. As a young drover, Drew would bring his cattle to the New York market, where he would pen them up with salt and no water. The next morning, before he sold them, he would drive them into a creek, where the groaning beasts bloated themselves. At market, they were fat, sleek, and largely phony.

(and Washington after 1889) made it impossible to attract private investors. Railroad building was expensive. To lay a mile of track required bedding more than 3,000 ties in gravel and attaching 400 rails to them by driving 12,000 spikes. Having built that mile in Utah or Nevada at considerable expense, a railroader had nothing to look forward to but hundreds more miles of arid desert and uninhabited mountains.

With no customers along the way, there would be no profits and, without profits, no investors. The federal government had political and military interests in binding California and Oregon to the rest of the Union, and, in its land, the public domain, the government had the means with which to subsidize railroad construction.

The Pacific Railway Act of 1862 granted to two companies, the Union Pacific and the Central Pacific, a right of way of 200 feet wide between Omaha, Nebraska, and Sacramento, California. For each mile of track that the companies built, they were to receive, on either side of the tracks, ten alternate sections (square miles) of the public domain. The result was a checkerboard-pattern belt 40 miles wide, of which the U.P. and C.P. owned half the territory. (The rest was reserved for disposition under the Homestead Act or by direct government sale.)

The railroads sold their land, thus raising money for construction and creating customers. Or, just as im-

NARROW GAUGE

The short, narrow-gauge feeder lines that snaked into canyons and around mountains to bring out ore or logs were not so colossal as the great trunk lines, but the engineering required to build them was often more demanding. For example, the California Western that brought redwood logs down to the port of Fort Bragg, California, was only 40 miles long but never ran in a straightaway for as much as a mile, crossed 115 bridges, and went through one tunnel 1,122 feet long.

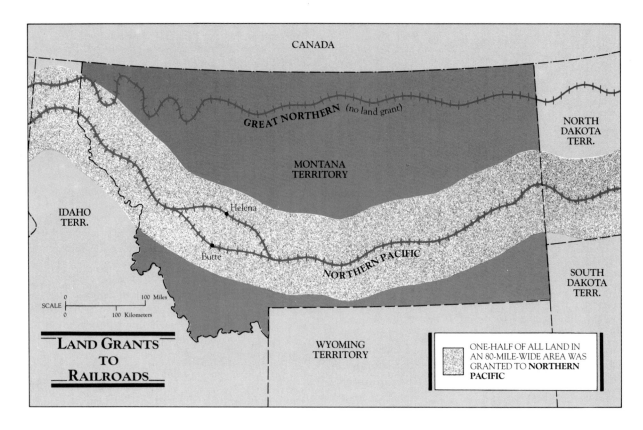

CANADA

GREAT NORTHERN *(no land grant)*

NORTH DAKOTA TERR.

MONTANA TERRITORY

IDAHO TERR.

Helena

Butte

NORTHERN PACIFIC

SOUTH DAKOTA TERR.

SCALE

0 — 100 Miles
0 — 100 Kilometers

LAND GRANTS TO RAILROADS

WYOMING TERRITORY

ONE-HALF OF ALL LAND IN AN 80-MILE-WIDE AREA WAS GRANTED TO **NORTHERN PACIFIC**

portant, they could use the vast real estate as collateral to borrow cash from banks. In addition, the government lent the two companies $16,000 per mile of track at bargain interest rates (and up to $48,000 in mountainous country).

The Romance of the Rails

As in the consolidation of eastern trunk lines, the business end of the transcontinental railroad was marred by crooked dealing as in the case of the Crédit Mobilier. However, the actual construction of the line was a heroic and glorious feat. The Union Pacific, employing thousands of Civil War veterans and newly immigrated Irish pick-and-shovel men, the "Paddies," laid over a thousand miles of track. The workers lived in shifting cities of tents and freight cars built like dormitories. They toiled by day, and bickered and brawled with gamblers, saloon keepers, and whores by night. Until the company realized that it was more efficient to hire professional gunmen as guards, the workers kept firearms with their tools in order to fight off those Indians who sensed that the iron horse meant the end of their way of life.

The builders of the Central Pacific had no trouble with Indians, but a great deal with terrain. Just outside Sacramento rose the majestic Sierra Nevada. There were passes in these mountains through which the line

could snake, but they were narrow and steep. Under the direction of a brilliant engineer, Theodore D. Judah, 10,000 Chinese chipped ledges into the slopes, built roadbeds of rubble in deep canyons, and bolted together trestles of timbers two feet square.

The snows of the Sierra proved to be a difficult problem, not only for the builders but for the eventual operation of the line. To solve it, the workers constructed snowsheds miles long. In effect, the transcontinental railroad crossed part of the Sierra Nevada indoors. Once on the Nevada plateau, the experienced C.P. crews built at a rate of a mile a day for an entire year.

LAND FOR SALE

In order to promote land that it owned in Nebraska, the Burlington and Missouri River Railroad offered a number of come-ons. A would-be purchaser had to pay his own fare to go out to look at the land, but the railroad would refund his fare if he bought. Once a landowner, he would receive a free railroad pass, as well as "long credit, low interest, and a twenty percent rebate for improvements." Prices were not extravagant. The Union Pacific disposed of pretty good Nebraska land at $3 to $5 an acre.

The U.P. and C.P. joined at Promontory Point, Utah, on May 10, 1869. The final days were hectic. Because the total mileage that each company constructed determined the extent of its land grants, the two companies raced around the clock. The record was set by the crews of the Central Pacific. They built 10.6 miles of more-or-less functional railroad in one day (just about the same length of track the company laid down during the whole of 1864). That involved bedding 31,000 ties, and connecting 4,037 iron rails to them with 120,000 spikes!

A Mania for Railroads

Seeing that the owners of the U.P. and C.P. had become instant millionaires, other ambitious men descended on Washington in search of subsidies. In the euphoria of the times, Congress in 1864 was doubly generous to the Northern Pacific, which planned to build from Lake Superior to Puget Sound. In the territories, the N.P. received 40 alternate sections of land for every mile of railway built! The Atchison, Topeka, and Santa Fe ran from Kansas to Los Angeles. The Texas Pacific and Southern Pacific linked New Orleans and San Francisco at El Paso, Texas. In 1884, the Canadians (who were even more generous with government land) completed the first of their two transcontinental lines, the Canadian Pacific. Never before had there been such an expenditure of effort and wealth to accomplish the same purpose in so short a time.

The costs were considerable. The federal government gave the land-grant railroads a total of 131 million acres. To this, the state governments added 45 million acres. Totaled up, an area larger than France and Belgium combined was given to a handful of capitalists. In addition, towns along the proposed routes

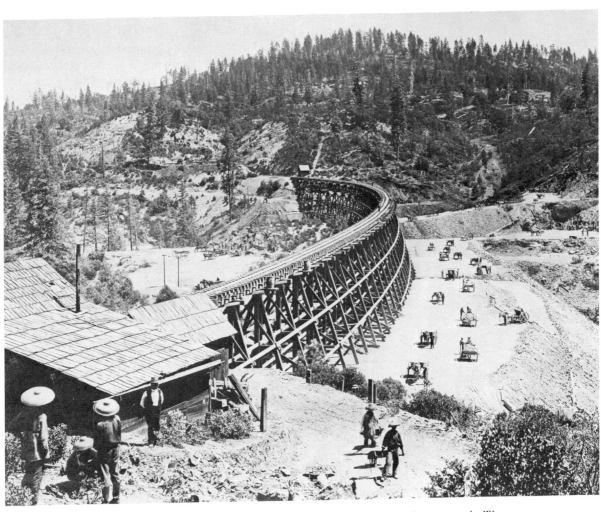

Ten thousand immigrant Chinese laborers built the Central Pacific Railway across the West. Here workers complete the Secrettown Trestle in the Sierra Nevada.

enticed the builders to choose them as sites for depots by offering town lots, cash bounties, and exemption from taxes.

These gifts were not always offered with a glad hand. If a railroad bypassed a town, that town frequently died. Aware of this, railroaders did not hesitate to set communities against one another like roosters in a cock fight. The Atchison, Topeka, and Santa Fe, popularly known as "the Santa Fe," did not enter that city until much later, and then on a spur line. Nearby Albuquerque offered the better deal and got the major depot.

The Panic of 1873

Western railroaders made money by building railroads with public and borrowed money, not by actually operating them. As a result, they built too many too soon. When the time came to pay the high operating costs and to pay off loans out of fees paid by shippers and passengers, many of the new companies found that there were just not enough customers to go around. In 1872, only one railroad in three made a profit.

On September 18, 1873, a Friday, the chickens came home to roost. Jay Cooke and Company, a bank that

A construction crew in the Montana Territory in 1887 is shown laying track for the Manitoba Railway which ran between Seattle, Washington and St. Paul, Minnesota.

BUILDING THE RAILROADS

"Track-laying is a science. A light car, drawn by a single horse, gallops up to the front with its load of rails. Two men seize the end of a rail and start forward, the rest of the gang taking hold by twos. They come forward at a run. At a word of command the rail is dropped in its place, less than thirty seconds to a rail for each gang, and so four rails go down to the minute: Close behind come the gangers, spikers, and a lovely time they make of it."

William Bell

had loaned heavily to western railroads, including the richly endowed Northern Pacific, announced that the firm was bankrupt. Jay Cooke and Company was not an ordinary bank. It was the most prestigious house of finance in the United States. During the Civil War, Jay Cooke had virtually managed the government's finances. So, its failure caused a panic: speculators rushed to sell their stocks and the market crashed. By the end of 1873, 5,000 businesses had declared bankruptcy and a half million workers were jobless. The depression of the 1870s was the worst in American history to that time.

It would not be the last. A by-product of fabulous economic growth was a wildly erratic "business cycle." For a time the industrial capitalist economy boomed, luring investment and speculation, encouraging expansion and production. Sooner or later, the capacity of railroads to carry freight and factories to produce goods outpaced the capacity of the market to absorb their services and products. When that happened, banks closed, investments and savings were wiped out, factories closed, workingpeople lost their jobs. After a depression, the cycle began anew.

THE ORGANIZERS

In a free economy, the cycle of boom and bust was inevitable and, since the age of Jackson, Americans as a people had been committed to the ideal of a free economy. They believed that their country's peculiar virtue lay in the fact that competition was open to everyone having the will and wherewithall to have a go at it.

Once a businessman reached the top of the economic pyramid, however, it was easy to become disenchanted with the competitive ideal. For the entrepreneur who was no longer scrambling but in charge of a commercial or industrial empire valued at millions

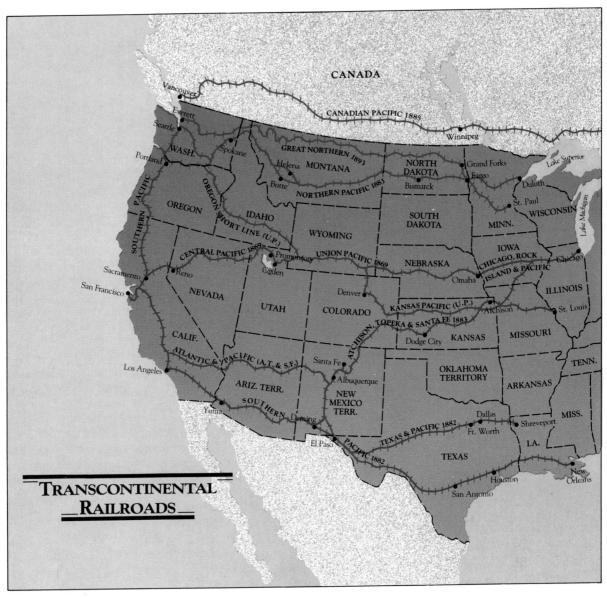

TRANSCONTINENTAL RAILROADS

of dollars, free-wheeling competitors threatened stability and order. In the late nineteenth century, Andrew Carnegie in steel, John D. Rockefeller in oil, and other canny businessmen devoted their careers to minimizing the threat of competition. Carnegie organized his company so efficiently that he could determine the price structure of the entire steel industry without regard to what other steel makers did. Rockefeller destroyed his competitors by fair means and foul, and simply gobbled them up.

Steel: The Bones of the Economy

Steel is the element iron from which carbon and other "impurities" are burned out at high temperatures. Although the means of producing this super iron was known for centuries, the expense involved was so great that steel was used to make only small, specialty items: knives, other cutting tools, precision instruments. Nevertheless, iron manufacturers were aware of its potential. Steel is much stronger than iron per unit of weight. Produced in quantity, steel could be used in buildings, bridges, and, of particular interest in the late nineteenth century, superior rails for trains.

By the time of the Civil War, working independently of each other, two ironmakers, Henry Bessemer of England and William Kelly of Pennsylvania and Kentucky, developed a method by which steel could be made in quantity at a reasonable price.

Andrew Carnegie, an immigrant from Scotland who, beginning as a telegrapher, became a high-rank-

Andrew Carnegie, steel manufacturer and master of vertical integration.

ing executive of the Pennsylvania Railroad, understood that steel plate, girders, and rails were the bones of the industrial age. Already a rich man by the end of the Civil War as a result of speculations in oil and the manufacture of iron bridges (his company built the first span across the Mississippi), he decided to sell everything and concentrate on steel, "putting all his eggs in one basket, and then watching that basket." In 1873, he began construction of a huge Bessemer plant in Braddock, Pennsylvania, outside Pittsburgh.

A Head for Business

Carnegie knew apples as well as eggs—how to polish them. He named his factory after J. Edgar Thomson, his former boss and the president of the Pennsy, which would be a major customer of Carnegie Steel. But Carnegie also knew to locate the great works outside of Pittsburgh, which was served by the Pennsylvania Railroad alone. In Braddock, Carnegie could play several railroads against one another, winning the most favorable shipping rates.

Nor was it coincidence that Carnegie built his mill during the depression of 1873. For the next 25 years, he took advantage of hard times, when the price of everything was down, to expand his factories, scrap old methods, and introduce the latest technology.

Carnegie also prided himself on spotting talent and rewarding it. Charles Schwab, later the president of United States Steel and the founder of Bethlehem Steel, was an engineer's helper at Carnegie Steel whom Carnegie promoted and made a partner.

"Vertical Integration"

Carnegie's major contribution to business organization was "vertical integration." That is, in order to get a leg up on his competitors, he expanded his operation from a base of steel manufacture to include ownership of the raw materials from which steel was made and the means of assembling those raw materials at the factory. For example, Bessemer furnaces were fueled by coke, which is to coal what charcoal is to wood, a hotter-burning distillation of the mineral. Rather than buy coke from independent operators, Carnegie absorbed the 5,000 acres of coalfields and 1,000 coke ovens owned by Henry Clay Frick, who became a junior partner in Carnegie Steel. Carnegie and Frick then added iron mines to their holdings.

While never completely independent of trunk-line railroads, Carnegie controlled as much of his own shipping as he could. He owned barges that carried iron ore from Michigan and the Mesabi to his own port facilities in Erie, Pennsylvania. He owned a short-line railroad that brought the ore from Erie to Homestead. By eliminating from his final product price the profits of independent suppliers, distributors, and carriers, Carnegie was able to undersell competing companies that were not vertically integrated and, therefore, had to include the profits of independent suppliers in their final product price.

Vertical integration served Andrew Carnegie very well. His personal income rose to $25 million a year. He lived much of the time in a castle in Scotland not far from where his father had worked as a weaver. In 1901, 66 years old and bored with business, he threatened a new combination of steel companies organized by J. P. Morgan with all-out price war, then sold out to Morgan for $500 million. The new company Morgan created was the first billion dollar corporation, United States Steel.

The Corporation

Although a pioneer in many ways, Andrew Carnegie was curiously old fashioned in that he organized his company as a partnership. The chief agency of business consolidation in the late nineteenth century was not the partnership or individual ownership but the corporation.

The corporate structure—selling small "shares" in a company on the open market—was advantageous to both investors and business organizers. Widely dis-

INC. AND LTD.

In the United States, a limited liability corporation is distinguished by the word "Corporation" in its name or the abbreviation "Inc.," meaning "incorporated." in Great Britain, the comparable designation is "Ltd.," meaning "limited."

persed ownership meant widely dispersed risk. The investor who owned some shares in a number of companies did not lose everything if one of those companies failed. American corporation law also provided investors with the privilege of "limited liability." That is, the corporation's legal liability was limited to the assets of the corporation and did not extend to the assets of shareholders. (If a partnership went bust, creditors could seize the assets of the partners too, even home and personal property.)

These inducements made it possible for entrepreneurs to raise the huge amounts of capital needed to finance expensive industrial enterprises. However, by reserving controlling interest to themselves, they did not have to share decision making with investors. Abuses were common enough. Pirates like the Erie Ring could drain a corporation of its assets, enrich themselves personally through their control of corporate policy, allow the company to go bankrupt (as the Erie did), and still hold on to their ill-gotten personal fortunes.

New Uses for Equal Rights

The Fourteenth Amendment to the Constitution, designed to secure equality under the law to all citizens, proved to be more valuable to corporations than to black people. After dodging the question for several years, the Supreme Court ruled in *Santa Clara County v. The Southern Pacific Railroad* (1886) that a corpo-

A ladle used in a nineteenth-century steel mill dwarfs the men standing nearby.

ration was a "person" under the meaning of the Fourteenth Amendment. The states were forbidden to pass laws that applied specifically to corporations and not to flesh-and-blood persons because those laws would deny the corporate person the civil rights that were granted to others.

While a corporation could legally be granted the civil rights of a human being, it was difficult to exact the same responsibilities of it. A walking and talking man or woman could be sent to jail for violating the law. A corporation could not. Because the amendment required that laws applied equally to all persons, it was difficult even to levy an effective fine on businessmen. A man or woman might be deterred from breaking the law by the threat of a $50 fine; a railroad would not.

John D. Rockefeller

While thousands of businessmen organized corporations, they all disappear in the shadow of the solemn, muscular, splendiferously dressed, and deeply religious person of John Davison Rockefeller. Beginning his career as an accountant, Rockefeller avoided service in the Civil War by hiring a substitute. He made a small fortune selling provisions to the Union Army but a small fortune was only an appetizer to a man with a voracious appetite for riches. Rockefeller had such an appetite. He talked of little but money. After

John D. Rockefeller and his attorneys.

STEEL AT ONE CENT A POUND

Just as John D. Rockefeller liked to point out that kerosene was cheaper after Standard Oil came to monopolize the refining industry, Andrew Carnegie had a neat justification of his organization of the steel industry:

Two pounds of ironstone mined upon Lake Superior and transported nine hundred miles to Pittsburgh; one pound and one half of coal, mined and manufactured into coke, and transported to Pittsburgh; a small amount of manganese ore mined in Virginia and brought to Pittsburgh—and these four pounds of materials manufactured into one pound of steel, for which the customer pays one cent.

swinging a lucrative deal as a young man, he danced a two-step jig and exclaimed "Bound to be rich! I'm bound to be rich!" He disapproved of smoking and drinking, in part because he was a devoted Baptist, but in part because cigars and whiskey cost money that could be invested to make more money. He carefully recorded how he spent every dime; he spent few frivolously.

Black Gold

Rockefeller would have succeeded no matter what his business. The one he chose, oil, proved to be as basic to industrial society as steel.

Crude oil had been seeping to the surface of the earth in some parts of the world as long as anyone remembered. Europeans used it as a lubricant. Some Indians used it as a laxative. That classical American huckster, the snake-oil salesman, bottled the stuff, flavoring it with sugar and spices and tossing in a healthy shot of alcohol, thence claiming it cured everything from smallpox to a rainy day. The farmers of western Pennsylvania were more likely to hate the gunk. It fouled the soil, polluted the waterways, and, if it caught fire, filled the air with billows of noxious smoke.

In 1855, an organic chemist, Benjamin Silliman, discovered that by "breaking" crude oil into its component parts, superb lubricants could be made. Most useful of all was kerosene, an oil used for heating, cooking, and illumination. It was an intriguing discovery because, in the 1850s, overharvesting had devastated the world's population of whales, and caused the price of whale oil to soar. In 1859, Edwin Drake, a former army officer, devised at Titusville a drill and pump system by which western Pennsylvania's crude could be extracted in commercial quantities.

The Pennsylvania oil rush was as wild a scramble as the California gold rush of 1849. Drilling for oil, like

Canning peaches in Fresno, California, around 1900.

The pioneers of centralized meatpacking were Gusta-vus Swift (1839–1903) and Philip D. Armour (1832–1901). Armour perfected the "disassembly line," a continuously moving chain in which hogs ran in one end under their own power, and pork packed for retailing came out the other. Armour kept his prices down by using what previously had been waste: bones, blood, hides, and even bristle (which was made into hairbrushes). It was said that he made money on every part of the pig but its squeal, and he was working on that.

Gustavus Swift pioneered the use of ice and, later, refrigerator cars to ship fresh sides of beef from Chicago to the east coast. He had to overcome popular suspicions of any meat from animals that had been slaughtered more than a few days before it was set on the table and the resistance of local butchers. By opening his own shops in the major cities of the East and underselling even locally raised steers with his Texas, Wyoming, and Montana beef, Swift had his way.

By the end of the nineteenth century, a middle-class family in Portland, Maine, would likely sit down to a loaf of bread baked with flour from Minneapolis, a beefsteak from Chicago seasoned with Heinz ketchup from Pittsburgh, and oranges from Florida or California for dessert. Vegetables alone were local. Maine produced plenty of potatoes, and it was only in the twentieth century that the food revolutionaries shipped greens any considerable distance.

For Further Reading

Overviews and Classics

Thomas C. Cochran and William Miller, *The Age of Enterprise* (1942)

Vincent P. DeSantis, *The Shaping of Modern America, 1877–1916* (1973)

John A. Garraty, *The New Commonwealth, 1877–1890* (1968)

Samuel P. Hays, *The Response to Industrialism, 1885–1914* (1957)

Matthew Josephson, *The Robber Barons* (1934)

Glenn Porter, *The Rise of Big Business, 1860–1910* (1973)

Robert H. Wiebe, *The Search for Order* (1967)

Valuable Special Studies

Roger Burlingame, *Engines and Democracy: Inventions and Society in Mature America* (1940)

———, *The Visible Hand: The Managerial Revolution in American Business* (1977)

Thomas C. Cochran, *Railroad Leaders, 1845–1890* (1953)

Robert W. Fogel, *Railroads and American Economic Growth* (1964)

Edward C. Kirkland, *Dream and Thought in the Business Community, 1860–1900* (1956)

———, *Men, Cities, and Transportation* (1948)

Gabriel Kolko, *Railroads and Regulation* (1965)

James McCague, *Moguls and Iron Men* (1964)

Samuel T. McSeveney, *The Politics of Depression: Political Behavior in the Northeast, 1893–1896* (1972)

Eltin E. Morison, *From Know-How to Nowhere: The Development of American Technology* (1974)

Walter T. K. Nugent, *Money and American Society, 1865–1880* (1968)

George R. Taylor and R. D. Neu, *The American Railroad Network, 1861–1900* (1956)

Biographies and Autobiographies

Robert V. Bruce, *Alexander Graham Bell and the Conquest of Solitude* (1973)

Matthew Josephson, *Edison* (1959)

Harold C. Livesay, *Andrew Carnegie and the Rise of Big Business* (1975)

Allan Nevins, *A Study in Power: John D. Rockefeller* (1953)

J. F. Wall, *Andrew Carnegie* (1971)

29

Coming to Terms with Leviathan
Americans React to Big Business and Great Wealth

In *Democracy in America*, written more than twenty years before the Civil War, Alexis de Tocqueville admired the equity with which wealth was distributed in the United States. Except for the slaves of the South, no Americans seemed so poor that they could not hope to improve their situation; no Americans were so rich that they formed an aristocracy, a distinct social class permanently established above the mass of the population and enjoying privileges denied to the rest. Indeed, the wealthy people whom Tocqueville observed seemed to feel that a single stroke of bad luck would send them tumbling down into the world of hard work, sore backs, and calloused hands. In the land of opportunity, it was as easy to fail as to succeed. American society was as fluid as it was egalitarian.

In the late nineteenth century, this was no longer so. Industrialization and the growth of big business had created a class of multimillionaires whose fortunes were so great that it was absurd to imagine them slipping into the anonymous masses ever again. A fortune of $5 million invested at 10 percent yielded an annual income of $500,000 a year—an amount difficult to spend in that era without throwing it away.

Members of America's leisure class flaunted their wealth and devoted themselves to idle pursuits. This detail from John Singer Sargent's painting, The Daughters of Edward Darley Boit, portrays some young members of this privileged class.

Moreover, 10 percent was a moderate yield and $5 million was a comparatively modest fortune. Cornelius Vanderbilt left $100 million in 1877. His son William doubled that to $200 million in a few years. By 1900, Andrew Carnegie was able to pocket $480 million in a single transaction. John D. Rockefeller gave that much away within a few years, all the while his family grew richer.

Just as important, the industrial and financial aristocracy's control of technology, transportation, industry, and money seemed to prevent others from succeeding—fulfilling their American Dream. It is not surprising that Americans should protest and attempt to harness the new elite. Given the egalitarian streak in the American character, it is perhaps surprising only that Americans came so easily to terms with a society that was both richer and poorer than that which they had known and, with Alexis de Tocqueville, prized.

REGULATING THE RAILROADS AND TRUSTS

The first critics of the railroads were poets and philosophers who saw "the machine in the garden" as a defilement of what was good and vital in American life. In some cities, people banded together to fight plans to run tracks down their streets. Unlike today, many railways ran into city centers on residential streets, and the wood-burning locomotives were noisy, dirty, and dangerous, throwing sparks and running over people and animals.

But the nay-sayers were a small group. Most Americans welcomed the iron horse, especially those who lived in isolated rural areas. To them the railroad offered the possibility of shipping their produce to lucrative markets, thereby earning money with which to enjoy a fuller life.

A Short Honeymoon

Even in areas that actually were opened up by railroads, the honeymoon was a short one. It was not difficult to see that pirates like Drew, Fisk, and Gould made money only to the extent that they destroyed the railroad as a means of transportation. Town dwellers discovered that the railway barons' arrogance did not end with their demands for free sites for their depots. Along the transcontinental lines, virtually every important piece of business had to be "cleared" with the local railway manager. Farmers learned that

the railroads were less their servants, carting their produce to market, than the masters of their fate.

California's "Big Four"—Collis P. Huntington, Leland Stanford, Mark Hopkins, and Charles Crocker—were popularly said to "own" California and that was not absurdly far from the truth. Their Southern Pacific Railroad, which absorbed the Central Pacific, was the most lucrative of their properties. Whereas the bulk of the land that had been given to the transcontinental lines was sold quite cheaply, at $3 to $5 per acre, the S.P.'s land grants in the fertile central valley of California were worth tens and occasionally a hundred times that much. Instead of disposing of its California holdings, the S.P. held tight, driving up the value of the real estate. By the end of the nineteenth century, the railroad was the single biggest landowner in California.

The successors of the Big Four sometimes used the railroad's leverage to drive small farmers and ranchers out of business. The line's political officer at the turn of the century, William F. Herrin, was widely considered to be the boss of the state legislature, monitoring every law that was passed in the interests of the S.P. Novelist Frank Norris summed up the Southern Pacific for many Californians when he called it *The Octopus* (1901), its tentacles reaching into and gripping every aspect of life in the Golden State.

The Farmers' Grievances

In the Mississippi Valley, farmers also discovered that the railroad did not necessarily usher in a golden age. If there were too many western railroads in general, in most regions there was no competition among railroads; one line handled all the traffic. As a result, the rates at which farmers shipped their wheat, corn, or livestock to markets in the city were at the mercy of the shippers. All too often, farmers saw their margin of profit consumed by transportation costs.

Most infuriating was the railroads' control of storage facilities, the grain elevators that stood close to the depot in every railway town. The farmer had to pay the company storage fees until such time as the railroad sent a train to haul away his grain. Obviously, it was

---

LELAND STANFORD

When he was president of the Southern Pacific Railroad, Leland Stanford ordered that all employees of the company stand at attention in a line along the track when his private trains passed through. All Southern Pacific locomotives traveling in the other direction were to blow their whistles in salute.

often to the railroad's interests to delay scheduling a train as long as possible. The company determined how long a farmer had to store his products and, thus, how large his fee was. Within a few weeks, a railroad could gobble up a year's income.

Attempts to Regulate

In the early 1870s, an organization of farmers, the Patrons of Husbandry (or Grangers, as members were called) won control of the state legislature of Illinois and considerable influence in adjoining states. Allied with small businessmen who also felt squeezed by big business, they passed a series of "Granger laws" that set maximum rates that railroad companies could charge both for hauling and storing. Other state governments followed Illinois's lead and the railroad barons launched a legal counterattack, hiring high-powered corporation lawyers like Richard B. Olney and Roscoe Conkling to question state regulatory legislation before the Supreme Court.

At first the Grangers prevailed. In the case of *Munn v. Illinois* (1877), a Supreme Court dominated by old-fashioned midwestern agrarians and Whiggish Republicans declared that when a private company's business

Gift for the Grangers, *a lithograph made in 1873 celebrates the Patrons of Husbandry, a farmers' organization.*

affected the public interest, the public had the right to regulate that business.

Nine years later, times and the membership of the Supreme Court had changed. In 1886, justices who had come cordially to terms with the new order wrote several prorailroad doctrines into the law of the land. In the Wabash case (*Wabash, St. Louis, and Pacific Railway Co. v. Illinois*), the Court broadly extended the interstate-commerce clause of the Constitution to protect the railroads. That is, the Constitution provides that only Congress can regulate commerce between and among states. The Court ruled that because the Wabash, St. Louis, and Pacific Railroad ran through Illinois into other states, the state of Illinois could not legally regulate freight rates even between points within the state! In the age of consolidation, when a handful of syndicates controlled all important American railroads, this decision left state governments with authority over only those short, generally insignificant local lines (at most, a quarter of the track in the United States) that were rarely exploitative in the first place.

The Interstate Commerce Commission

There was a hellish uproar. Rural politicians and urban reformers condemned the Court as the tool of the railway barons. If only Congress could bridle the iron horse, they shouted from Grange halls and from the stages of city auditoriums, let Congress do so. In 1887, Congress did, enacting the Interstate Commerce Act.

On the face of it, the law brought the national railroads under control. Discriminatory rates were outlawed, and Congress created an independent regulatory commission, the Interstate Commerce Commission, to keep an eye on railroad charges. Ostensibly, railroads were to publish their rates and were not to discriminate against small shippers by giving rebates to the larger ones. They were not to charge less for long hauls along routes where there was competition than for short hauls in areas where a railroad had a monopoly. The act also outlawed the pooling of business by railroads, a practice by which, shippers believed, they were controlled and fleeced.

However, the Interstate Commerce Act did not forbid mergers or interlocking directorates, both of which were far more effective means of avoiding competition than were the pools. Moreover, the Commission was given little real power; it had to take its decisions to the same courts that had favored the railroads over the state legislatures, and within a few years railroaders and lawyers friendly to them held a majority of seats on the I.C.C.

Indeed, the principal effect of the landmark law was to mute the popular appeal of the antirailroad movement by creating nominal government control. Its secondary effect was to provide, through the auspices of the federal government, the means for the further consolidation of power by an even smaller group of men than the eastern consolidators and the western railway builders.

The Money Power

By the early 1890s, the trunk lines of the country had been consolidated into five great systems. By 1900, these had fallen under the effective control of two large New York investment banks, J. P. Morgan and Company and Kuhn, Loeb and Company, the latter in league with Union Pacific president, Edward H. Harriman.

When the government ceased to subsidize railway construction, the railroads had to look to other sources in order to mobilize the huge amounts of capital needed to lay second tracks, modernize equipment, and buy up competitors. The companies often needed more money than their profits provided. Capital was even more serious a problem during the recurrent business depressions of the period when income sank, while fixed costs (such as maintenance) remained the same.

The traditional means of raising capital—offering shares of stock to the public—was simply not up to these needs, particularly during depressions. Into the gap stepped the investment banks. These institutions served both as sales agents, finding moneyed buyers for railway stock at a commission, and as buyers themselves. In return for these services, men like John Pierpont Morgan insisted on a say in the formation of railroad policy, placing a representative of the bank on the client's board of directors.

Because every large railroad needed financial help at one time or another—every transcontinental but the Great Northern went under during the depression of 1893 to 1897—Morgan's and Kuhn-Loeb's men soon sat on every major corporate board, creating an interlocking directorate. Like all bankers, their goal was a steady, dependable flow of profit, and their means to that end was to eliminate wasteful competition. They called a halt to the periodic rate wars among the New York Central, Pennsylvania, and Baltimore and Ohio railroads in the eastern states. In 1903, J. P. Morgan tried to merge the Northern Pacific and the Great Northern, two systems with essentially parallel lines between the Great Lakes and the Pacific Northwest. Competing for traffic, he believed, hurt them both.

Banker control had its benefits. No more did unscrupulous pirates like the Erie Gang ruin great transportation systems for the sake of short-term killings. The integration of the nation's railways resulted in a gradual but significant lowering of fares and freight rates. Between 1866 and 1897, the cost of shipping a hundred pounds of grain from Chicago to New York dropped from 65 cents to 20 cents, and the rate for shipping beef from 90 cents per hundred weight to 40 cents.

J. P. Morgan

But the control of so important a part of the economy by a few men with offices on Wall Street called into question some very basic American ideals. Where was individual freedom and opportunity, many people asked, when a sinister "money power" headed by the imperious J. P. Morgan could decide on a whim the fate of millions of farmers and workingpeople?

A resplendent and cultivated man who owned yachts that were larger than the ships in most countries' navies and collections of rare books and art that were superior to those in most countries' national museums, Morgan never attempted to disguise his power or his contempt for ordinary mortals. In return he was feared, held in awe, and hated.

Morgan shook off all those reactions. In the end, he was vulnerable only to ridicule. An affliction of the

Banker John Pierpont Morgan, as photographed by Edward Steichen in 1906.

*An overfed monopoly demands tribute from workers, farmers, and merchants in the cartoon
from the British magazine* Puck.

skin had given him a large, bulbous nose that swelled and glowed like a circus clown's when he was angry. Making fun of it, however, was the only foolproof way to make it light up, and Morgan rarely rubbed elbows with the kind of people who would notice his single human weakness.

An Age of Trusts

In addition to railroaders, Morgan found plenty of company among the industrialists whose trusts and other devices for doing business he organized for personal fees of a million dollars and more. The trust was most useful in industries in which, like oil, there was a single critical stage of manufacture that involved relatively few companies. Some of John D. Rockefeller's most successful imitators were in sugar refining (the sugar trust controlled about 95 percent of the nation's facilities) and whiskey distilling. In 1890, James Buchanan Duke of Durham, North Carolina, founded the American Tobacco Company, which co-ordinated the activities of practically every cigarette manufacturer in the United States. In effect, he dictated the terms by which tens of thousands of tobacco growers did business.

By 1890, many Americans had become convinced that when a few men could control a whole industry, the principle of economic opportunity was mocked and the very foundations of American democracy were jeopardized.

The Sherman Antitrust Act

Responding to public pressure in that year, Congress passed the Sherman Antitrust Act, which declared that "every contract, combination, in the form of trust or otherwise, or conspiracy, in restraint of trade or commerce among the several states, or with foreign nations, is hereby declared to be illegal." The Sherman Act authorized the Attorney General to move against such combinations and force them to dissolve, thus reestablishing the independence of the companies that had formed them.

The law was no more successful in halting the consolidation movement than the Interstate Commerce Act was in controlling the power of the railroads. Critics said that the Sherman Act was a sham from the beginning, designed to quiet unease but not to hurt big business. In fact, the weakness of the law lay in the inability of congressmen to comprehend this new economic phenomenon. Real monopoly was so unfamiliar to the lawmakers that they were unable to draft a law that was worded well enough to be effective. The language of the Sherman Act was so ambivalent that a shrewd lawyer—and the trusts had the best—could usually find a loophole.

Moreover, while congressmen could take fright at a popular uproar, the courts were immune to it. The Santa Clara County and Wabash cases were only the first of a series of decisions by the Supreme Court that ensured the survival of the biggest of businesses. In the first major case tried under the Sherman Act, *U.S. v. E. C. Knight Company* in 1895, the Court found that a nearly complete monopoly of sugar refining in the United States did not violate the law because manufacture, which the sugar trust monopolized, was not a part of trade or commerce, even though its sugar was sold in every state.

Nor was the executive branch keen to attack big business. President Grover Cleveland's Attorney General, Richard B. Olney, was a former corporation lawyer. Under Benjamin Harrison and William McKinley, the other presidents of the 1890s, the Justice Department was similarly probusiness. During the first ten years of the Sherman Act, only eighteen cases were instituted and four of these were aimed at labor unions, also "conspiracies in restraint of trade."

Consequently, rather than heralding doomsday for the trusts, the years between 1890 and 1901 were a golden age. The number of state chartered trusts actually grew from 251 to 290. More telling, the amount of money invested in trusts rose from $192 million to $326 million. By the end of the century, there was no doubt that the demands of modern manufacturing meant that massive organizations were here to stay. But whether they would continue to be the private possessions of a few Bells, Morgans, Carnegies, and Rockefellers was still open to debate.

RADICAL CRITICS OF THE NEW ORDER

The Interstate Commerce and Sherman Antitrust laws were enacted by mainstream politicians who believed that the individual pursuit of wealth was a virtue and wished only to restore the opportunity to succeed and the possibility of competing that the big business combinations had apparently destroyed. Outside the mainstream, sometimes radical critics of the new industrial capitalism raised their voices and wielded their pens in opposition to the new order itself. At least briefly, some of them won large followings.

Henry George and the Single Tax

A lively writing style and a knack for simplifying difficult economic ideas made journalist Henry George and his single tax the center of a briefly momentous social movement. In *Progress and Poverty*, which was published in 1879, George observed the obvious. Instead of freeing people from onerous labor, as it had promised to do, the machine had put millions to work under killing conditions for long hours. Instead of making life easier and fuller for all, the mass production of goods had enriched the few in the House of Have, and had impoverished the millions in the House of Want.

George did not blame either industrialization or capitalism as such for the misery he saw around him. Like most Americans, he believed that the competition for comfort and security was a wellspring of the nation's energy. The trouble began only when those who were successful in the race grew so wealthy that they could live off the "rents" from their property.

George called income derived from mere ownership of property "unearned increment" because it required no work, effort, or ingenuity of its possessors; the property grew more valuable and its owners richer only because other people needed access to it in order to survive. Such value was spurious, George said. Government had every right to levy a 100 percent tax on it. Because the revenues from this tax would be quite enough to pay all the expenses of government, George called it the single tax. All other taxes would be abolished. The idle rich would be destroyed as a social class. The competition that made the country great would take place without the handicaps of taxation. Everyone would compete on an equal basis.

George was popular enough that in 1886 he narrowly missed election as mayor of New York, a city where real-estate values and "unearned increment" from land were higher than anywhere in the world.

Edward Bellamy and Looking Backward

Another book which became the Bible of a protest movement was Edward Bellamy's novel of 1888, *Looking Backward, 2000-1887*. Within two years of publication, the book sold 200,000 copies (the equivalent of about 1 million in the 1980s) and led to the founding of about 150 "Nationalist clubs," made up of people who shared Bellamy's vision of the future.

The story that moved them was rather simple. A proper young Bostonian of the 1880s succumbs to a mysterious sleep and awakes in the United States of the twenty-first century. There he discovers that technology has produced not a world of sharp class divisions and widespread misery (as in 1887), but a utopia that provides abundance for all. Like George, Bellamy was not opposed to industrial development in itself.

Capitalism no longer exists in the world of *Looking Backward*. Through a peaceful democratic revolution—won at the polls—the American people have abolished competitive greed and idle unproductive living because they had become at odds with true American ideals. Instead of private ownership of land and industry, the state owns the means of production and administers them for the good of all. Everyone contributes to the common wealth. Everyone lives decently, and none wastefully, on its fruits.

Bellamy's vision was socialistic. Because he rooted it in American values rather than in the internationalism of the Marxists, he called it "Nationalism." The patriotic quality of his message made his gospel more palatable to middle-class Americans who, while troubled by the growth of fantastic fortunes and of wretched poverty, found foreign ideologies and talk of class warfare obnoxious and frightening.

Socialists and Anarchists

Socialists who believed in class conflict were, for the most part, followers of the German revolutionary living in London, Karl Marx. Marx influenced some old-stock Americans, but found most of his support in the United States among immigrants and the children of immigrants. Briefly after 1872, in fact, the General Council of the First International, the official administration of world socialism, made its headquarters in New York, where Marx sent it to prevent the followers of his anarchist rival, Mikhail Bakunin, from winning control of it.

The Marxists believed that capitalist labor arrangements—workers laboring for wages in the employ of a capitalist class that owned the means of production, the factories and machines—would fall under their own weight to socialism and then communism, under which, respectively, the state and the workers themselves would own the factories and machines, administering them for the good of all. Some Marxist socialists held that in democratic countries like the United States, this social revolution would be voted in peacefully. Such social democratic movements flourished in a number of cities. Most notably, an Austrian immigrant, Victor L. Berger, built up a social democratic party in Milwaukee, Wisconsin, that after 1900 would govern the city for several decades. Other socialists held that the overthrow of capitalism would be violent. The most extreme of these revolutionaries were the anarchists, some of whom held that individuals could hasten the great day through "the propaganda of the deed," acts of terrorism against the ruling

American writer Edward Bellamy, author of the widely read novel, Looking Backward.

class. Anarchists figured prominently in an incident in Chicago in 1886 in which, ironically, they were not responsible for the bloodshed that occurred.

Haymarket

In May 1886, workers at the McCormick International Harvester Company, the world's largest manufacturer of farm machinery, were on strike. The Chicago police were blatantly on the side of the employers, and over several days they killed four workers. On May 4, a group of anarchists, mostly German but including a Confederate Army veteran of some social standing, Albert Parsons, held a rally in support of the strikers at Haymarket Square, just south of "the loop," or city center.

The oratory was red-hot; but the speakers broke no laws, and the crowd was orderly. Indeed, the rally was about to break up under the threat of a downpour when a platoon of police entered the square and demanded that the people disperse. At that instant, someone threw a bomb into their midst, killing seven people and wounding 67 officers. The police fired a volley, and four workers fell dead.

A New York tenament photographed by Jacob Riis.

News of the incident fed an antianarchist hysteria in Chicago. Authorities rounded up several dozen individuals who were known to have attended anarchist meetings, and authorities brought eight to trial for the murder of the officers. Among them was Parsons and a prominent German agitator, August Spies.

The trial was a farce. No one on the prosecution team knew or even claimed to know who had thrown the bomb. (His or her identity is still unknown.) Nor did the prosecution present evidence to tie any of the eight to the bombing. One, a deranged young German named Louis Lingg, was a bomb maker, although even he had a plausible alibi. Several of the defendants had not been at the rally. Parsons had been ill in bed that evening and, indeed, had been ill since before the rally was called.

All these facts were irrelevant. Chicago was determined to have scapegoats, and, although the charge was murder, the Haymarket anarchists were tried for their ideas and associations. Four were hanged. Lingg committed suicide in his cell. Three were sentenced to long prison terms. Not only was the McCormick strike broken in the aftermath, the incident frightened Americans away from "European ideologies."

The Social Gospel

Taking a more moralistic approach to the tensions of the late nineteenth century were a number of influ-

ential Protestant clergymen. Troubled by the callousness of big business, preachers of the "Social Gospel" emphasized the Christian's social obligations, his duty to be his brother's keeper.

Walter Rauschenbusch began his ministerial career on the edge of Hell's Kitchen, one of New York City's worst slums. "One could hear human virtue cracking and crushing all around," he wrote in later years. Poverty was the cause of crime and sin, and mass poverty was the result of allowing great capitalists a free hand in enriching themselves. Later, as a professor at Rochester Theological Seminary, Rauschenbusch taught the obligation of the churches to work for both the relief of the poor and a more equitable distribution of wealth.

Washington Gladden, a Congregationalist, called unrestricted competition "antisocial and anti-Christian." He did not propose the abolition of capitalism, but he did call for regulation of its grossest immoralities. He was highly moralistic. Late in life, Gladden described John D. Rockefeller's fortune as "tainted money" and urged his church not to accept contributions from the millionaire.

The Social Gospel appealed to many middle-class people, often modestly well-to-do themselves, who did not suffer directly from the power of the very wealthy but who were offended by the extravagance and idleness of their life. William Dean Howells, the editor of the *Atlantic Monthly,* wrote a novel about a successful industrialist (*The Rise of Silas Lapham,* 1885) who finds the idleness of his new life discomfiting. He "rises," finds purpose and happiness again, only when he loses his fortune and is forced to return to productive work. Howells even convinced an old friend from Ohio, former president Rutherford B. Hayes, to go on record late in his life as an advocate of the peaceful abolition of capitalism.

THE DEFENDERS OF THE SYSTEM

Such an array of criticism did not, of course, go unanswered. At the same time that great wealth was taking its knocks, it was reaping the praise of defenders. In part, like the critics, they drew on traditional American values to justify the new social system. In part, also like the critics, the defenders created new philosophies, original with the era of industrial capitalism.

Social Darwinism

Thoughtful and reflective people who were at peace with their era found a justification for great wealth and dubious business ethics in a series of books, essays, and lectures by the British philosopher Herbert Spencer. Because Spencer seemed to apply Charles Darwin's celebrated biological theory of evolution to human society, his theory is known as "Social Darwinism." According to Spencer, as in the world of animals and plants, where species compete for life and those best adapted survive, the "fittest" people rise to the top in the social competition for riches. Eventually, in the dog-eat-dog world, they alone survive. "If they are sufficiently complete to live," Spencer wrote, "they do live, and it is well that they should live. If they are not sufficiently complete to live, they die and it is best they should die."

The intellectual toughness of Social Darwinism made Spencer immensely popular among American businessmen who were proud of their hard-headedness. The Englishman was never so celebrated in his own country as he was in the United States. Although a vain man, Spencer was frequently embarrassed by the adulation heaped on him at banquets sponsored by American academics and rich businessmen. Social Darwinism accounted for brutal business practices and underhand methods, justifying them as the natural "law of the jungle."

The language of Social Darwinism crept into the vocabulary of both businessmen and politicians who represented business interests. John D. Rockefeller, Jr., told a Sunday school class that "the growth of a large business is merely the survival of the fittest. The American Beauty Rose can be produced in the splendor and fragrance which bring cheer to its beholder only by sacrificing the early buds which grow up around it. This is not an evil tendency in business. It is merely the working out of a law of nature and a law of God."

But few American millionaires were true Social Darwinists. The very ruthlessness of the theory, which made it more consistent than the Success Gospel, also made it unpalatable to rich families who, in their personal lives, were committed to traditional religious values (like the Rockefellers). Moreover, businessmen are rarely intellectuals, and Spencer's philosophy and writing style were as thick and murky as crude oil. Understanding him demanded careful study, such as businessmen rarely had the time to do. As a result, his explanation of the new society was more influential among scholars.

William Graham Sumner

The most important of these was a Yale professor, William Graham Sumner. He was as uncompromising as his master in his opposition to aiding the poor, putting government restrictions on business practices, and interfering in any way whatsoever with the law of the jungle.

Sumner's consistency also led him to oppose the high protective tariff and government intervention in labor disputes. To protect and even to subsidize American industry by taxing imports was just as unnatural to him as was regulating the growth of trusts. If American manufacturers were not fit to compete with European manufacturers in a free market, Sumner said, they were not fit to survive. Likewise, Sumner opposed government intervention in strikes on behalf of employers. He believed that the strike was a natural test of the fitness of the employers' and the workers' causes. The outcome of a strike determined which side was "right." To businessmen who used government trade policy and courts to their own purposes, Sumner's applications of "natural law" were going too far.

After the turn of the century, the principles of Social Darwinism were turned on their head by the sociologist Lester Frank Ward of Brown University. Whereas Sumner argued that nature must be allowed to work without restraint, Ward suggested that human society had evolved to a point where natural evolution could be guided by government policy. Just as farmers improved fruit trees and ranchers improved livestock through selective breeding, government could improve society by intervening in the naturally slow evolutionary process. Ward's "Reform Darwinism" influenced two generations of twentieth-century liberals, but it appealed to few nineteenth-century businessmen.

The Success Gospel

It was the Success Gospel that touched their hearts. The United States had been built on the desire to prosper, Success Gospellers said. Therefore, if competition for riches was a virtue, what was wrong with winning? Far from a source of anxiety, as the critics said, or evidence of social immorality, the fabulous fortunes of America's wealthy families were an index of their virtue. The Rockefellers, Carnegies, and Morgans deserved their money.

Success manuals, books that purported to show how anyone could become a millionaire, were read as avidly as the books of George and Bellamy and the sidelong swipes of the scandal sheets. All pretty much the same, the manuals drew on the widespread assumptions that hard work, honesty, frugality, loyalty to employers and partners, and other "bourgeois virtues" drawn from Benjamin Franklin inevitably led to success. Having succeeded, America's millionaires deserved not resentment but admiration and imitation.

Shrugging off his enemies, John D. Rockefeller said flatly, "God gave me my money." A Baptist minister from Philadelphia, Russell B. Conwell, made a fortune delivering a lecture on the same theme. In "Acres of Diamonds," which the eloquent preacher delivered to paying audiences more than 6,000 times, Conwell said that great wealth was a great blessing. Not only could every American be rich, but every American *should* be rich.

If a person failed, it was his own fault. "There is not a poor person in the United States," Conwell said, "who was not made poor by his own shortcomings." The opportunities, the "acres of diamonds," were everywhere, waiting to be collected.

Conversely, those who already were rich were by definition virtuous. "Ninety-eight out of one hundred of the rich men of America are honest. That is why they are rich." Conwell's own extraordinary success indicated that many Americans believed what he said.

Horatio Alger and "Ragged Dick"

Through the 130 boys' novels written by another minister, Horatio Alger, the Success Gospel was conveyed to the younger generation. Alger's books sold 20 million copies between 1867 and 1899, and a battalion of imitators doubtless accounted for millions more.

Alger was no writer. His prose was wooden, and his characters were snipped from cardboard. The plots of all the short novels are variations on two or three

Thrifty, hard-working, idealized boys were the staple of Horatio Algers novels.

simple themes. Based on the assumption that the purpose of life is to get money, the most popular plot tells of a poor lad who is honest, hard working, loyal to his employer, and clean living. "Ragged Dick," Alger's first hero and the prototype for "Tattered Tom," "Lucky Luke Larkin," and dozens of others, is insufferably courteous and always goes to church.

Curiously, the hero does not get rich slowly through hard work. At the beginning of the final chapter, he usually is as badly off as on page one. Then, however, Ragged Dick is presented with what amounts to a visitation of grace, a divine gift that rewards his virtues. The daughter of a rich industrialist falls off the Staten Island Ferry; or she stumbles into the path of a runaway brewery wagon drawn by panicked horses; or she slips into the Niagara River just above the falls. Because he acts quickly, rescuing her, the heroic lad is rewarded with a job, marriage to the daughter, and eventually the grateful father's fortune. While appealing to the adolescent boy's yen for adventure, the novels also touched the American evangelical belief in divine grace. Just as he did with Rockefeller, God gave Ragged Dick his money as reward for his virtues.

Philanthropy

The flaw in the Success Gospel as a justification of great fortunes was the obvious fact that many rich men got their money by practicing the opposite of the touted virtues: dishonesty, betrayal of partners and employers, reckless speculation rather than thrift; and they grew richer while living a life of sumptuous ease. Rockefeller's unethical practices were probably exaggerated, but there was no question that he cut corners. Similar suspicions surrounded practically every rich family in the country.

To compensate for the negative marks on their reputations, wealthy businessmen turned to philanthropy as a kind of retroactive justification of their fortunes. Horatio Alger supported institutions that housed homeless boys in New York City. Russell B. Conwell founded Temple University, where poor young men could study very cheaply and improve themselves. Rockefeller and other industrial millionaires gave huge sums to their churches and to universities. Leland Stanford built a wholly new "Harvard of the West" in California. In retirement, Rockefeller took particular interest in helping American blacks to break out of the prison that their race had built around them.

Andrew Carnegie devised a coherent theory that justified fabulous fortunes on the basis of stewardship. In a widely publicized essay entitled "Wealth," he argued that the unrestricted pursuit of riches made American society vital and strong. The man who succeeded became a steward, or trustee. He had an obli-

Booker T. Washington (center) won the support of many wealthy benefactors with his "Atlantic Compromise." To his left is steel magnate Andrew Carnegie at the dedication of Tuskegee Institute.

BELMONT'S WINE CELLAR

While many millionaires outspent August Belmont, New York associate of the Rothschild banking interests, few of them spent their money as gracefully as did the European-born banker. It was said of Belmont that his monthly wine budget was $20,000.

Conspicuous Consumption

Having much more money than they could possibly put to good use, the very rich competed in spending it by hosting lavish parties for one another, by building extravagant palaces, by purchasing huge yachts that were good for little but show, by adorning themselves with costly clothing and jewelry, and by buying European titles for their daughters.

Some high-society parties lasting but a few hours cost more than $100,000. At one, hosted by the self-proclaimed prince of spenders, Harry Lehr, 100 dogs dined on "fricassee of bones" and gulped down shredded dog biscuit prepared by a French chef. The guests at one New York banquet ate their meal while mounted on horses (trays balanced on the animals' withers); the horses simultaneously munched oats out of sterling-silver feedbags. At a costume affair, guests boasted that they had spent more than $10,000 each on their fancy dress.

gation to distribute his money where it would provide opportunities for poor people to join the competition of the next generation. Indeed, Carnegie said that the rich man who died rich, died a failure. He retired in 1901 and devoted the rest of his life to granting money to libraries, schools, and useful social institutions. He was so rich, however, that despite extraordinary generosity, he died a multimillionaire.

HOW THE VERY RICH LIVED

Probably nothing reconciled ordinary Americans to the existence of the new multimillionaires more than the sheer fascination of the multitudes with the splendor in which the very rich lived. As Thorstein Veblen, an eccentric sociologist of Norwegian origin, observed in several books written at the end of the century, the very wealthy literally lived to spend money for the sake of proving that they had money. Veblen called this showy extravagance "conspicuous consumption," and the propensity to practically throw it away, "conspicuous waste."

There could be only one reason for dining on horseback: the diners could afford to do it. This was at Sherry's Ballroom in New York in 1903.

The lavish interior of "The Breakers," built by Cornelius Vanderbilt as his summer house, in Newport, Rhode Island.

It was the golden age of yachting. Cornelius Vanderbilt's *North Star* was 250 feet long. Albert C. Burrage's *Aztec* carried 270 tons of coal; it could steam 5,500 miles without calling at a port for fuel. As on land, J. P. Morgan was champion at sea. He owned three successively larger, faster, and more opulent yachts called *Corsair.* (Morgan had a sense of humor; *corsair* means "pirate.") At least Morgan used his—at every opportunity. Other millionaires bought yachts simply so they could say that they owned one.

Nowhere was consumption more conspicuous and lavish than at upper-class resorts such as Newport, Rhode Island. A summer "cottage" of 30 rooms, used for only three months a year, cost $1 million. Coal baron E. J. Berwind spent $1.5 million to build "The Elms." William K. Vanderbilt outdid everyone with "Marble House." That cottage cost $2 million; the furniture inside, $9 million.

Those places were for vacations. At home in the cities, the millionaires created neighborhoods of mansions such as New York's Fifth Avenue, a thoroughfare given over to grand houses for twenty blocks; Chicago's Gold Coast, which loomed over the city's lakeshore; and San Francisco's Nob Hill, from which palaces looked down on the city like the castles of medieval barons.

A Lord in the Family

A fad of the very rich that aggravated many Americans was the rush during the 1880s and 1890s to marry daughters to European nobles. Nothing more clearly dramatized the aristocratic pretensions of the new elite. Wealthy families took pride in the price that they paid to have an earl or a prince as a son-in-law.

It was a two-way bargain. An American daughter got a title to wear to Newport along with her diamonds. An impoverished European aristocrat got money with which to maintain himself in his accustomed life of fine wines and fox hunts.

Thus, heiress Alice Thaw was embarrassed on her honeymoon as countess of Yarmouth when creditors seized her husband's luggage. She had to wire her father for money to get it out of hock. Helena Zimmerman, the daughter of a coal and iron millionaire from Cincinnati, married the duke of Manchester. For twenty years their bills were paid by the father of the duchess out of the labor of workers living on subsistence wages.

The most famous American aristocrats were the heiresses of two of the original robber barons, Jay Gould and Cornelius Vanderbilt. Anna Gould became the Countess Boni de Castellane. Before she divorced the count so that she could marry his cousin, the higher-ranking Prince de Sagan, the count extracted more than $5 million from Jay Gould's fortune. Consuelo Vanderbilt was married against her wishes into the proudest family in England. Both when Consuelo married the duke of Marlborough and when she divorced him, the payoff ran to several million. The duke may have been the only individual ever to get the better of the Vanderbilt family. American businessmen could handle their own kind easily enough, but they had trouble with their status-symbol sons-in-law.

Women as Decor

The role of young heiresses as pawns in the game of conspicuous waste helps to illustrate the curious role of women in the new social class. They were more idle

YOU CAN TAKE IT WITH YOU

At the Vanderbilt family tomb on Staten Island, watchmen punched a time clock every hour on the hour around the clock. William Vanderbilt, son of the Commodore, had a deathly fear of graverobbers.

Consuelo Vanderbilt's marriage to the Duke of Marlborough marked the epitome of "buying titles" among American millionaires. The unhappiness of the Duchess, which led to divorce, is obvious even in this first photograph of her in her robes.

PRIVATE CARS

Partial to yachts, J. P. Morgan never owned a private railroad car, which was one of the status symbols of the late nineteenth century. In George Gould's, guests for dinner were expected to dress formally; Gould's liveried waiters served the food on solid gold plates. The Vanderbilt family's car, called the "Vanderbilt," could not accommodate all the guests whom they wished to entertain, so they had a new one built and called it "Duchess" after Consuelo. At Palm Beach, a favorite pleasuring ground of the rich, twenty to thirty private cars were sometimes parked in a special section of the train yard. When Morgan wished to go to a place he could not reach by water, he had to rent an opulent private car. On one occasion, he rented a whole train of private cars to transport east coast Episcopalian bishops to a conference in San Francisco.

revolved around the moments when she entered ballrooms, all eyes on her pearls.

Women's fashions were designed to emphasize their wearers' complete idleness. Fashion, by its very nature, is conspicuously wasteful. In keeping up with changes, the whole point of fashion, the wealthy woman was demonstrating that it made no dent in her husband's fortune if she annually discarded last year's expensive clothing to make room in her closet for the latest from Paris.

Fashion reflects social status in other ways. When wealthy women laced themselves up in crippling steel and bone corsets, which made it difficult for them to move, let alone perform any physical work, they were making it clear that they did not have to do such work and were purely decorative. They had servants to care for every detail of their lives.

Men's clothing reflected social status, too. The tall silk hat, the badge of the capitalist, was a completely useless headgear. It offered neither protection nor warmth. But it did prevent a man from so much as

than the men; denied an active role in business and public life, they were also spared the homemaking duties of the middle-class wife and daughter.

They were, in effect, their families' chief consumers. Woman's role was to reflect her husband's accomplishment in amassing wealth; she was a glittering display piece for costly clothing and jewelry. Mrs. George Gould, daughter-in-law of the crusty Jay, went through life known exclusively as the owner of a single pearl necklace that was worth $500,000. No one ever mentioned Mrs. Gould in any other context. Her life

HAVING HER CAKE AND EATING IT TOO

At least one American heiress actually improved her finances by marrying European aristocrats. Alice Heine, daughter of a wealthy New Orleans banker, married the French Duc de Richelieu. When the duke died in 1879, he left her $15. She later married Prince Albert of Monaco, thus becoming the wife of a prince who actually ruled and was himself quite comfortably fixed.

THE LAST DANCE OF THE IDLE RICH: THE BRADLEY MARTIN BALL OF 1897

In the winter of 1896/97, Americans were wrestling with a depression greater than the depression of the 1870s, bad times that would be exceeded only during the Great Depression of the 1930s. Businesses had failed by the thousands. Several million people were out of work. People had been evicted from farms and homes by the hundreds of thousands. The treasuries of charitable organizations were strained to the breaking point; some had given up in despair and closed their doors. Jobless people had marched on Washington; others had rioted; yet others plodded on day by day—gathering coal along railroad tracks, or picking through the garbage pails behind expensive restaurants. In November 1896, a presidential candidate who was called the Great Commoner, William Jennings Bryan, was defeated by William McKinley, who, fairly or not, was widely described as a tool of the moneyed interests. It was an unhappy time, with class sensibilities keen, resentments explosive.

Sometime during that winter, at breakfast in his Fifth Avenue mansion, Bradley Martin, one of high society's grandest adornments, had an idea. "I think it would be a good thing if we got up something," he told his wife and brother, Frederick. "There seems to be a great deal of depression in trade; suppose we send out invitations to a concert."

Mrs. Martin complained that a concert would benefit only foreigners. Most professional musicians in the country at that time were German and Italian, and she wanted to do something for Americans. "I've got a far better idea," she said. "Let us give a costume ball at so short notice that our guests won't have time to get their dresses from Paris. That will give an impetus to trade that nothing else will."

The conversation was recorded by Frederick Townshend Martin with no intention of making his brother and sister-in-law look either vicious or ridiculous. In fact, he justified their economic theories, explaining that "many New York shops sold out brocades and silks which had been lying in their stockrooms for years."

The ball was held on February 10, 1897, in the ballroom of the Waldorf-Astoria Hotel, which had been decorated to resemble the palace of the French kings at Versailles. To the Martins' set, it was a glorious success. According to experts, there was never such a display of jewels in New York. Financier August Belmont came in gold-inlaid armor that cost him $10,000. The costumes of others were inferior only by comparison. One woman said that in order to help the particularly hard-pressed Indians, she had had native Americans make her Pocohontas costume. Bradley Martin himself made a curious selection. As the host at Versailles, he had first claim to be Louis XIV, the Sun King, who had built the great palace and was universally conceded to be the most glorious of the French monarchs. But Bradley chose to be his great-grandson, Louis XV. He would not have wanted to be Louis XVI, who had been beheaded because of his and his predecessors' extravagance in a country where the poor suffered wretched misery.

"Everyone said it was the most brilliant of the kind ever seen in America."

Not quite everyone. Even before the first waltz, Martin and his "idle rich" friends were being vilified from pulpit, editorial desk, and political platform for their callous decadence in a difficult time. Much more significant, the ball was criticized by more than one business leader. If idle heirs such as the vapid Martin did not know that such affairs caused resentment, class hatred, and (in more than one instance in the past) social revolution, sensible businessmen did. Two years after the ball, in his book *The Theory of the Leisure Class*, sociologist Thorstein Veblen would give a name to Bradley Martin's life style, "conspicuous consumption." However, already by that time, America's wealthy were learning to enjoy their riches quietly. Indeed, looking back after several decades, two distinguished historians, Charles and Mary Beard, called the Bradley Martin ball of 1897 the "climax of lavish expenditure" in the United States. "This grand ball of the plutocrats astounded the country, then in the grip of a prolonged business depression with its attendant unemployment, misery, and starvation."

It was not only the fear of social upheaval that wrote an end to conspicuous consumption on a grand scale. To a large extent, high-society affairs like the ball were the doings of women, the wives and daughters of rich businessmen. After the turn of the century, many of them rebelled against their enforced idleness and frivolity and began to take an interest, even a leading role, in social and political causes: votes for women, of course, but also prohibition, suppression of the white-slave racket (prostitution), amelioration of lower-class suffering, and other social programs of the Progressive era.

Not Mrs. Bradley Martin and her husband, of course. Unreconstructable denizens of the ballroom, they carried on as before. But not in New York. The ball was so unpopular there that city hall slapped a large tax increase on the Martin mansion on Fifth Avenue. In a huff, the Martins moved to London. Brother Frederick Townshend Martin wrote of this relocation with an air of despondency: the United States had lost two valuable citizens.

The Waldorf-Astoria Hotel was decorated to resemble the palace at Versailles for the Bradley Martin Costume Ball. It was held, according to Mrs. Martin's brother, to provide employment to seamstresses during the depression of the 1890s.

Mrs. George Gould's identification with her half-million dollar pearl necklace was so total that she was never photographed without it.

bending down to dust his patent-leather shoes. "White collar," displaying clean linen at wrist and neck, made it clear that the wearer did no work that would soil his clothing.

Unlikely Neighbors

For the most part, ordinary Americans knew of the shenanigans of the very rich only through hearsay and the popular press. Farmers and factory workers did not vacation at Newport or attend costume balls and ducal weddings at Blenheim palace. The nature of urban life in the late nineteenth century was such, however, that the idle rich could not completely conceal their extravagance from the middle and lower classes.

The rich employed legions of servants to maintain their mansions. The grandeur and waste of upper-class life was well known to these poorly paid people. (Two million women worked in domestic service at the end of the century.) More important, because it was im-

possible to commute long distances in the congested cities, whether for business or social life, the wealthy lived not in isolated suburbs but close to the centers of New York, Boston, Philadelphia, Chicago, and other great cities.

The tradesmen who made daily deliveries of groceries, meat, vegetables and fruit, ice, coal (for heating), and other necessities, not to mention repairmen and those who delivered durable goods, were intimately familiar with the kind of wealth that their customers enjoyed. Marginal workers who were employed by the service and the light manufacturing industries of the center city walked daily past palaces and saw the rich come and go in lacquered carriages tended by flunkies in livery.

Popular Culture

In newspapers aimed at a mass readership, in popular songs, and in the melodramas favored by workingpeople, the idleness and extravagance of the "filthy rich" were favorite themes. The wealthy were depicted with

Readers of sensationalist newspapers were awed by the beauty of Evelyn Nesbit and titillated by the sex scandal in which she was involved.

a mixture of envy and resentment. New York's Tin Pan Alley, the center of the sheet-music industry, preached a combination of pity for the "bird in a gilded cage," the wealthy woman, and the traditional moral that because poor people worked, they were more virtuous.

In the popular melodramas of the day, simple plays with no subtlety of character and a completely predictable plot, right-living poor people were pitted against an unscrupulous rich villain. "You are only a shopgirl," said the high-society lady in a typical play. "An honest shopgirl," replied the heroine in stilted language, "as far above a fashionable idler as heaven is above earth!" (The poor but virtuous shopgirl was often rewarded in the final act by marriage to a rich young man; she consequently took up the life of idleness that she had condemned through two and a half acts.)

Juicy Scandals

Ordinary people studiously followed the scandals that periodically rocked high society. In 1872, "Jubilee Jim" Fisk was shot to death by a rival for the affections of his showgirl mistress, Josie Mansfield. Newspaper readers took satisfaction in the fact that Fisk's great wealth and power could not save him from a violent death at the comparatively young age of 38. Nevertheless, a good part of the story's appeal were the details of Fisk's sumptuous personal life, on which the newspapers lovingly dwelled.

Even more sensational was the 1906 murder of architect Stanford White by millionaire Harry Thaw. During his trial, Thaw accused White of having seduced his beautiful fiancée, Evelyn Nesbit. Her testimony concerning the famous White's peculiarities behind closed doors simultaneously titillated the public and served as a moral justification for the murder. (Thaw went free.) Such scandals were the stock in trade of nationally circulated periodicals, such as *Police Gazette* and *Frank Leslie's Illustrated Newspaper*, that appealed to the working classes. By the end of the century, many large daily papers also took to bumping conventional news to the back pages when an upper-class scandal came up in the courts.

For Further Reading

Overviews and Classics

Vincent P. DeSantis, *The Shaping of Modern America, 1877–1916* (1973)

John A. Garraty, *The New Commonwealth, 1877–1890* (1968)

Samuel P. Hays, *The Response to Industrialism, 1885–1914* (1957)

Glenn Porter, *The Rise of Big Business, 1860–1910* (1973)

Thorstein Veblen, *The Theory of the Leisure Class* (1899)

Valuable Special Studies

John G. Cawelti, *Apostles of the Self-Made Man in America* (1966)

Sigmund Diamond, *The Reputation of American Businessmen* (1959)

Sidney Fine, *Laissez-Faire and the Welfare State: A Study of Conflict in American Thought, 1865–1901* (1956)

Richard Hofstadter, *Social Darwinism in American Thought* (1944)

Edward C. Kirkland, *Dream and Thought in the Business Community* (1956)

Gabriel Kolko, *Railroads and Regulation* (1965)

Samuel T. McSeveney, *The Politics of Depression: Political Behavior in the Northeast, 1893–1896* (1972)

John L. Thomas, *Alternative America: Henry George, Edward Bellamy, Henry Demarest Lloyd* (1983)

Irwin Wyllie, *The Self-Made Man in America* (1954)

Biographies and Autobiographies

C. A. Barker, *Henry George* (1955)

A. E. Morgan, *Edward Bellamy* (1944)

Andrew Sinclair, *Corsair: The Life of J. Pierpont Morgan* (1981)

30

Factories and Immigrant Ships
The People Who Built Modern America

Leland Stanford and James J. Hill thought of themselves as the men who had built the railroads. So did most Americans. John D. Rockefeller took pride in the majesty of the Standard Oil Company as his personal creation, and, whether they liked the results or not, Americans agreed with him. Newspapers and magazines referred to Andrew Carnegie as the nation's greatest steelmaker. In the popular mind, vast industries were associated with powerful individuals, just as battles were identified with generals: Sherman had marched across Georgia; Grant had taken Richmond; Vanderbilt ran the New York Central. J. P. Morgan even spoke of his hobby, yachting, in personal terms. "You can do business with anyone," he huffed, "but you can only sail a boat with a gentleman."

In reality, Morgan and his friends merely decided when and where the boat was to go. It took 85 grimy stokers and hard-handed sailors to get Morgan's *Corsair* out of New York harbor and safely into Newport or Venice. In the same way, Stanford, Hill, Rockefeller, Carnegie, and other great businessmen supervised the creation of industrial America, but the edifice was built by anonymous millions of men and women who wielded the shovels and needles and tended the machines that whirred and whined in the factories and mills.

Immigrants, identification tags pinned to their clothes, arrive at Ellis Island, New York, in 1907.

A NEW WAY OF LIFE

America's workingpeople could not be kept below decks like the crew of the *Corsair.* While the population of the United States rose rapidly during the last part of the nineteenth century, more than doubling between 1860 and 1900, the size of the working class quadrupled. In 1860, 1.5 million Americans made their living in workshops and mills, and another 700,000 in mining and construction. By 1900, 6 million people worked in manufacturing and 2.3 million in mining and construction, increases of four times and 3.3 times, respectively. Wageworkers, previously a minor part of the American population, now constituted a distinct and significant social class.

Bigger Factories, Better Technology

The size of the work place also grew, a fact of profound importance for the quality of workingpeople's lives. In 1870, the average workshop in the United States employed eight people and was owned by an individual or by partners who lived nearby and who personally supervised the business, sometimes working at the bench side by side with their employees. Like it or not, generous or cruel, such bosses were personally involved in the lives of their workers. They heard of events in their lives ranging from the birth of a child to the death of a parent, and they discussed matters such as wages, hours, and shop conditions face to face with the people who were affected by them.

By 1900, the average industrial worker labored in a shop with 25 employees, and many worked in large factories with hundreds of co-workers. In 1870, not one American factory employed as many as a thousand men and women. By 1900, such gigantic plants were common, and a few companies listed 10,000 people on the payroll. The typical employer of 1900 was a large company that was directed by men who rarely stepped onto the floor of a shop. They were interested in wages, hours, and conditions only insofar as these figures were entered in the ledgers that lined the walls of their offices.

The increased application of steam power—few mills were still water driven by 1900—and constantly improved machinery affected workers in other ways. The highly skilled craftsman, trained for years in the use of hand tools, ceased to be the backbone of the manufacturing process. Not many crafts actually disappeared (as they would in the twentieth century), and some, like the machinist's trade, increased in importance. But in almost every area, steam-powered

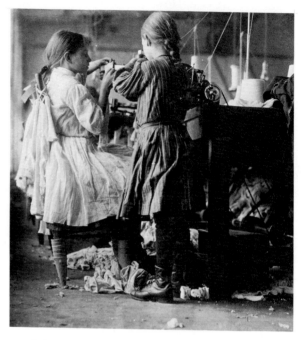

Girls work at a thread-winding machine at the Loudon Hosiery Mill in Loudon, Tennessee, in 1910.

machines took over from artisans and "mechanics," performing their jobs more quickly and usually better.

Into their places came the unskilled or semiskilled machine tenders—men, women, and children who merely guided the device at its task. Unlike craftsmen, these workers were interchangeable, easily replaced because their jobs required little training. For this reason, they were poorly paid, and they commanded scant respect from employers, small businessmen, professionals, politicians, and skilled workers.

Wages

The cash wages of workingpeople remained the same or declined during the final decades of the nineteenth century. However, *real wages,* or purchasing power, actually rose. The cost of food, clothing, and housing dropped more radically than did hourly pay during the deflationary final decades of the nineteenth century. Taken as a whole, the industrial working class enjoyed almost 50 percent more purchasing power in 1900 than in 1860.

But this statistic can be misleading because the skilled "aristocracy of labor"—locomotive engineers, machinists, master carpenters, printers, and other highly trained craftsmen—improved their earnings much more than did the unskilled workers at the bottom of the pyramid. The average annual wage for manufacturing workers in 1900 was only $435, or $8.37 a week. Unskilled workers were paid about ten

AVERAGE ANNUAL EARNINGS FOR SELECTED OCCUPATIONS—1890

Farm laborers	$233
Public school teachers	256
Bituminous coal miners	406
Manufacturing employees	439
Street railway employees	557
Steam railroad employees	560
Gas & electricity workers	687
Ministers	794
Clerical workers in manufacturing & Steam RR	848
Postal employees	878

cents an hour on the average, about $5.50 a week. A girl of twelve or thirteen, tending a loom in a textile factory, might take home as little as $2 a week after various fines (for being late to work, for example) were deducted from her pay. As late as 1904, sociologist Robert Hunter estimated that one American in eight lived in poverty, and he almost certainly hit below the true figure.

Hours and Conditions

Hours on the job varied as widely as wages. Most government employees had enjoyed an eight-hour day since 1840. Skilled workers, especially in the building trades (bricklayers, carpenters, plumbers), generally worked ten. Elsewhere, such humane hours were rare. A factory worker was counted lucky if he or she worked a twelve-hour day. During the summer months, many mills ran from sunup to sundown, as long as sixteen hours—with only one shift.

The average workweek was 66 hours in 1860, and 55 hours in 1910. It was usually five and a half or six days long. (Half-day Saturday was considered a holiday.) In industries that were required to run around the clock, such as steel (the furnaces could not be

JOHN HENRY

Ironically, considering that few blacks held industrial jobs in the nineteenth century, a black man became the symbol of the decline of the skilled worker in the face of the new machines. "The Ballad of John Henry," written about 1872 and immediately popular among workingpeople, told the story of a black miner's contest with the newly introduced steam drill. There are several versions. Most of them end in tragedy for the human being. John Henry might defeat the steam drill in a contest to sink steel in rock, but he dies from the pace, "with his hammer in his hand."

shut down), some gangs were divided into two shifts on seven-day schedules. Each shift worked for twelve hours. At the end of a two-week period, the day workers switched shifts with the night workers. This meant a "holiday" of 24 hours once a month. The price of this luxury was working for 24 hours two weeks later while the other shift enjoyed its vacation.

Except to skilled workers, regular holidays were virtually unknown. Because of the erratic swings in the business cycle of the period, however, factory workers had plenty of unwanted time off. Some industries were highly seasonal. Coal miners, for example, could expect to be without wages for weeks or even months during the summer, when city people did not heat their homes. In times of depression, of course, unemployment was worse. During the depressions of the 1870s and 1890s, about 12 percent of the working population was jobless.

While some employers attended carefully to safety conditions, a safe work place was by no means the rule. Liability law provided that an employer could be sued by an injured worker only if the worker was not responsible for an accident. Short of the collapse of a factory roof, this was rarely the case. If a worker was hurt because his machine was dangerous, the employer was not liable, even if the worker could prove that he would have been fired had he refused to tend the machine. Railroads had a particularly horrid record. Every year, one railroad worker in 26 was injured seriously, and one in 400 was killed. Textile workers without some fingers and ex-textile workers without hands were fixtures in every mill town.

Between 1880 and 1900, 35,000 American workers were killed on the job, an average of one about every two days. In many cases, their wives or dependents received nothing. In most, employer compensation amounted to little more than burial expenses. In the coal fields, the mine owners thought themselves generous if they allowed a dead miner's teenage son, who was younger than the regulation age, to take a job in the mines in order to support his family.

What compensation there was applied only to accidents. Occupational diseases—the coal miner's "black lung," the cotton-mill worker's "white lung," and the hard-rock miner's silicosis—were not recognized as the employer's responsibility. Poisoning resulting from work with chemicals was rarely identified as related to the job.

WHO WERE THE WORKERS?

Skilled workers inclined to be males of old-stock British or Irish origin. Unskilled jobs were generally filled

Mostly women and children, these cannery workers prepare beans under the strict eyes of the supervisor.

by children, women, and recent immigrants. But that was only the norm.

Child Labor

In 1900, the socialist writer John Spargo estimated that 1,752,187 children under 16 years of age were employed full time. They did all but the heaviest kinds of work. Girls as young as twelve tended dangerous looms and spinning machines in textile mills. "Bobbin boys" of ten hauled heavy wooden boxes filled with spindles from spinning rooms to weaving rooms and back again. Children swept filings in machine shops. Boys as young as eight were found working the "breakers" at coal mines, hand picking slate from anthracite in filthy, frigid wooden sheds.

In city tenement "sweat shops," whole families and their boarders sewed clothing or rolled cigars by hand, and children worked as soon as they were able to master the simplest tasks. In cities, children practically monopolized messenger-service work, light delivery, and some kinds of huckstering. Apprenticeship in

some skilled trades largely amounted to low-paying menial labor for long hours.

In part, child labor was the fruit of greed. On the grounds that children had no nonworking dependents to support, employers paid them less than adults. The justification was not always convincing, however. In southern textile towns, the "Mill Daddy" became a familiar figure. Unable to find work because his own children could be hired for less, the Mill Daddy was reduced to carrying lunches to the factory and tossing them over the fence each noon.

But the widespread character of child labor also provides an example of "cultural lag." It took time for society to face up to the reality that industrial life was something new in the world; factory work was different from work on a family farm or in a small workshop. Children had always worked. But where relations in the work place were personal, as in the small shop, the limited capacity of the immature person, especially a child's fatigue when set to tedious, repetitive tasks, was easy to recognize and take into account. Placed

Rural vs Urban

The change from a rural to an urban environment was a gradual process that gained increasing
momentum as the population of the country increased. Landscape (detail) by Thomas Cole
(1825) depicts an early pioneer's homestead. The Minneapolis Institute of Arts.

Philadelphia was the largest colonial city with a population of over 28,000 by 1770. This print by William Birch views Second Street North from Market with Christ Church.

During the heyday of steamboats, St. Louis became the gateway to the West for thousands of settlers.

Tranquil rural life before the Civil War was portrayed by William Mount in Eel Spearing at Setauket (above) and Long Island Farmer Husking Corn (right).

Although it was the capital of the nation, in 1851 Washington, D.C., was still a small southern town.

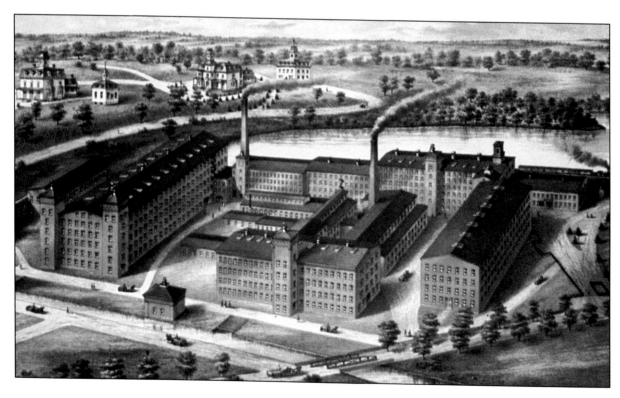

As factories grew, they often became the sole source of employment for people living in the area.

Gift for the Grangers, *a lithograph made in 1873, celebrates the virtues of the Patrons of Husbandry, a farmer's organization.*

An elevated train moves above street traffic in this 1895 painting by W. Louis Sontag, Jr.,
The Bowery at Night.

Alexander Hogue captures the abandonment and despair of the Dust Bowl in Drought Stricken Area *(1934).* Dallas Museum of Art, Dallas Art Association Purchase.

American Gothic *by Grant Wood is a vivid study of determined, hardworking farm people and their entire way of life.* Art Institute of Chicago.

"Street Scene" from the mural Metropolitan Life *was painted by Victor Arnautoff in 1934 for the WPA.*

in a niche in a massive factory, the child laborer became nothing but a number on an accountant's sheet.

Women Workers

Cultural lag also played a part in the large numbers of women in industry. The *first* industrial workers had been female, partly because women had always been the mainstay of cloth making in western culture, partly because the founders of the first American textile mills had not been able to imagine factory work as a suitable lifetime career for the head of a family. Instead of recruiting men to work in their mills, the early cloth manufacturers had persuaded New England farmers to send their unmarried daughters to towns like Lowell, Massachusetts. The plan had been that they would work for a few years, save their money, and return to the farm to take up their true calling as wives of farmers, with a dowry that their fathers could not afford.

In devising the "Lowell system," the well-meaning pioneers of the factory system had believed that they had reconciled industrialization with the old way of life. But the increasing demands of growing industry, and the heavy nature of much factory work, soon resulted in a work force that was predominantly male. Nevertheless, Lowell paternalism survived here and there into the twentieth century. And the difficulty of supporting a family on one person's income forced working-class women to continue to labor for wages even after they married. In 1900, almost 20 percent of the total work force was female. About half the workers in textiles were women, and the percentage

A newsboy peddles papers in St. Louis, Missouri.

WEEKENDS OFF

The necessity of taking a break from toil was recognized at the dawn of history. The western tradition of one day off a week derives from the sabbath of the ancient Hebrews, a day—Saturday—when the Lord forbade work. The Christians made Sunday their sabbath, in part to distinguish themselves from their Jewish origins and the medieval church forbade "servile labor" on the sabbath as one of its precepts. The longer weekend is of English origin. In 958 A.D., the Saxon King Edgar ordered that peasants cease working at noon on Saturday. In the United States, the five-day workweek became general only in the twentieth century. Scheduling certain holidays—most notably Labor Day, a legal holiday since 1894—created the occasional "three-day weekend" but as high absenteeism rates on Fridays and "Blue Mondays" tell, personally proclaimed three-day weekends occur more frequently. During the 1970s, there was a flurry of enthusiasm in some industries for a four-day workweek and a three-day weekend as a means of saving jobs for more people in troubled industries, but the movement did not have much effect.

in the needle trades and other home manufactures was much higher.

With few exceptions, women were paid less than men, sometimes half as much for performing the same tasks for the same number of hours. Abysmally low pay was particularly characteristic of the largest female occupation. In 1900, 2 million women were employed for subsistence wages or less in domestic service: cooking, cleaning, and tending the vanities and children of the well-to-do.

DIVIDE AND CONQUER

A western lumber magnate explained that in order to have a tractable work force, an employer should hire from several ethnic groups: "Don't get too great a percentage of any one nationality. For your own good and theirs mix them up and obliterate clannishness and selfish social prejudices."

WOMEN IN THE WORK FORCE

There was at least one woman in each occupation listed by the Census Bureau in 1890. More than 225,000 were running farms, and 1,143 listed their occupation as clergyman. Women outnumbered men as teachers and as waiters (the latter by five to one). There were 28 female lumberjacks. In all the United States, however, out of 12,856 wheelwrights (makers and repairers of wagon wheels) there was only one woman.

Women factory workers, being paid less than men, were more economical to employ.

No Blacks Need Apply

Very few industrial jobs were open to blacks. While a few carved out places for themselves in the lowest-paying jobs, the prejudice of white workers as well as employers kept blacks concentrated in agriculture and in low-paying service occupations: domestic servants, waiters, porters, and the like. In 1900, more than 80 percent of the black population lived in the South, most of them on the land.

The industrial color line was most clearly drawn in the South. When the cotton textile industry moved south at the end of the century, the millowners drew on the poor white population for its work force. Implicitly, and sometimes explicitly, employees were informed that if they proved troublesome (that is, if they complained about wages, hours, and conditions), the companies could always tap the huge and poor black population. Racism served to keep southern workers the poorest industrial work force in the country. Rather than risk the loss of poorly paid jobs to blacks, they accepted their low wages and standard of living.

THE ORGANIZED LABOR MOVEMENT

However poorly industrial work paid, it was generally preferable to other alternatives open to people on the bottom of society and even a few steps up on the social scale. As a result, the majority of workers most of the time passively accepted unattractive wages, hours, and conditions of labor. They expressed their discontent (or desperation) as toilers have done since ancient times. For example, absenteeism was high in factories, particularly on Mondays after beery Sundays. They were unable to take holidays sufficient to health and sanity, and in good times, when getting another menial job was easy, workers simply quit on a minute's notice.

Sabotage was a word yet to be invented, but the practice was well understood. When the pace of work reached the dropping point, or a foreman stepped beyond the bounds of tolerable behavior, it was easy enough to clog or damage a machine so that it appeared to be an accident—and take a break while it was fixed. An angry worker who had made up his mind to quit might decide literally to "throw a monkey wrench into the works" or to slash the leather belts that turned the looms, drills, stampers, lathes—that ran the entire factory.

A Heritage of Violence

When workers were nearly powerless to remedy their conditions, violence was common in the work place. During the nationwide railroad strike of 1877, an unorganized, spontaneous outbreak that was caused by depression, workers did not merely walk off the job, but they stormed in mobs into railroad yards and set trains and buildings on fire. In a few places they fought pitched gun battles with company guards and, toward the end of the unsuccessful strike, with troops who had been called out to put them down.

At Andrew Carnegie's Homestead Works in 1892, a strike led by the Amalgamated Association of Iron and Steel Workers actually besieged the giant factory and forced the withdrawal of a barge bringing 300 armed guards into the town. Similar conflicts characterized labor disputes in many industries; they were nowhere more bloody and bitter than in the coal mines of Pennsylvania and in the hard-rock gold and silver mines of the mountain West.

The Molly Maguires

During the early 1870s, many Irish coal miners in northeastern Pennsylvania gave up on the possibility of improving the conditions of their unhealthful and dangerous work through peaceful means. Within the semisecret atmosphere of a fraternal lodge, the Ancient Order of Hibernians, they formed a secret society called the Molly Maguires. The Mollys then launched an effective campaign of terrorism against the mine owners and particularly the supervisors. They systematically destroyed mine property and murdered loyal

SABOTAGE

Sabotage is thought of as violent, but it is not necessarily so, and the origin of the word, at the end of the nineteenth century, is ambivalent. The word comes from the French word for the wooden shoes many peasants still wore, *sabots*. One explanation of its beginnings is that when a worker threw a sabot into a machine, like a monkey wrench, the machine would be damaged. Another is that sabotage was nonviolent: it meant the conscious withdrawal of efficiency; that is, angry French stevedores—men who load and unload ships—decided to work as if they were peasants in the clumsy *sabots*—in other words, not very well. In any case, while some American labor leaders called only for the peaceful form of sabotage, which they called "striking on the job," it was the other meaning that stuck.

company men rather than merely beating them up. (In which case, the victims could have identified their attackers.)

Because of the ethnic dimension of the conflict—almost all the miners were Irish; almost all the bosses were American or Cornish—the Molly Maguires were able to maintain an effective secrecy. Their enemies did not know who they were, how numerous they were, how much support they had in the community. To this day, historians are unable to discuss the Mollys in other than general terms, and some have suggested that the organization was largely a figment of the mine owners' imagination, created in order to provide an excuse for demoralizing the mining community as a whole.

In any event, the mine owners brought in an Irish-American undercover detective, James McParland. He was an employee of the Pinkerton Agency, which specialized in breaking up unions. McParland infiltrated the Mollys and gathered evidence that led to the hanging of several men and the destruction of the organization.

The Union Makes Us Strong

At best, violence is a risky mode of protest and resistance. In a stable and free society, organizing for strength seemed more appropriate and likely to yield results. "One out of many," "in numbers there is strength," the sacredness accorded to the federal union in the Civil War—all such American mottos and ideals fed the imaginations of workingpeople who were determined to have their contributions recognized.

The first American union dated from before 1800, an association of shoemakers in Philadelphia, the Knights of St. Crispin. Workingmen's associations had

been the backbone of the Jacksonian political movement in the eastern states. By the early 1870s, skilled workers such as machinists, iron molders, carpenters, and locomotive engineers and firemen had formed thousands of local trade groups that totaled about 300,000 members.

For the most part, these scattered organizations had little to do with one another. Developing at a time when industry was decentralized, the unions inevitably lagged behind the employers in recognizing the need for national organization. By the end of the Civil War, however, the outlines of the new industrial order were clearly sketched in. In 1866, William Sylvis, a visionary iron puddler (a man who made castings from molds), founded the National Labor Union and devoted the last three years of his life to its cause, traveling by foot around the northeastern states and rallying workers of every occupation in churches, in fraternal lodges, or under the stars.

Sylvis believed that the workers' future depended on political involvement. He formed alliances with a number of reform groups, including the woman-suffrage movement and farmers' organizations that were lobbying for a cheap currency. The National Labor party put up candidates in the presidential election of 1872. So poor was their showing, however, that the party and the NLU itself broke up, its members demoralized. From a membership of 400,000 in 1872, the NLU disappeared within two years.

The Knights of Labor

A different kind of national labor organization already had emerged to take the place of the National Labor Union. Organized in 1869 by a group of tailors led by Uriah P. Stephens, the Noble and Holy Order of the Knights of Labor spread its message much more quietly than Sylvis had done. Indeed the Knights spread it *secretly*. Stephens was aware that an employer's usual reaction, when he discovered a union man in his midst, was to fire him. When the Knights announced meetings in newspaper advertisements, they did not even reveal their name but identified the group as ✶✶✶✶✶✶.

The Knights of Labor also differed from the NLU in their disinterest in political action as an organization. Members were urged to vote, but Stephens believed that the interests of workingpeople would ultimately be served by solidarity in the work place in opposition to their enemies. Who those enemies were, however, was never clearly defined. Sometimes the Knights spoke of a conflict between producers and parasites—workers and farmers, on the one hand; capitalists, on the other—but they barred membership to only saloonkeepers, lawyers, and gamblers, hardly professions

Women delegates to a Knights of Labor convention held in 1886.

that included all the bosses of industrial America. In fact, Stephens disliked the idea of class conflict and looked forward to a day when men and women of good will in all social classes would abolish the wage system and establish a cooperative commonwealth. Women were welcome in the Knights; so were blacks and unskilled workers, who usually were overlooked as union material in the nineteenth century. However, the Knights failed to appeal to one group that was essential to the success of any labor organization; Roman Catholics, particularly Irish-Americans, were the single largest ethnic group in the working class.

As the name of his organization implies, Stephens surrounded the Knights of Labor with the mystery, symbolism, ritual, secret handshakes, and other riga-marole that was common to American fraternal orga-nizations. A lifelong Freemason, Stephens based the Knights' ritual on that of his own lodge.

The trouble was that in Europe, the Masons were an anti-Catholic organization, and the pope forbade members of the Church to join secret societies of any sort. The Catholic suspicion of the Knights was a serious drawback. Without Catholic support, no labor organization could prosper.

Enter Terence Powderly

In 1879, Stephens was succeeded as Grand Master Workman by Terence V. Powderly, a deceptively mild-looking man with a handlebar moustache. Himself a Roman Catholic, albeit not strictly observant, Pow-derly brought the Knights into the open and toned down the Masonic flavor of the ritual. He persuaded an influential Catholic bishop, James Gibbons, to pre-vail on the pope to approve Catholic membership in the union.

Then the Knights grew at a dazzling rate. By 1885, there were 110,000 members, and in only one year, the union grew to 700,000. Powderly disliked strikes, so it was ironic that the major impetus of this increase was a remarkable victory over Jay Gould's Missouri Pacific Railroad. Gould had vowed to destroy the union. "I can hire half the working class to kill the other half," he growled. But when he tried to cut wages, the Knights closed down his line and forced him to meet with their leaders and agree to their terms.

The easy victory and the explosive growth of the union proved to be a curse as well as a blessing. Pow-derly and the union's general assembly were unable to control the new members. Instead of working together according to a national policy, which was the rationale of a national labor organization, local leaders, who were often new to the concept of unionism, were encouraged by the victory in the Missouri Pacific strike to go it alone in a dozen unrelated directions. Powderly fumed and sputtered and refused to back the rash of strikes in 1885 and 1886. But he could not stop them.

Jay Gould got his revenge, completely crushing a strike against the Texas Pacific Railroad, another of his many properties. Then, in 1886, the Haymarket tragedy was unfairly but effectively imputed to the Knights. Membership plummeted. Workers wanted union; not many wanted chaos.

Samuel Gompers and the AFL

In the same year, a national labor organization dedi-cated to union and stability for some workers was put together by a few dozen existing associations of skilled workers. The American Federation of Labor's guiding spirit was a cigarmaker, born in London of Dutch-Jewish parents, an emigrant to the United States as a boy. Samuel Gompers astonished his fellow workers (and their employers) with his intelligence, learning,

THE YELLOW-DOG CONTRACT

Yellow-dog contracts, which were forced on employees by some companies, were meant to intimidate as much as anything else. The penalty for violating such a contract was dismissal, which employers did often enough without such documents. Employees had to agree that "in consideration of my present employ-ment I hereby promise and agree that I will forthwith abandon any and all membership, connection, or af-filiation with any organization or society, whether se-cret or open, which in any way attempts to regulate the conditions of my services or the payment there-for."

toughness in bargaining, and oratorical eloquence. He was a homely, even ugly man, squat and thick of body with a broad, coarse-featured face. But this uncomely character had very definite ideas about how organizations of labor could not only survive in the United States, but become one of the interlocking forces that governed the country.

No Unskilled Workers or Dreamers Need Apply

First of all, Gompers believed that only skilled craftsmen could effectively force employers to negotiate with them. When bricklayers refused to work, and all the bricklayers in a locality stuck together, the employer who wanted bricks laid had no choice but to talk. When the unskilled hod carriers (workers who carried the bricks to the bricklayers) went out, however, employers had no difficulty in finding other men with strong backs and empty stomachs to take their

Samuel Gompers was elected head of the American Federation of Labor every year but one until his death in 1924.

place. Therefore, Gompers concluded, the AFL would admit only skilled workers.

Second, the goal of the AFL unions was "bread and butter," higher wages, shorter hours, better working conditions. Gompers had no patience with socialistic or other utopian dreamers. What counted was the here and now, not "pie in the sky." Unions with utopian programs not only distracted workers from the concrete issues that counted, but were easy targets for suppression by the bosses who were able (as in the Haymarket incident) to convince Americans that labor organizations threatened the very stability of their society.

Third, while Gompers believed that the strike, as peaceful coercion, was the union's best weapon, he made it clear that AFL unions would cooperate with employers who recognized and bargained with them. Make union partners in industry, especially AFL unions that supported the capitalist system, and radical anticapitalist organizations would wither and die.

Conservative Unionism

Gompers, who lived until 1924, served as president of the AFL every year but one (when AFL socialists defeated him). He did not see his hopes come to fruition, but he made a start. With his carrot-and-stick approach to dealing with employers—striking against those who refused to deal with the AFL, cooperating with those who accepted unions—he saw the AFL grow from 150,000 members in 1888 to more than 1 million shortly after the turn of the century.

Most employers continued to hate him and the AFL as dearly as they hated socialists and revolutionary labor unions. "Can't I do what I want with my own?" Cornelius Vanderbilt had asked years before about his company's policies. The majority of American industrialists continued to believe that the wages they paid and the hours their employees worked were no one's business but their own. Their argument was that the worker who did not like his pay had the right to quit. In 1893, hard-nosed antilabor employers formed the National Association of Manufacturers to destroy unionism wherever it appeared. The NAM remained the most important antiunion organization into the twentieth century.

The Friends of Friends

In 1900, a more enlightened group of manufacturers led by Frank Easley and Marcus A. Hanna, a former Rockefeller associate, came to the conclusion that labor unions were a permanent part of the American industrial scene. The choice was not between unions and no unions. The choice was between conservative, procapitalist unions that were willing to cooperate with employers and desperate, revolutionary unions that were determined to destroy capitalism. They chose Gompers's AFL and joined with him in 1900 to form the National Civic Federation, which was to work for industrial peace through employer–union co-operation.

By 1900, there was no doubt that the AFL would survive. Nevertheless, and as much due to Gompers as were the successes of the AFL, the conservative trade-union movement failed to recognize some of the most serious questions that would face workingpeople in the twentieth century. The AFL remained inflexible in its opposition to organizing unskilled workers. On more than one occasion, Gompers used AFL unions to destroy unions formed by the unskilled.

By the turn of the century, this policy was not so much a tough practical decision as it was a reflection of the labor aristocracy's prejudice against the new immigrants who made up the mass of the unskilled work force. In part, the AFL wanted immigration re-stricted on economic grounds. By cutting off the supply of cheap labor from abroad, American workers would be better able to improve their own situation. How-ever, Gompers and many of his strongest supporters also harbored a racial dislike for the newcomers. Cu-riously, though of Jewish background (although per-sonally irreligious), Gompers was able to denounce Jewish immigrants from Eastern Europe as being in-capable of becoming good American citizens. His views concerning the Japanese and Chinese on the west coast were frankly racist.

The AFL unions also generally opposed the organi-zation of women (20 percent of the work force) and blacks, who were not numerically important outside of agriculture but were potentially of supreme interest to any working-class movement because they could be used as strikebreakers. The result was that while the lot of the skilled workers steadily improved in the late nineteenth and early twentieth centuries, only 3 per-cent of "gainfully employed" Americans were members of labor organizations. A union movement, the AFL was; a working-class organization, it was not.

THE NATION OF IMMIGRANTS

"So at last I was going to America! Really, really going at last!" These words were written by Mary Antin, recalling her feelings as a girl in a *shtetl*, a Jewish village in the Russian Empire, when her family decided that their future lay in the United States. "The boundaries burst!" she went on. "The arch of heaven soared! A million suns shone out for every star. The winds rushed in from outer space, roaring in my ear, 'America! America!' "

A sign in four languages helps immigrants at Ellis Island.

No one ever caught the thrill of moving to the New World with such exuberance. It may have been Mary Antin's genius with her adopted language. Americans thought so: they bought 85,000 copies of *The Promised Land* when it was published in 1912. Or her joy may have been because, as Jews, her mother and father had come to the United States not merely to improve their standard of living, but to survive.

In 1881, a czar who had relaxed anti-Jewish laws in Russia was assassinated. His dim-witted son, Alexan-der III, persecuted the Jews and encouraged Christian peasants to rampage through the *shtetls* on bloody po-groms (from the Russian word meaning "riot" or "dev-astation"). Frustrated by the poverty and desperation of their own lives in that oppressive and poor country, they beat and killed Jews with no fear of the law. As they had before and would again, the Jews moved on. Between about 1881 and 1914, fully one-third of the Jewish population of Russia left the country, most of them for the United States. It was one of the greatest relocations of a people in such a short period in the history of the world.

And the Jews were not the largest group of people to come to the United States during the late nine-teenth and early twentieth centuries. Between 1890 and 1914 (when the outbreak of the First World War temporarily choked off immigration), some 3.6 million Italians cleared the Immigration Service. And there were others: Irish, Scots, Welsh, English, Scandinavians, Germans—the so-called "Old Immigration" that continued in large numbers through the late nineteenth century—and Poles, Lithuanians, Ukrainians, Russians, Serbians, Croatians, Slovenes, Armenians, Greeks, and, from Asia, Chinese and Japanese.

Immigration Old and New

Immigration was and is part and parcel of the American historical experience. The word itself, meaning movement *to a place,* was coined by an American, as more appropriate to Americans than emigration, movement *from a place.* Not even the Indians, the "native Americans," had originated in the Western Hemisphere. Throughout most of the colonial period, immigrants were as important to American growth as the natural increase of population. The Revolution and the uncertain period that followed slowed down the flow of newcomers, but not even the dangers of sea travel during the War of 1812 could quite close it down. After 1815, Europeans came over in numbers that increased almost annually. Only during serious depressions, when jobs were scarce, and during the Civil War, when a young man might be drafted before he shook down his sea legs, did the influx slow down.

From 10,000 in 1825, immigration topped 100,000 in 1845. Except for the first two years of the Civil War, the annual total never dipped below that figure.

In 1854, a record 428,000 foreigners stepped ashore. It was broken in 1880, when 457,000 immigrants made landfalls in Boston, New York, Philadelphia, Baltimore, New Orleans, and dozens of smaller ports. Only a crippling depression during the 1890s pushed the total below 300,000. After the turn of the century, during each of six years, more than 1 million people arrived to make homes in the United States. Always an abundant stream, sometimes swollen, immigration had become a flood.

But there was more to the immigration after 1880 than a mere increase in numbers. Before 1880, a large majority of immigrants listed the British Isles (including Ireland), Germany, or Scandinavia as their place of birth. While these northern and western Europeans continued to arrive in large numbers after 1880, an annually larger proportion of newcomers after that year originated in southern Italy: the Ottoman (Turkish) Empire; Greece; and the Slavic, Hungarian, and Rumanian parts of the Austro-Hungarian Empire. And from Russia, which then included much of Poland, came both Christian and Jewish Russians, Poles, Lithuanians, Latvians, Estonians, and Finns.

Before 1880, only about 200,000 people of southern and eastern European origin *lived in* the United States. Between 1880 and 1910, about 8.4 million *arrived.* In 1896, this New Immigration exceeded the Old for the

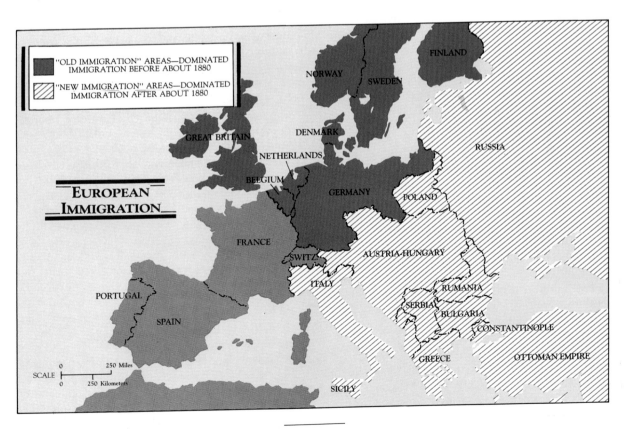

EUROPEAN IMMIGRATION

"OLD IMMIGRATION" AREAS—DOMINATED IMMIGRATION BEFORE ABOUT 1880

"NEW IMMIGRATION" AREAS—DOMINATED IMMIGRATION AFTER ABOUT 1880 first time. By 1907, New Immigrants were almost the whole of the influx. Of 1,285,349 legal immigrants who were registered that year, just about 1 million began their long, difficult journey in southern and Eastern Europe.

Birth Pains of a World Economy

Although only parts of Europe, North America, and Japan may be described as having been "industrialized" in the nineteenth century, the effects of this economic revolution were felt everywhere save the most remote jungles and mountain valleys. A decline in infant mortality and an increase in life expectancy, side effects of the new technology, resulted in a giant leap in population in agricultural lands as well as in the industrial countries. The world production of foodstuffs soared too, but unequally. The biggest gains were made where agriculture was itself becoming mechanized, as in the United States. In those parts of the world where peasants remained the agricultural work force, food production did not keep up with population growth. Thus, the grain from the broad American prairies and increasingly from Canada undersold grain raised on small plots by peasants in countries such as Italy and Poland, the granary of Eastern Europe. Even in Italy and Poland, American and Canadian grain was cheaper than the home-grown product.

This and increasing population knocked the bottom out of the standard of living in the industrial world's hinterlands. During the latter decades of the nineteenth century, southern Italian farm workers made between $40 and $60 a year, Polish farm workers about the same. The cash income of peasants in southern China was too small to be calculated. When large landowners in Europe attempted to consolidate and modernize their holdings, the result was to push people off the land even more efficiently than declining incomes had.

The Jews of Russia felt the effects of the worldwide Industrial Revolution in their own way. Generally forbidden by Russian law to own land, most of them were old-fashioned artisans who handcrafted goods. Others were peddlers, some fixed in one place, others wandered. Both craftsmen and peddlers found that their way of life was undercut by modernization. The shoes made by a Warsaw cobbler could not compete with cheap, machine-made shoes from England. The peddler who wandered around Russian Poland trying to sell handmade clothing learned the same lesson.

Fleeing Militarism

Finally, people on the bottom in Germany, in the Austro-Hungarian, Russian, and Ottoman empires, and in some smaller nations were cursed by the drive to build up modern military forces. In the period before the First World War, conscription into the army could mean a life sentence. Terms were ten to twelve years in Austria-Hungary, and sometimes 25 years in Russia. Even when the term of service was just a few years, army life was brutalizing. For generations, peasants and immigrants to the United States related chilling tales of self-mutilation by young men who were trying to escape the press gangs; they chopped off their toes or fingers, or blinded an eye.

Clearly it was better to go to South America, which became home to many Germans and Italians, or to Canada, which boasts a population as ethnically mixed as that of the United States. But most of all they emigrated to the United States, where the opportunities were greatest.

Promoting Immigration

American industrialists encouraged immigration. Until the Foran Act of 1885 made it illegal to do so, some companies paid immigrants' fares if they signed contracts agreeing to work for their patrons when they arrived in the United States. James J. Hill plastered every sizable town in Sweden and Norway with posters that described the richness of the soil along his Great Northern Railroad. (South Dakota was nicknamed the "Sunshine State" in a promotional campaign; some advertisements had palm trees swaying in the balmy Dakotan breezes.) The American Woolens Company circulated handbills in southern Italy that showed an immigrant worker with a sleek, perfumed handlebar moustache carrying a heavy sack of money from a mill to a *banco* across the street. In the West, railroaders and other employers encouraged Cantonese labor recruiters to import gangs of Chinese coolies to do heavy, low-paying construction work.

Employers liked immigrant labor because it was invariably cheaper than American labor; because immigrants would take menial, dirty jobs that Americans shunned; and because the newcomers were almost always more docile than old-stock Americans. So far from familiar surroundings and customs, they hesitated to complain. Since many intended to work in America only temporarily, a few months or a few years, and then return to their homelands, they were likely to accept very low wages, live on next to nothing, and take no interest in joining a union or going on strike.

From the national perspective, immigrant labor was pure asset. On the average, more than 60 percent of the arrivals on late nineteenth-century immigrant ships were able-bodied males; the percentage was higher among Italians and Greeks. The "old country" had borne the expense of supporting them during their

Posters like this—"Direct to America"—caught the eye of farmers in even the smallest villages of Scandinavia.

unproductive childhood years and was still, in part, supporting their women and children. In the United States, they were producers and consumed little. It was a very profitable arrangement.

ETHNIC AMERICA

In addition to the general push and pull that affected all immigrants to some degree, each ethnic group had its unique experience that strongly influenced both the decision to make a home in a new land and the reception that greeted them.

The Smooth Road of the British

It is sometimes forgotten that people from England, Scotland, Wales, and the Protestant north of Ireland continued to be among the major immigrant groups of the nineteenth century. Between the Civil War and the turn of the century, 1.9 million Britons came to the United States. They were almost immediately at home among a people who derived primarily from their stock: in appearance they were indistinguishable from the vast majority of white Americans; they practiced the religious faiths that were most common in the United States, were familiar with the basic culture and folkways, and spoke the language.

To be sure, they spoke with identifiable accents that distinguished them from native-born Americans. But those accents are so rarely mentioned in the historical sources that it seems clear that the foreign birth of English, Scottish, and Welsh immigrants separated them in no meaningful way from the mainstream of American society. Andrew Carnegie, Alexander Graham Bell, James J. Hill, and several of John D. Rockefeller's associates were British, but their places of birth were of no consequence to their careers or historical images.

Among the most significant as a group in the building of the American economy were the Cornish "Cousin Jacks." Miners in their homeland in England's southwest, the Cornish brought skills that were indispensable to the development of American mining: coal, iron, lead, and precious metals. The English and Scots and Welsh eased into positions at every level in every occupation and industry.

The Catholic Irish

The story is a little different for the people of southern Ireland, then officially a part of Great Britain but far from British in sentiment. Almost all of the 3.4 million Irish who came to the United States between

SUI GENERIS

The population of Ireland in 1840 was estimated to have been 8 million. In 1980, the population of the country was a bit less than 4 million. Surely the Emerald Isle is the only part of the world with fewer people today than 140 years ago, let alone less than half the number. Leaving is, perhaps, the central fact of Irish culture.

IRISH-AMERICAN PATRIOTISM

In 1835, John England, the Roman Catholic bishop of Charleston, provided an explanation of why the Irish took so adeptly to politics: "The Irish are largely amalgamated with the Americans, their dispositions, their politics, their notions of government; their language and their appearance become American very quickly, and they praise and prefer America to their oppressors at home."

1845 and 1900 spoke English (the Irish Gaelic language survived only in outlying regions), and they too were familiar with the rudiments of Anglo-American culture. However, they differed from the British in two important ways. First, they were members of the Roman Catholic Church, which many nineteenth-century American Protestants feared and hated out of historical memory. Indeed, in 1887 anti-Catholic prejudice was revived with the formation of the American Protective Association, which was especially strong in the Midwest. Members of the APA took an oath to "strike the shackles and chains of blind obedience" to the Roman Catholic Church from the minds of communicants, but their chief activity seemed to be discrimination against ordinary Catholics.

Second, the Irish arrived not only much poorer than most Britons, but practically starved. Their land had been exploited by England for centuries. Brutalized by poverty, the Irish were considered by their English lords to be semibarbaric, stupid, and addicted to drunken riot as their recreation. Many Americans, especially the WASPs (white Anglo-Saxon Protestants) who dominated American society, culture and economy, adopted the common English prejudice. Although Irish behavior was little different from the behavior of any people ground down by poverty, many of the idealistic Republicans who had fought against similar stereotypes when they had been applied to blacks were the most extreme Irish-baiters. Employers hung the sign "NINA" (No Irish Need Apply) on their gates and in their shop windows. Since they competed with blacks for the jobs at the bottom of the social

pyramid, Irish-Americans were often in the front line of antiblack agitation. The most notable example is the New York City draft riots of July 1863, when white mobs attacked individual blacks and burned down the city's Colored Orphanage.

The Great Famine

The massive Irish emigration began in the 1840s when the Emerald Isle was hit by one of the greatest natural disasters in modern history, the Great Potato Famine of the 1840s and early 1850s. The Irish people were almost completely dependent on the potato for their food. When the crop failed, the result was catastrophic. Within a few years, as many as 1 million people out of a population of 8 million died of starvation or nutrition-related diseases. People dropped dead on the roadsides and at work in the fields, digging up the black, gelatinous mass into which the blight turned potatoes. Another 3 million people left the Emerald Isle for good, emigrating all over the world but particularly to the United States. In no other country was getting out so central to the people's culture as it was in Ireland.

Because life in the United States was infinitely more comfortable than in Ireland, even though the Irish began with the most menial jobs, Irish-Americans took with enthusiasm and patriotism to their adopted home. Numerous enough that they could insulate their personal lives from anti-Catholic prejudice, the Irish parlayed their cohesiveness and natural bent for oratory into a formidable political force. By the time of the Civil War, the Democratic party organizations in heavily Irish cities such as Boston and New York were catering to the interests of the Irish community and reaping rewards in an almost unanimous Irish vote. By the 1880s, Irish immigrants and Irish-Americans dominated urban politics in much of the East and Midwest, and in San Francisco. Ironically, it was their considerable power on the west coast that led to the first legislation to restrict immigration—of the Chinese.

PADDY'S LETTER

A favorite Irish-American story that reflects the abundance that Irish immigrants found in the United States concerned "Paddy," who was writing to relatives back in Ireland with the help of his parish priest. (Most Irish immigrants were illiterate.)

"Why do you say you have meat on the table twice a week, Paddy," the priest asks, "when you know very well you have it twice a day."

"Because," Paddy replies, "if I said twice a day no one would believe me."

The Chinese and the Golden Mountain

In 1849, seamen brought the news to the Chinese port of Canton that a "Mountain of Gold" had been discovered in California. In a country plagued by overpopulation, flood, famine, epidemic disease, and civil warfare, the people of southern China listened avidly to the usual distortions of life across the ocean. "Americans are a very rich people," one promoter explained. "They want the Chinaman to come and will make him welcome. . . . It will not be strange company."

By the time the Chinese arrived in any numbers, the rich mines had been exhausted. Accustomed to working communally, they often made a living taking over diggings that Caucasians had abandoned and found employment in the menial jobs that whites disdained: cook, laundryman, farm worker, domestic servant. By 1860, there were 35,000 Chinese immigrants in California. Most of them were young men who

A Chinese immigrant posed with his possessions to prove to relatives back home that he had been successful in America.

hoped to return home after they had made their fortune; there were only 1,800 Chinese women in the state, a good many of them prostitutes. In San Francisco, Sacramento, Marysville, and most mining camps of any size, lively Chinatowns flourished.

Race and a radically different culture kept the Chinese separate. "When I got to San Francisco," wrote Lee Chew, later a wealthy businessman, "I was half-starved because I was afraid to eat the provisions of the barbarians. But a few days living in the Chinese Quarter and I was happy again."

Leaders of the Gum Shan Hok—the Guests of the Golden Mountain—also encouraged the immigrants to stick to themselves. "We are accustomed to an orderly society," explained a leader of the San Francisco Chinatown, "but it seems as if the Americans are not bound by rules of conduct. It is best, if possible, to avoid any contact with them."

After the construction of the transcontinental railroad began in 1864, Chinese immigration stepped up. Previously about 3,000 to 6,000 a year had come to California; after 1868, the annual number jumped to 12,000 and 20,000, peaking at 23,000 in 1872.

Keeping John Chinaman Out

As long as there was plenty of work, hostility to the Chinese was restrained. But in 1873, the West lapsed into a depression along with the rest of the country.

In 1877, when the Chinese represented 17 percent of California's population, a San Francisco teamster named Denis Kearney began to speak to white workingpeople at open-air rallies in empty sandlots. He blamed their joblessness not on impersonal economic forces but on the willingness of the Chinese to work for less than an American's living wage. Kearney led several rampages through Chinatown, but, much more important, the anti-Chinese movement inspired politicians to choke off the Asian immigration. In 1882, Congress enacted the Exclusion Act, which forbade the Chinese to come. A few hundred continued to enter legally every year (mostly women to become wives of Gum Shan Hok already here), and illegal immigration via Canada helped somewhat to augment the Chinese-American population.

To some extent, Filipinos and Japanese replaced the Chinese in the Asian immigration. Filipinos had free access to the United States after their country was made an American colony in 1898. Japanese began to trickle in, usually via Hawaii, where they were an important part of the agricultural labor force. Caucasians resented them as much as they had disliked the Chinese, but because Japan had a strong government that was sensitive to racial slights, the U.S. Congress

THE IMMIGRATION EXPERIENCE

The immigrants' trek began with a walk. Most of the people who came to the United States after 1880 were peasants, from rural villages that were far from a seaport or a railroad line. So they walked, a circumstance that put a stricter limit on the amount of baggage they could carry to America than did the rules of the steamship companies. Some might fill a handcart and sell it in a buyer's market when they reached their port of embarkation. More commonly, they carried a cheap suitcase or a bundle filled with their few possessions: clothing; a down-filled pillow or comforter; perhaps a favored cooking pot; a treasured keepsake; sometimes a vial of the soil of the native land that they would never see again.

In Italy, they usually walked all the way to the seacoast, to Genoa in the north or to Naples in the south. In Greece, which is made up of peninsulas and islands, there would usually be a ferry ride to Piraeus, the port of Athens. From deep within Russia, Lithuania, Poland, and Germany, there would be a train ride—more likely in boxcars than in passenger wagons. Even the Russians and Poles headed for a German port, Bremen or Hamburg, because while the czarist government provided both Christian peasants and Jews with excellent reasons to leave, the absence of a first-class commercial port in Russia prevented exploitation of the emigrant trade at home. Indeed, despite the threat of persecution, Russian and Polish Jews often had to enter Germany illegally, paying people who lived on the frontier to smuggle them across and secure a semblance of legal passports and exit visas.

Tickets, at least, were cheap. By the 1890s, heated competition among steamship companies in both northern and southern Europe pushed the price of transatlantic passage in steerage (the lowest class) below $20 and sometimes as low as $10. There were humiliating but important ceremonies on departure day: a rude bath and fumigation for lice on the docks, and a more than casual examination by company doctors for contagious diseases (especially tuberculosis), insanity, feeble-mindedness, and trachoma (an inflammation of the eye that leads to blindness and was common in Italy and Greece at the time). On the other side of the Atlantic, United States immigration authorities would refuse entry to anyone who suffered from these diseases, and the company that had brought them over was required to take them back. With paying passengers waiting in New York for passage home—there was a reverse migration too—captains were careful to make sure that they would not lose money on the return voyage. Moreover, while the horrors of shipboard epidemic were considerably reduced from what they had been in the age of sail, highly contagious diseases were not to be taken lightly.

The immigrants were crowded together. Immigrant ships held as many as a thousand people in steerage. There were no cabins, only large compartments formed by bulkheads in the hull. The only privacy was the minimum that could be created by hanging blankets around the few square feet of deck to which a family could enforce its claim. Bickering was constant, and fist fights were common. Except when the weather was bad, almost everyone preferred sitting on the open deck to huddling in the hold.

Most captains prohibited cooking of any kind, except perhaps the brewing of tea on the open deck. Meals were included in the price of passage and were taken in shifts; the last breakfast ran into the first dinner, and so on. Despite the efforts of the German and Italian governments to regulate the quality of food and cookery, the ship at sea was pretty much on its own, and emigrants were unlikely to complain about the quality of service once they arrived in America. Food was cheap, and the cause of constant complaint. Even when meals were good and prepared in sanitary galleys, the ship's cook could not please every passenger; the immigrants tended to be conservative in their culinary tastes, and devoted to a regional or village cuisine. Immigrant manuals recommended the smuggling on board of a sausage or two, or some fruit and vegetables, in order to escape from the poor fare.

Between meals the travelers chatted, sewed, played games, sang, danced, studied English in small groups, read and reread manuals and letters from friends and relatives who were already in the United States, exchanged information and misinformation about their new home, and worried that they might have made a mistake. Days could be interminable, but the voyage was not a long one by steamship. Depending on the port of embarkation and the size of the ship, it took from eight days to two weeks to arrive in New York harbor.

Indeed, an immigrant steamer that arrived at the same time as many others might lie at anchor in lower New York harbor for almost as long as it had taken to cross the Atlantic. In 1892, the United States Immigration Service opened a facility designed specifically for the "processing" of newcomers on Ellis Island, a landfill site in New York harbor that had served as an arsenal. Laid out so that a stream of immigrants would flow in controlled lines through corridors and examination rooms to be inspected by physicians, nurses, and officials. Ellis Island, its architects boasted, could handle 8,000 people a day. Fifteen thousand immigrants passed through on some days, and thousands more had to wait before they could be checked.

Processing at Ellis Island was an experience that few immigrants ever forgot. Crowds milled and shoved for position before they entered the maze of pipe railings that took them from station to station. Instructions boomed over loudspeakers in half a dozen languages;

Immigrants huddled on the steerage deck of the S.S. Pennland, *bound for the United States in 1893.*

children wailed; and anxious parents called for their lost children.

The first person to examine the immigrants was a doctor who was expected to make an instant diagnosis of afflictions for which the newcomers might be denied entry. If he saw a facial rash, he marked a large *F* on the immigrant's clothing with a piece of soft white chalk. People so marked were cut out of the herd and examined more closely. *H* meant suspected heart disease; *L* meant limp and examination for rickets (children were made to do a little dance); and a circle around a cross meant feeble-mindedness and thus immediate return to the ship. Thousands of families were faced with the awful decision, which had to be made within moments, whether to return to Europe with a relative who had been forbidden entry or to push on.

Those who pushed on were quickly examined for trachoma and other eye diseases and brusquely interviewed by an immigration officer. Everyone was prepared for the trick question: "Do you have a job waiting for you?" Immigrant manuals cautioned readers in capital letters *NOT* to reply in the affirmative. The Foran

Contract Labor Law of 1885 forbade the making of pre-arrival agreements to work. Previously—and surreptitiously after 1885—labor jobbers had impressed immigrants into jobs under virtually slavelike conditions, or, at least, many immigrants believed that they had no choice but to work for what the Italians called the *padrone,* or "master."

About 80 percent of those who had entered the building were given landing cards that enabled them to board ferries to the Battery, the southern tip of Manhattan Island. The United States government was through with them, and the horde of agents who made their living by offering "services" now took charge. Again in a babel of languages, previously arrived countrymen shouted that they could offer jobs, provide train tickets, change currency, recommend an excellent boarding house. Some, but not many, were honest. Every large ethnic group in the United States eventually founded aid societies to provide newcomers such services and to protect them from being swindled within hours of their arrival in the land of opportunity.

did not adopt a Japanese exclusion law until 1924, when most immigrant groups were shut out.

The Germans and the Political Motive

In general, the large German immigration to the United States owed to the same worldwide economic forces that displaced other peasant peoples. After 1848, however, there was also a strong political dimension to the German removal. The failure of a series of liberal revolutions in several German states—revolutions aimed at establishing a democratic system and individual rights much like those that existed in the United States—forced the exile of many leading German liberals. The most famous German exile in the United States was Carl Schurz, who became a senator from Missouri and a member of Rutherford B. Hayes's cabinet.

Many of the 4.4 million ordinary Germans who came to the United States between 1850 and 1900, an average of about 100,000 a year, were also influenced by fears that life would be intolerable under the new reactionary governments in their homeland.

Because many of them had been landowners in Europe, albeit not rich ones, German immigrants generally had enough money when they reached the United States to move west and take up free or cheap land. Wisconsin became heavily German in the last half of the nineteenth century. By 1900, more Milwaukeeans spoke German, at least as their first language, than spoke English. There were other heavily German areas in Missouri and Texas.

Adapting to America

Like the Germans, Scandinavians inclined to become farmers in the United States. Norwegians predominated in whole counties in Wisconsin and Minnesota. Swedes were numerous in other parts of Minnesota and in the Pacific Northwest. Finns, who speak an entirely different language from the Swedes but are historically tied to them in many respects, were important in yet other regions, particularly in logging country and in the iron mines of the Mesabi Range.

Ethnic groups that predominated over large areas found adaptation to the New World comparatively easy since they could approximate familiar Old World ways of life. They founded schools taught in their native languages, newspapers and other periodicals, European-style fraternal organizations (the Germans' athletically oriented *Turnverein*, or the Norwegians' musical Grieg Societies, named after their national composer), and so on. They continued to eat familiar food and raise their children by traditional rules. They

were numerous enough to deal with "Americans" from a position of strength.

The problems that such immigrants faced were common to all settlers of a new land. Ole Rolvaag, a gloomy Norwegian-American writer, focused on the loneliness of life on the northern prairies, an experience that was shared by all pioneers there regardless of ethnic background; he did not write about cultural alienation. Indeed, he wrote in Norwegian and, like Isaac Bashevis Singer in the late twentieth century, became known as an American novelist only in translation.

Sephardic and German Jews

Other immigrant groups had a comparatively easy time adapting because they were few and cosmopolitan. The best example is the Sephardic Jews (Jews descended from and still somewhat influenced by the customs of Spanish and Portuguese forebears). Small in numbers, generally well educated and well fixed, they eased into middle- and upper-class society even before the Civil War, particularly in Rhode Island, New York, Charleston, and New Orleans. Considering the fewness of their numbers, they contributed a remarkable number of prominent citizens. Jefferson Davis's strongest supporter in the Confederacy was Judah P. Benjamin, a Sephardic Jew who served in three cabinet posts. Supreme Court justice Benjamin Cardozo had a Sephardic background. So did the twentieth-century financier and presidential adviser, Bernard Baruch of South Carolina.

By 1880, there was also a small German Jewish community in the United States, perhaps 150,000 people. The majority were small-scale tradesmen or businessmen—rare was the southern town without its Jewish-owned drygoods store. Some German Jews pioneered in the founding of the ready-made clothing industry (Levi Strauss is a prime example); others carved out places for themselves in finance, usually independent of the long-established American banking community, which was WASP and generally closed to outsiders (August Belmont was the most successful). The Guggenheim syndicate was one of the nation's leading owners of metal mines by the turn of the century.

The German Jews clung to their religious heritage, but otherwise quickly adopted American mores and customs. Indeed, led by Rabbi Isaac Mayer Wise of Cincinnati, German Jews in the United States preferred Reform religious observance, which is highly secular and closely equivalent to liberal Protestantism, to the Orthodox, fundamentalist Judaism of the Jews of the New Immigration.

The Trauma of the New Immigration

Adapting to their new homes was not so easy for most of the New Immigrants who arrived after 1880. Very few of the newcomers from southern and eastern Europe had much money when they arrived. Most were illiterate, and their Old World experience in peasant village and *shtetl* did not prepare them for life in the world's greatest industrial nation during its era of most rapid development.

However serious the immigrants' reasons for leaving ancestral homes, the homes were still ancestral, the rhythms of life familiar, the customs second nature. Wherever their origins, the New Immigrants had been accustomed to a rural and traditional way of life that was the very antithesis of life in the United States, whether on a commercial farm or in the crowded streets of the big city.

Not only was the circle of friends and acquaintances small in the Old World, but the number of people with whom the peasant or Jewish shopkeeper dealt in the course of life was limited to a comparatively few who, in any case, spoke a familiar language and thought according to similar (or, at least, well understood) values.

In the United States, however, all but a very few *Landsmen* or *campagni* were alien, and everyone spoke incomprehensible languages. The immigrants, at home for better or for worse in Europe or Asia, were foreigners, a *minority* in the United States.

Strangest of all for people who came from traditional, preindustrial cultures where life was regulated and slowed by the seasons, the weather, the use of hand tools, American life was regulated and rushed by the tyrannical clock and powered by the relentless churning of the dynamo. In the industrial society of the late nineteenth century, Americans were even more self-driven than they had been when Alexis de Tocqueville's head had been set spinning by the American pace. This was particularly true in the big cities where a majority of the New Immigrants settled and which, in the minds of other Americans, were intimately associated with the newcomers.

For Further Reading

Overviews and Classics

Vincent P. DeSantis, *The Shaping of Modern America, 1877–1916* (1973)

John A. Garraty, *The New Commonwealth, 1877–1890* (1968)

Samuel P. Hays, *The Response to Industrialism, 1885–1914* (1957)

Robert Wiebe, *The Search for Order* (1968)

Valuable Special Studies

Rowland T. Berthoff, *British Immigrants in Industrial America* (1953)

David Brody, *Workers in Industrial America* (1979)

Robert V. Bruce, *1877: Year of Violence* (1959)

Leonard Dinnerstein and David Reimers, *Ethnic Americans: A History of Immigration and Assimilation* (1975)

Melvyn Dubofsky, *Industrialism and the American Worker, 1865–1920* (1975)

Foster R. Dulles and Melvyn Dubofsky, *Labor in America* (1984)

Nathan Glazer and Daniel P. Moynihan, *Beyond the Melting Pot* (1970)

Herbert G. Gutman, *Work, Culture, and Society in Industrializing America* (1976)

Oscar Handlin, *The Uprooted* (1951)

Marcus L. Hansen, *The Immigrant in American History* (1940)

John Higham, *Send These to Me: Jews and Other Immigrants in Urban America* (1975)

Maldwyn A. Jones, *American Immigration* (1960)

Harold C. Livesay, *Samuel Gompers and the Origins of the American Federation of Labor* (1978)

David Montgomery, *Workers' Control in America: Studies in the History of Work, Technology, and Labor Struggle* (1979)

Daniel Nelson, *Managers and Workers: Origins of the New Factory System in the United States, 1880–1920* (1975)

Henry Pelling, *American Labor* (1960)

Daniel T. Rogers, *The Work Ethic in Industrial America, 1850–1920* (1974)

Philip Taft, *The A.F. of L. in the Time of Gompers* (1929)

Philip A. M. Taylor, *The Distant Magnet* (1970)

Biographies and Autobiographies

Samuel Gompers, *Seventy Years of Life and Labor* (1924)

Terence V. Powderly, *Thirty Years of Life and Labor, 1859–1889* (1890)

31

Bright Lights and Squalid Slums
The Growth of Big Cities

Once in the United States, the New Immigrants discovered that their most ordinary practices—even the way they looked!—were not only foreign but exotic. Americans who had grown accustomed to the restrained Roman Catholic worship of the Irish and the Germans found themselves introduced to the mystical Roman Catholicism of the Poles and the demonstrative emotionalism of the Italians. Irish bishops joined Methodists in worrying about the paganism implied in the magnificently bedecked statues of the Madonna and the gory, surrealistic depictions of the crucified Christ that peasants from Sicily and the Campania carried through the streets of San Francisco, Chicago, New Orleans, and New York accompanied by the music of brass bands.

The Orthodox religion of the Greeks, Russians, some Ukrainians, Serbians, and other Slavic peoples featured even more ornate vestments and mystifying rituals than did the Catholicism of the Poles and Italians. The Jews and the Chinese, of course, were not even Christian and therefore all the more exotic to Americans.

The newcomers looked different from Americans. The Greeks, Armenians, Assyrians, Lebanese, and Italians were swarthy in complexion, a formidable handicap in a nation that had

The first step for an independent-minded immigrant was a rent-free peddler's cart parked by the curb as in this view. They lined the streets in the ethnic communities.

long since drawn a sharp color line. Polish women often arrived clad in colorful babushkas, aprons, and billowing ground-length skirts of the eastern European peasant.

The impoverished Jews dressed drably enough for late-nineteenth-century American taste, but the men, if religious, wore full beards and never removed their hats. Their Saturday sabbath attracted attention principally because the Jews then turned Sunday into a combination holiday and major market day, which offended the sabbatarian sensibilities of some Protestants.

Americans who visited immigrant neighborhoods were unsettled because the smells in the air were alien. Clinging to their traditional diets, which were often based on pungent seasonings and the use of much more onion and garlic than old-stock Americans deemed humane, the immigrants seemed determined to resist American ways all the while they lived in the country.

A Russian immigrant in native dress, photographed by R. F. Turnbull in 1900.

CITIES AS ALIEN ENCLAVES

In his novel of 1890, *A Hazard of New Fortunes*, William Dean Howells sent Basil March, a genteel and educated middle-class American, on a ride on an elevated train in New York City. March "found the variety of people in the car as unfailingly entertaining as ever" but he felt like a foreigner in his own country. Even the Irish, who ran the city, were outnumbered by "the people of Germanic, Slavonic, of Pelasgic [Mediterranean], of Mongolian stock. . . . The small eyes, the high cheeks, the broad noses, the puff lips, the bare, cue-filleted skulls, of Russians, Poles, Czechs, Chinese, the furtive glitter of Italians, the blonde dullness of Germans; the cold quiet of Scandinavians—fire under ice—were aspects that he identified, and that gave him abundant suggestion for the . . . reveries in which he dealt with the future economy of our heterogeneous commonwealth."

A Patchwork of Ghettos

The cities, particularly the metropolises of the Northeast and Midwest, where 80 percent of the New Immigrants settled, seemed to be salients established and secured by invading armies. By 1890, one-third of the population of Boston and Chicago had been born abroad, one-quarter of Philadelphia's people. When their children, who seemed to old-stock Americans as obdurately foreign as their parents, were added to this

total, the anxiety of "American" residents and visitors to the cities is easy to understand.

In fact, the immigrants threatened no one. Members of each ethnic group clustered together into "ghettos" that were exclusively their own. A map of New York, wrote journalist and photographer Jacob Riis, himself a Danish immigrant, "colored to designate nationalities, would show more stripes than the skin of a zebra

MELTING POT OR VEGETABLE SOUP?

Israel Zangwill, 1908: "There she lies, the great Melting Pot—listen! Can't you hear the roaring and the bubbling? . . . Celt and Latin, Slav and Teuton. Greek and Syrian—black and yellow—Jew and Gentile . . . how the great Alchemist melts and fuses them with his purging flame! Here shall they unite to build the Republic of Man and the Kingdom of God."

Jesse Jackson, 1969: "There is talk about [America] being a melting pot. But it is really more like vegetable soup. There are separate pieces of corn, meat, and so on, each with its own identity."

and more colors than the rainbow." Jane Addams sketched a similar patchwork in the poor part of Chicago, where she established one of the first American settlement houses, agencies to help the immigrants, Hull House. The same was true of most large eastern and midwestern cities and of many smaller industrial towns. In Lawrence, Massachusetts, a woolens manufacturing town, more than twenty languages and probably twice that many distinctive dialects were spoken.

There were ghettos within ghettos. In New York City's Greenwich Village, an Italian community, people from the region of Calabria effectively controlled housing on some streets, immigrants from Sicily on others. On such regional blocks, Italians from a specific village would sometimes be the sole occupants of an "Agrigento tenement," and so on. Grocery stores and restaurants advertised themselves not as Italian but as purveyors of Campanian or Apulian food. Priests frequently ministered to the same people whom they

had known back in Italy; lawyers often represented the same clients.

The same held true for Jewish neighborhoods, where Galician Jews (Galicia was a province of Poland) looked with suspicion on Jews from Russian-speaking areas. Rumanian Jews fastidiously set up their own communities, and the better established and assimilated German Jews wondered what the world was coming to.

Germans divided on the basis of religion (Lutheran or Catholic). Serbians and Croatians (from what is now Yugoslavia), while never a large immigrant group, nevertheless separated according to their faiths (Orthodox or Catholic) and to whether they wrote their language in the Latin or the Cyrillic alphabet.

The Impulse to Assimilate

The desire to assimilate, to become American, varied in intensity from group to group, and among individuals within a group. Some immigrants found solace in

Early Chinese immigrants to San Francisco, most of them men, lived in a segregated section of town dubbed Chinatown, shown here in a photograph by Arnold Genthe.

Hester Street in New York City was home to a large community of Jewish immigrants in the early 1890s.

the familiar language, familiar customs, familiar foods, and fellowship within "Little Italy," "Jewville," and "Polack Town," and clung tenaciously to the neighborhood. The ethnic ghetto was a buffer against the prejudice of old-stock Americans, and frequently, the hostility of other ethnic groups with whom its inhabitants competed for the lowest-level jobs. Even an educated immigrant from the Austro-Hungarian Empire found himself disoriented in his attempts to "shift" from old to new ways of thinking and reacting.

> I never knew if my reactions would be in line with the new code of conduct and had to think and reflect. Whenever I decided on the spur of the moment I found myself out of sympathy with my environment. I did not feel as they felt and therefore I felt wrongly according to their standards. To act instinctively in an American fashion and manner was impossible, and I appeared slow and clumsy. The proverbial slowness of foreigners is largely due to this cause.

Others seized avidly on what they took to be "American" ways with an extraordinary enthusiasm. This was perhaps best illustrated in the large jewish community of New York's Lower East Side, which in its earliest years was sharply divided between those who clung to the medieval ways of the Russian and Polish *shtetls* and the big city-wise and sophisticated younger immigrants and children of immigrants who often scorned their elders' "greenhorn" ways.

Avenues of Advancement

Hard work at menial jobs was the economic lot of most immigrants. The urban political machine, which had room at or near the top for anyone who could deliver votes, provided an avenue of advancement for a few who recognized the opportunities it provided for the "boss" of the ethnic ghetto. Others joined the American quest for material success by pursuing careers in areas that were not quite respectable, and, therefore, less attractive to members of established social groups —show business, professional sports, and organized crimes, that is, illegal business. The roster of surnames of leading entertainers, boxers, baseball players, and gangsters over a period of decades reads almost like the strata of a canyon that geologists read, each layer dominated by members of a new, aspiring ethnic group.

Immigrant Aid Institutions

The ethnic groups themselves established institutions to assist their countrymen in adjusting to the new life. Some encouraged assimilation, some clannishness. Sephardic and German Jewish families who were comfortably established in the United States founded the Hebrew Immigrant Aid Society to minister to the needs of the penniless eastern European Jews who flocked into the cities. The Young Men's and Young Women's Hebrew Associations, dating back to 1854, expanded several times over during the last decade of the century.

Among the Catholic population, which grew from 6 million in 1880 to 10 million in 1900 (making it the country's largest single denomination), traditionally charitable religious orders such as the Franciscans and the Sisters of Mercy established hospitals and houses of refuge in the slums. The St. Vincent de Paul Society functioned much like the Salvation Army, but without the military trappings.

Curiously, a sort of ethnic prejudice helped to hamstring the older Jewish and older Catholic communities in responding to the needs of the New Immigrants. Sephardic and German Jews worried that the numbers, poverty, and provincialism of the eastern European newcomers would arouse an anti-Semitic spirit among Christians that would be turned on them too. The American Catholic Church was dominated by Irish-Americans who were no more cordial toward Italians, Poles, and other Catholic nationalities than were old-stock Protestants. Only after an encyclical of 1891, *Rerum Novarum*, in which the pope proclaimed a Catholic Social Gospel, did the Church hierarchy take much interest in the material well-being of its communicants.

Then the Church was torn between serving as an agency of assimilation and maintaining its high standing among Catholic immigrants—who often clung to their religion with more piety than they had in Europe—by encouraging a "fortress mentality" toward the dominant Protestant culture.

Settlement Houses

Old-stock Americans created the settlement house, patterned after Toynbee Hall, in a notorious London slum, to assist immigrants in coming to terms with their new country.

During the 1880s, a number of middle-class Americans who were imbued with the New England conscience that dictated concern for others traveled to England to learn how Toynbee worked. They found that the house provided food and drink to the disinherited, as traditional charities had, but also child care for working mothers, recreational facilities, and courses of study in everything from household arts (which were not generally known among the very poor) to the English language and social skills needed for self-improvement. Most important of all, the young men and women who worked at Toynbee Hall told the Americans that they had been morally elevated by their sacrifices and exposure to a misery that they had not known in their own lives.

The first American settlement house was the Neighborhood Guild, set up in New York City in 1886. More famous, however, because of the intelligence and powerful personalities of their founders, were Jane Addams's Hull House in Chicago (1889), Robert A. Woods's South End House in Boston (1892), and Lillian Wald's Henry Street Settlement in New York (1893). From comfortable middle-class backgrounds, well educated, and finely mannered, Addams, Woods, and Wald were exemplars of the American middle class who were determined to fight the materialism of their own people, the misery suffered by poor city dwellers, and to keep traditional American values alive. What they did not always understand was that in the great metropolises that took shape in the late nineteenth century, a new American culture and code of values was emerging.

OF THE GROWTH OF GREAT CITIES

Americans had an ingrained prejudice against cities that dated back to Thomas Jefferson, but they were also, by the end of the nineteenth century, one of the world's most urban peoples. The proportion of city dwellers in the total population, the number of cities, and the size of cities all increased at a faster rate in the United States than in any other country in the world.

In 1790, when the first national census was taken, only 3.4 percent of Americans lived in towns of 8,000 people or more. By 1860, the eve of the Civil War, 16 percent of the population was urban, and by 1900, 33 percent.

The increase in the number of cities is rather more striking. In 1790, only 6 American cities boasted populations of 8,000 or more. The largest of them, Philadelphia, was home to 42,000 people. In 1860, 141 municipalities had at least 8,000 people within their limits; by 1890, 448 did (and by 1910, 778!). Fully 26 cities were larger than 100,000 in 1900, and 6 of them topped 500,000. Philadelphia counted 1.3 million people at the turn of the century and, at that, had slipped to third place behind New York and Chicago.

From Country to City

Although the influx of immigrants was largely responsible for the tremendous growth of cities at the end of the century, Americans migrated from country to city too. Dismayed by the isolation of farm life, ground down by the heavy tedious labor, and often as not reaping few rewards for their toil, they heard of well-paying jobs for literate, mechanically inclined people. Or they visited cities and were dazzled by the bright lights, the abundance of company, the stimulation of a world in constant motion, and the stories of the fortunes that might be made in business.

Parents, rural ministers, and editors of farm magazines begged, threatened, and cajoled in an effort to keep the children of the soil at home, but their efforts met with limited success. While the total number of farm families grew during the late nineteenth century, the proportion of farmers in the total population declined, and in some regions, with a nearby city beckoning, even the numbers dropped. During the 1880s, more than half the rural townships of Iowa and Illinois declined in population, while Chicago underwent its miraculous growth. In New England, while the overall population of the region increased by 20 percent, three rural townships in five lost people to the dozens of bustling mill towns that lined the fast-moving rivers and to the metropolises of Boston and New York.

For the most part, the American migration from farm to city was a white migration. Only 12 percent of the 5 million blacks in the United States in 1890 lived in cities. Nevertheless, about 500,000 moved from the rural South to the urban North during the

final decade of the century, foreshadowing one of the most significant population movements of the next century.

The Walking City

While rapid growth was the rule in cities large and small, the most dramatic phenomenon of American urbanization in the late nineteenth century was the emergence of the gigantic metropolises, the six cities of more than 500,000 people that dominated the regions in which they sat like imperial capitals. Philadelphia doubled in size between 1860 and 1900, when William Penn's "green countrie towne" claimed 1.3 million people. New York, with 33,000 people in 1790, and over 1 million in 1860, quadrupled its numbers until, by 1900, 4.8 million lived within its five "boroughs." New York was the second largest city in the world, smaller only than London.

Chicago's crazy rate of growth as the hub of the nation's railroad system amazed Americans and foreigners alike. With only a little more than 100,000 people in 1860, Chicago increased its size twenty times in a generation, numbering 2.2 million inhabitants in 1900.

Before the 1870s, cities so vast were unimaginable. When the mass of a city's population moved around by foot, city growth was limited in area to a radius of a mile or two, as far as a worker could walk to work or a housekeeper could walk to market in an hour or so. To be sure, the well-to-do owned horses and carriages in the walking city and could, therefore, live a greater distance from their places of business and entertainment. But not too far. A horse moves only marginally faster than a pedestrian and not a bit faster when the streets are choked with people making their way to and fro. Indeed, the most common layout of a mill town was a factory or two at the geographical center of the city and residential areas surrounding it in concentric circles or, more likely, because mills were generally located near rivers, in semicircles fronting

POPULATION OF TEN LARGEST AMERICAN CITIES—1880	
New York	1,773,000
Philadelphia	847,000
Chicago	503,000
Boston	363,000
St. Louis	351,000
Baltimore	332,000
Cincinnati	255,000
Pittsburgh	235,000
San Francisco	234,000
New Orleans	216,000

POPULATION OF TEN LARGEST AMERICAN CITIES—1900	
New York	3,437,000
Chicago	1,699,000
Philadelphia	1,294,000
St. Louis	575,000
Boston	561,000
Baltimore	509,000
Pittsburgh	452,000
Cleveland	382,000
Buffalo	352,000
San Francisco	343,000

Grid-lock in the horsedrawn age. Because a horse could panic or collapse, traffic jams in the late nineteenth century were often worse than they are today.

the water. The workers clustered close by; with a twelve-hour day to work, there was little time for commuting. The small businessmen who owned the shops lived behind them. The millowners, their top supervisors, and professionals lived on the outskirts. They were not strangers to the crowding, noise, dirt, and turmoil of the walking city, but when the opportunity to flee presented itself, they were quick to seize it.

Farthest out of all, beyond the built-up neighborhoods, paved streets, and sewers, were ramshackle shantytowns inhabited by people with only a marginal role to play in the city's life, if that. Unlike today, when the unemployed crowd into the core cities, the limitations inherent in foot and horse travel left the suburbs, a form of banishment, to them.

Getting Around

The first means by which wealthy and middle-class people could put some considerable distance between their residences and center city was the horsecar line. With charters from city hall, entrepreneurs strung light rails down major thoroughfares and ran horse-drawn streetcars with seats open to the public. Cheap as the fares were, five cents and occasionally less, they were still too expensive for many workingpeople, who continued to walk to work. However, skilled artisans, white-collar workers, and small businessmen took advantage of the quick, cheap transportation to move away from their places of business—north on the island of Manhattan in New York, west across the Schuylkill River in Philadelphia, north and west in Chicago, and west out of Boston, a migration that absorbed once distinct towns and villages.

Allowing even more distant residential neighborhoods was the steam-powered elevated train, or El, which ran at high speeds above the crowded streets on ponderous and ugly steel scaffolding. In 1870, New York completed the first El on Ninth Avenue, and the range of the trains, soon up to the northern tip of Manhattan, encouraged the middle classes to move even farther away from Wall Street and the once leafy, now crowded Bowery. In making the suburbs more accessible, the Els also served to begin the process of pushing the residents of the shantytowns into inner-city housing abandoned by the middle classes.

Electric Trolleys

The utility of elevated trains was limited by the high cost of constructing them. Only the richest, largest (and most corrupt) cities were able and willing to shoulder the expense. Moreover, no sooner did the Els stimulate residential construction along their routes, where they ran at ground level, than the noisy, dirty, and dangerous locomotives roused the ire of the very people who rode on them to work and recreation.

Consequently, it was the electric trolley car, pioneered by inventor-businessman Frank J. Sprague, that really turned the walking city into a memory and ensured the sprawl of the great metropolises. Economical, fast but easy to stop, clean, quiet, even melodious in their rattling and ringing of bells, the trolleys were the key to the growth of big cities and assets to smaller ones. Richmond was the first to build a system in 1887. By 1895, fully 850 lines crisscrossed American cities on 10,000 miles of track. They were as important to the urbanization of the United States as the railroads were to the settlement of the West.

Building Up

By enabling the construction of residential neighborhoods miles from city business districts, the trolleys made it possible for many more people to congregate in city centers for work, business, and entertainment. This caused real-estate values to soar to absurd heights.

SUBWAYS

The electric-powered subway train was to nurture the sprawl of cities even more than did surface trolleys and Els. Underground trains moved faster than trolley cars in traffic but they did not, like the Els, make life intolerable along the line. The subway was a twentieth-century development in the United States. London had a line by 1886, but America's first, in Boston, did not open until 1897. In New York City, where the subway was to become supreme, the first line began operating in 1904.

The practical solution was obvious enough: multiply the square footage of midtown properties by building multistoried structures such as the electric-powered elevator theoretically made possible.

Elevator or not, there was still a catch in vertical construction. In order to support the weight of huge towering structures, the bearing walls of a conventional structure had to be so thick on the lower floors, virtually solid like the pyramids of Egypt, as to defeat the whole purpose of building up.

Once again, technology provided the solution in the form of extremely strong I-shaped steel girders. With these at their disposal, architects were able to abandon the very concept of weight-bearing walls and design skeletons of steel on which, in effect, they hung decorative siding of cast iron or of stone. The potential

Elevated trains, or Els, were unsightly, noisy, and dirty, but they enabled cities to expand by providing fast, unimpeded transit.

The Flatiron Building, an early skyscraper, photographed around 1905. Today it is dwarfed by its neighbors.

height of steel buildings seemed almost limitless. They could rise so high as to scrape the sky. Indeed, once the method was perfected, corporations competed to erect the tallest tower, as medieval cities had competed to build the tallest cathedral spire.

In time, New York was to become the most dramatic of the skyscraper cities; but Chicago architects pioneered in the design of "tall office buildings," as Louis H. Sullivan, the most thoughtful of architects, rather prosaically described his graceful structures. In an article in *Lippincott's* magazine in 1896, Sullivan explained how through the use of "proud and soaring" vertical sweeps, "a unit without a single dissenting line," the artistic form of the skyscraper reflected the essence of its construction. In the twentieth century, Sullivan's even more imaginative protégé, Frank Lloyd Wright, was to apply the principle of "form follows function" to a wide variety of structures.

Building Over

Another technological innovation that contributed to the expansion of cities was the suspension bridge, which erased wide rivers as barriers to urban growth. Its pioneer was a German immigrant, John A. Roebling, who came to the United States in 1831 as a canal engineer and set up the first American factory for twisting steel-wire into cable. Roebling's associates scoffed at his contention that if a bridge were hung from strong cables instead of built up on massive pillars that had to stand in the water, much broader rivers could be spanned. Obsessed with the concept of a suspension bridge, Roebling devoted his life to perfecting a design. Before the Civil War, he had several to his credit, including an international bridge over the Niagara River near the Falls.

Roebling planned his masterpiece for the East River, which separated downtown New York, which was beginning to burst at the seams, from the roomy seaport of Brooklyn on Long Island. While working on the site in 1869, he was injured, contracted a tetanus infection, and died. Without delay, his equally devoted son, Washington A. Roebling, carried on the work. He too received serious injuries; he was crippled from the "bends," later associated with deep-sea divers, as a result of working too long below water level on the foundations of the towers. Nevertheless, from a chair in a room overlooking the great span, now called the Brooklyn Bridge, he saw it completed in 1883. It was admired for its beauty as well as its engineering.

In providing easy access to Manhattan—33 million people crossed it each year—the bridge ignited a residential real-estate boom in Brooklyn; within a few years, it was the fourth largest city in the United States, but the bridge also spelled the end of Brooklyn as an independent city. A satellite of New York in

BROOKLYN'S ENDLESS WOES

Brooklyn, New York, had a proud independent heritage, being among other things the home of poet Walt Whitman. That was before the construction of the Brooklyn Bridge. Although the people of Brooklyn prospered as a result of the access to New York, the suspended highway also led to the deincorporation of the city in 1898 and its annexation to New York as a borough.

Brooklyn became a butt of jokes, in part because of the "Brooklyn accent" that comedians found ultimately urban and therefore useful for stereotypical quips. Nevertheless, Brooklynites held on to a kind of pride in the borough's identity that fixed itself most dramatically on Brooklyn's major league baseball team, the Dodgers (originally the Trolley Dodgers). If not officially a city, Brooklyn was urban with bells on.

Then, just as New York, the American city of cities, robbed Brooklyn of its independence, the great American conurbation of the mid-twentieth century, Los Angeles, robbed Brooklyn of its identity in 1958 by buying the Dodgers with its promise of larger television revenues. Now, as Gertrude Stein said of Oakland, California, another great city overshadowed by a more exciting neighbor, "There is no there there."

This 1877 engraving from Harper's Weekly *depicts construction of the Brooklyn Bridge. As skyscrapers allowed cities to expand vertically, suspension bridges allowed cities to sprawl even beyond rivers.*

fact, Brooklyn was incorporated into the city by law in 1898.

The Great Symbol

The Brooklyn Bridge was dedicated with a mammoth celebration. President Chester A. Arthur proclaimed it "a monument to democracy"; sides of beef were roasted in the streets; oceans of beer and whiskey disappeared; brass bands competed in raising a din; races were run; prizes were awarded; dances were danced; and noses were punched. A fireworks display of unprecedented magnificence topped off the festivities, illuminating the labyrinthine silhouette from both sides of the East River. The Brooklyn Bridge was a celebration of the city.

It was also an indictment of the city. On the morning of the gala, one dissenting newspaper editor groused that the Brooklyn Bridge had "begun in fraud" and "continued in corruption." It was no secret to anyone that much of the $15 million that the project had cost had gone not into concrete, steel, and Roebling cable but into the pockets of crooked politicians.

The glories of the bridge were also marred by its cost in human lives. At least twenty workers were killed—others just vanished, probably falling unnoticed—and many more were maimed. Then, just a few days after the dedication, a woman stumbled while descending the stairs that led to the ground, and someone shouted, "The bridge is sinking!" In the stampede that followed, twelve people were trampled to death.

THE EVILS OF CITY LIFE

City people died at a rate not known in the United States since the seventeenth century. At a time when the national death rate was 20 per 1,000 (20 people in each 1,000 died annually), the death rate in New York City was 25. In the slums, it was 38, and for children under 5 years of age, 136 per 1,000. The figures were only slightly lower in the other big cities, and in parts of Chicago they were higher. In one Chicago slum as late as 1900, the infant mortality rate was 200; 1 child in 5 died within a year of birth. By way of comparison, the infant mortality rate in the United States today is less than 20 per 1,000, and the total death rate is less than 9.

Too Many People, Too Little Room

City people died primarily because of impossibly crowded living conditions, another consequence of high real-estate values. In Philadelphia and Baltimore, the poor crowded into two- and three-story brick "row houses" that ran for 200 yards before a cross street broke the block. In Boston and Chicago, typical housing for the New Immigrants was in old wooden structures that had been comfortable homes for one family; in the late nineteenth century, they were crowded by several families, plus boarders. In New York, the narrow confines of Manhattan Island made the crowding even worse. Former single-family residences were carved into tenements that housed a hundred and more people.

In 1866, the New York Board of Health found 400,000 people living in overcrowded tenements with no windows, and 20,000 living in cellars below the water table. At high tide, their "homes" filled with water. The board closed the cellars and ordered 46,000 windows cut in airless rooms; but in 1900, people whose memories dated back to 1866 said that conditions were even worse than ever.

Jacob Riis, a newspaper reporter who exposed urban living conditions in a book of 1890, *How the Other Half Lives,* estimated that 330,000 people lived in a square mile of slum; 986.4 people an acre. New York was more than twice as crowded as the London that had turned Charles Dickens's stomach, and parts of it were more populous than Bombay, the American's image of a living hell. On one tenement block in the Jewish section of the Lower East Side, just a little larger than an acre, 2,800 people lived. In one apartment of two tiny rooms there, Riis found a married couple, their twelve children, and six adult boarders.

When architect James E. Ware designed a new kind of building to house New York's poor, he worsened the situation. His "dumbbell" tenement, named for its shape, ostensibly provided 24 to 32 apartments, all with ventilation, on a standard New York building lot of 25 by 100 feet.

However, when two dumbbells were constructed side by side, the windows of two-thirds of the living units opened on an air shaft, sometimes only two feet wide, that was soon filled with garbage, creating a threat to health worse than airlessness. Nevertheless, the dumbbells met city building standards, and by 1894, there were 39,000 of them in New York, housing about half the population of Manhattan.

Health

Such crowding led to epidemic outbreaks of serious diseases like smallpox, cholera, measles, typhus, scarlet fever, and diphtheria. Quarantining of patients,

the indispensable first step in dealing with highly contagious diseases in the nineteenth century, was out of the question in slums: where were the unafflicted people to go? Even less dangerous illnesses like chicken pox, mumps, whooping cough, croup, and the various influenzas were killers in the crowded cities. Common colds were feared as the first step to pneumonia.

In his famous book, Jacob Riis took readers on a tour of a tenement: "Be a little careful, please! The hall is dark and you might stumble. You can feel your way, if you cannot see it. Close? Yes! What would you have? All the fresh air that enters these stairs comes from the hall-door that is forever slamming." He paused at the entrance to a windowless apartment. "Listen! That short, hacking cough, that tiny, helpless wail. . . . The child is dying of measles. With half a chance it might have lived; but it had none. That dark bedroom killed it."

Sanitation

The crowding itself was the chief cause of poor sanitation. Whereas free-roaming scavengers—chickens, hogs, dogs, and wild birds—handily cleaned up the

Lewis W. Hine's photograph of a rear tenement bedroom on New York's Lower East Side shows the crowded conditions in which poor city dwellers lived.

BIG CITY SWEATSHOPS

In the early nineteenth century, four Americans in five wore clothing that had been made to order. The wealthy took their wants to the little shops in every town and city where fine garments were expertly made by hand from fabric to finished product. With great skill, tailors and seamstresses worked not from patterns, as someone interested in sewing would do today, but from fashion plates, carefully drawn pictures in magazines of people dressed in the latest styles. By the early nineteenth century, Paris was already considered the authority in such matters.

The middle classes, which began to pay more attention to "fashion" in the nineteenth century, depended on their womenfolk for their garb. That is why needlecraft learned at a mother's knee was such an important part of a young girl's education; clothing her family would be one of her most important duties as a wife and mother.

As for the poor, they made do with castoffs either scavenged or purchased from merchants who specialized in buying and reconditioning used clothing. The fact that most garments were made to fit an individual did not mean that any particular item had been made to fit the person who, at a given time, was wearing it.

Only sailors, slaves, and—after 1849—miners in the West were likely to wear clothing such as virtually everyone does today, ready-made in quantity to standard sizes and sold "off the rack." Sailors were not generally in a port long enough to be fitted and a garment sewn. (The first ready-made clothing stores were called "sailors' shops.") The slaves had no choice in the matter of what they put on their backs, and their owners, wanting to provide them some protection from the elements at a minimum cost, became an attractive market for enterprising tailors who abandoned the custom trade and took to producing rough, cheap garments in quantity. Miners, like sailors, were in a hurry, and they lived in an almost entirely masculine society. Their demand for sturdy, ready-made clothing provided the impetus for the founding in 1850 of the Levi Strauss Company of San Francisco, today perhaps the best-known manufacturer of ready-made clothing in the world.

By 1900, things had changed. Nine Americans in ten were wearing ready-made togs. A "Clothing Revolution," as historian Daniel Boorstin has called it, had taken place as a consequence of technology with, curiously, a boost from the American Civil War.

The technology was supplied by inventions such as the sewing machine, patented by Elias Howe in 1846, and powered scissors that could cut through eighteen pieces of fabric at once, thus making the parts for eighteen garments of exactly the same size. The standard sizes were provided by the United States government when the Civil War made it necessary to buy uniforms for hundreds of thousands of men. The army's Quartermaster Corps measured hundreds of recruits and arrived at sets of proportions that provided a fit for almost all. It was a simple step to do the same for women's sizes after the war ended, and ready-made clothing shops began to displace tailors and seamstresses. The department store, which appeared at the end of the century, was built around its selection of every kind of clothing. The great mail-order houses such as Montgomery Ward and Sears Roebuck were able, with everyone knowing his or her size, to sell garments by mail.

How were the new ready-made clothes manufactured? Not, ironically, in factories. There was little outsize machinery involved in the making of garments (sewing machines were treadle or electrically powered) and a great deal of handwork (finishing buttonholes, installing linings). Thus it was possible to farm out the work to people in their homes, just as, before the invention of cloth-making machinery, spinning and weaving had been farmed out.

Whereas the old putting-out system usually had involved the wives and daughters of farmers, leaving people on the land, the new putting-out system engaged people who lived in city slums and who depended exclusively on needlework for their livelihood.

The system was called "sweating," and the places in which the garmentmakers worked were called "sweatshops" because of the peculiarly exploitative character of the system. A manufacturer of clothing kept a small headquarters; at the most, the material was cut to pattern in his "factory." Then, the pieces of a garment were handed out on a weekly or daily basis to people, usually Jewish or Italian immigrants, who took them home to their tenement apartments. There the whole family—perhaps some boarders, perhaps even some neighbors—sat down during all the daylight hours to make up the garments. Sometimes a household saw a coat (usually called a cloak in the nineteenth century) or a gown through from components to completion. Other households specialized in different phases of the process, such as roughing the garment in, or finishing work. Some sweatshops made buttonholes, others sewed pockets, and so on.

The key to the system was that everyone involved was paid by the piece—so much per jacket, so much per lining. A complex hierarchy of subcontracting developed in which it was to the interest of all to pay those below them in the chain as little for their work as possible. That is, a man who provided finished cloaks to the manufacturer received a fixed rate for each garment that he delivered. In order to make a profit, he had to pay less than that rate to those households that had done the work. If the head of a household sweatshop had boarders or neighbors sewing, he had to pay them even less. Everybody was "sweating" their income out of somebody else.

Moreover, just as in factories, employers were inclined to cut the piece rate as a worker's productivity

The tenement sweatshop was an avenue out of poverty for a few, but a squalid, oppressive, unhealthy workplace for most. Here workers make neckties in this photograph by Jacob Riis.

increased or when someone else told the manufacturer whom he supplied (who sweated him) that others were willing to work for less. In order to compete, he sweated the people under him.

In turn, everyone in the chain had to take less for their work. The operator of a Chicago sweatshop explained the results to a Congressional committee in 1893:

Q. *In what condition do you get the garments?*
A. *They come here already cut and I make them up.*
Q. *What is the average wage of the men per week?*
A. *About $15 a week.*
Q. *How much do the women get?*
A. *About $6. They get paid for extra hours. . . .*
Q. *Are wages higher or lower than they were two years ago?*
A. *Lower. There are so many who want to work.*
Q. *How much do you get for making this garment?*
A. *Eighty cents.*

Q. *How much did you get for making it two years ago?*
A. *About $1.25.*
Q. *Is the help paid less now?*
A. *Yes, sir.*

A cloakmaker, Abraham Bisno, told the same panel that he had earned about $20 a week in 1885 for completing fewer garments than he had sewn in 1890, when he had made $13 to $14 a week. In 1893, he was being paid $11 a week for even greater productivity.

As the rate per piece fell, sweatshop workers increased their hours in the unhealthful, poorly ventilated tenements. Only when urban states such as New York and Illinois passed laws that forbade such work in residences was there any improvement in conditions. But, often as not, the driving exploitation of the sweat system was merely transferred to an unhealthful, poorly ventilated factory that was little different from a tenement flat.

Dead horses left to rot in the streets compounded New York's growing sanitation problems at the turn of the century.

garbage in small towns, and backyard latrines were adequate in disposing of human wastes, neither worked when more than a hundred people lived in a building and shared a single privy. City governments provided for waste collection, but even when honestly administered (which was the exception), sanitation departments simply could not keep up.

Horses compounded the problem. They deposited tons of manure on city streets daily, and special squads could not begin to keep pace. Moreover, on extremely hot and cold days, old and poorly kept horses keeled over by the hundreds; sometimes in New York the daily total topped 1,000. Although by law the owner of the dead beast was required to dispose of the carcass, this often meant dumping it into the river. More often, because the task was so formidable, owners of faltering nags cut their horses out of harness and disappeared. In summer, the corpses bloated and began to putrefy within hours.

In the poorest tenements, piped water was available only in shared sinks in the hallways, which were typically filthy. Safe water had been so heavily dosed with chemicals that it was barely palatable. The well-to-do bought bottled "spring water" that had been trucked into the cities. Other people depended on wells in the streets that were inevitably fouled by runoff.

Tenement apartments did not have bathrooms. Children washed by romping in the water of open fire hydrants or by taking a swim in polluted waterways. If you did not come home tinged gray or brown, one survivor of New York's Lower East Side remembered, you had not washed. When a bath was necessary, adults went to public bathhouses where there was hot, clean water at a reasonable price. Many of these establishments were quite respectable. Others became known as dens of immorality.

Vice and Crime

As they always are, slums were breeding grounds of vice and crime. With 14,000 homeless people in New York in 1890, many of them children—"street Arabs"—and work difficult to get and uncertain at the best of times, many found the temptations of sneak thievery, pocket picking, purse snatching, and, for the bolder, violent robbery too much to resist. As early as the 1850s, police in New York were vying with (or taking bribes from) strong-arm gangs that were named after the neighborhoods where they held sway: the Five Points Gang, Mulberry Bend, Hell's Kitchen, Poverty Gap, the Whyo Gang. They occasionally struck outside their areas, robbing warehouses and the like, and preying on the middle- or upper-class fops who took to slumming in these neighborhoods. But the gangs' typical victims were slum dwellers struggling to survive and escape the slum: the workingman who paused for a beer before he took his pay envelope home, the small businessmen who were forced to make regular payments or risk physical violence. Whereas the homicide rate declined in German and British cities as they grew larger, it tripled in American cities during the 1880s. Although the prison population rose by 50 percent, the streets in some sections grew more dangerous.

By the end of the century, the more sophisticated gangs moved into vice, running illegal gambling operations, opium dens, and brothels. Prostitution flourished at every level in a society where sex was repressed, and there was a plentiful supply of impoverished girls and young women who had no other way to survive. The lucky ones set themselves up as mistresses or in fancy houses that catered to the wealthy. More common was the wretched slattern who plied her trade in the slums under the "protection" of a gang.

An Urban Culture

And yet, for all the horror stories, which no one savored more than the people who lived in the cities, for all the lurid accounts of urban life in books, newspapers, magazines, sermons, lectures, plays, and scandalized reports by people who visited New York, Chicago, Kansas City, or other "dens of pestilence," a vital, exciting, and excited urban culture developed in American cities. City people compared rural "yokels" and "hayseeds" unfavorably to themselves. Once established, city people were unlikely to move to the country or even to be attracted by jobs beyond the municipal limits.

The cities continued to grow at an extraordinary rate, both from immigration and the influx from the towns and countryside. Indeed, had it not been for the existence of a more traditional American frontier larger than any that had gone before, it is likely that the rural population would have declined in the late nineteenth century, as it was to do in the twentieth century.

For Further Reading

Overviews and Classics

Vincent P. DeSantis, *The Shaping of Modern America, 1877–1916* (1973)

John A. Garraty, *The New Commonwealth, 1877–1890* (1968)

Nathan Glazer and Daniel P. Moynihan, *Beyond the Melting Pot* (1970)

Oscar Handlin, *The Uprooted* (1951)

Samuel P. Hays, *The Response to Industrialism, 1885–1914* (1957)

A. M. Schlesinger, *The Rise of the City, 1878–1898* (1933)

Valuable Special Studies

Robert H. Bremner, *From the Depths: The Discovery of Poverty in America* (1956)

Thomas N. Brown, *Irish-American Nationalism* (1966)

Howard Chudakov, *The Evolution of American Urban Society* (1975)

Leonard Dinnerstein and David Reimers, *Ethnic Americans: A History of Immigration and Assimilation* (1975)

John B. Duff, *The Irish in the United States* (1971)

John Higham, *Send These to Me: Jews and Other Immigrants in Urban America* (1975)

Irving Howe, *World of Our Fathers* (1976)

Alan Kraut, *The Huddled Masses: The Immigrant in American Culture, 1880–1921* (1982)

Blake McKelvey, *The Urbanization of America, 1860–1915* (1962)

Zane Miller and Patricia Melvin, *The Urbanization of Modern America* (1987)

Humbert Nelli, *The Italians of Chicago* (1970)

Thomas L. Philpott, *The Slum and the Ghetto* (1978)

Moses Rischin, *The Promised City: New York's Jews* (1962)

Barbara Rosenkrantz, *Public Health and the State* (1972)

Thomas Sowell, *Ethnic America: A History* (1981)

Stephan Thernstrom, *The Other Bostonians: Poverty and Progress in the American Metropolis* (1973)

Sam B. Warner, *Streetcar Suburbs: The Process of Growth in Boston, 1870–1900* (1971)

———, *The Urban Wilderness: A History of the American City* (1972)

Virginia Yans-McLaughlin, *Family and Community: Italian Immigrants in Buffalo* (1977)

Biographies and Autobiographies

Jane Addams, *Twenty Years at Hull House* (1910)

The Last Frontier
Winning the Rest of the West, 1865–1900

In long-settled parts of the world, the frontier is the place where the territory of one sovereign state comes to an end and the territory of another state begins. In Europe, the crest of the Pyrenees mountains marks the frontiers of Spain and France, the Rhine River the frontiers of France and Germany. The novelist's and film-maker's vision of a frontier that is not a natural boundary is a place of locomotives hissing on sidings, customs guards interrogating travelers, zebra-striped barricades lowered across tracks and roadway.

European frontiers have been moved about frequently enough as a consequence of dynastic marriages, wars, and treaties. But redrawing a frontier in Europe has long meant detaching from one country lands that are already populated, often densely, and attaching them to another sovereignty.

In the United States, the word *frontier* came to mean something entirely different. To Americans, the frontier was the vaguely demarcated zone where the nation's settled lands ended and its undeveloped region began. Because the course of American expansion had begun on the eastern rim of the continent, the frontier usually took the shape of a line that ran from north to south and that was more or less constantly moving westward. On and beyond that line was not a sovereign state but a rival in the form of nature to be developed, what Americans called "the West."

The typical crew of cattle-herding cowboys included black and Mexican cowboys.

THE LAST FRONTIER

The Census Bureau's definition of "settled land" was not very rigorous. While Americans of the late twentieth century would consider a square mile on which only 2, 3, or 4 people lived to be something on the order of howling wilderness, the Census Bureau defined a square mile as settled if 2.5 persons lived there. Even at that, at the time of the Civil War, the part of the United States that was *unsettled* comprised roughly half the total area of the nation. With the exception of California, Oregon, and Washington Territory on the west coast, where 440,000 people lived; the Great Salt Lake basin, where the Mormon Zion had grown to be home to a population of 40,000; and New Mexico, which was the seat of a gracious culture and home to 94,000 mostly Spanish-speaking citizens, the American frontier ran north to south about 150 to 200 miles west of the Mississippi River. Settlement barely spilled over the far boundaries of Minnesota, Iowa, Missouri, and Arkansas. Half of the state of Texas was still not settled at the end of the Civil War.

An Uninviting Land

Rather more striking in view of what was to happen in the late nineteenth century, few Americans believed that this West would ever be settled. Americans thought agriculturally; pioneering meant bringing land under tillage, and, except for isolated pockets of fertile, well-watered soil, none of the three geographical regions of the West was suitable to agriculture. Quite as discouraging, those isolated pockets of good land were too far from the markets and the sources of manufactured goods that any settlers would need in order to prosper.

In the middle of the last West lay the majestic Rocky Mountains, which range from Alaska to New Mexico. The snowy peaks of the Rockies were familiar to easterners from landscape paintings by artists who had accompanied the transcontinental wagon trains or military expeditions, or, having learned of the natural glories of the American landscape, had traveled west on their own, easel and canvases packed in their lumbering wagons. The very grandeur of the Rockies, however, told Americans that the mountains could not support a population living as people did in the older regions.

West of the Rockies and east of California's Sierra Nevada lay the high desert and the Great Basin—the mountainous and arid home of birds, snakes, rodents, coyotes, antelope, the grotesque Gila monster and comical armadillo, cactus, creosote bush, sagebrush, and tumbleweed. The soil was rocky, thin, and often alkaline. This region is called a basin or sink because its rivers lost heart in their search for an outlet and pooled up in the desert, disappearing into the earth and evaporating in the sun. The Mormons had worked miracles in one of those sinks, the Great Salt Lake basin. But no part of the West seemed less inviting to Americans than this genuine desert.

East of the Rockies stretched the Great Plains, also a land of little rain and no trees. A short grass carpeted the country, and rivers like the Missouri and the Platte meandered through it, making the Great Plains less forbidding than the Great Basin. Nevertheless, there was simply not enough rainfall on the plains to support staple agriculture as Americans knew it.

The Native Peoples of the West

Some people did live in this last great region, of course. In addition to the Mormons and the people of the Mexican borderlands, Indians living according to traditional, sometimes ancient ways survived throughout the country. Even the most forbidding parts of the Great Basin supported a few thousand Ute, Paiute, and Shoshone who coped with the torrid summers by

Navajo weaving techniques predated white settlement in the Southwest.

dividing into small wandering bands and seeking higher elevations.

Farther south, in the seemingly more hostile environment of present-day Arizona and New Mexico, the Pima, Zuñi, and Hopi had developed methods for farming the desert intensively. They lived in pueblos, communal houses or groups of houses, sometimes perched high on sheer cliffs, where a delicately integrated urban culture evolved. The Navajo, more numerous than the other peoples in the desert south of the Grand Canyon (and comparative newcomers there) lived in family groups spread out over the country, but they too came together on special tribal occasions. The Navajo were skilled weavers of cotton when the introduction of Spanish sheep provided them with the opportunity to raise their craft into a durable art. Both the Navajo and the Pueblo Indians feared the warlike raiders of the Apache tribes, who dwelled farther south but ranged widely in search of booty.

In what was then called Indian Territory, present-day Oklahoma, the "civilized tribes," which had been forced out of Georgia and Alabama during the age of Jackson, had rebuilt their amalgam of native and European cultures: an intensive cash-crop agriculture; a town life; a written language; a school system; and newspapers. Indian Territory came to loom large in the American imagination after the Civil War because, beyond the pale of state and effective federal law, it was an attractive sanctuary for some of the most famous "outlaws" and "badmen" of the era.

But the Indians who most intrigued easterners were, curiously, those who were most determined to resist the whites and their ways, the tribes of the Great Plains. Thanks to the writings of intrepid travelers such as historian Francis Parkman and painters Alfred J. Miller, Karl Bodmer, and George Catlin, the Comanche, Cheyenne, and Arapaho peoples of the central and southern plains, and the Mandan, Crow, Sioux, Nez Percé, and Blackfoot peoples of the northern half of the grasslands were a source of awe and admiration to easterners and of apprehension to those whites who came into their country to compete with them.

Plains Culture

Everything in the lives of the Plains Indians—economy, social structure, religion, diet, dress—revolved around two animals: the native bison and the horse, which was introduced to the West by the Spanish and Mexicans. The bison not only provided food, but its hides were made into clothing, footwear, blankets, portable shelters (the conical tepees), bowstrings, and canvases on which artists recorded heroic legends, tribal histories, and genealogies. The bison's manure

Whose Land?

Bear Rib, chieftain of the Hunkpapa Sioux, during treaty talks at Pierre, South Dakota, in 1866: "To whom does this land belong? I believe it belongs to me. If you asked me for a piece of it I would not give it. I cannot spare it, and I like it very much. . . . I hope you will listen to me."

made a tolerable fuel for cooking and warmth in a treeless land where winters were harsh.

The Plains Indians were nomadic. Except for the Mandan, they grew no crops but trailed after the herds of bison on their horses—to southern grazing grounds in the winter, and back north to fresh grass in the summer. It was by no means an ancient way of life. Runaway horses from Mexican herds had been domesticated only about 150 years before the Plains Indians were confronted by Americans. Nevertheless, in that short time the Indians had developed their stirrup-less, saddle-less, and bit-less mode of riding, which was quite independent of Mexican example and awe-inspiring to American observers. "Almost as awkward as a monkey on the ground," wrote painter George Catlin in 1834, "the moment he lays his hand upon a horse, his face even becomes handsome, and he gracefully flies away like a different being."

The wandering ways of the Plains tribes brought them into frequent contact with one another and with Indians who had developed different cultures. While they traded and could communicate with remarkable subtlety through a common sign language, the tribes were just as likely to fight one another. Since the Indians had no concept of private ownership of land, their wars were not aimed at territorial conquest, but at capturing horses, tools, and sometimes women, and at demonstrating bravery, the highest quality of which a Great Plains male could boast. The English word *brave*, as used to define Indian warriors, was not chosen on a whim.

With only about 225,000 native Americans roaming the Great Plains in 1860, war was not massive, but it was chronic. A permanent peace was as foreign to the Indians' view of the world as the notion that an individual could claim sole ownership of eight acres of good grassland.

By 1860, every Plains tribe knew about the "pale-faces" or "white-eyes." They did not like the wagon trains that had traversed their homeland for two decades, and they occasionally skirmished with the white wayfarers. But the outsiders did move on and were welcome to the extent that they traded, abandoned,

Sioux Indians, camouflaged by animal skins, stalk buffalo in this painting by George Catlin.

or neglected to secure horses, textiles, iron tools, and rifles, all of which improved the natives' standard of living.

The Destruction of the Bison

This uneasy coexistence began to change when Congress authorized the construction of a railroad to the Pacific. The crews that laid the tracks of the Union Pacific and Kansas Pacific across the plains were not interested in staying. But unlike the California and Oregon emigrants, their presence led to the destruction of the bison, the basis of the native peoples' way of life.

The killing began harmlessly enough. In order to feed the big work crews cheaply, the Union Pacific Railroad hired hunters like William F. "Buffalo Bill" Cody to kill bison. The workers could hardly consume enough of the beeflike meat to affect the size of the herds, which numbered perhaps 15 million bison in 1860. However, when a few of the hides that were shipped back east caused a sensation as fashionable "buffalo robes," wholesale slaughter began.

A team of marksmen, reloaders, and skinners could down and strip a thousand of the great beasts in a day. Living in huge herds, the animals were not startled by loud noises and stood grazing, pathetically easy targets, as long as they did not scent or see human beings. With dozens of such teams at work, the bison population declined at a startling rate.

The railroad companies encouraged the slaughter because, merely by crossing over the flimsy iron tracks, a herd of bison could obliterate the line. To apply the finishing touches, wealthy eastern and European sportsmen chartered special trains to take them to the plains where, sometimes without stepping to the ground, they could shoot trophies for their mansions and clubs. By the end of the century, when preservationists stepped in to save the species, only a few hundred buffalo remained alive. It was the most rapid extinction of a species in history, but no more rapid than the extinction of the culture of the people whose fate was tied to the bison.

The Last Indian Wars

The United States cavalry accompanied the railroad's construction crews, ostensibly to enforce the Indians' treaty rights as well as to protect the workmen. Some of these troops were captured Confederate soldiers who elected to take an oath of loyalty and serve in the West as preferable to languishing in prisoner camps. After the war, they were joined by blacks, former slaves who had enlisted and found army life preferable to hard-scrabble farming and menial jobs back home.

Some soldiers and officers learned to respect the tribes and tried to deal fairly with them. For example, General George Crook, who is remembered as the most able of the army's Indian fighters, preferred being known for his respect for the tribes and his just dealings with them. Others shared the opinion of General

An advertisement for buffalo robes, which were fashionable in the 1870s.

Philip H. Sheridan, who was reputed to have told a Comanche chief at Fort Cobb in 1869, "The only good Indian is a dead Indian." The sympathies of the army were with the whites—the railroaders, miners, cattlemen, and eventually farmers who intruded on Indian lands. They believed that because the Indians used the land so inefficiently, their claim to it was not equal to their own. From 1862, when the final era of Indian wars began with a Sioux uprising in Minnesota, to 1890, when the power of the last untamed tribe was shattered at Wounded Knee, South Dakota, the United States cavalry joined with the buffalo hunters to destroy a way of life.

Indian war remained a war of small skirmishes and few pitched battles. Between 1869 and 1876, for example, the peak years of the fighting, the army recorded 200 distinct "incidents," a number that did not include many unopposed Indian raids and confrontations between civilians and the tribes, but the total casualties on the army's side (and possibly the Indians') was less than in any of several Indian-white battles in the 1790s.

The army preferred to fight decisive battles. But the Indians generally clung to traditional hit-and-run attacks that exploited their mobility and allowed them to escape fights in which, with their inferior arms and numbers, they were at a disadvantage. The result was frustration and a cruelty toward the enemy such as had not been seen in the Civil War. In 1871, Commissioner of Indian Affairs Francis Walker explained that "when dealing with savage men, as with savage beasts, no question of national honor can arise. Whether to fight, to run away, or to employ a ruse, is solely a question of expediency."

Custer's Last Stand

By 1876, the army's victory seemed complete. Little by little, the soldiers in dust-blue had hemmed in the wandering tribes and whittled away at their ability to subsist. The typical state of a surrendering tribe was near-starvation, with a goodly proportion of the young men dead. But Indian resistance was not quite at an end.

In June of the centennial year, an audacious Civil War hero and colonel of the Seventh Cavalry, George Armstrong Custer, led 265 men into a battle with the Sioux on Montana's Little Bighorn River. In a rare total victory for the Indians, every one of Custer's men was killed. Although a completely unexpected defeat, "Custer's Last Stand" thrilled Americans. Denied in life the advancement that he believed his record and talents had merited, "Yellow Hair," as the Sioux called him, became a romantic hero in death. A brewery

A drawing of the battle of Little Bighorn by Red Horse, 1881.

commissioned an imaginative painting of the Battle of the Little Bighorn by Cassilly Adams and within a few years distributed 150,000 reproductions of it.

Senior officers who had disapproved of the flamboyant and impetuous Custer, and thought him to blame for the disaster, kept their mouths shut. Only in the next century would the episode be fully appreciated from the Indians' point of view, as a final great military victory brilliantly engineered by Sioux war chiefs. At the time, however, the tribes' joy was short-lived. Most of the victors were under control within the year.

Good Intentions, Tragic Results

In 1881, a Colorado writer, Helen Hunt Jackson, published *A Century of Dishonor*, which became a best-selling book. In meticulous detail and with little distortion of fact, she detailed the cynical immorality with which the United States government had dealt with the Indians since independence. The broken treaties were almost too numerous to be listed. Time and again, according to Jackson, "Christian" whites had cheated "savage" Indians of their land, had herded them onto reservations on lands judged to be the least useful, and then had chipped away at those.

By 1876, the government had ceased to make treaties with the Indians. Those Indians who did not resist American control were defined as wards of the federal government; they were not citizens but were under Washington's protection and enjoyed a few special privileges. After the publication of *A Century of Dishonor*, many easterners demanded that the government use wardship in a just manner.

A CENTURY OF DISHONOR

"It makes little difference . . . where one opens the record of the history of the Indians; every page and every year has its dark stain. The story of one tribe is the story of all, varied only by differences of time and place; but neither time nor place makes any difference in the main facts. Colorado is as greedy and unjust in 1880 as was Georgia in 1830, and Ohio in 1795; and the United States Government breaks promises now as deftly as then, and with added ingenuity from long practice."

Helen Hunt Jackson,
A Century of Dishonor (1881)

In 1887, Congress approved the Dawes Severalty Act. Intentions were of the best. Assuming that the traditional Indian life was no longer feasible, the supporters of the Dawes Act argued that the Indian peoples must be Americanized; that is, they must become self-sustaining citizens through adoption of the ways of the larger society. Under the Dawes Act, the tribes were dissolved and the treaty lands were distributed, homestead-style, 160 acres to each head of the family (itself not a plausible concept to most tribes), and an additional 80 acres to each adult member of the household. Lands left over were sold to whites; in order to avoid further despoliation, remaining Indian land could not be sold or otherwise disposed of for 25 years.

The supporters of the Dawes Act overlooked a number of facts. First, few of the western Indians were farmers; traditionally they had been hunters, gatherers, and traders. Second, the reservation lands were rarely suited to agriculture; they had been allotted to the Indians precisely because they were unattractive to white farmers. Third, tracts of a few hundred acres in the arid West were rarely enough to support efficient white farmers. Finally, no western tribe thought in terms of private ownership of land as vested in a nuclear family. The tribe, which the Dawes Act aimed to relegate to the dustheap, was the basic social unit to which the native Americans looked. The defeated Indians were demoralized by the forced disintegration of their culture and individuals too often were debauched by idleness and alcohol. When it was again permitted by law, they would be stripped of much of their land too.

Wounded Knee

Among these people appeared a religious teacher in the tradition of Tecumseh's brother, The Prophet. Jack Wilson, or Wovoka, a Paiute who had lived with a white Christian family and had been fascinated by the doctrine of redemption, wandered the West preaching a religion that appealed to thousands of Indians. His message was that by performing a ritual dance, the Indians, who were God's chosen people, could prevail on the Great Spirit to make the white man disappear. This "Ghost Dance" would bring back to life the buf-

Helen Hunt Jackson, *author of* Ramona *and* A Century of Dishonor.

falo herds and the many Indians who had been killed in the wars. The old way of life, which in the 1880s all adult Indians vividly remembered, would be restored. This sort of belief, simultaneously edifying and pathetic, is common among peoples who have seen their world turned upside down. In parts of the Southwest that were untouched by Wovoka's religion, defeated Indians turned to peyote, a natural hallucinogenic drug, as a way to escape a bewildering, intolerable reality. To understand the appeal of the

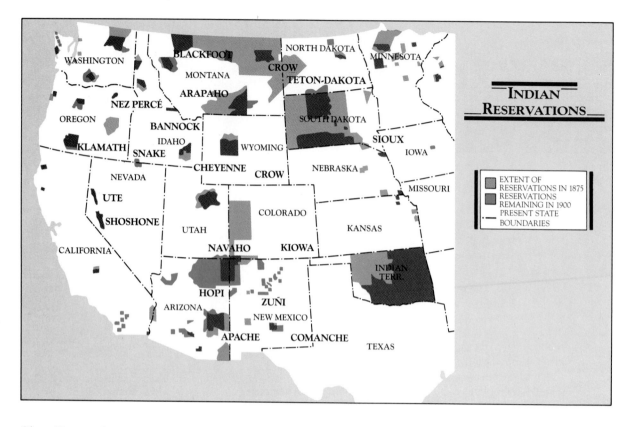

INDIAN
RESERVATIONS

EXTENT OF
RESERVATIONS IN 1875
RESERVATIONS
REMAINING IN 1900
PRESENT STATE
BOUNDARIES

Ghost Dance religion, it is necessary to recall just how rapidly the culture of the Plains Indians was destroyed.

The Dakota Sioux did not go to war with the whites until the end of the 1860s. Within another decade, the survivors had been herded on the Pine Ridge Reservation in South Dakota. There, on Wounded Knee Creek, when the Dakotas took avidly to the Ghost Dance religion, and the soldiers guarding them heard that there were guns in the camp, a war of nerves set in. In December 1890, after a shoving incident, the soldiers opened fire with rifles and artillery. About 200 people, half of them women and children, were killed. For the Indians there was no escape, even in religion.

THE CATTLE KINGDOM

As the Indians lost the West, the Americans won it. Indeed, the final decades of the nineteenth century stand as the greatest era of economic expansion in American history.

In 1870, American forests yielded about 12.8 billion board feet of lumber. By 1900, this output had almost tripled to about 36 billion. Although this increase reflects in part the development of forest industries in the southern states, the region of greatest expansion was a new one, the Pacific Northwest.

In 1870, Americans were raising 23.8 million cattle. In 1900, 67.7 million head of the stupid, bawling creatures were fattening on grasslands, mostly in the West, and in western feedlots.

Annual gold production continued only slightly below the fabulous levels of the gold-rush era, until the end of the century, it was nearly double the totals of 1850. Annual silver production, only 2.4 million troy ounces in 1870, stood at 57.7 million in 1900.

Beginnings

Acre for acre, cattlemen won more of the West than any other group of pioneers. They were motivated to bring the vastness of the Great Plains into the American economy by the appetite of the burgeoning cities for cheap meat, and they were encouraged in their venture by the disinterest in the rolling arid grasslands of anyone save the Indians. Their story thrills Americans to this day (and other people) partly because it was romanticized, partly because the cattle kingdom was established so quickly and just as quickly destroyed.

The cowboy first rode into American legend just before the Civil War. In the late 1850s, enterprising Texans rounded up herds of the half-wild longhorns that ranged freely between the Nueces River and the Rio Grande and drove them north over a trail that had been blazed by Shawnee Indians to Sedalia, Missouri, a railroad town with connections to Chicago. Although the bosses were English-speaking, many of the actual workers were Mexican. They called themselves *vaqueros*.

Vaquero, which translates roughly as "cowboy," entered the English language as *buckaroo*. Indeed, while Anglo-Americans soon comprised the majority of this mobile work force, and former black slaves were a substantial minority of it, much of what became part of American folklore and parlance about the buckaroos was of Mexican derivation. The cowboy's colorful costume was an adaptation of functional Mexican work dress. The bandana was a washcloth that, when tied over the cowboy's mouth, served as a dust screen, no small matter when a thousand cattle were kicking up alkali grit. The broad-brimmed hat was not selected for its picturesque qualities but because it was a sun and rain shield. Manufactured from first-quality beaver felt, the sombrero also served as a drinking pot and washbasin.

The pointed, high-heeled boots, awkward and even painful in which to walk, were designed for riding in the stirrups, where a *vaquero* spent his workday. The "western" saddle was of Spanish design, quite unlike the English tack that Americans in the East used.

Chaps, leather leg coverings, got their name from chaparral, the ubiquitous woody brush against which they were designed to protect the cowboy.

Meat for Millions

The Civil War and Missouri laws against importing Texas cattle (because of hoof-and-mouth disease) stifled the first long-distance commerce in cows before it was fairly started. However, in 1866, when the transcontinental railroad reached Abilene, Kansas, a wheeler-dealer from Illinois, Joseph G. McCoy, saw the possibilities of underselling steers raised back East with Texas longhorns. McCoy built a series of holding pens on the outskirts of the tiny Kansas town, arranged to ship cattle he did not then have with the Kansas Pacific Railroad, and dispatched agents to southern Texas to induce Texans to round up and drive cattle north to Abilene on a trading route called the Chisholm Trail.

In 1867, McCoy shipped 35,000 "tall, bony, coarse-headed, flat-sided, thin-flanked" cattle to Chicago. In 1868, 75,000 of the beasts, nearly worthless in Texas, passed through Abilene with Chicago packers crying for more. In 1871, 600,000 "critters" left the pens of several Kansas railroad towns to end up on American dinner tables.

The Sioux camp near Pine Ridge, South Dakota, in 1891.

Skills now exhibited at rodeos were once the cowboy's everyday activity.

The profits were immense. A steer that cost about $5 to raise on public lands could be driven to Kansas at the cost of one cent a mile ($5 to $8) and sold for $25 or, occasionally, as much as $50. Investors from as far as England went west to establish ranches that were as comfortable as big-city gentlemen's clubs. The typical cattleman at the famous Cheyenne Club never touched a gun and sat on a horse only for the photographer. Instead, he sank into plush easy chairs, ignited a Havana cigar, and discussed account books, very often in an English accent, with his fellow businessmen.

The railhead continued to push westward, and with it went the destination of the cowboys, who were soon arriving from the North as well as the South. The migration of the trailhead was alright with most of the citizens of towns like Abilene. They concluded after a few seasons that the money to be made as a cattle-trading center was not worth the damage done to their own ranches and farms by hundreds of thousands of cattle. The wild atmosphere given their towns by the rambunctious cowboys, many of them bent on a blowout after months on the trail, was even less conducive to respectable civic life. As a cow town grew, its "better element" demanded churches and schools in place of saloons, casinos, and whorehouses. The stage was set for the "taming" of a town, which is the theme of so many popular legends.

THE GREAT LOCOMOTIVE CRASH

A bizarre illustration of just how fast the West was "developed" took place in Waco, Texas, on September 15, 1896. William Crush, general passenger agent of the Missouri, Kansas, and Texas Railroad (which was called the "Katy"), had two obsolete locomotives at his disposal. He decided to put on a show, which, among other things, sold a lot of tickets. One engine was painted red and the other, green, and they were parked facing each other at either end of a four-mile stretch of track. They were fired up and the throttles tied back. By the time they collided, they were each traveling at 90 miles per hour. Over 15,000 people witnessed the spectacle. Several were killed and hundreds were injured by the flying steel.

Never, though, did the cowboys lack for someplace to take their herds. There were always newer, smaller towns to the west to welcome them. In Kansas alone, Ellsworth, Newton, Wichita, Dodge City, and Hays had their "wide-open" period.

Disaster

The cattle kingdom lasted only a generation, ending suddenly as a result of greed with the assistance of two natural disasters.

The profits to be made in cattle were so great that exploiters ignored the fact that grassland has its limits as the support of huge herds. Vast as the plains were, they were overstocked by the mid-1880s. Clear-running springs were trampled into unpotable mud holes. Weeds never before noticed replaced the grasses that had invited overgrazing. Hills and buttes were scarred by cattle trails. Some species of migratory birds that once passed through twice a year simply disappeared; the beefsteaks on hoof had beaten them to their food.

Then, on January 1, 1886, a great blizzard buried the eastern and southern plains. Within three days, three feet of snow drifting into 20- and 30-foot banks suffocated the range. Between 50 and 85 percent of the livestock froze to death or died of hunger. About 300 cowboys could not reach shelter and were killed; the casualties among the Indians never were counted. When spring arrived, half the American plains reeked of death.

The summer of 1886 brought ruin to many cattlemen who had survived the snows. Grasses that had weathered summer droughts for millennia were unable to do so in their overgrazed condition; they withered and died, starving cattle already weakened by winter. Then, the next winter, the states that had escaped the worst of the blizzard of 1886 got sixteen inches of snow in sixteen hours and weeks more of intermittent fall.

The blizzard of 1886 froze millions of cattle. This illustration is from Harper's Weekly.

The End of a Brief Era

The cattle industry recovered, but only when more prudent and methodical businessmen took over the holdings of the speculators of the glory days. Cattle barons like Richard King of southern Texas foreswore risking all on the open range. Through clever manipulation of land laws, King built a ranch that was as large as the state of Rhode Island. If not quite so grandiose in their success, others imitated King's example in Texas, Wyoming, Montana, and eastern Colorado.

Even more important in ending the days of the long drive and the cowboy as a romantic knight-errant was the expansion of the railroad network. When new east-west lines snaked into Texas and the states on the Canadian border, and the Union Pacific and Kansas Pacific sent feeder lines north and south into cow country, the cowboy became a ranch hand, a not-so-freewheeling employee of large commercial operations.

The Cowboy's Life

Even in the days of the long drive, the world of the cowboy bore scant resemblance to the legends that came to permeate American popular culture. Despite the white complexion of the cowboys in popular literature and in Western films of the twentieth century, a large proportion of cowboys were Mexican or black. In some cases, these workers and the whites acted and mixed as equals. Just as often, however, they split along racial lines when they reached the end of the trail, frequenting segregated restaurants, barber shops, hotels, saloons, and brothels.

The appellation "boy" is more accurate. Photographs that the buckaroos had taken in cow towns like Abilene and Dodge City (as well as arrest records, mostly for drunk and disorderly conduct), show a group of very young men, few apparently much older than 25. The life was too hard for anyone but youths—days in the saddle, nights sleeping on bare ground in all weather. Moreover, the cowboy who married could not afford to be absent from his own ranch or farm for as long as the cattle drives required.

The real buckaroos were not constantly engaged in shooting scrapes such as made novels and movies so exciting. Their skills lay in horsemanship and with a rope, not with the Colt revolver that they carried to signal co-workers far away. Indeed, toting guns was forbidden in trailhead towns. With a drunken binge on every cowboy's itinerary, the sheriff or marshal in charge of keeping the peace did not tolerate shooting irons on every hip. Those who did not leave their revolvers in camp outside town checked them at the police station.

No. 577   NEW YORK, JUNE, 1, 1912   5 CENTS

The BUFFALO BILL STORIES

Devoted To Far West Life

BUFFALO BILL AND THE SILK LASSO

OR PAWNEE BILL'S MASQUERADE
BY THE AUTHOR OF "BUFFALO BILL"

Suddenly the tables were turned, and the masked outlaw found himself
underneath the famous scout and looking into the ominous
barrel of Pawnee Bill's revolver.

Primarily a showman, "Buffalo Bill" Cody was transformed into a chivalric hero in pulp novels.

acters he invented; others were highly fictionalized real people. Called pulps after the cheap paper on which they were printed or dime novels after their price, the books by Judson and his many competitors were devoured chiefly but not exclusively by boys. Indeed, the mythical world appealed to those who knew much better. During the 1880s, while living as a rancher in North Dakota, future president Theodore Roosevelt helped capture two young cowboys who had robbed a grocery store. In their saddlebags, Roosevelt found several Ned Buntline novels that no doubt featured outlaws who were unjustly accused.

The tiny town of Palisade, Nevada, on the Central Pacific railroad line, won the reputation in eastern newspapers as a den of cutthroats because brawls and gunfights broke out so regularly when passengers left the train for refreshment. In fact, the fights were staged by locals in part to twit eastern fantasies, in part because they were just plain bored.

Legendary Characters

In the pulps and later in films, Americans discovered that the bank and train robbers Jesse and Frank James, and several cohorts from the Clanton family, were really modern-day Robin Hoods who gave the money they took to the poor. When Jesse was murdered, his mother made a tourist attraction of his grave, charging admission and explaining that her son had been a Christian with an inclination to read the Bible in his spare time.

Belle Starr (Myra Belle Shirley) was immortalized as "the bandit queen," as pure in heart as Jesse James was socially conscious. Billy the Kid (William Bonney), a

THE WILD WEST IN AMERICAN CULTURE

The legend of the cowboy as a romantic, dashing, and quick-drawing knight of the wide-open spaces was not a creation of a later era. On the contrary, all the familiar themes of the Wild West were well formed when the cold, hard reality was still alive on the plains. Rather, the myths of the Wild West were embraced not only by easterners in their idle reveries, but by the cowboys themselves.

The most important creator of the legendary Wild West was a shadowy character named E. Z. C. Judson. A former Know-Nothing who was dishonorably discharged from the Union Army, Judson took the pen name Ned Buntline, and between 1865 and 1886, churned out more than 400 romantic, blood, guts, and chivalric novels about western heroes. Some of his char-

A WOMAN OF THE WILD WEST

In several instances during the Civil War, women were discovered posing as men—soldiers in the army. No doubt, many more maintained such an imposture throughout the war. "Charlie" Parkhurst was a woman who lived as a man in one of the West's toughest professions. Beginning in 1851, Charlie drove a stage coach through the California gold country. During "his" career, Charlie built a reputation as an expert with the whip. He chewed tobacco, squandered money at the gaming tables, and put in as hard a day's work as was expected of any man. Charlie shot at least one would-be bandit who stopped the stage. In 1879, Charlie's neighbors in Watsonville, California, remarked on his absence and went to his cabin where they found the old teamster dead. Only then was it discovered Charlie Parkhurst was a woman.

Brooklyn-born homicidal maniac, was romanticized as a tragic hero who had been forced into a life of crime by a callous society. James Butler "Wild Bill" Hickok, a gambler and clothes-horse who killed perhaps six people before he was shot down in Deadwood Gulch, South Dakota, in 1876, was attributed with dozens of killings, all in the cause of making the West safe for women, children, and psalmbooks. Calamity Jane (Martha Cannary), later said to have been Wild Bill's paramour, wrote her own romantic autobiography in order to support a drinking problem.

Calamity Jane and other "living legends" of the West personally contributed to the mythmaking by appearing in Wild West shows that traveled to cities in the East and in Europe, where they dramatized great gun battles. The most famous of these shows was the creation of "Buffalo Bill" Cody, who had begun his career as a buffalo hunter for the Union Pacific. Among his featured players was Sitting Bull, the Hunkpapa Sioux chief who had overseen the defeat of George Custer. Reality and myth were implausibly confused. After a successful career in show business, Sitting Bull returned to the Rosebud Reservation where, during the Ghost Dance excitement, he was

accidentally killed by two Indian policemen who were arresting him on suspicion of fomenting rebellion.

Some creators of the legendary West were conscientious realists; Frederic Remington, whose paintings and bronze statues of cowboys and Indians are studiously representative, is a fine example. Others, while romantics, were talented artists; Owen Wister, an aristocratic easterner, created the prototype of the western knight without armor in *The Virginian*, published in 1902. But for the most part, the Wild West was the invention of highly commercial merchandisers of popular entertainment.

THE MINING FRONTIER

The folklore of the precious-metal mining frontier is second only to the legend of the cowboy in the American imagination. Deadwood Gulch, for example, where Wild Bill Hickok was gunned down and Calamity Jane spent much of her life, was no cow town but a gold-mining center.

Gold and Silver Rushes

After the richest of the California gold fields played out, prospectors in search of "glory holes" fanned out over the mountains and deserts of the West. For more than a generation, they discovered new deposits almost annually and very rich ones every few years. In 1859, there were two great strikes. A find in the Pike's Peak area of Colorado led to a rush that was reminiscent of that of 1849. At about the same time, gold miners in northern Nevada discovered that a "blue mud" that had been fouling their operations was one of the richest silver ores ever discovered. This was the beginning of Virginia City and the Comstock Lode, which, before it pinched out in the twentieth century, yielded more than $400 million in silver and gold.

In 1862, Tombstone, Arizona, was founded on the site of a gold mine; in 1864, Helena, Montana, rose atop another. In 1876, rich placer deposits were discovered in the Black Hills of South Dakota (then forbidden to whites by Indian treaty). The next year, silver was found at Leadville, Colorado, almost two miles above sea level in the Rockies.

During the 1880s, the Coeur d'Alene in the Idaho panhandle drew thousands of miners, as did the copper deposits across the mountains in Butte. In 1891, the Cripple Creek district in Colorado began to outproduce every other mining town. In 1898, miners rushed north to Canada's Klondike, Alaska's Yukon, and then to Nome, where the gold was on the beach. As late

Sitting Bull, a squaw, and three of his children pose with two white visitors to the Standing Rock reservation in 1882.

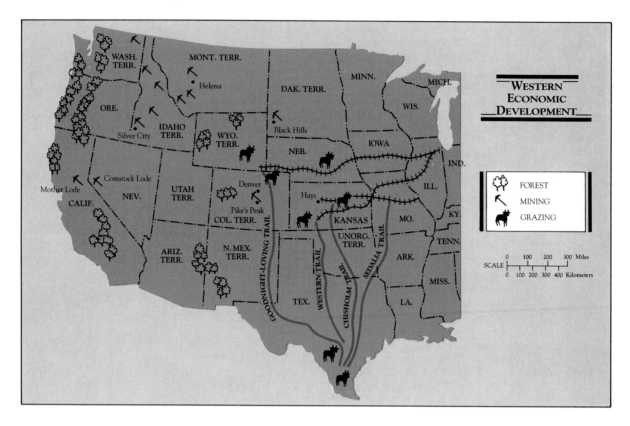

as 1901, there was an old-fashioned rush when the classic grizzled old prospector in a slouch hat, Jim Butler, drove his pick into a desolate mountain in southern Nevada and found it "practically made of silver." From the town of Tonopah, founded on its site, prospectors discovered rich deposits in Goldfield, a few miles away.

Of Mining Camps and Cities

Readers of the dime novels of the time and film viewers since have avidly savored the vision of boisterous, wide-open mining towns, complete with saloons rocking with the music of tinny pianos and the shouts of bearded men. The live-for-today miner, the gambler, the prostitute with a heart of gold are permanent inhabitants of American folklore. Nor is the picture altogether imaginary. The speculative mining economy fostered a risk-all attitude toward life and work.

However, efficient exploitation of underground (hard rock) mining required a great deal of capital and technical expertise, both to finance the operation and to build the railroads that hauled ore out. Consequently, the mining camps that were home to from 5,000 to even 10,000 people within a short time of their founding were also cities with a variety of services and a social structure more like that of older industrial towns than the towns of the cattleman's frontier.

In 1877, only six years after gold was discovered on its site, Leadville, Colorado, boasted several miles of paved streets, gas lighting, a modern water system, thirteen schools, five churches, and three hospitals. Leadville was hardly the tiny, false-front set that is used to represent mining towns in Hollywood films.

Towns like Virginia City in Nevada, Deadwood Gulch in South Dakota, and Tombstone in Arizona are best remembered as places where legendary characters like Wild Bill Hickok and Wyatt Earp dis-

SOLID GOLD

Observing the centennial year (1976) of America's richest and longest-lived gold mine, the Homestake of Lead, South Dakota, historian T. H. Watkins calculated that if all the gold that the Homestake had produced "could somehow be gathered together, melted, and poured into a solid cube, that cube would measure only a little over twelve feet to a side. Yet that hypothetical cube, hardly large enough to fill an average bedroom, would weigh more than 1,093 tons, or 35 million ounces." At the time that Watkins wrote, this bauble was worth $4,725 million. According to the average price of gold in 1985, the price tag was $11 billion.

charged their revolvers; but they were also the sites of huge stamping mills (to crush the ores) that towered over the landscape, and of busy exchanges where mining stocks were traded by agents of San Francisco, New York, and London bankers.

In Goldfield, the last of the wide-open mining towns, one of the most important men in the camp was the urbane Wall Street financier Bernard Baruch (who may have been outdressed by some of the locals). The Anaconda Copper Company of Butte, Montana, was one of the nation's ranking corporate giants. The Guggenheim mining syndicate was supreme in the Colorado gold fields. Rockefeller's Standard Oil was a major owner of mines in the Coeur d'Alene. If it was wild, the mining West was no mere colorful diversion

for readers of dime novels, but an integral part of the national economy. In fact, the gold and silver that the hard-rock miners tore from the earth stood at the very center of a question that divided Americans more seriously than any other after the end of Reconstruction—what was to serve as the nation's money.

The miners and mine owners alone could not make an issue of the precious metals from which coins were minted, goods bought and sold, and debts incurred and paid off—or not paid off. There were too few of them. However, as the century wound to a close, the money question became of great interest to a group of people who formed a major part of the American population, and who had once been its most important segment, the farmers on the land.

Mining was a dangerous occupation in the West. Here a mucker moves a load of silver ore to the surface.

PUNCHING COWS

It took three or four months to drive a herd of cattle from the vicinity of San Antonio, Texas, to a rail-head town in Kansas and to be asked to join a trail crew was a coveted honor among the young men of the country. The wages were low, only $1 a day plus board and as good a bed as the sod of the Great Plains provided. But because a lot of money and many lives rested on every member of a crew, only those who had impressed a trail boss with their skills and reliability were invited to go.

A trail crew consisted of the trail boss, usually the owner of the cattle; his *segundo*, or assistant; a cook; a wrangler, who was in charge of the *remuda*, or herd of horses that accompanied the expedition; and a hand for each 250 to 300 cattle. Most herds were made up of between 2,500 and 3,000 cattle, so 10 to 12 cowpunchers, or buckaroos, was typical. (The "cows" were really steers, males that had been castrated at their first roundup; the "punchers" got their name because one of their jobs was to punch the cows into corrals and loading chutes—using poles.)

A herd moved about ten to fifteen miles a day, the animals grazing as they got the chance. The usual procedure for getting a herd along was for two men to ride "lead," or "point," one on either side of the milling steers; two to ride "swing" and "flank," in pairs at regular intervals alongside the herd; and two or three to ride "drag," behind the herd to hurry up stragglers.

Each position had its peculiarities and was assigned in rotation or with an eye to a particular cowpuncher's abilities or his personal standing at the moment in the trail boss's graces. Riding point was the most dangerous in the event of a stampede, but it was also the most prestigious and most pleasant in terms of dust and odor (unless there was a powerful tailwind). Conversely, riding drag was the safest but also the least desirable job, not only because of the quality of the air that 3,000 animals left behind, but also because there was not a moment in which some independent-minded "dogies" were not determined to set off on their own.

The day's drive started at first light and ended as late toward dusk as the trail boss could find satisfactory grass and water, but the cowboy's work was not done. After a big dinner at the chuck wagon, the hands had to "ride night." In two-hour shifts, pairs of riders circled the herd in opposite directions, looking out for preda-

When cattle roamed the unfenced range, unique "brands" burned into the animals' hides identified their owners.

tors and soothing the nervous steers. Some folklorists (and some old cowpunchers) say that the western singing and guitar-playing tradition developed as a means of keeping a herd calm; music soothed the generally docile if not the savage beast. Indeed, night riding was as dangerous as it was detested for its theft of sleep. Almost all stampedes started at night, tripped by a bolt of lightning, a steer dodging a coyote, or, to human reckoning, no reason whatsoever. Except for river crossings—there were four major and numerous minor watercourses between Texas and Kansas—the stampede was the most frequent cause of death written on the wooden markers that dotted the Shawnee, Chisholm, and Goodnight-Loving trails. (Indians were not a serious threat to the cow puncher's life, although they stole his cattle when they could.)

There would be no strumming guitar in the pouring rain that came often enough. Then the night riders donned their yellow oilskin slickers that covered their whole saddle, and gently cursed, or slept. It was said that a cowpuncher who had a good night horse could sleep in the saddle, since his mount even knew to wake him at the end of the two-hour shift.

Cowboys on the long drive might bring along a horse or two of their own, but the boss supplied the tough, wiry work ponies. They were geldings, about seven to ten for each hand. (Stallions fought, and mares were considered too temperamental for the job.) Each had a unique identity and job. There were morning horses and afternoon horses. The night horse had singular qualities already noted. The cowboy used the strong rope horse to help pull a stray out of a bog or for some other problem involving a lasso. A highly specialized but important horse was the water horse, a good swimmer on which a cowboy could count to get him across as much as a mile of strong current with steers rolling their wild, pink-rimmed eyes and thrashing about on every side. The most talented mount was the cutting horse, which knew exactly how a steer would act without the rider's instructions. The best were as agile as sheepdogs.

The cowboy's attachment to his horses, the butt of many Hollywood jokes, was nevertheless genuine. The cowpuncher was a horseman; he shunned work that had to be done on foot. Everyone had stories of crews that quit rather than slop hogs or milk dairy cows.

If passionate in general, however, the cowboy's attachment to horses in the particular was fickle. He did not own the mounts on which he worked, and at the end of the trail they were sold off along with the cattle. Only a few hands returned home to Texas overland. After they had spent most of their money on liquor, women, and cards, cowboys climbed aboard an eastbound train, rode it to the Mississippi River, and struck south by riverboat.

For Further Reading

Overviews and Classics

Ray A. Billington, *Westward Expansion: A History of the American Frontier* (1967)

Thomas D. Clark, *Frontier America: The Story of the Westward Movement* (1969)

Frederick Merk, *History of the Westward Movement* (1978)

Frederick Jackson Turner, *The Frontier in American History* (1920)

Robert A. Wiebe, *The Search for Order* (1968)

Valuable Special Studies

Allan C. Bogue, *From Prairie to Corn Belt* (1963)

Dee Brown, *Bury My Heart at Wounded Knee* (1970)

E. E. Dale, *The Range Cattle Industry* (1930)

David Day, *Cowboy Culture: A Saga of Five Centuries* (1981)

Robert R. Dystra, *The Cattle Towns* (1968)

J. B. Frantz and J. E. Choate, *The American Cowboy: The Myth and the Reality* (1955)

William S. Greever, *The Bonanza West: The Story of the Western Mining Rushes* (1963)

William T. Hagan, *American Indians* (1961)

E. S. Osgood, *The Day of the Cattleman* (1929)

Rodman W. Paul, *Mining Frontiers of the Far West, 1848–1880* (1963)

J. M. Shagg, *The Cattle Trading Industry* (1973)

Fred A. Shannon, *The Farmer's Last Frontier* (1967)

Duane A. Smith, *Rocky Mountain Mining Camps* (1967)

Henry Nash Smith, *Virgin Land: The American West as Symbol and Myth* (1950)

J. R. Swanson, *The Indian Tribes of North America* (1953)

Robert M. Utley, *Last Days of the Sioux Nation* (1963)

Wilcomb E. Washburn, *The Indian in America* (1975)

Thomas H. Watkins, *Gold and Silver in the West* (1960)

Biographies and Autobiographies

Ray A. Billington, *Frederick Jackson Turner* (1973)

Charles K. Hofling, *Custer and the Little Bighorn: A Psychobiographical Inquiry* (1981)

The Revolt of the Farmers
The Struggle to Save Agrarian America

Ever since the first farmer poked a hole in the ground and inserted a seed, tillers of the soil have understood that they were engaged in a game of chance with nature. Farming involved gambling a year's living on such uncertainties as winter's final frost, summer's yield of sunshine and rain, and an autumn storm's driving winds and hailstones. Farmers accepted the fact that they were at the mercy of capricious insects and birds. They knew that illness when the harvest was begun might result in twelve months of privation.

But farmers have also known that they were the people who performed the job that distinguished civilization from savagery, that made all other kinds of work possible. They knew that they produced the first necessity of life after air and water, and that the farmer was the man, in the words of a song of the 1890s, "who feeds them all." They believed that farmers would always be society's most valuable citizens. In the United States, Thomas Jefferson and four generations of politicians had told them that those who toiled in the earth were the "bone and sinew" of the republic.

Then, in the final decades of the nineteenth century, the farmers of the West and South discovered that these old truisms were not necessarily so. In industrial America the powers of nature came to pale in comparison with the power of people whom the farmers considered to be far from valuable to society. Railroad barons, industrial millionaires, landlords, bankers (most of all), lawyers, newspaper editors, and politi-

The grandeur and isolation of a plains farm are captured in this traveling photographer's masterpiece.

cians—all of them the farmers came to see as parasites who sucked a rich living from the marrow of the bones of hard-working producers.

The farmers found that they were no longer the most valuable citizens, but just one interest group among many. And, in an urban and industrial America, they were not a particularly important group. The new America was apt to view cultivators as ludicrous people, hayseeds and yokels to be mocked on the vaudeville stage and in the traveling salesman's joke books.

THE PARADOX OF AMERICAN AGRICULTURE: ITS FINEST HOUR IS ITS WORST

Farmers rarely led the way on America's last frontier. They generally followed miners, loggers, cattlemen, and soldiers when the population of a region was large enough to provide a local market for foodstuffs. Large-scale commercial agriculture was not feasible in the last West until the railroad arrived to carry crops in quantity to hungry eastern and foreign cities.

Once settled, farmers sometimes clashed with other westerners. In California, farmers of the Central Valley demanded that the state legislature take action against hydraulic miners who, in washing down whole mountainsides to win their grains of gold, polluted the rivers with mud so that the water was unfit for irrigation.

On the Great Plains, homesteaders, who were called "nesters" by open-range cattlemen, fenced in their holdings with barbed wire, which prevented cattle from reaching streams and water holes. The cattlemen retaliated by damming up streams before they reached

the nesters' lands and by cutting fence wire. In Johnson County, Wyoming, a shooting war erupted. However, as in the conflict between farmers and miners in California, most of these disputes were resolved in the legislatures and courts. As long as the conflicts were local, the more numerous farmers usually had their way. On the national level, numbers mean less than concentrated power and influence, and the story had a different plot.

A Success Story

Never in the history of the world have people put new land to the plow as quickly as Americans did in the final three decades of the nineteenth century. As of 1870, when the takeoff occurred, Americans had brought 408 million acres of land under cultivation, an average of 1.6 million acres of new farmland a year. Between 1870 and 1900, a single generation of farmers put 431 million acres of virgin soil to the plow, an average of 14.4 million acres each year!

Crop production increased just as sharply. By 1900, American farmers were producing up to 150 percent more of the staples—cotton, corn, wheat—than they had in 1870. Hogs, which may be considered a by-product of corn, numbered 25 million in 1870 and 63 million in 1900.

The ravenous appetites of American and foreign city dwellers encouraged this amazing growth, and the expansion of the railroads made it possible for crops raised by a Great Plains farmer to feed the inhabitants of Chicago and New York, London and Warsaw. Even at that, however, the pioneer farmers of the West had to overcome formidable difficulties to accomplish what they did.

New Methods for a New Country

Farming the land west of 98° longitude, with its paucity of rain, called for innovations in traditional farming methods. The absence of trees, except for scrub cottonwood and poplar on riverbanks, made the cost of fencing prohibitive. But because millions of cattle roamed the open range, protection of crops was more urgent than it was back east. The solution came in 1872 when Joseph Glidden of Illinois perfected a machine that mass-produced cheap barbed wire, the makings for an extremely efficient steel "hedge" that could be erected on the flimsiest of scavenged fenceposts.

Traditional wood-frame houses could be built only after a family had harvested a few crops and squirreled away enough money to buy lumber. In the meantime, pioneers lived in sod houses, which were constructed by piling blocks cut from the tangled plains sod as though they were bricks. Sod houses were snug enough in the winter, but dripped mud in the spring thaw and

---

THE FARMER FEEDS THEM ALL

When the Lawyer hangs around and the Butcher cuts
   a pound,
Oh the farmer is the man who feeds them all.
And the preacher and the cook go a-strolling by the brook
And the farmer is the man who feeds them all.

Oh the farmer is the man, the farmer is the man,
Lives on credit 'till the fall.
Then they take him by the hand and they lead him from
   the land
And the middle man's the one that gets them all.

Song of the 1890s

Wearing masks so they won't be recognized, settlers cut fifteen miles of Brighton Ranch fence in 1885. Note the fencepost, a mere brittle branch of a tree.

A couple stand with their prized possessions in front of their sod house in Custer County, Nebraska, about 1886.

became hellholes of choking dust during the long arid summers.

Dearth of water was the chief obstacle to farming on the Great Plains. In part, the pioneers overcame it with improved windmills that pumped water for irrigation from far below the surface. In part, however, "dry farming" depended on a self-serving delusion. The summers of the 1870s and 1880s, when much of the Great Plains was settled, were untypically wet. When normal conditions returned, a few experts warned in advance, the deep wells would run dry and crops would wither. The pioneers airily waved away these warnings. They believed that they had permanently altered the rainfall patterns of the region; when they broke the sod, moisture was liberated from the earth and would return indefinitely in the form of heavier rains and snows.

A Mechanized People

Improvements in farm machinery furthered agricultural expansion. Equipped with chilled steel plows that sliced through sod that could shatter iron, disc harrows that cultivated wide swaths with each pass, and machines that planted seeds, shucked corn, threshed wheat, bound shocks, and shredded fodder to make food for livestock, farmers were able to cut down on waste, raise more animals, and tend to more acreage than earlier generations had dreamed possible.

The value of farm machinery in use in the United States increased from $271 million in 1870 to $750 million in 1900. The meaning of this statistic for an individual can be appreciated if it is translated into the number of hours that a hand had to devote in a season to produce wheat on an acre of land. By plowing and seeding by hand, harvesting with a sickle, and threshing the wheat by flailing it, a farmer had to spend between 50 and 60 hours to harvest about 20 bushels of wheat per acre. With a gang plow and a horse-drawn seeder, harrow, reaper, and thresher—all of which were in widespread use by 1890—a farmer produced a much larger crop after only eight to ten hours of work per acre. Potentially, a single man could cultivate six times as much land in 1890 as his father had farmed before the Civil War.

Hard Times

Expansion and mechanization disrupted the ways of the farmers of the Northeast and the Ohio Valley, but in the end their fate was a kind one. They ceased growing the staples that were grown more cheaply farther west and specialized in perishable crops such as dairy goods, poultry and eggs, and garden vegetables to supply nearby urban markets.

But the western raisers of wheat, corn, and livestock, and the southern growers of cotton, watched their incomes sag beginning about 1872, and collapse by the 1890s. A crop that in 1872 had brought a farmer $1,000 in real income (actual purchasing power) was worth only $500 in 1896. A man who was 48 years of age in 1896, still an active working farmer, had to produce precisely twice as many hogs or two times the bushels of corn or wheat as he had produced as a young man of 24 just to enjoy the same standard of living that he had known in 1872.

With their machinery, many farmers were doing just that. But it was not comforting to know that a quarter

Mechanization on the farm—horse-drawn reapers like this did the work of many men.

century of backbreaking toil and openness to new methods yielded nothing but more struggle. By the 1890s, the price of corn was so low (eight cents a bushel) that some farmers had to forgo buying coal and burn their grain for winter warmth.

Because it is in the nature of commercial farming to borrow money, declining prices meant bankruptcy for many. Between 1889 and 1893, some 11,000 Kansas farm families lost their homes, foreclosed by the banks for failing to make their mortgage payments. In several western counties of Kansas and Nebraska during the same period, nine out of every ten farmsteads changed hands; thousands lay vacant until after 1900, houses and barns decaying amidst thistles and dust. The number of farm tenant families—those who did not own the land they worked—doubled from 1 to 2 million between 1880 and 1900, most of the increase coming after 1890.

The South: Added Travails

In the South, the wholesale price of cotton fell to six cents a pound (to below five cents in 1893). Fortunately for the people who grew it, for their crop did not burn as well as corn, and firewood was abundant. In every other particular, however, southern farmers were worse off than farmers anywhere save in the wretched western counties of Kansas and Nebraska. Whereas landowners outnumbered tenants three to one in the North and West, owners and tenants were equal in number in the South, and among blacks, tenants and sharecroppers outnumbered landowners by almost five to one. Nothing better illustrates the benighted condition of southern farmers than the fact that pellagra, a fatal niacin-deficiency disease unknown even in slavery times, was endemic in the rural South by the turn of the century.

Just as in the West, these difficulties accompanied a success story. Southern agriculture made a remarkable recovery after the Civil War. The land survived, and the work force remained. (Few of the South's 4 million black people went north or west.) Cotton production reached the 1860 level in 1870 and exceeded the prewar record (1859) within a few more years. This was accomplished by means of a system of cultivation that was born of expediency and survived only by exploitation of the people on the bottom of southern society.

Tenants and Sharecroppers

The challenge facing southern agriculture after the Civil War lay in three interrelated facts: the blacks were free and would no longer work for nothing; the Radical Republicans passed up an opportunity to make them independent farmers when, instead of dividing

---

STOVEPIPING

In the autumn of 1893 there was so much rain in the wheatbelt of eastern Washington State that much of the year's crop was ruined. Some farmers tried to stave off disaster by means of a technique called "stovepiping." A length of stovepipe was inserted into an upright sack and filled with the rotten grain. Then the rest of the sack—top and sides—was filled with good wheat, and the stovepipe was removed. When the purchasing agent opened the sack, the grain looked good. It did not work for long. Buyers learned to use their own hollow tube to dig for samples deep within each sack.

---

the old plantations into homesteads for former slaves, they left the land in the possession of its prewar owners; the landowners had no cash with which to pay wages to black (and white) farm laborers. Indeed, even if a gang-labor system based on wages had been financially possible, the blacks would have resisted it because its patterns too closely resembled the way they had lived under slavery, sleeping in "quarters" and working in groups.

The solution was the share-tenant or the sharecropper system. Plantation owners partitioned their land into family-farm-size plots on which a cabin, usually

In southern agriculture, a system of sharecropping replaced slavery. Here, sharecroppers pick cotton in the 1890s.

quite rude, was constructed. In return for the use of the house and the land, share tenants, who provided their own daily bread, mule, plow, and seed, turned over to the landlord one-quarter to one-third of each year's crop.

Sharecroppers, who were likely to be black, were tenants who were too poor to supply their own mule, plow, and seed. The landlord provided everything in return for one-half of the crop. No money changed hands. In theory, tenant and landlord marketed their shares of the crop independently of one another.

In practice, the landlord or sometimes an independent merchant took the tenant's share too. In order to live day by day, the sharecropper bought on credit from a general merchandiser, using as collateral a lien on his share of the fall's harvest. All too often, with the price of cotton and corn declining steadily during the late nineteenth century, the sharecropper family found that it had no share left to sell when the books were balanced at the store. All the family had was an open line of credit, and maybe a lien on a crop that was not yet in the ground.

There was, of course, an element of security in this debt bondage; the cropper who owed money to the landlord was not likely to be evicted. But there had been an element of security in slavery too.

Hayseeds

A more subtle blow to farmers was the decline in their political power and status. Not only did the proportion of agriculturalists in the population go down annually, but the legislators whom they sent to Washington and the state capitals often seemed to forget about their constituents once they made the acquaintance of lobbyists for the railroading, industrial, and banking interests.

A newly confident urban culture depicted the man of the soil in popular fiction, songs, and melodramas as a thick-skulled yokel, a ridiculous figure in a tattered straw hat with a hayseed clenched between his teeth. White southern farmers labored under the scorn northeasterners had held them in since the days Yankee masters threatened to sell troublesome servants "to Virginia." Southern blacks, of course, were virtually forgotten by their former northern friends after 1877.

Serious writers such as Hamlin Garland understood the hardships of the agricultural life but also rejected them. In his popular book of 1891, *Main-Travelled Roads,* Garland depicted farm life as dreary and stultifying. State insane asylum statistics bore out this dismal picture. In states that were both industrial and agricultural, such as Ohio and Indiana, farm people were proportionately more numerous than city people in the institutions, and farm women (who lived a more isolated life than their husbands) outnumbered the men.

Tens of thousands of farmers' sons and daughters followed Garland in his flight to the city. In part, they despaired of ever making a living on the land. In part, they were lured by the social and cultural attractions of the city. "Who wants to smell new-mown hay," playwright Clyde Fitch wrote in 1909, "if he can breathe gasoline on Fifth Avenue instead?" With each son and daughter who opted for urban fumes, farmers who clung to the Jeffersonian image of themselves became further dejected and agitated.

A GROWING PROTEST

Against jokes and jeers the farmers could defend themselves by reaffirming their confidence that they were peculiarly valuable to society. This was done in speech and sermon, in the pages of magazines aimed at a rural leadership. In sturdy pillars of American popular culture, like the McGuffey's *Readers* in which urban and rural schoolchildren alike learned their ABCs and morals, the ennoblement of farm life remained alive and well.

But what of the depression? What—or who—was to blame for the sliding prices and fitful but inexorable decline in farm income? Because the agricultural depression was so widespread and lasted so long, the

Mary Elizabeth Lease, one of America's first women lawyers and a leader of protesting farmers.

"Sockless Jerry" Simpson reveled in his homey nickname, but he was no "hick." He was a sophisticated thinker and shrewd politician.

explanations were many and sometimes contradicted one another.

Too Many Farmers, Too Much Crop

At bottom, economists said, there were too many farmers producing too much grain, livestock, and fiber than the marketplace could absorb. Because too many transcontinental railroads had been built too quickly, the supply of farm products far exceeded the demand for them.

Many leaders of the protesting farmers agreed. Fiery Mary Elizabeth Lease of Kansas, one of the country's first woman lawyers, told listeners at a hundred county fairs to "raise less corn and more hell." Canadian-born Jerry Simpson, who also settled in Kansas and was known as "Sockless Jerry" in recognition of his folksy

SAYINGS OF MOTHER LEASE

"The people are at bay, let the bloodhounds who have dogged us thus far beware."

"The farmers of Kansas should raise less corn and more hell."

manners, urged the federal government to create new markets abroad.

But "Mother" Lease also wondered aloud how overproduction alone could be blamed for the crisis when American cities were teeming with hungry people. She was also famous for saying that "the makers of food are underclad, and the makers of clothes are underfed"; in other words, the problem lay not in production but in the means by which American society exchanged foodstuffs for industrial goods.

The World Market

Nor was Simpson's call for expanded foreign markets an answer in itself. In fact, American sales abroad expanded steadily during the late nineteenth century, and integration within an international economy brought its own problems. The weather in western China affected the price that a South Dakota wheat grower sold at in Rapid City; the decision of a British colonial administrator in Bombay influenced the quotations buyers shouted out on the Mobile cotton exchange.

When major banks failed, like Jay Cooke and Company in 1873, or even eastern railroads folded, like

POPULIST ANTI-SEMITISM?

The hatred of farmers for bankers sometimes took the form of anti-Semitism, hatred of Jewish bankers. One book that blamed Jews particularly for the ruination of the American farmer was Ignatius P. Donnelly's novel *Caesar's Column*. One character's explanation of why Jewish bankers were exploiting farmers is curious: past anti-Semitism with a Darwinian twist:

Christianity fell upon the Jews, originally a race of agriculturists and shepherds, and forced them, for many centuries, through the most terrible ordeal of persecution the history of mankind bears record of. Only the strong of body, the cunning of brain, the long-headed, the persistent, the men with capacity to live where the dog would starve, survived the awful trial. Like breeds like; and now the Christian world is paying, in tears and blood, for the sufferings inflicted by their bigoted and ignorant ancestors upon a noble race. When the time came for liberty and fair play the Jew was master in the contest with the Gentile. . . . They were as merciless to the Christians as the Christians had been to them.

the Reading Railroad which served Philadelphia, in 1893, the Nebraska corn grower lost money too. Financial collapse meant unemployment for thousands of factory workers who cut down on food expenditures. During the depression of the 1870s, the wholesale price at which farmers sold their crops slipped 30 percent, more than enough to ruin a family with mortgage payments to meet. The slide of the 1890s was just as bad and began during times that, for farmers, were already hard.

The farmers were willing to accept the uncertainty that the blessings of a worldwide economy brought. But, it seemed, they bore the brunt of misfortunes. When a New York banker stumbled in his office, they said, it was the Iowa pig raiser or the Mississippi sharecropper who broke a leg.

THE FARMERS ORGANIZE

One of the greatest obstacles American farmers faced in attempting to serve their own interests was a reluctance to face the fact that they lived in an age of organization. At the center of the American agrarian mystique was the vision of Jefferson's independent yeoman. The American farmer stood on his own two feet, beholden to no one. In owning his own land, he was the lord of his fief. Only the compilation of evidence all around them—from corporation to labor, from temperance movement to woman-suffrage movement—

that they lived in an organizing age, changed the farmers' ways.

The Grange

The Patrons of Husbandry, or Grangers, who sponsored the state laws regulating railroads in Illinois and elsewhere in the Midwest during the 1870s, had actually been founded to serve social purposes. Oliver H. Kelley, a farmer and land speculator turned Washington bureaucrat, longed nostalgically for an idyllic agrarian America that never quite existed. In 1867, along with several other former farmers living in the national capital, he founded the Grange to preserve the vitality of the family farm and to serve as a social center where farm families living in isolation could attend lectures and parties, converse and dance.

After the Wabash decision of 1886 nullified the Granger Laws, the Patrons of Husbandry became once again a cultural and social institution which survives as a focal point of farmer activity to this day. However, the Grangers never again took the lead in confronting the farmers' economic plight.

The Co-op Movement

During the 1880s, numerous kinds of cooperatives arose to serve this purpose. In consumer cooperatives, farmers banded together to purchase essential machinery in lots and therefore more cheaply.

Money pools, associations much like contemporary credit unions, sprouted all over the Midwest. Through these associations, which were capitalized by members and operated on a nonprofit basis, farmers hoped to eliminate their dependence on the hated banks. While many survived to serve the credit needs of their members for generations, money pools suffered from the opposition of the banks and the inexperience of amateur administrators. Distrusting professionalism almost as much as exploitation, farmers too often put friends rather than experts in charge of the money pools, and the rate of mismanagement and embezzlement was sadly high. Failed farmers who were suddenly entrusted with large sums of money frequently found the temptation to steal and abscond too difficult to resist.

Producer cooperatives were designed to counter the great power of the railroads. Again after the Supreme Court's decision in the case of *Wabash, St. Louis, & Pacific Railway Co. v. Illinois* effectively permitted railroads to set their own rates for storing and carrying grain, corn-belt farmers built their own grain elevators. Members of producer co-ops believed that with their own storage facilities, they could not only circumvent the high costs of holding their crops until the railroads were ready to move them, but also withhold their products from the market until they liked the selling price.

State and Regional Organization

To the extent that individual co-ops succeeded, they were of inestimable aid to their members. But their effect was limited. During the late 1880s, western and southern farmers moved increasingly to politics as essential to their survival.

At first, farmer organizations such as the Agricultural Wheel, the Texas State Alliance, and the Colored Farmers' National Alliance and Cooperative Union contented themselves, as had the Grangers before them, with endorsing politicians of any party who agreed to support their programs. But once many of these congressmen and state assemblymen began to be seduced by lobbyists for opposing interests, the state and regional organizations opted for independent political action.

By 1889, the various alliances and wheels had merged into three large associations—one representing mostly western farmers; another of southern white farmers, tenants, and sharecroppers; and the third of southern black farmers. In December 1890, delegates representing all three gathered in Ocala, Florida, to draw up a list of grievances.

The Populists

Although the Ocala Conference was constructive, it took more than a year for the farmers to make the break with the Republican party (to which the blacks and most midwesterners belonged) and the Democratic party (traditionally the party of white southerners). At Omaha, Nebraska, in February 1892, they organized the People's party, or, as it was commonly known from the Latin word for "people" (*populus*), the Populist party. Once the new movement was proclaimed, however, a virtually religious enthusiasm swept over the delegates. Far from just a pressure group or a political organization, the Populists believed that they were engaged in a sacred cause. Not only would they capture the American government, but they would remake the republic of democratic virtue that the Founding Fathers had envisioned.

To symbolize the fact that farmers from both North and South had bridged the sectional chasm that had separated them, the Populists nominated former Union General James B. Weaver for president and former Confederate General James G. Field for vice president.

A Far-Reaching Program

At Omaha, the Populists drafted a comprehensive platform that, had it been enacted, would have sig-

Thomas E. Watson, a Populist from Georgia, advocated the principle that social class was more important than race. He had a knack for inflammatory journalism and oratory.

nificantly altered American history. Overproduction was addressed only obliquely in a call for the prohibition of land ownership by aliens. Aliens were the only people who, constitutionally, could be denied the right to farm. The plank was designed to prevent further large land purchases by British investors and to win support for the new party from the trade-union movement, which inclined to be anti-immigrant.

As a means of restoring a democracy that the Populists believed was corrupted by well-organized lobbies, the new party demanded a series of political reforms. Senators, who were elected by state legislatures, should be chosen in popular elections. The Populists also endorsed the adoption of the secret "Australian" ballot. (In many states at that time, particularly in the South, a voter's choice was a matter of public record; the Populists believed that this practice led to intimidation by employers and landlords.)

The new party also introduced the concepts of the initiative, recall, and referendum. The initiative allows voters, through petition, to put measures on the ballot independent of action by legislatures and thus free of manipulation by professional lobbyists and their accomplices. The recall allows voters, also through petition, to force a public official to stand for election before his or her term is up. The Populists hoped that the recall would discourage politicians from backing down on campaign pledges. The referendum allows voters to vote directly on laws rather than indirectly through their representatives; it is the means by which initiative measures and recall petitions are decided.

The most controversial Populist demands were for the abolition of national banks and for government ownership of railroads and the telegraph. The Populists were not socialists. Since so many of them were landowners, they could hardly advocate state ownership of all productive property. But they did believe that "natural monopolies," enterprises that could be run efficiently only under a single management, should not be in private hands. Decisions that affected the interests of all should be made democratically, not by combinations of individuals who were interested only in their own enrichment. The "socialistic" parts of the Populist program were actually designed to protect the property of the common man and his opportunities to improve himself.

The party also called for a postal savings system, so that ordinary people might avoid depositing their money in privately owned banks, and for a graduated income tax. In 1892, the federal income tax was 2 percent for all, and the Populists wanted the wealthy to pay a higher percentage of their income than the modest farmer or wageworker paid. Finally, the Populists demanded an increase in the money in circulation of $50 per capita. This inflation was to be accomplished through the free and unlimited coinage of silver, its value pegged to that of gold.

THE MONEY QUESTION

Money is a subject that bores those who have enough of it and obsesses those who have too little. Neither circumstance is friendly to true understanding and, in the late nineteenth century, like today, money was a commodity that everybody handled and few people really understood. Nevertheless, the question of just what would be money in the United States became the most significant issue in American politics after Reconstruction. It engendered passions that were religious in intensity. It nurtured and then helped to destroy the Populist party, and contributed to the emergence of a new era in the national history. The

---

THE POLLOCK CASE

In the Wilson-Gorman Tariff of 1894, provision was made for an income tax of 2 percent on all incomes of $4,000 or more, a pretty modest tax by today's standards. It was widely condemned by men of means, and in the case of *Pollock v. Farmers' Loan and Trust Co.* (1895), the Supreme Court ruled that because the tax was a direct tax that did not fall on all equally, it was unconstitutional. Only after the Sixteenth Amendment was adopted in 1913 was it constitutional to tax the wealthy at a higher rate than the poor.

---

money question of the nineteenth century—boring or obsessing—must be examined in some detail.

What Is Money?

Money is a medium of exchange, a token that the people of a society agree represents value. It makes the exchange of goods and services—jobs done—more workable than simple barter: so much grain, for example, in return for so many pairs of shoes or so many hours of labor. Obviously, money is essential to all but the most primitive economies.

The value of money can change. In the first days of European settlement in North America, many Eastern Woodlands tribes used *wampum*, or strings of beads made of shell, to represent value when they exchanged grain, hides, and other goods. When Europeans were able to introduce sparkling, desirable glass beads into this economy at little cost to themselves, buying valuable hides for a pittance, but refusing to accept the trinkets in return when the Indians tried to purchase iron tools and weapons and other European products, *wampum* soon became worthless to everyone. It was no longer available in a limited, more-or-less known quantity, which is essential to the idea of money.

Gold Was the Standard

This is why, until very recently, the economically sophisticated nations of the world based their money on the metallic element, gold. In addition to being durable (and beautiful), gold was limited in supply. This made the value it represented stable and dependable. The farmer who received gold for his crop knew that the suppliers of the goods his family needed would accept the gold in return. In the age of the gold standard, it did not much matter which country's emblem was stamped on a coin. The weight of the gold token determined its value. In the United States, the Treasury minted gold coins of large denominations,

$5, $10 (called "eagles"), $20 ("double eagles"), and so on.

Coins of smaller denomination (dimes, quarters, dollars) were minted in silver, which was also available worldwide in a quantity that, until the era of the Civil War, increased only slowly. Because about sixteen times as much silver as gold was available in the United States, silver's value was pegged by law to the value of gold at a ratio of 16 to 1. That is, an ounce of gold was legally worth 16 ounces of silver.

Larger transactions were carried out in paper money, mostly issued by banks. The value of paper money depended upon people's confidence in the ability of the bank in question to hand precious metal over the counter when presented with its own notes.

The Greenbacks

During the Civil War, finding itself with too little gold and silver and bank notes to support the army, the Lincoln administration issued a new kind of money, some $433 million in a paper money. These bills, called "greenbacks" because they were printed on the obverse in green ink, were not redeemable at face value in gold or silver. They were "fiat money." Their value depended upon the government's proclamation, or *fiat*, that they would be accepted in payment of most financial obligations, such as taxes. This gave them value in ordinary business transactions too.

However, because the capacity of a government's well-oiled presses to print bills far exceeded the stubborn earth's yield of gold and silver, the value of the greenbacks fluctuated, sometimes wildly. Naturally, people preferred to be paid in gold and silver coin, "hard money." At a bank at the end of the Civil War, it took $157 in greenbacks—"soft money"—to buy $100 in coin. This rate generally determined all transactions. Throughout the economy, it was usually specified if a deal was to be closed in paper or coin.

Inflation versus Deflation

Nevertheless, more money in circulation meant generally higher wages and prices for farmers, higher selling prices for their crops. So, the greenbacks had many devotees, people who associated soft money with prosperity. They came to believe that the federal government should regulate the amount of money in circulation, by means of its power to issue greenbacks, in order to accommodate the needs of a dynamic, growing economy. The supply of gold and silver did not expand rapidly enough to keep up with the explosive economy of the United States.

Bankers and big businessmen generally thought otherwise. They dealt in large sums of money and feared having the value of their vast properties, and the money others owed to them, reduced in value any time politicians decided to curry favor with voters. These monetary conservatives argued that money had absolute, natural value, determined by the amount of gold in existence and, until the 1870s, by the amount of silver.

With close ties to the executive branch of the government in the wake of the Civil War, the conservatives had their way. By February 1868, $45 million in greenbacks had been withdrawn from circulation. At the rate of $4 million a month, the Secretary of the Treasury destroyed greenbacks that had been paid to the government in taxes. Money grew scarcer and therefore more valuable. The trend was deflationary. Wages and prices, including the prices at which farmers sold their crops, declined. Particularly because they were debtors, now expected to repay loans in money that was harder to get than the money they had borrowed, farmers inclined to be inflationists. They wanted more money in circulation. Through the 1870s and into the 1880s, they wanted more greenbacks printed.

The Ups and Downs of the Greenbackers

Throughout the 1860s and 1870s, congressional policy toward the greenbacks shifted from inflationary to deflationary depending upon shifts in popular sentiment. In October 1868, when the rapid retirement of the greenbacks was accompanied by an economic downturn, Congress ordered the Treasury Department to cease burning the notes. In 1875, ascendant conservatives ordered that for every $100 issued by banks (money theoretically backed by gold), $80 in greenbacks be retired. In 1879, the "Gold Bug" Secretary of the Treasury John Sherman, ordered that all payments to the government be made in specie, or coin. Generally, the trend was deflationary. Between 1865 and 1878, the amount of money in circulation in the United States shrunk from $1.08 billion to $773,370,000. Whereas in 1865 there had been $31.18 in circulation for every American, in 1878 there was $16.25.

Fighting a losing battle against this triumph of monetary conservatism were "Greenbackers" within both major parties and a third party, the Greenback Labor party, which was dedicated to the single issue of inflating the currency. Like most third parties in American history, the Greenbackers attracted few voters. In 1880, Civil War General James B. Weaver of Iowa won 308,578 votes, enough to deny Republican James A. Garfield an absolute majority, but in 1884, Greenbacker candidate Benjamin F. Butler won 175,370 votes, only marginally more than the Prohibitionist party candidate that year. By 1884, people who wanted the currency inflated had turned to another, once conservative form of money—silver coin.

The Silver Issue

Silver became a political issue at first because it was too scarce and, therefore, too expensive for the government to buy. So little silver was mined during the 1860s that silver producers sold their ingots not to the government but to private buyers. Whereas the government was required by law to pay only one ounce of gold for sixteen ounces of silver, jewelry makers and other consumers of silver would take fourteen and even fewer ounces of the lesser metal for the same price. In the Demonetization Act of 1873, Congress reacted to the disappearance of silver sellers at the mint by ceasing the purchase of silver. The silver dollar was dropped from the list of coins the government minted.

Already, however, new silver discoveries and new methods of mining it had resulted in a vast increase in production. In 1861, only $2 million worth of silver was mined in the United States compared to $43 million worth of gold. In 1873, the value of silver and

Loading silver bullion into a freight car in Leadville, Colorado, a silver boomtown until the Sherman Act was repealed.

gold mined was about equal, $36 million each. During the 1870s, silver production increased rapidly so that the price of silver on the private market, the only market now open to miners, collapsed.

Politician friends of mining interests like the excitable Democrat Richard "Silver Dick" Bland of Missouri and Senator Henry W. Teller of Colorado described the Demonetization Act as "The Crime of '73." The implication was that government had conspired to punish silver miners for their success. There was no "crime." No one could anticipate the explosive growth of silver mining in 1873 but the most sanguine western prospector. Still, it was undoubtedly true that when silver production soared, the Gold Bugs were relieved that the government was not buying it, cheapening money, and reducing the value of their property. They began to look upon silver as a threat to monetary conservatism as serious as the greenbacks.

By themselves, mine owners and miners would have been powerless to force the Secretary of the Treasury to resume the purchase of silver. Even after the admission of mineral-rich Colorado in 1876, mining interests were significant in only a handful of states. However, inflationist congressmen from agricultural states—mostly southern and western Democrats—seized on the resumption of silver coinage as a way to get more money in circulation. In the depression year of 1878, they forced conservatives to agree to a compromise. The Bland-Allison Bill of that year required the Secretary of the Treasury to purchase between $2 and $4 million of silver each month for minting into money. The silver dollar was back.

Politics Becomes Religion

The silver dollar was back, but whether the administration was Republican or Democratic, the Treasury remained in the hands of conservatives dedicated to the gold standard. The government almost invariably bought the minimum $2 million required by law while the national production of silver continued to grow. Therefore, the market price of silver was pushed ever downward. By 1890, it took nearly 20 ounces of silver to buy a single ounce of gold. In the minds of inflationists and silver producers, the old ratio of 16 to 1 took on a sacred significance.

In 1889 and 1890, the balance of power tipped to the side of the inflationists. Six new states in which silver was an important commodity entered the Union—the two Dakotas, Montana, Washington, Idaho, and Wyoming—bringing 12 silver senators to Washington. In the midterm elections of 1890, the Democrats, who were friendlier to inflation than Republicans, won a big victory, sending 235 representatives to Washington compared to only 88 Republicans, some of them free silverites. The inflationists were joined by nine Populists in the House, who were also committed to the free coinage of silver as one plank in their platform.

The Sherman Silver Purchase Act

The result was the Sherman Silver Purchase Act of 1890. Like Bland-Allison, it was a compromise. It required the Secretary of the Treasury to purchase 4.5 million ounces of silver each month, which was approximately the entire output of the nation's silver mines. However, the government bought at the market price, which continued to decline, from a ratio of 20 to 1 in 1890 to 26.5 to 1 in 1893. As a result, the act failed to relieve discontent in the mining regions and led to violent strikes as mine owners attempted to cut costs by forcing down wages.

The Sherman Act indirectly tied the legal value of silver to gold by providing that paper notes issued by the government be redeemable in silver or gold. However, both Presidents Benjamin Harrison and Grover Cleveland, who succeeded Harrison in March 1893, were devoted to the gold standard. Cleveland called the Sherman Act "dangerous and reckless" and insisted on meeting all the government's obligations in gold.

As depression descended in 1893, this caused a crisis. Foreign and domestic creditors of the government rushed to redeem their bonds in gold while there was still gold to be had. The government's gold reserve—the actual metal in its vaults—sunk to below $100 million, regarded by conservatives as the absolute minimum for maintaining the government's credit. Shortly after undergoing a secret operation for cancer (carried out on a yacht in New York's East River), Cleveland called for the repeal of the Sherman Act, "to put beyond all doubt or mistake" the commitment of the United States to the gold standard. A frightened Congress obliged him.

The Crisis

The result was a dramatic upsurge in the popularity of the Populists, who were joined in the Midwest by both Republicans and Democrats who believed that the federal government was firmly in the hands of the bankers. (It did not help matters that Cleveland had to turn personally to J. P. Morgan for help in increasing the gold reserve.) Within the Democratic party, Cleveland retained only minority support from eastern conservatives. The southern and western wings of the party, in part out of fear that the Populists would steal their voters from them, renounced the president. By 1894, it was clear that they would control the party's national convention in 1896.

All over the country, farmers and workers seemed to be in rebellion. An Ohioan, Jacob S. Coxey, led a march of the unemployed on Washington. It came to nothing. Coxey was arrested for walking on the grass when he tried to read a statement at the Capitol, but the news of thousands of angry men on the march frightened conservatives.

A nationwide and sometimes violent railroad strike, led by the exciting Eugene V. Debs of Terre Haute, Indiana, was crushed only when Cleveland's attorney general, corporation lawyer Richard B. Olney, jailed Debs on the trumped-up charge of interfering with the delivery of the mail. In the mining west, strikes resembled small wars more than industrial disputes. Miners were imprisoned by the thousands in improvised stockades they called "bull pens." In the farm belt of the plains, "hayseeds" gathered to talk of a new order and to jostle people who were well-dressed. The word "revolution" was being voiced in gatherings of "the bone and sinew of the republic."

Coxey and his secretary leading his army to Washington, D.C.

THE NEW SOUTH: THE PROPHET AND THE BUILDER

In speech after speech throughout the South, he told the story of a funeral that he had attended in rural Georgia. "They buried him in a New York coat and a Boston pair of shoes, and a pair of breeches from Chicago and a shirt from Cincinnati." The coffin, continued Henry W. Grady (1851–89), the wisecracking editor of the Atlanta *Constitution*, was made from northern lumber and hammered together with northern-forged nails. "The South didn't furnish a thing on earth for that funeral but the corpse and the hole in the ground."

Grady's point, to which he devoted most of his short life, was that the South must abandon its traditional reliance on agriculture and promote industrialization. The North's industry explained why the Confederacy had been defeated and why, in the wake of the war, the South suffered in company with the agricultural Plains. Only by accepting the realities of the modern world would the South prosper and escape its status as a backwater.

Although Grady lived to see few of his ideas come to fruition, during the very period that southern agrarians like Thomas E. Watson were vilifying urban, industrial America, southerners scored the kind of successes that Grady had called for. Beginning with a federal grant of almost 6 million acres of forest land in 1877, southern syndicates laid the basis of a thriving lumber and turpentine industry in the vast pine woods of the section. Birmingham became the "Pittsburgh of the South," the center of a booming steel industry, following the discovery of coal and iron in northern Alabama in the early 1870s. By 1890, Birmingham was making more pig iron than was Pittsburgh. ("Pigs" are iron ingots, intermediate products ready for further processing.)

The southern oil industry was largely a twentieth-century development; the great Texas gusher, Spindletop, came through in 1901. Likewise the southern textile industry. Most of the New England textile mills migrated to the South after 1900, although, even before Grady died in 1889, the trend of "bringing the factory to the fields" was to some degree under way.

The southerner who was most successful in bringing the factory to the fields was not a maker of cloth but a maker of cigarettes and bad habits. James Buchanan "Buck" Duke (1856–1925) started out as a tobacco grower, a good southern agrarian on the face of it. In 1881, he was shown a new machine that rolled cigarettes by the hundreds per minute, and his head began to spin in contemplation of its possibilities. All cigarettes were then rolled by hand, mostly by the smoker. Like a chess player, Duke had to see several moves ahead. To make money from manufacturing cigarettes, it was necessary not only to mass-produce them cheaply, but also to change Americans' tobacco habits.

In the late nineteenth century, "decent" women did not smoke (at least in public), upper- and middle-class

Newspaper editor Henry W. Grady.

men smoked cigars or pipes, and workingmen and the lower classes in the South were inclined to chew tobacco. Cigarettes were around. The soldiers in the Civil War had taken to them because they could carry papers and a pouch of tobacco but not cigars. After the war, however, the white cylinders were considered to be effete, a boy's smoke behind the barn. Duke would have to change that image, and he did.

Buying the patent to the cigarette-rolling machine, he encouraged adolescents to cultivate the habit by selling a pack of twenty for only a nickel and by including inside each pack a "trading card" that featured pictures and brief biographies of military heroes and popular athletes, mostly boxers and baseball players. No one better understood the wisdom in putting together a long-term market than "Buck" Duke. All the while he created his consumers, he improved machinery and bought out competitors. By 1889, his company accounted for half the cigarettes sold in the United States, and Duke had only begun.

In 1890, he set up a trust along the lines laid out by John D. Rockefeller. Through it he gained control of his major competitors, R. J. Reynolds and P. J. Lorillard, and built an almost perfect monopoly. Indeed, through loose arrangements with British cigarette manufacturers, Duke had a major say in the tobacco-processing industry on two continents. Only federal antitrust action in 1911 forced him to disband his gigantic corporation. By that year, he controlled 150 factories, and, even at that, his reputation as the South's greatest home-grown business mogul was being challenged by the directors of the recently founded Coca-Cola Company of Atlanta.

Like the Yankee moguls whose methods he adopted, "Buck" Duke was a generous philanthropist. His most enduring monument is Duke University, which had been a small, local college before it received an endowment from Duke and changed its name; it is now an architecturally magnificent Gothic-style campus in Duke's hometown of Durham, North Carolina. Until the militant antismoking campaigns of the 1970s, Duke was one of the few universities in the United States where students and faculty could light up the "coffin nails" that had built the institution wherever and whenever they chose. That practice has been abandoned, but his statue, which stands in front of the university's cathedral-size chapel, portrays James Buchanan Duke gently tapping the ash from his cigar.

James Buchanan "Buck" Duke, the father of the modern cigarette industry and the philanthropist after whom Duke University is named.

For Further Reading

Overviews and Classics

Vincent P. DeSantis, *The Shaping of Modern America, 1877–1916* (1973)

Gilbert C. Fite, *The Farmer's Frontier, 1865–1900* (1966)

Fred A. Shannon, *The Farmers' Last Frontier: Agriculture 1860–1897* (1945)

Robert H. Wiebe, *The Search for Order, 1880–1920* (1967)

Valuable Special Studies

Solon J. Buck, *The Granger Movement* (1913)

Everett Dick, *The Sod-House Frontier, 1854–1890* (1937)

R. F. Durden, *The Climax of Populism* (1965)

Lawrence Goodwyn, *Democratic Promise: The Populist Movement in America* (1976)

John D. Hicks, *The Populist Revolt* (1931)

Richard Hofstadter, *Age of Reform* (1955)

J. Morgan Kousser, *The Shaping of Southern Politics: Suffrage Restriction and the Establishment of the One-Party South, 1880–1910* (1974)

Walter T. K. Nugent, *Money and American Society, 1865–1880* (1968)

———, *The Tolerant Populists: Kansas Populism and Nativism* (1963)

Norman Pollock, *The Populist Response to Industrial America* (1966)

Theodore Saloutos, *Farmer Movements in the South, 1865–1933* (1960)

Irwin Unger, *The Greenback Era: A Social and Political History of American Finance, 1865–1879* (1964)

Allen Weinstein, *Prelude to Populism: Origins of the Silver Issue, 1867–1878* (1970)

C. Vann Woodward, *The Strange Career of Jim Crow* (1974)

Biographies and Autobiographies

P. E. Coletta, *William Jennings Bryan: Political Evangelist, 1860–1908* (1964)

Louis W. Koenig, *Bryan: A Political Biography of William Jennings Bryan* (1971)

Martin Ridge, *Ignatius Donnelly* (1962)

Francis B. Simkins, *Pitchfork Ben Tillman: South Carolinian* (1949)

C. Vann Woodward, *Tom Watson: Agrarian Rebel* (1938)

Bryan, McKinley, and a New Era

The United States Becomes a World Power, 1896–1903

Few presidential elections have been held amidst such anxiety as swirled about the election of 1896. Even as the year began, almost everyone who was active in politics recognized that the contest was more important than any since 1860, when the Union hung in the balance. The deep depression, the "revolt of the hayseeds," the violent strikes, and the passions the silver issue engendered meant that the campaign would not be fought by more or less similar parties on the basis of personalities, slogans, and the competition for patronage. It would be fought on issues dressed up to look like holy causes and under the cloud of the fears with which one social class looked at another. When the election was over, the political era that had begun with the end of Reconstruction would be dead, and a new one underway. No one knew what the new era would be like. That depended upon which party and which candidate won the electoral college in November. Thus the anxiety. Thus the importance of the election of 1896.

Taking It Easy During a Lull, *a photo of American troops in the Philippines taken around 1899 by Perley Freemont Rockett.*

THE WATERSHED ELECTION OF 1896

Meeting in St. Louis in June, the Republican convention was deceptively placid. Most of the G.O.P.'s agrarian rebels had long since said goodbye to join the Populists. A small free silver contingent from the mining states, led by Senator Teller of Colorado, walked out after failing to win more than token concessions from a convention dominated by industrialists and bankers who were convinced that the gold standard was sacred. The Teller group later supported the Democratic party candidate.

The remaining delegates were not only monetary conservatives. They were uneasy amidst the agitation and militance that hard times had loosed in the country. They chose as their candidate a man who was a model of conservatism, prudence, and sobriety. Or, rather, as the opposition was soon to claim, they sat back and allowed a beefy Cleveland industrialist, Marcus Alonzo Hanna, to choose their candidate for them.

Mark Hanna and Bill McKinley

Bald, scowling Mark Hanna was nearly 60 years of age in 1896. He had made a fortune in coal and iron, was intimate with the Rockefellers, and was well known in industrial circles as a feisty spokesman for moderation and flexibility in dealing with employees and labor unions. Hanna railed against exploitative capitalists and labor radicals alike.

Only in the 1890s, particularly after the descent of the depression, did Hanna cast his eyes toward a wider horizon, presidential politics. In fact, he found his candidate before he thought much about the White House. The man was former Ohio representative and governor William McKinley of Canton, the Republican party's leading expert on the benefits of a high tariff. The very high McKinley tariff of 1890 had established "Bill" as a friend of industry. His less enthusiastic support for gold money—the issue never really excited McKinley—made him acceptable to other conservative Republicans.

William McKinley was ambitious. Theodore Roosevelt later said that the Ohioan looked into every introduction and conversation for the advantage it might mean to him. And yet, without Hanna clearing the way and pushing him on, it is unlikely that McKinley would have won higher office than a cabinet post. McKinley lacked the presence and personality that made people stand aside and applaud. He was too restrained, too dignified, too proper in the midwestern way. (McKinley refused to smoke cigars in public lest young men emulate his bad habit; William Allen

Industrialist Marcus Alonzo Hanna was the kind of man who walked into an office and got what he wanted.

White said that "he was destined for a statue in the park and he was practicing the pose for it.") McKinley was easy to overlook.

Mark Hanna, by way of contrast, was the fellow who walked into an office, cigar blazing, and planted a hefty haunch on the desk of the person he wanted to see. Republicans and Democrats alike assumed that McKinley was his puppet.

Actually, while McKinley agonized over big decisions, he was quite capable of making them on his own. Nevertheless, when he agreed with Hanna that 1896 was the target year, he probably had no idea that the election would be as momentous as it was. When it turned out that 1896 was a crucial year, it was a lucky accident of fate that the Republicans had the solemn McKinley and the energetic Hanna to lead them.

The Frightening Boy Bryan

The partnership of energy and solemnity was indispensable to the Republicans in 1896 because the Democratic party candidate, nominated at a frenzied convention in July, was a tornado of energy with a singular lack of dignity. William Jennings Bryan, scarcely beyond the 35 years of age the Constitution requires a president to be, was a two-term congressman from Nebraska, a newspaperman, and regionally famous as a platform orator. His one and only subject for four years had been the free coinage of silver and Bryan had polished a single speech, the "Cross of Gold," to a mathematical perfection in phrasing, timing, and theatrical gesture.

Deeply religious himself, Bryan enlisted God in the cause of silver coinage. He identified the gold standard with the crucifiers of Christ, silver with democracy and Christianity. If the intensity with which he spoke was set aside, Bryan was a rather conservative man. He did not, as the nation soon learned, approve of much of what the Populists held dear except for free silver. But his language and apparently irresponsible youth were enough to frighten Republicans. They called him "Boy Bryan" and "the boy orator of the Platte," scornfully but with trepidation. The Democrats, committed to the cause of silver when the Chicago convention was planned, gladly scheduled him and his Cross of Gold to close out the debate on the currency question.

Later it would be said that when Bryan spoke he transformed himself from an obscure delegate into a presidential candidate by acclamation. In fact, he and his supporters had paved the way for his nomination as carefully as Mark Hanna had worked for McKinley. Nevertheless, his speech and the Democratic party's ringing endorsement of free silver were so electrifying

William Jennings Bryan was famous for his impassioned oratory.

THE CROSS OF GOLD

The following lines are the first and last from William Jennings Bryan's electrifying speech at the 1896 Democratic convention:

I would be presumptuous, indeed, to present myself against the distinguished gentlemen to whom you have listened if this were a mere measuring of abilities; but this is not a contest between persons. The humblest citizen in all the land, when clad in the armor of a righteous cause, is stronger than all the hosts of error. I come to speak to you in defense of a cause as holy as the cause of liberty—the cause of humanity. . . .

If they dare to come out in the open field and defend the gold standard as a good thing, we will fight them to the uttermost. Having behind us the producing masses of this nation and the world, supported by the commercial interests, the laboring interests, and the toilers everywhere, we will answer their demand for a gold standard by saying to them: you shall not press down upon the brow of labor this crown of thorns, you shall not crucify mankind upon a cross of gold.

William Jennings Bryan carries a cross of gold in this cartoon by Grant Hamilton, who viewed Bryan as a despoiler of the Bible.

that the western farmers began to celebrate a November victory in July. For, late in the month, the Populists nominated Bryan too.

The Populists Join the Democrats

Meeting in St. Louis, the Populists were presented with a difficult decision. If they maintained their independence by nominating a candidate of their own, they would split the free silver vote and put Bill McKinley in the White House. If they nominated Bryan—and just about everyone but Mark Hanna agreed on this in July—they would easily elect a man whose evangelical style suited them and whose position on free silver was perfect.

However, Bryan was pointedly clear in his opposition to the rest of the comprehensive Populist program for reform. For the sake of a silverite president, the Populists would throw away their grand plans for America and, fused to the older, larger Democratic party, their very identity.

Urban Populists like Henry Demarest Lloyd urged the party to think in long-range terms. He told the Populists to maintain their integrity, accept their loss in 1896, and work toward 1900. Some southern Populists like Tom Watson of Georgia had another reason for opposing fusion. In the South, the conservative enemy was not Republican but Democratic. To fuse with the Democrats in the South meant suicide, and breaking what binds had been tied to black Republicans.

But Populism was impatient and sanguine. The party nominated Bryan and, in a request for Democratic confirmation of the partnership, nominated Tom Watson for vice president. Instead of accepting Watson as the Democrats' vice-presidential candidate too, however, dropping Arthur Sewall from his ticket, Bryan merely accepted the nomination. It was a gratuitous insult to Populist pretensions. It would not be the last.

Fury versus a Rock of Stability

Campaigning for votes was Bryan's forte. Handsome, tireless, and completely at home among ordinary, hardworking farm people—whether exhorting them or gobbling up potato salad and chowchow after a speech—Bryan revolutionized the presidential campaign. With a few exceptions, presidential nominees had been quiet, as though it were an insult to the dignity of the office to woo votes like a candidate for town councilman in an Appalachian hollow.

Not Bryan. His speaking tour took him more than 13,000 miles by train. He delivered 600 speeches in 29 states in only fourteen weeks (over six speeches a

Candidate William McKinley between speeches on his front porch in Canton, Ohio.

day). The roaring enthusiasm of the crowds that greeted him, at least in the West and South, confirmed him in his zeal and threw eastern bankers and industrialists into a panic.

This was exactly what Mark Hanna wanted to see. He pressured wealthy Republicans (and more than a few conservative Democrats) into making large contributions to McKinley's campaign. By the time of the election, Hanna had spent more on posters, buttons, rallies, picnics, advertisements, and a corps of speakers who dogged Bryan's steps than had been spent by both parties in every election since the Civil War. (The Republicans printed five pamphlets for every American voter.) Hanna was so successful that, before election day, he began to return surplus contributions.

Knowing that the phlegmatic McKinley could not rival Bryan on the stump, Hanna kept his candidate at his modest home in Canton, Ohio. Republican speakers compared McKinley's sense of self-respect with Bryan's salesmanlike hustling. A steady stream of Republican delegations traveled to Canton, where they marched through the town behind a brass band and gathered on McKinley's front lawn. McKinley delivered a short speech from the porch, answered a few prearranged questions, and invited "all his friends" to join him for lemonade or beer, depending on the delegation's attitude toward alcohol (which had been discreetly ascertained by party workers when the visitors arrived at the railroad depot).

Momentous Results

Bryan won more votes, 6.5 million, than any candidate in any previous election. But McKinley won 7 million easily and in the electoral college gathered 271 votes to Bryan's 176. It was the first time in a quarter of the century that any presidential candidate had won an absolute majority. What happened? As late as September, professional politicians believed that Bryan was well ahead.

First, although Bryan's supporters were noisy, his appeal was fatally limited to Democrats from the Solid South, hard-pressed staple farmers of the West, and to a few numerically insignificant groups like western metal miners. McKinley swept the Northeast, including the swing states, and also the largely agricultural states of North Dakota, Minnesota, Wisconsin, Iowa, Michigan, and Illinois. Many farmers whose conditions were not desperate accepted the Republican contention that Boy Bryan was a dangerous radical, never a desirable label in American politics.

More important, Bryan could not win substantial support among factory workers and city people gener-

ally. He hardly tried. Imbued with common rural prejudices against big cities and the "foreigners" who lived there, he made only one speaking tour in vital New York State and was quoted as having called New York City "the enemy's country," as though it were inhabited solely by bankers and grain speculators. Fourteen of the fifteen biggest cities were controlled by Republican machines and they delivered their blocs to William McKinley.

Some industrialists tried to intimidate their employees into voting for the Republican candidate. The Baldwin Piano Works posted notices on the eve of election day to the effect that if Bryan won, the plant would close for good the next day. But Bryan's weakness in the industrial districts was not due to such tactics. His single-issue free-silver campaign offered little to factory workers. They found more convincing the Republican claim that a high-tariff policy protected their jobs.

Finally, Mark Hanna shrewdly judged the instincts of a newly important element in American politics, the growing middle class of small businessmen, professional people, salaried town dwellers, and highly skilled, well-paid workingmen. Preoccupied with their respectability and considering themselves to be the

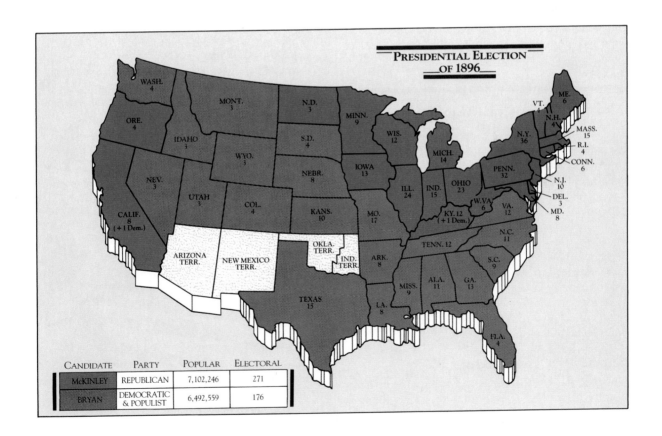

CANDIDATE	PARTY	POPULAR	ELECTORAL
McKINLEY	REPUBLICAN	7,102,246	271
BRYAN	DEMOCRATIC & POPULIST	6,492,559	176

new bone and sinew of the American republic, they were frightened by Bryan and the ragged, restive farmers whom he represented. These people committed themselves to the Republican party as "the party of decency." For 40 years after 1896, they helped to make it the majority party.

The End of Populism

As Watson and Lloyd had feared, fusion with the Democrats meant extinction for the Populists. Having sacrificed their comprehensive reform program for the chance of winning free silver with Bryan, they had nothing left when the votes were counted against him. In the South, Populists who had worked to build a party based on interracial cooperation turned against the blacks (who voted Republican in 1896) to become prominent exponents of white supremacy. In the West, the party withered away, in part because of the electoral rebuke, and in part because, slowly under McKinley, the wholesale prices of farm products began to rise.

The agricultural depression lifted for a number of reasons. Newly discovered gold deposits in Canada and Alaska inflated the currency somewhat and helped raise prices. Several poor growing seasons in Europe created an increased demand for American farm products. Finally, farmers, like most of the American people, were distracted in 1898 by the McKinley administration's decision to win the United States a place among the empires of the world.

AMERICAN IMPERIALISM

McKinley hoped to have a presidency as relaxing as his front-porch campaign had been. He was a man who liked peace and quiet, and his confidence in American business convinced him that prosperity was just around the corner. All he had to do was wait patiently.

McKinley got his prosperity. Even before he was inaugurated in March 1897, the economic indicators began to show improvement. Peace and quiet were more elusive. Little as the role suited him, McKinley led the American people into a series of overseas adventures that transformed a nation that had been born in an anticolonial revolution into an empire with colonies in both hemispheres.

The Myth of Isolationism

Not that the United States had been an isolationist country before McKinley became president. Far from it. The American government maintained busy missions in all important capitals, had fought a war with

Mexico in the interests of expansion, and several times came close to war in defense of American prestige. In 1889, only a typhoon that had sunk German and American warships in the Samoan harbor of Apia prevented a full-scale naval encounter in the South Pacific.

Trade made the United States an active participant in world affairs. American ships and sailors were a common sight in the world's most exotic ports. As early as 1844, the United States had signed a trade treaty with the Chinese Empire, as far off and foreign a place as Americans could imagine. In 1854, a naval squadron under Commodore Matthew Perry had anchored off Yokohama, Japan, and had threatened to bombard the city unless the Japanese agreed to abandon their country's genuine isolationism and begin to purchase American goods.

By 1870, American exports had totaled $320 million, mostly agricultural produce bound for Europe. By 1890, $857 million in goods was sold abroad, with American manufacturers competing with European industrialists in peddling steel, textiles, and other products in Pacific countries, Latin America, and Europe itself.

A pro-expansion cartoon shows a sword-bearing Uncle Sam rolling up his sleeves for a fight.

Anticolonialism

If Americans were not isolationists, neither were they imperialists. Neither the people nor most statesmen wanted anything to do with the scramble for colonies that engrossed Europe and newly powerful Japan. To Americans, there was a difference between establishing suzerainty over densely settled lands with long cultural traditions and taking the West from the handful of Indians there, and they wanted nothing to do with the former. With the exceptions of Alaska and the tiny Pacific island of Midway, both acquired in 1867 and neither with much population, the United States possessed no territory that was not contiguous to the states.

Two deep convictions worked against the occasional proposals that the United States take such colonies. First, the country had been founded in a war against imperial control. Could the heirs of the first great anticolonial rebellion take over other peoples? Most Americans thought not. Second, the vastness of the American continent provided a more than adequate outlet for American energies. There was plenty of work to be done at home. William McKinley shared these assumptions. In all sincerity, he said in his inaugural address that "we must avoid the temptation of territorial expansion."

The Nature of Imperialism

But times were changing. By 1897, the United States was the single most important industrial power in the world. Consciousness of this greatness stirred many people to believe that the United States should assume its rightful place among the great nations, and in the 1890s, the great nations were empires.

The European powers had partitioned Africa so that only two countries there maintained their independence, ancient Ethiopia and Liberia, a republic that had been founded by former American slaves. Indochina was a French colony. The Dutch flag flew over Indonesia. The Japanese were in the process of securing Korea and the Chinese island province of Taiwan, which they renamed Formosa. Russia had designs on northern China. Germany and Italy, latecomers to the scramble, looked in Africa and Asia for areas to annex. India, the biggest prize of all, save China, was British.

The initial impulse toward empire was economic. Colonies were a source of raw materials and a market for the products of the mother country. Colonialism also generated an emotional justification of its own. Colonies were a source of pride. British imperialists took pleasure in seeing "all that red on the map." (Mapmakers usually colored British possessions in red.) The Germans seized parts of Africa that had little economic value just for the sake of having colonies.

In England and later in the United States, this bumptious chauvinism was known as "jingoism." To the jingoes, being strong enough to overcome less advanced peoples was reason enough to do so. "We do not want to fight," ran a British song of 1877. "But, by jingo, if we do . . ." Finally, imperialism fed on itself like a sport. Nations seized colonies simply to prevent competitors from doing so.

Some young American politicians such as Henry Cabot Lodge of Massachusetts and Theodore Roosevelt of New York itched to join the scramble. They worried publicly that, in their wealth and prosperity, Americans were becoming soft and flabby. The country needed war in order to toughen up. Roosevelt, a bodybuilding enthusiast, often drew analogies between individuals and nations, between boxing matches and wars.

Anglo-Saxons

Lodge, Roosevelt, and other expansionists were influenced by a theory of race that evolved out of Darwinism. Whereas Herbert Spencer had applied his doctrine of "survival of the fittest" to relationships within a society, disciples such as Harvard historian John Fiske and Congregationalist minister Josiah Strong applied it to relationships among races and cultures. In separate publications of 1885, Fiske and Strong wrote that the Anglo-Saxons (British and Americans) were obviously more fit to govern than were other peoples. According to Strong's *Our Country*, the Anglo-Saxons were "divinely commissioned" to spread their institutions. It was not a betrayal of American ideals to take over other lands. There was a racial and religious duty to do so.

Strong believed that inferior races eventually would die out. An influential political scientist at Columbia University, John W. Burgess, stated flatly in 1890 that the American principle of self-government was irrelevant to dark-skinned people both at home and

---

AMERICAN EMPIRE

"The West Indies drift toward us, the Republic of Mexico hardly longer has an independent life, and the city of Mexico is an American town. With the completion of the Panama Canal all Central America will become part of our system. We have expanded into Asia, we have attracted the fragments of the Spanish dominions, and reaching out into China we have checked the advance of Russia and Germany."

Brooks Adams,
The New Empire (1902)

abroad. He wrote that "there is no human right to the status of barbarism."

Alfred Thayer Mahan

Also in 1890, the expansionists found a highly calculating spokesman in naval captain Alfred Thayer Mahan. In his book *The Influence of Sea Power Upon History,* Mahan argued that the great nations were always sea-faring nations possessing powerful navies. He chided Americans for having allowed their own fleet to fall into decay. (In 1891, jingoes who wanted war with Chile had to quiet down when they were informed the Chilean navy was superior to the American.) Mahan urged a massive program of ship construction, and Congress responded with large appropriations.

A modern steam-powered navy needed coaling stations at scattered points throughout the world. That in itself required taking colonies, even if they were only dots on the globe like Midway, or building bases in ostensibly independent countries like Hawaii, where in 1887, the United States cleared a harbor at the mouth of the Pearl River on the island of Oahu.

Fears for an America Without a Frontier

Another theory of history that fired up the expansionist movement was based on the announcement of the Director of the Census in 1890 that the frontier no longer existed. In 1889, Congress opened Oklahoma to white settlement; the last large territory that had been reserved for the sole use of Indians was occupied by whites literally overnight.

At the 1893 meeting of the American Historical Association, a young historian named Frederick Jackson Turner propounded a theory that the frontier had been the key to the vitality of American democracy, social stability, and prosperity. Turner was interested in the past, but the implication of his theory for the future was unmistakable. With the frontier gone, was the United States doomed to stagnation and social upheaval? To some who found Turner convincing, the only solution was to establish new frontiers abroad. Throughout the 1890s, American financiers pumped millions of dollars into China and Latin America because they felt investment opportunities within the United States to be shrinking.

By 1898, America's attitude toward the world was delicately balanced. Pulling in one direction was the tradition of anticolonialism. Tugging the other way were jingoism, Anglo-Saxonism, and apprehensions for the future. All it took to decide the direction of the leap was a sudden shove. That was provided by a Cuban war for independence that began in 1895.

THE SPANISH-AMERICAN WAR

On a map, Cuba looks like an appendage of Florida, a geographical curiosity that frequently aroused the interest of American expansionists. Cuba was also a historical curiosity because, alone of the old Spanish possessions, the rich sugar island and Puerto Rico remained under Spanish rule. Rebellion was chronic in Cuba, but weak as Spain was, the archaic monarchy was able to hold on to its last American jewel.

The uprising of 1895 was more serious. Smuggling in arms and munitions provided by Cuban exiles in the United States, the rebels won the support of a large number of ordinary Cubans, perhaps the majority. Until the 1890s, the island had been rather prosperous, exporting sugar to the United States, but the Wilson-Gorman Tariff of 1894 practically shut out Cuba's sole export and caused an economic crisis.

It was a classic guerrilla war. The Spanish army and navy controlled the cities of Havana and Santiago and most large towns. By day, Spanish soldiers moved with little trouble among a seemingly peaceful peasantry. By night, however, docile field workers turned into fierce rebels and sorely punished the Spanish troops. As in most guerrilla wars, fighting was bitter and cruel. Both sides were guilty of atrocities.

Americans were generally sympathetic to the Cubans. Their interest in the conflict was excited into near hysteria when two competing newspaper chains decided that the rebellion could be used as ammunition in their circulation war.

The Yellow Press

William Randolph Hearst's *New York Journal* and Joseph Pulitzer's New York *World* were known as the "yellow press" because they relied on gimmicks to appeal to readers. The nickname came from one of those gimmicks: "The Yellow Kid," the first comic strip to appear in a newspaper.

The Hearst and Pulitzer chains also could squeeze the most lurid details out of celebrated murder and sex cases, and they pioneered the "invented" news story. In 1889, Pulitzer's *World* sent Elizabeth S. "Nellie" Bly around the world in an attempt to break the record of the fictional hero of Jules Verne's *Around the World in Eighty Days.* (She did beat it, completing the trip in 72 days, six hours, and eleven minutes.)

It was easy to move from this kind of promotionalism to exploiting Spanish atrocities. The Spanish military commander in Cuba, Valeriano Weyler, was called "The Butcher" for his repressive policies, which include the establishment of the first concentration camps. Warring against a whole population, he tried to stifle the uprising by herding whole villages into camps; thus the people could be watched, and everyone who was found outside the camps could be defined as enemies to be shot on sight. This method was inevitably brutal, and Cubans died by the thousands from malnutrition, disease, and abuse.

But real atrocities were not enough for Hearst and Pulitzer. They transformed innocuous incidents into horror stories and invented others. When Hearst artist Frederic Remington wired from Havana that everything was peaceful and he wanted to come home, Hearst ordered him to stay: "You furnish the pictures. I'll furnish the war." One sensational drawing showed sinister Spanish officials leering at a naked American woman. In fact, the woman had been searched quite properly in private by female officers.

McKinley's Dark Hour

McKinley tried to pursue a peaceful policy. The business community had substantial investments in Cuba, about $50 million in railroads, mines, and sugar-cane plantations, and they feared the revolutionaries more than the Spanish. McKinley and his advisers wanted Spain to abandon its harsh policies and placate both Cubans and bellicose Americans by liberalizing government on the island.

The Spanish responded to the pressure, but the war came anyway. In 1898, a new government in Madrid withdrew Weyler and proposed autonomy for Cuba within the Spanish Empire. McKinley's administration was satisfied. Two events caused a complete change in policy.

On February 9, Hearst's New York Journal published a letter that had been written by the Spanish ambassador in Washington, Enrique Dupuy de Lôme. In it, Dupuy told a friend that McKinley was "weak, a bidder for the admiration of the crowd." It was by no means an absurd assessment of the president, but it was insulting. McKinley himself was riled, and war fever flared higher.

Six days later, on February 15, 1898, the battleship U.S.S. Maine exploded in Havana harbor with a loss of 260 sailors. To this day, the cause of the disaster is unknown. The explosion may have been caused by a coal fire that spread to the magazine. A bomb may have been planted by Cuban rebels in an attempt to provoke the United States into declaring war on their behalf. Or it may have been the work of Spanish diehards who opposed the new liberal policy in Cuba. So charged was the atmosphere that some people suggested that William Randolph Hearst had planted the bomb for the sake of a headline!

In any case, with the yellow press raging, many Americans accepted the least credible explanation: the

The February 17, 1898, edition of William Randolph Hearst's New York Journal *reported the destruction of the U.S.S.* Maine *and suggested it was sunk by Spaniards.*

Spanish government, which was trying to avoid war at all costs, had destroyed the Maine.

McKinley vacillated for a month and a half. He flooded Spain with demands for a change of policy. As late as March 26, Mark Hanna urged him to keep the peace, and on April 9, in a last desperate attempt to avoid war, the Spanish government gave in on every count. In the meantime, fearing that to continue resisting the war fever would cost the Republicans control of Congress in the fall elections, McKinley caved in. With the Democratic party still led by William Jennings Bryan and the agrarians, the risk was not worth taking. On April 11, practically ignoring the Spanish capitulation, the president asked Congress for a declaration of war and got it.

The "Splendid Little War"

Declaring war was one thing. Fighting the Spanish was quite another. The United States Army, which numbered only 28,000 men, most of whom were in the West supervising Indians, was not up to launching an invasion even just a hundred miles away.

The navy was ready, however. It struck first not in Cuba but halfway around the world in Spain's last Pacific colony, the Philippines. On May 1, acting on the dubious instructions of Undersecretary of the Navy

Theodore Roosevelt and his "Rough Riders" cavalry unit.

Theodore Roosevelt (the Secretary of the Navy was ill), Commodore George Dewey steamed a flotilla into Manila Bay and completely surprised the Spanish garrison. He destroyed most of the Spanish ships before they could weigh anchor.

But Dewey had no soldiers with which to launch an attack on land. For more than three months, he and his men sat outside Manila harbor, baking in their steel ships, while Filipino rebels struggled with the Spanish garrison. In August, newly arrived troops finally took the capital. Although they did not know it, a peace treaty had been signed the previous day.

By that time, American troops had also conquered Cuba and Puerto Rico. Secretary of State John Hay called their campaign a "splendid little war" because so few Americans died in battle. In order to celebrate so gaily, however, it was necessary to overlook the more than 5,000 soldiers who died from typhoid, trop-

ical diseases, and poisonous "embalmed beef," tainted meat that had been supplied to the soldiers because of corruption or simple inefficiency.

Although the Spanish army in Cuba outnumbered the Americans until the last, both commanders and men were paralyzed by defeatism. They might have been overcome more easily than they were but for the ineptitude of the American commanders, General Nelson A. Miles and General William R. Shafter, who was so fat that he had to be helped into the saddle of an extremely large horse when it was time to move.

Despite shortages of food, clothing, transport vehicles, medical supplies, ammunition, and horses, an army of 17,000 was landed in Cuba in June and defeated the Spanish outside Santiago at the battles of El Caney and San Juan Hill. (With 200,000 soldiers in Cuba, the Spanish foolishly stationed only 19,000 in Santiago.)

The latter victory allowed Americans to forget the poor management of the war and gave them a popular hero. Theodore Roosevelt had resigned from the Navy Department to accept a colonelcy in a volunteer cavalry unit called the "Rough Riders." It was a highly unmilitary group, made up of cowboys from Roosevelt's North Dakota ranch, men in show business, upper-class polo players and other athletes, and even some ex-convicts. The Rough Riders had to fight on foot because the army had been unable to get their horses out of Tampa, Florida, but they fought bravely in the hottest action on San Juan Hill.

THE EMPIRE CONFIRMED

In August, the Spanish gave up. American troops occupied not only Manila in the Philippines and much of Cuba, but also the island of Puerto Rico, which had been seized without resistance. But what should be done with these possessions? Suddenly, the imperialism controversy was no longer an academic debate. It involved three far-flung island countries that were inhabited by millions of people who spoke Spanish, who clung to traditions very different from those of Americans, who were not Caucasian for the most part, and who did not want to become part of the United States.

To the dismay of the imperialists, the independence of Cuba had been guaranteed before the war had begun. In order to get money from Congress to fight Spain, the administration had accepted a rider drafted by Senator Henry Teller of Colorado. The Teller Amendment forbade the United States to take over the sugar island. Therefore, the great debate over imperialism centered on Puerto Rico and the Philippine Islands.

The Debate

The anti-imperialists were a disparate group, and their arguments were sometimes contradictory. In Congress, they included idealistic old Radical Republicans like George Frisbie Hoar of Massachusetts and former Liberal Republicans like Carl Schurz and much of the old Mugwump wing of the party. Some Republican regulars also opposed taking colonies; among them was Thomas B. Reed of Maine, the no-nonsense, dictatorial Speaker of the House who otherwise despised reformers. Finally, a substantial part of the Democratic party, led by William Jennings Bryan, opposed annexation of any former Spanish lands. Henry Teller became a Democrat in 1900 because of his opposition to imperialism.

The anti-imperialists reminded Americans of their anticolonial heritage. "We insist," declared the American Anti-Imperialist League in October 1899, "that the subjugation of any people is 'criminal aggression' and open disloyalty to the distinctive principles of our government. We hold, with Abraham Lincoln, that no man is good enough to govern another man without that man's consent."

Some of the anti-imperialists appealed to racist feelings. With many people ill at ease because of the nation's large black population, was it wise to bring millions more nonwhite people under the flag? When Congress finally decided to take the Philippines and pay Spain $20 million in compensation, House Speaker Reed resigned in disgust, grumbling about "ten million Malays at two dollars a head."

But racist feelings worked mostly in favor of the imperialist group. Shrewd propagandists like Roosevelt, who was now governor of New York; Henry Cabot Lodge; and the eloquent Albert J. Beveridge, senator from Indiana, preached that the white race had a duty and a right to govern inferior peoples. "God has not been preparing the English-speaking and Teutonic peoples for a thousand years for nothing but vain and idle self-contemplation and self-admiration," Beveridge told the Senate. "No! He has made us the master organizers of the world to establish system where chaos reigns."

Well-grounded fear that if the United States abandoned the Philippines, Japan or Germany would seize them motivated other politicians to support annexation. Such anxiety was especially significant in deciding McKinley's mind on the question. But most of all, the American people were in an emotional, expansive

THE WHITE AMERICAN'S BURDEN

"The White Man's Burden," a poem by the British writer Rudyard Kipling, was often quoted by imperialists to justify governing nonwhite peoples as a duty. Kipling had subtitled the poem "The United States and the Philippines," and the final stanza was addressed specifically (and some think sarcastically) to the young American nation:

Take up the White Man's Burden—
*   Have done with childhood days—*
The lightly-proffered laurel,
*   The easy, ungrudged praise.*
Comes now to search your manhood
*   Through all the thankless years,*
Cold, edged with dear-bought wisdom,
*   The judgement of your peers!*

"The White Man's Burden" from the COLLECTED WORKS OF RUDYARD KIPLING. Reprinted by permission of Doubleday and Co., Inc.

mood. Coming at the end of the troubled, depressed, and divided 1890s, annexation of colonies seemed a way to unite the country.

This idea undoubtedly swayed McKinley. There is some reason to believe that two years before he came out for annexing the Philippines, the president could not have located the islands on a map. The ignorance with which he acted is evident in one of the reasons that he gave for supporting annexation. He said that the United States had a duty to Christianize the natives of the islands. McKinley was unaware that the majority of Filipinos had been Christian before the first church bell had rung in his native state of Ohio.

Hawaii: The First Colony

McKinley found it easier to come out for annexation of the Philippines and Puerto Rico because the United States already had taken its first real overseas colony. In July 1898, shortly after the Spanish-American War began, Congress had annexed the seven main islands

and 1,400 minor ones that made up the mid-Pacific nation of Hawaii. Shortly thereafter, Guam, Wake, and Baker islands were added as coaling stations for the navy.

The annexation of Hawaii was long in the making. The descendants of American missionary families in the islands had grown rich by exporting sugar to the United States, and they had won the confidence and support of the Hawaiian king, Kalakaua. Until 1890, they were more than content with their independent island paradise.

Then, the McKinley Tariff introduced a two-cent-per-pound bounty on American-grown sugar. This encouraged enough mainland farmers to produce cane or sugar beets that Hawaiian imports declined sharply. Unable to affect American tariff policy from outside, the Hawaiian oligarchy concluded that it must join the islands to the United States and benefit from the bounty.

The plan was squelched before it got started. In 1891, Kalakaua died and was succeeded by his anti-

Sanford B. Dole, a businessman and the first governor of the territory of Hawaii, seated next to Queen Liliuokalani, the last monarch of Hawaii.

imperialist sister, Liliuokalani. Weighing 200 pounds, with a will to match her bulk, "Queen Lil" was devoted to Hawaiian culture and independence. She announced that the theme of her reign would be "Hawaii for the Hawaiians" and introduced a series of reforms aimed at undercutting the *haole* or white control of the economy and legislature.

Alarmed, the oligarchy acted quickly with help from the American ambassador in Honolulu. He declared that American lives and property were in danger and landed marines from the U.S.S. *Boston* who quickly took control of the peaceful islands. Back home, imperialists in the Senate introduced a treaty of annexation. But before they could push it through, Grover Cleveland was sworn in as president (March 4, 1893), and he withdrew the proposal.

Cleveland was not opposed to annexation on principle. But he wanted to know how the Hawaiian people felt, and he sent an investigator, James H. Blount, to the islands. Blount reported that very few nonwhite Hawaiians wanted to be part of the United States; they wanted independence and the restoration of Queen Liliuokalani. Cleveland ordered the marines to return to their ships and to the naval base at Pearl Harbor.

However, the Hawaiian whites had gone too far to chance restoring Queen Lil. They maintained control and declared Hawaii a republic. As long as Cleveland sat in the White House, they bided their time and quietly cultivated Republican senators. Annexation was probably inevitable under McKinley whatever happened with Spain. As it was, the thrill of overseas war allowed easy annexation by means of a joint resolution of the American Congress and Hawaiian legislature, the same device under which Texas had joined the Union.

Many Hawaiians continued to resent the takeover. Liliuokalani spent much time in the United States trying to win financial concessions for herself and the islands' natives. But as the white population grew and the islands attracted Japanese and Chinese immigrants, the native Hawaiians declined into a weak minority. Like the American Indians, they became foreigners in their own homeland. The famous islands' anthem, *Aloha Oe*, which was written by Liliuokalani, translates as "Farewell to Thee."

The Philippine Insurrection

Incorporating the Philippines was not so easy. If the war with Spain had been something like splendid, the war that followed was a great deal like ugly. Like the Cubans, the Philippine people were experienced in guerrilla warfare. Led by Emilio Aguinaldo, a well-educated patriot who was as comfortable in the jungle

Fighting the insurrectos *in the jungles of the Philippines was new to American soldiers and the result was brutal atrocities on both sides.*

as he was in the library, the rebels withdrew from the American-occupied cities to the jungle and fought only when the odds favored them.

In response, the American army was expanded to 65,000 men by early 1900, but made little progress outside the cities. The American commanders were unable to draw the *insurrectos* into a conventional battle in which superior fire power told the tale.

The fighting took a vicious turn. The Filipinos frequently decapitated their victims. The Americans, frustrated by their failures, the intense tropical heat, insects, and diseases, retaliated by slaughtering whole villages that were thought to be supporting the rebels. The army never did defeat the Filipinos. The rebellion ended only when, in March 1901, General Arthur MacArthur succeeded in capturing Aguinaldo. Weary of the bloodshed, Aguinaldo took an oath of allegiance to the United States and ordered his followers to do the same. (He lived quietly and long enough to see Philippine independence established in 1946.) More than 5,000 Americans died in the cause of suppressing a popular revolution, a queer twist in a conflict that had begun, three years before, in support of a popular revolution.

The China Market

Having raised the flag in several far-flung islands, not even the most exuberant imperialists could point to other countries the United States might reasonably colonize. The largest part of the non-Western world not occupied or dominated by imperial nations was China.

On the face of it, the "Middle Kingdom" was ripe for plucking. The emperor was weak; powerful regional warlords battled one another; and most of the imperialistic nations of Europe, plus Japan, had carved out "spheres of influence" in which their own troops maintained order and their own laws governed their resident citizens' behavior.

However, the most powerful of all the occupying powers, Great Britain, opposed the partition of China. Longer an imperial power and therefore more conscious than Japan, Russia, Germany, and Italy of the headaches and expense that attended imperial glory, the British believed that with their efficient industrial complex they could dominate the market of an independent China.

American businessmen disagreed with the British assessment of how economic competition in China would turn out, believing that they would win the lion's share of the prodigious purchases 160 million Chinese were capable of making. However, this projection put them in complete agreement with the British policy of preventing their imperial competitors from turning their spheres of influence into colonies and shutting the door on all competition.

The Open Door Policy

Just as John Quincy Adams had beaten the British to promulgating the Monroe Doctrine, McKinley's Secretary of State, John Hay, rushed ahead of Great Britain to circulate a series of memoranda called the "Open Door notes," which pledged the imperial powers to respect the territorial integrity of China and to grant equal trading rights in their spheres of influence to all other countries.

An anticolonialist monument, the Open Door policy was by no means a statement on behalf of Chinese self-determination. In 1900, when antiforeign rebels known as Boxers (the Chinese name of their religious movement was "Righteous Harmonious Fist") besieged 900 foreigners in the British legation in Peking, American troops joined the soldiers of six other nations in defeating them. The victory encouraged beliefs in white superiority (despite the Japanese contribution) and convinced other nations that cooperation in maintaining the Open Door was the best policy in China.

McKinley Reelected, McKinley Murdered

In 1900, the Democrats again nominated William Jennings Bryan to run against McKinley. Bryan tried to make imperialism the issue but the campaign fizzled. Americans were either happy with their overseas pos-

Chinese Boxers captured by soldiers of the U.S. Cavalry in Tianjin, China.

sessions or simply did not care. McKinley sidestepped the issue and pointed to the prosperity of the country; the Republican slogan was "Four More Years of the Full Dinner Pail." Several states that had voted for Bryan in 1896 went Republican in 1900, including even Bryan's home state of Nebraska.

A new vice president stood at McKinley's side on Inauguration Day. Theodore Roosevelt had moved quickly from his exploits in Cuba to the governorship of New York. He immediately alienated the Republican boss of the state, Thomas C. Platt, by refusing to take orders and even attacking some corrupt members of Platt's machine. When McKinley's vice president, the obscure Garrett Hobart of New Jersey, died in 1899, Platt saw a chance to get rid of the troublesome Rough Rider. He would banish him to the political burial ground of the vice presidency. Mark Hanna had his reservations. What would happen to the country, Hanna asked McKinley, if something happened to him? The president was almost 60 at a time when that was a ripe old age.

Something did happen to McKinley. On September 6, 1901, the president paid a ceremonial visit to the

Pan-American Exposition in Buffalo. Greeting a long line of guests, he found himself faced by a man who extended a bandaged hand. The gauze swathed a large-bore pistol. Leon Czolgosz, an anarchist who "didn't believe one man should have so much service and another man should have none," shot the president several times in the chest and abdomen. Eight days later, McKinley died. "Now look," Hanna shook his head at the funeral, "that damned cowboy is president."

A Flexible Imperialist

Unlike every "accidental president" who preceded him, "Teddy" Roosevelt was to leave an indelible mark on the office. Completely unlike any of his predecessors as far back as Lincoln, the young New Yorker (42 years old when he took office) knew only one way to do anything: take the lead. Nowhere was his assertive personality more pronounced than in his foreign policy, a peacetime extension of the zest that had taken him shouting up San Juan Hill.

Roosevelt's actions varied according to the part of the world with which he was dealing. With the European nations he insisted that the United States be accepted as an equal, active imperial power. Although friendship between Great Britain and the United States had been long in the making, Roosevelt sped it along by responding cordially to every British request for cooperation. Toward Latin America, however, he

was arrogant. He told both Latin Americans and Europeans that the whole Western Hemisphere was an American sphere of influence. Toward Asia, Roosevelt continued to practice the "Open Door."

During his presidency, American capital poured into China. International consortia developed mines, built railways, and set up other profitable enterprises. In 1905, the president applied his policy of equilibrium in China by working through diplomatic channels to end a war between Russia and Japan. Much to the surprise of most Europeans, Japan handily defeated Russia and threatened to seize complete control of Manchuria and other parts of northern China. Through a mixture of threats and cajolery, Roosevelt got both sides to meet at Portsmouth, New Hampshire, to work out a treaty that maintained a balance of power in the area and continued Chinese independence.

High-Handedness in Latin America

In Latin America, Roosevelt was not so compromising. He made it clear to the European nations that the United States held a preeminent position in the Western Hemisphere. In 1904, when several European nations threatened to invade the Dominican Republic to collect debts owed to their citizens, Roosevelt proclaimed what came to be called the Roosevelt Corollary to the Monroe Doctrine. In order to protect the independence of American states, the United States

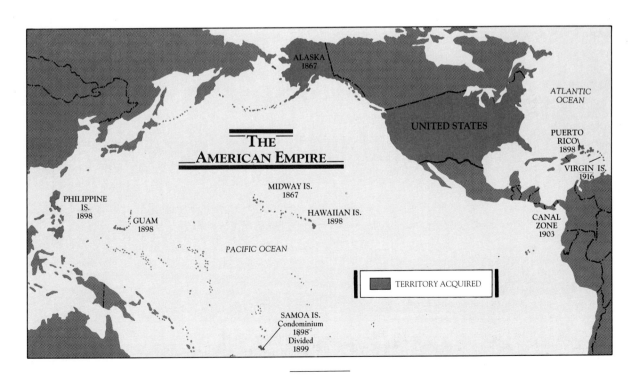

REMEMBERING THE *MAINE*: SOLDIERS IN THE SPANISH-AMERICAN WAR

Secretary of State John Hay called it "a splendid little war." Undersecretary of the Navy Theodore Roosevelt resigned his post in order to fight in it. William Allen White remembered the glad excitement with which the declaration of war had been received in the Midwest: "Everywhere over this good, fair land, flags were flying, . . . crowds gathered to hurrah for the soldiers and to throw hats into the air." The celebrants' favorite cry was, "Remember the *Maine*; to hell with Spain." Americans regarded the occasion as an opportunity to prove the arrival of the United States as a world power and, at home, as a chance to seal the reunion of North and South by having northern and southern boys join together to fight Spain. While McKinley would not allow political rival William Jennings Bryan to go abroad and make a military reputation, he was delighted to appoint old Confederate officers like Fitzhugh Lee and General Joseph Wheeler to active command.

But, as historian Frank Freidel points out, for the soldiers in the ranks "it was as grim, dirty, and bloody as any war in history." He adds: "Only the incredible ineptitude of the Spaniards and the phenomenal luck of the Americans" kept the Spanish-American War small and short—splendid.

While the navy proved ready to fight on an instant's notice, the army was not ready for anything. In 1898, the army was only 28,000 strong, and those troops were scattered the length and breadth of the country. Congress had authorized increasing this force to 65,700 in wartime, but despite a rush of enlistments, the army never grew this large. The young men who rallied to arms in every state preferred to join the state militias or new units of volunteers, in which enlistments were for two years unless discharged earlier (as almost all would be).

In 1898, the militias numbered 140,000 men, but regular army officers justly suspected their training and equipment and generally preferred volunteer units in the regular army. Indeed, training was generally inadequate across the board because of the rush to get into action, and supplies were worse. Companies mustering, mostly in the southern states, were issued heavy woolen winter uniforms and Civil War-vintage Springfield rifles. Much meat that was provided the recruits was tainted and sanitary conditions in the crowded camps were such that filth-related diseases such as typhoid and dysentery ravaged them. When the dead were counted at the end of 1898, 379 men were listed as killed in combat, while 5,083 men were listed as dead of disease.

There was no difficulty in getting volunteers. While 274,000 eventually served in the army, probably an equal number were turned down. Among these rejects were Frank James, brother of the late train robber Jesse

James, and William F. "Buffalo Bill" Cody, who annoyed the War Department by writing a magazine article entitled "How I Could Drive the Spaniards Out of Cuba with Thirty Thousand Indian Braves." Martha A. Chute of Colorado was discouraged in her offer to raise a troop of women, as was William Randolph Hearst in his suggestion to recruit a regiment of professional boxers and baseball players. "Think of a regiment composed of magnificent men of this ilk," the editor of the *New York Journal* wrote "They would overawe any Spanish regiment by their mere appearance." Nevertheless, the "Rough Riders," a motley collection of cowboys, athletes, and gentlemen like Colonel Theodore Roosevelt, was mustered. But because of shipping problems, the Riders had to leave their horses in Florida when they sailed for Cuba and fight on foot.

In fact, there were few battlegrounds in Cuba or in the Philippines that were suited to cavalry attack. Both are tropical countries, and most of the fighting was done in summer and much of it in jungle. The army tried to prepare for jungle warfare by authorizing the recruitment of up to 10,000 "immunes," young men who were thought to be immune to tropical diseases. However, medicine's comparative ignorance of the nature of tropical diseases combined with racism to make the immune regiments no more serviceable than any others. Whereas the original idea had been to fill these units with men who had grown up in marshy areas of the Deep South, within months recruiters were turning away white Louisianians from the bayous and accepting blacks from the upcountry South and even urban New Jersey. They were believed to possess a genetic immunity to malaria, yellow fever, and other afflictions of the tropics.

Blacks played a large part in both the Cuban and the Philippine campaigns. When the war broke out, there were four black regiments in the regular army: two infantry and two cavalry, the Ninth and the Tenth Horse Regiments. All four saw action. In fact, while Theodore Roosevelt was describing the capture of San Juan Hill as an accomplishment of the Rough Riders, other witnesses believed that the Rough Riders would have been devastated had it not been for the Tenth Negro Cavalry, which was immediately to their left during the charge. While the Rough Riders made a lot of noise, the Tenth simply did their job. In the words of the restrained report of their commander, later to be General of the Armies, John J. "Black Jack" Pershing: "The 10th Cavalry charged up the hill, scarcely firing a shot, and being nearest the Rough Riders, opened a disastrous enfilading fire upon the Spanish right, thus relieving the Rough Riders from the volleys that were being poured into them from that part of the Spanish line."

Black soldiers, members of the Twenty-fourth U.S. Infantry Division assigned to battle in Cuba, in an 1898 stereographic image by B. L. Singley.

About 10,000 blacks served in the war, 4,000 of them in the "immunes." A study done of white regiments indicates that the Spanish-American War was generally a poor man's fight and, rather more surprising, a city man's fight.

From largely rural Indiana, for example, of those volunteers who listed their occupation, only 296 were farmers. There were 322 common laborers, 413 skilled laborers, and 118 white-collar workers (clerks). Only 47 in the regiment were professional men, and 25 were merchants. A survey of a Connecticut volunteer unit reveals similar figures. Several historians state that the army was far less representative of the occupations of the general population than were the armies of the two world wars.

In age, it was typical, however. The average age of the soldiers was 24. Their average height was 5 feet 8 inches, and their average weight was 149 pounds, both less than the averages today.

DEWEY'S BLUNDER

Commodore George Dewey became a national hero by virtue of his victory at Manila Bay during the Spanish-American War. A group of conservative Democrats hoped to nominate him for the presidency in 1900 in order to head off William Jennings Bryan, who was still regarded as something of a radical. At first Dewey refused because he did not believe that he was qualified for the office. He later changed his mind, explaining that "since studying the subject, I am convinced that the office of the president is not such a very difficult one to fill." As a result of his candor, Dewey lost the support of virtually everyone, and Bryan was nominated once again.

would, if necessary, exercise an "international police power" in the Western Hemisphere. In other words, while European nations still had to keep out of the Americas, the United States could intervene south of the border.

Roosevelt immediately put his corollary to work. United States marines landed in the Dominican Republic and took over the collection of customs, seeing to it that European creditors were paid off. From 1904 until the 1930s, the United States intervened in a number of Latin American countries: Cuba, Nicaragua, the Dominican Republic, and Haiti. These actions may have pleased European investors, but they created a reservoir of ill will among Latin Americans who felt bullied by the great "Anglo" power to the north. No action offended Latin Americans more than Roosevelt's high-handed seizure of the Panama Canal Zone, which was the president's proudest foreign accomplishment.

In 1911, when the construction of the canal was nearly complete, Roosevelt reflected (quite accurately)

PROMOTING THE PANAMA ROUTE

On May 8, 1902, Mount Pelée on the French West Indian island of Martinique erupted, killing 30,000 people. A month later, Nicaragua's Mount Momotombo also blew its top, albeit without such tragic results. Nevertheless, the shrewd and ever alert promoter of the Panama route for an isthmian canal, Philippe Bunau-Varilla, seized the opportunity by sending Nicaraguan postage stamps depicting a smoking Mount Momotombo to members of the U.S. Congress and other individuals who would play an important role in choosing between the proposed Nicaraguan route and Bunau-Varilla's Panama route.

that only his decisiveness had moved the project along. "If I had followed traditional, conservative methods," he said, "the debates on it would have been going on yet. But I took the Canal Zone and let Congress debate; and while the debate goes on the Canal does also."

The Need for a Canal

Naval officers had long recognized the value of a quick route between the Atlantic and the Pacific. During the Spanish-American War, this was brought home with new urgency when it took American warships more than two months to steam from San Francisco to Cuban waters.

In 1881, a French company had started to dig across the Isthmus of Panama, which was then a part of Colombia. But the project was abandoned because of financial difficulties and the ravages of tropical diseases among the laborers. By 1900, the French company's rights to continue construction were about to expire, and an agent of the company, Philippe Jean Bunau-Varilla, began to prod American expansionists into buying its titles.

Most political leaders, including anti-imperialists, realized that the United States needed the canal in order to protect and supply its scattered possessions. However, some preferred to allow the existing rights to expire, whence negotiations could be reopened with

Theodore Roosevelt took immense personal satisfaction in securing American rights to dig the Panama Canal and in 1906 traveled to Panama to inspect the construction project.

Colombia. Others argued that a route across Nicaragua was preferable to the Panamanian plan.

Roosevelt Takes Panama

When the Colombian government turned down an American offer to buy construction rights for $10 million and pay an annual rental of $250,000 (the Colombians wanted $25 million), Roosevelt conspired with Bunau-Varilla to start a revolution in Panama. On November 2, 1903, the president moved several warships to the vicinity, and the next day, the province erupted in riots and declared its independence. On November 6, the United States recognized the new republic of Panama. On November 18, the first foreign minister of Panama, none other than Philippe Jean Bunau-Varilla, signed a treaty with the United States that granted perpetual use of a ten-mile-wide "canal zone" across the isthmus on the terms that Colombia had refused.

None of Roosevelt's successors in the presidency were quite so arrogant in dealing with Latin America. For example, Roosevelt's hand-picked successor, William Howard Taft, tried to replace "gunboat diplomacy" with "dollar diplomacy," the attempt to influence Latin America (and China) through investment rather than armed force. In 1921, over the protests of Roosevelt's old ally Henry Cabot Lodge, the United States attempted to make amends to Colombia for Roosevelt's high-handed actions by paying the $25 million that the Colombians originally had demanded for the right to dig the Panama Canal.

But such gestures could not change America's "big brother" behavior or the simmering resentment of the Latin American people. The plunge into imperialism established intervention as an essential part of American diplomacy. Every president from Theodore Roosevelt to Herbert Hoover (1929–33) used troops to enforce the American will in Latin America.

For Further Reading

Overviews and Classics

Vincent P. DeSantis, *The Shaping of Modern America, 1877–1916* (1973)

H. Wayne Morgan, *From Hayes to McKinley: National Party Politics, 1877–1896* (1971)

Robert H. Wiebe, *The Search for Order, 1880–1920* (1967)

Valuable Special Studies

Howard K. Beale, *Theodore Roosevelt and the Rise of America to World Power* (1956)

Robert L. Beisner, *From the Old Diplomacy to the New, 1865–1900* (1975)

C. S. Campbell, *The Transformation of American Foreign Relations, 1865–1900* (1976)

Robert F. Durden, *The Climax of Populism: The Election of 1896* (1965)

Frank Freidel, *The Splendid Little War* (1958)

Lloyd Gardner, Walter Le Feber, and Thomas McCormick, *The Creation of the American Empire* (1973)

Ray Ginger, *Altgeld's America: The Lincoln Ideal and Changing Realities* (1958)

Paul F. Glad, *McKinley, Bryan, and the People* (1964)

———, *The Trumpet Soundeth* (1960)

G. Grunder and W. E. Livezey, *The Philippines and the United States* (1951)

S. L. Jones, *The Presidential Election of 1896* (1964)

Walter R. Le Feber, *The New Empire: An Interpretation of American Expansion, 1860–1898* (1963)

Ernest R. May, *Imperial Democracy: The Emergence of America as a Great Power* (1961)

Dwight C. Miner, *Fight for the Panama Canal* (1966)

Thomas J. Osborne, *American Opposition to Hawaiian Annexation, 1893–1898* (1981)

J. W. Pratt, *America's Colonial Experiment* (1950)

———, *Expansionists of 1898: The Acquisition of Hawaii and the Spanish Island* (1936)

William A. Russ, Jr., *The Hawaiian Republic, 1894–98* (1961)

Theodore Saloutos, *Farmer Movements in the South, 1865–1933* (1960)

William A. Williams, *The Tragedy of American Diplomacy* (1959)

C. Vann Woodward, *The Strange Career of Jim Crow* (1974)

Biographies and Autobiographies

P. E. Coletta, *William Jennings Bryan: Political Evangelist, 1860–1908* (1964)

Louis W. Koenig, *Bryan: A Political Biography of William Jennings Bryan* (1971)

Margaret Leech, *In the Days of McKinley* (1959)

H. Wayne Morgan, *William McKinley and His America* (1963)

Edmund Morris, *The Rise of Theodore Roosevelt* (1979)

Gay Nineties and Good Old Days
American Society in Transition, 1890–1917

In the final months of 1899, editors and writers of letters to editors bickered in print about the significance of the New Year's Day that was rapidly approaching. One group declared that New Year's Day 1900 would mark the beginning of a new century. Another rushed to point out that the first century A.D. had not ended with the last day of A.D. 99, but with the last day of A.D. 100. Therefore, the twentieth century would begin at the stroke of midnight on January 1, 1901, a year in the future.

They were quite right, of course. The year 1900 was the last year of the nineteenth century, not the first year of the twentieth. Nevertheless, the titillation of writing such a portentously sounding date as 1900 on their next letter to the editor meant more to people than did the dictates of arithmetic. Americans would ring out the old century on December 31, 1899, and ring in the new in the wee hours of January 1, 1900.

The newspapers say that the celebrations were particularly festive that night, cold as it was over much of the nation; and historians since, who focus on economic and political issues find 1900 a convenient date for dividing two eras: depression before, prosperity after; conservative hegemony in the 1890s, reform during the 1900s.

Men and women bicyclists riding at the turn of the century.

Culturally and socially, however, 1900 seems less a watershed year than the midpoint in a quarter-century era when the American middle class, as we know it, came into its own and brimmed with confidence.

THE BIRTH OF MIDDLE AMERICA

To a black, to an Indian of the Plains or a Mexican of the Southwest, to a white workingman in a marginal job, or to many of the nearly 12 million immigrants who came to the United States between 1890 and 1910, the decades that spanned the year 1900 were not so rosy. During most of the 1890s, the United States languished in hard times. It was the decade of Wounded Knee, bloody labor battles, grinding prejudice, an era when the lynching of blacks in the South reached epidemic proportions. In 1899, a mob in Palmetto, Georgia, could announce in advance that a man would be burned alive so that thousands could flock aboard special excursion trains to witness the spectacle.

Life expectancy at birth for most white Americans was about 45 years, lower for blacks and immigrants. Infant mortality in New York City was worse than it had ever been. Nationwide, people were six times more likely to die of influenza than they are today, sixty times more likely to die of syphilis, and more than eighty times more likely to die of tuberculosis. Diseases that are minor health problems in the late twentieth century—typhoid, scarlet fever, strep throat, diphtheria, whooping cough, measles—were common killers in the 1890s and 1900s.

And yet, when we think of the years around the turn of the century, we are not apt to remember them as the worst of times. On the contrary, the final decade of the nineteenth century has come down in the popular consciousness as the "Gay Nineties," a decade of nickelodeon music and Coney Island, of a night of vaudeville and a week at the seaside, of beer gardens and ice cream parlors, of the bicycle craze and winsome Gibson Girls.

The years that preceded American intervention in the First World War have lived on in the national memory as the original "good old days." The prewar period is the slice of time to which popular novelists and filmmakers repair when they want to portray an America that is recognizable but unmistakably better.

Life was less complex then. The summer sun was warmer; the hot dogs, tastier; the baseball, more exciting; the cars truly adventurous; the boys, more gallant; the girls, prettier; the songs, lilting and cheering

A white mob preparing to lynch a black man in Paris, Texas, in 1893.

the heart with melody and innocent lyrics. Even historians, who are trained to be skeptical of such images, have referred to the generation that lived before the First World War as the last to enjoy basking in an "age of American innocence."

A Golden Age

The turn of the century has cast such an alluring glow over time because middle-class values and aspirations have dominated American culture in the twentieth century, and in the 1890s and early 1900s the modern middle class came into its own. The troubles of poor farmers, most industrial workers, blacks, Indians, Mexicans, and recent immigrants were real and often tragic. But the class of people who, while not rich, did not have to struggle in order to survive reached unprecedented numbers at the turn of the century. The middle class became numerous enough to create and sustain a distinctive lifestyle and to support a bustling consumer economy and technology devoted to physical comfort, convenience, individual self-improvement, and the enjoyment of leisure time.

Increasingly well educated, the new middle class quietly shelved the zealous, religious piety of their parents and grandparents. They embraced instead the material world and its pleasures. The people of the "good old days" were by no means oblivious to social evils. Far from it; they were also the citizens of the "Progressive era." But because war and revolution were not yet constant companions, and because the very idea that the world itself could be destroyed was preposterous fantasy, the middle class of the turn of the century could look their problems in the eye with confidence and optimism.

Teddy

The buoyant temper of the period was personified in the young New Yorker who, in September 1901, succeeded William McKinley as president. Theodore Roosevelt was climbing a mountain in the Adirondacks when he received the news of McKinley's death. He rushed to Buffalo, took the oath of office, and confided to a friend, "It is a dreadful thing to come into the presidency in this way. But it would be a far worse thing to be morbid about it." Roosevelt intended to enjoy the presidency, as his fellow Americans intended to make the most of life. And no other chief executive before or since has had such a "bully" time living at 1600 Pennsylvania Avenue.

Both critics and friends of the president poked fun at his personal motto: "Walk softly and carry a big stick." They said that they observed Roosevelt wildly waving clubs around often enough, but rarely knew

By 1896, cheap trolley fares made Coney Island a popular destination with middle- and working-class people.

him to walk softly. Quite the contrary. Everything that Roosevelt did was accompanied by fanfare. He seemed to swagger and strut about like an exuberant adolescent, hogging center stage and good naturedly drowning out anyone who dared to compete for the spotlight. He insisted on being, in the words of a son, the bride at every wedding and the corpse at every funeral.

Roosevelt shattered the image of solemn dignity that had been nurtured by every president since Rutherford B. Hayes. He stormed about the country far more than had any predecessor, delivering dramatic speeches, mixing gleefully with crowds of all descriptions, camping out, climbing mountains, and clambering astride horses and atop farm and industrial machines. When a motion-picture photographer asked him to move around for the ingenious new camera, Roosevelt picked up an ax and furiously chopped down a tree.

The Strenuous Life

Of an old aristocratic Dutch family, Roosevelt had been sickly as a youth. He was hopelessly nearsighted and suffered from asthma. But he built up his body through a regimen of difficult exercise. He fought on the Harvard boxing team, and rode with cowboys on his North Dakota ranch. As Police Commissioner of New York City, he accompanied patrolmen on night beats as dangerous as any in the world. When the war with Spain broke out, he left his office job and joined the army. In dozens of articles and books, he wrote of the glories of "the strenuous life."

Roosevelt liked to show off his large, affectionate, and handsome family with himself at stage center, a stern but generous patriarch. He sported a modest paunch (fashionable at the turn of the century), a close-snipped moustache, and thick pince-nez that dropped from his nose when he was excited, which was often. His teeth were odd, all seemingly incisors of the same size and about twice as many as normal. He displayed them often in a broad grin that he shed only when he took off after enemies whom middle-class Americans also found it easy to dislike: Wall Street bankers, Socialists, impudent Latin Americans.

Unlike McKinley, Roosevelt had no compunctions about smoking cigars in public. What was the harm in a minor vice that brought a man pleasure? More than any other individual, he taught Americans to believe that their president should be a good fellow and part showman.

The Symbol of His Age

Roosevelt had many critics. But most Americans, especially those of the vibrant new middle class, found him a grand fellow. They called him "Teddy" and

RETAIL PRICES: 1900–1910

Junction City, Kansas—population 5,000

Bacon (per pound)	$0.12
Beef (per pound)	.10
Butter (per pound)	.18
Eggs (per dozen)	.12
Ice cream soda	.10
Oranges (per dozen)	.20
Ladies' shoes (per pair)	1.50
Men's suit	9.00
Sewing machine	12.00

named the lovable animal doll they bought for their children, the teddy bear, after him. He was the first president to be routinely identified in newspapers by his initials, T.R., another signal of affection. Even Elihu Root, a stodgy eastern aristocrat who served as both Secretary of War and Secretary of State, waxed playful when he congratulated the president on his forty-sixth birthday in 1904. "You have made a very good start in life," Root said, "and your friends have great hopes for you when you grow up." The British ambassador quipped, "You must remember that the president is about six years old."

Kansas journalist William Allen White, the archetype of the middle-class townsman, wrote that "Roosevelt bit me and I went mad." White remained a lifelong devotee of "the Colonel," as did Finley Peter Dunne, the urbane Chicagoan who captured the salty, cynical humor of the big-city Irish in his fictional commentator on current events, Mr. Dooley. Radical dissenters hated Roosevelt (who hated them back with interest). But they were at a loss as to how to counter his vast popularity. Labor leaders and Socialists stuck to the issues when they disagreed with him. There was no advantage in attacking Teddy Roosevelt personally.

Although Roosevelt was a staunch believer in Anglo-Saxon superiority, blacks liked him because he ignored the squeals of southern segregationists and invited Booker T. Washington to call on him in the White House. Woman suffragists, gearing up for the last phase of their long battle for votes, petitioned rather than attacked him. Elizabeth Cady Stanton addressed him from her deathbed in 1901 as "already celebrated for so many deeds and honorable utterances."

Much mischief was done during Theodore Roosevelt's nearly eight years in office. He committed the United States to a role as international policeman that damaged the nation's reputation in many small countries. He was inclined to define his opponents in moral

terms, a recurring and unfortunate characteristic of American politics since his time.

But the happy symbiosis between the boyish president and the majority of the American people may be the most important historical fact of the years spanning the turn of the century. Like the man who was their president between 1901 and 1909, the worldly middle class of the Gay Nineties was confident, optimistic, and glad to be alive.

An Educated People

The foundation of middle-class vigor was wealth. American society as a whole had grown so rich that despite the disproportionate wealth controlled by a small number of multimillionaires, millions of people in the middle could afford to indulge interests and pleasures that had been the exclusive property of tiny elites in earlier epochs and other countries. Among these was education beyond "the three r's"—"readin', 'ritin', and 'rithmetic." During the final third of the nineteenth century, and especially after 1890, the American educational system expanded and changed to accommodate the numbers and aspirations of the new class.

There were no more than about 300 secondary schools in the United States in 1860 (a country of 31.4 million people), and only about 100 of them were

Horseback riding was one of Theodore Roosevelt's many athletic pursuits.

Stanford University, constructed by railroad baron Leland Stanford in memory of his son.

free. While girls were admitted to most public elementary schools, very few attended beyond the first few grades.

Colleges and universities—about 560 in 1870—catered to an even more select social set. They offered the traditional course in the liberal arts (Latin, philosophy, mathematics, and history) that was designed to polish young gentlemen rather than to train people for a career. The handful of "female seminaries" and colleges that admitted women before the Civil War also taught the ancient curriculum mixed with a strong dose of evangelical religion.

After about 1880, educational facilities rapidly multiplied and changed character. By 1900, there were 6,000 free public secondary schools in the United States, and by 1915, there were 12,000, educating 1.3 million pupils. Educational expenditures per pupil increased from about $9 a year in 1870 to $48 in 1920. Secondary schools no longer specialized in preparing a select few for university, but offered a wide range of courses leading to jobs in industry and business, from engineering and accounting to agriculture and typing.

New Kinds of Universities

The Morrill Land Grant Act of 1862 and the philanthropy of millionaires combined with the middle class's hunger for learning to expand the opportunities for higher education. The Morrill Act provided federal land to the states for the purpose of serving the educational needs of "the industrial classes," particularly in "such branches of learning as are related to agriculture and mechanic arts." Thus it not only fostered the founding of technical schools in which middle-class youth might learn a profession, but put liberal-arts training within the reach of those who sought it. Many of the great state universities of the West owe their origins to the Morrill Act.

Gilded Age millionaires competed for esteem as patrons of learning by constructing buildings and by endowing scholarships and professorial chairs at older institutions. Some even founded completely new universities. The story was told that railroad king Leland Stanford and his wife traveled to Harvard with the notion of erecting a building in memory of their son, who had died. As President Charles W. Eliot was explaining how much it had cost to construct each of Harvard's magnificent stone buildings, Mrs. Stanford suddenly exclaimed, "Why, Leland, we can build our own university!" And they did; Stanford University in Palo Alto, California, was founded in 1885.

Cornell (1865), Drew (1866), Johns Hopkins (1876), Vanderbilt (1872), and Carnegie Institute of Technology (1905) were universities that bear the names of the moguls who financed them. In Philadelphia, Success Gospel preacher Russell B. Conwell established Temple University in 1884 explicitly to educate poor boys ambitious to rise in social station. John D. Rockefeller pumped millions of dollars into the University of Chicago (1890), making it one of America's most distinguished centers of learning within a decade. George Eastman, who made a fortune from Kodak cameras, gave to the University of Rochester.

The midwestern and western state universities, beginning with Iowa in 1858, generally admitted women to at least some programs. In the East, however, separate women's colleges were founded, again with the support of wealthy benefactors. Georgia Female College (Wesleyan) and Mount Holyoke dated from before the Civil War. In the later decades of the century they were joined by Vassar (1861), Wellesley (1870), Smith (1871), Radcliff (1879), Bryn Mawr (1880), and Barnard (1889). Vassar's educational standards rivaled those of the best men's colleges, but it was necessary to maintain a kind of "head start" program in order to remedy deficiencies in the secondary education provided even well-to-do girls.

Studying for Careers

The transformation of higher education was not simply a matter of more colleges, universities, and students. While some institutions, such as Yale, clung tenaciously to the traditional liberal-arts curriculum, the majority of schools adopted the "elective system" that was pioneered by the College of William and Mary, Washington College in Virginia, and the University of Michigan and most effectively promoted by President Eliot of Harvard. Beginning in 1869, Eliot abandoned the rule that every student follow precisely the same sequence of courses. Instead, he allowed individuals to choose their field of study. "Majors" included traditional subjects but also new disciplines in the social sciences, engineering, and business administration. The new emphasis on university education as preparation for a career unmistakably revealed the interests of middle-class students who had not yet arrived financially and socially.

From Germany, educators borrowed the concept of the professional postgraduate school. Before the 1870s, young people who wished to learn a profession at-

tached themselves to an established practitioner. A would-be lawyer agreed with an established attorney to do routine work in his office, sweeping floors and helping with deeds and wills, in return for the right to "read law" in the office and to observe and question his teacher. After a few years, the apprentice hung out his own shingle. Many physicians were trained the same way. Civil and mechanical engineers learned their professions "on the job" in factories. All too often, teachers received no training and were miserably paid, about $200 a year in rural states.

Women, Minorities, and the New Education

Exceptional women who were dauntless enough to shake off the ridicule of their male classmates could be found in small numbers at every level of the new system. By the mid-1880s, the word *coeducational* and its breezy abbreviation, *coed*, had become part of the American language. The first female physician in the United States, Elizabeth Blackwell, was accredited only in 1849. In 1868, she established a medical school for women in New York City. By that date, the Woman's Medical College of Pennsylvania already was recognized, however grudgingly, as offering one of the nation's most effective programs of medical education.

Female lawyers were unusual at a time when women were not considered equal to men before the law. In 1873, the Supreme Court approved the refusal of the University of Illinois to admit women by declaring that "the paramount mission and destiny of women are to fulfill the noble and benign offices of wife and mother." By the end of the century, dozens of women practiced law, among them wife and "Mother" Mary Elizabeth Lease. Antoinette Blackwell, sister-in-law of Elizabeth, paved the way for the ordination of women ministers, and by the turn of the century, the more liberal Protestant denominations, such as the Unitarians and Congregationalists, had ordained some women.

Also in small numbers, well-to-do Jews and Catholics began to take advantage of the new educational opportunities. The Sephardic and German Jews were a secular people who preferred to send their sons to established institutions rather than found their own. The Catholic Church, on the other hand, the largest

CONSUMER GOODS

By 1909, thirteen of the largest industrial firms in the United States were involved in the production of consumer goods, including tobacco, whiskey, meat, petroleum products, and tires for automobiles.

religious denomination in the United States but mainly a church of the lower classes, preferred to found its own colleges. Church policy was to prepare the sons and daughters of the Catholic middle class for active careers in business and the professions while simultaneously shoring up their loyalty to their faith by means of rigorous schooling in Church doctrine, history, and observance.

The most famous Catholic colleges dated from before the Civil War: Notre Dame had been founded in 1842; Holy Cross (1843) and Boston College (1863) were explicitly designed as foils to aristocratic Harvard. Thomas Jefferson's and John Quincy Adams's dream of a national university was fulfilled by the Roman Catholic Church with the founding in 1889 of the Catholic University of America in Washington, D.C. It is difficult to imagine either the Virginian or the New Englander quite happy about it.

On a much smaller scale, educational opportunities for blacks also expanded. The traditional universities in New England and many of the sectarian colleges of the Ohio Valley continued to admit a small number of very well-qualified blacks. W. E. B. Du Bois, a founder of the National Association for the Advancement of Colored People, earned a Ph.D. at Harvard.

In the North as well as the South, philanthropists and state governments founded institutions for blacks only. Beginning with Lincoln University in Pennsylvania (founded as the Ashmun Institute in 1854),

W. E. B. Du Bois, a founder of the National Association for the Advancement of Colored People.

idealistic benefactors supported schools to train a black elite such as Howard University in Washington (1867) and Fisk in Nashville (1866). After Booker T. Washington's Atlanta Compromise speech of 1895 and the Supreme Court's decision in *Plessy v. Ferguson* (1896) gave the go-ahead to segregation at all levels of education, southern state governments founded "agricultural and mechanical" schools patterned after Alabama's Tuskegee Institute (1881), at which blacks could train for manual occupations.

The accomplishments of these institutions should not be underestimated. Few scientific researchers of the time were more productive than Tuskegee Institute's great botanist, George Washington Carver. Nevertheless, the educational level of blacks lagged so far behind that of whites that in 1910, when only 7.7

Thomas Eakins' The Gross Clinic, painted in 1875, shows young physicians learning their trade from more experienced colleagues.

WOMEN IN GOVERNMENT

Just as the black cowboy virtually has been forgotten, few historians have noted that women played an important part in government long before they could vote. At the turn of the century, nearly one government worker in three was female. The federal bureaucracy was very much a woman's world.

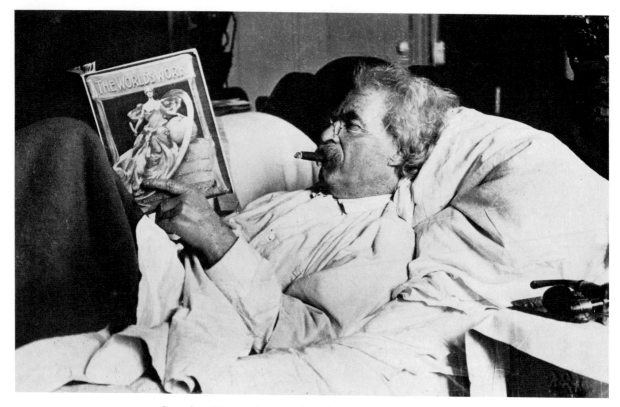

Samuel L. Clemens, known to his wide readership as Mark Twain.

percent of the American population was illiterate (the figure includes the millions of recent immigrants), one black in three above the age of ten could neither read nor write.

A LIVELY CULTURE

Increasing numbers of white Americans could read, however, and they did. They continued to buy the books of European authors and the works of the older generation of American writers—Emerson, Longfellow, Whitman, Whittier—while supporting new ones. Nevertheless, the greatest poet of the period was virtually unknown until after her death. Emily Dickinson, who led a life of quiet gentility in Amherst, Massachusetts, published only two of her haunting verses before she died in 1886.

By way of contrast, the finest novelists of the period—some say in all American literary history—grew famous and some rich from the demand for their books. Samuel L. Clemens, or Mark Twain, was quintessentially and comprehensively American. A southerner by birth, he deserted a Confederate militia unit to go west to Nevada, and eventually settled in Hartford,

Connecticut, when he became able to choose his style of life. Brilliantly capturing both the hardships and ribald humor of frontier life in *Roughing It* (1872), he earned an international reputation with *The Adventures of Tom Sawyer* (1876) and *The Adventures of Huckleberry Finn* (1885). Readers sometimes missed the profound and subtle social criticism in Twain's work (as an old man, he grew melancholy, cynical, and bitter), but they read him with pleasure for his rich wit and mastery of the American language.

Twain's favorite settings and themes were robustly western. The other great novelist of the period, Henry James, settled in England because he found American culture stultifying, and he set most of his novels in the Old World and peopled them with cultivated, cosmopolitan characters. But like Twain, he was determined to define America. In *The American* (1877), *The Europeans* (1878), and *Daisy Miller* (1879), James dealt with the relationship of open, albeit less cultivated American characters with a jaded and decadent European culture.

Realism and Naturalism

An able novelist in his own right, William Dean Howells presided over the American literary establishment as editor of the *Atlantic Monthly*. Like *Harper's*, *Forum*, and *The Arena*, the *Atlantic* published a mix of poetry, stories, and elegant essays that sometimes dealt with contemporary issues but usually at a fastidious distance.

Howells was a realist. He had no patience with the high-flown, preposterous motives and beliefs that romanticist and sentimentalist writers imputed to their characters. In *The Rise of Silas Lapham* (1885), a novel about a successful industrialist, when one sister loses a suitor to another, she does not react selflessly, nor does the sister who gets her man think seriously of sacrificing herself. Nevertheless, neither Howells nor the *Atlantic* would have considered dealing explicitly with sexual matters or graphically with the degradation that poverty and squalor created. Because the proper upper and middle classes themselves considered such discussions unacceptable, the writings of realists like Howells are sometimes lumped with romanticism and sentimentalism as "the genteel tradition."

Naturalistic writers defied the taboos, some of them with considerable success. In *Maggie: A Girl of the Streets* (1893), Stephen Crane depicts the poor not as noble and selfless but as miserable and helpless. In *The Red Badge of Courage* (1895), the Civil War is described as something other than glory, bugles, bravery, and flying colors (if anything, a more daring venture than a book about a prostitute). In *McTeague* (1899) and *The Octopus* (1901), Frank Norris deals with people driven almost mechanically by animal motives.

The most successful of the naturalists was Jack London, who also depicts a universe in which human beings were shaped by nature and their natures rather than in control of the environment and themselves. His *Call of the Wild* (1903) is comparable to *Huckleberry Finn* in that it is simultaneously a fine adventure story (about a dog) and, at a deeper level, a profound commentary on the human condition. Theodore Dreiser broke with a literary convention (that nevertheless survived) by allowing characters like *Sister Carrie* (1900) to enjoy rich lives despite sinful pasts. Dreiser's success was doubly remarkable because, from a midwestern German household, his treatment of the English language was adversarial at best, and more often downright cruel.

A Hunger for Words

The genteel tradition was also challenged by a new type of magazine that made its appearance in the 1880s and 1890s. Catering to the new, hungry, but not so ethereally intellectual middle classes, these periodicals illustrate the interaction of industrial technology, the larger reading public, and the emergence of modern advertising that was first exploited in 1883 by Cyrus H. K. Curtis and his *Ladies' Home Journal*.

Improved methods of manufacturing paper, printing, and photoengraving, as well as the cheap mailing privileges that had been established by Congress in 1879, inspired Curtis to found a magazine for women who were hungry for a world beyond the kitchen and parlor but who found few opportunities in business and the professions. *Ladies' Home Journal* sold for only ten cents (compared with the thirty-five-cent *Atlantic* and *Harper's*) and emphasized women's interests. It was not a feminist publication. On the contrary, editor Edward Bok preached a conservatism that reassured homemakers that their conventional prejudices were proper and right and middle-class people generally that they were a "steadying influence" between "unrest among the lower classes and rottenness among the upper classes."

Somewhat more daring were the new general-interest magazines of the 1890s, such as *McClure's*, *Munsey's*, and *Cosmopolitan*. They too cost a dime, thus putting them within reach of a large readership. (*The*

THE LADIES' HOME JOURNAL

ROMANCE NUMBER

JULY 1910 · THE CURTIS PUBLISHING COMPANY, PHILADELPHIA · FIFTEEN CENTS

The cover of a 1910 copy of The Ladies' Home Journal.

Saturday Evening Post, which Cyrus Curtis bought in 1897, sold for only a nickel.) Without stooping to sensationalism, they presented readers with a livelier writing style than the established journals and a lavish use of photographs and illustrations.

McClure's and *Munsey's* pioneered the curious but successful economics of selling their publications for less than it cost to print and mail them. They made their profit from building up big subscription lists and selling advertising to manufacturers of consumer goods wanting to reach people who had extra money to spend. The subscribership of *McClure's* increased from 8,000 in 1893 to 250,000 in 1895, and that of *Munsey's* grew from 40,000 to 500,000 during the same two years. By 1900, the combined circulation of the four largest magazines totaled 2.5 million per month, more than all American magazines combined only twenty years earlier.

Libraries and Lyceums

The cultural hunger of the middle class was also expressed in the construction of free public libraries. Again, men suddenly grown rich gave millions to build them. Enoch Pratt donated $1 million to Baltimore for its library. Wealthy lawyer and presidential candidate Samuel J. Tilden gave New York City $2 million, and William Newberry founded one of the nation's greatest collections of books and valuable manuscripts in Chicago with a munificent bequest of $4 million. Beginning in 1881, the self-taught Andrew Carnegie made libraries his principal philanthropy. Before his death in 1919, Carnegie helped found 2,800 free public libraries.

The old lyceum idea of sending lecturers on tour to speak to people who lived far from big cities was revived in 1868 by James Redpath. Offering large fees, Redpath persuaded the most distinguished statesmen, ministers, and professors of the day to deliver highly moral and usually informative addresses in auditoriums and specially erected tents in hundreds of small cities and towns.

Chautauqua

The lyceum movement was a throwback to the antebellum period, when only the very wealthy traveled away from home and the middle class still held fast to the Calvinist beliefs that constant work was the human fate and idleness such as casual travel was a sin. The lyceum scheduled programs in the evening, when the day's toil was done.

The phenomenon that was born in 1874 at Lake Chautauqua in New York's Allegheny Mountains was more characteristic of the new age. The "Chautau-quas" originally were eight-week summer training programs for Sunday-school teachers. During the 1890s, however, cheap excursion fares on the trains made it feasible for people who had little interest in active church work to make the trip for the sake of the cool mountain air and relaxation. To accommodate them, the Chautauqua organizers broadened their program to include lecturers on secular subjects. By the turn of the century, a middle-class family spending a few weeks at Lake Chautauqua could expect to hear lectures by individuals as prominent as William Jennings Bryan and to watch "magic-lantern" (slide) shows about the Holy Land, Persia, or China presented by professional world travelers. Distinguished professors (including quacks) expounded on their theories about human character, happy marriage, or childrearing. German oom-pah bands, Hawaiian dancers, trained dogs, Italian acrobats, and Indian fire-eaters provided lighter entertainment.

AMERICANS AT PLAY

Promoters founded more than 200 Chautauqua-type resorts, some in the mountains, some at the seaside. Enough people could afford to take a holiday from work that a flourishing tourist economy based on leisure time soon grew up.

Nevertheless, old assumptions died hard. Resort promoters found it advisable to provide at least the appearance of "usefulness" for the vacations they offered. If the middle class trekked to Lake Chautauqua or Lake George in New York and to Long Beach or Atlantic City in New Jersey primarily for rest and relaxation, they could tell others and convince themselves of the cultural and educational aspects of their holiday. They were not just wasting time.

Taking the Cure

A similar conjunction of relaxation and constructive use of time underlay the resorts that were devoted to good health. Owners of mineral springs claimed miraculous powers for their waters. Baths in naturally heated mineral waters or in hot mud were prescribed as nostrums for dozens of afflictions. "Hydropathy," a nineteenth-century medical fad, taught that virtually constant bathing and drinking water improved health. For decades, the wealthy had made prosperous summer resorts of places like Saratoga Springs in New York and White Sulphur Springs in Virginia where "taking the cure" could be done in pleasant natural surroundings among congenial people. Now thousands of middle-class people followed them, again rationalizing

M. A. LESEM'S
Kneipp Sanitarium
FOR THE CURE OF ACUTE AND
CHRONIC DISEASES

2467 First Street   San Diego, Cal.

*An advertisement for M. A. Lesem's Kneipp Sanitarium
in San Diego.*

their desire for relaxation by extolling the health benefits of their holiday.

Leisure and the Working Class

Workingpeople could not afford to take off a week for the mountains or seaside. However, leisure came to play a part in their lives, too. Great urban greens, beginning with New York's magnificent Central Park, provided free relief on weekends for the teeming masses of the city's slums. Workingpeople in large cities were also able to enjoy themselves at the commercial "amusement parks" that sprang up as a means by which trolley car companies could exploit their investments to the fullest.

Traction companies made a profit only from those parts of their lines that traversed the crowded parts of the cities and then only on workdays. However, the expense of center-city real estate required them to build their sprawling car barns (storage and repair facilities) outside the city. If they were not required by law to run trolleys on Saturday and Sunday, they still wanted to make constant use of their expensive equipment.

In order to encourage people to ride the trolleys beyond the city centers, the traction companies encouraged the construction of amusement parks "at the end of the line" or, in many cases, built "playlands" themselves. Perhaps the most famous was New York's Coney Island, located on the ocean in Brooklyn. The

fare from downtown New York was five cents with children riding free. Once there, for a dollar or two, a large family could ride the mechanical amusements, such as George C. Tilyou's Bounding Billows, Barrel of Love, and Human Roulette Wheel. They could imitate Buffalo Bill at shooting galleries, visit sideshows and exotic "Somali Villages," or simply loll on the beach with a picnic lunch or "a weird-looking sausage muffled up in two halves of a roll."

These homely pleasures were as exciting to workingpeople as was a trip to Saratoga to the new middle class. Most important, Coney Island, Philadelphia's Willow Grove, Boston's Paragon Park, and Chicago's Cheltenham Beach represented an organized industry. Since the amusement parks manufactured and merchandised leisure time, they marked a sharp break with traditional forms of recreation.

Working-class leisure was more frankly devoted to simple "fun" than were the middle-class Chautauquas. Nevertheless, insistence that even a day at Coney Island was educational and healthful demonstrated the pervasiveness of traditional ideals. Sordid sideshows were touted with moralistic spiels. Knocking over weighted bottles for a prize of a Kewpie doll was defined as honing a valuable skill. Even suggestive dancing by "hoochie-koochie girls" such as Fatima, the sensation of the Chicago World's Fair of 1893 who toured the country for a decade, was described as glimpses into the culture of the Turkish Empire. A writer in prim *Harper's Weekly* approved of the "trolley parks" because they were "great breathing-places for millions of people in the city who get little fresh air at home." In a nation that was not yet free of its Calvinistic past, every hour must have a purpose.

The First Fitness Craze

Good health was also the rationale for a series of sporting manias that swept over the United States at the turn of the century. To some extent, the concern for bodily health was a contribution of German immigrants, whose *Turnvereins*, clubs devoted to calisthenics, were old-country carry-overs like democratic socialism and beer gardens. However, it was obvious as early as the mid-nineteenth century that the urban population walked less and got less exercise generally than had its farmer forebears. In the first issue of the *Atlantic Monthly* in 1858, Thomas Wentworth Higginson asked, "Who in this community really takes exercise? Even the mechanic confines himself to one set of muscles; the blacksmith acquires strength in his right arm, and the dancing teacher in his left leg. But the professional or businessman, what muscles has he at all?" Only a society with plenty of spare time could ask such a question.

Croquet, archery, and tennis, all imported from England, enjoyed a vogue in the 1870s. Roller skating was even more popular. Great rinks like San Francisco's Olympian Club, with 5,000 pairs of skates to rent and a 69,000-square-foot floor, charged inexpensive fees that were within reach of all but the poorest people. But no sporting fad was so widespread as bicycling.

Bicycles

Briefly during the 1860s, French "dandy horses" were seen on American city streets. These crude wooden vehicles were powered by pushing along the ground. About 1876, the "bone crusher," with its six-foot-high front wheel, made its appearance; by 1881, when the League of American Wheelmen was founded, more than 20,000 intrepid young Americans were devoting their idle hours to pedaling furiously about parks and city streets.

While some praised bicycling as a "health-giving outdoor exercise," moralists condemned the sport for promoting easy, informal relations between young people of the opposite sex. While young men and ladies might leave home for a Sunday ride in proper groups of their own sex, they found it easy to strike up casual acquaintances in parks far from the eyes of parents and chaperones. More than one worried preacher thought that the bicycle was a first step toward moral chaos.

Indeed, it was on the pneumatic tires of the bicycle that many emancipated young women of the 1890s escaped into a refreshing new freedom. The "safety bicycle," which had much the same design as bicycles today, took the risk of broken bones out of the sport. On Sundays, the streets were full of them, and a goodly number carried young women in candy-striped blouses with billowing sleeves, sporty broad-brimmed hats, and full free-flowing skirts.

The Gibson Girl

The "new look" woman of the 1890s took the name of the "Gibson Girl" after the popular magazine illustrator, Charles Dana Gibson, who "invented" her. Gibson's vision of ideal American womanhood charmed the nation from Newport high society to working-class suburbs. The Gibson Girl was by no means a feminist. She took little interest in woman suffrage or other political issues. Essentially she remained an object of adoration—fine-featured, trim, coy, flirtatious, even seductive.

The Gibson Girl was novel: she was no shrinking violet. She did not faint after the exertion of climbing a staircase. She played croquet, golf, and tennis. She rode a bicycle without chaperones. She was quite able to take care of herself; one of Gibson's favorite themes was the helplessness of young men in the hands of his self-assured young ladies.

Theodore Roosevelt's daughter, Alice, who became a national sweetheart when the popular waltz "Alice Blue Gown" was named for her, might have been sculpted by Gibson, and middle-class women adopted her style. Photographs of mill girls leaving textile factories in Massachusetts and of stenographers in offices in New York reveal an air of Gibson Girl self-assurance. The new independence of women was also indicated by the fact that they were marrying later. In 1890, the average age for a woman on her wedding day was 22, two or three years older than it had been in 1860.

Technology and the Lives of Women

Technology played a part in creating the new, active, and independent woman. The telephone, for example, permitted a familiarity with men that was forbidden to "young ladies of breeding" face to face.

Also much noted by people of the time was the fact that Bell's American Telephone and Telegraph Company turned to young ladies to handle the job of con-

New York's Coney Island amusement park in 1896.

necting callers to each other. The company fired the young men whom it originally had hired because their conversation on the wires was flippant and occasionally obscene; also anticipating the future, they took advantage of anonymity to shock or insult proper middle-class subscribers.

Unlike factory work, which was menial and "dirty," a job as an operator was socially acceptable for middle-class girls. In addition to finding an escape from the plush and velvet prison of the parlor, thousands of women earned an income independent of their parents' or husbands'. Alexander Graham Bell, unknown to both parties, was a partner with American feminists in their movement to emancipate women.

The Changing Office

Another invention that created jobs for women, and therefore a sense of independence, was the typewriter. Because handwriting was often illegible, and potentially costly in business, dozens of inventors had taken a stab at creating a "writing machine." But the first practical—easily manufactured and reliable—typewriter was perfected only in 1867 by Christopher Latham Sholes, and first marketed in 1874 by the Remington Arms Company, a firearms manufacturer in search of a product with which to diversify its interests.

Before the use of the machine became standard in business, almost all secretaries were men. They not only wrote letters for their employers, but they ran various errands and sometimes represented the boss. The typewriter made it possible for businessmen to split the secretarial profession into assistant and typist. Men continued to perform the more responsible and better-paid job, rising to a status that would be described as "junior executive" today. The mechanical task of transcribing letters and business records into type went to women.

Like the job of telephone operator, that of typist did not require the higher education that was available to only the wealthiest women. It was not heavy labor, an important consideration in an age that defined respectable young ladies as "delicate." And the job did not usually involve much responsibility, which nineteenth-century men were disinclined to allot to women.

The typewriter created secretarial jobs for women in large business offices where formerly all employees were male.

classes avidly followed the fortunes of the nearest "Ivy League" team. Basketball, which was invented in 1891 by Dr. James Naismith, a physical-education instructor who was looking for a sport that his students could play during the rigorous Massachusetts winter, was still in its infancy. The spectator sports that obsessed Americans were baseball and boxing. Both had evolved from traditional folk recreations, but by the end of the nineteenth century, both already were organized as money-making enterprises.

SPORTS

The turn of the century was also a golden age of organized sport. Although football (with somewhat different rules from today) was a game played almost exclusively by university students, people of all social

---

DAMN TELEPHONE!

Bell's telephone company quickly opted for young ladies as operators because it was assumed that they would be more refined and less mischievous than the boys whom Bell first hired for the job. Soon, the burden for polite language was on the customer. On December 26, 1882, A. H. Pugh of Cincinnati was angered by his inability to get a connection and told the operator, "If you can't get the party I want you to, you may shut up your damn telephone." The company canceled Pugh's service and took his phone. He sued to get it back, but the court ruled that it was reasonable and legal to penalize a man who said "damn" to a young lady on the phone.

SCOTT JOPLIN (1868–1917)

Ragtime composer Scott Joplin.

The music of the good old days at the turn of the twentieth century was ragtime, and its foremost practitioner and composer was a Texarkana-born black man named Scott Joplin. Many of the popular histories do not say that. They attribute the birth of the syncopated style of music that both delighted and enraged Americans to Irving Berlin and his "Alexander's Ragtime Band" of 1911. But Berlin was rather late in composing ragtime, and it was not even he who popularized it. Scott Joplin put the music into more than 1 million American parlors with the "Maple Leaf Rag," which was published by John Stark in Sedalia, Missouri, in 1899. "Maple Leaf Rag" sold over 1 million copies of sheet music, perhaps more than any other piece of purely instrumental music. (Joplin wrote words to the song only later.)

Both the Texas and Arkansas sides of the state-line town of Texarkana claim to be Joplin's birthplace. His father was an ex-slave who urged his children to learn a trade, which was about the only realistic means that a black person had of ensuring comfort and security in the South or the North in the late nineteenth century. It was the course of action that, during the 1890s, Booker T. Washington codified into a gospel.

By the 1890s, however, Scott Joplin's life had taken another turn, which he attributed to the fact that his mother, who had been born free in Kentucky, worked as a laundress for several white families in Texarkana.

It was through his mother that Scott's reputation as a musical prodigy became known among the city's whites. The Joplin family was musical; there were any number of cheap instruments around their house, and all the children learned to play at least one. Before he was seven years old, Scott had mastered the bugle and guitar. Then he discovered the piano, and within months he was the talk of his mother's employers. A German music teacher who heard him play was so impressed that he gave Scott lessons for free. It was through his teacher, Joplin said, that he was introduced to and instilled with love for the great European composers for piano, a professional expertise rare among blacks of the era.

By the time he was fourteen, Scott's single-minded dedication to music caused a violent rift between him and his father that may never have been healed. Rather than give up the piano and take up a trade, Scott left home. Thus began an obscure period of his life that, however, can be conjectured.

There was only one class of establishment in which a black musicmaker could make a living. Through the 1880s and early 1890s, Joplin was "the professor," as pianists were called, in saloons, gambling casinos, and brothels (then called honky-tonks) up and down the Mississippi Valley and as far west as Oklahoma City. He played in the fanciest and highest-priced houses, such as Lulu White's famous "high yellow house" in New Orleans and Mother Johnson's lavish brothel in St. Louis. He also remembered playing some wretched dives that were run by madams with names like Ready Money, Suicide Queen, and Scarface Mary. What was just a living for many "professors," however, was an education for Joplin. Already a capable classical pianist and familiar with the black musical tradition, he mastered the sentimental themes that were popular among whites and became acquainted with other southern regional forms from other black professors.

For a few years during the early 1890s, Joplin toured with a group that included two of his brothers and appeared as far east as Syracuse, New York, where he published one of several waltzes. Then, however, he went to Sedalia, Missouri, to attend the George R. Smith College for Negroes (probably to sharpen his knowledge of the classics, for such institutions regarded the folk music of the black people as beneath them). While a student, Joplin continued to play the honky-tonks, and it was after a Sedalia honky-tonk, the Maple Leaf Club, that he named the composition that made him financially independent.

Already by 1900, when Joplin and his publisher struck it rich and moved to St. Louis, ragtime was sweeping the nation, displacing the waltzes of the Gay Nineties as naturalism displaced romanticism in literature. Only a few people realized, however, that the form was more than a novelty, particularly in the hands of Scott Joplin. With his formal training in the classics, Joplin did precisely what Mozart, Chopin, Brahms, and Dvořák had done. He applied his knowledge to the rhythms and structures of folk dances, especially the cakewalk and two-step favored by southern blacks. English music critic Arnold Bennett understood Joplin's intent and acidly criticized his American colleagues for condemning ragtime as "nigger whorehouse music." The trouble, Bennett wrote, was that "the American dilettanti never did and never will look in the right quarters for vital art. A really original artist struggling under their very noses has small chance of being recognized by them, the reason being that they are imitative with no real opinion of their own." Indeed, the name *ragtime* (which Joplin did not particularly like) was originally pejorative, signifying music that had been carelessly stitched together.

While he continued to write rags, tangos, and waltzes, in order to support himself, Joplin was developing ideas with which to overcome the prejudices of American critics and make a lasting contribution to American music. In music critic Rudi Blech's words, Joplin was aiming at a musical form that was "respectful of but not subservient to European music, a racially balanced music."

In 1902, he wrote a folk ballet, *The Ragtime Dance,* which was performed once in Sedalia, and then forgotten. In 1913, he applied for a copyright for an opera, *A Guest of Honor,* but either because he never found a libretto that satisfied him or because he quarreled with his friend and publisher John Stark, the opera was never published and has been lost.

In 1916, when his second wife was forced to commit him to an insane asylum (Joplin had contracted syphilis, probably as a professor), he was said to have been working on a symphony that synthesized European form with melody and rhythm of African origin. If so, this symphony also has been lost. However, *Treemonisha,* another unfinished opera, did survive. Following the revival of interest in Joplin's music after the popular movie *The Sting* used another of his compositions, "The Entertainer," as a theme, *Treemonisha* was produced in Atlanta. The unpolished opera excited many music critics with its bold attempt to use rag, barbershop-quartet harmonies, "country music," spirituals, and Negro work chants in an operatic setting. And yet, it was unfinished and unpolished. In the end, Joplin failed in his great mission.

Oddly, Joplin died just as the musical form that had supported him well, if not lavishly, was dying out. By the end of the First World War, ragtime had gone out of style in the United States. Essentially European musical comedy replaced it in eastern music halls, while driving New Orleans jazz, known today as "Dixieland," came into vogue among blacks and the venturesome white "flaming youth" of the 1920s. Because New Orleans jazz was more sophisticated than ragtime, allowing considerably more room for creativity, it is impossible not to wonder what Joplin might have done had he not died in 1917 at the age of 49.

The first World Series in 1903 was played between Boston and Pittsburgh.

The National Pastime

Baseball developed out of two ancient children's games, rounders and town ball, which had been brought to the United States by English immigrants. According to Albert G. Spalding, a professional pitcher for clubs in Boston and Chicago, systematic rules for the sport were first drafted by Abner Doubleday of Cooperstown, New York, in 1839. The story appears to be poppycock. Doubleday may never have invested a minute thinking about the game, and the tale may have been devised by Spalding to promote the sporting goods manufacturing company that made him a millionaire. In reality, there was little agreement on a number of important rules until after the Civil War.

While many towns organized teams to play neighbors on special occasions, the professional sport emerged from upper-class baseball "clubs" such as the New York Knickerbockers. Soon concerned more with defeating rivals than with enjoying an afternoon of exercise, the clubs began to hire (at first secretly and despite noisy protest) long-hitting and fast-pitching working-class boys to wear their colors. In 1869, however, the first openly professional team, the Cincinnati Red Stockings, went on tour and defeated all comers.

When people proved willing by the thousands to pay admission fees to see the difficult game played well, businessmen in most eastern and midwestern cities organized other professional teams, and in 1876, the National League was founded. Other major leagues came and went, including one in which the players themselves, feeling exploited, tried to organize a co-operative association. The American League, "the junior circuit," dates from 1901, and the first World Series was played in 1903.

Teams became focal points of civic pride. Important games often received more attention in the newspapers than did foreign wars. After Brooklyn became a borough of New York City in 1898, its baseball team, the Trolley Dodgers, became the former city's sole symbol of an independent identity, its antidote to the Brooklyn Bridge.

Boxing and American Society

Watching a fight between two strong men may be humanity's oldest diversion. In 1867, because boxing was becoming a "manly art" practiced by the upper class, an English sportsman, the marquis of Queensberry, devised a code of rules that was quickly adopted throughout Europe and the United States. The Queensberry rules hardly made for a gentle sport. One read that "all attempts to inflict injury by gouging or tearing the flesh with the fingers or nails and biting shall be deemed foul."

As with baseball, the opportunities to make money from paid admissions encouraged promoters to search out popular heroes. The first to win a national reputation was a burly Boston Irishman named John L. Sullivan, who started out by traveling the country and offering $50 and later $1,000 to anyone who could last four rounds with him. Between 1882 and 1892, "the Boston Strong Boy" bloodied one challenger after another, personally collecting as much as $20,000 a fight and making much more for the entrepreneurs who organized his bouts.

The crowds that watched great championship bouts and most baseball games included comparatively few workingpeople. However, they followed their heroes in the new sports pages of the newspapers, which, as with baseball, devoted column after column to important fights. Because Sullivan and his successor as heavyweight champion, Gentleman Jim Corbett, were Irish, they became objects of ethnic pride. So entangled in the culture did the sport become that when a black boxer rose to the top, he caused an anxiety that reached into the halls of Congress.

Jack Johnson

Blacks played baseball with whites during the earliest professional years. The catcher on a team that toured the world in the 1880s was black. However, the same wave of racism that initiated the Jim Crow Laws in the 1890s led to the segregation of the sport. It was a first baseman from Iowa, Adrian "Cap" Anson, who led the fight to keep black players out of major league ball.

Black boxers did fight whites and, in 1908, Jack Johnson won the heavyweight crown and proceeded to batter every challenger who stepped forth. Such a feat by a black man rankled many white Americans. Johnson aggravated the hatred for him by gleefully insulting every "great white hope" who emerged. A tragically indiscreet man, he flaunted his white mistresses at a time when the color line was being clearly drawn in every American institution.

Southern states, which has been the most hospitable to professional prize fights, forbade Johnson to fight within their borders. Politicians raved at every Johnson victory and gaudy public appearance. Congress actually passed a law that prohibited the interstate shipment of a film of Johnson's victory over former champion Jim Jeffries in Reno in 1910. Finally, in 1912, racism defeated him not in the ring but through an indictment under the Mann Act, which forbade "transporting women" across state lines "for immoral purposes." (Johnson had taken his common-law wife to another state.)

Johnson fled to Europe, and then to the West Indies. But he was unhappy away from home and agreed to fight the white boxer Jess Willard in Havana in 1915. He lost, and it was widely believed that he threw the match as part of a deal with the Justice Department by which he could reenter the United States without fear of arrest. A famous photograph of the knockout shows Johnson on his back, apparently relaxed and unhurt, and shielding his eyes from the Caribbean sun. Jack had his last jibe at good-old-days society, but the days were good enough for the white middle class that few people noticed.

For Further Reading

Overviews and Classics

Vincent P. DeSantis, *The Shaping of Modern America, 1877–1916* (1973)
Ray Ginger, *The Age of Excess* (1965)
William L. O'Neill, *The Progressive Years: America Comes of Age* (1975)
Mark Sullivan, *Our Times* (1926–35)
Robert H. Wiebe, *The Search for Order, 1880–1920* (1967)

Valuable Special Studies

Frederick Lewis Allen, *The Big Change* (1952)
Van Wyck Brooks, *The Confident Years, 1885–1915* (1952)
G. W. Chessman, *Governor Theodore Roosevelt* (1965)
Carl M. Degler, *At Odds: Women in the Family in America from the Revolution to the Present* (1980)
Ann Douglas, *The Feminization of American Culture* (1977)
Foster R. Dulles, *America Learns to Play* (1940)
Ray Ginger, *Altgeld's America: The Lincoln Ideal and Changing Realities* (1958)

Otis L. Graham, Jr., *The Great Campaigns: Reform and War in America, 1900–1928* (1971)
Jack D. Kirby, *Darkness at the Dawning: Race and Reform in the Progressive South* (1972)
J. R. Krout, *Annals of American Sport* (1924)
Margaret Leech, *In the Days of McKinley* (1959)
Henry F. May, *The End of American Innocence* (1959)
H. Wayne Morgan, *William McKinley and His America* (1963)
George E. Mowry, *The Era of Theodore Roosevelt* (1958)
Steven A. Reiss, *Touching Base: Professional Baseball and American Culture in the Progressive Era* (1980)
C. Vann Woodward, *The Strange Career of Jim Crow* (1973)

Biographies and Autobiographies

John M. Blum, *The Republican Roosevelt* (1954)
W. H. Harbaugh, *Power and Responsibility: The Life and Times of Theodore Roosevelt* (1961)
Henry F. Pringle, *Theodore Roosevelt* (1931)

The Reform Impulse
The Emergence of the Progressives After 1900

In 1787, when many of his political cronies were launching the Constitution, in part because they feared social turmoil, Thomas Jefferson wrote several letters in which he said that periodic revolution was essential to the health of a free society. "A little rebellion, now and then, is a good thing," he wrote to James Madison, "as necessary in the political world as storms in the physical." To another friend a few months later he added, "The tree of liberty must be refreshed from time to time with the blood of patriots and tyrants."

Was Jefferson correct? Is significant change in the way government works brought about only when there has been a tumult among the people? Some historians have thought so. They have written that political progress depends upon the success of revolutionaries or the quaking fear of revolution among the people in power.

Other historians have looked at the history of the United States and discounted the importance of riot and rebellion. They have emphasized the stability that has characterized the American experience during an epoch of world history that has been anything but stable. Only once in two centuries has the United States been shaken by a revolution, the secession of the southern states in 1861, and it was neither progressive nor successful.

Some historians have attributed American political stability to the fact that a mechanism for

Members of the Women's Trade Union League demonstrating in New York.

change was written into the Constitution in the form of the amendment process. In the United States, as in few other countries, strict adherence to the basic instrument of government includes—or should include—an openness to change.

Just as important, for the Constitution is—or should be—amended only in matters of basic law, Americans as a people have periodically felt an impulse to rid themselves of political and social abuses, to prune the deadwood and plant anew. They have been positively impelled to change the relationship of government to society. Such a period of impulsive, even compulsive reform was the "Progressive era," the first wo decades of the twentieth century.

THE PROGRESSIVE ERA

The far-reaching changes the people called progressives demanded and, for the most part, put into effect after 1900, were not original with the new century. The movement inherited impulses and ideas from the Mugwumps, the preachers of the Social Gospel, woman suffragists, urban social workers, even the exponents of various socialistic theories of the preceding era. William Allen White oversimplified the ancestry of the reform movement he supported, but he made a point worth noticing when he wrote that the progressives "caught the Populists in swimming and stole all of their clothing except the frayed underdrawers of free silver."

What was new about the progressives was the fact that they did succeed where the Populists and the others had failed. The progressives succeeded because they appealed to a much larger and more broadly dispersed constituency than their forebears had. Indeed, the heart of the progressive constituency was the new, comparatively well educated middle class of small businessmen, professionals, and managers that industrialization had enlarged so grandly.

Who Were the Progressives?

Few progressives came from the industrial and financial elite. Few rose from the masses of laboring people and poor farmers. For the most part, the progressives were people in the middle. Those who took to the stump or typewriter and those who ran for public office were lawyers, physicians, ministers, teachers, journalists, social workers, small businessmen, white-collar managers, and the wives and daughters of the middle classes whose first reform was personal: to break free

of the nursery, parlor, and chapel in order to play a part in public life.

The progressives were acutely aware that they were "in between." Eternally knocking about in the back of the progressive mind were the assumptions that what was good about America was its middle class and that the middle class was threatened by both plutocrats from above and the potentially dangerous mob from below.

Thus, progressives objected to the immense power of the great corporations or, at least, to the way that power was used. They wanted the Rockefellers and the Morgans to be forced to behave in ways that were compatible with the good of society, as the progressives defined it.

While the progressives were concerned with the material and moral welfare of those below them on the social ladder, they also feared the masses. In the cities, progressive reformers often voiced concern that the slums were tinderboxes of anger, ready to explode in destructive anarchy. In the Midwest and West, most progressive leaders had been staunch enemies of the

The Progressives came from the new middle class such as the Drummond family, posing on the back porch of their New York home.

REFORM

What is reform? One dictionary defines it as "to change into a new and improved condition; removal of faults or abuses so as to restore to a former good state, or bring from bad to good." In the context of American history, *reform* has also come to mean peaceful, usually gradual change, as opposed to violent and sudden change, which Americans define as *revolution*.

Populists during the 1890s. William Allen White, an activist in the independent Progressive party between 1912 and 1916, had made his name as the author of a scathing manifesto of anti-Populist propaganda called "What's the Matter with Kansas?" Years later, a little sheepishly, White explained that he had written not because an idea had occurred to him in his study, but because he had been jostled on a street corner in Emporia, Kansas, by "lazy, greasy fizzles," impoverished farmers whose crudeness and vulgarity, fruits of their poverty, had offended him as their program, which had been around for years, had not.

Of Towns, WASPs, and Righteousness

The progressives' disdain for "hayseeds" also revealed their urban character. Progressivism was a movement of the cities and towns, not of the countryside. It is no coincidence that the progressive President Theodore Roosevelt remains the only chief executive in American history to have been born in a large city, New York. Even those progressives who represented rural states, such as Robert M. La Follette of Wisconsin and George Norris of Nebraska, had grown up in small towns. As boys, they had rubbed elbows with farmers, but they had not walked behind plows or milled about anxiously next to their wagons as agents weighed, graded, and put a price on the year's crop.

FILTHY LUCRE

Progressives were morally appalled by money grubbing. When he was president, Theodore Roosevelt expressed this sentiment when he tried to have "In God We Trust" deleted from American coins. "It seems to me," he wrote, "eminently unwise to cheapen such a motto by use on coins, just as it would be to cheapen it by use on postage stamps and advertisements." A few coins were struck without "In God We Trust," but Congress, failing to appreciate T.R.'s point, restored it.

A few progressive leaders were members of minority groups. Louis Brandeis, a Louisville, Kentucky lawyer who helped design the Democratic party program for reform, was Jewish. Alfred E. Smith and Robert F. Wagner, progressive politicians in New York State, were Irish and German, respectively, and devoted Roman Catholics. W. E. B. Du Bois, who supported most progressive reforms and helped to found the National Association for the Advancement of Colored People, was black. But they were exceptions. Most progressive leaders were old-stock Americans of northern European origin.

They were not a particularly broad-minded lot. The progressives inclined to be moralistic to the point of pompous self-righteousness, ever searching for the absolute right and absolute wrong in every political disagreement—and finding them. California's Hiram Johnson irked even his strongest supporters with his clenched-teeth sanctimony. Robert M. La Follette did not know what a sense of humor was. To "Fighting Bob" and to many other progressives, life was one long, holy crusade for what was right.

Theodore Roosevelt described the beginning of an election campaign in biblical terms: "We stand at Armageddon and do battle for the Lord." Lantern-jawed, unsmiling Woodrow Wilson, a Calvinist in wing collar and pince-nez could be frivolous in private. But he eventually destroyed himself because he would not yield even a little on minor disagreements with his critics in order to save the most important cause of his life.

Statism

Almost all progressives believed in the state—the government—as the chief means of improving the way America worked. Unlike many traditional American reformers who considered strong government to be part of the problem, the progressives believed that an active, assertive state was the only force that could bring the corporations to heel and provide for the welfare of the weak and unfortunate. In *The Promise of American Life,* published in 1909, Herbert Croly called for serving "Jeffersonian ends," the good of the common people, by the use of "Hamiltonian means," the power of the state. What *business* was to the industrialists, *democracy* to the Jacksonians, and *liberty* to the Founding Fathers, *government* was to the progressives: the single word that summed up the central spirit of the age.

A Coat of Many Colors

Beyond this general inclination, however, progressivism was variety, a frame of mind rather than a single

TRAINING LOBSTERS

Finley Peter Dunne, who wrote a column in Irish dialect for a Chicago newspaper, was a friend to reform, but shared few of the illusions of the progressives that improvement was an easy matter of appealing to human nature. According to his commentator, Mr. Dooley: "A man that'l expict to thrain lobsters to fly in a year is called a loonytic; but a man that thinks men can be tur-rned into angels by an iliction is called a rayformer, an' remains at large."

coherent movement. Indeed, some progressives differed from other progressives as radically as they differed from their enemies, whom they generally called "conservatives" or the "Old Guard."

For example, while many progressives believed that labor unions had the right to exist and fight for the betterment of their members, others opposed unions for the same reason that they disliked powerful corporations: organized special-interest groups were at odds with the American ideal of serving the good of the whole. On one occasion, a few leaders of the National American Woman Suffrage Association said that women should work as strikebreakers if by so doing they could win jobs currently held by men. It was a statement that would have warmed the heart of Jay Gould.

The progressives sometimes disagreed about social action such as laws that regulated child labor. By 1907, about two-thirds of the states, governed or influenced by progressives, forbade the employment of children under fourteen years of age. However, when progressives in Congress passed a federal child-labor law in 1916, the progressive President Woodrow Wilson expressed grave doubts before signing it. Wilson worried that to forbid children to work infringed on their rights as citizens. This was essentially the same reasoning

PROGRESSIVES

It makes a difference whether the word *progressive* is written with a lowercase *p* or a capital *P*. In the lowercase, *progressive* refers to the broad impulse that motivated all the many kinds of reformers during the first couple of decades of the twentieth century. A *Progressive*, however, was a member of the Progressive party, an offshoot of the Republican party, which was organized in 1912. Because there were progressives in the Democratic party—and some historians consider the Socialist party to be part of the movement—not every progressive, in a word, was a Progressive.

that was offered by the conservative Supreme Court in *Hammer* v. *Dagenhart* (1918), which struck down the law.

Many, perhaps most, progressives could not imagine blacks as full citizens. How, they asked, could a population that was 45 percent illiterate, as blacks were in 1900, contribute to an America that was based on educated citizenship? The increased oppression of blacks that began during the 1890s continued unabated during the Progressive era, sometimes furthered by white politicians who were otherwise committed to reform, such as Governor James K. Vardaman of Mississippi and Governor Jeff Davis of Arkansas.

Other progressives regarded racial prejudice and discrimination as among the worst evils afflicting America. Journalist Ray Stannard Baker wrote a scathing and moving exposé of racial segregation in a series of articles entitled "Following the Color Line." In 1910, white progressives, including Jane Addams, joined with the black Niagara Movement to form the National Association for the Advancement of Colored People. Except for his race, W. E. B. Du Bois, the guiding spirit of the Niagara Movement, was an ideal progressive: genteel, middle class, university educated, and devoted to the idea that an elite should govern. As far as blacks were concerned, a "talented tenth" would lead them to civil equality in the United States.

Some progressives were ultranationalists. Others clung to a humanism that embraced all people of all countries. Some progressives were expansionists. Senator Albert J. Beveridge of Indiana saw no conflict in calling for broadening democracy at home while urging the United States to rule colonies abroad without regard to the will of their inhabitants. Theodore Roosevelt brought reform to the White House, but he was also more of a militarist than any president who preceded him, including those who had been career generals. Other progressives were anti-imperialists. Many were isolationists who looked on Europe as a fount of corruption. Most were antimilitaristic. And a few, such as Jane Addams and William Jennings Bryan, were pacifists.

Forebears

Such a diverse movement had a diverse ancestry. From the Populists, the progressives adopted the demand for the direct election of senators; a graduated income tax that would hit the wealthy harder than the poor and middle classes; the initiative, referendum, and recall; government regulation of big business; and government ownership of local public utilities such as water, gas, and electric companies.

The progressives also hearkened back to the "good government" idealism of the Liberal Republicans and

Progressive journalist Ida Tarbell. Standard Oil executives assumed she was a gullible female reporter, but learned otherwise after she attacked John D. Rockefeller's business practices in McClure's *magazine.*

Mugwumps. Indeed, in the progressives' intense moralism, their compulsion to stamp out personal sin as well as social and political evils, they sometimes sounded like the evangelical preachers of the early nineteenth century.

In exalting expertise and efficiency, and in their belief that a new social order must be devised to replace the social chaos of the late nineteenth century, the progressives owed a debt to people whom they usually considered their enemies. Marcus A. Hanna, described as a conservative when he died in 1904, had spent half his life preaching collaboration between capital and labor as an alternative to dangerous class conflict. This was also a progressive ideal.

John D. Rockefeller, an archvillain to progressive propagandists, was the leading nineteenth-century spokesman for the rational, coordinated operation of industry. In her influential magazine articles on the "History of the Standard Oil Company," which were published in 1904, progressive journalist Ida M. Tarbell ruthlessly exposed Rockefeller's dubious business practices. But despite a deep personal antipathy for the billionaire (who had ruined her father), Tarbell could not help but admire the efficiency of his company.

Frederick W. Taylor, the inventor of "scientific management," was rarely described as a progressive and

personally took little interest in politics. Nevertheless, in his conviction that the engineer's approach to solving problems could be fruitfully applied to human behavior, he was a forebear of the progressive movement. The progressives believed that society could be engineered as readily as Taylor engineered machine tools and the way a man wielded a shovel.

PROGRESSIVES IN ACTION

Progressivism began on the municipal level. In the last years of the nineteenth century, capitalizing on widespread disgust with the corruption that had become endemic to American city government, a number of reform mayors were elected. They were not, as had been their predecessors, easily ousted after a year or two.

"Good Government"

One of the first of the new city reformers was Hazen S. Pingree, a shoe manufacturer who was elected mayor of Detroit in 1890. He spent seven years battling the corrupt alliance between the owners of the city's public utilities and Detroit councilmen.

In nearby Toledo, Ohio, another businessman, Samuel M. Jones, ran for mayor as a reformer in 1897. Professional politicians mocked Jones as an addleheaded eccentric. He ran his factory on the basis of fair treatment of employees, and shared profits with them. Other capitalists laughed at "Golden Rule" Jones, a nickname that stuck. But it did him no harm at the polls. He won the election and proved to be a skillful administrator. Within two years, he rooted graft out of Toledo's city hall.

Another progressive mayor from Ohio was Cleveland's Thomas L. Johnson. A former single-tax advocate, Johnson was elected in 1901. Not only did he clean up a dirty government, but he actively supported woman suffrage, reformed the juvenile courts, took over public utilities from avaricious owners, and put democracy to work by presiding over open "town meetings" at which citizens could make known their grievances and suggestions.

Lincoln Steffens, a staff writer for *McClure's* magazine, called Cleveland "the best-governed city in the United States," and Steffens was the expert. In 1903, he authored a sensational series of articles for *McClure's* called "The Shame of the Cities." Researching his subject carefully in the country's major cities, he named grafters, exposed corrupt connections between elected officials and dishonest businessmen, and demonstrated how ordinary people suffered from corrupt government in the quality of their daily lives.

Journalist Lincoln Steffens, pioneer of investigative journalism, exposed corrupt practices in America's big cities.

Steffens's exposés hastened the movement for city reform. Joseph W. Folk of St. Louis, whose tips put Steffens onto the story, was able to indict more than 30 politicians and prominent Missouri businessmen for bribery and perjury as a result of the outcry that greeted "The Shame of the Cities." Hundreds of reform mayors elected after 1904 owed their success to the solemn, bearded journalist.

The Muckrakers

No single force was more important in spreading the gospel of progressivism than the mass-circulation magazines. Already well established by the turn of the century thanks to their cheap price and lively style, journals such as *McClure's, The Arena, Collier's, Cosmopolitan,* and *Everybody's* became even more successful when their editors discovered the popular appetite for the journalism of exposure.

The discovery was almost accidental. Samuel S. McClure himself had no particular interest in reform. He just wanted to sell more magazines so that he could woo more paying advertisers. He hired Ida M. Tarbell

and Lincoln Steffens at generous salaries not because they were reformers, but because they wrote well. But when Tarbell's and Steffens's exposés caused circulation to soar, McClure and other editors were hooked.

The mass-circulation magazines soon brimmed with sensational revelations about corruption in government, chicanery in business, social evils like child labor and prostitution, and other subjects that lent themselves to indignant, excited treatment. In addition to his series on racial segregation, Ray Stannard Baker dissected the operations of the great railroads. John Spargo, an English-born Socialist, discussed child labor in "The Bitter Cry of the Children." David Graham Phillips, who later succeeded as a novelist dealing with social themes, revealed that the United States Senate, elected by state legislatures, had become a kind of "millionaires' club."

Theodore Roosevelt called the new journalists "muckrakers" after a character in John Bunyan's religious classic of 1678, *Pilgrim's Progress.* The writers were so busy raking through the muck of American society, he said, that they failed to look up and see its glories in the stars.

He had a point, especially when after a few years the quality of exposure journalism deteriorated into sloppy research and wild, ill-founded accusations made for the sake of attracting attention. During the first decade of the century, no fewer than 2,000 articles and books of exposure were published. Inevitably, the conscientious muckrakers ran out of solid material, and muckraking as a profession attracted incompetent hacks and sensation-mongers.

But the dirt could be real enough, and the early reform journalists were as determined to stick to the facts as to arouse their readers' indignation. Their work served to transmit the reform impulse from one end of the country to the other. The ten leading muckraking journals had a combined circulation of 3 million. Because the magazines were also read in public libraries and barbershops, and just passed around, the readership was many times larger.

In the Jungle with Upton Sinclair

Upton Sinclair was probably the most influential muckraker of all. A young, obscure socialist, in 1906 he wrote a novel about how ethnic prejudice and economic exploitation in Chicago turned a Lithuanian immigrant into a revolutionary who was determined to smash the capitalist system. *The Jungle* was too radical for the mass-circulation magazines, and Sinclair had to turn to a Socialist party weekly newspaper, the *Appeal to Reason,* to find an audience. Even the *Appeal* had a large subscription list. One issue sold over 1 million copies, and *The Jungle* was a mighty success, reaching even the desk of President Roosevelt. It sold 100,000 copies in book form, an extraordinary figure at the time.

Sinclair's book may have converted a few of its readers to socialism although its literary quality decayed rapidly in the final chapters when the character, Jurgis, makes his momentous decision. However, the passages that made it a best seller were those that luridly described the conditions under which meat was processed in Chicago slaughterhouses. *The Jungle* publicized well-documented tales of rats ground up into sausage, workers with tuberculosis coughing on the meat they packed, and filth at every point along the disassembly line.

"I aimed at the nation's heart," Sinclair later said ruefully, "and hit it in the stomach." He meant that within months of the publication of *The Jungle*, a federal meat-inspection bill that had been languishing in Congress was rushed through under public pressure and promptly signed by President Roosevelt. It and a second Pure Food and Drug Act, which forbade food processors to use dangerous adulterants (the pet project of a chemist in the Agriculture Department, Dr. Harvey W. Wiley), expanded government power in a way that had been inconceivable a few years earlier.

Efficiency and Democracy

The spread of the city-manager system of government was scarcely less dramatic. The first town to adopt the plan was Staunton, Virginia, in 1908. The small city abolished the office of mayor. The voters elected a city council, which then hired a nonpolitical, professionally trained administrator to serve as city manager. The progressives reasoned that democracy was protected by the people's control of the council; and because the daily operations of the city were supervised by an executive who was free of political influence, they would be carried out without regard to special interests.

It was an original notion, but did not prove universally successful. Nevertheless, by 1915, only seven years after Staunton's experiment, over 400 mostly medium-size cities had adopted it.

The "Oregon system" was the brainchild of one of the first progressives to make an impact at the state level. William S. U'ren, a former Populist and single taxer, believed that the remedy for corruption in government was simple: more democracy. The trouble lay in the ability of efficient, well-organized, and wealthy special interests to thwart the good intentions of the people. Time after time, U'ren pointed out, elected officials handily forgot their campaign promises and worked closely with the corporations to pass bad laws or defeat good ones.

In 1902, U'ren persuaded the Oregon legislature to adopt the initiative, recall, and referendum. The Oregon system also included the first primary law. It took the power to nominate candidates for public office away from the bosses and gave it to the voters. Finally, U'ren led the national movement to choose United States senators by popular vote rather than in the state legislatures.

U'ren lived to the ripe old age of 90, long enough to see 20 states adopt the initiative and 30, the referendum. A number of progressive states also instituted primaries of one kind or another, but until the 1970s, the primary was a less popular idea. In the South, the "white primary," by which Democratic party candidates were chosen, was used in the interests of racism: since most whites were Democrats, the primary was the contest that counted; and because the primary was an election within a private organization, blacks could be legally excluded from it.

"Fighting Bob" and the Wisconsin Idea

The career of Wisconsin's "Fighting Bob" La Follette is almost a history of progressivism in itself. Born in 1855, he studied law and served three terms as a Republican in Congress before 1890. He showed few signs of the crusader's compulsion until a prominent Republican offered him a bribe to fix the verdict in a trial. La Follette flew into a rage at the shameless audacity of the suggestion, and he never quite calmed down for the rest of his life.

In 1900, he ran for governor in defiance of the Republican organization, attacking the railroad and lumber interests that dominated the state. He promised to devote the resources of the government to the service of the people and his timing was perfect. A state that recently had rebuffed the Populists was ready for reform, and La Follette was elected.

As governor, he pushed through a comprehensive system of regulatory laws that required every business that touched the public interest to conform to clear-cut rules and submit to close inspection of its operations. He went beyond the negative, or regulatory, powers of government to create agencies that provided positive services for the people. La Follette's "Wisconsin idea" held that in the complex modern world, people and government needed experts to work on their behalf. A railroad baron could not be kept on a leash unless the government had the support of knowledgeable specialists who were as canny as the railroad men. Insurance premiums could not be held at reasonable levels unless the state was able to determine what

Robert La Follette speaking to a crowd in Cumberland, Wisconsin, in 1897.

profit was just and what was rapacious. The government could not intervene to determine what was fair in a labor dispute unless it had the help of the labor experts and economists.

La Follette formed a close and mutually beneficial relationship with the University of Wisconsin. His organization generously supported the institution, making it one of the nation's great universities at a time when most state-supported schools were little more than poorly funded agricultural colleges. In return, distinguished professors like Richard Ely, Selig Perlman, and John Rogers Commons put their expertise at La Follette's disposal. The law school helped build up the first legislative reference library in the United States so that assemblymen would no longer have to rely on lobbyists to draft their laws.

The university's School of Agriculture not only taught future farmers, but carried out research programs that addressed problems faced daily in Wisconsin's fields and barns. La Follette even made use of the football team. When enemies hinted there would be trouble if he spoke at a political rally, he showed up in the company of Wisconsin's burly linemen, who folded their arms and surrounded the platform. There was no trouble.

Perhaps La Follette's most original contribution to progressivism was his application of machine methods to the cause of reform. He was idealistic. But he was not naive. In order to ensure that his reforms would not be reversed, he built an organization that was more finely integrated than Boss Tweed's. Party workers in every precinct got out the vote, and if they did not violate La Follette's exacting demands for honesty in public office, they were rewarded with government patronage.

In 1906, La Follette took his crusade to Washington as a United States senator. He held that office until his death in 1925, and made several unsuccessful tries at winning the presidency. In Wisconsin and elsewhere he was loved as few politicians have been. He was "Fighting Bob," incorruptible and unyielding in what he regarded as right. La Follette's thick, neatly cropped head of brown hair combed straight back, which turned snow white with years, waved wildly during his passionate speeches. He looked like an Old Testament prophet, and, in a way, La Follette devoted his life to saving the soul of American society, as Jeremiah had done for Israel.

Progressives in Other States

In New York State, Charles Evans Hughes came to prominence as a result of his investigation into public utilities and insurance companies. Tall, erect, dignified, with a smartly trimmed beard such as was going out of fashion at the turn of the century, he lacked the charisma of La Follette and other progressives. If they were humorless in their intensity, Hughes was "a cold-blooded creature" (in the words of the hot-blooded Theodore Roosevelt). But he was unshakably honest as governor of New York between 1906 and 1910.

William E. Borah was not elected to the Senate from Idaho in 1906 as a progressive. On the contrary, his career in politics had been characterized by a close and compliant relationship with the mining and ranching interests that ran the state.

Once in the Senate, however, Borah usually voted with the growing progressive bloc. This record and his isolationism—like many westerners, Borah believed that the United States was corrupted by close association with foreign powers—guaranteed his reelection until he died in office in 1940. It was discovered only a generation later that the old lion had accepted gifts of money from unlikely donors under rather dubious circumstances.

Progressivism in California

It is impossible to imagine Hiram Johnson of California accepting money other than in a spotlight so as to emphasize the perfect honesty of the transaction. He came to progressivism by much the same path as had La Follette. A prim, tight-lipped lawyer of no partic-

ATTEMPTED MURDER?

In late May 1908, Robert La Follette led a filibuster against a financial bill of which he disapproved. He spoke for nearly seventeen hours before giving up. Through much of this time, La Follette sipped a tonic of milk and raw eggs prepared in the Senate dining room. After he had been taken violently ill on the floor, it was discovered that there was enough ptomaine in the mixture to kill a man. Because no one else suffered from eating in the Senate dining room that day, many assumed that La Follette's enemies had tried to kill him.

ular distinction, Johnson won notoriety after he took over the prosecution of the corrupt political machine of Abe Ruef in San Francisco.

At first it appeared to be an ordinary graft case such as was all too common at the time. Ruef and his ally, Mayor Eugene E. Schmitz, collected payoffs from brothels, gambling dens, and thieves in return for running a wide-open city. In the wake of the great San Francisco earthquake and fire of 1906, Ruef set up a system by which all those who wished to profit from the rebuilding had to clear their plans with him. Scarcely a street could be rebuilt or a cable-car line laid out until money changed hands. On one occasion, Ruef pocketed $250,000, of which he kept one-quarter, gave one-quarter to Schmitz, and distributed the remainder among the aldermen whose votes were needed to authorize public works. Like other city bosses, Ruef also bought and sold judges in lawsuits.

Johnson discovered that Ruef not only was associated with vice and petty graft, but was intimately allied with the most powerful corporation in the state, the Southern Pacific Railroad. The distinguished and ostensibly upright directors of the Southern Pacific, men whom Johnson had admired, were tangled in a web that stretched to include profiting from the misfortune of the wretched syphilitic whores on the city's notorious Barbary Coast.

Johnson turned into "a volcano in perpetual eruption, belching fire and smoke." Never again would he assume that great wealth and a varnish of propriety indicated a decent man. His sense of personal rectitude was so great that it cost him a chance to be president. In 1920, Republican party bosses such as Johnson loathed asked him to run as vice president in order to balance the conservative presidential nominee, Warren G. Harding. Johnson turned them down in a huff. As a result, when Harding died in office in 1923, he was succeeded by the phlegmatic Calvin Coolidge instead of the volcano from California. Coolidge adulated the big businessmen whom Johnson reflexively distrusted. If ever there was an example of an individual's decision profoundly affecting the course of history, Johnson's was it.

American Socialist Eugene V. Debs speaking in Canton, Ohio.

ON THE FRINGE OF PROGRESSIVISM

Most progressives advocated municipal ownership of public utilities, but they were staunchly opposed to socialism. Indeed, progressive politicians like La Follette and Johnson warned that the reforms they proposed were necessary to preserve the institution of private property from a rising Red tide in American politics.

This message had a special urgency in the early years of the twentieth century because the Socialist party of America, founded in 1900, came very close to establishing itself as a major force in American politics. Pieced together by local Socialist organizations and embittered former Populists, the Socialist party nominated labor leader Eugene V. Debs for president in 1900, and he won 94,768 votes. In 1904, running again, Debs threw a scare into progressives and conservatives alike by polling 402,460.

The Socialists

Personally, Debs resembled progressive leaders. He was a fiery, flamboyant orator, a master of the theatrical and gymnastic style of public speaking that not only was necessary in an age when sound amplification was primitive, but was favored by Americans in their preachers and politicians. He was highly moralistic rather than intellectual. In fact, Debs freely admitted that he had little patience with the endless ideological hairsplitting with which Socialists were commonly associated. He was, however, orthodox enough a Marxist to believe sincerely that socialism was inevitable.

Debs' followers worshiped him as progressives worshiped La Follette, Borah, and Roosevelt. The adulation and loyalty accorded him made him a presidential candidate five times between 1900 and 1920. In 1912, he won almost 1 million votes, 6 percent of the total.

But Debs was not a progressive under a different name. He did not seek to smooth over the conflict between classes, but to exhort the working class to take charge. If he was more Christian than Marxist, he nevertheless agreed with Karl Marx that the class that produced wealth should decide how that wealth was to be distributed.

Victor Berger of Milwaukee linked socialism and progressivism more closely. An Austrian middle-class immigrant, Berger forged an alliance among Milwau-

kee's large German-speaking population, the labor movement, and the city's reform-minded middle class. His Social Democratic party (a part of Debs' Socialist party) soft-pedaled revolutionary rhetoric and promised Milwaukee honest government and efficient city-owned public utilities. Once he and Debs were speaking to a newspaperman, and Debs said that capitalists would not be compensated when their factories were taken from them; their "property" had been stolen from workingpeople, and theft would not be rewarded. They would be compensated, Berger interrupted. Property might well be theft; he would not frighten Americans with the specter of wild confiscation.

In 1910, Berger was elected to the House of Representatives and Socialist candidates for mayor and city council were swept into office. To more radical members of the party, Berger's "sewer socialism," a reference to his emphasis on city ownership of utilities, was nothing more than progressivism. Berger thought otherwise. He insisted that by demonstrating to the American people the Socialists' ability to govern a large city, the Socialist party would win their attention to the revolutionary part of its program.

Labor's Quest for Respectability

Berger also hoped to advance the fortunes of socialism by capturing the American Federation of Labor. Socialists were a large minority in the union movement, a majority among members who were not Roman Catholic. At the AFL's annual conventions, the Socialists challenged the conservative leadership of Samuel Gompers and several times came close to ousting him from the presidency.

In the end they always failed. Presenting a moderate face to the American people was also central to Gompers' strategy for establishing the legitimacy of the labor movement, and his version of moderation included a growing support of progressive capitalism. His glad willingness to cooperate with employers won him many friends among progressives (and some conservatives such as Mark Hanna). In 1905, President Theodore Roosevelt intervened in a strike by coal miners in effect on the strikers' side. During the William Howard Taft administration (1909–13), progressives established a Commission on Industrial Violence with a membership that was skewed in a pro-union direction. Progressive Democratic President Woodrow Wilson named Samuel Gompers to several prestigious government posts and appointed a former leader of the AFL's United Mine Workers, William B. Wilson, to be Secretary of Labor.

The union movement grew in the favorable climate of the Progressive era, but by no means sensationally. Membership in the AFL rose from about 500,000 in 1900 to 1.5 million in 1910, with some 500,000 workers holding cards in independent organizations. This was a pittance among a nonagricultural labor force of almost 20 million. The labor movement had its reformer friends, but the Progressive era was not a workingman's era.

The "Wobblies"

The most important unions outside the AFL were the very conservative Railway Brotherhoods (of Locomotive Engineers, Firemen, Brakemen, etc.) and the very radical Industrial Workers of the World, or, as members were called, "the Wobblies." Founded in 1905 by Socialists and other radicals who were disgusted by Gompers' conservatism and his reluctance to organize unskilled workers, the IWW also found friends among progressives, but more often, sent chills racing down their spines.

Progressives supported west-coast and wheatbelt Wobblies when, between 1909 and 1913, the hobo members of the union waged a series of "free speech fights" to protect their right to recruit members by speaking from streetcorner soapboxes. Progressive sensitivity to traditions of personal liberty and common

Strikers—both men and children workers—march in Lawrence, Massachusetts, 1912.

WOBBLIES

Members of the IWW were called Wobblies by both friends and enemies. There are several explanations of the origin of their name; according to one, they were so strike prone that they were "wobbly" workers. The story the IWW favored told of a Chinese restaurant operator in the Pacific Northwest who would give credit only to Wobblies because they could be depended on. When someone asked for a meal on credit, the restaurant owner, unable to pronounce the name of the letter W, asked, "I-Wobbly-Wobbly?"

A Suffragette posting bills to advertise their cause.

decency was agitated when policemen assigned to destroy the union arrested Wobblies for reading publicly from the Declaration of Independence and the Constitution. In 1912, progressive organizations, particularly women's clubs, helped the IWW win its greatest strike victory among immigrant textile mill workers in Lawrence, Massachusetts. They publicized the horrendous living conditions in Lawrence, lobbied congressmen, and took the children of strikers into their homes, a masterful public-relations ploy.

The capacity of middle-class progressives to back the Wobblies could not, however, go much beyond well-wishing. The Wobblies called loudly and gaily for revolution, precisely what progressives were determined to avoid. Although the IWW officially renounced violence, including violent sabotage, members spoke glibly about driving spikes into logs bound for sawmills and throwing hammers into the works of harvesters, threshers, and balers. And, although the first blow was more often thrown by employers than workers, fistfights, riots, and even murder characterized enough Wobbly strikes to besmirch the union's reputation.

Nor were middle-class progressives alone in considering the IWW beyond the pale. No one used fiercer language in denouncing the organization than Samuel Gompers. In 1913, Victor Berger and a prominent New York Socialist, Morris Hillquit, led a movement within the Socialist party that successfully expelled the leader of the IWW, William D. "Big Bill" Haywood, from the party's National Executive Committee.

Feminism and Progressivism

Another "-ism" with an ambivalent relationship to the progressive movement was feminism. In 1900, the struggle on behalf of equal rights for women was more than 50 years old. Despite the tireless work of leaders like Elizabeth Cady Stanton and Susan B. Anthony, the victories had been few. In their twilight years at the beginning of the Progressive era, Stanton and Anthony could look back on liberalized divorce laws, women voters in six western states, a movement unified for the moment in the National American Woman Suffrage Association, and the initiation of a new generation of leaders including Carrie Chapman Catt and Anna Howard Shaw, a British-born physician.

But the coveted prize, a constitutional amendment that would guarantee women the right to vote, seemed as remote as it had at Seneca Falls in 1848. Most articulate Americans, women as well as men, continued to believe that women's delicacy and fine moral sense made it best that they remain in a separate sphere from men. If women participated in public life, they would be sullied as men had been and lose their vital moral influence in the home.

In fact, when Anthony died in 1906, success was fewer than fifteen years away. The democratic inclinations of the progressives made it increasingly difficult for them to deny the franchise to half the American people. Even progressive leaders who had little personal enthusiasm for the idea of female voters publicly supported the cause.

The Suffrage Movement Becomes Respectable

Much more important in accounting for the victory of the suffrage movement was a fundamental shift in its appeal. Under the leadership of Carrie Chapman Catt, the National American Woman Suffrage Association came to terms with progressive prejudices and quietly shelved the comprehensive critique of women's status in American society that the early feminists had developed, including strong doubts about the institution of marriage. The suffragists also downplayed the traditional argument that women should have the right to vote because they were equal to men in every way.

A few "social feminists" clung to the old principles. Charlotte Perkins Gilman, an independently minded New Englander, argued in *Women and Economics* (1898) that marriage was itself the cause of women's inequality. Alice Paul, a Quaker like many feminists before her, insisted that the suffrage alone was not enough to solve "the woman question."

But most of the middle-class suffragists argued that women should have the right to vote precisely because

Feminist Carrie Chapman Catt, leader of the National American Woman Suffrage Association.

VOTES FOR WOMEN? T.R. SAYS: IT DOES NOT MATTER

"Personally, I believe in woman's suffrage, but I am not an enthusiastic advocate of it, because I do not regard it as a very important matter. I am unable to see that there has been any special improvement in the position of women in those states in the West that have adopted woman's suffrage, as compared to those states adjoining them that have not adopted it. I do not think that giving the women suffrage will produce any marked improvement in the condition of women. I do not believe that it will produce any of the evils feared, and I am very certain that when women as a whole take any special interest in the matter they will have suffrage if they desire it."

---

they were more moral than men. Their votes would purge society of its evils. Not only did the suffragists ingeniously turn the most compelling antisuffrage argument in their favor, but they told progressives that in allowing women to vote they would be gaining huge numbers of allies. In fact, women were in the forefront of two of the era's most important moral crusades, the struggle against prostitution and the prohibition movement.

White Slavery

To earlier generations, prostitution had been an inevitable evil that could be controlled or ignored by decent people, but not abolished. Most states, counties, and cities had laws against solicitation on the grounds that streetwalking "hookers" were a public nuisance. Somewhat fewer governments declared the quiet sale of sex to be a crime. Even where prostitution was nominally illegal, it was common to tolerate "houses of ill repute" that were discreetly operated (and usually made contributions to worthy causes such as the welfare of the police).

VOTES FOR WOMEN? A WOMAN SOCIALIST SAYS: NOT IMPORTANT

"You ask for votes for women. What good can votes do when ten-elevenths of the land in Great Britain belongs to 200,000 and only one-eleventh to the rest of the 40,000,000 population? Have your men with their millions of votes freed themselves from this injustice?"

Helen Keller to a British suffragist, 1911

THE CASUAL WORKERS

"Home, a permanent place of abode, respect of others, the decencies of right living, have neither meaning nor attraction for them," wrote the editor of the *Record*, a newspaper in the northern California farm town of Chico. He was talking about people who were familiar to everyone who lived west of the Mississippi in 1910—the hobos, otherwise known as migrant workers or casual laborers.

Most of these wandering workers were men who had no homes, families, or ties to the sort of proprieties to which the editor referred. They were essential to the economic life of the western states. They brought in the wheat from the Mississippi to Oregon; picked the fruit in the Pacific states from Washington to the Mexican border; and manned the construction crews on projects far from any town, such as the aqueduct that rerouted the Owens River 300 miles across the Mojave Desert to the thirsty metropolis of Los Angeles in southern California. They worked in canneries and lumber mills, and those with the skills were the lumberjacks in the great redwood, spruce, and Douglas fir forests of the Northwest.

Almost all this work was seasonal or temporary; a mammoth construction job like the aqueduct took years to complete, but the day came when hands were no longer needed. Therefore, the kind of worker who made his way to a job at his own expense and disappeared when the job was done was precisely the kind of worker who was called for.

Of course, the casual worker did not disappear into thin air. When there was no work, as in winter, or when he did not feel like working, the casual laborer headed for a town in which he could expect to find a "main stem" or "skid row" on which were located cheap restaurants, cheap saloons, cheap hotels, pawnshops, second-hand clothing stores, brothels, and "missions" run by evangelical religious groups.

Here was a big part of their problem. On the main stem, the hobos rubbed elbows with derelicts, and it took a practiced eye to distinguish between the two groups. The casual workers knew the difference. Whereas "tramps" wandered but did not work and "bums" did little but drink, hobos were self-sufficient workers. They held tough jobs, albeit only as long as they chose to work, and when they were down on their luck, they chopped wood, hauled water, or mowed a lawn in return for a meal. They did not beg for handouts. Hobos explained to dozens of investigators that they could usually be identified by the bedroll or "bindie" that they carried. Most of the jobs they took required them to furnish their own bedding, whereas tramps and bums had little use for it. One of the terms used to describe casual workers was "bindle-stiff."

Nevertheless, the hobos looked much the same as tramps and bums. When they were traveling by freight train (which was illegal but generally tolerated), they were dirty, in clothing just a few notches above rags, unshaven, and ripe to the nose. And they patently did not live as the "respectable classes" believed people should live. The "hobo jungle" on the outskirts of every railroad town, a camp where casual workers gathered to eat and sleep while waiting for a train, was a dangerous and forbidden place in the imagination of children and many adults as well.

The hobos believed that they were the builders of the West. "It is we," one of their songs had it, who

> Dug the mines and built the workshops, endless miles of railroad laid.
> Now we stand outcast and starving, 'mid the wonders we have made. . . .

A hobo poem caught the same sense of resentment that society should scorn them:

> He built the road,
> With others of his class, he built the road,
> Now o'er it many a mile he packs his load,
> Chasing a job, spurred on by hunger's goad,
> He walks and walks, and wonders why
> In Hell he built the road.

The casual worker considered himself to be the last frontiersman—freewheeling, independent, not "afraid of his job" but quick to quit when something about it displeased him. In other words, he was the kind of American who, already by the turn of the century, was enshrined in nostalgic myth as the best kind of American.

At the very least they were not afraid to stand up for their rights when they believed that those rights were threatened. In 1894, when Jacob Coxey led his march of the unemployed from Ohio to Washington, the "petition in boots" demanding federal action to create jobs during the depression, a contingent of western casual laborers called "Kelley's Army" set off from Oakland, traveling to Washington by freight trains that they virtually commandeered.

After the turn of the century, western migrant workers turned in large numbers to the Industrial Workers of the World to voice their grievances. Between 1909 and 1914, they fought a number of "free-speech fights" in such western towns as Missoula, Spokane, and San Diego. These actions, directed against laws that forbade street speaking on the main stem, anticipated the protest tactic of nonviolent civil disobedience that later was employed by Mohandas Gandhi in India and Martin Luther King, Jr., in the United States. By deliberately disobeying the obnoxious laws but peacefully submitting to arrest, the free speechers put the burden of law enforcement on the shoulders of the authorities.

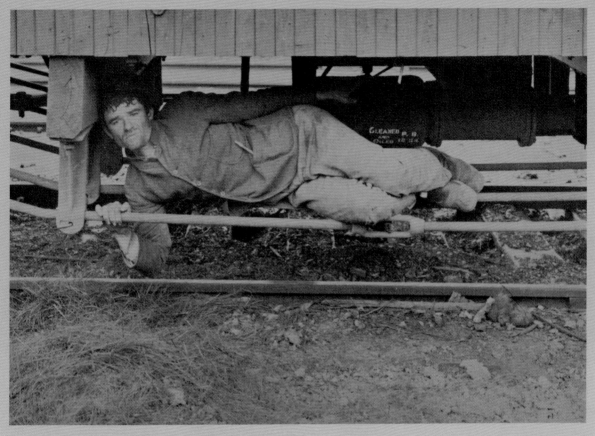

Seasonal workers and hobos used trains as a free form of transportation.

They were happy to be arrested. As long as they were in jail, the city governments had big bills to feed them, and the judicial calendars were clogged because every free speecher demanded a separate jury trial. Most of the cities in which free-speech fights were joined found it preferable to repeal the ordinances.

What happened to the army of casual workers? The virtual completion of the western railroad system eliminated many jobs. Mechanization of harvesting wheat or even picking fruit destroyed other jobs that had been filled by hobos. So did the practice of sound forestry: by farming trees and harvesting a forest in order to have a steady supply of timber ("sustained yield"), lumbermen could maintain a permanent, more reliable work force rather than send out the call for migrant workers.

Perhaps as important as anything else was the advent of the cheap automobile. By the 1920s, the used Model T Ford, which almost everyone could afford, led to the family's becoming the chief unit of the migrant work force. A family of five or six, including children, was cheaper to hire than were the homeless men who rode the rails. Moreover, with children to feed, the family was more stable as employees than was the vagabond adventurer who was not "afraid of his job."

By the 1930s, when the Great Depression caused a big jump in the number of people who were tramping the country, the working hobo was already a vanishing figure. Indeed, the work of harvesting fruit and vegetables on the west coast was becoming increasingly dependent on Mexicans who, coming from extreme poverty, could be hired even more cheaply than the solitary hobo.

Communities in which men vastly outnumbered women—cow towns, mining camps, seaports, migrant farm-worker and logging centers—typically tolerated red-light districts in a back corner of town. A stock figure of small-town folklore was the woman on the wrong side of the tracks who sold favors to those sly or bold enough to knock on her door. In the large cities, prostitution ran the gamut from lushly furnished and expensive brothels for high-society swells, such as Sally Stanford's in San Francisco, to "the cribs," tiny cubicles rented by whores who catered to working men. Because their pay was so low, thousands of New York working women moonlighted as prostitutes at least part of the time. Novelists Stephen Crane (*Maggie: A Girl of the Streets,* 1892) and Upton Sinclair (*The Jungle*) both dealt with the theme of tacitly forced prostitution.

The world's oldest profession had affronted proper people long before the Progressive era. In most places, the middle class was content to declare the trade illegal and then tolerate it out of their sight. Some cities restricted prostitution to neighborhoods far from middle-class residential areas, such as New Orleans's Storyville, San Francisco's Barbary Coast, and Chicago's South of the Loop.

The progressives, spearheaded by women's organizations, determined to wipe out the institution. During the first decade of the twentieth century, most states and innumerable communities passed strict laws against all prostitution and enforced them rigorously. In 1917, prodded by the army when it established a big training camp nearby, even wide-open Storyville, the birthplace of jazz, was officially closed. By 1920, all but a few states had an antiprostitution law on the books. Within a few more years, only Nevada, with its stubborn mining frontier outlook, continued to tolerate the institution within the law.

The Limits of Progressive Moralism

Action on the federal level was more complicated. Prostitution was clearly a matter for the police powers of the states and localities. However, progressives were

so convinced that government held the key to social reform and must act at every level that, in 1910, they joined with some conservatives to put the interstate commerce clause of the Constitution to work in the cause. Senator James R. Mann of Illinois sponsored a bill that struck against the probably exaggerated practice of procurers luring poor girls from one part of the country to become prostitutes elsewhere. The Mann Act forbade transporting women across state lines "for immoral purposes." It was this law under which boxer Jack Johnson was prosecuted.

Of course, neither local, state, nor federal law abolished prostitution. The campaign may be the best example of the progressives' excessive faith in the powers of the government. Brothels continued to operate, albeit less openly and probably with more police graft than before. Streetwalkers, previously the most despised and degraded of whores, became the norm be-

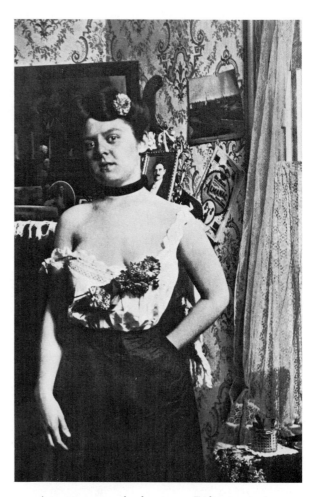

A prostitute poses for the camera. Ending prostitution became a goal of the progressives and members of the women's movement in the early 1900s.

cause they were less easily arrested. Wealthy men continued to maintain paid mistresses and created the "call girl," a prostitute who stayed at home until "called" by a hotel employee or pimp who worked the streets and hotel lobbies.

Prohibitionism

The nineteenth-century impulse to combat the evils of drink never quite died. Temperance advocates and outright prohibitionists had battled back and forth with the distillers of liquor and with ordinary people who simply enjoyed a cup of good cheer. By 1900, however, anti-alcohol crusaders were emphasizing social arguments over their moral distaste for drunkenness and, in so doing, won widespread progressive support.

The prohibitionists pointed out that the city saloon was often the local headquarters of the corrupt political machines. Close the saloons, the reasoning went, and the bosses would be crippled. Moreover, generally overlooking the fact that poverty caused a widespread drinking problem among the working classes, the prohibitionists argued that the misery of the working classes was the result of husbands and fathers spending their wages on demon rum and John Barleycorn. Because the public bar was then an all-male institution, the temperance movement formed a close alliance with feminists.

Carry Nation of Kansas was one woman who suffered her whole life with a drunken husband and poverty. Beginning in 1900, she launched a campaign of direct action, leading hatchet-wielding women into saloons where, before the bewildered eyes of saloonkeeper and customers, they methodically chopped the place to pieces.

Frances Willard, head of the Woman's Christian Temperance Union, opposed such tactics. She and her followers also entered saloons, but instead of breaking them up, they attempted to shame drinkers by kneeling to pray quietly in their midst. In addition, the WCTU turned to politics, supporting woman suffrage for its own sake as well as for the purpose of winning the final victory over liquor.

Increasing numbers of progressives adopted the reform. Only in the big cities, mostly in the eastern states, did socially minded politicians like Alfred E. Smith and Robert Wagner of New York actively fight the prohibitionists. The large Roman Catholic and Jewish populations of the cities had no religious tradition against alcohol; on the contrary they used wine as a part of religious observance. Elsewhere, libertarian progressives argued that the government had no right to interfere with the individual decision of whether or not to drink.

Nevertheless, the possibilities of moral improvement, of striking a blow against poverty, and of joining battle against the political manipulations of the big distillers and brewers converted many progressives to prohibition, and in the waning days of the movement (though they were not thought to be waning at the time), they had their way.

For Further Reading

Overviews and Classics

Vincent P. DeSantis, *The Shaping of Modern America, 1877–1916* (1973)

William L. O'Neill, *The Progressive Years: America Comes of Age* (1975)

Robert H. Wiebe, *The Search for Order, 1880–1920* (1967)

Valuable Special Studies

John D. Buenker, *Urban Liberalism and Progressive Reform* (1973)

D. M. Chalmers, *The Social and Political Ideas of the Muckrakers* (1964)

Carl M. Degler, *At Odds: Women in the Family in America from the Revolution to the Present* (1980)

Arthur Ekirch, *Progressivism in Practice* (1974)

Louis Filler, *Crusaders for American Liberalism* (1939)

Lewis L. Gould, *Reform and Regulation: American Politics, 1900–1916* (1978)

Otis L. Graham, Jr., *The Great Campaigns: Reform and War in America, 1900–1928* (1971)

Samuel T. Hays, *Conservation and the Gospel of Efficiency: The Progressive Conservation Movement, 1890–1920* (1959)

Richard Hofstadter, *The Age of Reform* (1955)

David M. Kennedy, *Birth Control: The Career of Margaret Sanger* (1970)

Jack D. Kirby, *Darkness at the Dawning: Race and Reform in the Progressive South* (1972)

Gabriel Kolko, *The Triumph of Conservatism* (1963)

Christopher Lasch, *The New Radicalism in America* (1965)

Roy Lubove, *The Progressives and the Slums* (1962)

George E. Mowry, *The California Progressives* (1951)

William L. O'Neill, *Everyone Was Brave: The Rise and Fall of Feminism* (1969)

Jean Quandt, *From the Small Town to the Great Community: The Social Thought of Progressive Intellectuals* (1970)

James H. Timberlake, *Prohibition and the Progressive Movement, 1900–1920* (1963)

James Weinstein, *The Corporate Ideal in the Liberal State, 1900–1918* (1968)

Robert H. Wiebe, *Businessmen and Reform* (1962)

Biographies and Autobiographies

John M. Blum, *The Republican Roosevelt* (1954)

W. H. Harbaugh, *Power and Responsibility: The Life and Times of Theodore Roosevelt* (1961)

R. S. Maxwell, *La Follette and the Rise of Progressivism in Wisconsin* (1956)

Henry F. Pringle, *Theodore Roosevelt* (1931)

Standing at Armageddon
The Progressives in Power, 1901–1916

By 1904, the impulse to reform had coalesced into a potent political movement. Progressivism commanded the allegiance of a large bloc of senators and congressmen from both major parties and could claim as a leader none other than the chief executive, Theodore Roosevelt.

The irony that he, a scion of an old and privileged family, should lead a popular protest movement was not lost on T.R. In a letter to his equally aristocratic and decidedly nonprogressive friend, Senator Chauncey Depew of New York, who was at the same time chairman of the New York Central Railroad, Roosevelt wrote in mock weariness: "How I wish I wasn't a reformer, Oh Senator! But I suppose I must live up to my part, like the Negro minstrel who blackened himself all over!"

In fact, it was not so bizarre that T.R. should have disdained the newly rich and powerful industrial capitalists who were the progressives' villains. Roosevelt recognized their energies and organizational skills as essential in a healthy, dynamic society, but as an heir to "old money" (and not so very much of it) the president believed that the "malefactors of great wealth" occasionally needed a brusque reminder that they had better. Moreover, despite the sigh of fatalism in his letter to Depew, Roosevelt loved to be in the thick of things, and during T.R.'s nearly eight years in the White House, reform was the bully, tangled thick.

Theodore Roosevelt speaking at Newcastle, Wyoming, in 1903.

T.R. TAKES OVER

Roosevelt moved cautiously at first. He knew that the Republican bosses regarded him as a "damned cowboy" and that through 1901, at least, they were more powerful than he. Mark Hanna made no secret of the fact that he was discussing the possibility of contesting the 1904 Republican nomination with T.R., and the Republican machine remained in the hands of bosses like Tom Platt.

By February 1904, when Hanna died suddenly, he had already been outridden by the cowboy and Platt's power was on the decline. Not only was the president's personal popularity immense, but Roosevelt quietly had replaced members of the Old Guard with his own men in middle-level government positions, eased out the McKinley-Hanna mediocrities in his cabinet, and won the loyalty of the able holdovers by reorganizing their departments in a way that gave them an authority and autonomy that they previously had not enjoyed. Among those whom he kept in office were Secretary of State John Hay; Secretary of War Elihu Root, who succeeded Hay in the State Department in 1905; Attorney General Philander C. Knox; Secretary of the Interior E. A. Hitchcock; and Secretary of Agriculture James Wilson. All were competent men. Roosevelt had an eye for competence in his subordinates.

Busting Taboos and Trusts

Unlike presidents who have been insecure personally, feared ability in others, and tried to attend to day-to-day administration, T.R. was a Mississippi of self-confidence. He was happy and able to delegate responsibility because there was no doubt in the public mind about who was in charge. Gaily he lambasted whoever annoyed him. He crossed the color line by lunching at the White House with the prominent black educator, Booker T. Washington. He named a Jew to the cabinet, Oscar S. Straus, as Secretary of Commerce and Labor.

Nor were his actions all symbolic. In April 1902, T.R. conspicuously directed Attorney General Knox, a former corporation lawyer, to take on the most powerful corporate organizers in the United States. His target, the Northern Securities Company, had been designed by J. P. Morgan and railroaders Edward H. Harriman and James J. Hill to end struggles for control of the railroads in the northern quarter of the country. Funded by the nation's two richest banks, Northern Securities was a holding company that was patterned after Morgan's United States Steel Corporation.

Theodore Roosevelt aggressively enforced antitrust laws. In this cartoon he is depicted as a powerful lion tamer whipping the trusts into shape.

Morgan was shocked. Under McKinley (and pre-Roosevelt Knox) the Sherman Antitrust Act had nearly died from disuse. In a pained and revealing moment, the great financier wrote to Roosevelt, "If we have done anything wrong, send your man to my man and we can fix it up." In other words, let the president of the United States do his job while holding hands in a quiet room with big business.

Roosevelt blithely ignored the proposition and pushed on in the courts. In 1904, he won. The Supreme Court ordered the Northern Securities Company to dissolve, and progressives cheered. When Roosevelt instituted other antitrust suits, 40 in all, of which he won 25, progressives nicknamed him the "trust-buster."

It was an overstatement. Roosevelt did not believe that bigness was itself the evil, and he continued to socialize with business leaders. In 1907, he allowed Morgan's United States Steel to gobble up a major regional competitor, Tennessee Coal and Iron. His criteria for determining what made one trust "good" and another "bad" were vague. Essentially, Roosevelt wanted to show big business and the American people that he and the United States government were boss. In order to take over Tennessee Coal and Iron, Morgan had to send his man to see T.R.'s man and not vice versa.

The Workingman's Friend

Much more startling than trust-busting was Roosevelt's personal intervention in the autumn of 1902 in a strike by 140,000 anthracite miners. The men's demands were moderate. They wanted a 20 percent increase in pay, an eight-hour day, and their employers to recognize and negotiate with their union, the United Mine Workers. The mine owners refused to yield. Theirs was a competitive, unstable business; with so many companies in it, the price of coal fluctuated so radically and unpredictably that they feared long-term contracts with their employees. Moreover, most of them were entrepreneurs of the old hard-nosed school. Their property was their property and that was that. They would brook no interference in their use of it, least of all by grimy employees. George F. Baer, a leader of the

operators, stirred up a furious public reaction when he told a newspaper reporter that he would never deal with the UMW because God had entrusted him and the other owners with control of the mines of Pennsylvania.

By way of contrast, union leader John Mitchell seemed to be a modest likable man who Roosevelt knew was constantly fighting Socialists for control of the UMW. In October, the president let it be known that if the strike dragged on through the winter with no settlement, he might use federal troops to dispossess the owners and open the mines. Knowing enough to believe that the Rough Rider was capable of so rash an action, J. P. Morgan pressured the mine owners to go to Washington to work out a settlement.

The result was a compromise. The miners got a 10 percent raise and a nine-hour day, but the owners did not recognize the UMW. (They refused to meet face to face with Mitchell.) The miners were elated any-

Striking miners, members of the United Mine Workers, parade silently in their Sunday best during the 1902 coal strike.

way. So were people who counted on coal to ward off winter's cold. But the big winner, as in most of his chosen battles, was Theodore Roosevelt. He had reversed the tradition of using federal troops to help employers break strikes and had forced powerful industrialists to bow to his will on behalf of a "square deal" for workingmen.

As with his reputation as a "trust-buster," Roosevelt's image as the workingman's friend was overblown, what the slang of a later generation would call "hype." T.R. never concealed the fact that in any showdown between workers and employers he would side with his own social class. Short of a showdown, however, the president had a nose for popular action and he believed, quite correctly, that personal popularity in a president translated into real political power.

Teddy's Great Victory

By 1904, T.R. was basking in the warmth of nationwide adulation. He was unanimously renominated by the Republicans and presented with a huge campaign chest. The Democrats, hoping to capitalize on the grumbling of some conservatives over the president's stinging remarks about business, did a complete about-face from the party's agrarianism of 1896 and 1900 and named a Wall Street lawyer with a record of sympathy for labor, Judge Alton B. Parker, to oppose him.

Parker was hopelessly stodgy, but even the second most colorful politician in the country would have looked like a cardboard cutout next to T.R. Not even Parker's Wall Street friends voted for him. If they disliked T.R.'s antitrust adventures, they recognized that Roosevelt hewed to conservative lines in advocating an anti-inflationary money policy and a high tariff, which were of far greater importance to business interests than was anything else. J. P. Morgan, recently stung in the Northern Securities case, donated $150,000 to Roosevelt's campaign.

The president won a lopsided 57.4 percent of the vote, more than any candidate since popular totals had begun to be recorded. His 336 to 140 electoral sweep was the largest since Grant's in 1872, and he did it without the help of the southern states. Building on the coalition of money and respectability that had been put together by McKinley and Hanna in 1896, T.R. enlarged the Republican majority by appealing to progressives.

THE PRESIDENT AS REFORMER

The only sour note for the Republicans in a giddy election week was the remarkable showing of the So-cialist party candidate, Eugene V. Debs. His 400,000 votes amounted to only 3 percent of the total, but represented an astonishing fourfold increase over what he had won in 1900. Roosevelt did not like it. He took every opportunity to denounce anticapitalist radicals, even if it meant sounding rather lawless. For example, late in 1905, Charles Moyer and Big Bill Haywood, then the two chief leaders of the militant Western Federation of Miners, were arrested and illegally extradited—in effect, kidnapped—to be indicted for murder in Idaho. Roosevelt dismissed the irregularity of the incident because the two were "undesirable citizens." Moyer and Haywood's lawyer, Clarence Darrow, justifiably complained that with the president of the United States making such statements, a fair trial was not likely. (Nevertheless, neither man was convicted.)

More important, Roosevelt set out to co-opt the Socialists by unleashing a whirlwind of reform. In part, he was determined to eliminate the abuses that gave the Socialists their easiest targets.

The Railroads Derailed

As they had been for 30 years, the railroads remained a focus of popular resentment. The freewheeling arrogance of their directors and the vital role of transportation in the national economy preoccupied progressives at every level of government. Prodded by regional leaders, most notably Senator Robert La Follette, Roosevelt dove into a long, bitter struggle with the railroad companies. In 1906, he won passage of the Hepburn Act. The new law authorized the Interstate Commerce Commission to set maximum rates that railroads might charge their customers, and forbade them to pay rebates to big shippers. This prohibition had been enacted before but had not been effectively enforced; the Hepburn Act gave the ICC some teeth. More than any of T.R.'s previous actions, it blasted the railroaders' traditional immunity from government interference.

Also in 1906, Congress passed an act that held railroads liable to employees who suffered injuries on the job. By European standards, it was a mild compensation law, but in the United States, it marked a sharp break with precedent, which held employees responsible for most of their injuries.

Pure Food and Drugs

Several Pure Food and Drug Acts crippled the patent-medicine industry, which marketed dangerous and addictive opiates as "feel-good" nostrums, the laws struck at the adulteration of foods with sometimes toxic preservatives and fillers, and provided for federal inspection of meat-packing plants and other food-processing industries.

While such wholesale federal interference annoyed some big businessmen, others quietly supported it. They realized that strict sanitary standards could work to their benefit at the expense of smaller competitors, for with their greater resources, big companies were better able to comply. For example, as early as 1902, the gigantic Coca-Cola Company of Atlanta, striving for a monopoly of soft-drink production, had come up with a substitute for cocaine as the "kick" in its beverage. With its vast national apparatus and huge purchasing capacity, Coca-Cola was able to contract with drug manufacturers to buy the residue from processed coca leaves (what was left *after* drug companies had extracted cocaine) and to incorporate caffeine, an acceptable stimulant, into its secret recipe. Small cola companies trying to compete with "coke" found it difficult to match the big company's advanced technology and later to conform to federal standards.

Although it had been the giant meat packers that Upton Sinclair had attacked in *The Jungle,* only the smaller abattoirs found federal inspection to be an impossible burden. Swift, Armour, Wilson, and other large packers quickly came to terms with the ubiquitous government officials and their notebooks. They even made advertising hay of the inspection stamps on their products: the government approved of them. Behind-the-butcher-shop slaughterhouses, on the other hand, could not comply and survive; it was too expensive. The only alternative to closing up was to restrict their sales of meat to the states in which they were located. (Like all national reforms, federal meat inspection applied only to firms involved in interstate commerce.) The opportunity to challenge the big packers was forever closed. Roosevelt the trust-buster did not object to the consolidation that the Meat Inspection Act tacitly encouraged. It was not bigness itself to which he objected, but irresponsibility in business.

The Need to Conserve Resources

No progressive reform gave Roosevelt more personal satisfaction than the movement to conserve natural resources. As a lifelong outdoorsman, he loved camping, riding, hiking, climbing, and hunting. As a historian, he was more sensitive than most of his contemporaries to the role of the wilderness in forming the American character. He sought and gained the friendship of John Muir, the adopted Californian and Alaskan who had founded the Sierra Club in 1892. Muir's interest in nature was aesthetic, cultural, and spiritual. He wanted to protect from development such magnificent areas of untouched wilderness as Yosemite Valley,

Theodore Roosevelt and Sierra Club founder John Muir in Yosemite National Park.

which he had helped to establish as a national park in 1890.

The motives of progressive conservationists such as T.R.'s tennis partner and America's first trained forester, Gifford Pinchot of Pennsylvania, were somewhat different. While by no means oblivious to the cultural and aesthetic values of wilderness, Pinchot's major concern was protecting natural resources from rapacious exploiters interested only in short-term profits. He wanted to ensure that future generations of Americans would have their share of nonrenewable natural resources such as minerals, coal, and oil to draw on and the continued enjoyment of renewable resources like forests, grasslands, and water for drinking and generating power.

Pinchot and Roosevelt had good reason to worry on both counts. Lumbermen in the Great Lakes states mowed down forests, moved on, and left the land behind them to bloom in useless scrub and shoddy. Western ranchers put too many cattle on delicate grasslands, turning them into deserts. Coal and phosphate mining companies and drillers for oil thought in terms of open account books and never of the fact that, in a century, the United States might run out of these vital resources. Virtually no one in extractive businesses worried that they were destroying watersheds vital to urban water supplies, polluting rivers, and sending good soil into the sea.

Americans had always been reckless with the land, none more so than the pioneers of legend. But there was a big difference between what a few frontiersmen could do to it with axes and horse-drawn plows and the potential for destruction of irresponsible million-dollar corporations.

A Revolution in Conservation Policy

The National Forest Reserve, today's National Forest System, dates from 1891, when Congress empowered the president to withhold forests in the public domain from private use. Over the first ten years of the law, Presidents Harrison, Cleveland, and McKinley had declared 46 million acres of virgin woodland off limits to loggers without government permission.

Enforcement had been desultory until, prodded by Pinchot, Roosevelt began to prosecute "timber pirates" who raided public lands and cattlemen who abused government-owned grasslands. Within a few years, Roosevelt also added 125 million acres to the national forests, as well as 68 million acres of coal deposits, almost 5 million acres of phosphate beds (vital to production of munitions), a number of oil fields, and 2,565 sites suitable for the construction of dams for irrigation and generation of electrical power.

Exploiters howled; progressives cheered. Some of the "multiple uses" to which the national forests were dedicated—recreation, preservation—won the plaudits of groups like the Sierra Club. Others—flood control, irrigation, development of hydroelectric power—pleased social planners. The principle of "sustained yield"—managing forests to ensure an adequate supply of lumber into the indefinite future—appealed to heavily capitalized lumbermen and encouraged them to employ foresters on their own lands.

In the West, however, an angry opposition developed. Cattlemen, clear-cut loggers, and private power companies banded together in an anticonservation movement that succeeded, in 1907, in attaching a rider to an appropriations bill that passed Congress. It forbade the president to create any additional national forests in six western states.

Roosevelt had no choice but to sign the bill; the Department of Agriculture could not have functioned otherwise. But he had one last go at what he called the "predatory interests." Before he wrote his name on the bill, he reserved 17 million acres of forest land in the interdicted states.

Concern for the Farm

Theodore Roosevelt's conservation campaign remains one of the single most important contributions of his presidency. Nevertheless, his policies could hurt ordinary people as well as special interests. For example, he and Pinchot helped Los Angeles, the burgeoning metropolis of southern California, to grab the entire Owens River, 300 miles to the north, for its water supply. The president regarded the mammoth construction project, now known as the Los Angeles Aqueduct, as a showpiece of resource development and public control of electrical power. In the process, however, he helped to destroy the fertile Owens Valley. Then a land of prosperous, self-reliant small farmers, it would become by 1930 an arid, desolate region of sagebrush, dust storms, and tarantulas.

Had Roosevelt lived to see its results, he might well have regretted his action. He was a devotee of the family farm as one of the essential American institutions. He established the Country Life Commission, which lamented the steady disappearance of this way of life and submitted to Congress a number of recommendations designed to help family farmers. Conservative congressmen who had soured on their progressive president refused even to publish the report.

The Reformer Retires

Congress sidestepped most of Roosevelt's legislative proposals for 1908. In two major speeches he called for a comprehensive, even radical, program that included federal investigation of major labor disputes and close regulation of both the stock market and businesses that were involved in interstate commerce.

Roosevelt could be ignored in 1908 because he was a "lame duck." It was a presidential election year. Four years earlier, celebrating the great victory of 1904, T.R. had impulsively declared that "a wise custom which limits the President to two terms regards the substance and not the form, and under no circumstances will I be a candidate for or accept another nomination." Having served three and a half years of McKinley's term, Roosevelt had defined himself as a two-term president.

In 1908, he almost certainly regretted his vow. Roosevelt loved his job as no other president has. He was a marvelous success in it. He was not yet 50 years of age and as popular as ever in 1908 with the voters. Roosevelt undoubtedly would have won reelection in 1908 had he been willing to forget his pledge of 1904.

But he kept his word and settled for hand-picking his successor, which no president had been able to do since Andrew Jackson in 1836. That William Howard Taft, then Secretary of War, was not the man whom either conservative or progressive Republicans would have chosen indicates just how powerful Roosevelt was.

BIG BILL TAFT, A CONSERVATIVE PRESIDENT IN A PROGRESSIVE ERA

Taft never would have been nominated without Roosevelt's blessing. He would not have dreamed of running for president. Regularly in his correspondence he dashed off the exclamation "I hate politics!" and meant it. He was a lifelong functionary, not a politician. His only elective post prior to 1908 was as a judge in Ohio. Taft remembered that job as the most congenial he had ever held, for his temperament was judicial. Sober, cautious, reflective, dignified, Taft was an excellent administrator, but no showman.

Even physically, Taft was ill fit to follow Roosevelt's gymnastic style. he weighed over 300 pounds, and was truly at ease only when he settled into a swivel chair behind a desk or sank into an overstuffed couch with other easygoing men. His single form of exercise, golf, did not help his image; batting a little white ball around an oversize lawn was considered a sissy's game in the early twentieth century.

Taft was no reactionary. He had loyally supported Roosevelt's reforms, and T.R. calculated that he, more than anyone else, would carry out the Square Deal. So did other progressives. They supported him, as did the conservative wing of the Republican party. Anyone was preferable to the man whom they had begun to refer to privately as "the mad messiah."

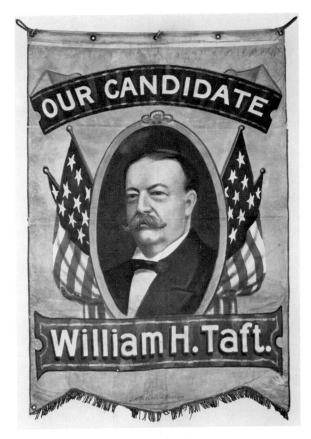

William Howard Taft on a Republican campaign banner of 1908.

The Election of 1908

The election was an anticlimax. The Democrats returned to William Jennings Bryan as their candidate, but the thrill was gone. The Boy Orator of the Platte, no longer young, was shopworn beyond his years. He had grown jowls and a paunch as penance for his lifelong vulnerability to the deadly sin of gluttony, and was rapidly losing his hair.

Moreover, his loyal supporters, the staple farmers of the Midwest, were no longer struggling to survive. They were beginning to dress like the townsmen they had jostled in 1896 and to build substantial homes. Even the issue of 1900, imperialism, was dead. Taft, who had served as American governor of the Philippines, could claim credit for having transformed the anti-American Filipinos, whom he called his "little brown brothers," into a placid and apparently content colonial population. Puerto Rico was quieter. Hawaiians did the hula for increasing numbers of American tourists. Central America simmered but the spectre of American power kept the lid on. Thousands of men were digging their way across Panama. The upshot was that a lethargic Bryan won a smaller percentage of the popular vote than in either of his previous tries, although several western states returned to the Democratic column.

The Socialist party was even more disappointed in the results. Optimistic at the start of the campaign, they chartered a private train, the "Red Special," on which candidate Debs crisscrossed the country. His crowds were big and enthusiastic. But Debs's vote was only 16,000 higher than in 1904 and represented a smaller percentage of the total. It appeared that Roosevelt's tactic of undercutting the socialist threat with a comprehensive reform program had worked.

Taft Blunders

Taft lacked both the political skills and the zeal to keep the campaign going. For example, even though he initiated 90 antitrust suits during his four years as president, twice as many as Roosevelt had launched in seven and a half years, no one complimented him as a trust-buster. Taft had alienated the progressives immediately after taking office when he stumbled over the obstacle that T.R. had danced around so nimbly—the tariff.

In 1909, duties on foreign goods were high, set at an average 46.5 percent of the value of imports by the Dingley Tariff of 1897. Republican conservatives insisted that this rate was necessary in order to protect the jobs of American factory workers and to encourage industrial investment by capitalists. Some midwestern progressives disagreed. They believed that American industry was strong enough to stand up to European competition. To maintain the Dingley rates was to subsidize excessive corporate profits by allowing manufacturers to set their prices inordinately high. Farmers were twice stung because the European nations, except Great Britain, retaliated against the Dingley Tariff by levying high duties on American agricultural products.

Roosevelt had let the conservatives have their way on the tariff, placating progressives by moving on other reforms. By 1908, that was no longer possible, and Taft pledged during the campaign to call Congress into special session for the purpose of revision. He did so in March 1909, and the House of Representatives drafted a reasonable reduction of rates in the Payne bill. In the Senate, however, Nelson Aldrich of Rhode Island, a trusty ally of industrial capitalists, engineered 800 amendments to what became the Payne-Aldrich Act. On most important commodities, the final rate was higher than under the Dingley Tariff.

Taft was in a bind. Politically, he was committed to lower rates. Personally, however, he was more comfortable with the aristocratic Aldrich and the five corporation lawyers in his cabinet than with low-tariff men in the Senate who were Democrats or excitable progressives like La Follette, Albert Beveridge of Indiana, and Jonathan Dolliver of Iowa. After equivocating, Taft worked out what he thought was a compromise in the Roosevelt tradition. The conservatives got their high tariff but agreed to a 2 percent corporate income tax and a constitutional amendment that legalized a personal income tax. (It was ratified in 1913 as the Sixteenth Amendment.) Instead of emphasizing the progressive aspects of his arrangement, as T.R. surely would have done, Taft described the Payne-Aldrich Act as "the best tariff that the Republican party ever passed."

The Insurgents and a Wounded Pinchot

This angered the midwestern Republican progressives, especially after Taft came out in favor of a trade treaty with Canada that threatened to dump Canadian crops on the American market. But they broke with the new president only when he sided with the reactionary Speaker of the House of Representatives, Joseph G. Cannon of Illinois, against them.

Illinois congressman "Uncle Joe" Cannon, a hard-bitten Republican conservative.

"Uncle Joe" Cannon offended the progressive Republicans on several counts. He was so hidebound a conservative as to be a ludicrous stereotype. As Speaker of the House and chairman of the House Rules Committee, he put progressives on unimportant committees and loaded the meaningful ones with "Old Guard" friends. Finally, while the progressives inclined to be highly moralistic, even priggish in manner, Uncle Joe was a crusty tobacco chewer, a hard drinker who was not infrequently drunk, and a champion foulmouth.

The proper Taft also found Cannon's company unpleasant. However, the president believed in party loyalty, and when a number of midwestern Republican progressives, calling themselves Insurgents, voted with Democrats to strip Cannon of his near-dictatorial power, Taft joined with the Speaker to deny the Insurgents access to party money and patronage in the midterm election of 1910. The result was a Democratic victory and Cannon was out of the speakership, never to return.

Pinchot Forces a Break

It is impossible to say how Theodore Roosevelt would have handled the quarrel between Cannon and the Insurgents. But he assuredly would not have done what Taft did in a dispute between Secretary of the Interior Richard A. Ballinger and Chief Forester Gifford Pinchot.

When Ballinger released to private developers a number of hydroelectric sites that Pinchot had persuaded Roosevelt to reserve, Pinchot protested to Taft and won the president's grudging support.

However, when Pinchot leaked his evidence against Ballinger to *Collier's* magazine, which was still in the muckraking business, Taft fired him. This was exactly what Pinchot wanted. Almost immediately he booked passage to Italy, where his friend and patron, former president Roosevelt, was vacationing. Pinchot brought with him an indictment of Big Bill Taft as a traitor to the cause of reform.

Enter Stage Left the Conquering Hero

Roosevelt was having a bully time on his extended world tour. He had left the country shortly after Taft's inauguration to give his successor an opportunity to function outside his predecessor's aura. First Roosevelt traveled to East Africa, where he shot a bloody swath through the still abundant big game of Kenya and Tanganyika (Tanzania). He bagged over 3,000 animals, many of which he had stuffed for the trophy room of his home at Oyster Bay, Long Island.

Then he went to Europe to bask in an adulation that was scarcely less fierce than he enjoyed at home. He hobnobbed with aristocrats and politicians, who thought of him as the ultimate American, much as Benjamin Franklin had been considered in eighteenth-century France. Roosevelt topped off his year-long junket by representing the United States at the funeral of King Edward VII, shining in the greatest collection of royalty ever assembled.

And yet, something was missing. Roosevelt longed for the hurly-burly of politics, and he was all too willing to believe Pinchot's accusations. When he returned to the United States in June 1910, he exchanged only the curtest greetings with the president. He spoke widely on behalf of Republican congressional candidates, at first playing down the split between regulars (conservatives) and Insurgents (progressives). Then, at Osawatomie, Kansas, in September 1910, Roosevelt proclaimed what he labeled the "New Nationalism," a comprehensive program for further reform. To Republican conservatives, it was frighteningly radical.

Among other proposals, Roosevelt called for woman suffrage, a federal minimum wage for women workers, abolition of child labor, strict limitations on the power of courts to issue injunctions in labor disputes, and a national social-insurance scheme that resembled present-day Social Security. He struck directly at Taft's policies by demanding a commission that would set tariff rates "scientifically" rather than according to political pressures. He supported the progressive initiative, recall, and referendum, including a new twist, a referendum on judicial decisions. This was enough in itself to aggravate the legalistic Taft, but in demanding a national presidential-primary law under which the people, and not professional politicians, would make party nominations, Roosevelt also hinted that he was interested in running for the presidency again.

Fighting Bob and Teddy Challenge Big Bill Taft

Taft was not the only politician who worried about Roosevelt's presidential plans. Robert La Follette believed that he had a chance to win the Republican nomination from Taft *if* Roosevelt did not run. He sent mutual friends to ask Roosevelt his intentions, and Teddy responded that he was not interested in the White House. Tacitly encouraged, in January 1911, the Wisconsin senator organized the Progressive Republican League as the vehicle of his campaign.

Most progressive Republicans supported La Follette, including Roosevelt backers who not so secretly hoped that their real hero would change his mind. In fact, Roosevelt was itching to run. In March 1912, La Follette collapsed from exhaustion during a speech, and Roosevelt announced, "my hat is in the ring."

La Follette was not seriously ill, and he never forgave T.R. for having used him as a stalking-horse. But he was no match for the old master when it came to stirring up party activists, and his campaign fell apart. Roosevelt swept most of the thirteen state primary elections, winning 278 convention delegates to Taft's 48 and La Follette's 36. If La Follette was beaten, however, the suddenly aroused Taft was not, and he held a powerful weapon.

Taft controlled the party organization. As president, he appointed people to thousands of government jobs, wedding their careers to his own success. In the Republican party, this power of the patronage was particularly important in the southern states, where the party consisted of little more than professional office-holders, including many blacks, who made their living as postmasters, customs collectors, agricultural agents, and the like. While the Republicans won few congressional seats and fewer electoral votes in the South, a substantial bloc of delegates to Republican conventions spoke with a Dixie drawl. They were in Taft's pocket.

Consequently, when the convention voted on whether Taft or Roosevelt would be awarded 254 disputed seats, Taft delegates won 235 of them. Roosevelt's supporters shouted "Fraud!" and walked out. They formed the Progressive party, or, as it was nicknamed for the battle with the Republican elephant

THE LATEST ARRIVAL AT THE POLITICAL ZOO

DRAWN BY E.W. KEMBLE

A Harper's Weekly *cartoon depicting Theodore Roosevelt as a bull moose that relies on a trust for survival.*

and the Democratic donkey, the Bull Moose party. (In a backhanded reference to La Follette's allegedly poor health and Taft's obesity, Roosevelt had said that he was "as strong as a bull moose.")

DEMOCRATIC PARTY PROGRESSIVISM

The Republican party was not the majority party when it was split in two, and the Democrats smelled victory. When the convention assembled in Baltimore, there was an abundance of would-be nominees. As at the Republican convention, but for a rather different reason, the key to winning the party's presidential nomination lay in the southern state delegations.

Because the South was "solid" in delivering electoral votes to the Democratic column, it held a virtual veto power over the nomination as a result of the two-thirds rule. In order to be nominated, a Democrat needed the votes of two-thirds of the delegates; no

one could win two-thirds if southern delegates solidly opposed him. The trouble in 1912 was that none of the leading candidates was offensive to the South, and each had southern supporters; thus the usual southern bloc was split.

The Democratic Hopefuls

William Jennings Bryan was still popular in the South, but as a three-time loser, he was not an attractive candidate. Although he hoped to be selected as a compromise candidate in case of a deadlock, few Democrats wanted to risk sure victory for the sake of old times.

Oscar Underwood of Alabama was another minor hopeful; he commanded the support of the southern "Bourbon" conservatives, but for that reason he was unacceptable to southern progressives, who might more accurately be described as Populists who preached racism along with attacks on big business. Some progressives supported Judson Harmon of Ohio. Others backed Champ Clark, the "Old Hound Dawg" of Missouri, which was as much a southern as a western state. In fact, Clark went into the convention confident of winning. The man who left it a winner, however, was New Jersey governor Woodrow Wilson, who was nominated on the forty-sixth ballot.

A Moral, Unbending Man

Wilson was actually a southerner; he had been born in Virginia and had practiced law in Georgia as a young man. He had abandoned the law, however, earned a Ph.D. degree, and ended up as a professor of political science at Princeton University. In 1902, he had been named president of Princeton, the first non-minister to hold that post at the still strongly Presbyterian school.

And yet, Wilson had more than a little of the Presbyterian clergyman in him. His father and both grandfathers were parsons. So was his wife's father. He had been raised to observe an unbending Calvinist morality, and his stern sensitivity to the struggle between good and evil in the world was reflected in an ascetic, lean figure and a sharply chiseled, thin-lipped face. With his family and a few intimate friends, Wilson was fun-loving and playful, a fan of the cinema, liable to erupt in horseplay with his daughters, who adored him. Publicly, he was formal, even icy. A less talented man with such a personality would never have risen half so high as Wilson did.

Indeed, his meteoric rise in politics was almost accidental. In 1910, he was merely an honored educator, the president of Princeton University. He had transformed the college from an intellectually lazy finishing school where rich young men made social contacts into a nationally respected university. But Wilson's stubbornness caught up with him. Clashing repeatedly with trustees and alumni, he quit academic life.

There was no loss of face involved. He had been offered the Democratic nomination for governor of New Jersey, and in winning in the traditionally Republican state, Wilson became a national figure overnight. He was more an honest-government progressive than a social reformer, and, like Theodore Roosevelt in New York a decade before, he proved to be a nuisance to some of New Jersey's political bosses. They were delighted when he decided to seek the presidency. Ironically, in terms of what followed, he first offered himself as a safe and sane conservative alternative to William Jennings Bryan and Champ Clark.

Woodrow Wilson was the president of Princeton University before entering political life.

The Campaign of 1912

In fact, Wilson's "New Freedom," as he called his program, was a decidedly less ambitious blueprint for reform than was Roosevelt's "New Nationalism." Wilson emphasized states' rights to the extent that he opposed the Progressive party's comprehensive social program as strongly as Taft did. He considered Roosevelt's proposals to be a dangerous expansion of government powers.

The two men differed even more sharply on the question of the trusts. Whereas T.R. concluded that consolidation, even monopoly, was inevitable in an industrial society, and that the federal government should supervise the operations of the big corporations in the public interest, Wilson condemned this vision as "a partnership between the government and the trusts." Wilson believed that competition in business was still possible in modern America. In his view, the government's task was to ensure free competition by breaking up the trusts and then letting the economy function without direction. In 1912, he opposed the huge, permanent government apparatus that Roosevelt endorsed.

With the Republican organization in tatters and Taft practically dropping out of the race, it would have been difficult for Wilson to have lost the election. Nevertheless, he campaigned tirelessly and skillfully. Articulate, as a college professor is supposed to be, Wilson was also exciting—as few are. Lifelong dreams of winning public office flowered in eloquent speeches that left no doubt that the Presbyterian schoolmaster was a leader.

Wilson won only 41.9 percent of the popular vote but a landslide in the electoral college, 435 votes to Roosevelt's 88 and Taft's 8. Eugene V. Debs, making his fourth race as the Socialist party nominee, won 900,000 votes, 6 percent of the total. The big jump after four years of a conservative president seemed to indicate that it was necessary to reform in order to stifle the socialist challenge. Taft, the only conservative candidate, won but 23.2 percent of the vote.

Tariff and Taxes

T.R. had governed by outflanking Congress, interpreting the president's constitutional powers in the broadest possible terms. Taft had deferred to congressional leaders, ultimately collapsing before the most persuasive of them. Wilson's style was to act as a prime minister. He was not a member of Congress, as the British prime minister is a member of the House of Commons, but he could and did address Congress personally as though he were. When soon after his

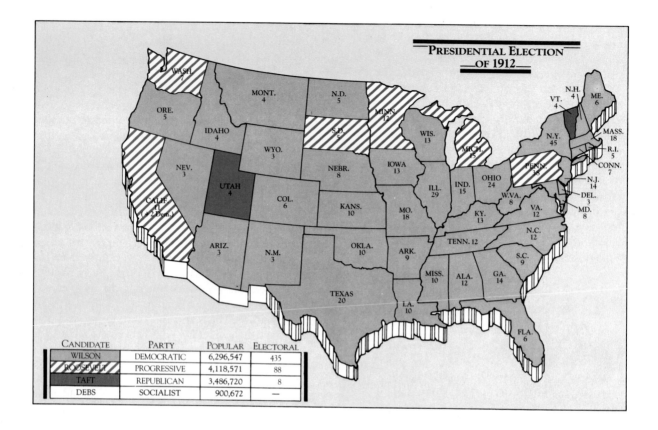

PRESIDENTIAL ELECTION OF 1912

Candidate	Party	Popular	Electoral
WILSON	DEMOCRATIC	6,296,547	435
ROOSEVELT	PROGRESSIVE	4,118,571	88
TAFT	REPUBLICAN	3,486,720	8
DEBS	SOCIALIST	900,672	—

inauguration he asked the House and Senate for sharp reductions in the tariff, he was the first president to appear on Capitol Hill since John Adams. Adams's successor, Thomas Jefferson, had suffered from a stammer and had set the precedent of communicating with Congress only through written messages.

Wilson's short but dramatic address was aimed less at persuading congressmen than at inspiring their constituents to put pressure on them, and it worked. A number of Democratic senators who had been dragging their feet on tariff revision fell into line. The Underwood-Simmons Tariff reduced the Payne-Aldrich rates by 15 percent and put on the free list several commodities that were controlled by trusts—iron, steel, woolens, and farm machinery—thus lowering prices on them.

The lower tariff reduced revenue for the government. To make up the losses, Wilson sponsored both a corporate and a personal income tax. It was not high by late-twentieth-century standards. People who earned less than $4,000 a year paid no tax. On annual incomes between $4,000 and $20,000, a tidy sum in 1913, the rate was only 1 percent. People in the highest bracket, $500,000 and up, paid only 7 percent, a fraction of the low brackets today. Nevertheless, by forcing the rich to pay proportionately more toward

supporting the government, the tax provisions of the tariff law represented a triumph of progressivism.

Wilson's Cabinet

Wilson designed his cabinet in order to unite the Democratic party behind him. The president never had liked William Jennings Bryan, but he named him Secretary of State because Bryan had helped to nominate him and still owned the affection of many western Democrats.

Most other appointments rewarded key components of the party, especially the South and, through Secretary of Labor William B. Wilson, the labor movement, whose support the president needed. The most valuable member of the cabinet was William G. McAdoo. As Secretary of the Treasury, he provided the president with shrewd advice on banking policy. When McAdoo married Wilson's daughter, he became a kind of heir apparent.

Three confidants did not sit in the cabinet. Joseph Tumulty, a canny Irish politician, served as Wilson's private secretary and reminded the president of the sometimes sordid realities involved in keeping together a political machine. Colonel Edward M. House, a Texas businessman, was a shadowy, but not sinister figure. Self-effacing and utterly devoted to the president, House neither desired nor accepted any official position. Instead, he traveled discreetly throughout the United States and abroad, informally conveying the president's views and wants, to businessmen and heads of state.

Louis D. Brandeis, a corporation lawyer become antitrust progressive, provided Wilson with both economic principles and a social conscience. The father of the New Freedom, Brandeis turned Wilson away from the limitations of the program after 1914 and toward a broader progressivism. In 1916, Wilson rewarded him by naming him to the Supreme Court, on which Brandeis served as one of the most influential liberal justices of the twentieth century.

The New Freedom in Action

Two laws that reflected Brandeis's influence were the Federal Reserve Act of 1913 and the Clayton Antitrust Act of 1914. The first was designed both to bring order to the national banking system and to hobble the vast power of Wall Street. The law established twelve regional Federal Reserve Banks, which dealt not directly with people but with other banks. The Federal Reserve System was owned by private bankers who were required to deposit 6 percent of their capital in it. However, the president appointed the majority of the directors, who sat in Washington, theoretically putting the government in control of the money supply.

The greatest power of the Federal Reserve System was (and is) its control of the discount rate, the level of interest at which money is lent to other banks for lending to private investors and buyers. By lowering the discount rate, the Federal Reserve could stimulate investment and economic expansion in slow times. By raising the prime rate, the Federal Reserve could cool down an overactive economy that threatened to blow up in inflation, financial panic, and depression.

The Federal Reserve Act did bring some order to the national banking system. But it did not, as many progressives hoped, tame the great bankers. Indeed, because representatives of the private banks sat on the Federal Reserve Board, the long-term effects of the law were to provide Wall Street with an even more efficient, albeit more accountable, control of national finance.

In 1914, Wilson pushed his antitrust policy through Congress. The Clayton Antitrust Act stipulated that corporations would be fined for unfair practices that threatened competition, forbade interlocking directorates (the same men sitting on the boards of "competing" companies and thereby coordinating policies), and declared that officers of corporations would be held

WILSONIAN HORSEPLAY

Stern and forbidding in person, Woodrow Wilson's private personality was rather the opposite. On the morning after his wedding to his second wife in 1915, he was seen in a White House corridor doing a dance and singing, "Oh, you beautiful doll." His daughters by his first wife, Margaret, Jessie, and Eleanor, certainly showed no signs of moralistic browbeating. One of their amusements in the White House was to join tourists who were being shown around by guides and make loud remarks about the homeliness and vulgarity of the president's daughters.

personally responsible for offenses committed by their companies. Another bill that was passed at the same time created the Federal Trade Commission to supervise the activities of the trusts. This agency looked more like T.R.'s New Nationalism than the New Freedom Wilson had plumped for in 1912.

Wilson Changes Direction

After the congressional elections of 1914, Wilson shifted far more sharply toward the reforms that Teddy Roosevelt had promoted. Although the Democrats retained control of both houses, many progressives returned to their Republican voting habits in 1914 and cut the Democratic margin in the House. It was obvious to both the president and Democratic congress-

THE FATHER OF THE AMUSEMENT PARK: GEORGE C. TILYOU, 1862–1914

George C. Tilyou was born to Irish-American parents in 1862. When he was three years old, his father leased a lot on the beach in the then independent community of Coney Island for $35 a year. It was a brilliantly timed act. The end of the Civil War was the signal for the runaway growth of resorts in the United States, and Coney Island was strategically located, far from the congestion of New York City but close enough to be convenient for a stay of a few days. The wealthy came first, sometimes by yacht, but also middle-class people to whom Newport, Rhode Island, and Palm Beach, Florida, were just names. Tilyou's hotel, the Surf House, catered to the middling sort. In fact, because Tilyou, Sr., was active in Democratic party politics, at any time his hostelry was likely to be filled with ward heelers and other political bosses from Manhattan and Brooklyn.

So George Cornelius Tilyou grew up, as they said at Coney, with sand in his shoes. Like two generations of Coney natives, he found it difficult to leave the place, and when he did, as on a wedding trip to the Columbian Exposition in Chicago in 1893, it was to pick up ideas for how to develop the Beach as a resort.

It developed as a resort for the middle and working classes, soon abandoned by the yachting and horsey sets, and Tilyou recognized the opportunities in providing mass, cheap entertainment. He was one of the first and by far the most successful operators of amusement parks, as shrewd a psychologist as Phineas T. Barnum and, when he died, a rich man.

Tilyou's first venture into the vacation business came in 1876 when the Centennial Exposition in Philadelphia attracted people from all over the nation to the east coast. Calculating that they had money to throw away, the 14-year-old Tilyou filled old medicine bottles with sea water and cigar boxes with Coney beach sand which he sold for 25 cents each. He made enough from dubious but classic resort "gifts" with which to dabble in beachfront real estate. The township did not sell land on the beach but, instead, leased it to people who were part of the political machine, who then sublet choice business locations to others, sometimes at extraordinary profits. Because of his contacts, Tilyou was able to open a theater that featured some of the leading vaudeville acts of the era.

Then he made what appeared to be a fatal mistake. He broke with the political boss of Coney, John Y. McKane, who protected brothels and illegal gambling dens and organized a party devoted to the policy that Coney's future rested on becoming a wholesome family resort. Tilyou denounced McKane for his grafting and when the boss weathered the attack, Tilyou found himself shut out of the profitable leasing deals.

In 1893, however, McKane was jailed for stuffing ballot boxes and Tilyou was back in business. In that same year he discovered the Ferris wheel at the Chicago World's Fair and the young impresario's career took off.

The Ferris wheel was the hit of the fair. It was 250 feet in diameter, almost as high when it was mounted as a football field is long. Suspended on the gigantic circle were 36 "cars," like railroad carriages, each of which held 60 people. The most nominal admission fee promised tremendous profits.

Although he was on his honeymoon, Tilyou was obsessed with the fantastic toy and only briefly disconcerted when he learned that its inventor had already sold it. He contracted with Ferris to build another for Coney. It was only half the size of the original, 125 feet in diameter with 12 cars holding 36 people each but the sign Tilyou erected back home in Coney Island was: "ON THIS SITE WILL BE ERECTED THE WORLD'S LARGEST FERRIS WHEEL!" Tilyou was making money before it was built. He sold concessions around it to various vendors, including one to a purveyor of a frankfurter sausage on a white milk roll, the first hot dog. Then Tilyou built a number of other "amusements," at first simple gravity devices such as giant sliding boards and seesaws but soon enough the electrically powered forerunners of devices still active on boardwalks and at fairs today. From another Coney entrepreneur, Paul Boyton, Tilyou copied the idea of fencing in a large "amusement park" and charging a single admission fee. Coney's clientele did not have the means for extravagant spending; better to commit them to a whole day at Steeplechase Park where they would have to buy their food and other extras rather than having them wander over to Steeplechase's competitors, Luna Park and Dreamland.

Steeplechase Park opened in 1897. Its centerpiece was a gravity driven "horse race" ride imported from England. People mounted wooden horses—a beau and his belle could ride on the same one—which rolled on tracks over a series of "hills" and entered the central pavilion at the Park where, upon exiting, the customers were mildly abused by a clown and costumed dwarf. The biggest hit of the Steeplechase was the jet of compressed air which shot out of the floor blowing young ladies' skirts into the air amidst great shrieking and guffawing.

Innocent sexual horseplay was the idea in many of the mechanical amusements Tilyou constructed. Airjets were everywhere. Other amusements were designed to throw young ladies in such a position that their ankles were exposed or they landed in the laps of their escorts or, perhaps, someone whom they were interested in meeting. In an age when polite society was warily trying to come to terms with sex, dwelling on it through romantic euphemisms in popular songs, Tilyou's formula worked. For a time after the turn of the century, Steeplechase Park lost ground to newer amuse-

Steeplechase Park on Coney Island provided cheap entertainment for the middle and working classes.

ment parks, Luna Park (featuring "a trip to the moon") and Dreamland, where holiday-makers could stroll through the streets of an Egyptian city, a Somali village, among Philippine headhunters, or see the eruption of Mount Pelée, the Johnstown flood, the Galveston tidal wave, or other natural disasters.

But it was Tilyou who really had the sand in his shoes. When Steeplechase Park burned to the ground in 1907—every wooden Coney Island attraction burned at one time or another—he simply hung up a sign:

I have troubles today that I didn't have yesterday.
I had troubles yesterday that I have not today.
On this site will be erected shortly a better, bigger, greater Steeplechase Park.

Admission to the Burning Ruins—10 cents.

Tilyou also built Steeplechase Pier in Atlantic City, a New Jersey oceanfront town that competed with Coney. He died in 1914, only 52 years of age. Coney's Steeplechase Park closed in 1967.

President Woodrow Wilson conferring with aides.

men that if they were to survive the election of 1916 against a reunified Republican party, they would have to woo these progressive voters.

Consequently, Wilson agreed to support social legislation that he had opposed through 1914. He did not like laws that favored any special interest, farmers any more than bankers, but in order to shore up support in the West, he agreed to the Federal Farm Loan Act of 1916, which provided low-cost credit to farmers. Early in his administration, Wilson had opposed a child-labor law on constitutional grounds. In 1916, he supported the Keating-Owen Act, which severely restricted the employment of children in most jobs.

The Adamson Act required the interstate railroads to put their workers on an eight-hour day without a reduction in pay. Wilson even moderated his antiblack sentiments, although Washington definitely took on the character of a segregated southern city during his tenure. Despite a lifelong opposition to woman suffrage, the president began to encourage states to enfranchise women and to hint that he supported a constitutional amendment that would guarantee the right nationwide.

By the summer of 1916, Wilson could say with considerable justice that he had pushed progressive reform farther than had any of his predecessors. He enacted or supported much of Theodore Roosevelt's program of 1912, as well as his own. By 1916, however, Americans' votes reflected more than their views on domestic issues. They were troubled about their nation's place in a suddenly complicated world. Simultaneous with Wilson's enactment of progressive reforms, Europe had tumbled into the greatest war in history.

For Further Reading

Overviews and Classics

Vincent P. DeSantis, *The Shaping of Modern America 1877–1916* (1973)

Arthur S. Link, *Woodrow Wilson and the Progressive Era* (1954)

William L. O'Neill, *The Progressive Years: America Comes of Age* (1975)

Robert H. Wiebe, *The Search for Order, 1880–1920* (1967)

Valuable Special Studies

D. F. Anderson, *William Howard Taft: A Conservative's Conception of the Presidency* (1973)

Lewis L. Gould, *Reform and Regulation: American Politics, 1900–1916* (1978)

Otis L. Graham Jr., *The Great Campaigns: Reform and War in America, 1900–1928* (1971)

Samuel T. Hays, *Conservation and the Gospel of Efficiency: The Progressive Conservation Movement, 1890–1920* (1959)

Richard Hofstadter, *The Age of Reform* (1955)

Gabriel Kolko, *The Triumph of Conservatism* (1963)

———, *The Era of Theodore Roosevelt* (1958)

Robert H. Wiebe, *Businessmen and Reform* (1962)

Biographies and Autobiographies

John M. Blum, *The Republican Roosevelt* (1954)

———, *Woodrow Wilson and the Politics of Morality* (1956)

P. E. Coletta, *The Presidency of William Howard Taft* (1973)

John A. Garraty, *Woodrow Wilson* (1956)

W. H. Harbaugh, *Power and Responsibility: The Life and Times of Theodore Roosevelt* (1961)

Arthur S. Link, *Woodrow Wilson* (1947–65)

Henry F. Pringle, *Theodore Roosevelt* (1931)

America Discovers Europe
The Path to World War, 1914–1918

A few days before his inauguration in 1913, Woodrow Wilson was reminded of some difficulties in American relations with Mexico. He thought about the problem for a moment and set it aside, remarking, "It would be the irony of fate if my administration had to deal chiefly with foreign affairs."

Wilson did not fear such a challenge. Although it was more restrained, his self-confidence was as sturdy as Theodore Roosevelt's. But his academic and political careers had been devoted to domestic concerns. He had paid scant attention to the thorny snarls in which relations among nations could be tangled, and he never had been particularly interested in them. When Wilson considered the rest of the world, it was on the basis of assumptions and sentiments rather than with careful thought and in terms of a coherent, deliberate policy.

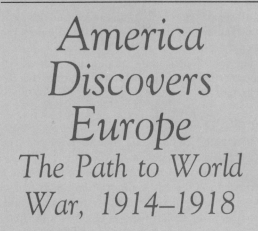

Soldiers man the trenches that zigzagged across the French countryside during the First World War.

WILSON, THE WORLD, AND MEXICO

Like most Americans, the president was proud that because of its population and industrial might, the United States ranked with only a handful of nations as a great world power. Also like other Americans, he believed that the United States was unique among great and lesser powers alike. Protected from Europe by a broad ocean, the United

States required no huge armies to defend its security but, instead, expended its resources in constructive ways. Founded on the basis of an idea in men's minds rather than on inheritance of a common culture and territory, the American nation should act toward other countries in accordance with principles rather than out of narrow self-interest.

Moral Diplomacy

As a moralist, Wilson had roundly criticized Teddy Roosevelt's gunboat diplomacy. To bully small nations was to betray the American ideal of self-government. He proclaimed that his administration would deal with the weak and turbulent Latin American countries "upon terms of equality and honor." As a progressive who was suspicious of Wall Street, Wilson also disapproved of Taft's dollar diplomacy. Shortly after he took office, Wilson canceled federal support of an investment scheme in China because it implied the government had an obligation to intervene in the event that the investor's profits were threatened.

Wilson was influenced by the Christian pacifism toward which Secretary of State William Jennings Bryan also leaned. Bryan believed that war was justified only in self-defense. If nations would act cautiously and discuss their problems, they would not have to spill blood. With Wilson's approval, Bryan negotiated conciliation treaties with 30 nations. The signatories pledged that in the event of a dispute, they would wait and talk for one year before declaring war. Bryan believed that during this "cooling-off" period, virtually every dispute between nations could be resolved without the use of force.

Race and the Missionary's Mind

High ideals. Once in the cockpit, however, Wilson found that applying them consistently was more difficult than flying the recently invented airplane. In part this was because he was also impelled by assumptions that conflicted with his moral and progressive principles. Raised to believe in the superiority of the white race, an academic in a time when racism permeated the university, he found it difficult to act as an equal in dealing with the Japanese and the racially mixed Latin Americans.

His commitment to diplomacy by good example was complicated by a missionary's impulse to dictate proper behavior. When weaker nations did not freely emulate American ways of doing things, Wilson could wax arrogant, patronizing, and demanding. If other peoples did not realize what was good for them, Wilson would teach them.

So he raised no objections to a California state law that insulted racially sensitive Japan by restricting the

Wilson shakes his finger at Mexico in rebuke in this cartoon from Punch.

right of Japanese-Americans to own land. In 1915, he ordered the marines into black Haiti when chaotic conditions there threatened American investments, and the next year, he landed troops in the Dominican Republic under similar circumstances. These actions angered Latin Americans, but they were minor irritants compared with Wilson's prolonged and blundering interference in Mexican affairs.

¡Viva Madero!

In 1911, the Mexican dictator for 35 years, Porfirio Díaz, was overthrown following a revolution supported by practically every Mexican social group save the tiny elite that Díaz had favored. Foreign investors, who had reaped rich rewards by cooperating with the dictator, waited and fretted, none more so than the British and Americans. The leader of the revolution spoke of returning control of Mexican wealth to Mexicans, and Americans alone owned $2 billion in property in Mexico, most of the country's railroads, 60 percent of the oil wells, and more of the mines than Mexicans controlled. About 50,000 Americans lived in Mexico.

Francisco Madero was the reflective idealist who headed the revolution. He and Wilson would have disagreed, but they might also have gotten along. Madero was cultivated, educated, and moderate, not given to acting rashly. Moreover, he shared Wilson's liberal political philosophy and admired American institutions.

They never had to chance to communicate. Quietly encouraged by the Taft administration, a group of Díaz's generals led by Victoriano Huerta staged a coup. Apparently making their plans in the American embassy, the rebels struck shortly before Wilson was inaugurated, murdered Madero, and seized control of the federal government.

¡Viva Carranza!

The murder offended Wilson. He said that he would not deal with "a government of butchers," and he pressured England to withdraw its hasty recognition of the Huerta government. When peasant rebellions broke out in scattered parts of Mexico and a Constitutionalist army took shape behind a somber, long-bearded aristocrat, Venustiano Carranza, Wilson openly approved.

In April 1914, the United States intervened directly in the civil war. Seven American sailors on shore leave in Tampico were arrested by one of Huerta's colonels. They were freed almost immediately, but Huerta refused the demand of Admiral Henry T. Mayo for a twenty-one gun salute as an appropriate apology. Claiming that American honor had been insulted (and seeking to head off a German ship that was bringing arms to Huerta), Wilson ordered troops into the important port of Vera Cruz.

To Wilson's surprise, ordinary Mexicans joined the fight against the Americans, and street fighting in Vera Cruz claimed more than 400 lives. Wilson failed to understand that while Huerta was unpopular, the Mexican people resented gringo interference as an attack on the nation itself. Even Carranza, in control of the north of Mexico, condemned the American landing. Somewhat alarmed, Wilson agreed to an offer by Argentina, Brazil, and Chile to mediate the crisis.

Pancho Villa Versus the United States

Before anything could be settled, Carranza ousted Huerta. However, he then quarreled with one of his own generals, a bizarre, charismatic character who was born Doroteo Arango, but was universally known as Pancho Villa. Alternately jovial and vicious, half ban-

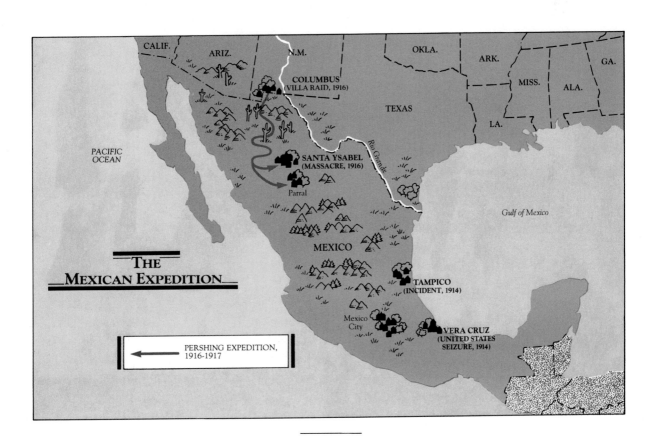

THE MEXICAN EXPEDITION

PERSHING EXPEDITION, 1916-1917

dit and half social revolutionary, Villa was romanticized by the young American journalist John Reed as "The Robin Hood of Mexico." For a time even Wilson was convinced that Villa represented democracy in Mexico, and would be friendlier to American interests than was Carranza.

But Wilson wanted stability most of all. When Carranza took Mexico City in October 1915, Wilson recognized his de facto control of the government. This stung Villa, prompting him to show his seamier side. Calculating that if he provoked American intervention he could unsettle Mexico again and make a play for power, Villa stopped a train carrying American engineers invited by Carranza to reopen several mines, and shot all but one. Early in 1916, he led a raid across the border into the dusty little desert town of Columbus, New Mexico, where his brigands killed 17 people.

Instead of allowing Carranza to root out and punish Villa, as was proper with neighboring nations that were sovereign equals, Wilson ordered General John J. Pershing and 6,000 troops, including the Tenth Cavalry, one of the last black regiments, to capture the bandit guerrilla. They were humiliated. In the arid mountainous state of Chihuahua that was his home, Villa easily evaded the Americans, leading them on 300 miles of a zigzag route during which time they never gained sight of Villa's main force. Pershing's men did, however, exchange shots several times with Carranza's troops. In one skirmish, 40 died. While accomplishing nothing, Wilson had succeeded in alienating every political faction in Mexico.

In January 1917, he finally gave up and ordered "Black Jack" Pershing to return home. Only because Americans were faced by a more formidable enemy, the German Kaiser, were they able to make light of their humiliation at the hands of a man whom they considered an illiterate *bandido*.

EUROPE'S GREAT WAR

By the beginning of 1917, Europe had been at war for two and a half years. In June 1914, a Serbian (Yugoslavian) nationalist, Gavrilo Princip, had assassinated

Bandit and revolutionary Pancho Villa (center) with the leader of agrarian revolt in Mexico, Emiliano Zapata (right).

an archduke of Austria, which ruled several provinces peopled by Serbs. At first the incident appeared to be minor; the turn of the century was a time when assassination was epidemic in Europe. Then, however, Austria-Hungary's sensitivity to the decline of its once great empire, obligations among the great powers written into secret treaties, the weakness of the Russian Czar and the irresponsibility of the German Kaiser, and the reckless arms race in which the European nations had been engaged for a generation, plunged the Continent into war.

Tangled Alliances

Serbia was an ally of Russia, which backed the little country in defying Austria. Austria-Hungary looked to powerful Germany for encouragement, and got it. France became involved because of French fears of German industrial might, which had led to secret agreements promising mutual support to Russia. England, traditionally aloof from European wrangles, had been frightened by Germany's construction of a world-wide navy (larger than America's and second only to Britain's) and, early in the century, had signed mutual-assistance treaties with both France and Russia. Many of the smaller nations of Europe were associated with either the Central Powers (Germany, Austria-Hungary, Bulgaria, Turkey) or the Allied Powers (England, France, Russia, eventually Italy). By August 1914, most of Europe was at war. Soon, 33 nations would be involved.

Americans React

The American people reacted to the explosion with a mixture of disbelief and disgust. For a generation, European rulers had filled the air with the sounds of saber rattling. Americans were used to that; their own Teddy Roosevelt was a master of noisy bluff. But T.R., it seemed, had understood the difference between a bully show and a catastrophe. Until 1914, so had the Europeans. Even Kaiser Wilhelm II of Germany, an absurd and broadly ridiculed figure with his extravagant military uniforms, golden spiked helmet, comic-opera waxed moustache, and penchant for bombast, had acted prudently in the crunch. Like most Europeans, Americans concluded that the constant talk about war without going to war would continue indefinitely. They did not really believe that powerful, civilized countries would turn their terrifying technology for killing on one another.

Once European nations had done just that, Americans consoled themselves that their nation, at least, remained above such savagery. Politicians, preachers, and editors quoted and praised the wisdom of George Washington's and Thomas Jefferson's warning against

Kaiser Wilhelm's love of militarism bordered on the ludicrous and did nothing to help his image in the United States.

"entangling alliances." They blamed Europe's tragedy on Old-World corruptions, its kings and princes, religious intolerance, nationalistic hysteria, and insane stockpiling of armaments that were superfluous if they were not used, suicidal if they were.

Never did American political and social institutions look so superior. Never had Americans been more grateful to have turned their backs on Europe's ways. As reports of hideous carnage on the battlefield began to hum over the Atlantic Cable, Americans shuddered and counted their blessings. No prominent person raised an objection when President Wilson proclaimed absolute American neutrality. However, when the president also called on Americans to be "neutral in fact as well as in name, . . . impartial in thought as well as in action," he was, as he was wont to do, demanding too much of human nature.

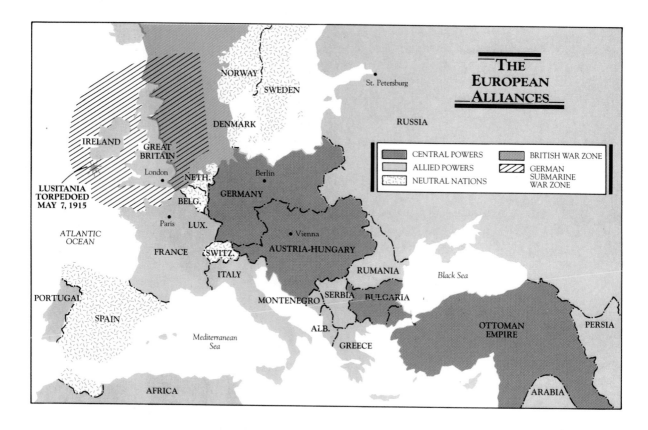

Sympathy for the Allies

A large proportion of Americans looked to England as their ancestral as well as cultural motherland, and they were naturally sympathetic to Britain's cause. Wilson himself was an unstinting Anglophile. Before becoming president, he had vacationed regularly in England. He frankly admired the British parliamentary form of government, and in his first year in office, he had resolved the last minor points of difference between England and the United States: a border dispute in British Columbia, a quarrel between Canadian and American fishermen off Newfoundland, and British objections to discriminatory tolls on the Panama Canal.

Hardly noted at first, but ominous in the long run, American and British capitalists were closely allied. British investments in the United States were vast, and when the cost of purchasing everything from wheat to munitions required that these holdings be liquidated, sold to Americans at bargain rates, the relationship grew warmer. Banking houses like the House of Morgan lent money to the English, at first with Wilson's disapproval, and acted as agents for Allied bond sales. By 1917, Great Britain owed American lenders $2.3 billion. It was a strong tie, when

compared with the meager $27 million that the Germans managed to borrow in the United States. Wall Street had good reason to favor an English victory or, at least, to pale at the thought of an English defeat.

Old-stock Americans were also sympathetic to France. The land of Lafayette was America's "oldest friend," the indispensable ally of the Revolution. Americans never had formally gone to war with the French. And France was, except for the United States, the only republic among the world's great powers, constitutionally pledged to civil equality and representative institutions.

Sympathy for the Central Powers

But Americans were by no means unanimously in favor of the Allies. One American in three was either foreign-born or a first-generation citizen, many of them with strong Old-World sentiments that made them pro-German or unfriendly toward the Allied Powers. Millions of Americans traced their roots to Germany or Austria-Hungary. While they had come to the United States for its economic opportunities, many of them clung to their old culture. Few German-, Austrian-, or Hungarian-Americans seriously believed or suggested that their adopted country take the side of the fatherland. But they did hope for American neutrality, and in heavily German areas like Wisconsin and other parts of the Midwest, they said so loudly. The National German League numbered 3 million members and actively worked against intervention.

German-Americans joined with Irish-Americans in the German-Irish Legislative Committee for the Furtherance of United States Neutrality and the Labor's National Peace Council. Many of the nation's 4.5 million people of Irish descent hated England. They wished England ill in every venture, and when Germany aided Irish rebels in 1916, and England summarily crushed the "Easter Rising," many Irish-Americans expressed strong pro-German loyalties.

Similarly, many Russian and Polish Jews, who had suffered brutal persecution under the czars, supported Germany. They thought of Germany and Austria as countries where Jews enjoyed nearly equal citizenship. Socialists, who were an important minority within the Jewish community in New York, hated Russia above all other countries because of the cruelty of the czar's secret police.

With such a diverse population and tangle of conflicting loyalties, Wilson's policy of neutrality not only was idealistic, but was the only practical alternative, especially for a Democratic party politician who depended on ethnic voters. And it might have worked if Europe's "Great War" (as the First World War was called until the Second broke out in 1939) had been fought for clearly stated and limited goals, and had been concluded with an early victory by one side or the other.

The Deadly Stalemate

A quick victory was what the German General Staff had in mind. Germany's "Schlieffen Plan" was to knock the modern French army out of the war by flanking its powerful defenses. This meant invading France through neutral Belgium. In control of the Channel coast, German troops would keep the British army from landing in Europe and sweep down on Paris. In the meantime, weaker German forces in the east would take a beating from the Russians. However, once France and Britain were neutralized, troops from the western front could speed to meet the Russians on railroads designed for just that purpose.

The Schlieffen Plan failed because, instead of providing a broad avenue into France, the Belgians resisted heroically. Capturing the single fortress city of Liège took the Germans twelve days, longer than they expected to be in Belgium. Frustrated, the invaders treated the Belgians with a chilling ferocity, earning a reputation as "the savage Hun," which profoundly in-

fluenced public opinion in the United States and elsewhere.

The delay enabled the Russians to advance deeply into German territory and the German high commanders lost their nerve. At a critical moment, they weakened the army on the western front in order to stop the Russians. The result was stalemate on both fronts. Enemy armies dug entrenchments and earthworks and faced one another—along 475 miles in the west—across a "no man's land" of moonscape craters, spools of barbed wire, and the smell of death. For three years men on both sides would hurl themselves "over the top" and die by the tens of thousands for the sake of advancing the trenches a few miles.

The Technology of Killing

A revolution in military technology, and the inability of the generals to comprehend it, made the war unspeakably bloody. Although the airplane, first flown at Kitty Hawk, North Carolina, in December 1903, captured the imagination of romantics, it was of little importance in battle. (Ordinary soldiers considered pilots playboys; in fact, the life expectancy of British pilots at the front was two weeks.) Nor was poisonous mustard gas, used by both sides, very effective. Its results were devastating, but a slight shift in the wind blew the toxic fumes back on the army that had loosed it.

The machine gun, on the other hand, made the old-fashioned mass infantry charge, such as had dominated battle during the American Civil War, an exercise in suicide. When one army charged out of its trenches, enemy machine guns filled the air with a hurricane of lead that mowed down soldiers by the thousands. On the first day of the Battle of the Somme in July 1916, 60,000 young Britons were slaughtered or wounded, the majority of them within the first half hour. By the time the campaign sputtered to a meaningless end, British losses totaled 400,000; French, 200,000; and German, 500,000.

The British developed the tank as a means of neutralizing German machine guns. Armored vehicles could drive unharmed directly into gun emplacements. But the generals never used their edge intelligently. They attached the tanks to infantry units, thus slowing them to a walk, rather than sending groups of the steel monsters in advance of the foot soldiers.

Incompetence at the top of every army contributed substantially to the bloodshed. Petty personal jealousies among generals of the the Allies, especially between the English and the French, resulted in decisions that had nothing to do with the welfare of the common soldier or even the winning of the war.

The War at Sea

Americans were sickened by the news from Europe, but it was the war at sea that directly touched American interests. As in the past, naval war was economic war; it was aimed at destroying the enemy's commerce and, therefore, its ability to carry on the fight. Its naval superiority allowed Great Britain to strike first, proclaiming a blockade of Germany.

According to the "rules of war," all enemy merchant ships were fair game for seizing or sinking, although tradition required that crews and passengers be rescued. The ships of neutral nations, however, retained the right to trade with any nation as long as they were not carrying contraband (at first defined as war materiel).

The laws of blockade, which had caused friction between the English and the Americans in the past, were more complicated, and in 1914 Great Britain introduced several new wrinkles. The British "blockaded" Germany by mining some parts of the North Sea. Ships, including those of neutrals, would risk being destroyed merely by attempting to trade with Germany. The Royal Navy stopped many American ships on the high seas and took them to English ports for search. England redefined *contraband* to mean almost all trade goods, including some foodstuffs. When neutral Holland, Denmark, and Sweden began to import goods for secret resale to Germany (pastoral Denmark, which never before purchased American lard, imported 11,000 tons of it in the first months of the war), England slapped strict regulations on trade with those countries.

American objections were mild. The German market never had been important to American shippers, and wartime sales to England and France rose so dramatically that exporters needed no extra business. Trade with the Allies climbed from $825 million in 1914 to $3.2 billion in 1916, a fourfold increase in two years.

At first the Germans were indifferent to the British blockade. Their plan had been to win a quick victory on land, which rendered economic warfare moot. When the war stalemated, however, the German General Staff recognized the necessity of throttling England's import economy. Germany's tool for doing this was another creation of the new military technology, the *Unterseeboot* (undersea boat, or U-boat), or submarine.

Submarine Warfare

Ironically, the modern submarine was the invention of two Americans, John Holland and Simon Lake. When the navy rejected their device as frivolous, however, they took their plans to Europe. The Germans recog-

With a large flotilla of submarines, Germany turned British waters into a war zone during World War I.

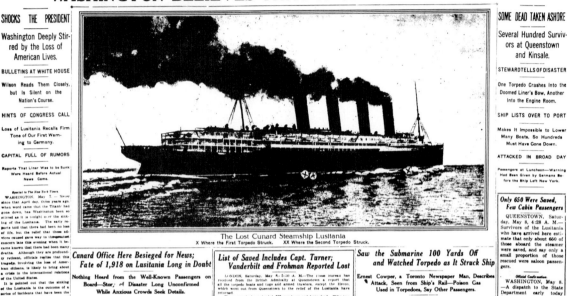

"All the News That's Fit to Print."

The New York Times.

EXTRA
5:30 A.M.

VOL. LXIV...NO. 20,923. ..... NEW YORK, SATURDAY, MAY 8, 1915.—TWENTY-FOUR PAGES. ONE CENT In Greater New York, Jersey City and Newark. | Elsewhere TWO CENTS.

LUSITANIA SUNK BY A SUBMARINE, PROBABLY 1,260 DEAD; TWICE TORPEDOED OFF IRISH COAST; SINKS IN 15 MINUTES; CAPT. TURNER SAVED, FROHMAN AND VANDERBILT MISSING; WASHINGTON BELIEVES THAT A GRAVE CRISIS IS AT HAND

SHOCKS THE PRESIDENT

Washington Deeply Stirred by the Loss of American Lives.

BULLETINS AT WHITE HOUSE

Wilson Reads Them Closely, but Is Silent on the Nation's Course.

HINTS OF CONGRESS CALL

Loss of Lusitania Recalls Firm Tone of Our First Warning to Germany.

CAPITAL FULL OF RUMORS

Reports That Liner Was to be Sunk Were Heard Before Actual News Came.

Special to The New York Times.
WASHINGTON, May 7.—Never since that April day, three years ago, when word came that the Titanic had gone down, has Washington been so stirred as it is tonight over the sinking of the Lusitania. The early reports told that there had been no loss of life, but the relief that these advices caused gave way to the gloomiest concern late this evening when it became known that there had been many deaths. Although this is profoundly rational, officials realize that this tragedy, involving the loss of American citizens, is likely to bring about a crisis in the international relations of the United States.

It is pointed out that the sinking of the Lusitania is the outcome of a series of incidents that have been the cause of concern to this Government

The Lost Cunard Steamship Lusitania
X Where the First Torpedo Struck.   XX Where the Second Torpedo Struck.

Cunard Office Here Besieged for News; Fate of 1,918 on Lusitania Long in Doubt

Nothing Heard from the Well-Known Passengers on Board—Story of Disaster Long Unconfirmed While Anxious Crowds Seek Details.

List of Saved Includes Capt. Turner; Vanderbilt and Frohman Reported Lost

LONDON, Saturday, May 8-5:30 A. M.—The Press Bureau has received from the British Admiralty at Queenstown a report that all the torpedo boats and tugs and trawlers, except the Heron, which went out from Queenstown to the relief of the Lusitania have returned.

These vessels have landed 500 survivors and forty dead. Fifty-two

Saw the Submarine 100 Yards Off and Watched Torpedo as It Struck Ship

Ernest Cowper, a Toronto Newspaper Man, Describes Attack, Seen from Ship's Rail—Poison Gas Used in Torpedoes, Say Other Passengers.

SOME DEAD TAKEN ASHORE

Several Hundred Survivors at Queenstown and Kinsale.

STEWARD TELLS OF DISASTER

One Torpedo Crashes Into the Doomed Liner's Bow, Another Into the Engine Room.

SHIP LISTS OVER TO PORT

Makes It Impossible to Lower Many Boats, So Hundreds Must Have Gone Down.

ATTACKED IN BROAD DAY

Passengers at Luncheon—Warning Had Been Given by Germans Before the Ship Left New York.

Only 650 Were Saved, Few Cabin Passengers

QUEENSTOWN, Saturday, May 8, 4:28 A. M.—Survivors of the Lusitania who have arrived here estimate that only about 660 of those aboard the steamer were saved, and say only a small proportion of those rescued were saloon passengers.

Official Confirmation
WASHINGTON, May 8.—A dispatch to the State Department early today

The front page of the New York Times *on May 8, 1915, announcing the sinking of the* Lusitania, *an English luxury liner.*

nized the submarine's potential and launched a large-scale construction program. By February 1915, Germany had a large enough flotilla of the vessels, each armed with nineteen torpedoes, to declare the waters surrounding the British Isles to be a "war zone." All enemy merchant ships within those waters were liable to be sunk, and the safety of neutral ships could not be absolutely guaranteed. Within days, several British vessels went to the bottom, and President Wilson warned the Kaiser of Germany's "strict accountability" for American lives and property lost to U-boats.

Because submarines were so fragile, the kind of warfare that they engaged in appeared to be particularly inhumane. On the surface, the submarine was helpless; a light six-inch gun mounted inconspicuously on the bow of a freighter was enough to blow a U-boat to bits. Because submarines could dive only slowly, British merchant vessels were instructed to ram them. Therefore, German submarines had to strike without warning, giving crew and passengers no opportunity to escape. And since submarines were tiny, their crews were cramped, and there was no room to take aboard those who abandoned ship. Survivors of torpedoed boats were on their own in the midst of the ocean.

Many Americans grumbled that if the English blockade was illegal, the German submarine campaign was immoral. The English were thieves, but the Germans were murderers. They drowned seamen by the score. And more than seamen. The issue came to a head on May 7, 1915, when the English luxury liner *Lusitania* was torpedoed off the coast of Ireland, and 1,195 people were killed, including 128 Americans. What kind of war was this, Americans asked, that killed innocent travelers? The *New York Times* described the Germans as "savages drenched with blood."

Wilson Wins a Victory

The Germans replied that they had warned Americans against traveling on the *Lusitania* through advertisements in major New York and Washington newspapers. They pointed out that the *Lusitania* had not been merely a passenger ship. It had been carrying 4,200 cases of small arms purchased in the United States and some high explosives. So many people had drowned because the *Lusitania* had gone down in only eighteen minutes, blown wide open not by the torpedo but by a secondary explosion. The British had been using innocent passengers as hostages for the safe conduct of war materiel.

Wilson was well aware of this and did not hold the British blameless in the tragedy. Nevertheless, Germany's military right to use the new weapon was less important to him than the principle of freedom of the seas for those not at war. He sent a series of strongly worded notes to Germany. The second was so antagonistic that the pacifistic Bryan feared it meant war. He resigned rather than sign it, and Wilson replaced him in the State Department with Robert Lansing, an international lawyer.

While making no formal promises to Wilson, the Germans stopped attacking passenger vessels, and the uproar faded. Then, early in 1916, the Allies announced that they were arming all merchant ships, and Germany responded that the U-boats would sink all enemy vessels without warning. On March 24, 1916, a French channel steamer, the *Sussex*, went down with an American among the casualties. Wilson threatened to break diplomatic relations with Germany, the last step before a declaration of war, if "unrestricted submarine warfare" were continued.

The German General Staff did not want the United States to enter the war. Plans for a major offensive on all fronts were afoot, and the German navy did not have enough U-boats to launch a full-scale attack on British shipping. In the Sussex Pledge of May 4, 1916, the German foreign office promised to observe the rules of visit and search before attacking enemy ships. It meant effectively abandoning the use of the submarine, but it kept the United States out of the war.

AMERICA GOES TO WAR

Wilson had won a spectacular diplomatic victory at the beginning of his campaign for reelection. He was enthusiastically renominated at the Democratic convention, and his campaign was given a theme that did not entirely please him. The keynote speaker designed his speech around the slogan "He Kept Us Out of War."

He Kept Us Out of War—While Preparing for It

Wilson did not like the slogan because, as he confided to an aide, "I can't keep the country out of war. Any little German lieutenant can put us into war at any time by some calculated outrage." He meant that a

---

WHAT'S IN A NAME?

The British called it the European War, and Americans were inclined to use that term until the United States intervened in April 1917. Then, a few idealistic but awkward tags were tried: War for the Freedom of Europe, War for the Overthrow of Militarism, War for Civilization, and—best known—Woodrow Wilson's War to Make the World Safe for Democracy. Only after 1918 did the Great War and the World War become standard—until 1939 when the outbreak of another great worldwide war made it World War I.

---

submarine commander, acting on his own, could bark out the order that would torpedo the Sussex Pledge. Like many national leaders before and since, Wilson had trapped himself in a position where control over a momentous decision was out of his hands, and he knew it.

Wilson began to prepare for the possibility of war as early as November 1915, when he asked Congress to beef up the army to 400,000 men and fund a huge expansion of the navy. He was pushed into this "preparedness" campaign by his political enemy Theodore Roosevelt, who jabbed and poked at the fact that American forces totaled fewer than 100,000; that the Quartermaster Corps (entrusted with supply) had only recently begun using trucks; that at one point in 1915 the American artillery had only enough ammunition for two days' fighting with cannon that were a generation obsolete.

Wilson also had to contend with an antipreparedness Congress led by Representative Claude Kitchin of North Carolina. With widespread backing among the western and southern progressives, on whom Wilson depended for support, the antipreparedness forces pointed out that it had been "preparedness" that had led to Europe going to war in the first place. If the United States had the means to fight, they argued, it was all the more likely that the United States *would* fight. Wilson had to settle for a compromise.

The Election of 1916

While Wilson wrestled with the preparedness issue, the Republicans patched up their split of 1912. Progressives who were able to stomach T.R.'s aggressiveness wanted to maintain the Bull Moose party's independence. They met and nominated the Colonel to run. Roosevelt wanted the Republican nomination too, however, and when he could not get it, he favored his friend, Henry Cabot Lodge, who was warlike enough, but no progressive. So easily, in the heat of war, he had lost sight of the ideal of 1912. When the

A flag-waving preparedness parade of 1916.

Trying and Failing to Keep the Peace

Elated but still nervous about the "little German lieutenant" who could plunge the United States into war, Wilson tried to act as a mediator. Only by ending the war in Europe could he be sure of keeping the United States out. During the winter of 1916/17, he believed that he was making progress, at least with the Germans. For a time, the British seemed to be the major obstacle to peace.

On January 22, 1917, Wilson outlined his peace plan to Congress. Only a "peace without victory," a "peace among equals" with neither winners nor losers, could solve the problem. The progressive idealist did not call for a mere cessation of hostilities. He proposed to pledge the warring powers to uphold the principles of national self-determination and absolute freedom of the seas, and to establish some kind of international mechanism for resolving future disputes.

But it was all an illusion. He and the American people were in for a rude awakening. The proposal was not even half-digested when, a week later, the German ambassador informed Wilson that on February 1, German submarines would begin sinking neutral as well as enemy ships in the war zone around Great Britain. With a fleet of 100 submarines, the German military planners believed that they could knock Great Britain out of the war within a few months. They knew that breaking the Sussex Pledge meant almost certain American intervention. But because the United States was unprepared, the German leaders calculated that the war would be over before more than a token American force could be landed in Europe.

Wilson was crestfallen, then irate. He broke off diplomatic relations with Germany, as he had threatened to do, and asked Congress for authority to arm American merchant ships. When former progressive allies such as La Follette and Borah filibustered to prevent this, he denounced them as "a little group of willful men, representing no opinion but their own."

Republicans actually nominated Supreme Court Justice Charles Evans Hughes, progressive in the past but a moderate on the war issue, T.R. lost heart and dropped out. William Allen White wrote that the Progressives were all dressed up with nowhere to go.

Hughes's integrity was unimpeachable. In dignity and presidential bearing, he was more than a match for Wilson. His distinguished gray beard was a reminder of the simpler days before the Great War. He spoke in high-sounding phrases. But Hughes was also a dull fellow on the speaker's platform, and he lacked Wilson's moral toughness. His views on the war issue actually differed little from the president's. He wanted to avoid war if he could. But thanks to Theodore Roosevelt, who stormed about the country sounding like the German Kaiser, the Republican choice came to be known as the war candidate.

This undeserved reputation cost Hughes just enough votes to give the election to Wilson. It was very close. Hughes carried every northeastern state but New Hampshire and every midwestern state but Ohio. He went to bed on election night believing that he was president.

Then one antiwar western state after another turned in majorities for Wilson. When he carried California by a paper-thin margin, he was elected, 277 electoral votes to 254. The election was on Tuesday. Not until Friday did the American people know for certain who would lead them for the next four years.

THE TWENTY-EIGHTH PRESIDENT

When Republican candidate Charles Evans Hughes went to bed early on election night, 1916, he believed he had carried California and with it the election. Shortly after midnight, tradition has it, a newspaper reporter phoned him at his home and was informed "the president cannot be disturbed." The caller, who had late results from California that gave the state to Woodrow Wilson by a few thousand votes, replied, "Well, when he wakes up tell him he isn't president anymore."

For the first time, the president was the leader of the war party. Nevertheless, Wilson did not abandon all hope of staying out until German submarines sent three American freighters to the bottom. On the evening of April 2, mourning that "it is a fearful thing to lead this great peaceful people into war," a solemn Wilson asked Congress for a formal declaration.

For four days a bitter debate shook the Capitol. Six senators and about fifty representatives fought to the end, blaming Wilson for having failed to be truly neutral and claiming that the United States was going to spill its young men's blood in order to bail out Wall Street's loans to England and to enrich the munitions manufacturers, the "merchants of death." In one of the most moving speeches, freshman Senator George Norris of Nebraska said, "We are going into war upon the command of gold. . . . We are about to put the dollar sign on the American flag."

Why America Went to War

In later years, some historians would say that Norris had been right. With varying emphases, they agreed that special interests had methodically maneuvered the United States into a war that did not concern the country. To the extent that Wall Street favored a British victory for the sake of its own profits and that the "merchants of death" fed off the blood of soldiers, they were correct.

But to say that certain interest groups wanted to go to war is not to say that they got their way. In fact, Wilson was as unlikely to take his policy from Wall Street and munitions manufacturers as he was to seek advice from Theodore Roosevelt. To Wilson, the free-

dom of the seas was sacred, a right on which Americans had insisted since the 1790s. Moreover, the president shared in the profound shift in public sentiment from 1914 and even 1915, when virtually no American dreamed of declaring war, to the spring of 1917, when the majority favored entering the conflict. The reasons for this about-face lie in the growing belief that Germany represented a force for evil in the world and the skillful propaganda of the British and pro-British Americans in encouraging this perception.

The Hun and His Kultur

The depiction of Germans as barbaric "Huns" practicing a diabolical "*Kultur*" (German for *culture*) had its origins in the German violation of Belgian neutrality. Figuratively at first, the British and French called the invasion "the rape of Belgium" and soon discovered the propaganda value of the word. In fact, the German occupation of the little country, while harsh, was generally no more brutal than the wartime controls the British slapped on the ever-rebellious Irish. But wall posters representing the broken body of a young girl being dragged away by a bloated, beastlike German soldier in a spiked helmet elicited all the horrible implications that rape connotes.

German insistences that their troops observed all due proprieties toward civilians were undermined in October 1915, when the German army executed Edith Cavell, the British head of the Berkendael Medical Institute in Brussels. Although Cavell was guilty of acts that were considered espionage in international law (she helped a number of British prisoners escape), the execution of a woman for charitable acts was pro-

A banner headline on the New York American *reported the beginning of war between the United States and Germany, April 6, 1917.*

foundly stupid when women were only rarely executed for murder.

The submarine war further angered Americans. Not everyone agreed with Wilson that the rights of neutrals during modern war could be absolute. But repeated incidents of unarmed merchant seamen and innocent passengers drowning in the dark, cold waters of the North Atlantic touched a delicate nerve. Artists brilliantly aroused basic human fear in posters that showed seamen fighting vainly to swim while their ship sank in the moonlit background.

German saboteurs were probably not so active in the United States as British and pro-British propagandists claimed. Nevertheless, several German diplomats were caught red-handed in 1915 when a bumbling agent left incriminating papers on a train, and in 1916, the huge Black Tom munitions stores in New Jersey was completely destroyed in a suspicious "accident."

But the real blockbuster was a mere piece of paper. On February 25, 1917, while Wilson was searching for a last chance to avoid war, the British communicated to him a message that the German foreign minister, Arthur Zimmermann, had sent to the Mexican government. In the event that the United States declared war on Germany, Zimmermann had proposed, Germany would finance a Mexican attack on the United States. Assuming Germany won, Mexico would be rewarded after the war with the return of some of the territory that it had given up in the Mexican War 70 years earlier, specifically the "lost provinces" of New Mexico and Arizona.

It was a foolish proposal. Mexico was still wracked by civil turmoil, and was in no condition to make war on the United States. Nevertheless, with the American people already angered, the Zimmermann Telegram persuaded many that the unprincipled Hun must be stopped.

The American Contribution

The Germans provoked the American intervention on a gamble. German leaders bet that their all-out U-boat attack would starve England into surrender before the Americans could contribute to the war effort. For three frightening months, it appeared as though they had guessed right. In February and March 1917, German submarines sank 570,000 tons of shipping bound to and from England. In April, the total ran to almost 900,000 tons. A quarter of the British merchant fleet lay at the bottom of the sea. At one point, England had enough food on hand to feed the island nation for only three weeks. Starving people cannot fight a war.

But the Germans lost their wager. The major American contribution to the war was precisely in keeping

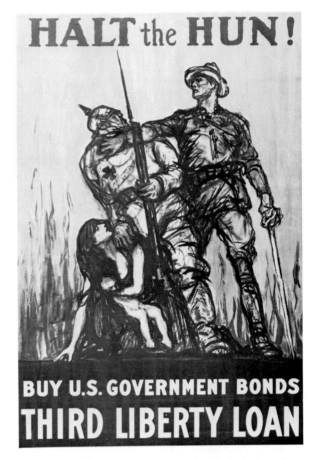

HALT the HUN!

BUY U.S. GOVERNMENT BONDS
THIRD LIBERTY LOAN

The art of the poster—expressing a thought instantly and forcefully—reached its apogee during World War I.

England and the other Allies supplied. At the insistence of Admiral William S. Sims, merchantmen ceased to travel alone. Guarded by naval vessels, particularly the small, fast, and heavily armed destroyers (the nemesis of the U-boats), merchant ships crossed the Atlantic in huge convoys.

Over the objections of the Royal Navy (but with the support of Prime Minister David Lloyd George), Sims succeeded in building his "bridge of ships." As early as May 1917, U-boat kills dropped drastically, far below what the German navy claimed it could do. By July, the American navy took over most defense operations in the Western Hemisphere and sent 34 destroyers to Queenstown (present-day Cóbh), Ireland, to assist the British. So successful was the well-guarded convoy system that not one of the 2 million American soldiers sent to France in 1917 and 1918 was drowned on the way. In the meantime, by commandeering more than a hundred German ships that were in American ports at the time war was declared

American troops head for the front in 1918.

(including the behemoth *Vaterland,* renamed the *Leviathan*) and by launching a massive shipbuilding program, the Americans were soon producing two ships for every one that the Germans sank.

The Fighting Over There

Soldiers went too. General John Pershing arrived in Paris in July 1917 with the first units of the American Expeditionary Force, the First Infantry Division. This was primarily a symbolic gesture. Because Pershing refused to send poorly trained men to the front, the Germans were proved right in gambling that American reinforcements could not in themselves turn the tide. The first Americans to see action, near Verdun in October, were used merely to beef up decimated French, British, and Canadian units.

The autumn of 1917 went poorly for the Allies. The Germans and Austrians defeated the Italians in the

south and, in November, knocked Russia out of the war. A liberal democratic government that had deposed the czar in March 1917 proved unable to keep a mutinous Russian army supplied, and a group of revolutionary Communists, the Bolsheviks, led by Vladmir Ilyich Lenin, seized power on the basis of promises of "Peace and Bread." The Treaty of Brest-Litovsk, which the Germans forced on the Russians, was vindictive and harsh. News of it convinced many Americans that they had done well in going to war to stop the Hun's hunger for world conquest. By closing down the eastern front, the Germans were able to throw a bigger army than ever into France.

In May 1918, Germany launched a do-or-die offensive. The Allies fell back to the Marne River, close enough to Paris that the shelling could be heard on the Champs Elysées. But by this time there were 250,000 fresh American troops in France, including about 27,000 at Château-Thierry, near the hottest of the fighting. By the middle of July, when the Germans attempted one last drive toward the capital, about 85,000 Americans helped hurl them back at Belleau Wood.

The Supreme Allied Commander, Field Marshal Ferdinand Foch, wanted to incorporate American

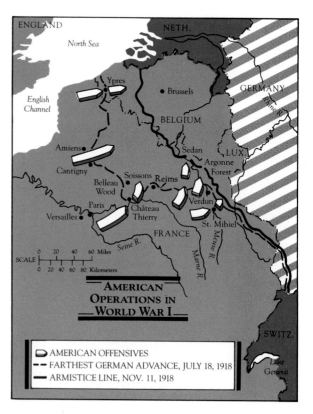

American soldiers move supplies during the Argonne offensive, the last large battle involving Americans before World War I came to an end.

By the summer of 1918, the Americans in France represented the margin of victory over the Germans. In July, the Americans took over the attack on a bulge in the German lines called the St. Mihiel Salient, and succeeded in clearing it out. The final great American battle was along a 24-mile line in the Argonne Forest, a naturally rugged country just short of the border between France and Germany that had been transformed into a ghostly wasteland by four years of digging and shelling. It was in that position that over 1 million "doughboys" were sitting when, on November 11, 1918, the Germans surrendered.

Armistice

In the trenches and back home, Americans celebrated deliriously. Millions of people gathered in city centers throughout the country, dancing and whooping. They believed that the Yanks had won the war. After all, the Germans had stalemated the French and British until the boys had gone "over there," in the words of a popular song of the time. Then, just a year after the Americans had begun to fight, it was over.

The American intervention was invaluable to the Allied victory, but the unmitigated joy in the United States was possible only because the American sacrifice was a comparatively minor one. Over 100,000 Americans were dead, more than half of them from disease (particularly the influenza that swept the world in 1918) rather than from bullets. By comparison, 1.4 million French and almost 1 million British soldiers died. Three-quarters of all the Frenchmen who served in the armed forces were casualties. Never again would France be truly a great power, and Great Britain was also badly maimed. Germany and Russia were defeated. If it was not true that the United States had "won the war," it was certainly true that the United States was the only nation whose people could feel like victors.

troops into exhausted British and French units. Pershing stubbornly insisted that the Yanks fight as a unit. This was important to him not only for reasons of morale, but because Wilson had made it clear that the United States was not an "ally" of Britain and France but merely their "associate." In order to ensure his "peace without victory," Wilson was determined to play an independent role at the peace conference that would follow the war. Foch had no choice but to give in and grumble.

WORLD WAR I CASUALTIES				
	Total mobilized forces	Killed or died	Wounded	Prisoners & missing	Total casualties
United States	4,791,000	117,000	204,000	5,000	326,000
Russia	12,000,000	1,700,000	4,950,000	2,500,000	9,150,000
France	8,410,000	1,358,000	4,266,000	537,000	6,161,000
British Commonwealth	8,904,000	908,000	2,090,000	192,000	3,190,000
Italy	5,615,000	650,000	947,000	600,000	2,197,000
Germany	11,000,000	1,774,000	4,216,000	1,153,000	7,143,000
Austria-Hungary	7,800,000	1,200,000	3,620,000	2,220,000	7,020,000
TOTAL	58,520,000	7,707,000	20,293,000	7,187,000	35,187,000

WILLIAM D. HAYWOOD
1869–1927

Big Bill Haywood was famous during the years before the Great War. As the head of the IWW, the Industrial Workers of the World, he came close to wielding real power as a leader of the unskilled industrial and agricultural working people so vital in the economy. But the war was to destroy Haywood's career and shatter his vision of what America should mean. Within a few years after the guns were stilled, he was a lonely exile who would never come home.

William D. Haywood was born in Salt Lake City in 1869. He became a miner in northern Nevada while still a teenager. Several times he turned to other work, cowboying, prospecting for a mine of his own, homesteading on the site of an abandoned army post. Haywood was a quintessential westerner, looking for the chance to improve himself, an implicit believer in the American gospel of opportunity that said the West was the place a man could best do such a thing.

Bad luck and the attractive wages gold and silver miners took home brought Haywood back to the mines of Silver City, Idaho. There he found his opportunity to rise within the Western Federation of Miners, the militant labor union of the miners, mill, and smelter workers of the region. His forceful personality and aptitude for running an organization brought him to the attention of the WFM's leadership in Denver. At the turn of the century, Haywood moved to the metropolis as the WFM's Secretary-Treasurer.

In Silver City, Haywood had supervised an orderly union local, negotiating wages and conditions across a table from the owners of the mines. Elsewhere in the West, union miners fought violent strikes with their employers, which were increasingly large corporations with headquarters in San Francisco, New York, and London.

The miners resented absentee control of the gold and silver they believed they had found and which they won from the earth. They worked daily with explosives and were apt, when pushed, to fight back with dynamite and guns. The bosses, when they sensed a chance to break the miners' unions and gain uncontested control of labor in the mining camps, were equally quick to use violence in the form of hired thugs and pliant local and state authorities. Bill Haywood found himself one of the leaders of an organization engaged in what was unmistakeably class warfare. He did not disdain the role. During the 1890s, he had concluded that some form of socialism, common rather than private ownership of the means of production, was the only way to achieve social justice in the United States.

The miner owners and their allies in government considered Haywood one of an "Inner Circle" of sinister conspirators whom they held responsible for the disorder. If he could be removed from the scene, they believed they could gain the upper hand in labor rela-

Bill Haywood and Elizabeth Gurley Flynn of the IWW march with striking textile workers in Paterson, New Jersey.

tions. In 1906, when a ne'er-do-well known as Harry Orchard confessed that he had murdered a former governor of Idaho on the orders of the "Inner Circle," Haywood was brought to trial in Boise.

The prosecution's case relied heavily on the testimony of the unsavory Orchard. Haywood's lawyer, Clarence Darrow, seized on this and defended him by prosecuting Orchard's character. Haywood was acquitted.

His career in the WFM was at an end. Other leaders of the union believed Haywood's tough talk was responsible for the trial (and may have believed him guilty of the crime). It mattered little to Haywood. The publicity had made him an eminent man. Intellectuals, particularly in New York's Greenwich Village, lionized him as a primal, exemplar of the working masses. He lectured widely, building his image with a simple, eloquent platform manner. He was elected to the Socialist party's National Executive Committee and twice represented the party at international conferences. He became an organizer for the IWW, the revolutionary union of unskilled workers he had helped found in 1905. He was in the headlines during strikes the IWW led in Lawrence, Massachusetts, in 1912 and Paterson, New Jersey in 1913.

In 1914, Haywood became Secretary-Treasurer of the IWW, in effect its leader. He introduced a degree of order to an organization that had been almost guerrilla-like in its operations. He regularized dues collections, set up an efficient national office in Chicago, and perfected a system for enrolling the dispersed casual workers who brought in the nation's grain harvest, previously a virtually unorganizable workforce.

Haywood's IWW opposed American entrance into World War I. Haywood was, however, very cautious in the issue. He believed that the workers' business lay "at the point of production," in the factory, field, forest, and mine, not in fighting causes that, however noble, were beyond their power to effect. He attempted to soft-pedal the IWW's antiwar line. He dropped bitterly sardonic antiwar lyrics from the IWW's songbook and said that it was a matter of personal choice whether or not members registered for the draft.

To no avail. In the fall of 1917, federal authorities launched nationwide raids of IWW headquarters. Either because they believed that the IWW was really treasonous, because they feared what the union's strength in the critical areas of agriculture, lumber, and copper could mean to the war effort, or simply because they saw a chance to use wartime hysteria as an opportunity to crush the anticapitalist IWW and Big Bill Haywood, the federal prosecutors did just that.

Long trials for sedition drained the IWW's resources and distracted its leaders from the business of running a union. Vigilante action against the IWW in the field reduced its membership. For all his cynical comments about the capitalist enemy, Haywood was shocked that he and more than a hundred other IWW leaders were found guilty of charges that bordered on the absurd.

By 1921 he was stunned by the shattering of the IWW. Like many American socialists, Haywood found consolation only in the success of the Bolsheviks in far-off Russia. Instead of reporting to prison, he slipped aboard a ship and sailed for the Soviet Union.

For a few years, while the Russian Communists deluded themselves that international revolution was just around the corner, Haywood acted like a leader of that campaign, appearing at ceremonies in Moscow. When the capitalist order proved far from dead in Europe and America, and the Soviet leaders engrossed themselves in domestic affairs, Haywood was first put in charge of a factory (he was apparently a failure at the job) and then pensioned off in a small apartment in the Russian capital.

He was delighted to receive American visitors but was miserable as an exile. There was no alternative. To return to the United States meant prison. In 1927, he suffered a stroke and died.

For Further Reading

Overviews and Classics

Vincent P. DeSantis, *The Shaping of Modern America, 1877–1916* (1973)

Arthur S. Link, *Woodrow Wilson and the Progressive Era* (1954)

William L. O'Neill, *The Progressive Years: America Comes of Age* (1975)

Robert H. Wiebe, *The Search for Order, 1880–1920* (1967)

Valuable Special Studies

A. E. Barbeau and F. Henri, *The Unknown Soldiers* (1974)

E. H. Buehrig, *Woodrow Wilson and the Balance of Power* (1955)

Foster R. Dulles, *America's Rise to World Power, 1898–1954* (1955)

Lewis L. Gould, *Reform and Regulation: American Politics, 1900–1916* (1978)

Otis L. Graham, Jr., *The Great Campaigns: Reform and War in America, 1900–1928* (1971)

P. Edward Haley, *Revolution and Intervention: The Diplomacy of Taft and Wilson with Mexico, 1910–1917* (1970)

George F. Kennan, *American Diplomacy, 1900–1950* (1951)

David Kennedy, *Over Here: The First World War and American Society* (1980)

N. G. Levin, Jr., *Woodrow Wilson and World Politics: America's Response to War and Revolution* (1968)

A. S. Link, *Wilson the Diplomatist* (1957)

———, *Woodrow Wilson: War, Revolution, and Peace* (1979)

Ernest R. May, *The World War and American Isolation, 1914–1917* (1959)

Walter Millis, *The Road to War* (1935)

R. E. Quirk, *An Affair of Honor: Woodrow Wilson and the Occupation of Vera Cruz* (1962)

Lawrence Stallings, *The Doughboys* (1963)

C. C. Tansill, *America Goes to War* (1938)

Russell Weigley, *The American Way of War: History of United States Military Policy and Strategy* (1973)

William A. Williams, *The Tragedy of American Diplomacy* (1959)

Biographies and Autobiographies

John M. Blum, *Woodrow Wilson and the Politics of Morality* (1956)

John A. Garraty, *Woodrow Wilson* (1956)

Arthur S. Link, *Woodrow Wilson* (1947–65)

Jubilant American soldiers prepare to depart for Europe, *"over there."*

39

Over Here
The First World War at Home, 1917–1920

"Every war," said the Irish playwright George Bernard Shaw, "is a reign of terror." In earlier times, simple peasants and town folk in the paths of marching armies were at the mercy of hard, immoral men who regarded anyone and anything within their reach as fair game. When armies were professionalized and brought under tight discipline, the worst of the marauding was brought under control.

By the 1910s, however, when Shaw made his remark, the expense of waging war—the prodigious cost of weapons and huge armies—meant that for a country to fight, the entire society and economy had to be mobilized. When national leaders concluded, as they all did during the First World War, that their very survival was at stake, then they felt justified in moving quickly against anyone and anything that stood in the way of winning, including the doubts of their own citizens. When the warring nation was free and democratic, like the United States, Great Britain, and France, war meant that leaders must often be less than candid. In war, another saying had it, the first casualty is truth.

President Wilson understood this. On the one hand, he called the First World War a war to make the world safe for democracy. On the other hand, he told a newspaper reporter in April 1917, "Once lead this people into war, and they'll forget there ever was such a thing as tolerance. To fight you must be ruthless and brutal, and the spirit of ruthless brutality will enter into the very fiber of our national life." It was to be one of the tragic ironies of Wilson's career that he was to initiate many of the policies that made his prophecy come true.

THE PROGRESSIVE WAR

Equally ironic, the First World War was simultaneously the apogee of progressivism, when reformers had a free hand in turning their beliefs into policy, and the undoing of the progressive movement. For two years, progressive moralists and social planners of the New Nationalist stripe had their way in Washington. Within two years of the conclusion of the war, there was no progressive movement, only a few isolated voices crying in the wilderness of a congressional minority and getting no replies but echoes from the past.

The Movement Splits

The war split the progressives. A few of them itched to fight. The most famous was Theodore Roosevelt, a pathetic shrill figure in his waning years. When the United States finally intervened, T.R. asked for a command in Europe. Prudently, for this was no splendid little war, Wilson ignored him, but in doing so permanently embittered many of Roosevelt's devotees.

Other Republican progressives, mostly westerners such as La Follette, Norris, Borah, and Hiram Johnson, held out to the bitter end for American neutrality. After the declaration of war, they toned down their rhetoric in the interests of national unity. (And in order to save their careers: some newspaper cartoonists depicted them accepting medals from the German kaiser.) But they never changed their opinion that going to war was a tragic blunder that had been foisted on the country by munitions makers and bankers. They prolonged the debate on the Conscription Act of 1917 for six weeks, finally forcing Congress to exempt men under 21 from the draft. Any warmth they felt toward Wilson before April 1917 quickly dissipated thereafter.

Not so with most progressives. In Congress and out, the majority of them wholeheartedly supported the war. Like Wilson, they had come to believe that imperial Germany represented a deadly threat to free institutions all over the world. Moreover, in the task of mobilizing resources in order to fight the war, and in the wave of patriotic commitment that swept the country, the progressives saw a golden opportunity to put their ideas for economic and social reform to work.

They were right on one count. It was impossible to wage modern total war and cling to the nineteenth-century vision of a free, unregulated economy. Armies that numbered millions of men could not be supplied with food, clothing, shelter, medicine, and arms by companies that were free to do as their owners chose.

This poster reminded men to register for the draft.

France and England had clamped tight controls on their factories and farms. American progressives believed that the United States would have to do the same.

The progressives were not disappointed. Suggestions for regulation of business that had been rejected as too radical proved, in the emergency of wartime, to be less than was necessary. The federal government virtually took over the direction of the economy.

The Planned Economy

Some 5,000 government agencies were set up during the twenty months that the United States was at war, a statistical average of more than eight new agencies a day! Some were useless, wasteful bureaucracies that were established without careful thought and served little purpose save to provide desks, chairs, paper clips, and salaries for the functionaries who ran them. A few were failures. The Aircraft Production Board was commissioned to construct 22,000 airplanes in a year. That figure was unrealistic (and unnecessary). But the 1,200 craft and 5,400 replacement motors that the board actually delivered to France were far fewer than a crack hustler with a bank loan could have supplied.

Other agencies were more successful. The Shipping Board, actually founded in 1916 before the declaration of war, produced vessels twice as fast as the Germans could sink them. Privately run shipbuilding companies, loaded with deadwood in management, were not up to that herculean task.

The United States Railway Administration, headed by Wilson's son-in-law and Secretary of the Treasury, William G. McAdoo, was created early in 1918 when the owners of the nation's railroads proved incapable of moving the volume of freight the war created. The government paid the stockholders a rent equal to their earnings in the prosperous prewar years and simply took over. McAdoo untangled a colossal snafu in management within a few weeks, and reorganized the railroads into an efficient system such as the nation had never known. About 150,000 freight cars short of what was needed to do the job in 1917, American railroads enjoyed a surplus of 300,000 by the end of the war.

The various war production boards were coordinated by a superagency, the War Industries Board, which was headed by a Wall Street millionaire, Bernard Baruch. His presence at the top of the planning pyramid indicated that the progressives had not won their campaign for a directed economy without paying a price. American industry and agriculture were regulated, indeed regimented, as never before. But democratically elected officials and public-spirited experts with no stake in the profits were not in the driver's seat. Businessmen were.

Herbert Hoover:
The Administrator as War Hero

The task given to Food Administrator Herbert C. Hoover was even more difficult than McAdoo's, and his success was more spectacular. He was assigned to organize food production, distribution, and consumption so that America's farms could feed the United States, supply the huge Allied armies, and help maintain many European civilians.

Only 43 years old when he took the job, Hoover already was known as a "boy wonder." An orphan when still a boy in Iowa, Hoover moved to California and worked his way through Stanford University. A mining engineer who spent his young adulthood abroad, he had an eye for assets as well as adits. Shrewd investments made him a millionaire—and bored him

with making money when he was still young. Being besieged in China during the Boxer Rebellion was exciting, but Hoover's ambitions lay in public service. Like Andrew Carnegie, he believed that able, wealthy men had special responsibilities to society. Unlike Carnegie, who gave money away, Hoover meant to devote his talents for administration and organization to public service.

He got his chance when, before American intervention, he was asked to take over the problem of getting food to devastated Belgium. He jumped at the challenge, liquidated his business, and undoubtedly saved tens of thousands, if not hundreds of thousands, of lives.

He did it without charm or personal flash. Hoover was intense, humorless—all business. His method was to apply engineering principles to the solution of human problems. Progressives admired just such expertise, and the cool, methodical Hoover was a refreshing contrast to other humanitarians who moved about in a cloud of pious self-congratulation. It is an insight into the spirit of the times that he became a war hero comparable to Black Jack Pershing and America's most dashing ace pilot, Eddie Rickenbacker.

Hooverizing America

Hoover preferred voluntary programs to coercion. Food was not rationed during the First World War, as a few items would be during the Second. Instead, Hoover sponsored colorful publicity campaigns that urged American families to observe Wheatless Mondays, Meatless Tuesdays, Porkless Thursdays, and so on. This was shrewd psychology. Making do without a vital commodity one day a week was an easy sacrifice, but it made civilians feel as though they were part of the fighting machine. Moreover, when observed by millions, the savings were enormous.

Hoover also encouraged city dwellers to plant "Victory gardens" in their tiny yards. Every tomato that was raised at home freed commercially produced food for the front. His agency promoted classes in economizing in the kitchen and distributed cookbooks on how to prepare leftovers. The impact was so great that, half-seriously, Americans began to use the word *hooverize* to mean "economize." Chicago proudly reported that the housewives in that city had hooverized the monthly production of garbage down by a third.

Hoover increased farm production through a combination of patriotic boosting and cash incentives. He helped increase wheat acreage from 45 million in 1917 to 75 million in 1919. American exports of foodstuffs to the Allies tripled over already high prewar levels. Hoover was called "the Miracle Man," and another

Will you have a part in Victory?

WRITE TO THE NATIONAL WAR GARDEN COMMISSION ~ WASHINGTON, D.C. for free books on gardening, canning & drying.

"Every Garden a Munition Plant"

Charles Lathrop Pack, President

A National War Gardens Commission poster encouraged citizens to plant home vegetable gardens, thus freeing commercial producers to concentrate on providing goods for the war effort.

young Washington administrator, Undersecretary of the Navy Franklin D. Roosevelt, wanted the Democratic party to nominate him for president in 1920.

Managing People

People were mobilized too: workers and ordinary citizens as well as soldiers. In May 1917, Congress passed the Selective Service Act, the first draft law since the Civil War. Registration was compulsory for all men between the ages of 21 and 45. (In 1918, the minimum age was lowered to 18.) From the 10 million who registered within a month of passage (24 million by the end of the war), local draft boards selected able-bodied recruits according to quotas assigned them. Some occupational groups were deferred, but no one was allowed to buy his way out, as had been done during the Civil War. Indeed, authority to make final

selections was given to local draft boards in order to silence critics who said that conscription had no place in a democracy. About 3 million young men were inducted through selective service in addition to the 2 million who volunteered.

About 21,000 draftees claimed to be conscientious objectors on religious grounds, although, in the end, only 4,000 insisted on being assigned to noncombatant duty, as medics or in the Quartermaster Corps. Approximately 500 men refused to cooperate with the military in any way (some for political rather than religious reasons). Under the terms of the Selective Service Act, they were imprisoned and, generally, treated poorly. Camp Leonard Wood in Missouri had an especially bad reputation. In Washington State, a man who claimed that Jesus had forbidden him to take up arms was sentenced to death. He was not executed, but the last conscientious objector was not freed from prison until 1933, long after most Americans had come to agree with him that the war had been a mistake.

Labor Takes Its Seat

In order to keep the factories humming, Wilson made concessions to the labor movement that would have been unthinkable a few years earlier. He appointed Samuel Gompers, the patriotic president of the American Federation of Labor, to sit on Baruch's War Industries Board. In return for this recognition, Gompers pledged the AFL unions to a no-strike policy for the duration of the conflict.

Because wages rose during the war, there were comparatively few work stoppages. Business boomed, and employers dizzy with bonanza profits did not care to jeopardize them by resisting moderate demands by their employees. Most important, the National War Labor Board, on which five AFL nominees sat, mediated industrial disputes before they disrupted production and, in many cases, found in favor of the workers.

The quiet incorporation of organized labor into the decision-making process made the AFL "respectable," as it never had been before. From 2.7 million members in 1914, the union movement (including independent unions) grew to 4.2 million in 1919.

Blacks in Wartime

Like Gompers, leaders of American blacks hoped that by proving their patriotism in time of crisis, blacks would win an improved status. About 400,000 young black men enlisted or responded to the draft; proportionately, more blacks than whites donned khaki.

It was difficult to ignore the contradiction between Wilson's ringing declaration that the purpose of the war was to defend democracy and liberty and the sec-

Members of the 369th Infantry, a black regiment, returned to the United States in 1919
wearing medals given to them by the French government commending them
for gallantry in battle.

ond-class citizenship suffered by black people. W. E. B. Du Bois, the leader of the NAACP, pointedly reminded the president of the dichotomy, and Wilson did go so far as to issue a strong condemnation of lynching. Nevertheless, mere war could not destroy deeply rooted racist sentiments. Black soldiers were assigned to segregated units and usually put to menial tasks such as digging trenches and loading trucks behind the lines. Only a few black units saw combat, although one regiment that did was awarded the Croix de Guerre for gallantry in battle by the French government.

Military segregation had its advantages for some blacks. In order to command the black units, the army trained and commissioned more than 1,200 officers. This was particularly gratifying to Du Bois, who staked his hopes for the future on the creation of a black elite.

Race Riot at Home

More important in the long run than service in the army was the massive movement of blacks from the rural and strictly segregated South to the industrial centers of the North. Before 1914, only about 10,000 blacks a year drifted from the South to cities like New York, Philadelphia, Detroit, and Chicago. After 1914, when the risks of ocean travel choked off immigration from abroad while factories filling war orders needed workers, 100,000 blacks made the trek each year. It was not so great a leap in miles as the European immigration, but it was just as wrenching socially. From a Mississippi delta cabin to a Detroit factory and slum was a big change in life.

Those who served in the army, and most of those who moved north, were young people. They were less inclined to accept the daily humiliations that accompanied being black in white America. This was particularly true of the men in uniform, who believed that their service entitled them to respect.

The result was that 1917 was a year of racial conflict, with a frightening race riot in industrial East St. Louis, Illinois. In Houston, white civilians fought a pitched battle with black soldiers, and twelve people were killed. Although both sides shared the blame for the riot, thirteen black soldiers were hanged and fourteen were imprisoned for life. Du Bois and the NAACP were only partly correct in their analysis of how the war would affect blacks. Society made economic concessions to blacks in the interests of winning the war, but it did not grant civil equality.

It's a Woman's War

The woman-suffrage movement, on the contrary, skillfully parlayed wartime idealism and fears into final victory for the long-fought cause. Imitating British and French examples, the armed forces inducted female volunteers, mostly as nurses and clerical workers. More important was the same labor shortage that created opportunities in industry for blacks. Working-class women began doing factory work and other jobs that had been closed to them. Women operated trolley cars, drove delivery trucks, cleaned streets, directed traffic, and filled jobs in every industry from aircraft construction to zinc galvanization. Middle-class women took the lead in organizing support groups. They rolled bandages, held patriotic rallies, and filled the holds of ships with knitted sweaters and socks and home-baked cookies for the boys in France. With women's contributions to waging the war so obvious, it was increasingly difficult for patriotic politicians to oppose suffrage with the argument that women belonged in the nursery minding infants.

Voting At Last

By 1917, the feminist movement was split once again into radical and conservative wings. Curiously, while the "radicals" and "conservatives" were hostile toward each other, their different approaches both contributed to final victory. Thus, when the aggressive Women's Party led by Alice Paul demonstrated noisily in Washington, burning a copy of Wilson's idealistic Fourteen Points and chaining themselves to the fence in front of the White House, many politicians went scurrying for reassurance to the more polite National American Woman Suffrage Association.

Led by Carrie Chapman Catt, the association shrewdly obliged them. Not only did most American women oppose such irresponsible behavior, Catt argued, but social stability and conservative government could be ensured only by granting women the vote. Their numbers would counterbalance the increasing influence of radicals and foreigners at the polls, not to mention the blacks who were demanding their rights.

The suffrage movement was too long in the field and too large to be denied. Even Wilson, who instinctively disliked the idea of women voting, announced his support. On June 4, 1919, a few months after the Armistice, Congress sent the Nineteenth Amendment to the states. On August 18, 1920, ratification by Tennessee put it into the Constitution. "The right of citizens . . . to vote," it read, "shall not be denied or abridged by the United States or by any State on account of sex." Carrie Chapman Catt had no doubt about what had put it over. It was the war, the former pacifist said, that liberated American women.

The Moral War

Another long progressive campaign already had been brought to a victorious end. Like the suffragists, the

Women riveters in a Puget Sound shipyard in 1918.

In 1920, for the first time, women in every state were eligible to vote.

prohibitionists appeared to be stalled permanently on the eve of the war. In 1914, only one-quarter of the states had prohibition laws on the books, and many of those were casually enforced. With American intervention in the war, however, the antidrinking forces added a new and decisive argument to their armory: the distilling of liquor consumed vast quantities of grain that were needed as food. Shortly after the declaration of war, Congress passed the Lever Act, a section of which forbade the sale of grain to distilleries.

Because many breweries were run by German-Americans, they were doubly handicapped in fighting the prohibitionists. Although Americans had developed a taste for cold lager beer, the beverage was still associated with Germans. Moralism, hooverizing, and the popular insistence on 100 percent Americanism all combined to bring about, in December 1917, the passage of the Eighteenth Amendment, which prohibited "the manufacture, sale, or transportation of intoxicating liquors" in the United States. It was ratified in 1919 and put into effect by the Volstead Act.

War usually leads to relaxation of sexual morality, as young men are removed from the social restraints of family and custom. The First World War proved to be no exception. However, well-meaning moralists in Wilson's administration hoped to take advantage of the mobilization of millions in order to instill high moral standards in the young men under their control. Josephus Daniels, the deeply religious Secretary of the Navy, thought of his ships as "floating universities" of moral reform. He gave orders to clear out the red-light

districts that were a fixture in every naval port, and the army did the same in cities near its bases.

Prostitution was not eliminated by these orders any more than whiskey and beer drinking were abolished by the Eighteenth Amendment. But the short-term victories encouraged reformers in their belief that, among the horrors, the First World War was a blessing on reformers.

CONFORMITY AND REPRESSION

It was not a blessing on civil libertarians. As Wilson had predicted, white-hot patriotism scorched the traditions of free political expression and tolerance of disparate ways of life. Of course, free speech, religious expression, and ethnic variety had been violated before the First World War. But never had violation of the Bill of Rights been so widespread as during the war, and never had the federal government so stridently supported, even initiated, repression.

The Campaign Against the Socialists

The Socialist party of America was the only national political institution to oppose American intervention. In April 1917, in the wake of the declaration of war, the party met in emergency convention in St. Louis and proclaimed "unalterable opposition" to a conflict that killed workingpeople and paid dividends to capitalists. Rather than hurting the party at the polls, its stance earned an increase in votes as many non-Socialists cast ballots for the Socialist party as the only way to express their dissent on the issue.

Government moved quickly to head off the possibility of an antiwar bandwagon. The state legislature of New York expelled seven Socialist assemblymen simply because they objected to the war. Not until after the war did courts overrule the unconstitutional action. Victor Berger was elected to Congress from Milwaukee, but denied his seat. When he also beat the candidate supported by both the Democratic and Republican parties in the special election to fill the vacancy, Congress again refused to seat Berger. The seat remained empty until 1923 when Berger filled it. In the meantime, Berger's *Social Democratic Herald* and a number of other Socialist papers were denied cheap mailing privileges by Postmaster General Albert S. Burleson. Most of them never recovered from the blow.

The most celebrated attack on the Socialists was the indictment and trial of longtime leader Eugene V. Debs for a speech opposing conscription. In sending Debs to prison, the Wilson administration was taking a chance. The four-time presidential candidate was loved and respected by many non-Socialists. At his trial in September 1918, Debs's eloquence lived up to his reputation. "While there is a lower class I am in it; while there is a criminal element I am of it; while there is a soul in prison, I am not free," he told the jury. But in prosecuting and jailing him and other prominent Socialists such as Kate Richards O'Hare, the government also made it clear that dissent on the war issue would not be tolerated.

The Destruction of the Industrial Workers of the World

The suppression of the IWW was more violent. There was a paradox in this because while the radical union officially opposed the war, Secretary-Treasurer "Big Bill" Haywood tried to play down the issue. For the first time since its founding in 1905, the IWW was enrolling members by the tens of thousands every month, and Haywood hoped to ride out the patriotic hysteria and emerge from the war with a powerful organization.

But the government did not move against the IWW because of its paper position on the war. Most of the union's members were concentrated in three sectors of the economy that were vital to the war effort: among the harvest workers who brought in the nation's wheat; among loggers in the Pacific Northwest; and in copper-mining towns like Globe and Bisbee in Arizona and Butte in Montana. And the "Wobblies" refused to abide by the AFL's no-strike pledge.

The IWW was crushed by a combination of vigilante terrorism and government action. In July 1917, a thousand "deputies" wearing white armbands in order to identify one another rounded up 1,200 strikers in Bisbee, loaded them on a specially chartered train, and dumped them in the Mexican desert, where they were without food for 36 hours. The next month, IWW organizer Frank Little was lynched in Butte, probably by police officers in disguise. In neither case was any attempt made to bring the vigilantes to justice. President Wilson pointedly ignored Haywood's protest of the Bisbee deportation and his demand for action in the case of Little's murder.

In the grain belt, sheriffs and farmers had a free hand in dealing with suspected Wobblies. In the Sitka spruce forests of Washington and Oregon (spruce was the principal wood used in aircraft construction), the army organized the Loyal Legion of Loggers and Lumbermen to counter the popularity of the IWW. There, at least, conditions were improved as the union was repressed, but attacks on the IWW were consistently vicious. Local police and federal agents winked at and even participated in everyday violations of civil rights and violence against Wobblies and their sympathizers.

Civil Liberties Suspended

The fatal blow fell in the autumn of 1917, when the Justice Department raided IWW headquarters in several cities, rounded up the union's leaders, and indicted about 200 under the Espionage Act of 1917. Along with the Sedition Act of 1918, the Espionage Act outlawed not only overt treasonable acts, but made it a crime to "utter, print, write, or publish any disloyal, profane, scurrilous, or abusive language" about the government, the flag, or the uniform of a soldier or sailor. A casual snide remark was enough to warrant bringing charges, and a few cases were based on little more than that.

In *Schenck v. the United States* (1919), the Supreme Court unanimously upheld this broad, vague law. Oliver Wendell Holmes, Jr., the most liberal minded and humane Justice on the Court, wrote the opinion, which established the principle that when "a clear and present danger" existed, such as the war, Congress had the power to pass laws that would not be acceptable to normal times.

Even at that, the government did not prove that the IWW was guilty of sedition. In effect, the individuals who were sentenced to up to twenty years in prison were punished because of their membership in an unpopular organization. Many liberals who had no taste for IWW doctrine but who were shocked at the government's cynical policy of repression fought the cases. In 1920, led by Roger Baldwin, they organized the American Civil Liberties Union to guard against a repetition of what almost all historians regard as a shameful chapter in the evolution of American law.

SHOUTING "FIRE!" IN A THEATER

Charles Schenck was a Philadelphia Socialist who was imprisoned for having violated the Espionage Act of 1917. He had circulated 15,000 pamphlets that attacked the government for going to war and criticized the draft. Schenck appealed his conviction to the Supreme Court but lost his case. In the words of the Court's leading liberal, Oliver Wendell Holmes, Jr., his attack constituted "a clear and present danger" to the nation. Schenck was no more entitled to his freedom of expression in wartime than a person falsely shouting "Fire!" in a crowded theater was entitled to that expression.

While acknowledging the validity of the "clear and present danger" principle, Harvard law professor Zechariah Chafee said that it did not apply to Schenck. His act had been more along the lines of someone informing the manager of the theater between the acts that there were not enough fire exits.

We will NEVER be sunk!

From the day of the birth of this Nation we have stood for, and will always stand steadfastly, for those Principles that will ultimately bring LIBERTY to all the WORLD.

A wartime poster that was one of many used to encourage Americans to support their government's involvement in World War I.

Manipulating Public Opinion

The attack on the Socialists and the Wobblies was only one fulfillment of Wilson's prediction that a spirit of ruthless brutality would enter the fiber of American life. Americans in general were stirred to believe that they were engaged in a holy crusade, "a war to end war" against a diabolical foe. Violent acts against German-Americans and the very idea of German culture were commonplace.

Some of the innumerable incidents of intolerance that marred the wartime years were spontaneous; for example, a midwestern mob dragged a German-American shopkeeper from his home, threw him to his knees, forced him to kiss the American flag, and made him spend his life savings on war bonds. But the fire of intolerance that burned from coast to coast was also instigated and abetted by the national government.

The agency that was entrusted with mobilizing public opinion was the Committee on Public Information. It was headed by George Creel, a progressive newspaperman who had devoted his career to fighting the very intolerance and social injustice he now encouraged.

With the same energy, Creel now devoted himself to a twofold task. First, to avoid demoralization, the CPI censored the news from Europe. The CPI dispatches emphasized victories and suppressed or played down stories of setbacks. With most editors and publishers solidly behind the war, Creel had little difficulty in convincing them to censor their own correspondents.

Crushing Kultur

Second, and far more ominously, the CPI took up the task of molding public opinion so that slight deviations from full support of the war were considered disloyal. Obviously, all German-Americans could not be imprisoned. (Only 6,300 were actually interned compared with 45,000 of Great Britain's much smaller German community.) However, the CPI could and did launch a massive propaganda campaign that depicted German *Kultur* as intrinsically vile.

The government employed pamphlets, editorials, posters, massive rallies, parades, a corps of 75,000 "Four-Minute Men" who delivered patriotic speeches of that length at movie theaters during intermission, and, for the first time, the infant film industry itself.

The new but sophisticated techniques of advertising could be used to sell attitudes as well as corn flakes and Coca-Cola. Brilliantly painted CPI posters depicted a powerful and sinister network of German spies in the United States and urged loyal patriots to be vigilant. After a Hollywood film company was prosecuted in 1917 for having released a film about the American Revolution that depicted British troops unfavorably, Hollywood got the point and churned out movies with titles like *The Barbarous Hun*. Film stars such as Douglas Fairbanks, Charlie Chaplin, and Mary Pickford ("America's Sweetheart") appeared at Liberty Bond rallies and spoke anti-German lines written by the CPI.

Liberty Hounds and Boy Spies

The anti-German hysteria could take laughable form. Restaurants revised their menus so that sauerkraut became "liberty cabbage," hamburgers became "Salisbury steak" (after a liberal British lord), and frankfurters and wiener sausages, named after German and Austrian cities, became widely known as "hot dogs."

The real dog, the dachshund, had to be transformed into a "liberty hound." Towns with names of German origin chose more patriotic designations. German measles, then a common childhood disease, became "patriotic measles." Hundreds of schools and some colleges dropped the German language from their course offerings. Dozens of symphony orchestras refused to play the works of German composers, which left rather gaping holes in the repertoire. Prominent German-Americans who wished to save their careers found it advisable to imitate the opera singer Ernestine Schumann-Heinck. She was a fixture at patriotic rallies, her ample figure draped with a large American flag and her magnificent voice singing "The Star-Spangled Banner" and "America the Beautiful."

But the firing of Germans from their jobs, discriminating against German farmers, burning of German books, and beating and occasional lynching of German-Americans were not so humorous. Nor was the treatment of conscientious objectors by organizations of self-appointed guardians of the national interest with names like "Sedition Slammers," "Terrible Threateners," and even "Boy Spies of America." The

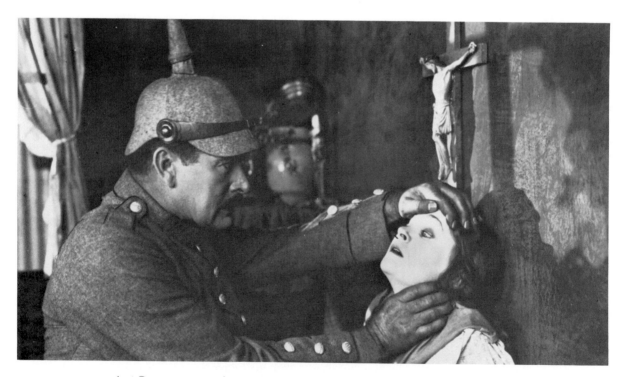

Anti-German sentiment became part of Hollywood movies after the United States entered World War I. In the film Stake Uncle Sam to Play Your Hand, *actress Mae Marsh was shown under the threatening grasp of an evil German soldier, played by A. C. Gibbons.*

FOUR-MINUTE RHETORIC

Four minutes was not enough time for developing subtle arguments, so the "Four-Minute Men" who spoke at theaters were as melodramatic as the films they interrupted:

The man who stands back now is lost; lost to the ranks of citizenship; lost to the father who gave him a name; lost to the flag that protects him; lost to the Nation that calls him. His day of birth is henceforth a day of dishonor. He can never name it without a lie. His time has come and he has denied it. He is a man without a country, an outcast.

members of such organizations stopped men on the streets and demanded to see their draft cards. The largest of these groups, which were responsible for hundreds of illegal acts, was the American Protective League. At one time it numbered 250,000 members, many of whom probably had signed up simply to avoid having their loyalty questioned.

WILSON AND THE LEAGUE OF NATIONS

Why did Woodrow Wilson, a Jeffersonian liberal before the war, tolerate and even encourage such behavior? The answer lies in the fact that the president's dream of building a new and just world order became an obsession. Like no president before him (like several since), he lost interest in domestic events except insofar as they affected his all-consuming foreign concerns. The one-time opponent of big government presided over its extraordinary expansion. Repression of dissenters, even unjust and illegal repression, appeared to hasten the defeat of the kaiser, so Wilson abandoned values that had guided his life.

The President's Obsession

In January 1918, Wilson presented to Congress his blueprint for the postwar world. It consisted of "Fourteen Points," which, Wilson insisted, were to be incorporated into the eventual treaty. Mostly, they dealt with specific European territorial problems to be resolved, but several general principles were woven through the plan.

First, Germany must be treated fairly and generously in order to avoid the deep resentments that could lead to another war. In practical terms this meant that Germany must not be saddled with huge reparations payments—"fines" as punishment for the war—such

as British and French leaders had told their people would be paid.

Second, the boundaries of European countries must conform to nationality as defined by language. Like many other people, Wilson believed that the aspirations of people to govern themselves had been a major cause of the war. No such concessions were to be made to the nonwhite peoples in Europe's colonies, however, although Wilson called for Germany's colonies to be disposed of on some basis other than as spoils of war divided among the victors.

Third, Wilson demanded "absolute freedom upon the seas, . . . alike in peace and in war." This was a reference to the German submarine campaign that Wilson blamed for American intervention, but it also challenged Britain's primacy on the waves. Fourth, Wilson called for disarmament. It was obvious to all parties that the arms race of the two decades preceding the war had not been a deterrent but a major cause of the tragedy.

Most important toward avoiding a repetition of the Great War, Wilson insisted on the establishment of "a general assembly of nations," a kind of congress of countries, to replace the old system of alliances and secret treaties. More than any other aspect of his program, the dream of a League of Nations came to obsess the president.

Wilson Fools Himself

As ultimate victory was ensured by an Allied breakthrough during the summer of 1918, Wilson turned virtually all his energies to planning for the peace conference in Paris. He announced that he would personally head the American delegation, the first president to do such a thing.

But Wilson mistook his own enthusiasm for the mood of the American people. In the congressional elections of 1918, voters returned Republican majorities of 240 to 190 to the House and of 49 to 47 to the Senate, but Wilson ignored the unmistakable signal that Americans wanted to cool off. The new Congress not only was Republican, but had a decidedly unidealistic tinge. Old bosses and professional politicians who had struggled against the reformers for a decade were returning to power. They were not all hidebound reactionaries by any means. They were the kind of men who were willing to make deals. But Wilson did not try to appeal to them by including a prominent Republican among the delegates with whom he sailed to Europe on December 4.

Wilson's reception in England, France, and Italy increased his blindness to political realities. Everywhere he went he was greeted with blizzards of flowers and confetti thrown by adoring crowds who thought of him as the savior of Europe. They were welcoming a conqueror. However, Wilson believed that they were expressing their support for "a peace without victory" and the principles of his Fourteen Points.

The Peace Conference

He could not have been more mistaken. The men with whom Wilson sat down in Paris had a much more realistic view of what the four dreadful years of war had meant to Europe. People wanted to forget the bitterness of sacrifice by tasting the sweetness of victory. The other three members of the "Big Four" paid lip service to Wilson's ideals, but once behind the closed doors of the conference room, they put their national interests first.

Georges Clemenceau, the prime minister of France, was a cagey, tough, and bitter infighter who was determined to hang the blame for the war on Germany and to ensure that France would never again be attacked. He was committed to stripping Germany of valuable territory and saddling the conquered nation with huge reparations payments. "God gave us the Ten Commandments and we broke them," he quipped in private. "Wilson gives us the Fourteen Points. We shall see."

David Lloyd George of Great Britain was personally more cordial to Wilson. But he was a chronic backroom manipulator given to inconstancy, and he too had political demands to meet. His country had suffered dreadfully from the bloodletting and wanted reparations. Moreover, Britain had no intention of giving up its dominance on the high seas.

Vittorio Orlando of Italy was only casually interested in the larger questions. He went to Versailles to make sure that Italy was rewarded with Austrian territory, including several regions of the Alps that were home to 200,000 German-speaking people, and the port of Fiume on the Adriatic, a city that was largely Serbian in population. His goals directly contradicted Wilson's Point Nine. The Japanese delegate, Count Nobuaki

None of his three fellow heads of government at the Versailles Conference shared Wilson's ideals or hopes for the future.

Makino, was determined to retain the German colonies in the Pacific that Japan had seized. So much for Point Five.

Bit by bit the Allies whittled away at Wilson's program. When the president revealed how all-important the League was to him by insisting that its Covenant (constitution) be acted on early in the proceedings, they knew that he would give in on other questions in order to save it. He did. The terms of the Treaty of Versailles, which Wilson brought home in July 1919, bore only a general resemblance to the Fourteen Points.

Article 10

Europe's rejection of Wilson's call for national self-determination in Europe and just treatment of Germany did not much concern the senators who had the constitutional responsibility to approve or reject the treaty. On the contrary, 12 of the 49 Republican senators, mostly the western progressives who had opposed going to war in 1917, announced themselves to be "irreconcilable" in their opposition to the pact that ended it. Still fuming because the United States went to war in the first place, they wanted to isolate themselves from corrupt Europe once again.

In March 1919, before Wilson returned from Versailles, the other 37 Republican senators signed a round robin declaring themselves to be "reservationists" on the issue. While they considered the Treaty of Versailles as it stood to be unacceptable, they put the president on notice that they would vote to ratify if Wilson made some changes in it or agreed to their reservations. What worried them most was Article 10 of the League Covenant, which pledged all member states to "preserve against external aggression the territorial integrity and . . . political independence of all members." Article 10 seemed to commit the United States to go to war if any other member of the League were attacked.

Wilson replied that Article 10 was merely a moral obligation on the part of members, and, long after his day, he would be proved correct; throughout its history, the League was unable to enforce its decisions.

ROUND ROBIN

A round robin is a petition or statement that is signed by several people with no one of them identified as the leader or instigator. All sign around the text of the document in order to disguise the order of signing. The intent of the round robin is precisely the opposite of that of John Hancock in signing his name so prominently to the Declaration of Independence.

Nevertheless, having said that the article had little concrete meaning, Wilson refused to make a single concession to the worried senators. In his stubbornness, he created an opportunity for the chairman of the Senate Foreign Relations Committee, an old friend of Theodore Roosevelt who despised everything about the president, to destroy his dream.

The Fight for the League

Henry Cabot Lodge was a dapper, aristocratic, and ill-tempered senator from Massachusetts who was not very popular with his colleagues. As stubborn and demanding as Wilson, he lacked a shred of Wilson's greatness. Nevertheless, Lodge proved in the battle over the League to be a much shrewder politician. Perceiving that Wilson was growing less flexible, Lodge became open and cooperative with senators who disliked the League less avidly than he did. Understanding that the longer the debate dragged on, the less the American people would be interested in the League, Lodge played for time and welcomed every one of Wilson's refusals to compromise. He read the entire 264 pages of the treaty into the record of his committee's hearings, even though it already had been published and placed on every senator's desk.

Lodge guessed right, and Wilson, less reasonable with every day, guessed wrong. Whereas the majority of Americans doubtless favored the League in the first months of 1919, their interest waned slowly but perceptibly as the months passed.

The climax came in September. With the treaty about to come before the Senate, Wilson undertook an exhausting 8,000-mile speaking tour. He believed that by rallying the people behind him, he could pressure wavering senators to support the treaty. By September 25, when he moved into Colorado, the crowds seemed to be with him. At Pueblo, however, his speech was slurred, and he openly wept. Wilson either suffered a mild stroke at that time or was on the verge of a nervous breakdown. His physician hastily canceled the remainder of the tour and rushed him back to Washington. A few days later he crumpled to the floor of his bedroom, felled by a cerebral thrombosis, a blood clot in the brain.

The Invisible President

No one really knows just how extensively Wilson was disabled over the next several months. His protective and strong-willed wife isolated him for six weeks from everyone but his physicians. She screened every document brought to him and returned them with shaky signatures at the bottom. When suspicious advisers insisted on seeing him, they discovered that his left side was paralyzed and his speech was halting. How-

H O W   T H E Y   L I V E D

"They Dropped Like Flies": The Great Flu Epidemic of 1918

About 10 million people died as a result of battle during the four years of the First World War. Small wonder that the event staggered the confidence and morale of the European nations.

But the war was a modest killer compared with the "Spanish flu." During only *four months* late in 1918 and early in 1919, a worldwide flu epidemic, or pandemic, killed 21 million people. The American army in Europe lost 49,000 men in battle and 64,000 to disease, the majority of them to the flu. At home, fully 548,452 American civilians died, 10 times as many as soldiers felled in battle.

In the United States, the yet unnamed disease first appeared in March 1918, at Fort Riley, Kansas. After a dust storm, 107 soldiers checked into the infirmary complaining of headaches, fever and chills, difficulty in breathing, and miscellaneous aches and pains. Most curious to them, the illness had befallen them in an instant; one moment they were feeling fit, the next they could barely stand. Within a week, Fort Riley had 522 cases, and in a little more than a month, when the affliction abruptly disappeared, 8,000 cases. Almost 50 of the sick men died, not too disturbing a rate in an age when any number of contagious diseases forgotten today were considered deadly. Some doctors noted that these flu victims were in the prime of life and, presumably after basic training, in excellent condition. Moreover, most of them were strapping farm boys, who usually shook off such ailments as though they were colds.

It was wartime, however, and the soldiers from Fort Riley were shipped to Europe in May. The flu made a brief appearance in the cities of the eastern seaboard, but did not rival any of a number of epidemics, including a serious one in the United States in 1889 and 1890.

In Europe, the disease was far more deadly. In neutral Switzerland alone, 58,000 died of it in July. The deaths in the trenches on both sides of the line were enough, according to the German general Erich von Ludendorff, to curtail a major campaign. By June, the flu was sweeping Africa and India, where the mortality was "without parallel in the history of disease." That could be attributed to the wretched poverty of the subcontinent. But what of Western Samoa, where 7,500 of the island's 38,000 people died?

The total figures had not been calculated when the flu began a second and even more destructive tour of the world. The war had created ideal conditions for such a pandemic. People moved about in unprecedented numbers; 200,000 to 300,000 crossed the Atlantic to Europe each month, and many were carrying the unidentifiable germ. Moreover, war crowded people together so that conditions were also perfect for the successful mutation of viruses. With so many handy hosts

to support propagation, the emergence of new strains was all the more likely.

That is apparently what happened in August, in western Africa, France, or Spain, which got the blame. A much deadlier variation of the original swept over the world, and this time the effects in the United States were cataclysmic.

In Boston, where it struck first, doubtless carried in by returning soldiers, 202 people died on October 1. New York City reported 3,100 cases in one day; 300 victims died. Later in the month, 851 New Yorkers died in one day, far and away the record. Philadelphia, which was particularly hard hit, lost 289 people on October 6; within one week, 5,270 were reported dead. The death rate for the month was 700 times its usual rate. Similar figures came in from every large city in the country. Just as worrisome, the disease found its way to the most obscure corners of the country. A winter logging camp in Michigan, cut off from the rest of humanity, was afflicted. Oregon officials reported finding sheepherders dead by their flocks.

Most public officials responded about as well as could be expected during a catastrophe that no one understood. Congress, many of its members laid low, appropriated money to hire physicians and nurses and set up clinics. Many cities closed theaters, bars, schools, and churches, and prohibited public gatherings such as parades and sporting events. Others, notably Kansas City, where the political boss frankly said that the economy was more important, carried on as usual. Mystifying moralists, Kansas City was no harder hit than were cities that took extreme precautions. (Nationwide and worldwide, about one-fifth of the population caught the Spanish flu, and the death rate was 3 percent.)

Several city governments required the wearing of gauze masks and punished violators with fines of up to $100. Many photographs that were taken during the autumn of 1918 have a surreal quality because of the masks. San Franciscans, their epidemic at a peak on Armistice Day, November 11, celebrated wearing gauze. Some wretched poet wrote the lines:

Obey the laws
And wear the gauze
Protect your jaws
From septic paws

Philadelphia gathered its dead in carts, as had been done during the bubonic plague epidemics of the Middle Ages. The city's A. F. Brill Company, a maker of trolley cars, turned over its woodshop to coffinmakers. The city of Buffalo set up its own coffin factory. Authorities in Washington, D.C., seized a trainload of coffins headed for Pittsburgh.

*An office worker wears a facemask to protect herself
during the deadly flu epidemic of 1918.*

Then, once again, the disease disappeared. There was a less lethal wave (perhaps another mutation) in the spring of 1919, with President Wilson one of the victims; and a leading historian of the phenomenon, Alfred W. Crosby, suggests that another minor epidemic in 1920 may have been a fourth wave. But the worst was over by about the time that the First World War ended, leaving physicians to reflect on the character of the disease and to wonder what they could do if it recurred.

There were some things to reflect on. The first has already been noted: the Spanish flu struck very suddenly, offering individuals no way to fight it except to lie down and wait.

Second, the disease went fairly easy on those people who are usually most vulnerable to respiratory diseases, the elderly; and it was hardest on those who usually shake off such afflictions, young people. In the United States, the death rate for white males between the ages of 25 and 34 was, during the 1910s, about 80 per 100,000. During the flu epidemic it was 2,000 per 100,000. In a San Francisco maternity ward in October, 19 out of 42 women died. In Washington, a college student telephoned a clinic to report that 2 of her 3 roommates were dead in bed and the third was seri-

ously ill. The report of the police officer who was sent to investigate was "Four girls dead in apartment." Old people died of the flu, of course, but the death rate among the elderly did not rise a point during the epidemic!

Third, people who had grown up in tough, poor, big-city neighborhoods were less likely to get the disease and, if they got it, less likely to die of it than were people who had grown up in healthier environments.

These facts eventually led scientists to conclude that the Spanish flu was a mutation of a common virus that caused a flu that was nothing more than an inconvenience. It was postulated, although never proved, that the deadly germ was the issue of an unholy liaison between a virus that affected humans and another that affected hogs. Spanish flu became "swine flu."

Thus, poor city people, who were more likely to suffer a plethora of minor diseases, had developed an immunity to the virus that farm people had not. Because old people were spared in 1918 and 1919, it has been said that the Spanish or swine flu was related to the less fatal virus that had caused the epidemic of 1889 to 1890. Having been affected by it, the elderly were relatively immune to its descendant.

A weakened Woodrow Wilson relied on a cane and the aid of an escort following a massive stroke.

ever, he appeared to be in complete control of his wits. To a group of senators who told him, "We've all been praying for you," he replied, "Which way, Senator?"

Wilson did not meet officially with his cabinet for six months, and photographs of that occasion show a haggard old man with an anxiety in his eyes that cannot be found in any earlier picture. The clarity of his thinking undoubtedly was affected. But since Wilson in the best of health had refused to consider compromising with Lodge, the president's removal from the scene probably had little effect on the final outcome of the battle.

That outcome was defeat. In November, on Wilson's instructions, the Democratic senators voted with the irreconcilables to kill the treaty with the Lodge reservations by a vote of 55 to 39. When the treaty was introduced without the reservations, the reservationists and the irreconcilables defeated it against the Democrats. In March, over Wilson's protest, 21 Democrats worked out a compromise with the reservationist Republicans and again voted on the treaty. The 23 Democrats who went along with Wilson's insistence that he get the original treaty or no treaty at all made the difference. They and the irreconcilables defeated it.

The Election of 1920

Wilson believed that he could win the Treaty of Versailles and the League of Nations in the presidential election of 1920. Incredibly, considering his shaky health and the tradition against a third term, he also wanted to be the Democratic party's nominee. That was too much for even the most faithful Democrats to swallow. They chose Governor James M. Cox of Ohio, a lackluster party regular who looked like a traveling salesman. For vice president the Democrats nominated a staunch young Wilsonian, the athletic and aristocratic Undersecretary of the Navy, Franklin D. Roosevelt. The Democrats were pessimistic. But perhaps the Roosevelt name on the Democratic ticket would win enough progressive votes to put the party across.

The Republicans expected to win. The congressional elections of 1918 had seemed to show that despite six years of Democratic government, the Republicans remained the majority party. As is common when parties are optimistic, there was a fight for the nomination between General Leonard Wood, an old comrade of Theodore Roosevelt (but no progressive) and Illinois governor Frank O. Lowden, who had a reputation as an innovative scientific farmer. Both arrived in Chicago with large blocs of votes, but neither had a majority.

Early in the proceedings, a group of reporters cornered a political wheeler-dealer from Ohio named Harry M. Daugherty and asked him who he thought would be nominated. Daugherty replied genially:

> Well boys, I'll tell you what I think. The convention will be deadlocked. After the other candidates have failed, we'll get together in some hotel room, oh, about 2:11 in the morning, and some 15 men, bleary-eyed with lack of sleep, will sit down around a big table and when that time comes Senator Harding will be selected.

Senator Harding was Warren G. Harding. A Daugherty crony, Harding was a handsome, likable man who was considered one of the least competent figures in Congress. Perhaps because of that, he was acceptable to almost everyone. Because Harding had been a "mild reservationist" on the treaty issue, as usual taking an innocuous stand, Henry Cabot Lodge (in whose "smoke-filled room" at the Blackstone Hotel the nomination took place) undoubtedly believed that he could control him.

The Great Bloviater

During the campaign, Harding waffled on the treaty, sometimes appearing to favor it with reservations and at other times hinting that he would let the issue quietly die. If there was a theme to his campaign, it was the need for the country to cool off after almost two decades of experimental reform and white-hot wartime crusading. This circumstance allowed Harding to implement his technique of "bloviation." Bloviating was "the art of speaking for as long as the occasion warrants, and saying nothing." In Boston, in September, Harding said that "America's need is not heroism but healing, not nostrums but normalcy, not agitation but adjustment, not surgery but serenity, not the dramatic but the dispassionate, not experiment but equipoise, not submergence in internationality but sustainment in triumphant nationality."

The acerbic journalist H. L. Mencken said that Harding's speech reminded him of "stale bean soup, of college yells, of dogs barking idiotically through endless nights." But he added that "it is so bad that a sort of grandeur creeps through it." A Democratic politician remarked that the speech "left the impression of an army of pompous phrases moving over the landscape in search of an idea."

But Harding did have an idea. The great bloviater had sensed that no specific issue, including the League of Nations, was as important to the American people in 1920 as "a return to normalcy," and he was right. He won 61 percent of the vote, more than any candidate who preceded him in the White House since popular votes were recorded and the landslide record until 1964.

Wilson lived on quietly in Washington until 1924, a semi-invalid specter out of the past, frustrated and bitter. Unlike the pedestrian Harding, he was a giant who loomed over an age. His intelligence, dignity, steadfastness, and sense of rectitude overshadowed even Theodore Roosevelt, something T.R. himself must have sensed in his final, pathetic years. Wilson's end was therefore more tragic than that of any other president, including those who were assassinated. For Wilson, like the tragic heroes of great drama, was murdered by his own virtues.

For Further Reading

Overviews and Classics

William E. Leuchtenburg, *The Perils of Prosperity, 1914–1932* (1958)
Arthur S. Link, *Woodrow Wilson and the Progressive Era* (1954)
Preston Slosson, *The Great Crusade and After* (1930)
Robert H. Wiebe, *The Search for Order, 1880–1920* (1967)

Valuable Special Studies

Thomas A. Bailey, *Woodrow Wilson and the Lost Peace* (1944)
———, *Woodrow Wilson and the Great Betrayal* (1945)
A. E. Barbeau and F. Henri, *The Unknown Soldiers* (1974)
Robert Cuff, *The War-Industries Board: Business-Government Relations During World War I* (1973)
Maurine Wiener Greenwald, *Women, War, and Work: The Impact of World War I on Women Workers in the United States* (1980)
Ellis W. Hawley, *The Great War and the Search for a Modern Order: A History of the American People and their Institutions, 1914–1920* (1979)
David Kennedy, *Over Here: The First World War and American Society* (1980)
N. G. Levin, Jr., *Woodrow Wilson and World Politics: America's Response to War and Revolution* (1968)
Arthur S. Link, *Woodrow Wilson: War, Revolution, and Peace* (1979)
Frederick C. Luebke, *Bonds of Loyalty: German Americans and World War I* (1974)
Harold Nicholson, *Peacemaking: 1919* (1939)
Frederick L. Paxson, *American Democracy and the World War* (1948)
William Preston, Jr., *Aliens and Dissenters: Federal Suppression of Radicals, 1903–1933* (1953)
Daniel M. Smith, *The Great Departure: The United States in World War I, 1914–1920* (1965)
Lawrence Stallings, *The Doughboys* (1963)
Ralph Stone, *The Irreconcilables: The Fight Against the League of Nations* (1970)
Russell Weigley, *The American Way of War: History of United States Military Policy and Strategy* (1973)

Biographies and Autobiographies

John M. Blum, *Woodrow Wilson and the Politics of Morality* (1956)
John A. Garraty, *Henry Cabot Lodge* (1953)
———, *Woodrow Wilson* (1956)

The Age of Harding
Troubled Years of Transition, 1919–1923

The ten years between 1919 and 1929 have come down to us with a ready-made personality, a nickname that seems to capture the flavor of a decade. In the popular imagination, the 1920s are the "Roaring Twenties." Exhausted by the prolonged fervor of progressivism and disillusioned by a righteous war that failed to save humanity from itself, the American people set out to have a little fun, and ended up by having a lot.

Images of the Roaring Twenties, lovingly recreated in novels, stories, films, and television programs, easily flood the mind: speakeasies (illegal saloons), college boys and flapper girls defying traditional morality during breaks between dancing to the exciting new jazz music played by happy blacks; bootleggers and gangsters, somehow menacing and engaging at the same time.

The 1920s were the golden age of sport: Babe Ruth's Yankees and John McGraw's Giants were the superteams of baseball; Harold "Red" Grange was the saint of the regional religion of football; Jack Dempsey and Gene Tunney were prizefighters as mythic as Odysseus and Hercules. Robert T. "Bobby" Jones of Georgia made golf a popular sport for both participants and spectators, and William "Big Bill" Tilden did the same for tennis.

Radio made its debut: the first commercial broadcast told of Warren G. Harding's landslide victory in the presidential election of 1920. The movies became a part of life in the cities and

Bound to uphold Prohibition, federal agents smash barrels of beer and empty them in the gutter.

towns. So did the automobile, the modern world's amulet of personal freedom, from the homely, accessible Model T Ford to the Stutz Bearcat, Dusenberg, and Cord, still among the most glorious creations of the auto maker's technology and craft.

The list can go on, but at any length it will be a distortion. Only a small proportion of the American population—the wealthy and the comfortably fixed middle classes who lived in cities and sizable towns—enjoyed even a semblance of the legend's roaring good times. And the gravy years were not ten, but five or six in number, beginning only after Calvin Coolidge became president in 1923.

THE WORST PRESIDENT

During the four years that preceded the reign of "Silent Cal," American life was beset more by contradictions, uncertainties, and fears than by diverting good times. In fact, during the two years immediately before and the two immediately after the inauguration of President Harding in March 1921, American society was on edge, and so was the man whom many historians consider to have been the worst president.

Warren G. Harding

A newspaperman, Warren Gamaliel Harding worked his way up in politics on the basis of a friendly smile, a firm handshake, the reliable support of the Republican party line in his newspaper (the *Marion Star*), and the happy discovery by Ohio's political bosses that whenever they asked favors, and whatever favors they asked, Warren G. Harding said yes.

He loved the Senate, where voters sent him in 1914; the job suited his temperament. Being a senator called for making the occasional speech—Harding was good at that—but as only one senator among 96, he was not expected to take the lead in anything.

No one objected that Harding helped old cronies find government jobs that they were unfit to perform, and the affable Ohioan had plenty of time to enjoy the all-night poker and bourbon parties with his pals that were his second most favorite recreation. Because newspaper reporters were more restrained in dealing with the private lives of public officials than they are today, Harding could carry on his favorite recreation with a minimum of discretion. He had a series of mistresses and even fathered an illegitimate daughter by one, Nan Britton, without scandal.

"He looked like a president." Warren G. Harding *won the election with his impressive appearance and likeable manner.*

A Decent Man

Harding had no illusions about his intelligence or his moral capacity for leadership. However, after the sour experience with the brilliant and imperious Wilson, neither he nor the American people regarded an ordinary mind as a handicap in a president. Harding was genuinely kind and decent. If he could not hope to be "the best president," he could, in his own words, try to be "the best liked," a distinction that was beyond the reach of the icy Wilson.

He displayed his humanity when, at Christmas 1921, he pardoned Eugene V. Debs and other Socialists who had opposed the war. (Vindictively, Wilson had refused to do so.) Harding personally pressured the directors of United States Steel to reduce the workday in their mills to eight hours. Most striking was Harding's reaction when political enemies whispered that he was part black. In an era when most white people thought in at least mildly racist terms, that kind of talk could ruin a career. Other politicians would have responded with a lawsuit or an indignant racist diatribe that outdid their accusers for spleen. But Harding merely shrugged, an extraordinary response in that era.

Hoover

Unfortunately, the presidency called for more than personal decency. Because Harding simply did not understand many of the problems that were suddenly thrust on him, he left policy making to his cabinet and to other appointees. No harm was done in the cases of Secretary of Commerce Herbert C. Hoover and Secretary of State Charles Evans Hughes. They were able men whose policies shine all the more because the Harding administration's record is otherwise so murky.

As he had done during the First World War, Hoover worked quietly, encouraging the formation of private trade associations in industry and agriculture. His hope was that these organizations would eliminate waste, develop uniform standards of production, and end "destructive competition." His success was limited, but to a large extent, Hoover anticipated the corporate liberal system that Americans would adopt for half a century as their preference in government policy.

The Treaty of Washington

Charles Evans Hughes first terminated the state of war with Germany that still formally existed because the United States had not ratified the Treaty of Versailles. At his behest, Congress merely resolved that the war was over. Then the Secretary of State presented his alternative to the League of Nations as a means of keeping the peace, calling nine nations to an international conference in Washington to discuss naval disarmament. The delegates, who expected the usual round of receptions and meaningless pieties that most such conferences involved, were shocked when Hughes proposed that all the great powers scrap their capital ships (battleships and battle cruisers) and cancel plans for future naval construction.

Because every diplomat agreed that the arms race had been instrumental in bringing on the First World War, the delegates in Washington had little choice but to listen, particularly when Hughes reminded them that by limiting the size of their navies, the powers could save millions: the construction of even a single capital ship was a major line item in a national budget.

In the Treaty of Washington of 1921, the five major naval powers agreed to limit their fleets according to a ratio that reflected their interests and defensive needs. For each five tons that Great Britain and the United States floated in capital ships, Japan would have three, and France and Italy would have somewhat smaller fleets. Each nation gave up ships, but each benefited too. Great Britain maintained naval equality with the United States, a primacy that American plans for ship construction would have destroyed. (The United States scrapped 30 battleships and cruisers that were under construction or on the drawing boards.) The American government cut the budget, a high Republican priority. Japan, which needed only a one-ocean navy whereas Britain and the United States had worldwide interests, got parity (or even superiority) in the Pacific. Italy and France, still reeling from the war, were spared the strain of an arms race, but retained naval strength in the Mediterranean.

The Harding Scandals

Unfortunately, the work of Hoover and Hughes just about sums up the accomplishments of the Harding administration. The other men in the administration were either servants of narrow special interests or blatant crooks. Secretary of the Treasury Andrew Mellon pursued tax policies that extravagantly favored the rich and helped bring on the disastrous depression that would end the Roaring Twenties. More dismaying in the short run were those old cronies whom Harding appointed to office. No sooner were they settled in their jobs in Washington than they set about filling their pockets and ruining their generous friend.

Attorney General Harry Daugherty winked at violations of the law by political allies. Probably with Daugherty's connivance, Jesse L. Smith, a close friend of the president, sold favorable decisions and public offices for cold cash. Charles R. Forbes, the head of the Veterans Administration, pocketed money intended for hospital construction. Grandest of all, Secretary of the Interior Albert B. Fall leased the navy's petroleum reserves at Teapot Dome, Wyoming, and Elk Hills, California, to two freewheeling oilmen, Harry Sinclair and Edward L. Doheny. In return, Fall accepted "loans" of about $300,000 from the two. Fall also tarred Harding with his corruption because, some time earlier, he had persuaded the president to transfer the oil reserves from the navy's authority to that of the Interior Department.

By the summer of 1923, Harding realized that his administration was shot through with thievery. When he set out on a vacation trip to Alaska, he knew that it was only a matter of time before the scandals hit the newspapers and destroyed his name. His health was already suffering; the famous handsome face is haggard and gray in the last photographs.

Nevertheless, a weak and obliging man to the end, Harding allowed his friend Forbes to flee abroad, and he took no action against the others. Jesse Smith killed

A cartoon showing a teapot that looks suspiciously like an embarrassed elephant illustrated the Republican party's uncomfortable involvement in the Teapot Dome scandal.

himself. Mercifully, perhaps, Harding died too, before he got back to Washington. Only later did Americans learn of the secrets that plagued him, from the corruption in his administration to the irregularities in his personal life, which Nan Britton described in her book, *The President's Daughter.* So tangled were the affairs of the Harding administration that scandalmongers suggested that Harding's wife had poisoned him, and they were widely believed. Actually, the president suffered a massive heart attack, possibly brought on by the realization that he had failed on so colossal a scale.

SOCIAL TENSIONS: LABOR, RADICALS, IMMIGRANTS

If Harding's poignant tale is symbolic of his time, the social tensions that strained and snapped while he was in the White House ran far deeper than the personality of an unhappy man from Marion, Ohio. Had Harding been a pillar of moral strength and probity, the years he presided over would have been much the same as they were. Indeed, the troubled half of the 1920s began two years before Harding was inaugurated. As far as most Americans were concerned, the social conflicts that first broke into the open then were quite closely related: labor, political radicalism, and the presence of so many immigrants in an idyllic America that had never really existed.

1919: A Year of Strikes

During the First World War, the conservative trade unions of the American Federation of Labor seemed to become part of the federal power structure. In return for recognition of their respectability, most unions agreed not to strike for the duration of hostilities. Unfortunately, while wages rose slowly during 1917 and 1918, the prices of consumer goods, including necessities, increased quickly and then soared during a runaway postwar inflation. The end of the war also led to the cancellation of government contracts; tens of thousands were thrown out of work, and the inevitable occurred: 3,600 strikes during 1919 involving 4 million workers.

Striker grievances were generally valid, but, to the surprise of many workers, few Americans outside the labor movement were sympathetic. When employers described the strikes of 1919 as revolutions, aimed at destroying middle-class decency, much of America agreed. In Seattle, a dispute that began on the docks of the busy Pacific port turned into a general strike involving almost all the city's 60,000 workers. Most of them were interested in nothing more than better pay. However, the concept of the general strike was associated in the popular mind with class war and revolution. Mayor Ole Hanson was able to depict the dispute as an uprising that had been inspired by dangerous foreign "Bolsheviks" like those who had taken over Russia during the war. With the help of the marines, he crushed the strike.

Steelworkers Walk Out

Steel-industry magnates employed similar methods to fight a walkout in September by 350,000 workers, largely in the Great Lakes region. The men had good reason to strike. Many of them worked a twelve-hour day and a seven-day week. It was not unusual for individuals to put in thirty-six hours at a stretch. That is, if a man's relief failed to show up, he was told to stay on the job or lose it. When the extra shift ended, his own began again.

For this kind of life, steelworkers took home subsistence wages. For some Slavic immigrants in the industry, that home was not even a bed to themselves. They contracted with a landlord to rent half a bed. After their wearying shift and a quick, cheap meal, they rolled under blankets still warm and damp from the body of a fellow worker who had just trudged off to the mill.

These wretched conditions were well known. And yet, the heads of the industry, Elbert Gary of United States Steel and Charles Schwab of Bethlehem Steel, easily persuaded the public that the strike was the work of revolutionary agitators like William Z. Foster. Because Foster had a radical past (and future as the leader of the American Communist party) and because many steelworkers had ethnic roots in Eastern Europe, the nursery of Bolshevism, the strikers were almost universally condemned.

The Boston Police Strike

The Boston police strike of 1919 frightened Americans more than any of the other conflicts. While the shutdown of even a basic industry like steel did not immediately affect daily life, the absence of police officers from the streets caused a jump in crime as professional hoodlums and desperately poor people took advantage of the situation.

Boston's policemen, mostly Irish-Americans, were underpaid. They earned prewar wages, not enough to support their families decently in a city where many prices had tripled. Nevertheless, they too commanded little public support. When Massachusetts governor Calvin Coolidge ordered the National Guard into Boston to break the strike, the public applauded. When Samuel Gompers asked Coolidge to restore the beaten workers to their jobs, the governor replied "there is no right to strike against the public safety by anybody, anywhere, anytime," and he became a national hero. His hard-line policy won him the Republican vice-presidential nomination in 1920 when the California progressive, Hiram Johnson, refused to balance the ticket by running with the conservative Harding.

Some of the strikes of 1919 ended in victory. Most failed and the debacle ushered in a decade of decline for the labor movement. The membership of unions stood at over 5 million in 1919, but at only 3.6 million in 1929, despite the expansion of the nonagricultural working class during the same years.

Red Scare

Public reaction to the strikes of 1919 revealed widespread hostility toward recent immigrants and second-generation Americans. This xenophobia took more virulent form in the Red scare of 1919. Even before the Armistice was signed, a new stereotype had replaced the "bloodthirsty Hun" as the villain whom Americans had most reason to fear: the seedy, bearded, and wild-eyed Bolshevik. American newspapers exaggerated the many real atrocities that took place during the civil war that followed the Russian Revolution and invented tales of mass executions, torture, children turned against their parents, and women declared the common property of all men. Already in an uneasy mood, Americans were prepared to believe the worst about a part of the world from which so many immigrants recently had come.

Many Americans believed that foreign-born Communists were a threat to the United States. In March 1919, the Soviets organized the Third International, or "Comintern," an organization that was explicitly dedicated to fomenting revolution around the world. So it seemed to be no accident when, in April, the Post Office discovered 38 bombs in the mail addressed to prominent capitalists and government officials. In June, several bombs reached their targets. One bomber who was identified—he blew himself up—was a foreigner, an Italian. And in September, two American Communist parties were founded in Chicago, and the press emphasized the immigrant element in the membership. Many Americans concluded that the Red threat was closely related to the large number of immigrants and their children within the United States.

In reality, very few ethnic Americans were radicals, and most prominent Socialists and Communists boasted impeccable WASP origins. Max Eastman, the editor of the radical wartime magazine *The Masses*, was of old New England stock. John Reed, whose *Ten Days That Shook the World* remained for many years the classic English-language account of the Russian Revolution, Debs, Haywood, and William Z. Foster had no ethnic ties. Moreover, neither they nor the foreign-born radicals posed a real threat to established institutions. Within a few years, the combined membership of the two Communist parties and the Socialist party numbered only in the thousands.

But popular dread of Communists was real, and the temptation to exploit it for political gain was overwhelming. Wilson's attorney general, A. Mitchell Palmer, tried to ride the Red scare into a presidential nomination by ordering a series of well-publicized raids on Communist headquarters.

Although an investigation found that only 39 of those whom he had arrested could be deported according to the law, Palmer put 249 people on a steamship dubbed "the Soviet Ark" and sent them to Russia via Finland. On New Year's Day 1920, Palmer's agents again swooped down on hundreds of locations, arresting 6,000 people. Some of them, such as a Western Union delivery boy, merely had the bad luck to be in the wrong place at the wrong time. Others were arrested while merely peering into the windows of Communist storefront offices. Nevertheless, all were imprisoned for at least a short time.

Palmer's popularity fizzled in the spring of 1920. He predicted that there would be mass demonstrations on May Day, the international Communist holiday, and nothing happened. By midsummer, the great scare was over, but antiforeign feeling continued to affect both government policy and popular attitudes throughout the 1920s.

Sacco and Vanzetti

The two most celebrated victims of the wedding of antiradicalism to xenophobia were Nicola Sacco and Bartolomeo Vanzetti. In 1920, the two Italian immigrants were arrested for an armed robbery in South Braintree, Massachusetts, in which a guard and a paymaster were killed. They were found guilty of murder, and sentenced to die in the electric chair.

Before they could be executed, the American Civil Liberties Union, Italian-American groups, and labor organizations publicized the fact that the hard evidence against Sacco and Vanzetti was scanty and, at least in part, invented by the prosecution. The presiding judge, Webster Thayer, was obviously prejudiced because the defendants were radicals (anarchists); he was overheard speaking of them as "damned dagos."

At the same time, Sacco and Vanzetti won admiration by acting with dignity during their trial, steadfastly maintaining their innocence but refusing to compromise their political beliefs. "I am suffering," Vanzetti said in court,

because I am a radical and indeed I am a radical; I have suffered because I was an Italian, and indeed I am an Italian . . . but I am so convinced to be right that if you could execute me two times, and if I could be reborn two other times, I would live again to do what I have done already.

Despite a movement to save them that reached international proportions, Sacco and Vanzetti were finally executed in 1927. Although recent research has indicated that at least Sacco was probably guilty, that question was irrelevant during the 1920s. The case against them seemed less flimsy to many American intellectuals who accused the state of Massachusetts of judicial murder by bowing to popular prejudice against foreigners. The same prejudice also ended the great age of immigration.

Shutting the Golden Door

In 1883, the American poet Emma Lazarus had written, "Send these, the homeless, tempest-tost to me, I lift my lamp beside the golden door." Immigration

Nicola Sacco and Bartolomeo Vanzetti, immigrants and anarchists whose case became an international cause in the 1920s.

continued at high levels until 1915, when all-out naval war made the Atlantic too dangerous for large numbers of people to cross. By 1918, immigration into the United States was down to 110,000.

Long before the war, many Americans of WASP and "Old Immigrant" stock had become nervous about the large numbers of Eastern and southern Europeans among them—or rather, about the immigrants who clustered in ethnic ghettos in the larger cities. Unlike earlier arrivals, including the once-despised Irish, the "New Immigrants" seemed determined not to become Americans.

Around the turn of the century, this cultural anxiety took on racist overtones. Writers who claimed to be social scientists described significant racial divisions among Europeans. The most important of these writers was William Z. Ripley, whose *Races of Europe* was published in 1899. Ripley divided Caucasians into the Teutonic, Alpine, and Mediterranean races. While all three had their redeeming traits (the Mediterranean Italians, for example, were credited with a finely developed artistic sense), there was no question that Teutons—Britons, Germans, northern Europeans generally—were the ones who were committed to liberty and to the American way of life. (The Celtic race of the Irish caused these theorists no end of trouble with their categories.)

Moving Toward Restriction

In 1882, the Chinese were excluded from further immigration. In that same year, Congress determined that criminals, idiots, lunatics, and those likely to become a public charge (people with glaucoma, tuberculosis, and venereal disease were the chief targets) could no longer enter the United States. By 1900, pressure groups such as the Immigration Restriction League began to call for an immigration law that would discriminate against genetic inferiors—southern and Eastern Europeans, in brief, the New Immigrants.

But how to keep the "undesirables" out? On four occasions between 1897 and 1917, Congress enacted bills that required would-be immigrants to pass a literacy test. Four times, three times by Woodrow Wilson alone, the bills were vetoed. The importance of ethnic voters to the Democratic party, and the demand of a still expanding industry for cheap labor, stymied the restrictionists. Then, in 1916, a lawyer and natural scientist of some reputation, Madison Grant, published a popular book, *The Passing of the Great Race,* that held that New Immigrants were literally destroying, through dilution, the prized genetic heritage of old-stock Americans. In the wake of the war, when immigration soared again—to 805,000 in 1921—the restrictionists' moment had come.

In that year, Congress enacted and President Harding signed a law stipulating that 350,000 people could enter the United States each year. However, each European nation was allowed to send only 3 percent of the number of its nationals who had been residents of the United States in the base year of 1910. In 1924, an amendment reduced the number of immigrants from outside the Americas to 150,000, the quota to 2 percent, and changed the base year to 1890. Because most southern and Eastern Europeans had begun to emigrate to the United States after 1890, the quotas of such poor countries as Poland, Czechoslovakia, Hungary, Rumania, Yugoslavia, Bulgaria, Greece, and Italy were very low. For example, the annual quota for Italy was a minuscule 6,000, and was inevitably filled within the first few months of each year.

By way of contrast, the quotas for the comparatively prosperous countries of northern and Western Europe, the nations of the Old Immigration, were generous and rarely filled. The annual quota for Great Britain under the 1921 law was 65,000, one-fifth of the total. During the 1930s, however, an average of only 2,500 Britons emigrated to the United States each year.

SOCIAL TENSIONS: RACE, MORAL CODES, RELIGION

The 1920s were also a time of anxiety and tension in relations between the two major races, between people

ANTI-SEMITISM

The hatred of Jews that was to acquire nightmarish proportions in Germany had its counterpart in the United States, albeit never so vicious or significant as it was under Adolf Hitler. For a time during the 1920s, automobile millionaire Henry Ford sponsored a newspaper, the *Dearborn Independent,* that insisted, as Hitler did, that Jews in general were party to an "international conspiracy" to destroy Western Christian civilization. The most astonishing aspect of this kind of anti-Semitism was that it posited an alliance between wealthy, conservative Jewish bankers like the Rothschild family of Europe and their worst enemies, Jewish Socialists and Communists.

These allegations never were taken very seriously in the United States. However, anti-Semitism was acceptable and even respectable when it took the form of keeping Jews out of some businesses (banking, ironically) and social clubs. Moreover, a number of universities applied Jewish "quotas" when they admitted students. Jews were admitted, but only up to a certain percentage of each class.

who held fast to traditional moral codes and those who rejected them, and (closely allied to the moral issue) between rural people and urban people.

Black Scare

Having supported the war effort with extraordinary enthusiasm, blacks looked forward to a greater measure of equality after the Armistice. The 200,000 young black men who had served in the army in Europe had been exposed to a white society in which their color was not a major handicap. Although they had been segregated within the armed forces, they had found that the French people looked on them as Yanks of a different color, nothing more or less, and had been grateful for their help against Germany. At home, blacks who moved to northern cities experienced a less repressive life than they had known in the rural South and felt freer to express themselves.

But white America had not changed its mind about race. In 1919, of the 78 blacks who were lynched, 10 were veterans; several were hanged while dressed in their uniforms. Race riots broke out in 25 cities with a death toll of more than a hundred. The worst of the year was in Chicago, where a petty argument on a Lake Michigan beach in July mushroomed into vicious racial war. White and black gangs with guns roamed the streets shooting at anyone of the wrong color whom they stumbled across. In all, 38 people were killed and more than 500 were injured.

Black Nationalism

In this charged and disillusioning atmosphere emerged a remarkable leader. Born in the British colony of Jamaica, Marcus Garvey came to the United States in 1916. He concluded that whites would never accept blacks as equals, and, filled with a glowing pride in his own race, he rejected integration. Garvey's alternative to the violent racial conflicts of the postwar years was the joining together of blacks throughout the world to organize a powerful black nation in Africa.

Garvey's Universal Negro Improvement Association (UNIA) was based on pride in race, the strong organizing point of all racial-separatist movements. "When

A black man lies wounded at the base of a staircase, the victim of the Chicago race riot of 1919.

*Wearing ornate uniforms and commissioning
paramilitary orders, Marcus Garvey led a large black
nationalist movement that was born in response to the
violent racial conflict that scarred America in 1919.*

Europe was inhabited by a race of cannibals, a race of
savages, naked men, heathens, and pagans," Garvey
told cheering throngs in New York's Harlem, turning
white stereotypes of blacks upside down, "Africa was
peopled by a race of cultured black men who were
masters in art, science, and literature."

He made little headway in the South, but in the
North, urban blacks who already were uprooted found
his call for a return to Africa appealing, at least in the
abstract. Estimates of UNIA membership as high as 4
million were probably exaggerated, but many more
blacks than that listened to Garvey's message with
open minds and enjoyed the pageantry of nationhood
with which he surrounded himself.

Garvey decked himself in ornate, regal uniforms and
commissioned paramilitary orders with exotic names
such as "The Dukes of the Niger" and the "Black
Eagle Flying Corps." Even veterans in the fight for
racial equality were influenced by Garvey's magic.
W. E. B. Du Bois wrote, "The spell of Africa is upon
me. The ancient witchery of her medicine is burning
in my drowsy, dreamy blood."

The popularity of black nationalism unnerved whites
who were accustomed to a passive black population.
When Garvey ran afoul of the law with one of his
dozens of business enterprises, the authorities moved
against him with an enthusiasm that bore little relation
to the seriousness of his offense. Whether because of
mismanagement or fraud, Garvey's Black Star Line, a
steamship company, had sold worthless shares through
the mails at a mere $5 a share. Some 35,000 blacks
lost $750,000, a comparatively minor take during the
1920s. Nevertheless, the government pressed its case
for five years, draining the resources of the UNIA.

The Ku Klux Klan

Marcus Garvey's ritual, costume, and ceremony was
paralleled in a white racist organization of the same
era, the Ku Klux Klan. The twentieth-century KKK
was founded in 1915 by William Simmons, a Methodist minister. After viewing *Birth of a Nation*, a film
that glorified the antiblack movement of the post-Civil
War period, Simmons began organizing, first in the
South but, by 1919, in the North and West as well.

Under Hiram Wesley Evans, the KKK gave local
units and officials exotic names such as Klavern, Klea-
gle, Grand Dragon, and Exalted Cyclops. Evans was
a shrewder businessman than Garvey. The Klan's central office retained a monopoly of "official" bedsheet
uniforms that all members were required to buy. The
Klan provided a cash incentive for local organizers by
giving them a percentage of all money that they collected, a kind of franchised bigotry. By the mid-1920s,
membership may have risen as high as 4.5 million.

In the South, the KKK was primarily an antiblack
organization. Elsewhere, however, KKK leaders exploited whatever hatreds, fears, and resentments were
most likely to keep the bedsheet orders rolling in. In
the Northeast, where Catholics and Jews were numerous, Klan leaders inveighed against their religions.
Immigrants generally were a target.

In the Owens Valley of California, a region of small
farmers whose water was drained southward to feed
the growth of Los Angeles, the big city was the enemy.
In the Midwest, some Klaverns concentrated their
attacks on saloonkeepers who ignored Prohibition and
"lovers' lanes" where teenagers flaunted traditional
morality on weekend nights. Stripped of the hocus-
pocus and the mercenary motives of the central office,
the Klan represented the belief of generally poor, Protestant, and small-town people that the America they
knew was under attack by immigrants, cities, and modern immorality. Nevertheless, the Klan prospered in
cities too. The twentieth-century metropolis was an
unsettling phenomenon, but it continued to attract
people of every kind.

Ku Klux Klan members march in Washington, D.C., in August 1925, without the masks that concealed their identities.

Klan power peaked in 1924. In that year, the organization boasted numerous state legislators, congressmen, senators, and even governors in Oregon, Ohio, Tennessee, and Texas. In Indiana, state Klan leader David Stephenson was a virtual dictator. At the Democratic national convention of 1924, the Klan was strong enough to prevent the party from adopting a plank that was critical of its bigotry.

The KKK declined as rapidly as the UNIA. In 1925, Grand Dragon Stephenson was found guilty of second-degree murder in the death of a young woman whom he had kidnapped and taken to Chicago. In an attempt to win a light sentence, he turned over evidence showing that virtually the whole administration of the KKK was involved in thievery and that Indiana Klan politicians were thoroughly corrupt. By 1930, the KKK had dwindled to 10,000 members.

Wets and Drys

To some extent, the Klan was a manifestation of hostility between cities and country and small towns. This social conflict was also evident in the split that devel-

oped after the Eighteenth Amendment went into effect in 1920. Violation of the Prohibition law was nearly universal. While some bootleggers smuggled liquor into the country from Mexico, the West Indies, and Canada, individual liquor distillers in isolated corners of rural America continued to practice their ancient crafts, distilling "white lightning" and "moonshine" and battling government agents with guns as well as stealth.

Nevertheless, there was a clear geographical and social dimension to the political battle between "drys," people who supported Prohibition, and "wets," those who opposed it. The drys were strongest in the South and in rural areas generally, where the population was largely composed of old-stock Americans who clung to fundamentalist Protestant religions. The wets drew their support from the big cities, where ethnic groups of Roman Catholic and Jewish faith were powerful forces and often in control of local government.

Wet mayors and city councils often refused to help federal officials enforce Prohibition. Democratic Mayor James J. Walker of New York openly frequented fashionable speakeasies. Republican "Big Bill" Thompson of Chicago ran for office on a "wide-open-town" platform and won. As a result, smuggling, illegal distilleries and breweries, and theft of industrial and medicinal alcohol were commonplace and provided the basis for an extremely lucrative, if illegal, business. In Chicago by 1927, the Alphonse "Al" Capone bootleg ring grossed $60 million by supplying liquor and beer to the Windy City's speakeasies. (Capone also made $25 million that year from gambling and $10 million from prostitution.)

Gangsters as Symbols

As far as Capone was concerned, he was a businessman. He supplied 10,000 drinking houses and employed 700 people. He and other gangsters needed the administrative acumen of a corporation executive to run their affairs and the same kind of political influence that conventional businessmen courted. "What's

Al Capone done?" he told a reporter. "He's supplied a legitimate demand. . . . Some call it racketeering. I call it a business. They say I violate the prohibition law. Who doesn't?"

With incredible profits at stake, however, rival gangs engaged in open, bloody warfare for control of the trade. More than 400 "gangland slayings" made the name of Chicago synonymous with mob violence, although other cities had only scarcely better records.

Very few innocent bystanders were killed. Capone and his ilk tried to keep their violence on a professional level. But Americans were appalled by the carnage, and they did not overlook the fact that most prominent gangsters were "foreigners." Capone and his predecessors in Chicago, Johnny Torrio and Big Jim Colosimo, were Italians. Dion O'Bannion (Capone's rival), "Bugsy" Moran, and Owney Madden were Irish. Arthur "Dutch Schultz" Flegensheimer of New York was German. "Polack Joe" Saltis came from Chicago's

Renowned Federal agents, Izzy Einstein and Moe Smith (flanking an illegal still) became national celebrities by using comical tactics to trap bootleggers.

Al Capone, a gangster who supplied thousands of drinking houses with illegal liquor, regarded himself as a businessman fulfilling a public demand.

HOORAY FOR HOLLYWOOD

The first filmmakers set up shop wherever they happened to be. By the 1920s, however, the movie industry had become concentrated in Hollywood, one of the myriad communities that grew together to form greater Los Angeles. The official explanation of the choice of location was the weather; southern California is one of the sunniest parts of the nation, and early filmmakers depended on natural light. But there was another reason for choosing Hollywood. Like the organizers of many infant industries, filmmakers took considerable liberties with business law, particularly copyright and contract law. Everyone, it seemed, was engaged in a dozen lawsuits at all times. Hollywood was only a hundred miles from the Mexican border. If a case seemed to be getting serious, the filmmakers could make a quick dash out to Tijuana.

Polish West Side. Maxie Hoff of Philadelphia, Solly Weissman of Kansas City, and "Little Hymie" Weiss of Chicago were Jews.

"Illegal business" attracted members of groups on the bottom of the social ladder because success in it required no social status or family connections, no education, and, to get started, little money. With less to lose than respectable established people who patronized the speakeasies, ethnics had fewer compunctions about the high risks involved. But the majority of Americans were not inclined to take a sociological view of the matter. To them, organized crime was violent, and "foreigners" were the source of it.

Hollywood as Symbol

Show business was also a low-status enterprise that presented few competitive advantages to wealthy and established groups. The film industry, which was booming by 1919, had been largely dominated from the beginning by Jewish studio bosses such as Samuel Goldwyn and Louis B. Mayer, graduates of the Yiddish-language theater tradition of New York City. Consequently, when protest against nudity and loose moral standards in Hollywood films boiled over, it took on an ethnic flavor. Preachers who demanded that controls be slapped on filmmakers were not above attributing immorality on the screen to "non-Christian" influences that aimed to subvert Protestant America.

By 1922, Hollywood's nabobs feared that city and state governments would ban the showing of their films. They banded together to censor themselves and, sensitive to ethnic prejudice, hired a man who was the epitome of the small-town midwestern Protestant to be chief censor and film-industry spokesman. Will H. Hays of Indiana, Postmaster General under Harding, supervised the drafting of a code that forbade movies that allowed adultery to go unpunished or that depicted divorced people in a sympathetic light. The Hays Code went so far as to prohibit showing a married couple in bed together or, indeed, a double bed in the background of bedroom scenes. In the movies, couples slept in twin beds, and so powerful was the medium that separate beds became fashionable in the real society.

The Evolution Controversy

The clash between traditional values and the worldly outlook of the twentieth century was clearest cut in the controversy that surrounded the theory of the evolution of species as propounded half a century before by the English biologist Charles Darwin. Although many scientists insisted that there was no contradic-

Exotic themes and lavish sets characterized the escapist films of the 1920s. Americans were hooked.

tion between the biblical account of the creation of the world (if interpreted as literary) and Darwin's contention that species emerged and changed character over the eons, fundamentalist Protestants who insisted on the literal truth of every word of the Bible disagreed. Feeling threatened by fast-changing times and urged on by such influential leaders as William Jennings Bryan, the fundamentalists tried to prohibit the teaching of evolution in the public schools; in Tennessee, they succeeded in passing a law to that effect.

In the little Appalachian town of Dayton in the spring of 1925, a group of friends who had been arguing about evolution decided to test the new law in the courts. One of their number, a high school biology teacher named John Scopes, would deliberately break it. In front of adult witnesses, Scopes would explain Darwin's theory, submit to arrest, and stand trial. The motives of the men were mixed. Dayton businessmen thought of a celebrated trial as a way to put their town

on the map and to make money when spectators, including reporters for newspapers and radio stations, would flock to Dayton in search of lodgings, meals, and other services.

The "Monkey Trial"

Dayton's boosters succeeded beyond their dreams. The "Monkey Trial," so called because evolution was popularly interpreted as meaning that human beings were "descended" from apes, attracted sensation-hungry broadcasters and reporters by the hundreds; among them was the nation's leading iconoclast, Henry L. Mencken, who came to poke fun at the "rubes" of the Bible belt. Number-one rube in Mencken's book was William Jennings Bryan himself, aged now—he died shortly after the trial ended—who agreed to go to Dayton to advise the prosecution.

Bryan's advice was ignored. He wanted to fight the case on the strictly legal principle that, in a democracy,

HOW THEY PLAYED THE GAME

Originally, baseball was a gentleman's game, played by wealthy amateurs for the pleasure of competition. By the turn of the twentieth century, this had changed. Baseball became a business, potentially very lucrative. The players were paid for their skills by teams organized into two major leagues, the National and the American. The profits to the owners, who called themselves "sportsmen" and their properties "clubs," lay in paid admissions to games. Because the better the team, the more people willing to pay to attend, it stood to reason that clubowners would seek to build winning teams. However, it did not always work that way. While the players indeed competed with one another to win games, the sportsmen did not compete with one another to win the best players.

In order to avoid bidding wars among themselves for the services of star pitchers, hitters, and fielders, the clubowners devised the "reserve clause," an agreement that every player was required to sign. The reserve clause was based on the dubious assumption that a baseball player was a professional like a physician or lawyer and not a lowly employee. Unlike a machinist or miner who, of course, as industrial employers never tired of saying, were free at all times to quit their job and find another, the professional baseball player was not free to do so. In signing the reserve clause, he agreed that he could not leave to play with another team without the owner's consent. His services were reserved unless the clubowner "sold" or "traded" him to another owner with whom the player then had no choice but to come to terms—if he wanted to stay in baseball.

As in other businesses, practices varied from team to team, but perhaps the most frankly businesslike of the owners was Cornelius "Connie Mack" McGillicuddy, who also managed his Philadelphia Athletics of the American League. The dominant team in baseball in the years before the First World War, the A's won six league pennants and three world series. Mack twice built up powerhouse teams in that era and then broke them up, selling his star players off for a cash profit. And again by the end of the 1920s he created a team that was better than the New York Yankees of the era. Once again Mack cashed in, selling off his players.

There was no reconciling the concept of sportsmanship or a sense of civic responsibility with Mack's policies, and yet, simply because he continued to manage the A's into his 90s, he was touted as one of the grand old men of the "game."

Charles A. Comiskey, owner of the Chicago White Sox, was another kind of businessman. Until the First World War he was content with mediocre players to whom he paid the lowest salaries in either major league. Then, during the war, while attendance in all cities declined, the White Sox jelled behind such stars as hard-hitting outfielder Joseph "Shoeless Joe" Jackson

Chicago White Sox outfielder "Shoeless Joe" Jackson.

and third baseman George "Buck" Weaver. After finishing high in the standings in 1917 and 1918, the White Sox won the American League pennant in 1919 and were regarded by most sports journalists as unbeatable in the World Series, particularly because the National League champion was an old team but an upstart champion, the Cincinnati Red Stockings.

There was trouble in the White Sox team, however. While their sterling play had caused attendance and profits to soar, Comiskey had actually taken the lead in calling for a league-wide paycut. At a time when wages in almost every job were rising, the two leading White Sox pitchers, who won 50 games between them, were paid a combined salary of only $8,600. Adding insult to exploitation, Comiskey allowed his champion players considerably lower expenses when they were on the road than any other team in either league.

The White Sox lost the World Series to the Red Stockings 5 games to 3. (Only in 1922 was the Series reduced to 7 games.) An investigation during the winter and spring revealed that it was no mere upset. Eight White Sox players, including stars Weaver and Jackson, had conspired with gamblers to throw the match and make a killing on longshot bets.

It was rumored that Comiskey had been aware of the fix all along but was willing to sacrifice the Series for the chance to intimidate future players. Indeed, although the eight accused "Black Sox" were acquitted in criminal court for lack of hard evidence, they were banned from playing professional ball for life by a newly installed Commissioner with broad powers to regulate the business, Judge Kenesaw Mountain Landis. Like the head of a government commission, Landis showed no reluctance to discipline owners whose actions threatened the good of the whole, but he backed up the owners in disputes with players.

Not every club ownership was so cash-oriented as Mack or so exploitative as Comiskey. Indeed, during the same years that Landis was brushing up baseball's reputation for honesty at the top, an ugly, pot-bellied, spindly legged, and atrociously vulgar orphan from Baltimore was revolutionizing the game and winning huge salaries from ungrudging employers, the New York Yankees.

George Herman "Babe" Ruth started in baseball as a pitcher—quite a good one—for the Boston Red Sox. In 1919, the year of the Black Sox Scandal, while playing the outfield on days he did not pitch, Ruth hit 29 home runs, double that of any previous player. In fact, the major leagues did not even keep official home run statistics until 1921; baseball B. R.—before Ruth—was a game of tactics played by lithe, swift men who eked out runs one at a time with scratch hits off over-powering pitchers, and gritty base running. Tyrus J. "Ty" Cobb of the Detroit Tigers, a genuinely mean-spirited man whose specialty was sliding into second with file-sharpened cleats slicing the air, was the most respected player of the 1910s.

Now, with a single swing, the "Sultan of Swat" could put up to four runs on the scoreboard and the fans loved it. Purchased from the Red Sox by the Yankees for $100,000—itself an unprecedented windfall under the reserve clause—Ruth hit 59 home runs in 1921, the record until his own 60 in 1927. Rather than haggle with their godsend, the Yankee ownership paid him annually higher salaries. By the end of the decade when his pay was higher than that of the president of the United States, Ruth shrugged nonchalantly, "I had a better year than he did."

Not only did he make the Yankees the best team in baseball, Babe Ruth made them the richest. In 1923, New York opened the largest baseball stadium of the era, Yankee Stadium, which was properly nicknamed, "the house that Ruth built." Other owners and Commissioner Landis took notice too. If home runs sold tickets, they would have more home runs. The baseball itself was redesigned into a livelier "rabbit ball" and the slugger became the mythic figure in the game. Hack Wilson of the Chicago Cubs hit 56 home runs in 1930, setting the National League's record, and Jimmy Foxx of the Philadelphia Athletics was eclipsing Ruth himself by 1932 when he hit 58 (and was promptly sold by Connie Mack). The New York Yankees remained the team that most totally staked its fortunes on men who swung the heavy bat and the "club" that was the most liberal with a paycheck. It would not have much mattered to Connie Mack and Charles Comiskey, perhaps, but the Yankees were also, of course, the most successful team in the history of both the sport and the business.

Babe Ruth as a pitcher for the Boston Red Sox.

Clarence Darrow for the defense and William Jennings Bryan for the prosecution at the Scopes "Monkey Trial," which addressed the question of evolution and its instruction in classrooms.

the people had the right to dictate what might and what might not be taught in tax-supported schools. Unfortunately, their heads spinning from the crowds and the carnival atmosphere of the town, the Daytonians wanted to debate religion versus science.

The defense, which had been put together and funded by the American Civil Liberties Union, also intended to fight the case on the basis of two significant principles. Led by the distinguished lawyer and libertarian Arthur Garfield Hays, the attorneys planned to argue that the biblical account of creation was a religious doctrine and therefore could not take precedence over science (evolution) because of the constitutional separation of church and state. The defense also insisted that freedom of intellectual inquiry, including a teacher's right to speak his or her mind in the classroom, was essential to the health of a democracy.

Hays was assisted by the era's leading criminal lawyer, Clarence Darrow, who loved the drama of courtroom confrontation more than legal niceties. Darrow regarded the trial as an opportunity to discredit fun-

damentalists by making their leader, Bryan, look like a superstitious old fool. Against his better judgment, Bryan allowed Darrow to put him on the stand as an expert witness on the Bible. Under the trees—the judge feared that the tiny courthouse would collapse under the crowd—Darrow and Bryan talked religion and science. Was the world created in six days of twenty-four hours each? Was Jonah literally swallowed by a whale?

Supporters of Darrow rested content that Bryan himself looked like a monkey, but they lost the case; Scopes was found guilty and given a nominal penalty. It was a small consolation to the anti-evolutionists, who were crestfallen when Bryan admitted that some parts of the Bible may have been meant figuratively. In fact, the only winners in the Monkey Trial were Dayton's businessmen, who raked in dollars for almost a month, and the people in the business of ballyhoo. This was appropriate in itself, for by 1925, the second full year of Calvin Coolidge's "New Era," raking in money and ballyhoo were what America seemed to be all about.

Transportation

Transportation—the movement of people, goods, and ideas—has played a major role in shaping the United States. Here Irish immigrants disembark in New York City.

The Erie Canal, 364 miles long and originally four feet deep, took eight years to complete and connected the frontier to New York City.

This view of Lockport, New York, shows 10 of the 83 locks on the Erie Canal.

Where there were no waterways, the trip west was made by Conestoga wagon or prairie schooner.

*Chinese laborers cheer for the first passenger train through the Sierra Nevada on the western end
of the transcontinental railroad.*

Railroads quickly replaced canals and stagecoaches for transporting goods and passengers between cities.

Passengers and train crew shoot buffalo along the Kansas Pacific Railroad.

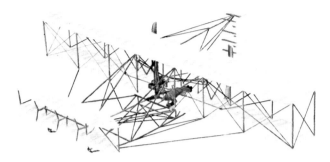

In 1903 Wilbur and Orville Wright successfully completed the first controlled, engine-powered flight with their homemade airplane.

With assembly-line production, Henry Ford transformed the automobile from a toy for the rich to an inexpensive transportation necessity. The Model T was first marketed in 1908.

Boomtown *by Thomas Hart Benton (1928) depicts life in the oil fields.*

Robots weld truck chassis in a modern assembly plant.

Beginning with the Interstate Highway Act of 1956, billions of dollars each year were used for highway construction, resulting in the grandiose Interstate freeway system.

Project Mercury, *the first U.S. manned space program of the early 1960s, led to the first moon landing by Apollo 11 astronauts on July 20, 1969.*

For Further Reading

Overviews and Classics

Frederick Lewis Allen, *Only Yesterday* (1931)
William E. Leuchtenburg, *The Perils of Prosperity, 1914–1932* (1958)
Robert K. Murray, *The Harding Era* (1967)
George Soule, *Prosperity Decade: From War to Depression, 1917–1929* (1947)

Valuable Special Studies

Wesley Bagby, *The Road to Normalcy* (1962)
Loren Baritz, *The Culture of the Twenties* (1969)
Irving Bernstein, *The Lean Years* (1960)
David Brody, *Labor in Crisis: The Steel Strike of 1919* (1965)
D. M. Chalmers, *Hooded Americanism* (1965)
N. H. Clark, *Deliver Us From Evil* (1976)
Robert L. Friedheim, *The Seattle General Strike* (1965)
Ray Ginger, *Six Days or Forever* (1958)
John Higham, *Strangers in the Land* (1955)
Nathan J. Huggins, *Harlem Renaissance* (1972)
Kenneth T. Jackson, *The Ku Klux Klan in the Cities, 1915–1930* (1967)
Don S. Kirschner, *City and Country: Rural Responses to Urbanization in the 1920s* (1970)
Isabel Leighton, *The Aspirin Age* (1949)
George M. Marsden, *Fundamentalism and American Culture* (1980)
Larry May, *Screening Out the Past* (1980)

Robert K. Murray, *The Politics of Normalcy* (1973)
———, *Red Scare* (1955)
Humbert S. Nelli, *The Business of Crime* (1976)
Burt Noggle, *Teapot Dome: Oil and Politics in the 1920s* (1962)
Gilbert Osofsky, *Harlem: The Making of a Ghetto, 1890–1930* (1966)
William Preston, Jr., *Aliens and Dissenters: Federal Suppression of Radicals, 1903–1933* (1963)
J. W. Prothro, *Dollar Decade: Business Ideas in the 1920s* (1954)
John Roe, *The Road and the Car in American Life* (1971)
Francis Russell, *A City in Terror: 1919, the Boston Police Strike* (1975)
Andrew Sinclair, *Prohibition: The Era of Excess* (1962)
Robert Sklar, *Movie-Made America* (1975)
William Tuttle, Jr., *Race Riot: Chicago and the Red Summer of 1919* (1970)
Theodore G. Vincent, *Black Power and the Garvey Movement* (1971)

Biographies and Autobiographies

Stanley Coben, *A. Mitchell Palmer: Politician* (1963)
Lawrence Levine, *Defender of the Faith: William Jennings Bryan, The Last Decade* (1965)
Francis Russell, *The Shadow of Blooming Grove: Warren G. Harding in His Times* (1968)
Andrew Sinclair, *The Available Man* (1965)

41

Calvin Coolidge and the New Era

When the Business of America Was Business, 1923–1929

Vice President Calvin Coolidge was visiting his father, a justice of the peace in rural Vermont, when he got the news of Harding's death. Instead of rushing to Washington to be sworn in by the Chief Justice of the Supreme Court, Coolidge walked downstairs to the darkened farmhouse parlor, where his father administered the presidential oath by the light of a kerosene lamp. To the very pinnacle of his political career, Coolidge was the image of simplicity and homey rectitude or, as some historians have suggested, of sloth and bewilderment.

Members of an organization of "boosters," the Minneapolis Commercial Club, gather for a meeting.

THE COOLIDGE YEARS

Coolidge was not a bit like his predecessor. Far from strapping and handsome, he was slight and had a pinched face that, even when he smiled, seemed to say that he wished he were somewhere else. Alice Roosevelt Longworth, the acidulous daughter of Theodore Roosevelt, said Coolidge looked as though he had been weaned on a pickle.

Whereas Harding's private life was tawdry, Coolidge was a man of impeccable, priggish, even dreary personal habits. His idea of a good time was a long sleep.

He spent twelve to fourteen hours out of twenty-four in bed except on slow days, when he was able to sneak in an extra nap. When in 1933 writer Dorothy Parker heard that Coolidge had died, she asked, "How could they tell?"

A Quiet Clever Man

Coolidge might have appreciated that. He may have been "Silent Cal," hesitant to say much of anything, but when he spoke he was often witty. In an attempt to break the ice at a banquet, a woman seated next to Coolidge told the president of a friend who had bet her that untalkative Cal would not say three words all evening. "You lose," Coolidge replied, and returned to his appetizer, resuming the blank stare that was his trademark. "I found out early in life," this fabulously successful politician once noted, "that you don't have to explain something you haven't said."

Coolidge took a curious pleasure in posing for photographers in costumes that were ludicrous on him: wearing a ten-gallon hat or a Sioux Indian war bonnet; strapped into skis on the White House lawn; dressed as a hard-working farmer at the haying, in patent-leather shoes with a Pierce Arrow in the background.

An old hand at grabbing publicity, Calvin Coolidge posed in an Indian headdress for photographers.

Perhaps the photos were Coolidge's quiet way of saying that he was at one with the American people of the 1920s in enjoying novelties and pranks. On being asked about the costume quirk, he said that he thought "the American public wants a solemn ass as President and I think I'll go along with them."

However that may be, he was assuredly at one with them in abdicating political and cultural leadership to the business community. Coolidge worshiped financial success and believed without reservation that millionaires knew what was best for the country. "The man who builds a factory builds a temple," he said. On another occasion, he put his faith with sublime simplicity: "The business of America is business."

Keep Cool With Coolidge

And so, while Coolidge quickly rid the cabinet of the racketeers and hacks whom he had inherited from Harding, he retained Harding's appointees from the business world, most notably Herbert Hoover (whom he did not like personally) and Secretary of the Treasury Andrew Mellon. He then sat back to preside over the most business-minded administration to his time, and, in return, business praised his administration higher than they built skyscrapers in New York and Chicago. The Republicans crowed about "Coolidge prosperity," which revived the erratic postwar economy beginning in 1923, and, thanks to the president's un-blemished record for honesty, the G.O.P. never suffered a voter backlash as a result of the Harding scandals.

On the contrary, the biggest of the scandals, Teapot Dome, hurt progressive Democrats. The Wilsonian, William G. McAdoo, a leading contender for the Democratic nomination in 1924, had been an attorney for the oilman Edward L. Doheny. Although McAdoo knew no more of the crooked transaction than did Coolidge, people associated him more closely with the wrongdoers than they did the Republicans. Montana Senators Thomas J. Walsh and Burton Wheeler, who had led the investigation into the oil leases, were squelched by the Republican slogan "Keep Cool With Coolidge." The president's supporters chastised them for ranting and raving about past crimes that Coolidge had remedied in his quiet way. By the summer of the election year of 1924, it was clear that Coolidge had the confidence of the country.

The Election of 1924

Then the Democrats obliged by tearing themselves apart. The convention, held in New York, pitted the Empire State's favorite son, Roman Catholic Alfred E. Smith, against William G. McAdoo, whose support came mostly from the South and the West. Although he was no bigot, McAdoo was backed by many Ku Kluxers who despised Smith because of his religion. So bitter was the split that neither candidate would yield for more than a hundred ballots, even though it was obvious neither could win the nomination.

Finally, the delegates chose a compromise candidate, Wall Street lawyer John W. Davis. He was not absent from his lucrative legal practice for long. He won only 29 percent of the vote to Coolidge's 54 percent. Aged Robert La Follette tried to revive the Progressive party in 1924. But he captured only 17 percent of the popular vote and carried no state but his native Wisconsin.

For four more years, Calvin Coolidge napped through good times. It was eight months after he left office, in October 1929, that what business called the "New Era" came crashing to an end. Ironically, in view of the impending Great Depression, Coolidge retired from office with great reluctance. It was whispered that when the Republican convention of 1928 took his coy statement, "I do not choose to run for president in 1928," as a refusal to run, and nominated Herbert Hoover to succeed him, Coolidge threw himself on his familiar bed and wept.

Mellon's Tax Policies

The keystone of New Era government was the tax policy sponsored by the Secretary of the Treasury, Andrew Mellon of Pittsburgh. Mellon looked less like the political cartoonist's stereotype of a big businessman—a bloated, fleshy moneybags—than like a sporting duke, but a moneybags he was. Trim, with chiseled aristocratic features, and dressed in deftly tailored suits and tiny pointed shoes that shone like newly minted coins, Mellon was one of the three or four richest men in the world, a banker with close ties to the steel industry.

Believing that economic prosperity depended on the extent to which capitalists reinvested their profits in economic growth, Mellon favored the rich by slashing taxes that fell most heavily on them. He reduced the personal income tax for people who made more than $60,000 a year, and by 1929, the Treasury was actually shoveling taxes back to large corporations. United States Steel received a nice refund of $15 million. Other big corporations were comparably blessed.

To compensate for the loss in government revenues, Mellon cut government expenditures. The costs of government that he conceded were indispensable were to be paid for by raising the tariff on imported products—a double benefit for industrial capitalists—and by modest increases in those kinds of taxes that were disproportionately paid by the middle and lower classes.

Andrew Mellon, a powerful businessman and a member of the Coolidge cabinet.

In the Fordney-McCumber Tariff of 1922, import duties reached levels that had been unheard of for a generation. Mellon also sponsored increases for some kinds of postal services, the excise (also a broadly paid consumer tax), and a new federal tax on automobiles. To those who complained that these measures penalized the middle classes and to some extent the poor, Mellon replied that the burden was small and that his overall scheme helped ordinary people as well as the rich.

Mellon's program was based on his belief that when businessmen reinvested their government-sponsored windfalls, they created jobs and the means of a better standard of living for all. The share of the middle and lower classes in Coolidge prosperity would "trickle down" to them. Moreover, the inducement to get rich, encouraged by government policy, would reinvigorate the spirit of enterprise among all Americans.

For six years, from late 1923 to late 1929, it appeared as though Mellon was indeed, as his friends called him, the greatest Secretary of the Treasury since Alexander Hamilton. Just how much damage his policies did to the national economy would not be known until after the collapse of the New Era in 1929. As early as 1924, however, the policy of subordinating everything to the short-term interests of big business and banking was helping to make a shambles of the international economy.

The Legacy of the Treaty of Versailles

The fundamental weakness of the international economy during the 1920s owed to the demands of Britain and France that Germany pay them $13 billion in reparations and the $10 billion the former Allies owed the United States for loans that had been made to them during the war. In short, international payments would flow from Germany to Britain and France (and other smaller countries) and from there to the United States. The trouble was that the flow drained too much money out of Germany for the economy of that important industrial nation to remain healthy. At home, paper marks inflated crazily; in time it took bundles, even wheelbarrows full of paper money to buy food. Expert observers warned that to continue to bleed Germany was to promote political extremism (including Adolf Hitler's Nazi party) and to threaten the economies of all the European nations.

The British and French governments acknowledged the point but insisted that as long as they were obligated to make huge debt payments to the United States, they had no choice but to insist on German payments to them. The burden of finding a remedy was on Americans.

New Era Foreign Policy

There were several ways out of the morass. First, the United States, the world's wealthiest nation, could invigorate European industry by importing more European products. The Fordney-McCumber Tariff, a vital part of Mellon's fiscal policy, shut the door on that idea. Alternatively, the United States could forgive Britain and France all or most of their debts, in return for which they would cancel reparations payments from Germany. The international economy would, so to speak, have a fresh start. Unfortunately, an administration that was closely allied with banking interests would not do that. "They hired the money, didn't they?" Coolidge said of the French and British war debts, as though he were talking about a grocer having trouble paying for his automobile.

In the Dawes Plan of 1924 (named for Budget Director Charles G. Dawes) and the Young Plan of 1929 (named for Owen D. Young), the United States agreed to a rescheduling of reparations payments, but not to a reduction of the total burden. Instead, American

bankers helped German industry and governments with the money that they made as a result of Mellon's tax policies. On the surface, money flowed in a circle: American bankers loaned it to Germany; Germany paid about $2.5 billion in reparations to Britain and France between 1923 and 1929; Britain and France paid $2.6 billion to American creditors. In reality, the European economy was steadily, if slowly, sapped, and the American economy was indirectly damaged: capital that was supposed to be reinvested at home to "trickle down" was devoted to a nonproductive balancing of international books that did nothing for American workers.

Isolationism

After the Treaty of Washington, the Harding and Coolidge (and Hoover) administrations resisted making meaningful cooperative cause with other nations; the foreign policy of the 1920s thus is described as "isolationist." The name is helpful in the sense that the United States remained isolated from the League of Nations, which had been an American invention. The nation did continue to pay lip service to the idea of maintaining the peace through international cooperation, and in 1928, Secretary of State Frank B. Kellogg joined with French Foreign Minister Aristide Briand in writing a treaty that "outlawed" war as an instrument of national policy. Eventually, 62 nations signed the Kellogg-Briand Pact, a clear indication that, as a broad and pious statement of unenforceable sentiment, the pact was meaningless.

The United States did not abstain from significant relations with non-European powers. In Latin America, American business investments climbed from about $800 million in 1914 to $5.4 billion in 1929. The United States replaced Great Britain as the chief economic force in South America, particularly in the nations of the Caribbean.

The poorer Latin American nations sorely needed capital, and to that extent every dollar invested there was potentially a boon—if the population of the host countries as a whole benefited from it. Unfortunately, American businessmen had little interest in how the Latin American countries were governed until their profits were threatened by political instability. They ignored the depredations of predatory elites until they were in trouble.

When dictators in the "banana republics" were unable to contain popular resentments, American investors turned to Washington for protection of their profits. By 1924, American officials directly or indirectly administered the finances of ten Latin American nations. For at least part of the decade, the marines occupied Nicaragua, Honduras, Cuba, Haiti, and the

Dominican Republic. The business of the entire Western Hemisphere was business too.

PROSPERITY AND BUSINESS CULTURE

Voters supported the Coolidge policies. The Republican party held comfortable majorities in every Congress between 1920 and 1930. Only in the South and some thinly populated western states, and in a few big cities, could the Democrats be sure of winning elections.

The Anticlimactic Election of 1928

In 1928, the 54 percent of the vote that Coolidge had won in 1924 rose to 58 percent. The victorious Republican candidate was Herbert Hoover, who was, in his energy and rather opaque written celebrations of business, even better an exemplar of the New Era than Silent Cal.

Hoover's opponent, Alfred E. Smith of New York, had spent four years mending fences with southern and western Protestants who had supported McAdoo in 1924. Smith was unable to win over the bigots, however. For the first time since Reconstruction, a number of prominent southerners, including Methodist bishop James Cannon, urged voters to support the Republican party. Their reason was partly Smith's Roman Catholic religion. But more often they drummed on Smith's opposition to Prohibition. Like many urban politicos, Smith not only urged repeal, he openly flaunted the law. Herbert Hoover probably disapproved of Prohibition personally, but in 1928 he called it "a great

Alfred E. Smith was popular among Montana farmers, but being Catholic he could not win support in the "Bible Belt."

social and economic experiment, noble in motive and far-reaching in purpose." He was the "dry" candidate, Smith the "wet."

Smith also invited hostility from southern, western, and rural voters with his nasal, tortured New York accent. Heard over the radio—or "raddio" as Smith called it—his voice elicited all the unsavory images associated with New York City for half a century.

Still, had he been a Kansas Presbyterian who never drank even patent medicines, Smith would have lost. Business and the Republican party reigned supreme in politics because of the general prosperity of the New Era and because a great many Americans were sincerely convinced that businessmen were the new messiahs Woodrow Wilson had tried so hard to be.

The Shape of Prosperity

Industrial and agricultural productivity soared during the 1920s, even though there was not much increase in the size of the industrial work force and the number of agricultural workers actually declined. Wages did not keep up with the contribution that the more efficient workers were making to the economy. While dividends on stock rose 65 percent between 1920 and 1929, wages increased only 24 percent.

Nevertheless, the increase in wages was quite enough to satisfy the workingpeople who enjoyed them, particularly because consumer goods were rela-

---

A BUSINESSMAN'S PRAYER

The following is not a parody, but a "prayer" that was quite seriously recommended to those in business during the 1920s:

God of business men, I thank Thee for the fellowship of red-blooded men with songs in their hearts and handclasps that are sincere;

I thank thee for telephones and telegrams that link me with home and office, no matter where I am.

I thank thee for the joy of battle in the business arena, the thrill of victory and the courage to take defeat like a good sport.

I thank thee for children, friendships, books, fishing, the game of golf, my pipe, and the open fire on a chilly evening.

AMEN.

---

tively cheap and business promoted an alluring new way for a family to live beyond their means—consumer credit.

Businessmen and farmers traditionally borrowed money, but their loans were invested in ways that were designed to increase their income, thus providing the means to retire their debts. In the 1920s, large numbers of Americans began to borrow in order to live more comfortably and more enjoyably. They borrowed not in order to produce and profit but to consume and enjoy.

Buy Now, Pay Later

A refrigerator that sold for $87.50 could be ensconced in a corner of the kitchen for a down payment of $5 and monthly payments of $10. Even a comparatively low-cost item like a vacuum cleaner ($28.95) could be had for $2 down and "E-Z payments" of $4 a month. During the New Era, 60 percent of all automobiles were bought on time; 70 percent of furniture; 80 percent of refrigerators, radios, and vacuum cleaners; and 90 percent of pianos, sewing machines, and washing machines. With 13.8 million people owning radios by 1930 (up from virtually none in 1920), the Americans who shared in Coolidge prosperity were also up to their necks in debt.

Defining the true meaning of the word "chic"

An advertisement for Crane bathroom fixtures encouraged consumers to buy on credit, a new marketing concept in the 1920s.

Moralists pointed out that borrowing in order to consume marked a sharp break with American ideals of frugality—the axioms of Benjamin Franklin—but others spoke louder and in more dulcet voices. They were the advertisers, members of a new profession dedicated to creating wants in people's minds—the advertising men called them *needs*—which people had never particularly noticed before.

Buy, Buy, Buy

The first advertisements were simple announcements: a merchant placed a tiny notice in a newspaper describing goods, perhaps unusual ones, available for purchase, or special "sale" prices on common products. During the 1870s, Robert Bonner, the editor of a literary magazine, the New York *Ledger*, learned by accident the curious effectiveness of repeating a message over and over. He intended to place a conventional one-line ad in a newspaper—"Read Mrs. Southworth's New Story in the Ledger"—and the

---

ANXIETY ADVERTISING

The text that follows was taken from a magazine advertisement of the 1920s for Listerine Antiseptic, a mouthwash. The illustration that accompanied it showed an elderly, attractive, poignantly sad woman sitting in a darkened parlor (with a photograph of Calvin Coolidge on the wall) pouring over old letters and a photograph album.

"Sometimes, when lights are low, they come back to comfort and at the same time sadden her—those memories of long ago, when she was a slip of a girl in love with a dark-eyed Nashville boy. They were the happiest moments of her life—those days of courtship. Though she had never married, no one could take from her the knowledge that she had been loved passionately, devotedly; those frayed and yellowed letters of his still told her so. How happy and ambitious they had been for their future together. And then, like a stab, came their parting . . . the broken engagement . . . the sorrow and the shock of it. She could find no explanation for it then, and now, in the soft twilight of life when she can think calmly, it is still a mystery to her."

The advertiser then went on so as to leave no doubt that "halitosis"—bad breath—was the source of the woman's tragedy.

---

compositor misread his instructions as "one page." The line ran over and over, down every column. To Bonner's surprise, the blunder did not bankrupt him; his magazine sold out in one afternoon.

By the 1920s, advertisers had long been plastering their repetitive messages on walls of barns and office buildings, making extravagant claims, telling outright lies, and using sexual titillation: suggestive young ladies in advertisements for such products as soda pop and tickets on railroads. Professional advertisers styled themselves as practical psychologists. They sold goods by exploiting anxieties and, in the words of Thorstein Veblen, "administering shock effects" and "trading on the range of human infirmities which blossom in devout observances, and bear fruit in the psychopathic wards." In the age of Coolidge, the makers of Listerine Antiseptic, a mouthwash, invented a disease, "halitosis," that the most trivial incident—a curt greeting—indicated that one suffered from. Listerine made millions of dollars from its concoction. Fleischmann's yeast, losing its market as people began buying instead of baking their bread, advertised yeast as excellent for curing constipation and adolescent pimples. The success of anxiety advertising resulted in the actual creation of underarm deodorants, a nicety without which humanity had functioned for millennia.

Chain Stores

With manufacturers of "low-ticket" items like toothpaste and mouthwash spending millions to create a

During the 1920s, Americans became accustomed to advertisements like this one appealing to middle-class America to follow the lead of "many people who can afford to pay far more."

In 1925 Sears, Roebuck opened its first retail store while continuing its catalogue sales.

demand for their products, it became advantageous to retail advertised goods on a nationwide basis too. Individual "Mom and Pop" grocery stores and locally owned and managed haberdasheries and sundries shops sold comparatively few cans of Chef Boy-Ar-Dee Spaghetti, Arrow shirts, and tubes of Ipana each month. Therefore, they paid the regional wholesaler a premium price. A centrally managed chain or franchise company, on the contrary, could buy the same goods for hundreds of stores at once, secure a better wholesale price, and keep shipping charges down through "vertical integration." The result was underselling "Mom and Pop" on the street corner and the lightning growth of retailing chains.

By 1928, 860 grocery chains competed for the dollars of a population that was eating better. Among the biggest success stories between 1920 and 1929 were the first supermarkets: Piggly-Wiggly (from 515 to 2,500 stores), Safeway (from 766 to 2,660 stores), and A & P (Atlantic and Pacific Tea Company, from 4,621 to 15,418 stores). Chains also came to dominate the sundries trade (F. W. Woolworth and J. C. Penney), auto parts (Western Auto), and, of course, the retailing of gasoline.

Image Advertising

"Image" advertising—associating a product with a certain kind of person—characterized the selling of automobiles at a time when dozens of manufacturers competed for a share of the market. Pierce Arrows and Lincolns implied, none too subtly, that possession of one of these automobiles indicated a person of high social standing. Stutz Bearcat was the car of the sport and the swell. Dodge affected a stodgy and stolid comfortable "old shoe" family image. Henry Ford insisted that his car be presented as common and democratic.

By the end of the decade, there were 27 million cars registered by state departments of motor vehicles. Indeed, everything related to automobiles, from publicly financed highway construction to those new features of the American landscape, service stations and the roadside motor hotel or "motel," flourished during the New Era.

THE TIN LIZZIE

Although Americans did not invent the automobile, they democratized it by putting cars within the reach of almost everyone. By striving for simplicity (shunning all "extras," including a choice of color), by adapting the assembly line to the manufacture of cars, and by refusing to change his design, Henry Ford managed to whittle the price of a brand-new Model T to $260 in 1925. That is more than $2,000 in today's dollars, but still considerably less than the cheapest new car on the market. By 1927, Ford had sold 15 million tin lizzies, as Model T Fords were affectionately known, more than all other auto makers combined.

The Limits of Prosperity

A few economists joined the moralistic critics of runaway consumption, pointing out that the time would come when everyone who could afford a car, a washing machine, and other consumer durables would have

Rows of parked automobiles lining a main street became a common sight in American cities in the 1920s.

them. They would no longer be buying, and the consumer industries would be in trouble. One of the major weaknesses of the economy was that significant numbers of Americans did not share in the good times and were shut out completely from the buying spree. The 700,000 to 800,000 coal miners and 400,000 textile workers and their dependents suffered depressed conditions and wages throughout the decade; they were not buying many cars and radios. Staple farmers struggled to stave off bankruptcy. Even those who did well often lived in places where there was no electricity; they were buying no appliances that had to be plugged in.

The southern states generally lagged far behind the rest of the country in income and standard of living. Blacks, Indians, Hispanics, and other minority groups tasted Coolidge prosperity only in odd bites.

Business Culture

But economically deprived groups are rarely politically articulate when the mainstream society is at ease in its world, and in the 1920s, mainstream America was. Business leaders hastened to take the credit for good times.

On a local level, businessmen's clubs such as the Rotary, Kiwanis, Lions, and Junior Chambers of Commerce seized community leadership and preached *boosterism*: "if you can't boost, don't knock." Successful manufacturers like Henry Ford were looked to for wisdom on every imaginable question. Any man who made $25,000 a day, as Ford did during most of the 1920s, must be an oracle on whatever subject he chose to speak about. Even that man once the most hated in America, John D. Rockefeller, then in his eighties and retired to Florida, became a figure of respect and affection, thanks to Coolidge prosperity and the skillful image building of the Rockefeller family's public-relations expert, Ivy Lee.

The career of an advertising man, Bruce Barton, showed just how thoroughly the business culture dominated the way Americans thought. In 1925, Barton published a book called *The Man Nobody Knows.* It depicted Jesus as a businessman, an entrepreneur and advertising genius whose religion was like a successful company. Instead of finding Barton's vision blasphemous or laughable, Americans bought *The Man Nobody Knows* by the thousands of copies. It was a best seller for two years.

John Jacob Raskob of General Motors promoted the worship of business in popular magazines such as *The Saturday Evening Post.* Because the value of many kinds of property was rising throughout the 1920s under the

---

LET'S HAVE A LOOK UNDER THE HOOD

Americans and Britons speak a different language when they talk about their cars. What Americans call the hood, the British call the bonnet. Some other differences:

American English	British English
clunker or junker	banger
gas	petrol
generator	dynamo
headlight	headlamp
muffler	silencer
station wagon	estate wagon
trunk	boot
windshield	windscreen

The different vocabularies provide a little case study in how languages develop. The automobile roared into history long after the United States and Great Britain had gone their separate political and cultural ways, but before instantaneous electronic communication allowed words coined on one side of the Atlantic to become immediately familiar on the other.

Because the early automobile was largely a French development, many American automotive terms were taken from the French language: *automobile* itself, *cabriolet* (later shortened to *cab*), *chassis, chauffeur, coupe, garage, limousine,* and *sedan.*

---

stewardship of business, Raskob said that it was a simple matter for workingmen to save a little money and invest it, thus becoming capitalists themselves. To an astonishing degree, middle-class Americans who had a small nest egg in the bank believed him. They plunged their savings into one get-rich-quick scheme after another, feeding but at the same time dooming the speculative economy.

GET RICH QUICK

The most colorful get-rich-quick craze of the decade centered on Florida, previously a backward and isolated agricultural state. Improved train connections with eastern and midwestern population centers, retirement in Florida by celebrities such as Rockefeller and Bryan, and the lively nationwide ballyhoo of promoters such as Wilson Mizner soon aroused people to the Sunshine State's possibilities as a vacation and retirement paradise.

MANUFACTURED HEROES

"Shakespeare, in the familiar lines, divided great men into three classes: those born great, those who achieve greatness, and those who have greatness thrust upon them. It never occurred to him to mention those who hire public relations experts and press secretaries to make themselves look great."

Daniel Boorstin, *The Image* (1962)

JESUS AS ADVERTISING MAN

He would be a national advertiser today, I am sure, as he was the greatest advertiser of his own day. Take any one of the parables, no matter which—you will find that it exemplifies all the principles on which advertising textbooks are written.

1. First of all they are marvellously condensed, as all good advertising must be. Jesus hated prosy dullness.

2. His language was marvellously simple—a second great essential. All the greatest things in human life are one-syllable things—love, joy, hope, child, wife, trust, faith, God.

3. Sincerity glistened like sunshine through every sentence he uttered. The advertisements which persuade people to act are written by men who have an abiding respect for the intelligence of their readers, and a deep sincerity regarding the merits of the goods they have to sell.

4. Finally he knew the necessity for repetition and practiced it. No important truth can be impressed upon the minds of any large number of people by being said only once.

Bruce Barton, *The Man Nobody Knows* (1925)

The Florida Land Boom

The development of cities like Orlando, Fort Lauderdale, and Miami Beach would take months or even years. The way to make money from their growth was to buy orange groves and sandy wasteland at bargain prices and hold the land for resale to the actual builders of vacation hotels and retirement homes. In 1925, however, enough people believed that they could make a fortune in Florida that the speculative fever began to feed on itself. As had happened in the early-nineteenth-century American West, prices of land rose as speculator bought from speculator, each convinced that someone else would soon buy from him at an even higher price. Some lots in Miami Beach changed hands dozens of times within a few months, the price climbing with every sale. At the height of the craze, one issue of a Miami newspaper ran more than 500 pages of advertisements of land for sale. At that time, there were over 2,000 real-estate offices in the little city.

Since the price of every acre in Florida seemed to be skyrocketing, many northerners were willing to buy sight unseen, and frauds were inevitable. More than a few snowbound speculators bought patches of alligator-infested swampland from fast-talking salesmen who assured them that they were purchasing the downtown of a major resort. Others purchased "beachfront lots" that were closer to the ocean than they counted on—underneath six feet of breakers at high tide. But the major fuel of the mania was not fraud. It was a foolishness born of a culture that exalted business and money-making above all else.

As with all speculative crazes, the day inevitably arrived when there were no more buyers, no one willing to bet on higher prices in the future. Then came the "crash." The speculators who were caught holding overpriced property were hurt; the banks that had lent them money to speculate failed; and the people who had trusted those banks to invest their savings sensibly lost those very savings.

The Florida crash was triggered by a hurricane that hit Miami and showed, as Frederick Lewis Allen put it, what a soothing tropical wind could do to a vacation paradise when it got a running start from the West Indies. The price of Florida land plunged within weeks to dollars per acre. Many citrus farmers who had cursed themselves for having sold their groves so cheaply at the beginning of the boom discovered that, thanks to a chain of defaults, they were back in possession of their land, only a little worse for the wear of speculators having tromped through it. Wilson Mizner, one of the architects of the boom and a big loser in the bust, was good humored about it. "Always be pleasant to the people you meet on the way up," he said, "because they are always the very same people you meet on the way down."

Playing the Market

Middle-class America was almost as nonchalant as Mizner. Even before Florida busted, they began to fuel another speculative mania, driving up the prices of shares on the New York Stock Exchange.

Speculation in stocks always had been a game for a few very rich people. However, the prosperity of the 1920s created savings accounts for the modestly fixed American, even after consumption, and the possibility of purchasing stock on very low "margins" stoked the fires. That is, a speculator was able to buy stock by paying out as little as 10 percent of its price (thus enabling him to hold title to ten times as many shares as he could actually afford). A bank or broker loaned the speculator the balance with the stocks themselves serving as collateral. This was the margin. When the shares were sold, presumably in the Coolidge years at

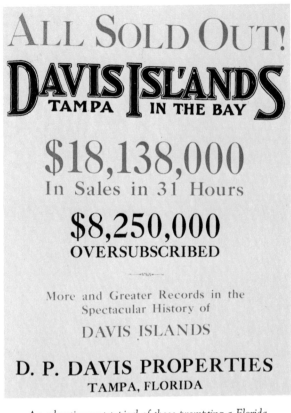

ALL SOLD OUT!
DAVIS ISLANDS
TAMPA · IN THE BAY

$18,138,000
In Sales in 31 Hours

$8,250,000
OVERSUBSCRIBED

More and Greater Records in the
Spectacular History of

DAVIS ISLANDS

D. P. DAVIS PROPERTIES
TAMPA, FLORIDA

An advertisement typical of those prompting a Florida land boom among real-estate speculators in the 1920s.

America rose during the late 1920s, it represented to some extent the extraordinary expansion of the automobile and radio industries.

During the speculative "Coolidge bull market," however, the prices of shares also reflected nothing more than the willingness of people to pay them because "greater fools" would buy from them in the belief that the prices would rise indefinitely. Moreover, speculators could buy on margin. It was immaterial that the companies they owned did not pay dividends or even use their capital to improve productive capacity. In fact, as in the Florida land boom, the rising prices of stocks fed on themselves. It became more profitable for companies to put their money into further stock speculation—making margin loans, for example—than into production. The face value of shares was absurdly inflated.

This is what accounted for much of the 300 percent rise in stock values between 1925 and 1929. Speculators bought in the belief that someone else would buy from them at a higher price. Banks and corporations put their capital into speculation. Politicians, either unable to understand what was happening or afraid to appear pessimistic in a time of buoyant optimism, reassured their constituents that there was nothing wrong. When a few concerned economists warned that the bubble eventually had to burst, with disastrous consequences, others scolded them. President Coolidge told people that he thought stock prices were cheap.

a big profit—the loan was paid off and the happy speculator pocketed the difference. At least that was how the 1.5 million Americans "playing the market" in 1926 understood margin to work.

Beginning in 1927, that was how it did work. Prices of shares began to soar beyond all reason. During the summer of 1929, values went crazy. American Telephone and Telegraph climbed from $209 a share to $303; General Motors went from $268 to $391, hitting $452 on September 3. Some obscure issues enjoyed even more dizzying rises. Each tale of a fortune made overnight, related with great satisfaction at a club or a social gathering, encouraged more people to carry their savings to stockbrokers, whose offices became as common as auto parts stores.

Empty Values

The value of a share in a corporation theoretically represented the earning capacity of the company. The money that a corporation realized by selling shares was expended, again theoretically, improving the company's plant and equipment. Thus, when the price of stock in General Motors or Radio Corporation of

The Inevitable

Joseph P. Kennedy, a Boston millionaire (and father of President John F. Kennedy), said in later years that he had sold all of his stocks during the summer of 1929 after the man who shined his shoes had mentioned that he was playing the market. Kennedy reasoned that if such a poorly paid person was buying stock, there was no one left to bid prices higher. The inevitable crash was coming soon.

Kennedy was right. On September 3, 1929, the average price of shares on the New York Stock Exchange peaked and then dipped sharply. For a month, prices spurted up and down. Then on "Black Thursday," October 24, a record 13 million shares changed hands, and values collapsed. General Electric fell forty-seven and a half points on that one day; other stocks dropped almost as much.

On Tuesday, October 29, the wreckage was worse. In a panic now, speculators dumped 16 million shares on the market. Clerical workers on Wall Street had to work through the night just to sort out the avalanche of paperwork. When the dust settled early the

N O T A B L E P E O P L E

THE LONE EAGLE: CHARLES A. LINDBERGH (1902–1974)

Charles Lindbergh standing beside his plane, the Spirit of St. Louis.

Raymond Orteig was a wealthy French restaurateur living in New York whose two enthusiasms were Franco-American friendship and aviation. He believed that airplanes had a much brighter future than, in 1926, seemed likely. During the 1920s, the fragile but ever improved crafts served as toys for rich hobbyists, as showpieces at state and county fairs where nomadic "barnstormers" did aerial tricks such as walking on the wing of a plane in flight, and, here and there in the United States, as vehicles to deliver "air mail," which the Post Office regarded as an experiment.

Even the prospects of military aviation were dim. Despite the publicity that had been given aerial dogfights during the First World War, planes had been more show than substance, playing no significant role in any action. In 1921 and 1923, General William Mitchell of the Air Service, a branch of the army, had proved in a series of tests that bombs dropped from planes could sink a capital ship (a captured German vessel); but in order to prove his point, Mitchell had disobeyed orders and won the enmity of his superiors. He was court-martialed, and his vision momentarily discredited.

But Orteig believed in the commercial potential, if not in the military uses, of airplanes. Partly to demonstrate the feasibility of long-distance trips, the only kind of transportation in which flying made sense, and partly because he enjoyed ballyhoo as well as most people in the 1920s, Orteig offered a $25,000 prize to the first plane to cross the Atlantic nonstop between France and the United States.

By the spring of 1927, a number of pilots, including First World War flying ace René Fonck, and polar explorer Admiral Richard A. Byrd, using huge biplanes powered by three motors, had tried and failed. Both survived their accidents, but in other attempts, including an east–west flight by two Frenchmen who almost made it to North America, six were dead and two were seriously injured.

In the meantime, in San Diego, California, another challenger for the prize had been making news. Charles A. "Slim" Lindbergh, Jr., a shy 25-year-old mail pilot from the Midwest, had a different approach to the problem. He had persuaded a group of St. Louis businessmen to finance the construction of a plane that would be capable of flying the Atlantic, and he had found a company, Ryan aircraft of San Diego, to build it. Instead of pinning his hopes on a massive machine powered by three large (and heavy) engines and flown by a crew (more weight), Lindbergh believed that the way to get to France was with a plane of the utmost simplicity, a machine designed to carry little more than gasoline and a single pilot.

Far from being the rickety wing and a prayer, as the press described the *Spirit of St. Louis*, it was the creation of careful calculation and engineering expertise that had no commercial value, but was designed down to the last rivet to do one thing: get off the ground with a maximum load of fuel. In effect, the *Spirit* was a flying gas tank. The press would dub the young pilot "Lucky Lindbergh" when he succeeded in his mission, but most of the luck involved in the venture was in the ease with which he persuaded his backers of his idea and found a builder who shared his confidence. Indeed, in getting the *Spirit* from San Diego to the airfield on Long Island from which he would depart, Lindbergh broke two aviation records: he made the longest non-stop solo flight to date (San Diego–St. Louis) and the fastest transcontinental crossing. It was no reckless experiment.

But that was how the press of the 1920s played it. Lindbergh was mobbed wherever he went in New York, and was depicted as the simple, plucky, American frontiersman sort of hero. He was not allowed to examine his plane without the presence of thousands of well-wishers, sensation-seekers, and even hysterics who wanted to touch him as though he were a saint. Historians have compared the fuss made over him with the adoration that Americans of the 1920s lavished on movie stars and boxing champions; but it seems more accurate to describe the preflight hoopla in terms of Daniel Boorstin's definition of a celebrity: a person who is well known for being well known.

On May 16, 1927, conditions for a takeoff were less than ideal. The airstrip was muddy from rains, which meant additional drag on the plane, and by the time that Lindbergh was ready to go, he was taking off with a tailwind, not recommended procedure even when the craft is not loaded to the utmost of its theoretical limi-

tations. (At the last minute, Lindbergh called for an additional 50 gallons of gasoline in the tanks.)

But Richard A. Byrd's plane was sitting at the same field, mechanically ready to go but stalled by legal complications; and another challenger was almost ready. Impatient, emotionally geared for the moment, perhaps influenced by the press notices of his singularity, Lindbergh packed five sandwiches into the tiny cockpit and took off. Once he was airborne, the riskiest part of the venture was behind him. Unless he fell asleep. That, and occasional threats of ice on the wings, which would add weight to the plane, were the worries he later recalled as most serious. At ten o'clock at night, two days after his departure, he landed amidst a screaming mob of 100,000 people at Le Bourget Field, Paris.

Americans were popular in Europe during the 1920s, and Lindbergh was exalted as the greatest of them. Back home it was the same thing: ticker-tape parades, thousands of invitations merely to appear in towns and cities. For a while, the soft-spoken hero luxuriated in the fame and money that came to him. In 1929, he married Anne Morrow, the daughter of the American ambassador to Mexico (Lindbergh was himself the son of a congressman), and as a team they continued to tour on behalf of the government and commercial aviation. The couple's infant son was kidnapped from their New Jersey home and, despite the payment of ransom, murdered. Police (and the Lindberghs) believed that the frenzied publicity surrounding the event contributed to the death of the child by frightening the abductor. After the trial, conviction, and execution of a carpenter, Bruno Hauptmann, which were criticized because of the relentless press coverage, the Lindberghs moved to Europe, where, they believed, they could escape the spotlight.

There, Lindbergh was impressed by the new German air force built up by Adolf Hitler and Hermann Goering, and he accepted a medal from the German dictator. After 1939, when he returned to the United States to lecture on behalf of the isolationist America First Committee, Lindbergh was criticized as being pro-Nazi. He was not, but he was an Anglophobe, and he believed that Germany would win the war that broke out in September 1939. Therefore, he opposed those who wanted to go to war before England fell.

Like most of the America Firsters, Lindbergh ceased his opposition to the war once the United States had entered it. He worked as a technical expert to aircraft companies, and, although over 40, he flew several missions in the Pacific theater. In the end, Lindbergh's accomplishment of 1927 overshadowed his politics of 1939 to 1941, and he was commissioned a general in the air force.

Businessmen crowd Wall Street on October 24, 1929, the day the stock market began to crash, sending America into economic depression.

next morning, more than $30 billion in paper value had been wiped out.

It was phony value, representing little more than the irrational belief that prices could rise indefinitely. Nevertheless, the eradication of so many dollars profoundly shattered the confidence of businessmen and belief in the business culture of the 1920s. The Great Crash eventually contributed to the hardship of millions of people who did not even know what a share in a company looked like.

Crash and Depression

The Great Crash of 1929 did not cause the Great Depression of the 1930s. That was the result of fundamental weaknesses in the economy that had little to do with the mania for speculation. But the crash helped to trigger the decline in the American economy that was well under way by New Year's Day 1930.

Middle-class families who had played the market lost their savings. Banks that had recklessly lent money to speculators went broke. When they closed their doors, they wiped out the savings accounts of frugal people.

Corporations whose cash assets were decimated shut down operations or curtailed production, thus throwing people out of work or cutting their wages. Those who had taken mortgages during the heady high-interest days of 1928 and 1929 were unable to meet payments and lost their homes; farmers lost the means by which they made a living. This contributed to additional bank failures.

Virtually everyone had to cut consumption, thus reducing the sales of manufacturers and farmers and stimulating another turn in the downward spiral: curtailed production to increased unemployment to another reduction in consumption by those newly thrown out of work.

For Further Reading

Overviews and Classics

Frederick Lewis Allen, *Only Yesterday* (1931)

Loren Baritz, *The Culture of the Twenties* (1969)

Paul A. Carter, *The Twenties in America* (1968)

Ellis W. Hawley, *The Great War and the Search for a Modern Order: A History of the American People and Their Institutions, 1917–1933* (1979)

John D. Hicks, *Republican Ascendancy, 1921–1933* (1960)

William E. Leuchtenburg, *The Perils of Prosperity, 1914–1932* (1958)

George Soule, *Prosperity Decade: From War to Depression, 1917–1929* (1947)

Valuable Special Studies

Irving Bernstein, *The Lean Years* (1960)

David Burner, *The Politics of Provincialism: The Democratic Party in Transition* (1968)

D. M. Chalmers, *Hooded Americanism* (1965)

John K. Galbraith, *The Great Crash* (1955)

Otis L. Graham, Jr., *The Great Campaigns: War and Reform in America, 1900–1928* (1971)

C. P. Kinderberger, *The World in Depression* (1973)

Donald Lisio, *The President and Protest* (1974)

E. A. Moore, *A Catholic Runs for President* (1956)

Humbert S. Nelli, *The Business of Crime* (1976)

J. W. Prothro, *Dollar Decade: Business Ideas in the 1920s* (1954)

Theodore D. Saloutos and John D. Hicks, *Twentieth Century Populism: Agricultural Discontent in the Middle West, 1900–1939* (1951)

Arthur M. Schlesinger, Jr., *The Crisis of the Old Order* (1957)

Biographies and Autobiographies

Oscar Handlin, *Al Smith and His America* (1958)

D. R. McCoy, *Calvin Coolidge: The Quiet President* (1967)

William Allen White, *A Puritan in Babylon* (1938)

Joan H. Wilson, *Herbert Hoover: Forgotten Progressive* (1975)

42

National Trauma
The Great Depression, 1930–1933

The Great Depression began in 1930. It did not really end until 1940, after the economy had been jolted into full activity by the outbreak of war in Europe. The depression was not only the most serious economic crisis in American history, it was a more jarring psychological and moral experience for the American people than any other event in their past except the Civil War.

The Great Depression was a national trauma. Americans who had lived through the First World War and the Roaring Twenties found their recollections of those periods vague and inconsequential after 1930. People who came of age during the 1930s would remember the anxieties and struggles of the decade more vividly than they would remember the Second World War, the return of prosperity, and the beginning of the nuclear age in the 1940s. So large did recollections of hard times loom over them that they passed on to their children, who were born in the 1930s and 1940s and never really experienced the depression, a sense that it was the most important event in their lives. Not until the late 1960s did a generation come of age for which the Great Depression was "ancient history." Not until 1980, half a century after the depression began, did voters in a national election repudiate the political "liberals" whom the Great Depression brought to the fore.

A mother and her children, victims of the Great Depression, in front of their makeshift home. This photograph, entitled "Children in a Democracy," was taken by Dorothea Lange as part of her work for the Farm Securities Administration.

THE FACE OF CATASTROPHE

Not every memory of the 1930s was a bad one. On the contrary, many people were proud that when times had been worst, they nevertheless had survived and, what is more, had carried on vital cultural, social, and personal lives. Negative or positive, however, the depression generation was the last American generation to date whose character and values were forged in an era of economic decline, denial, and insecurity.

The Depression in Numbers

During the first year after the crash of the stock market, 4 million workers lost their jobs. By 1931, 100,000 people were being fired each week. By 1932, 25 percent of the work force was unemployed, 13 million people with about 30 million dependents. Black workers, "the last hired and the first fired," suffered a higher unemployment rate than whites, 35 percent. In Chicago, 40 percent of those people who wanted work could not find it. In Toledo, 80 percent were unemployed. In coal-mining towns like Donora, Pennsylvania, virtually no one had a job.

Employees who held on to their jobs took cuts in pay. Between 1929 and 1933, the average weekly earnings of manufacturing workers fell from $25 to less than $17. The income of farmers plummeted from a low starting point. By the winter of 1933, some corn growers were burning their crop for heat because they could not sell it at a profit. Growers of wheat estimated that it took five bushels to earn the price of a cheap pair of shoes. The wholesale price of cotton dropped to five cents a pound, laughably low if the consequences were not so tragic.

Banks failed at a rate of 200 a month during 1932, wiping out $3.2 billion in savings accounts. When New York's Bank of the United States went under in December 1930, 400,000 people lost their deposits. Much of the money was in small accounts that had been squirreled away by workingpeople as a hedge against economic misfortune. When, understandably frightened, they withdrew their emergency funds, the downward spiral continued.

Hundreds of thousands of people lost their homes between 1929 and 1933 because they could not meet mortgage payments. One farm family in four had been pushed off the land by 1933, mainly in the cotton, grain, and pork belts of the South and Midwest. With their customers unable to buy, more than 100,000 small businesses went bankrupt, 32,000 in 1932 alone (88 per day). Doctors, lawyers, and other professionals reported huge drops in income. Some schools closed

On a Washington, D.C., sidewalk, a man sells apples to support himself while unemployed.

for lack of money; in others, teachers took sharp cuts or worked without pay. Some teachers in Chicago were not compensated for ten years. Others never were.

What Depression Looked Like

Even people who did not personally suffer were reminded of the depression at every turn. More than 5,000 people lined up outside a New York employment agency each week to apply for 500 menial jobs. When the city government of Birmingham, Alabama, called for about 800 workers to put in an eleven-hour day for $2, 12,000 applicants showed up. In 1931, a Soviet agency, Amtorg, announced openings for 6,000 skilled technicians who were willing to move to Russia; 100,000 Americans said they would go. Once-prosperous workers and small businessmen sold apples or set up shoeshine stands on street corners, claiming that they preferred any kind of work to accepting charity.

Charitable organizations were not up to the flood of impoverished people anyway. Philadelphia's social workers managed to reach only one-fifth of the city's unemployed in order to provide $4.23 to a family for a week, not enough to buy food, let alone pay for clothing, rent, and fuel. Soup kitchens set up by both religious and secular groups offered little more than a crust of bread and a bowl of thin stew, but for three years, they were regularly mobbed by people who waited in lines that strung out for blocks.

On the outskirts of most large cities (and right in the middle of New York's Central Park), homeless men and women built shantytowns out of scavenged lumber, scraps of sheet metal, flimsy packing crates, and cardboard boxes. The number of people who simply wandered the land brought the face of catastrophe to rural America. Because it was impossible to stay the flood, railroads gave up trying to keep people off the freight trains. The Missouri Pacific railroad counted 14,000 people hopping its freights in 1928; in 1931, 186,000 rode the same rails. Rough estimates indicate that 1.5 million people were moving about in search of casual work, and others were simply moving about; railroad officials noted ever increasing numbers of children in the trek.

SOUP LINE

A reporter for *The New Republic* described the soup line at the Municipal Lodging House in New York City in 1930:

There is a line of men, three or sometimes four abreast, a block long, and wedged tightly together—so tightly that no passer-by can break through. For this compactness there is a reason: those at the head of the grey-black human snake will eat tonight; those farther back probably won't.

This revelation plus increased desertion of their families by unemployed men, a rise in the divorce rate, and a decline in the birth rate—from more than 3 million births in 1921 to 2.4 million in 1932—convinced some moralists and sociologists that the depression was destroying the American family. Others responded that hardship was causing families to pull together.

Although the heart of the "Dust Bowl" was Oklahoma, dust storms suffocated placed like Baca County, Colorado, too.

NO ONE HAS STARVED

At the worst of times early in the Great Depression, it was common to say that "no one has starved." But some came close, as these two excerpts from the *New York Times* indicate:

MIDDLETOWN, N.Y., *December 24, 1931.*—Attracted by smoke from the chimney of a supposedly abandoned summer cottage near Anwana Lake in Sullivan County, Constable Simon Glaser found a young couple starving. Three days without food, the wife, who is 23 years old, was hardly able to walk.

DANBURY, Connecticut, *September 6, 1932.*—Found starving under a rude canvas shelter in a patch of woods on Flatboard Ridge, where they had lived for five days on wild berries and apples, a woman and her 16-year old daughter were fed and clothed today by the police and placed in the city almshouse.

This was true of the tragic odyssey of the "Okies" and "Arkies." In 1936 and 1937, the hardships of depression were compounded by a natural disaster in the arid regions of Oklahoma, Texas, Kansas, and Arkansas: dust storms literally stripped the topsoil from the land and blacked out the sun. Whole counties lost half their population as people fled across the desert to California, typically in decrepit Model T Fords piled with ragged possessions. Novelist John Steinbeck captured their desperation, and their plucky inner resourcefulness, in *The Grapes of Wrath*, which was published in 1939.

THE FAILURE OF THE OLD ORDER

Will Rogers, himself an "Okie" and the nation's most popular humorist, quipped that the United States would be the first country to go to the poorhouse in

Suffering from unemployment and poverty, these men constructed homes from scrap lumber at West Houston and Mercer Streets in New York. They were photographed by Berenice Abbott on October 25, 1935.

an automobile. He was trying to restore a sense of proportion to the way people thought about the Great Depression. No one was starving, President Hoover added in one of his many unsuccessful attempts to ease tension.

In the broadest sense, both men were right. There was no plague or famine. Indeed, to many people the troubling paradox of America's greatest depression was that deprivation was widespread in a country that was blessed with plenty. American factories remained as capable as ever of producing goods, but they stood silent or working at a fraction of capacity because no one could afford to buy their wares. Farms were pouring forth food in cornucopian abundance, but hungry people could not afford to consume it. One of the most striking images of the early 1930s transformed a mild, white-haired California physician into an angry crusader. Early one Saturday morning, Dr. Francis E. Townsend looked out his window to see old women picking through the garbage pails of a store that was heaped high with foodstuffs.

The Tragedy of Herbert Hoover

Business and the Republican party had reaped credit for the kind winds of prosperity. Now they took the blame for the whirlwind of depression, and the recriminations were aimed particularly at the titular head of the party, Herbert Clark Hoover. The shantytowns where homeless thousands dwelled were called Hoovervilles; newspapers used as blankets by men who were forced to sleep on park benches were Hoover blankets; a pocket turned inside out was a Hoover flag; a freight car was a Hoover Pullman.

Still remembered as a great humanitarian when he entered the White House in 1929, Hoover was the callous national villain a year later. Celebrated for his energy and efficiency as Secretary of Commerce, Hoover as president was perceived to be incompetent, paralyzed by the economic crisis. When Hoover made one of his rare public appearances, a motorcade through the hard-hit industrial city of Detroit, sidewalk crowds greeted him with dead silence and sullen stares. The president could not even take a brief vacation without arousing scorn. "Look here, Mr. Hoo-

Herbert Hoover entered the presidency with a reputation for humanitarianism. He left it unmourned and despised.

ver, see what you've done," an Appalachian song had it. "You went a-fishing, let the country go to ruin."

In truth, Hoover's self-confidence decayed rapidly during his four years in the presidency. If never a warm man, Hoover had always exuded confidence, beaming smugly for photographers. Now he sat subdued, withdrawn, and embittered in the White House. Sitting down to talk with him, an adviser remembered, was like sitting in a bath of ink.

Hoover was unjustly accused when critics called him uncaring, a do-nothing president, a stooge for the Mellons and other big businessmen. The president was moved by the suffering in the country. He gave much of his income to charity and urged others to do the same. Far from paralyzed, he worked as hard at his job as Woodrow Wilson and James K. Polk. Nor was he a Coolidge, letting business do as it pleased; Hoover led government to greater intervention in the economy than had any preceding president. It would soon be forgotten, but the man who replaced Hoover in the White House, Franklin D. Roosevelt, several times criticized Hoover for improperly *expanding* the powers of government. It would be forgotten because Roosevelt would recognize, as Hoover never did, that the Republican administration had not done enough.

Hoover's Program

Something had to be done. History taught that economic crisis as severe as that of the early 1930s was

A CHICKEN IN EVERY POT

The Republican party slogan in the election campaign of 1928 had been "A Chicken in Every Pot and Two Cars in Every Garage." In 1932, the advertising man who had coined it was out of work and reduced to begging in order to support his family.

apt to lead to social unrest, particularly because the disaster was not "natural," but economic, social, and not equally suffered: not everyone was struggling. Moreover, the progressives (of whom Hoover had been one) had established the precedent that government was responsible for guiding the economy. Only in flush times like the Coolidge era could an administration abdicate its obligations and remain popular.

Hoover did break with the Coolidge–Mellon policies of withdrawing the government from active intervention in the economy. He spent $500 million a year on public works, government programs to build or improve government properties. These projects created some jobs that would otherwise not have existed. The most famous of them was the great Boulder Dam, now called Hoover Dam, on the Colorado River southeast of Las Vegas. Ironically the most conspicuous consequence of this water conservation and power-generation project was to transform Las Vegas into a pleasure dome of casinos. Nevertheless, the great wall of concrete was the single most massive example of government economic planning to its time.

Hoover cut Mellon's consumer taxes in order to encourage purchasing and, therefore, production. In the Reconstruction Finance Corporation (RFC), established by Congress in 1932, he created an agency to help banks, railroads, and other key economic institutions stay in business. The RFC lent money to companies that were basically sound but were hamstrung by the shortage of operating capital.

The trouble was that cutting consumer taxes did nothing for those who were unemployed and paying few rates. Those who still had jobs inclined not to spend what little windfalls came their way but to squirrel them away against the day when they might be out of work. Moreover, there was a glut in the urban middle class of the "big ticket" consumer durables like appliances and automobiles, the sale of which might have put people to work.

The RFC was a positively unpopular program. People in trouble saw it not as a recovery policy but as relief for big business while individuals were told to shift for themselves. The RFC alone looked very much like an extension of Andrew Mellon's "trickle-down" economics, except in the arid early years of the Great Depression, little seemed to trickle down.

The Blindness of the Rugged Individual

More was needed—massive relief to get the poor, who were growing in numbers, over the worst of the crisis. This Hoover would not do. A self-made man himself, he had forgotten the role of talent and good luck in getting ahead. He believed that rugged individuals—he used the phrase—who looked to no one but themselves, were the secret of American cultural vitality. For the federal government to stimulate that trait of the national character was one thing; for the government to sponsor huge handouts was quite another. Federal relief measures were not, in Hoover's opinion, the first step in defeating the depression, but were the first step in emasculating the American spirit. There was indeed a difference between helping deprived Belgians and helping deprived Americans.

Hoover also clung to certain assumptions that prevented him from realizing just how much federal guidance was needed. Failing to recognize that state boundaries had no economic significance, he wanted the states to take the lead in fighting the depression. Viewing government as much like a business, he was particularly inflexible when it came to the ideal of a balanced budget and the government's power to manipulate the value of the currency.

Government, Hoover insisted, must spend no more money than it collected; the books must balance. As for money questions, Hoover knew that during every depression since the Civil War, only Greenbackers, Populists, and others regarded as radicals had proposed

A line of hungry men stretches into the darkness outside a soup kitchen in New York City.

increasing the supply of money (deliberately inflating prices) in order to stimulate the economy. Each time they had been defeated, and each time the country had emerged from hard times more prosperous than before. Hoover was positive that this cycle would be repeated if the old faith were kept: if the budget were balanced and the dollar remained rooted in gold.

The Depression Goes International

For a few months, in 1931, Hoover's prediction that "prosperity was just around the corner" seemed to be coming true. Most economic indicators made modest gains. Then the entire industrialized world followed the United States into the economic pit. In May, a major European bank, the *Kreditanstalt* of Vienna, went bankrupt, badly shaking other European banks that had supported it and toppling many. In September, Great Britain abandoned the gold standard. That is, the Bank of England ceased to redeem its paper money in bullion. Worried that all paper money would lose its value, international investors withdrew $1.5 billion in gold from American banks, further weakening the financial structure and launching a new wave of local failures.

But the worst consequence of the European collapse was what it did to Hoover's state of mind. It persuaded him that America's depression was not the fault of domestic problems that he might help remedy, but of foreigners over whom he had no power. The most cosmopolitan president since John Quincy Adams had sunk to the ignorant provincial's easy excuses. The result was that by 1932 his administration was genuinely paralyzed. The country merely drifted, and conditions worsened by the month.

AMERICANS REACT TO THE CRISIS

If Hoover's failure represented the inability of conservatives to cope with the depression, radicals were unable to offer a plausible alternative. Critics of capitalism believed that the crisis represented the death throes of the system and that they would soon be in power. To a remarkable extent, they simply waited for the forces of inevitability to summon them to power.

The Not-So-Red Decade

After polling only 267,000 votes in prosperous 1928, Socialist party presidential candidate Norman Thomas won 882,000 in 1932. Communist candidate William Z. Foster doubled his vote in those four years, from 49,000 to 103,000. But the combined anticapitalist vote of less than 1 million was minuscule compared with the 23 million cast for the Democrats in that

year and even the 16 million won by the discredited Hoover. Thomas's total in 1932 was less than the Socialists had won twenty years before, when the electorate was much smaller and the economy was in better health.

Later in the 1930s, American Communists made some gains among intellectuals and in the leadership of the labor movement. Distinguished writers such as Mary McCarthy, Edmund Wilson, and Granville Hicks joined the Communist party. Even F. Scott Fitzgerald, the chronicler of "flaming youth" during the 1920s, flirted with Marxist ideas that he did not really understand. Theodore Dreiser, the dean of American novelists, wanted to join the Communist party but was told by party leaders that he could do more good for the cause outside the organization than in.

The love of conspiracy and manipulation that this decision illustrated drove intellectuals out of the party as quickly as they had joined. It also prevented the Communists from establishing a base in the labor movement despite their indispensable contributions to its success. Wyndham Mortimer of the United Automobile Workers, labor journalist Len De Caux, lawyer Lee Pressman, and many other Communists and "fellow travelers" (sympathizers who were not members of the party) devoted their lives to building up the union movement. However, most Communist organizers either denied or thickly camouflaged their affiliation with the party and their anticapitalist ideology. The result was that few rank-and-file union members were exposed to, let alone converted to, Communist ideas. When anti-Communist leaders took the offensive, particularly in the 1940s, they found it easy to oust party members from the unions.

A Curious Response

Americans simply did not interpret the Great Depression as evidence that capitalism had failed. During prosperous times, Americans had believed that individual success was primarily due to individual initiative, and not to general social conditions. So their initial response to the depression was to blame themselves for the hardships that beset them. Sociologists and journalists reported on homeless hitchhikers who apologized for their shabby clothing. A walk through a big-city park revealed unsuccessful job seekers slumped on benches, heads in hands, elbows on knees, collars drawn up, wondering where they, not the system, had failed.

The Gillette Company, a manufacturer of razor blades, exploited the feeling of personal failure by running an advertisement that showed a husband reporting shamefully to his wife that he still had not found a job. The message was that employers had turned him down not because there were no jobs but because he cut a poor appearance with his badly shaved whiskers. A maker of underwear put the responsibility for the unemployment of a bedridden man squarely on his own shoulders. He was out of work not because 13 million others were, but because he wore an inferior brand of undershirt and so caught a cold that he well deserved.

Long after the depression ended, it was the proud boast of many families that however bad things had gotten, they never had gone "on the county," never had taken handouts from public-welfare agencies. The unmistakable message was that coping with hard times was a personal responsibility. The implication for radicals who sought to direct anger and frustration against the system was not encouraging.

Episodes of Violence

There was violence. Hungry, angry people rioted in St. Paul and other cities, storming food markets and clearing the shelves. Wisconsin dairy farmers stopped milk trucks and dumped the milk into ditches, partly in rage at the low prices paid by processors, partly to dramatize their need for help. In Iowa, the National Farmers' Holiday Association told hog raisers to withhold their products from the market—to take a holiday—and attracted attention by blockading highways. Eat your own products, Holiday Association leader Milo Reno told the Iowans, and let the money men eat their gold.

But these incidents were isolated and exceptional. For the most part, Americans coped with the depression peacefully and without a thought for revolution. In fact, the most violent episode of the early depression was launched not by stricken people but by the authorities. This was the demonstration and destruction of the "Bonus Expeditionary Force" in Washington during the summer of 1932.

The Bonus Boys were 20,000 veterans of the First World War who massed in Washington to demand that Congress immediately vote them a bonus for their wartime service as a relief measure. When Congress

The Bonus Marchers' encampment on Anacostia Flats was destroyed by troops led by Douglas MacArthur and sent by a frustrated President Hoover.

adjourned in July without having done so, all but about 2,000 men and women left the capital. Those who remained set up a Hooverville on Anacostia Flats on the outskirts of the city, policed themselves, cooperated with authorities, and were generally peaceful.

Hoover, thoroughly frustrated by the failure of his policies, persuaded himself that they were led by Communist agitators. (Actually, the most influential organization among the Bonus Boys was the American Legion.) He sent General Douglas MacArthur, who arrayed himself in his best dress uniform and ceremonial sword, to disperse them. Using armored vehicles and tear gas, MacArthur made short work of the protesters. However, when an infant died from asphyxiation and Americans mulled over the spectacle of young soldiers attacking old soldiers on presidential orders, Hoover's reputation sank even lower.

Midwestern Robin Hoods

Americans displayed their disenchantment with traditional sources of leadership in other, less direct ways. Businessmen, who had been almost universally lionized just a few years before, became objects of ridicule in films, on radio programs, and in the columns and comic strips of daily newspapers. Perhaps the most curious example of cynicism toward traditional values was the admiration lavished on one kind of criminal, the midwestern bank robber.

The combination of hard times, automobiles, good roads, wide-open spaces, and a sensationalist press created John Dillinger, "Pretty Boy" Floyd, "Machine Gun" Kelly, Bonnie Parker and Clyde Barrow, and "Ma" Barker and her family-centered gang. They were bank robbers who operated in the nation's heartland, where paved but lightly traveled roads allowed for rapid escape.

Unlike the businessmen-gangsters of the big cities, they were small-time, guerrilla operators who botched as many holdups as they pulled off. They were also reckless with their guns, killing bank guards and even innocent bystanders in their attempt to create an atmosphere of terror to cover their escape. But because they robbed the banks whose irresponsibility had ruined many poor people and because they came from poor rural (and WASP) backgrounds themselves, the outlaws elicited a kind of admiration among midwesterners.

Some of the gangsters themselves cultivated the image of Robin Hood. John Dillinger (who killed ten men) made it a point to be personally generous. "Pretty Boy" Floyd, who operated chiefly in Oklahoma, never had trouble finding people who would hide him from the authorities. Bonnie Parker actually sent doggerel epics that celebrated the exploits of

"Machine Gun" Kelly under arrest in 1933.

"Bonnie and Clyde" to newspapers, which greedily published them.

The Movies: The Depression-Proof Business

The film industry exploited this envy of a few who "beat the system" by making movies that slyly glamorized lawbreakers. Still fearful of censorship, the studios always wrote a moral end to their gangster films: the wrongdoer paid for his crimes in a hail of bullets or seated in the electric chair. But the message was clear: criminals played by George Raft, Edward G. Robinson, and James Cagney were pushed into their careers by poverty and often had redeeming qualities.

The film industry did not suffer during the depression. Movies flourished during the worst years, occupying the central position in American entertainment that they would hold until the perfection of television. Admission prices were cheap. Each week, 85 million people paid an average of 25 cents (10 cents for children) to see Marie Dressler, Janet Gaynor, Shirley Temple, Mickey Rooney, Jean Harlow, and Clark Gable in a dizzying array of adventures and fantasies.

The favorite themes were escapist. During the mid-1930s, Shirley Temple, an angelic, saccharine little blonde girl who sang and danced, led the list of moneymakers. Her annual salary was $300,000, and her films made $5 million a year for Fox Pictures. Royalties from Shirley Temple dolls and other paraphernalia

Edward G. Robinson as the gangster "Little Caesar."

In Dinner at Eight, *glamorous Jean Harlow made movie-goers forget the Depression—at least for a few hours.*

made her a millionaire. Choreographer Busby Berkeley made millions for Warner Brothers with his dance-sequence tableaux of dozens of beautiful starlets (transformed by mirrors and trick photography into hundreds). People bought tickets to Berkeley films to escape the gray rigors of depression life. For the same reason, they supported the production of hundreds of low-budget Westerns each year. The cowboy was still a figure of individual freedom in a world in which public events and private lives had become all too complexly interrelated.

Music, Music, Music

At first almost destroyed by the depression, the popular music business rebounded quickly to rank a close second behind the movies as the ordinary American's entertainment outside the home. Sales of records, about $50 million a year during the 1920s, collapsed in 1932 to $2.5 million. The chief casualties were the "hillbilly" and traditional black "blues" singers whose audiences were among the hardest hit social groups in the country. Companies like Columbia, Decca, and RCA discontinued their "race record" lines and only a few black and Appalachian artists, like Bessie Smith and the Carter Family, continued to make money.

The advent of the 78 rpm record, which cost only 35 cents, and the jukebox, that provided a play for a nickel, slowly revived the business. By 1939, there were 225,000 jukeboxes in the United States scratching up 13 million records a year. Sales of records increased from 10 million in 1933 to 33 million in 1938 (and then soared, with the return of prosperity, to 127 million in 1941).

The chief beneficiaries were the "big bands," which played "swing," an intricately harmonized orchestral jazz music intended for dancing. For 50 cents (and even less), a young "jitterbugger" or adolescent girl could dance for three or four hours to the music of Benny Goodman, Harry James, or dozens of other groups. It was not an every-evening diversion. The 50 cents needed for admission was precious enough that the big bands had to rush from city to city and to towns too, on a series of one-night stands. Even the most popular orchestras might find themselves appearing in 30 different ballrooms in as many nights. Nevertheless, they were lionized when they came to town. In the Palladium Ballroom in Hollywood, California, Harry James once drew 8,000 dancers in a single night, 35,000 in a week. At other capitals of swing music, like the Glen Island Casino in New Rochelle, New York, big bands earned extra revenue by playing for a radio audience. Because a good radio could be es-

Benny Goodman was the "King of Swing" during the big band era.

conced in the parlor for $10 or $20, and operated for the cost of electricity, it was far and away most depression-era Americans' favorite form of entertainment.

The Election of 1932

The nostalgic glow that could come to surround listening to a favorite radio program, or going to a ballroom or a movie palace decorated like a Turkish harem, meant that many people would think back about the Great Depression as quite a good time. In the summer of 1932, however, when the economy hit bottom, few people took the situation with a light heart. The country's mood during the presidential election campaign of that year was somber and anxious.

A Democratic victory was a foregone conclusion, and the Republicans quietly renominated Herbert Hoover to bear the brunt of the reaction against the New Era. The leading Democrats fought a tough fight. The chief candidates were John Nance Garner of Texas, who inherited the McAdoo Democrats from the South and West; Al Smith, the standard-bearer in 1928; and Governor Franklin D. Roosevelt of New York, Smith's former protégé.

When the beginnings of a convention deadlock brought back memories of 1924, a large number of Garner supporters switched to Roosevelt and gave him the nomination. With a nose for the dramatic, Roosevelt broke with tradition, according to which a nominee waited at his home to be informed of the convention's decision. He flew to Chicago (conveying a sense of urgency) and told the cheering Democrats that he meant to provide a "New Deal" for the American people. In so saying, Roosevelt simultaneously slapped at Republican policies during the 1920s (the New Era) and reminded people of both major parties that he was a distant cousin of the energetic president of the Square Deal, Theodore Roosevelt.

Hoover's campaign was dispirited. He was in the impossible position of having to defend policies that obviously had failed. Roosevelt, on the contrary, like any candidate who expects to win, avoided taking controversial stands. Any strong position on any specific question could only cost him votes. At times, indeed, he seemed to be calling for the same conservative approach to the crisis that Hoover already had applied; he warned against an unbalanced budget and reassured voters that he was no radical.

The only obvious difference between the president and his opponent was Hoover's gloomy personality and Roosevelt's buoyant charm. He smiled constantly. He impressed everyone who saw him as he whisked around the country as a man who knew how to take charge, liked to take charge, and was perfectly confident in his ability to lead the country out of its crisis. The theme song of Roosevelt's campaign, which was blared by brass bands or played over loudspeakers at every whistle stop and rally, was the cheery "Happy Days Are Here Again."

Only after his lopsided victory—472 electoral votes to Hoover's 59—did it become clear that Roosevelt had spelled out no program for recovery. Because Inauguration Day came a full four months after the election, there was one more long winter of depression under Herbert Hoover. The repudiated president, now practically a recluse in the White House, recognized that a void existed and attempted to persuade Roosevelt to endorse the actions he had taken.

Roosevelt nimbly avoided making any commitments either in favor of or opposed to Hoover's policies. He took a quiet working vacation. He issued no statements of substance, but he was not idle. During the interregnum, Roosevelt met for long hours with experts on agriculture, industry, finance, and relief. Organized by Raymond Moley, a professor at Columbia University, this "brains trust," as reporters called it, marked a rather significant shift in the minds of people who ran Washington. During the 1920s, the capital had been a businessman's town. Now they were turning over their apartments and selling their homes to intellectuals, men (and a few women) from universities who hungered to have a go at making policy.

H O W   T H E Y   L I V E D

WEEKNIGHTS AT EIGHT

A couple in Hidalgo, Texas, listening to the radio in 1939.

Although commercial radio broadcasting began in 1920 and the first radio network, the National Broadcasting Company, was founded in 1926, it was during the Great Depression of the 1930s that the new medium of communication and entertainment found a place in the lives of almost all Americans. Radio receivers were ensconced in about 12 million American households in 1930. By 1940, they were in 28 million. Fully 86 percent of the American people had easy daily access to radio sets. They were designed not to look like electronic equipment but as a prized piece of furniture, the twentieth-century equivalent of the wardrobe. Some were sleekly modern "art deco," others gothic with the pointed, vertical arches of a medieval cathedral.

Hard times themselves were a big reason for the dramatic expansion of radio. During the 1920s, the average price of a receiver was $75, far out of reach of most families. During the 1930s, a serviceable set could be bought for $10 or $20, an amount that, with sacrifices, all but the utterly destitute could scrape up.

The New Deal also played a part in the radio boom. While most cities and towns were electrified before 1933, very little of the countryside was. Private power companies were not interested in the small return to be had from stringing wire into the hinterlands. By putting the advantages of electrification for country people above profits, Roosevelt's Rural Electrification Administration brought isolated farm families into the mainstream of society. With more than 57 million people defined as living in "rural territory" in 1940, the signifi-

cance of radio to American culture may be said to have owed largely to New Deal reforms. Indeed, country people depended more on the crackling broadcasts of news, music, and dramatic programs for brightening their lives than did city dwellers.

Manufacturers that produced consumer goods rushed to advertise on the three networks: the Columbia Broadcasting System; the Mutual; and the National Broadcasting Company with its two chains, the red and the blue networks. (When antitrust proceedings forced NBC to dispose of one of its networks, the American Broadcasting Company was born.) In 1935, the first year for which there are reliable statistics, networks and local stations raked in $113 million from advertisers with operating expenses at an estimated $80 million. In 1940, expenses were up to $114 million, but advertising revenues had almost doubled to $216 million.

The manufacturers of Pepsodent toothpaste got the best bargain of all. In 1928, they contracted with two white minstrel-show performers who had a program in black dialect on Chicago station WGN. "Sam 'n' Henry" agreed to pick two new names and do their show nationally on the NBC network. The new show was called "Amos 'n' Andy," and from the start it won a popularity that, comparatively speaking, has probably never been duplicated in the history of the entertainment industry.

Basically, "Amos 'n' Andy" was a blackface minstrel show set in Harlem instead of on a southern plantation. One of the two performers, Freeman Gosden of Richmond, said that he based the character of Amos Jones on a black boyhood friend. Amos was the honest, hard-working proprietor and sole driver of the Fresh Air Taxi Company—his cab had no windshield. Neither during the program's 32 years on radio nor after it had moved to television was Gosden's character offensive. However, Amos came to play a comparatively small part in the series as the program evolved. The chief protagonist was George (Kingfish) Stevens, a fast-talking con man who usually bungled his stings and ended up outsmarting himself. During the 1950s, black groups began to protest that the Kingfish, who was rather stupid underneath his pretensions and self-estimation, was an insulting stereotype.

The character of the Kingfish's usual mark, Andrew "Andy" H. Brown, also caused trouble. Andy was infinitely gullible, a character whom even the Kingfish easily swindled. He depended for survival on the con man's own ineptitude or on Amos's intervention.

Everyone in America, it sometimes seemed, listened to the program, which ran on weeknights at eight o'clock. Particularly interesting plots were discussed each day. Few needed to be told what Amos, Andy, and the Kingfish were like, or even the minor characters (also played by Gosden and his partner, Charles Correll): Lightnin', who swept up the hall of the Mystic Knights of the Sea; the shyster lawyer Algonquin J. Calhoun; Ruby Jones; and Sapphire Stevens, who made life as miserable for George as he made it for Andy.

In November 1960, "Amos 'n' Andy" went from radio to television in a weekly half-hour format featuring black actors who mimicked the voices that had been created by Gosden and Correll. Already, however, the program was an anachronism. The civil-rights movement was in full swing by 1960, pushing toward victory in the long campaign to establish full equality for blacks. The National Association for the Advancement of Colored People denounced "Amos 'n' Andy" as "a gross libel on the Negro."

The show's sponsors believed that blacks enjoyed the program as much as whites (which appears to have been so until the 1960s), and Gosden insisted that "both Charlie and I have deep respect for black men"; he felt that the show "helped characterize Negroes as interesting and dignified human beings." Today, it is easy to see the point. Even the most ridiculous characters on "Amos 'n' Andy" were stock comic figures in traditional comedy, and there was nothing derogatory in the depiction of Amos and Ruby Jones. Nevertheless, the NAACP had a point too. The social effects of ridiculing members of an oppressed group are mischievous at best. It is easy to shrug off ridicule when it does not relate to reality or ignore stereotypes when the stereotyped group is well established. But in the fight in which blacks were engaged in the early 1960s, such ridicule and stereotypes stood in the way of justice. After 100 episodes, "Amos 'n' Andy" went off the air.

For Further Reading

Overviews and Classics

Ellis W. Hawley, *The Great War and the Search for a Modern Order: A History of the American People and Their Institutions, 1917–1933* (1979)

John D. Hicks, *Republican Ascendancy, 1921–1933* (1960)

William E. Leuchtenburg, *The Perils of Prosperity, 1914–1932* (1958)

Valuable Special Studies

Frederick Lewis Allen, *Since Yesterday* (1940)

Roger Daniels, *The Bonus March* (1971)

John A. Garraty, *Unemployment in History: Economic Thought and Public Policy* (1979)

Susan Estabrook Kennedy, *The Banking Crisis of 1933* (1973)

C. P. Kinderberger, *The World in Depression* (1973)

Donald Lisio, *The President and Protest* (1974)

Van L. Perkins, *Crisis in Agriculture* (1969)

Albert Romesco, *The Poverty of Abundance: Hoover, the Nation, and the Great Depression* (1965)

Theodore D. Saloutos and John D. Hicks, *Twentieth Century Populism: Agricultural Discontent in the Middle West, 1900–1939* (1951)

Arthur M. Schlesinger, Jr., *The Crisis of the Old Order* (1957)

————, *The Coming of the New Deal* (1959)

Jordan A. Schwarz, *The Inter-regnum of Despair: Hoover, Congress, and the Depression* (1970)

Robert Sklar, *Movie-Made America* (1975)

Peter Temin, *Did Monetary Forces Cause the Great Depression?* (1976)

Raymond Walters, *Negroes and the Great Depression* (1970)

Biographies and Autobiographies

James MacGregor Burns, *Roosevelt: The Lion and the Fox* (1956)

Frank Freidel, *Franklin D. Roosevelt* (1952–73)

Joseph P. Lash, *Eleanor and Franklin* (1971)

H. G. Warren, *Herbert Hoover and the Great Depression* (1956)

43

Rearranging America
Franklin D. Roosevelt and the New Deal, 1933–1938

A few days before his inauguration, Franklin D. Roosevelt made a public appearance in Miami. From the crowd that surged around him, a demented jobless worker named Joe Zangara stepped up and emptied a revolver at Roosevelt and Anton Cermak, the mayor of Chicago. Cermak died; the president-elect was lucky. He escaped without a scratch.

From the episode, the American people learned that they had chosen a leader who was cool in a crisis: Roosevelt barely flinched during the shooting. But what else did they know about him? Not a great deal, and that little was not altogether reassuring.

Franklin Roosevelt is sworn into office as president, March 4, 1933.

THE PLEASANT MAN WHO CHANGED AMERICA

Walter Lippmann, the distinguished political commentator, called Roosevelt "a pleasant man who, without any important qualifications, would very much like to be president." Others wondered if a person who had lived so pampered and sheltered a life as Roosevelt had was capable of appreciating what real suffering was.

Writer Gore Vidal later described him as an "aristosissy." He was born into an old, rich, and privileged New York family. Boyhood vacations were spent in

Europe and at elegant yachting resorts in Maine and Nova Scotia. He attended only the most exclusive private schools and was sheltered to the point of suffocation by an adoring mother. When Roosevelt matriculated at Harvard, Sara Roosevelt packed up, followed him, and rented a house near the university so that she could take care of her boy. F.D.R.'s wife, Eleanor Roosevelt, was from the same narrow social set. Indeed, she was his distant cousin.

Even the vaunted charm with which Roosevelt ran his campaign, the jaunty air, toothy smile, and smooth ability to put people at their ease with cheery small talk, was very much a quality of the fluffy socialite who was a popular satirical target in films and popular fiction.

Roosevelt's Contribution

And yet, from the moment he delivered his ringing inaugural address—"the only thing we have to fear is fear itself!"—the clouds over Washington parting on cue to let the March sun through, it was obvious that F.D.R. was a natural leader. Within a few months, Roosevelt dominated center stage, as Theodore Roosevelt had one 30 years earlier. Poor sharecroppers and slum dwellers tacked his photograph on the walls of their homes next to prints of Christ in Gethsemane. Within a few years, he was so intensely hated by many of the wealthiest people that they could not bear to pronounce his name. Much to the amused satisfaction

Franklin Roosevelt's cheery grin and ever-present cigarette holder became his trademarks.

of Roosevelt's supporters, they referred to him through clenched teeth as "that man in the White House." The "aristosissy" was a "traitor to his class." Long before he died in office in 1945, after having been elected four times, Roosevelt was ranked by historians as one of the greatest of the chief executives, the equal of Washington, Jackson, Lincoln, and Wilson (his one-time political idol).

Roosevelt's unbounded self-confidence was a major contribution to the battle against the depression. His optimism was infectious. The change of mood he brought to Washington and the country was astonishing, and shortly after assuming office he exploited his charisma by launching a series of radio-broadcast Fireside Chats. In an informal livingroom manner he explained to the American people what he was trying to accomplish and what he expected of them.

Roosevelt was more than a charmer. He was not afraid to make decisions or to accept responsibility. He acted. The day after he was sworn in, he called Congress into special session for the purpose of enacting crisis legislation, and he declared a "bank holiday." Calling on emergency presidential powers that are rarely used, he ordered all banks to close their doors temporarily in order to forestall additional failures. Although the immediate effect of the bank holiday was to tie up people's savings, the drama and decisiveness of his action won wide approval.

Roosevelt was by no means brilliant. He never fully understood the complex economic and social processes with which his administration had to grapple. But he recognized his limitations and sought the advice of experts, his "brains trust."

Roosevelt was open to everyone's suggestions. But because he never doubted his abilities and responsibilities as the elected "chief," he was able to maintain his authority over his stable of headstrong intellectuals, who themselves were often prima donnas. He soothed their vanities, played one brains truster against another, and retained the personal loyalty of even some of those whose advice he rejected. Faces changed. Friends became critics. But Roosevelt never lacked talented advisers.

In the end, Roosevelt's greatest strength was his flexibility. "The country needs bold, persistent exper-

AMERICAN ARISTOCRAT

Franklin D. Roosevelt was descended from or related by marriage to eleven presidents of the United States who had preceded him. Curiously, only one of them, Martin Van Buren, had been a Democrat.

imentation," he said. "It is common sense to take a method and try it. If it fails, admit it frankly and try another." Roosevelt's pragmatic approach to problems not only suited the American temperament, but contrasted boldly with Hoover's insistence on making policies conform to a discredited ideology.

A Real First Lady

Not the least of F.D.R.'s assets was his remarkable wife, Eleanor. Only much later did Americans learn that the personal relationship between the two had been chilled, and strained by F.D.R.'s love affair with Eleanor's personal secretary, Lucy Mercer. (Eleanor offered a divorce; Franklin declined; Eleanor said that Lucy had to go, and she did.) During the New Deal years, the homely, shrill-voiced First Lady was thought of by friend and foe alike as a virtual vice president, the alter ego of "that man in the White House."

Politically, she was. F.D.R. was a cripple. He had been paralyzed by polio in 1921 and unable to walk more than a few steps in his heavy steel leg braces, but Eleanor Roosevelt was a dynamo of motion. With

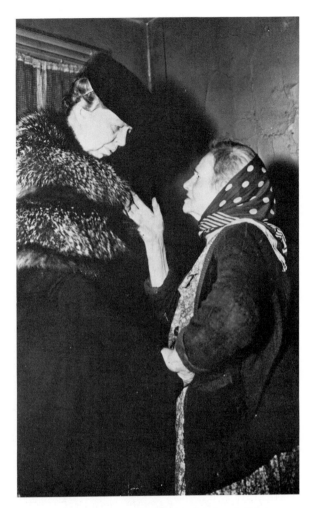

Although she grew up privileged and sheltered, Eleanor Roosevelt developed a genuine compassion for the disadvantaged.

no taste for serving as a social hostess, she raced about the country, both a political force in her own right and her husband's legs and eyes. She picked through squalid tenements and descended into murky coal mines. Whereas F.D.R. was a cool, detached, and calculating politician whom few ever got to know well, Eleanor was compassionate, deeply moved by the misery and injustices suffered by the "forgotten" people on the bottom of society.

She interceded with her husband to appoint more women to government positions. She supported organized labor when F.D.R. tried to waffle on the question. She made the grievous problems of black Americans a particular interest. Much of the affection that redounded to F.D.R.'s benefit in the form of votes was actually earned by his energetic wife, "that woman in the White House."

THE HUNDRED DAYS

Never before or since has the United States experienced such an avalanche of laws as Congress passed and the president signed during the spring of 1933. By nature a cautious and deliberate body, Congress was jolted by the crisis and by Roosevelt's decisive leadership to pass most of his proposals without serious debate, a few without even reading the bills through. During what came to be known as the Hundred Days, Franklin D. Roosevelt and his brains trusters were virtually unopposed. The most conservative congressmen simply shut up, cowed by their own failure and the decisiveness of the New Dealers.

Saving Banks, Farms, and People

The most pressing problems were the imminent collapse of the nation's financial system, the massive foreclosures on farm and home mortgages that were throwing people out on the streets and roads, and the distress of the millions of unemployed.

The Emergency Banking Act eliminated weak banks merely by identifying them. Well-managed banks in danger of folding were saved when the Federal Reserve System was empowered to issue loans to them. Just as important, when the government permitted banks to reopen, people concluded that they were safe. They ceased to withdraw their deposits and returned funds that they already had withdrawn and thereby taken out of circulation. Roosevelt also halted the drain on

In an effort to stave off panicky customers, President Roosevelt ordered banks to close their doors for emergency "holidays."

*The Civilian Conservation Corps was one of the New Deal's most popular relief
programs, in part because it allowed city boys to work in national parks and forests.*

the nation's gold by forbidding its export and, in April,
by taking the nation off the gold standard. No longer
could paper money be redeemed in gold coin. Instead,
the value of money was based on the government's
word, and the price of gold was frozen by law at $35
an ounce. ("Well, that's the end of western civilization," one of the New Era's financial experts said.)

The New Deal attempted to stop the dispossessing
of farmers through the establishment of the Farm
Credit Administration. This agency refinanced mortgages for farmers who had missed payments. Another
agency, the Home Owners' Loan Corporation, provided money for town and city dwellers who were in
danger of losing their homes.

Nothing better illustrates the contrast between Hoover and Roosevelt than the establishment of the Federal Emergency Relief Administration. Whereas Hoover had resisted federal relief measures, the FERA
quickly distributed $500 million to states so that they
could save or revive their exhausted relief programs.
The agency was headed by Harry Hopkins, a New
York sidewalk social worker with a cigarette dangling
from his lip and a fedora pushed back on his head.
Hopkins disliked the idea of handouts. He thought it
better that people work for their relief, even if the
jobs they did were not particularly useful. His point

was that government-paid jobs not only would get
money into the hands of those who needed it, but
would give those people a sense of personal worth.
Nevertheless, Hopkins recognized that the crisis of
1933 called for quick handouts, and he won F.D.R.'s
confidence through his administration of the FERA.

Alphabet Soup: CCC, CWA, WPA

The Civilian Conservation Corps (CCC) was a New
Deal measure that was more to Hopkins's liking. With
an initial appropriation of $500 million, the CCC
employed 250,000 young men between the ages of 18
and 25 and about 50,000 First World War veterans.
Working in gangs, they reforested land that had been
abused by lumbermen and took on other conservation
projects in national parks and forests. Ultimately,
500,000 people worked for the CCC, and it became
one of the New Dealers' favorite programs. The CCC
not only relieved distress (employees were obligated to
send part of their paychecks to their families), but
accomplished many needed conservation measures,
and got city people into the fresh air of the woods, a
moral tonic in which Americans place great faith.

Critics of the CCC disliked the strict military discipline with which the army ran the program, but the
idea of relief through jobs rather than through charity

remained a mainstay of the New Deal. The Civil Works Administration (CWA), which Harry Hopkins headed after November 1933, put 4 million unemployed people to work within a few months. They built roads, constructed public buildings—post offices, city halls, recreational facilities—and taught in bankrupt school systems.

When the CWA spent more than $1 billion in five months, F.D.R. shuddered and called a halt to the program. But private investors would not or could not take up the slack, and unemployment threatened to soar once again. In May 1935, the president turned back to Hopkins and Congress to establish the Works Progress Administration (WPA).

The WPA actually broadened the CWA approach. It hired artists to paint murals in public buildings, and writers to prepare state guidebooks that remain masterpieces of their kind and, in the South, to collect reminiscences of old people who remembered having been slaves. The WPA even organized actors into troupes that brought theater to people who never had seen a play. By 1943, when the agency was liquidated, it had spent more than $11 billion and had employed 8.5 million people. The National Youth Administration, part of the WPA, provided jobs for 2 million high school and college students.

Roosevelt's support of the Twenty-first Amendment, the repeal of Prohibition, might be listed as one of the New Deal's relief measures. On March 13, 1933, F.D.R. called for the legalization of weak beer, and when the amendment was ratified in December, most states quickly legalized stronger waters. Certainly many people looked on the possibility of buying a legal drink as relief. An Appalachian song praising Roosevelt pointed to repeal of Prohibition as his most important act:

> *Since Roosevelt's been elected*
> *Moonshine liquor's been corrected.*
> *We've got legal wine, whiskey, beer, and gin.*

The Blue Eagle

The New Deal's relief programs were a great success. Although direct benefits reached only a fraction of the people who were hurt by the depression, they were a godsend to the worst off, and the government's willingness to act in the crisis encouraged millions of other people. Nevertheless, relief was just a stopgap. F.D.R. and the New Dealers were also concerned with the problem of actual economic recovery, and in this area their accomplishments were less effective.

The National Industrial Recovery Act, which created the National Recovery Administration (NRA), was a bold and controversial attempt to bring order

---

CHRISTMAS SEASON

In 1939, in order to give retailers an extra week of Christmas shopping season, President Roosevelt moved Thanksgiving Day from the last Thursday in November to the next to last. (Some Republican states refused to observe the change for ten years.)

---

and prosperity to the shattered economy. The NRA was headed by General Hugh Johnson, something of a blowhard but also a peerless, inexhaustible organizer and cheerleader, and a committed believer in economic planning. Johnson supervised the drafting of codes for each basic industry and, before long, some less than basic industries too.

The codes set standards of quality for products, fair prices, and the wages, hours, and conditions under which employees would work. Section 7(a) was pathbreaking, requiring companies which signed the codes to bargain collectively with labor unions that had the backing of a majority of company employees.

The NRA was designed to eliminate waste, inefficiency, and destructive competition—the goal of industrial consolidators since Vanderbilt and Rockefeller. In making the federal government the referee among companies and between employers and employees, the NRA was the legatee of Theodore Roosevelt's New Nationalism of 1912, the mobilization of the economy during the First World War, and Herbert Hoover's trade associations. The difference was that the NRA codes were compulsory. A business was bound to its industry's code not by the moral suasion that Hoover had preferred, but by the force of law. Noncompliance led to prosecution by the government.

Critics of the NRA, including some within the New Deal administration, likened it to the Fascist system

---

THE REGULATED SOCIETY

Regulatory agencies are established by Congress and given authority to act as watchdogs over specific aspects of American life. For example, the Interstate Commerce Commission (ICC) regulates the movement of goods and people across state lines, assigning rights over certain routes to trucking companies, setting rates, settling disputes, and so on. The Federal Communications Commission (FCC) keeps an eye on the practices of radio and television broadcasters. Today, 55 major regulatory commissions in the United States government turn out 77,000 pages of decisions and rules each year.

Eight thousand children form an eagle at a National Recovery Administration rally in San Francisco.

that had been set up in Italy in 1922 by Benito Mussolini, and to the Nazi economy that was being instituted in Germany at the same time under Adolf Hitler. This was unfair. Mussolini and Hitler suppressed free labor unions; the NRA promised them a part in making industrial policy. More to the point was the criticism that the Blue Eagle functionaries went ridiculously far. There was even a code for the burlesque house "industry" that specified how long strip-tease dances might go on and quality standards for tassels and G-strings.

Such extremes were possible because of the enthusiasm with which Americans took to the NRA. Rooted on by the bombastic Johnson, 200,000 people marched in an NRA parade in New York, carrying banners emblazoned with the NRA motto, "We Do Our Part." The symbol of the NRA, a stylized blue eagle clutching industrial machinery and thunderbolts, was painted on factory walls, pasted on shop windows, and adopted as a motif by university marching bands.

For a brief time, Hugh Johnson seemed as popular as Roosevelt himself. He was certainly more conspicuous. Johnson stormed noisily about the country, publicly castigating as "chiselers" those businessmen who did not fall into line. He apparently inherited his bullying personality from his mother, who at an NRA rally in Tulsa said that "people had better obey the NRA because my son will enforce it like lightning, and you can never tell when lightning will strike."

THE NEW DEAL THREATENED; THE NEW DEAL SUSTAINED

In time, both Roosevelt's and the people's enthusiasm waned so that in 1935 when the Supreme Court unanimously ruled the NRA unconstitutional, few protested. The case that killed the Blue Eagle was not brought by a major corporation but by a small business involved in the slaughtering of chickens for use in the kosher kitchens of religious Jews. Schechter Brothers found the sanitary standards required by their industry's code in conflict with ritual requirements and proved that the regulations represented undue federal interference in *intra*state commerce. (Their business was carried out entirely within New York State.)

Farm Policy

Roosevelt may have been relieved to be rid of the Blue Eagle. He was not happy with its excesses. But he was not at all pleased when the Supreme Court struck down a number of other New Deal laws during 1935 and 1936. The most important of these casualties was the Agricultural Adjustment Act, which had established the Agricultural Adjustment Administration (AAA). Also passed during the Hundred Days, the act embodied the principle of "parity," for which farmers' organizations had fought throughout the 1920s. Parity was a system of increasing farm income to the ratio that it had borne to the prices of nonfarm products during the prosperous years of 1909 to 1914, a kind of golden age of agriculture as farmers looked back on it. The AAA accomplished this by restricting farm production. Growers of wheat, corn, cotton, tobacco, rice, and hogs were paid subsidies to keep some of their land out of production. The costs of this expensive program ($100 million was paid to cotton farmers alone in one year) was borne by a tax on processors—millers, refiners, butchers, packagers—which was then passed on to consumers in higher food, clothing, and tobacco prices.

Because the 1933 crops were already growing when the AAA was established in May 1933, it was necessary to destroy some of them. "Kill every third pig and plow every third row under," Secretary of Agriculture Henry A. Wallace said. The results were mixed. Many people were repelled by the slaughter of 6 million small pigs and 220,000 pregnant sows. Others not so sensitive, wondered why food was being destroyed when millions were hungry. (In fact, 100 million pounds of pork was diverted to relief agencies and inedible waste was used as fertilizer.) Nevertheless, the income of hog growers began to rise immediately.

Fully a quarter of the 1933 cotton crop was plowed under, the fields left fallow. Within two years, cotton (and wheat and corn) prices rose by over 50 percent. However, because cotton growers tended those fields still under cultivation more intensely, production actually rose in 1933.

A less desirable side effect of AAA restrictions on production was the throwing of people off the land. Landowners dispossessed tenant farmers in order to get the subsidies that fallow land would earn. Between 1932 and 1935, 3 million American farmers lost their livelihood. Most of them were very poor black and white tenants who already were struggling to survive.

REA and TVA

Despite its weaknesses, the loss of the Agricultural Adjustment Act in a Supreme Court ruling in January 1936 was a serious blow. The New Dealers fought back by salvaging what they could of the unconstitutional law. In the Soil Conservation and Domestic Allotment Act, parity and the limitation of production were saved under the guise of conserving soil. A similar strategy was followed in passing the Wagner Labor Relations Act or National Labor Relations Act of 1935. In fact, the Wagner Act went further than Section 7(a) of the NRA in putting the New Deal behind the efforts of workers to form labor unions. It set up the National Labor Relations Board to investigate unfair labor practices and to issue "cease and desist" orders to employers found responsible for them. Most important, the law guaranteed the right of unions to represent those workers who voted for those unions in NLRB-supervised elections.

But the New Dealers worried that they would be unable to respond if the Supreme Court overturned the Rural Electrification Act and the bill that had set up the Tennessee Valley Authority (TVA). The Rural Electrification Administration (REA) brought electricity to isolated farm regions that had been of no interest to private utility companies, and it was vulnerable to Court action because it put the government into the business of distributing power, indirectly competing with private enterprise.

The TVA was farther reaching yet. It was the brainchild of Senator George Norris of Nebraska, who was a longtime advocate of economic planning and regional development engineered by the government. Almost every year, the wild Tennessee River flooded its banks and brought additional hardship to southern Appalachia, one of the nation's poorest areas. Norris proposed that the government construct a system of dams both to control floods and to generate electricity and manufacture fertilizers. The mammoth facility would be owned and managed by the government. By getting so completely into the power business, Norris argued, the government would be able to determine the fairness of prices that were charged for electricity by private companies elsewhere in the country.

Although Norris had prevented the sale, during the 1920s, of valuable sites in the Tennessee Valley to Henry Ford, his dream of regional planning had been impossible during the pro-business administrations of Coolidge and Hoover. With the turnaround in Washington in 1933, the TVA became a reality and a major cause of the split between big business and the New

A dam under construction by the Tennessee Valley Authority.

generally had been close) and when a series of retirements and deaths allowed Roosevelt to appoint New Dealers to the bench without tampering with the traditional size of the Court. So furious was the "packing" controversy that, as late as the 1980s, when an increased workload justified enlarging the Court, presidents and Congress alike sidestepped the issue for fear of being accused of Rooseveltian manipulation.

THE SPELLBINDERS

F.D.R. made his court-packing proposal in 1937, at the beginning of his second term. For a while, however, it appeared that he might not win a second term. The threat came not from the American Liberty League or even the Republican party but from three popular demagogues whom Roosevelt and his political adviser, Postmaster General James A. Farley, feared, put the future of the New Deal at risk.

With the coming of depression, Charles E. Coughlin, a Canadian-born Roman Catholic priest, had transformed a religious radio program into a platform for his political beliefs. At first, Coughlin enlisted his mellow, baritone voice in support of Roosevelt. "The New Deal is Christ's Deal," he said in 1933. A year later, however, he became convinced that the key to solving the depression was a complete overhaul of the national monetary system, including the abolition of the Federal Reserve System. Despite his reputation among the rich as a radical, Roosevelt had no patience for such extreme proposals. But because Coughlin had a huge and devoted following—perhaps 10 million listeners to some programs—his scathing attacks were a source of worry to Farley and other tacticians.

Dr. Francis E. Townsend, a California physician, was also a threat. Himself 66 years old in 1933, Townsend was appalled by the plight of the nation's aged citizens. He proposed that the federal government pay a monthly pension of $200 to all people over 60 years of age, with two conditions. First, pensioners would be forbidden to work. Second, they would spend every cent of their pension within the month. His "Townsend Plan" not only would provide security for the nation's elderly, the kindly doctor told audiences all over the country, but would reinvigorate the economy by creating jobs for young men and women.

By 1936, 7,000 Townsend Clubs claimed a membership of 1.5 million. When Roosevelt rejected the plan as unworkable, Townsend went into the opposition and laid tentative plans to join his movement with those of Father Coughlin and of Roosevelt's most serious political rival, Senator Huey P. Long of Louisiana.

Dealers. By 1934, no longer reeling from their failure in 1929, big businessmen founded the American Liberty League, which accused Roosevelt of having destroyed free enterprise, instituted a socialist system, and set up an antidemocratic dictatorship. Among those public figures who spoke for the American Liberty League were the Democratic presidential nominees of 1924 and 1928, John W. Davis and Alfred E. Smith. Realizing that he would never be president, Smith had abandoned the streets of New York for a corporate office in the Empire State Building, headquarters of dozens of large concerns.

Roosevelt had little trouble with the opposition of those whom he called "economic royalists." Most Americans remained distrustful of big businessmen. But Roosevelt sincerely feared the power of the Supreme Court, and he proposed a scheme by which he would "pack" the Court with additional justices who would endorse the New Deal.

Reaction in both Congress and the nation was hostile. Fortunately, the crisis passed when the Court endorsed several reforms (the anti-New Deal votes

The Kingfish

Huey Long remains one of the most fascinating figures of the Great Depression decade. He rose from the poor farming people of northern Louisiana to educate himself as a lawyer. He never forgot the poor. He built a successful political career as a colorful and often profane orator who baited the railroad and oil industry elite that ran the state. Unlike most southern demagogues, however, Long did not also attack black people. Indeed, he enjoyed the support of those Louisiana blacks, mostly in New Orleans, who had held on to their right to vote.

As governor of Louisiana between 1928 and 1932, Long built roads and hospitals, provided inexpensive or free textbooks and lunches for schoolchildren, social benefits that were almost unknown in the South and were not universal in the North and West. Long was an ambitious and egotistic showman. He called himself the Kingfish after a clownish (and devious) character on the popular radio program "Amos 'n' Andy." He was the Kingfish, and all the other politicians were little fishes. He led cheers at Louisiana State University football games. He made the university the best in the South. Once, when a circus announced that it would open in Baton Rouge on the date of an impor-

tant LSU game, Long killed the competition by closing down the show on the grounds that lion tamers were cruel to animals.

The New Deal Supreme

People loved Huey Long, not only in Louisiana, which he continued to run even after entering the Senate in 1933, but all over the South and Midwest. He based his national ambitions on a plan called "Share the Wealth," which called for a heavy tax on big incomes and no personal incomes of more than $1 million a year. To people struggling for the necessities, it was an appealing program.

Because Long was the virtual dictator of the Pelican State ("I'm the Constitution around here," he said with a smile), Roosevelt considered him a threat to democracy as well as to his own reelection in 1936. In the end, however, he overcame him and Townsend and Coughlin by a combination of cooptation and good luck. Roosevelt undercut Coughlin's financial program through his own moderate monetary reforms. To steal Townsend's thunder, he supported the Social Security Act of 1935. Its pensions were tiny compared with the $200 a month for which Townsend called. Nevertheless, it was a revolutionary law; for the first time, the United States government assumed responsibility for the welfare of people who were disabled or too old to work. Also in 1935, Roosevelt supported a revision of the income tax law that did not abolish huge incomes but taxed people in the upper brackets much more heavily than those in the lower.

In every case, the New Deal reforms were half a loaf. In no case was the program of the critics adopted. But so great was Roosevelt's personal popularity that his would-be rivals lost support and, eventually, lost heart. Townsend's clubs declined slowly, as did Coughlin's radio audience. In the end, the "radio priest" discredited himself by turning to a Nazi-like anti-Semitism and praising Adolf Hitler. Long was assassinated in 1935 (the motive was personal, not political).

Thus in the election of 1936, Roosevelt had to face only the congenial and moderate Republican governor of Kansas, Alfred M. Landon. Offering no real alternative to the New Deal, Landon was swamped, winning majorities only in Maine and Vermont.

THE LEGACY OF THE NEW DEAL

Even before the election of 1936, Roosevelt had shifted the direction of his reforms. At first, he had viewed the New Deal as very much a new deal for everyone. With some reason, he believed he had saved the capitalist system from the kind of political extre-

Louisiana politician Huey Long demonstrates his flair for theatrical oratory.

*Father Charles Coughlin and Dr. Francis Townsend
each commanded broad support but never transformed it
into a political movement.*

the people on the bottom of society. Their response in the election of 1936 only heartened him to push on. It was in this break with "the classes" and partisanship on behalf of "the masses" that the legacy of the New Deal lies. Such phenomena have occurred without revolution only rarely in history.

The Roosevelts and the Blacks

Roosevelt emphasized the economic problems of disadvantaged groups almost to the exclusion of other problems. On the question of civil rights for blacks as members of a racial group, for example, F.D.R. was nearly silent. The Democratic party depended on its southern bloc for support, and southern politicians were committed to white supremacy and racial segregation. In deference to them, Roosevelt refused to support a federal antilynching bill, and he allowed the racial segregation of work gangs on government-supported building projects such as the TVA.

Under constant pressure from the NAACP (National Association for the Advancement of Colored People), from Eleanor Roosevelt, and from such individual black leaders as Mary McLeod Bethune, the New Dealers made sure that blacks shared in relief programs and blacks moved into more than a third of new housing units constructed by the federal government. As a result, the 1930s saw a revolution in black voting patterns. In 1932, about 75 percent of American black voters were Republicans. They still thought of the G.O.P. as the party of Lincoln and emancipation. For example, the only black congressman in 1932 was Oscar De Priest of Chicago, a member of the G.O.P. By 1936, more than 75 percent of registered blacks were voting Democratic—even De Priest was defeated by a black New Dealer—and the trend continued for 30 years. The Democratic party might not have been the friend of the blacks, but it was the friend of the poor, and most blacks were poor.

The Growth of the Unions

Roosevelt also won the organized-labor movement to the Democratic party. Left to his own prejudices, he would have remained neutral in disputes between unions and employers. However, when militant unionists such as John L. Lewis of the coal miners (a lifelong Republican) and Sidney Hillman and David Dubinsky of the large needle-trades unions made it clear that they would throw their influence behind the president only in return for administration support, Roosevelt gave in. Lewis raised a donation of $1 million to the president's campaign for reelection in 1936. In return, Roosevelt had to be photographed accepting the check, smiling with approval on the burly, bushy-browed Lewis.

mism that the depression was nurturing elsewhere in the world. He felt betrayed when big business, instead of recognizing his moderation, vilified him. Threatened by the spellbinders and encouraged by his compassionate wife, with her ties to disadvantaged groups, F.D.R. became, in varying degrees, the president of

AS MAINE GOES

In the nineteenth century, the people of Maine elected their governor in September, almost two months before the national presidential election. The saying "As Maine goes, so goes the nation" reflected the significance that was attributed to the results there. In the 28 presidential elections in which Maine voters participated, the state's record in picking the winner was 22 to 6, good but not foolproof, as Herbert Hoover learned in 1932: he won Maine, but few other states.

In 1936, Maine again looked to vote Republican. Democratic party campaign manager James Farley quipped, "As Maine goes, so goes Vermont." He was right on the button. F.D.R. won every state that year except Maine and Vermont!

United Mine Workers Union president John L. Lewis.

"The President wants you to join the union," the Committee on Industrial Organization told workers in basic industries after F.D.R. signed the Wagner Act. At first a faction within the American Federation of Labor, the committee left the AFL in 1937 to become the Congress of Industrial Organizations (CIO). Massive, colorful campaigns won recruits in unprecedented numbers. The Steel Workers' Organizing Committee, parent organization of the United Steel Workers, was founded in 1936. By May 1937, it had 325,000 members. The United States Steel Corporation, the nerve center of antiunionism in the industry, recognized the union as bargaining agent without a strike.

The United Automobile Workers enlisted 370,000 members in a little more than a year. The story was similar among workers in other basic industries: rubber, glass, lumber, aluminum, electrical products, coal mining, the needle trades, even textiles. "The Union" came to have a mystical significance in the lives of many workers. Workers fought for the right to wear union buttons on the job. The union card became a certificate of honor. Old hymns were reworded to promote the cause. Professional singers like Woody Guthrie, Pete Seeger, and Burl Ives lent their talents to organizing campaigns.

Employer Violence

The sit-down strike was a dramatic manifestation of worker militance. Beginning with automobile workers in the Fisher Body Plant of Flint, Michigan, in early 1937, workers shut down factories not by picketing outside the gates, but by occupying the premises and refusing to leave.

Not every employer responded so sensibly as United States Steel. Tom Girdler of Republic Steel called the CIO "irresponsible, racketeering, violent, communistic" and threatened to fight the union with armed force. In this heated atmosphere occurred the "Memorial Day Massacre" of 1937, so called because Chicago police attacked a crowd of union members, killing ten and seriously injuring about a hundred.

Although he eventually came to terms with the United Automobile Workers, Henry Ford at first responded to the new unionism as did Girdler. He employed an army of toughs from the underworld and fortified his factories with tear gas, machine guns, and grenades. At the "Battle of the Overpass" in Detroit, Ford "goons" (as antiunion strong-arm forces were called) beat organizer Walter Reuther and other UAW officials until they were insensible. Violence was so common in the coal fields of Harlan County, Kentucky, that the area became known in the press as "Bloody Harlan."

But such incidents, well documented in photographs and newsreel films, redounded to the benefit of the union movement, and by the end of the depression decade, organized labor was a major force in American life. In 1932, there were 3.2 million union members. In 1940, there were 9 million, and by 1944, more than 13 million.

The Results

The greatest positive accomplishment of the New Deal was to ease the economic hardships suffered by millions

UNION MEMBERSHIP (Includes Canadian members of U.S. unions)	
1900	791,000
1905	1,918,000
1910	2,116,000
1915	2,560,000
1920	5,034,000
1925	3,566,000
1930	3,632,000
1935	3,728,000
1940	8,944,000
1945	14,796,000

Police attack a crowd of union members during the "Memorial Day Massacre" in Chicago, 1937.

of Americans and, in so doing, to preserve their confidence in American institutions. In its relief measures, particularly those agencies that put jobless people to work, Roosevelt's administration was a resounding success.

As a formula for economic recovery, however, the New Deal failed. When unemployment dropped to 7.5 million early in 1937 and other economic indicators brightened, Roosevelt began to dismantle many expensive government programs. The result was renewed collapse, a depression within a depression. The recession of 1937 was not so serious as that of 1930 to 1933. But it provided painful evidence that for all their flexibility and willingness to experiment and spend, the New Dealers had not unlocked the secrets of maintaining prosperity during peacetime. Only when preparations for another world war led to massive purchases of American goods from abroad (and to rearmament at home) did the Great Depression end. By 1939, the economy was clearly on the upswing. By 1940, with Europe already at war, the Great Depression was history.

Through such programs as support for agricultural prices, rural electrification, Social Security, insurance of bank deposits, protection of labor unions, and strict controls over the economy, the federal government came to play a part in people's daily lives such as had been inconceivable before 1933. In the TVA, the government became an actual producer of electrical power and commodities such as fertilizers. It was not "socialism," as conservative critics of the New Deal cried, but in an American context it was something of a revolution.

Perhaps the most dubious side effect of the new system was the extraordinary growth in the size of government. Extensive government programs required huge bureaucracies to carry them out. The number of federal employees rose from 600,000 in 1930 to 1 million in 1940, a total that would rise more radically during the Second World War. To the extent that bureaucracies are concerned above all with their own survival and expansion, leading to the squandering of tax moneys and to aggravations in dealing with government, the New Deal represented a worrisome turn in American development.

A Political Revolution

In part, the elephantine growth of government was responsible for the first crack in the political alliance Roosevelt and Jim Farley forged: of Solid South, liberals, blue-collar workers (particularly urban white ethnics), and black voters. Beginning in 1937, old-fashioned small-government southern Democrats, who also disapproved of the New Deal's gestures toward blacks and the prominence in Washington of "Yankee" liberals, sometimes voted with Republicans against New Deal measures.

Roosevelt's charm and his refusal to push civil rights for blacks, plus grass-roots support for the New Deal among southern whites, prevented the crack from widening into a real split during his presidency. He shattered the secure Republican majority of the 1920s and replaced it with a Democratic party domination of national politics that lasted for half a century, longer than any other distinct political era in United States history. During the fifty years between 1930 and 1980, Republicans occupied the White House for sixteen years, but those presidents (Eisenhower, Nixon, and Ford) were moderates who had made their peace with New Deal institutions. Until 1980, no strongly anti-New Deal politician achieved more than a brief ascendancy on the national scene, and in 1980, Republican Ronald Reagan repeatedly quoted F.D.R. as though he were carrying on his work.

In Congress, the Democratic majority was even more obvious. During the same fifty years, Republicans held majorities in the Senate for only six years and in the House of Representatives for only four. The Republican party controlled presidency, Senate, and House at the same time for a mere two years (1953 to 1955).

HOW THE WEALTHY COPED

The Union Cigar Company was by no means an industrial giant, but the collapse of its stock in the Great Crash of 1929 nevertheless made history. When the price of Union shares plummeted from $113.50 to $4 in one day's trading, the president of the company jumped to his death from a hotel room that he had rented for that purpose. The incident helped fuel a legend that rich men shouting "Ruined!" were hurling themselves wholesale from high buildings during late 1929 and early 1930. Cartoonists in newspapers and magazines had a field day with the theme. But it was only wishful thinking. When a historian researched the matter, he discovered that the suicide rate was higher in the months just preceding the crash than it was thereafter.

While many, perhaps most, middle-class investors and speculators were "ruined" in the collapse, the very rich suffered little more than a loss in paper wealth (relative richness) and not poverty. Still, the moneyed classes, which had been so at home during the age of Coolidge, very confident of their right and duty to govern the country, were stunned and even paralyzed by their failure. "I'm afraid," said Charles Schwab, chairman of the United States Steel Corporation, "that every man is afraid." Franklin D. Roosevelt, celestially noncommittal during his campaign for the presidency, may have had as much support from the nation's financial elite as did Hoover. Certainly the attitude of Wall Street and corporate boardroom alike was to give him a chance.

It did not last. By 1936, Roosevelt was being called "a traitor to his class" in society circles. Some of the jokes told about him and his wife, Eleanor, were vicious and ugly. Others were simply lame, as was this attack on Roosevelt's programs for putting people to work as welfare in disguise:

Q. Why is a WPA worker like King Solomon?
A. Because he takes his pick and goes to bed.

By 1937, when most people were wrestling with the recession of that year, the very wealthy were living comfortably again. Stock prices were up—although far below 1929 levels—and a new kind of social whirl made its appearance. Unlike the society of Mrs. Astor, J. P. Morgan, and Bradley Martin, with its regal ballrooms, private railroad cars, club parlors, and yachts, the café society of the late 1930s centered in Prohibition era speakeasies that had come above ground with repeal as restaurants and as clubs in which to sit and to dance all night, to see and to be seen. In New York City, the undisputed capital of café society, the chief seats were El Morocco, the Stork Club, and the "21" Club, which reveled in its cryptic speakeasy designation.

The young always had played an important part in the social whirl. Marrying daughters to European noblemen had been a way to display wealth during the late nineteenth century; youth had set the pace of fashion during the 1920s. In café society, however, the "rich, young, and beautiful" became the center of the piece.

What was more remarkable about café society was the interest that ordinary Americans took in its doings. Whom Alfred Gwynne Vanderbilt was dating was

Wealthy customers lounge at a cafe.

breathlessly reported in syndicated "society columns" by hangers-on such as Walter Winchell and "Cholly Knickerbocker." It was a news item if the heiress of an industrial fortune dropped in at El Morocco several times a week in order to dance the rhumba with her "agile husband." Naughtier gossip made reference to blond hubbies dancing the rhumba with willowy debutantes.

Debutantes (or debs), young women who were "coming out" into society, when in fact they had been lounging around night clubs since they were fifteen or sixteen, were the queens of café society. The leading deb of 1937 was Gloria "Mimi" Baker, whose mother replied to someone who called her a decadent aristocrat: "Why Mimi is the most democratic person, bar none, I've ever known." Indeed, café society was "democratic" in ways that earlier high societies had not been. Because status depended on beauty, on what passed for wit and talent, and on simply being well known and rich, the café set admitted movie stars, athletes, and even impoverished but slickly mannered nobles from Europe. They, in turn, were delighted to rub shoulders and dance the rhumba with the very rich.

Indeed, international "playboys" jumped at the opportunity to do more than be photographed at night clubs and race tracks they could not afford, and therein lay the great morality play of the 1930s and, possibly, part of the explanation for the fascination of many Americans with the doings of café society. Like people who attend high-speed automobile races, they were interested in the collisions as much as in the running.

Barbara Hutton, who had to stick to spartan diets in order to keep her weight down, was sole heiress to $45 million made in the five-and-tens of F. W. Woolworth. In 1933, she married Alexis Mdivani, who claimed to be a dispossessed Russian prince. Almost immediately after the marriage, the debonair Mdivani began to make her miserable, railing particularly at her weight problem. Drawing on the $1 million that Barbara's father had given him as a wedding present, the prince spent much of his time in the company of other women. In 1935, Barbara won Mdivani's consent for a divorce by giving him $2 million.

Almost immediately, she married a Danish count, Kurt von Haugwitz-Reventlow. Hutton showered him with gifts, including a $4.5 million mansion in London, but divorced him in 1937. The same photographers who snapped pictures of laughing, dancing debutantes at the Stork Club rushed about to get shots of tearful Barbara Hutton, the "poor little rich girl."

Some of the people who pored over them were sympathetic. "She's made mistakes," wrote columnist Adela Rogers St. Johns, "been a silly, wild, foolish girl, given in to temptations—but she's still our own . . . an American girl fighting alone across the sea." Others took pleasure in her repeated comeuppances. "Why do they hate me?" Barbara asked. "There are other girls as rich, richer, almost as rich."

For Further Reading

Overviews and Classics

Paul Conkin, The New Deal (1975)
William E. Leuchtenburg, Franklin D. Roosevelt and the New Deal, 1932–1940 (1963)
Arthur M. Schlesinger, Jr., The Coming of the New Deal (1959)
——, The Politics of Upheaval (1960)

Valuable Special Studies

Frederick Lewis Allen, Since Yesterday (1940)
Irving Bernstein, Turbulent Years: A History of the American Worker, 1933–1941 (1970)
Allan Brinkley, Voices of Protest: Huey Long, Father Coughlin, and the Great Depression (1982)
Sidney Fine, Sit-Down: The General Motors Strike of 1936–1937 (1969)
Frank Freidel, F.D.R. and the South (1965)
Abraham Holtzman, The Townsend Movement (1963)
Irving Howe and Lewis Coser, The American Communist Party (1957)
Susan Estabrook Kennedy, The Banking Crisis of 1933 (1973)
C. P. Kinderberger, The World in Depression (1973)
Roy Lubove, The Struggle for Social Security, 1900–1935 (1968)
D. R. McCoy, Angry Voices: Left of Center Politics in the New Deal Era (1958)
Thomas K. McCraw, T.V.A. and the Power Fight, 1933–1939 (1971)
Richard D. McKinzie, The New Deal for Artists (1973)
Michael Parrish, Security Regulation and the New Deal (1970)
Richard Polenberg, Reorganizing Roosevelt's Government: The Controversy over Executive Reorganization, 1936–1939 (1966)
E. E. Robinson, The Roosevelt Leadership (1955)
Elliott Rosen, Hoover, Roosevelt, and the Brains Trust (1977)
Theodore D. Saloutos and John D. Hicks, Twentieth Century Populism: Agricultural Discontent in the Middle West, 1900–1939 (1951)
David A. Shannon, The American Socialist Party (1955)
Harvard Sitkoff, A New Deal for Blacks (1978)
Studs Terkel, Hard Times (1970)
George Tindall, The Emergence of the New South, 1914–1945 (1967)

Biographies and Autobiographies

James MacGregor Burns, Roosevelt: The Lion and the Fox (1956)
Frank Freidel, Franklin D. Roosevelt (1952–73)
Paul A. Kurzman, Harry Hopkins and the New Deal (1974)
Joseph P. Lash, Eleanor and Franklin (1971)
Raymond Moley, After Seven Years (1937)
C. J. Tull, Father Coughlin and the New Deal (1965)
T. Harry Williams, Huey Long (1969)

44

Headed for War Again
Foreign Relations, 1933–1942

In 1933, the year Franklin D. Roosevelt became president, Germany also got a new leader. Adolf Hitler, the head of the extreme right-wing National Socialist, or "Nazi," party, was named chancellor of the Weimar Republic.

The two paid little attention to each other during their first years in office. F.D.R. had his hands full fighting the Great Depression. Hitler was also preoccupied with the home front, feeling his way toward the day he could seize absolute power. Both men were virtuosos in using the radio and other modern forms of communication as a means to persuade. Roosevelt was at his best as a soothing voice in his Fireside Chats, quietly reassuring Americans that through reform they could preserve what was of value in their way of life. Hitler was at his best ranting through loudspeakers, whipping up Germans to a hatred of the democracy of the Weimar Republic, the foreigners who had humiliated Germans in the Versailles Treaty, and people whom he defined as enemies within: Socialists, Communists, and Jews.

Roosevelt and Hitler would eventually confront each other and clash, but only after Americans had experimented with a foreign policy designed to avoid another foreign war, and had failed.

Thousands of German soldiers listen to Adolf Hitler speak at the Nuremberg Rally, 1936.

NEW DEAL FOREIGN POLICY

At first Roosevelt seemed to be as casual as Woodrow Wilson about foreign policy. Like Wilson, he passed over professional diplomats in naming his Secretary of State and made a political appointment, the courtly senator from Tennessee Cordell Hull, whose elegant manner and bearing belied his log-cabin origins.

Hull and Roosevelt were generally content to follow the guidelines that had been charted by Hoover and his Secretary of State, Henry L. Stimson. Where they departed from blueprint, their purpose was to support the New Deal program for economic recovery at home.

The Good Neighbor

Roosevelt and Hull even adopted Hoover's phrase "good neighbor" to describe the role that they meant the United States to play in Central and South America. Following through on Hoover's intentions when he left office, Roosevelt withdrew marines from Nicaragua, the Dominican Republic, and Haiti. Like Hoover, he refused to intervene in Cuba despite the chronic civil war that plagued the island republic and America's legal privilege, under the Platt Amendment, to send in troops.

In 1934, when peace returned to Cuba under a pro-American president who later became dictator, Cordell Hull formally renounced the Platt Amendment. No longer would the "Colossus of the North" be a bully, using its overwhelming power to force its way in the Caribbean. As a result of the about-face, no president was ever so well liked in Central and South America as was Roosevelt. Even when, in 1938, Mexico seized the properties of American oil companies and offered very little compensation to the former owners, Roosevelt kept cool and took a conciliatory stand. A few years later, he worked out a friendly settlement. By then, the Good Neighbor Policy was reaping concrete benefits for the United States. The Second World War had begun, but despite German efforts to win a foothold in the Western Hemisphere, most Latin American nations backed the United States, and the few neutrals that cozied up to Hitler were very cautious. Had even a single South American country permitted Nazi Germany to establish bases, it would have seriously inhibited the American contribution to the war in Europe and Asia.

The Stimson Doctrine

Toward Asia, New Deal diplomacy also moved along paths that had been staked out during the Hoover administration. The problem in the East, as policymakers saw it, was to maintain American trading rights in China—the Open Door Policy—in the face of an ambitious and expansion-minded Japan. China was disorganized, inefficient, and increasingly corrupt, despite the efforts of Chiang Kai-shek to unify the country. Late in 1931, taking advantage of this chaos, Japanese military men detached the province of Manchuria from China and set up a puppet state that they called Manchukuo. Hoover considered but rejected Stimson's proposal that the United States retaliate against Japan by imposing severe economic sanctions, denying Japan the vital American exports it needed, particularly oil. Instead, Hoover announced that the United States would not recognize the legality of any territorial changes resulting from the use of force. Curiously, this policy became known as the Stimson Doctrine.

The Stimson Doctrine was little more than a rap on the knuckles, one of those cheap and painless statements of moralistic disapproval that came from critics of foreign policy, rather than from those responsible for making it. Japanese militarists, driven by a com-

A young Chinese survivor of the Japanese air attack on Shanghai, 1937.

pelling sense of national destiny, shrugged it off. In 1932, they launched an attack on Shanghai and casually tyrannized the population. In 1937, the Japanese bombed the city, one of the first massive bombings of a civilian population. Nevertheless, Roosevelt went no further than Hoover in 1932. Both he and the League of Nations responded to Japanese aggression with words alone. With economic problems so serious, no Western country would consider risking war in China.

New Directions

Where the Roosevelt administration parted ways with Hoover and Stimson, the cause was that all-pervasive reality, the depression at home. For example, in May 1933, Roosevelt scuttled an international conference that was meeting in London for the purpose of stabilizing world currencies. Delegates of 64 nations had gathered with Hoover's approval and, so they assumed, with Roosevelt's as well. Before discussions actually began, however, Roosevelt announced that he would not agree to any decisions that ran contrary to his domestic recovery program, specifically his decision to abandon the gold standard. The conference collapsed.

In November 1933, Roosevelt formally recognized the Soviet government, which four presidents had refused to do. In part this was a realistic decision that was long overdue. For good or ill, the dictatorship of Joseph Stalin was fully in control of the Soviet Union and its traditional territories. But Roosevelt was also swayed by the argument that the Soviet Union would provide a large and profitable market for ailing American manufacturers. This was an illusion. Soviet Russia was too poor to buy much of anything from the United States. Still, it was the hope of stimulating economic recovery at home that made possible the end of a pointless sixteen-year policy of nonrecognition.

Increased trade was also the motive behind Secretary of State Cordell Hull's strategy of reducing tariff barriers through reciprocity. With his southern Democratic distaste for high tariffs, Hull negotiated reciprocal-trade agreements with 29 countries. The high Republican rates were slashed by as much as half in return for other nations' agreements to lower their barriers against American exports.

Isolationism Supreme

Roosevelt probably would have liked his administration to take a more active part in the affairs of nations than the United States did. He admired his cousin Theodore Roosevelt's forcefulness, and he was an old Wilsonian, as was Hull. He had staunchly supported the League of Nations when it was first proposed and, while recovering from his polio attack during the early 1920s, had studied and written about foreign policy.

But F.D.R. was also a politician. He knew that it was political suicide for an elected official to wander too far from popular prejudices in any matter, and according to an authoritative public-opinion poll of 1935, 95 percent of all Americans were isolationists. They believed that the United States had no vital interests to protect in either Europe or Asia and wanted their government to act accordingly.

Suspicion of Europe was reinforced by the theory that the economic collapse of the Old World was responsible for the American depression. This feeling intensified between 1934 and 1936, when Senator Gerald Nye of North Dakota began a series of investigations into the political machinations of the munitions industry. Nye insisted that the United States had been maneuvered into the First World War by "merchants of death" such as the giant Du Pont Corporation and other companies, which had been only too willing to see young men slaughtered for the sake of bigger sales. This belief was popularized in a best-selling book of 1935, *The Road to War* by Walter Millis, and many academic historians took a similarly jaundiced view of the reasons why, in 1917, Americans had gone "over there."

Neutrality Policy

In a series of Neutrality Acts passed between 1935 and 1937, Congress said "never again." Taken together, the three laws warned American citizens against traveling on ships flying the flags of nations at war (no *Lusitanias* this time) and required belligerent nations to pay cash for all American goods they purchased and to carry them in their own ships. There would be no United States flagships sunk even by accident, and no American property lost because of a war among Europeans. Finally, belligerent nations were forbidden to buy arms in the United States and to borrow money from American banks. This law was designed to prevent the emergence of an active lobby of munitions makers and bankers with a vested interest in the victory of one side in any conflict.

Critics of the Neutrality Acts argued that they worked to the disadvantage of countries that were the innocent victims of aggression. Such nations would be unprepared for war, whereas aggressor nations would equip themselves in advance. This was certainly the message of Fascist Italy's invasion of Ethiopia in 1935 and of Japan's huge purchases of American scrap iron. But until 1938, Americans were interested only in avoiding a repetition of the events that had taken them into war in 1917. The majority wanted no part of trying to influence international behavior if it meant American involvement.

THE WORLD GOES TO WAR

Each year brought new evidence that the world was drifting into another bloodbath. In 1934, the Nazi government of Adolf Hitler began rearming Germany. In 1935, Hitler introduced universal military training and Italy invaded Ethiopia, one of the few independent countries of Africa. In 1936, Francisco Franco, a reactionary Spanish general, started a rebellion against the unstable democratic government of Spain and received massive support from both Italy and Germany, including combat troops who treated the Spanish Civil War as a rehearsal for bigger things.

In July 1937, Japan sent land forces into China and quickly took the northern capital, then called Peiping, and most of the coastal provinces. In March 1938, Hitler forced the political union of Austria to Germany in the *Anschluss* (union), increasing the resources of what Hitler called the Third Reich. In September, claiming that he wanted only to unite all Germans under one flag, Hitler demanded that Czechoslovakia surrender the Sudetenland to him.

The Sudetenland was largely populated by people who spoke German. But it was also the mountainous natural defense line for Czechoslovakia, the only dem-

ocratic state in central Europe. Nevertheless, in the hope that they could win peace by appeasing Hitler, England and France agreed to the takeover; Hitler mocked their good intentions only a few months later. In March 1939, he seized the rest of Czechoslovakia, where the people were Slavic in language and culture and were generally fearful of or hostile to Germans.

The Aggressor Nations

In some respects, the three aggressor nations of the 1930s were very different. Japan was motivated to expand into China primarily for economic reasons. A modern industrial nation, Japan was poor in basic natural resources like coal and iron. China was rich in these raw materials, and Japanese leaders hoped to displace the United States and Great Britain as the dominant imperial power on the Asian mainland.

Until the summer of 1941, Japanese policymakers were undecided about whether they could best serve their country's purposes by coming to an understanding with the United States or by going to war. American trade was important to Japan; indeed, the Asian nation was the third largest customer of the United States. Japan imported vast quantities of American cotton, copper, scrap iron, and oil.

Italy under the Fascists, however, seemed locked into chronic poverty. Dictator Benito Mussolini, a

Adolf Hitler and Francisco Franco giving the fascist salute.

strutting buffoon in his public posing but ruthless in his use of power, made do with the appearance of wealth and power. Ethiopia was an easy victim, a destitute and backward country that had to resist the invaders with antiquated muskets and even spears. Mussolini's own army was poorly trained and poorly armed. Tanks, which were designed for showy parades rather than for war, were sometimes made of sheet metal that could be dented with a rock or even a swift kick. By itself, Mussolini's Italy represented no real threat to world peace, and Americans either applauded what progress the Italian economy made under Fascist rule or laughed at newsreel films of Mussolini's slapstick antics.

Beyond his Charlie Chaplin moustache, there was nothing comical about the Nazi dictator of Germany. Adolf Hitler's strutting was all too serious because it took place in a potentially rich and powerful nation. Moreover, Hitler was far more cunning and deliberate than Mussolini. He knew what he wanted and had said as much in an autobiography entitled *Mein Kampf*, or *My Struggle*, German domination of the continent of Europe. While his strategy was not without flaws,

Japanese soldiers believed that Emperor Hirohito was divine and swore to fight to the death serving him.

Hitler brilliantly grasped just how much he could get away with in dealing with the other European powers and the United States.

Perverted Nationalism

In other ways, the three aggressor nations were much alike. Japanese militarists, Italian Fascists, and German Nazis were all bitterly antidemocratic. They sneered at the ideals of popular rule and individual liberties, regarding them as the sources of the world's economic and social problems. In the place of traditional principles of democratic humanism, they exalted the totalitarian state as mystically personified in a single person: Hirohito, the divine emperor of Japan; Mussolini, the Italian *Duce*; and Hitler, the German *Führer*.

The aggressor nations were militaristic. They worshiped armed force as the best means of serving their national purposes. If militarism could be less than ominous when practiced by a poor country like Italy, it was frightening when combined with fanatical Japanese nationalism and Nazi racism. The Japanese considered other Asians to be their inferiors. Westerners

Benito Mussolini loved military displays, but most of the Italian army was in fact poorly trained and armed.

Nazi repression included destroying ideas as well as people. Here, students burn "subversive" books in front of the Berlin Opera House, May 10, 1933.

who had for a century looked down on the Japanese found it intolerable that they were now moving toward domination of the economy of the Far East. Japanese soldiers were sworn to solemn oaths to die serving emperor and homeland.

Nazi racism was criminal from its inception. Calling on ancient Germanic mythology and nineteenth-century pseudoscience, as well as populist anti-Semitism, it taught that "non-Aryans" were subhuman degenerates who had no claims on the master race save to serve it. After disposing of, exiling, or silencing the German Communists, Socialists, and Democrats, Nazi paramilitary organizations routinely brutalized German Jews. Hitler's government stripped them of their civil rights and eventually, during the war, murdered those who had not fled in extermination camps along with millions of Jews from conquered lands, gypsies, handicapped persons, political dissidents, and resistance fighters.

And the War Came

Hitler had repeatedly pushed the Western democracies and gotten his way. In September 1939, when he invaded Poland, ostensibly to secure German-speaking country, as he had done in the Sudetenland, Britain

and France finally woke up and declared war. However, neither nation had prepared adequately to help Poland, and Hitler had neutralized the Soviet Union by signing a "nonaggression" pact with Communist dictator Joseph Stalin. Stalin knew that Russia was on Hitler's list but he distrusted England and France and needed time to prepare. *And territory for a buffer:* while Hitler's legions invaded Poland from the west, Russian soldiers streamed into eastern Poland, and the tiny Baltic Sea states of Latvia, Lithuania, and Estonia.

An uneasy quiet fell on Europe during the winter of 1939/40. Journalists spoke of a "phony war" in which

Two Different Worlds

In December 1940, Adolf Hitler told Germans that there could be no reconciliation between Germany, on the one hand, and Great Britain *and the United States,* on the other. They were "different worlds."

The next month, President Roosevelt accepted Hitler's dichotomy and said that his world was devoted to the Four Freedoms, "freedom of speech and expression, freedom of worship, freedom from want, freedom from fear."

neither side attacked the other with force. Whatever the French and British had in mind, the Germans were planning a *Blitzkrieg* (lightning war): massive land, sea, and air attacks with which, in the spring, the crack German armed forces overran Denmark, Norway, Luxembourg, Belgium, and the Netherlands. In June 1940, even France collapsed, and Britain managed to evacuate their troops and some French units from the little port of Dunkirk only by mobilizing virtually every ship and boat that was capable of crossing the English Channel. The motley fleet returned 300,000 demoralized men to England to await a German invasion.

"We shall fight on the beaches, we shall fight on the landing grounds, we shall fight in the fields and in the streets, we shall fight in the hills; we shall never surrender," said the new British prime minister, Winston Churchill, and his eloquence inspired Americans as well as Britons. But few were truly confident that the British alone could withstand a German onslaught.

Instead of invading Great Britain with land forces, Hitler ordered relentless aerial bombardment of the country while Germany expanded its power to the south. Mussolini's Italy had joined the war against France (forming with Germany the Rome–Berlin Axis) and faced British and Anzac (Australian and New Zealand Army Corps) troops in Libya in North

Winston Churchill stands amid the ruins of the bombed-out House of Commons, 1940.

Africa. Then in June 1941, the *Führer* made what is widely regarded as his greatest strategic blunder: he invaded the Soviet Union.

The Russians had prepared. While some Soviet armies disintegrated before the seasoned *Wehrmacht*, others met the German troops with their first real challenge. Hitler lost 750,000 men in the first year in Russia, more than in the entire war to that point. Nevertheless, the *Wehrmacht* nearly surrounded Leningrad in the north and threatened Moscow. The next year, 1942, the Germans advanced farther, with Stalingrad in the south the chief objective. There the campaign stalled.

THE UNITED STATES AND THE WAR IN EUROPE

The fall of France, the heroic resistance of Britain, and to a lesser extent the invasion of Russia changed American attitudes toward neutrality. With the exception of neutral Sweden, Switzerland, and Eire, Britain and France were the last democracies in Europe. France was America's oldest friend, and Britain, if the nation's oldest enemy, was still the cultural motherland. Moreover, ugly pro-Axis and racist rhetoric in the United States by small but noisy Nazi organizations such as William Dudley Pelley's Silver Shirts and Fritz Kuhn's German-American Bund, as well as German machinations in Latin America, persuaded Americans that Hitler had no intention of stopping in Europe. During the "phony war" in March 1940, only 43 percent of Americans thought that a German victory in Europe would threaten them in any way. By July, almost 80 percent thought so. They viewed Hitler as a madman who wanted to conquer the world.

Roosevelt Leads the Way

Franklin D. Roosevelt played no small part in shaping this change of opinion. As early as 1938, when few Americans could conceive of getting involved in a foreign war, and the French and British governments were appeasing Hitler in the belief that he wanted peace, Roosevelt concluded that only a show of force—or the use of it—would stop the *Führer*. In this opinion he was one with Winston Churchill, then a bellicose gadfly in Parliament, later the wartime prime minister and F.D.R.'s close personal friend.

But whereas Churchill was in opposition and could snipe at Britain's policy of appeasement, waiting for events to rally public opinion behind him, Roosevelt was president. He could not afford to get too far ahead of the country, least of all in calling for preparation for war. His technique was to float trial balloons by delivering militant anti-Nazi speeches. If the reaction was hostile, he backed down; if friendly, he moved ahead.

In 1939, at F.D.R.'s behest, Congress amended neutrality policy so that war materials could be sold on a cash-and-carry basis. (That is, American ships were still banned from the trade.) In 1940, with a large majority of Americans worried about how a Nazi victory would affect them, he announced that he was trading 50 old destroyers the British needed to counter German submarines for eight naval bases in Bermuda, Newfoundland, and British colonies in the Caribbean. Roosevelt described the deal as a defensive measure and not involvement in the war, which, strictly speaking, was true. Preparedness was also the justification for the Burke-Wadsworth Act of September 1940, which instituted the first peacetime draft law in American history (the term of service was one year) and appropriated $37 billion to build up the navy and army air corps.

It was comparatively easy to win support for these measures. Nevertheless, when Roosevelt decided to break with tradition in 1940 and run for a third term as president, he felt it necessary to assure the American people that "your boys are not going to be sent into any foreign wars."

The Third Term

Despite the shift in public opinion in favor of fighting Hitler, Roosevelt feared that an antiwar Republican candidate might eke out a victory against him. He remembered very well that Woodrow Wilson had won reelection in 1916 only by claiming the antiwar position for himself. In 1940, however, the war versus peace debate never materialized. The Republicans

chose a man who did not disagree with Roosevelt on any essentials. Indeed, utilities magnate Wendell Willkie had been a Democrat most of his life. An attractive and personable Indianian who had relocated to Wall Street, Willkie made it clear that he differed only in degree from the popular incumbent.

Thus, Willkie attacked the undisputed waste of many New Deal programs without calling for their abolition. He assailed the vast presidential powers that Roosevelt had assumed as bordering on dictatorship, but he did not propose to dismantle the huge executive apparatus that the New Deal had created. Willkie claimed that he was the better bet to keep the United States out of war, but he did not oppose either arming for defense or aiding Great Britain. In short, he offered Americans the kind of choice that was better resolved by sticking to the leader who was already tested.

Willkie ran strong. He captured Maine, Vermont, and eight midwestern states and more popular votes than any losing candidate to that time, 45 percent of the total. But Roosevelt's popularity was too great to overcome. The president ran an incumbent's campaign. He did his job while the exuberant challenger barnstormed the country. His landmark third-term reelection, which broke the tradition established by Washington and Jefferson and challenged by only Grant and Theodore Roosevelt, was an anticlimax, and it did not interrupt the nation's drift toward war.

Undeclared War on Germany

A few weeks after the election, Roosevelt responded to Winston Churchill's plea for additional aid by sending the lend-lease bill to Congress. As passed, the Lend-Lease Act provided that the United States would serve as the "arsenal of democracy," turning out arms of all sorts to be lent to Britain. Eventually, with lend-lease extended to the Soviet Union, such aid totaled $54 billion.

Because no amount of aid in materiel could help the British defend their shipping against "wolf packs" of German submarines, Roosevelt proclaimed a neutral zone that extended from North American waters to Iceland. He sent troops to Greenland, a possession of conquered Denmark, and ordered American destroyers to patrol the sea lanes, warning British ships of enemies beneath the waves. This permitted the British to concentrate their navy in the waters around their home islands.

The United States was at war in everything but name. Indeed, in August 1941, Roosevelt met with Churchill on two ships, the British *Prince of Wales* and the American *Augusta*, a cruiser, off the coast of Newfoundland. There they adopted what amounted to mutual war aims patterned after Wilson's Fourteen Points.

LEND-LEASE

Britain could not afford to pay for the destroyers that Winston Churchill requested at the end of 1940. Britain had spent $4.5 billion in the United States for arms, and in December 1940 had only $2 billion in reserve. Roosevelt explained the "loan" of the ships to Britain with the following parable:

Suppose my neighbor's house catches fire, and I have a length of garden hose. If he can take my garden hose and connect it up with his hydrant, I may help him to put out the fire.

Now what do I do? I don't say to him before that operation, "Neighbor, my garden hose cost me $15; you have to pay me $15 for it." What is the transaction that goes on? I don't want $15—I want my garden hose back after the fire is over.

Winston Churchill welcomes Franklin Roosevelt to the Atlantic Charter Conference, which took place off the Newfoundland coast, August 1941.

The Atlantic Charter provided for self-determination of nations after the war; free trade and freedom of the seas; the disarmament of aggressor nations; and some new means of collective world security, a provision that would evolve into the United Nations.

It was only a matter of time before guns were fired. After a few ambivalent incidents involving German submarines and American destroyers, the U.S.S. *Reuben James* was sunk in October 1941 with a loss of 100 sailors. Prowar sentiment flamed higher.

A Bitter Debate

Roosevelt still did not ask Congress for a formal declaration of war. He hoped that Britain and the Soviet Union could defeat Germany without the expenditure of American lives, a commodity with which every wartime American president had been cautious. More important, Roosevelt did not want to go to war without a unified nation behind him. By the autumn of 1941, he had his majority. Most Americans had concluded, without enthusiasm, that Hitler must be stopped at any cost. Even the Communist party, which had opposed American intervention until Hitler invaded the Soviet Union, was now in the prowar camp, and much of the eastern big-business establishment had concluded that Hitler represented a threat to American commercial primacy in the world.

There was, however, an opposition. Roosevelt did not worry about the antiwar agitation of extremist Hitler supporters such as Father Coughlin and members of the Bund and Silver Shirts. But he was concerned about the old-fashioned isolationists who formed the well-financed and active America First Committee. Former president Herbert Hoover, ex–New Dealer Hugh Johnson, and progressive intellectuals such as Charles A. Beard despised Hitlerism. Whatever hostility toward Great Britain they harbored was aimed at British imperialism; they feared that the United States would go to war to protect the British Empire, an unworthy goal. Their priority in supporting the America First Committee was to avoid making the mistake of 1917 as they saw it—pulling British chestnuts out of the fire.

The America First Committee's case was weakened because most of its members agreed that the United States should arm for defense. Roosevelt and the rival Committee to Defend America by Aiding the Allies described every contribution to the British cause in just such terms, and this justification confounded the isolationists. Nevertheless, Roosevelt hesitated. He confided to Winston Churchill that he would not ask for war until some dramatic incident—in other words, a direct attack on the United States—rallied the America Firsters to his cause.

As it turned out, the bitter debate over intervention missed the point. Both sides in the argument trained their eyes on Europe and the Atlantic as the crisis area. The dramatic incident was to occur in the Pacific, where Japan moved into the former French colonies of Indochina and continued its war against the indecisive government of Chiang Kai-shek. War in Asia was an old story. It seemed reasonable to conclude that it would go on indefinitely without a decisive turn in either direction. If Roosevelt took a tougher line toward Japan after the occupation of Indochina, negotiations with Tokyo continued too, into the summer and autumn of 1941.

AMERICA GOES TO WAR

All the while the Japanese "peace party," headed by Prince Fumimaro Konoye, continued to negotiate during the summer of 1941, the prowar faction of the imperial government, headed by General Hideki Tojo, increased its influence. When he was named premier in October 1941, Tojo gave the negotiators until early November to come up with a formula for peace that the United States would accept. But the minimum Japanese demand that Japan be recognized as the dominant economic power in China could not be reconciled with the Open Door Policy, to which the United States was committed.

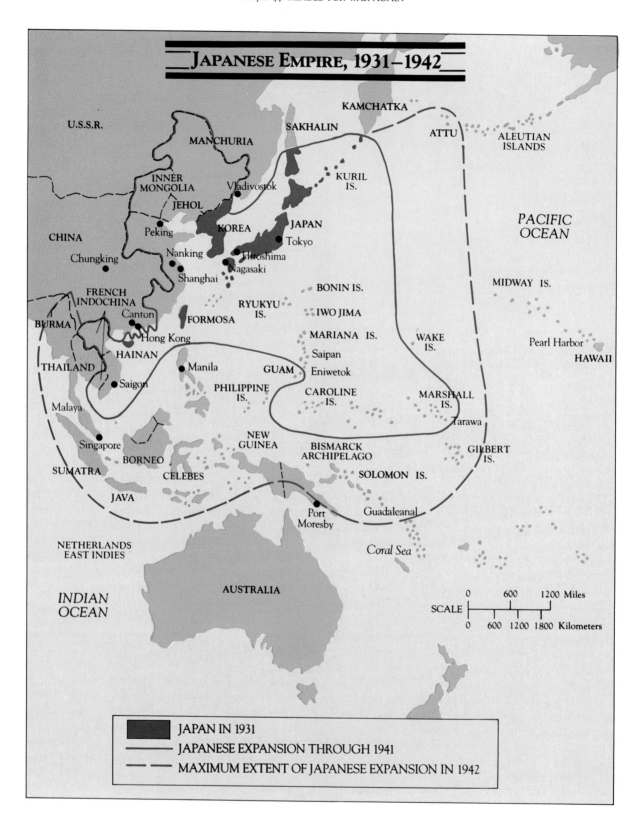

JAPANESE EMPIRE, 1931–1942

JAPAN IN 1931

JAPANESE EXPANSION THROUGH 1941

MAXIMUM EXTENT OF JAPANESE EXPANSION IN 1942

Pearl Harbor

Curiously, the Japanese and American governments concluded on the same day that they would never resolve their differences peacefully. Talks continued, as they always do, but Secretary of State Hull told the War Department that it should take over responsibility for Japanese-American relations, and military commanders in the Pacific were warned that hostilities could begin at any minute. In fact, the Japanese had initiated preparations for attack that could not easily be reversed.

On December 7, 1941, it was launched. Admiral Isoroku Yamamoto, a tragic figure who admired the United States and feared the result of a war he did not want, engineered a tactically brilliant aerial attack on Pearl Harbor, the huge American naval base on Oahu in the Hawaiian Islands. His planes sank or badly damaged 8 battleships, 7 other vessels, and 188 airplanes, and killed or wounded 3,435 servicemen. Yamamoto did not fully join in the celebrations that swept over his fleet and the people of Japan. The three American aircraft carriers that he believed would be at Pearl Harbor were at sea when the assault force arrived and thus escaped unscathed.

Yamamoto understood that air power was the key to war in the broad Pacific, and, in this area, the United States retained superiority over Japan. As a one-time resident of the United States, he also appreciated better than did the Tojo group how great American industrial might was compared with Japan's. "I fear we have only awakened a sleeping giant," he told his officers, "and his reaction will be terrible."

The Reaction

The wounded giant awakened with a start. Pearl Harbor was attacked on Sunday. The next day, Roosevelt

Destruction of the American fleet at Pearl Harbor, December 7, 1941.

Admiral Baron Isoroku Yamamoto opposed war with the United States.

was coming but withheld vital intelligence from Hawaii, sacrificing thousands of American lives for the political purpose of getting the United States into the war.

In truth, the lack of preparation at Pearl Harbor was stupid and shameful. As early as 1924, air-power advocate Billy Mitchell had said that Pearl was vulnerable to air attack. In 1932, Admiral Harry Yarnell had snuck two aircraft carriers and four cruisers to within bombing range of Oahu before he was detected. Had his force been hostile, an attack comparable to that of December 7, 1941, would have ensued. In early December 1941, numerous indications that something was brewing either were ignored or reached the appropriate commanders after unjustifiable delays. At Hickham Field, fighter planes were drawn up wing tip to wing tip so that they could be protected against sabotage on the ground. This made destruction from the air all the simpler, and, even after the attack began, it was difficult to get the fighters into the air. But to say that there was a deliberate conspiracy among the highest ranking officials in the United States government was absurd, an example of the paranoia that periodically curses American politics. The blunders of the military in Hawaii were just another example of the chronic incompetence in all large organizations, and the key to the stunning Japanese victory was the brilliant planning behind it.

went before Congress and described December 7, 1941, as "a day that will live in infamy." He got his unanimous vote, or very nearly so. In both houses of Congress, only Representative Jeannette Rankin of Montana, a pacifist who had voted against entry into the First World War, refused to endorse the declaration of war.

In every city in the nation during the next several weeks, the army's and navy's enlistment offices were jammed with stunned and angry young men. Pearl Harbor was so traumatic an event in the lives of Americans that practically every individual remembered exactly what he or she had been doing when news of the attack was announced.

Quietly at the time, more publicly later, Roosevelt's critics accused him and other top officials of having plotted to keep Pearl Harbor and nearby Hickham Field, an air base, completely unprepared for the attack. It was said that Washington knew the assault

Nevertheless, there is no doubt that Roosevelt was relieved to get officially into the conflict with a united people behind him. He was totally convinced by December 1941 that the survival of democracy, freedom, and American influence in the world depended on the total defeat of the aggressor nations, which only American might could ensure.

Getting the Job Done

Of all the nations that went to war, only Japan, whose participation in the First World War had been nominal, celebrated at the start of it. In Europe and the United States, there was very little of the exuberance with which people had greeted the first days of the fighting in the First World War. Among Americans, the attitude was that there was a job to be done.

The popular songs of the period were concerned with getting home again. There was a melancholy tenor to "I'll Be Seeing You" and "I'll Never Smile Again." The lyrics told of the sadness of separation, however

necessary it might be. Few people were attracted by the foot-stomping patriotism of George M. Cohan's "Over There," the American anthem during the First World War.

Once in the service, soldiers and sailors referred to the conflict as "W-W-2," a sardonically mechanical description of a war that was reminiscent of the name of a New Deal public works project. Indeed, because the country had been through it before, and because

Page boys of the New York Stock Exchange register for the draft in 1942.

the New Deal reforms had introduced the idea of government-supervised order to the national economy, mobilization of resources and people was far more orderly and effective than it had been 25 years earlier.

Organizing for Victory

The mobilization of fighting capacity began before Pearl Harbor. By December 1941, more than 1.5 million men were in uniform, most of them well trained. By the end of the war, the total number of soldiers, sailors, and airmen, and women in auxiliary corps in every service climbed to 15 million.

The draft accounted for the majority of these "GI's," a name that referred to the "government issued" designation of uniforms and other equipage. Boards made up of local civic leaders worked efficiently and with comparatively few irregularities to fill the armed forces. The "Friends and Neighbors" who informed young

men of their fate with the salutation "Greetings" exempted only the physically disabled and those with work skills designated as essential to the war effort, including farmers and agricultural workers. As time passed, another sad category of those exempted was adopted: "sole surviving sons," men of draft age all of whose brothers had been killed in action. In the windows of homes which lost a soldier, small red, white, and blue banners, with stars enumerating the loss, were sometimes hung. The lady of the house was called a "Gold Star Mother."

Money was mobilized too. When the war began, the government was spending $2 billion a month on the military. During the first half of 1942, the expenditure rose to $15 billion a month. By the time Japan surrendered in August 1945, the costs of the war totaled more than $300 billion. In less than four years, the American government spent more money than it had spent during the previous 150 years of national exis-

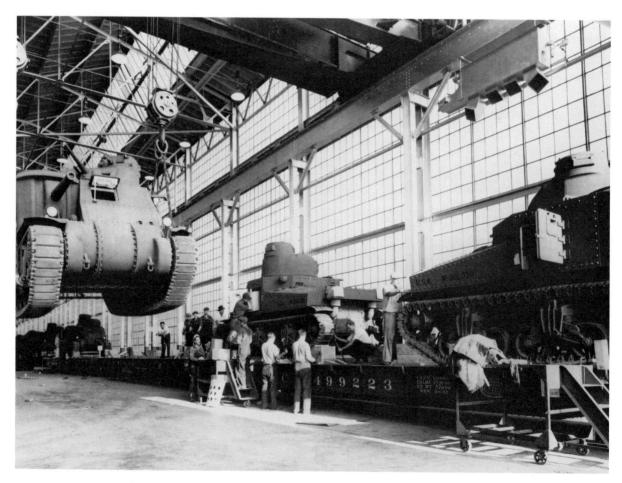

Instead of building automobiles, this Chrysler assembly line turned out tanks for the war effort.

tence. The national debt, already considered high in 1941 at \$48 billion, doubled and redoubled to \$247 billion in 1945.

A few businessmen continued to oppose government policy, particularly the wartime labor laws. One of the most graceless was Sewell L. Avery, head of the huge retail chain store Montgomery Ward. Roosevelt's policies had saved his company from bankruptcy, and during the war, full employment in the work force resulted in bonanza profits for retailers like him. But Avery had to be carried bodily to jail for refusing to obey a law that guaranteed his employees the right to join a union.

He was not typical. Most big businessmen, including former opponents of the administration, accepted unionization and rushed to Washington to assist the government. They were responding in part to the need for national unity. Corporation executives also recognized that wartime expenditures meant prosperity. General Motors, for example, received 8 percent of all federal expenditures between 1941 and 1945, *\$1 of every \$12.50* that the government spent. Few criticisms came from the General Motors boardroom. Indeed, General Motors president William S. Knudsen was one of the most prominent "dollar-a-year men," business executives who worked for Roosevelt in effect without pay. He headed the War Resources Board (WRB), which had been established in August 1939 to plan for the conversion of factories for military production in the event of war. There was a bit of cynical palaver about the patriotic sacrifice dollar-a-year men were making but the country did need their organizational skills.

New Alphabet Agencies

After the congressional elections of 1942, which brought many conservative Republicans to Washington, Roosevelt announced that "Dr. New Deal" had been dismissed from the country's case and "Dr. Win-the-War" had been engaged. He explained that since there was now full employment, social programs were no longer necessary.

However, the New Dealers' practice of establishing government agencies to oversee public affairs was vastly expanded. In addition to Knudsen's WRB, the Supplies Priorities and Allocation Board (SPAB), under Donald M. Nelson of Sears Roebuck and Company, was commissioned to ensure that raw materials, particularly the scarce and critical ones, were diverted to military industries. The Office of Price Administration (OPA) had the task of controlling consumer prices so that the combination of high wages and scarce goods did not lead to runaway inflation.

After Pearl Harbor, a National War Labor Board (NWLB) was set up to mediate industrial disputes. Its principal purposes were to guarantee that production was not interrupted and that wage increases were kept within government-set limits. This offended many of Roosevelt's former supporters in the labor movement, none of them more important than John L. Lewis of the United Mine Workers, who returned to the Republican party. But the NWLB also worked to ensure that employees were not gouged by avaricious employers. The board was reasonably successful. There were strikes, including a serious one led by Lewis in 1943. But labor relations were generally good, and union membership continued to rise.

The Office of War Mobilization (OWM) was the most important of the new alphabet agencies. Theoretically, it oversaw all aspects of the mobilized economy, as Bernard Baruch had done during the First World War. It was considered to be sufficiently important that James F. Byrnes of South Carolina resigned from the Supreme Court to head it as a kind of "assistant president." Many believed that Byrnes's contribution to the war effort earned him the right to a presidential nomination.

Success

In essentials, Dr. Win-the-War's treatment was an overwhelming success. The size of the federal government swelled at a dizzying rate, from 1.1 million civilian employees in 1940 to 3.3 million in 1945. (State governments grew at almost the same rate.) Inevitably there was waste (agencies doing the same thing), inefficiency (agencies fighting at cross-purposes with one another), and corruption (many unessential jobs). But with national unity and military victory constantly touted as essential, the few critics of wartime problems, such as Senator Robert A. Taft of Ohio, were unable to carry the day. The most effective check on waste, inefficiency, and corruption, the Senate War Investigating Committee, was headed by a Democratic New Dealer, Senator Harry S Truman of Missouri.

The lessons learned during the First World War and the administrative skills of dollar-a-year businessmen and bureaucrats trained in the New Deal worked wonders on production. New factories and those formerly given to the manufacture of America's automobiles canceled civilian production and churned out trucks, tanks, the versatile jeeps, and amphibious vehicles in incredible numbers. In 1944 alone, 96,000 airplanes (260 per day) rolled out of American factories. Industrialist Henry J. Kaiser perfected an assembly line for producing simple but serviceable freighters, the so-called Liberty ships. By 1943, his mammoth yards were

H O W   T H E Y   L I V E D

RATIONING AND SCRAP DRIVES

German submarines set a pair of four-man saboteur teams ashore in Florida and on Long Island. (They were immediately captured.) Japanese subs ran a few torpedoes up on California beaches, and several paper bombs, explosives held aloft and pushed by winds, detonated over Texas. Otherwise, the continental United States was physically untouched by the war that devastated most of Europe, half of China, and the cities of Japan. Considering the colossal scale of the American material contribution to the war, it is a remarkable testament to the nation's wealth that people on the home front experienced the war only in the form of shortages in consumer commodities and then not to a degree that could be called sacrifice.

Because the Japanese quickly gained control of 97 percent of the world's rubber-tree plantations in Malaya, automobile tires were the first consumer goods to be taken off the market. Washington froze the sale of new tires and forbade recapping early in 1942; the armed forces badly needed tires, and the national stockpile of rubber was only 660,000 tons, or just about what civilians consumed in a year. Huge quantities were collected in a scrap drive. One Seattle shoemaker contributed 6 tons of worn rubber heels that he had saved, and a Los Angeles tire dealer provided 5,000 tons of trade-ins. People cleared closets of old overshoes, and the Secretary of the Interior took to picking up rubber doormats in federal office buildings. Unfortunately, reclaimed rubber was not suitable to tire manufacture, and doormats were usually made of previously reclaimed rubber, so they were not particularly suitable for new doormats.

It was fear of a rubber rather than a gasoline shortage that accounted for the first controls on driving, although, on the east coast, which was dependent on tanker imports, gasoline was also short by the summer of 1942. The president proclaimed a nationwide speed limit of 35 miles per hour, and pleasure driving was banned. (Zealous officials of the Office of Price Administration jotted down license numbers at picnics, race tracks, concert halls, and athletic events.) In addition, the total miles a car could be driven was limited by the category of sticker issued to each owner. Ordinary motorists received "A" cards, entitling them to four gallons of gasoline a week, later three, and for a short time only two. A "B" card added a few gallons; these were issued to workers in defense plants for whom driving to work was necessary. Physicians and others whose driving was essential got "C" cards, a few more gallons. Truckers ("T") got unlimited gas, as did some others, including political bigwigs who got "X" cards (a source of resentment). Counterfeiting and selling of gas cards (usually "C" category) was common, as was theft from government warehouses. The OPA discovered that 20 million gallons' worth of cards were stolen in Washington alone.

A group of children, signaling a "V" for victory, display a pile of scrap metal collected for the war effort.

Surplus gasoline could not be collected, but just about every other commodity that was vital to the war effort could be and was. Community organizations like the Boy Scouts sponsored scrap drives through 1942 and 1943, collecting iron, steel, brass, bronze, tin, nylon stockings (for powder bags), bacon grease (for munitions manufacture), and waste paper. Many of these campaigns were more trouble than they were worth, but not those that collected iron, steel, tin, and paper. Scrap iron and steel made a significant contribution to the national output, and about half of the tin and paper products came not from mines and forests but from neighborhood drives. So assiduous were the Boy Scouts in their scrap-paper drive of 1942 that in June the government had to call a halt to it; the nation's paper mills simply could not keep up with the supply of "raw materials."

The tin shortage was responsible for the rationing of canned goods. In order to buy a can of corn or sardines, as well as coffee, butter, cheese, meat, and many other food items, a consumer had to hand the grocer ration stamps as well as money. These stamps were issued regularly in books and served as a second, parallel currency. In order to buy a pound of hamburger, a shopper needed stamps worth 7 "points" as well as the purchase price. A pound of butter cost 16 points; a pound of cheese, 8 points; and so on. The tiny stamps—which were color-coded red (meat, butter), blue (processed food), green, and brown—were a tremendous bother. More than 3.5 billion of them changed hands every month. In order to restock shelves, a grocer had to turn in the stamps to a wholesaler, who, in turn, had to deposit them with a bank in order to make additional purchases.

Everyone had a complaint of one sort or another, although, except for butter, the allotments were not stringent. For example, the weekly sugar ration was 8 ounces a person, about as much as a dentist would wish on a patient in the best of times. In 1943, the standard of living was 16 percent higher than it had been in 1939, and by 1945, despite rationing, Americans were eating more food and spending more money on it than ever before. Among the major foods, only butter consumption dropped appreciably, from seventeen to eleven pounds per capita per year, and some home economists believed that because of butter rationing, a larger proportion of the population was eating it.

In fact, the OPA noticed a curious fact about consumer habits in the cases of coffee and cigarettes. Coffee was rationed because of the shortage of ships available to carry it from South America. When rationing began in November 1942 (one pound a person per five weeks), people began to hoard it. At restaurants, some diners would trade their dessert for an extra cup. When rationing of coffee was dropped in July 1943, sales of coffee dropped! Then, in the autumn of 1943, when a coffee stamp was inadvertently included in ration books, Americans anticipated that coffee would be rationed again and stripped the market shelves bare. When the OPA announced that there would be no coffee ration, sales dropped again.

Cigarettes were rationed because 30 percent of the industry's production was reserved for the armed forces, which comprised only 10 percent of the population. The government was, in effect, subsidizing the smoking habit among the men and women in the service. At home, the operation of the principle that scarcity equals status may also have caused an increase in the incidence of the bad habit.

A much more salutary consequence of wartime shortages was the popularity of gardening. There was no shortage of fresh vegetables, and they were never rationed. But because canned vegetables were and because truck and train space was invaluable, the government encouraged the planting of Victory gardens. Some 20.5 million individuals and families planted them, and by 1945, consumers were raising between 30 and 40 percent of all the vegetables grown in the United States. Nutritionists recognized that this was paying dividends in the national diet, but when the war was over, Americans quickly shed their good taste. By 1950, they had returned to canned vegetables and to the frozen products of Clarence Birdseye.

christening a new one every day. Altogether, American shipbuilders sent 10 million tons of shipping down the ways between 1941 and 1945.

Such statistics would have been regarded as pipe dreams before the war. But they were duplicated in every basic industry, including steel, rubber, glass, aluminum, and electronics.

Workingpeople

Unemployment vanished as a social problem. Instead, factories running at capacity had difficulty finding people to fill jobs. There was a significant shift of population to the west coast as the demands of the Pacific war led to the concentration of defense industries in such ports as Seattle, Oakland, San Diego, and Long Beach. Among the new Californians (the population of the Golden State rose from 6.9 million in 1940 to 10.5 million in 1950) were hundreds of thousands of blacks. Finding well-paid factory jobs that previously had been closed to them, blacks also won a sense of security, which had been unknown to earlier generations, because of the generally antiracist policies of the young CIO unions and F.D.R.'s executive order in 1941 that war contractors observe fair practices in employing blacks.

Economic equality for blacks remained a long way in the future. Everywhere they went they found resentments and discrimination, and serious race riots in 1943. Nevertheless, prodded by Eleanor Roosevelt and pressured by influential black leaders such as A. Philip Randolph of the Brotherhood of Sleeping Car Porters, F.D.R. issued an executive order forbidding racial discrimination in companies that benefited from government contracts.

Women, including many of middle age who never had worked for wages, entered the work force in large numbers. The symbol of the woman performing "unwomanly" work was "Rosie the Riveter," assembling airplanes and tanks with heavy riveting guns. Indeed, women did perform just about every kind of job in the industrial economy. Rosie dressed in slacks, tied up her hair in a bandanna, and left her children with her mother. But off the job, she remained reassuringly feminine by the standards of the time.

Curiously, these genuinely independent women did not turn to traditional feminism. Comparatively little was heard of demands for equality during the war. On the contrary, woman after woman told newspaper reporters that she looked forward to the end of the war, when they could quit their jobs to return home as wives and mothers within the traditional family system. There were exceptions, of course. Many women enjoyed the economic and social freedom. For the most part, however, the female wartime workers were

Henry J. Kaiser mass-produced cheap Liberty ships that permitted the United States to fight a two-theater war.

an ideal wartime work force: intelligent, educated, energetic, impelled by patriotism, and generally uninterested in competing with the soldiers who eventually would come back and take their jobs.

Prosperity at a Price

Labor shortages inevitably produced a demand for higher wages. The unions grew stronger; membership rose from 10.5 million to 14.7 million. With a few exceptions, however, strikes were short and did not disrupt production. The NWLB mediated disputes, generally keeping raises within the limit of 15 percent over prewar levels that the government had set as an

acceptable standard. This made the task of the OPA all the easier.

The success of the OPA was remarkable. Coveted consumer goods—coffee, butter, sugar, some canned foods, meat, shoes, liquor, silk, rayon, and nylon—were scarce because of rationing, but high wages gave workers the money to spend on what there was. (Real wages rose 50 percent during the war.) There was a black market, or illegal sale of rationed goods, but it never got out of control, and prices rose only moderately between 1942 and 1945. Instead of consuming wholesale, Americans pumped their wages into savings accounts, including $15 billion in loans to the government in the form of war bonds. It became a point of patriotic pride with some women to paint the seam of a silk or nylon stocking on the calf of a naked leg (although a pair of stockings remained a treasure).

There was a kind of good-humored innocence about the way Americans fought the Second World War. If they did not believe that a world free of problems would follow victory, which few doubted lay ahead, Americans were confident that they and their allies were in the right. By the time the fighting was over, 290,000 Americans were dead. But shocking as that figure is at first glance, and bloody as some individual battles were, American suffering was insignificant compared with that of other nations. Indeed, keeping the casualty list short was one of Roosevelt's priorities throughout the conflict, and he succeeded. If Winston Churchill was right in describing the year 1940, when the British stood alone against Nazism, as "their finest hour," the Second World War was an hour of confidence and pride for Americans too, particularly in view of the difficult depression era that had preceded the war and the age of anxiety that was to follow.

For Further Reading

Overviews and Classics

Selig Adler, *Uncertain Giant: American Foreign Policy Between the Wars* (1966)
Charles A. Beard, *American Foreign Policy in the Making, 1932–1940* (1946)
Paul Conkin, *The New Deal* (1975)
Robert Dallek, *Franklin D. Roosevelt and American Foreign Policy, 1932–1945* (1979)
William E. Leuchtenburg, *Franklin D. Roosevelt and the New Deal, 1932–1940* (1963)
John E. Wiltz, *From Isolationism to War, 1931–1941* (1968)

Valuable Special Studies

Frederick Lewis Allen, *Since Yesterday* (1940)
Robert J. Burtow, *Tojo and the Coming of War* (1961)
W. S. Cole, *America First: The Battle Against Intervention* (1953)
Robert A. Divine, *The Illusion of Neutrality* (1962)
Herbert Feis, *The Road to Pearl Harbor* (1950)
R. H. Ferrell, *American Diplomacy in the Great Depression: Hoover-Stimson Foreign Policy, 1929–1933* (1957)
Lloyd C. Gardner, *Economic Aspects of New Deal Diplomacy* (1964)
Akira Iriye, *After Imperialism: The Search for a New Order in the Far East, 1921–1933* (1965)
Walter Johnson, *The Battle Against Isolationism* (1944)
Manfred Jonas, *Isolationism in America, 1935–1941* (1966)

Warren F. Kimball, *The Most Unsordid Act: Lend Lease, 1939–1941* (1969)
C. P. Kinderberger, *The World in Depression* (1973)
Gordon W. Prange, *At Dawn We Slept: The Untold Story of Pearl Harbor* (1981)
Basil Rauch, *Roosevelt: From Munich to Pearl Harbor* (1950)
E. E. Robinson, *The Roosevelt Leadership* (1955)
William A. Williams, *The Tragedy of American Diplomacy* (1962)
Robert Wohlsetter, *Pearl Harbor: Warning and Decision* (1962)
Bryce Wood, *The Making of the Good Neighbor Policy* (1961)

Biographies and Autobiographies

James MacGregor Burns, *Roosevelt: The Soldier of Freedom* (1970)
Wayne S. Cole, *Gerald P. Nye and American Foreign Relations* (1962)
Richard N. Current, *Secretary Stimson: A Study in Statecraft* (1954)
Frank Freidel, *Franklin D. Roosevelt* (1952–73)
Elting E. Morison, *Turmoil and Tradition: A Study of the Life and Times of Henry L. Stimson* (1960)
J. W. Pratt, *Cordell Hull* (1964)

45

America's Great War
The United States at the Pinnacle of Power, 1942–1945

In the histories of Europe, the First World War is the "Great War." The ferocious bloodletting of 1914 to 1918 badly shook a people who believed that their civilization had advanced far beyond such savagery. European artists and intellectuals voiced the fear that the First World War marked the beginning of the end of the Old World. In 1922, the German philosopher Oswald Spengler published *The Decline of the West:* European civilization would never recover morally from its great sin. After more than 60 years, it is easy to see that, at the least, the First World War signaled the decline of Western Europe's domination of world politics and economy.

For Americans, on the contrary, the First World War was a jarring experience but far from shattering. Casualties were minor compared with the horrible losses the Europeans suffered. The American material investment in the war stimulated rather than damaged the national economy. The United States emerged from the conflict unscathed physically and indisputably the world's richest and most powerful nation. Even the social divisions and tensions that the war brought into the open seemed to evaporate in the crisis of the Great Depression.

American troops on a Pacific beachhead during World War II.

STOPPING AND HOLDING JAPAN

America's great war was the Second World War. Even then the nation was not a battlefield, and casualties were fewer than those suffered by other combatant nations. But all Americans knew that they were in a fight between December 1941 and August 1945. Every adult at the time was to remember where he or she had been on the day Pearl Harbor was attacked, on D-Day when the invasion of Nazi-dominated Europe began, on the day Franklin D. Roosevelt died, on the days when Germany and Japan surrendered. Housewives saved tin cans for conversion into weaponry, and children saved tin foil and participated in scrap drives, collecting waste iron and steel for resmelting.

The American contribution in material and men was decisive in the outcome. Lend-lease kept the American allies—Great Britain, the Soviet Union, and China—afloat. American strategists designed the winning formula. American military administrators oversaw the huge and intricate apparatus of a modern military operation. American field commanders became heroes. American troops played an important part on the western front in Europe, and the Pacific war was their show. Without the United States, Germany and imperial Japan could not have been totally defeated.

It Began in Defeat

The first months of the war brought nothing but bad news. Immediately after paralyzing the American Pacific Fleet by the stunning blow at Pearl Harbor, the Japanese advanced easily into Malaya, Hong Kong, the Philippines, Java, Guam, and the two most distant islands of the Aleutians in Alaska. Within a few weeks, the dramatic Japanese battle flag, rays emanating from the rising sun, flew above Singapore, Burma, and present-day Indonesia.

There was heroism in defeat. On the island of Luzon, 20,000 crusty GI's under General Douglas MacArthur and their Filipino allies fought valiantly on the Bataan Peninsula and on the rocky island of Corregidor in Manila Bay. At first they thought they would be relieved or evacuated. Slowly the sickening truth sank in: they were alone, isolated, doomed, "the battling bastards of Bataan." Nevertheless, they grimly accepted their assignment of delaying the Japanese.

Roosevelt ordered MacArthur to flee to Australia. The general was an arrogant man, in fact an egomaniac who was given to posturing in a cool and collected version of the Mussolini show. "I studied

American soldiers surrender to the Japanese on the Philippine island of Corregidor in one of the bitterest military defeats in U.S. history.

dramatics under MacArthur," General Eisenhower said. F.D.R. did not like him; once he called MacArthur one of the two most dangerous men in the United States. Sunglasses, corncob pipe, and all, MacArthur was nevertheless one of the army's senior professionals and essential to winning the war against Japan. His connection with the Philippines was intimate; his father had been military governor of the colony. When MacArthur fled the islands, he promoted his mystique and made the Philippines a symbol with his parting words, "I shall return."

On May 6, the last ragged defenders of Corregidor surrendered. Humiliation in the worst military defeat in the nation's history gave way to furious anger when reports trickled into the United States of Japanese cruelty toward the prisoners on the infamous Bataan Death March. Of 10,000 men forced to walk to a prison camp in the interior, 1,000 died on the way. (Another 5,000 died in the camps before the war was over.)

Japanese Strategy

During the siege of Corregidor, the Japanese had moved on. Admiral Isoroku Yamamoto's plan was to establish a defense perimeter distant enough from Japan that the Americans could not bomb the homeland or force a decisive battle. By early May 1942, Japanese soldiers occupied the Solomon Islands and swarmed over most of New Guinea, threatening Port Moresby on Australia's doorstep. There, however, the advance was stopped.

On May 6 and 7, 1942, the Japanese and American fleets fought a stand-off battle in the Coral Sea off Australia's northeastern coast. It was a unique naval encounter. The ships of the opposing forces never came within sight of one another; carrier-based aircraft did the attacking. Yamamoto claimed victory in terms of ships sunk and planes lost, but he knew better. He had been forced to abandon his plan to cut the supply lines between Hawaii and Australia. Japan's defense perimeter would not extend to the subcontinent "down under." Instead, Yamamoto steamed into the central Pacific, hoping to capture the island of Midway, located about a thousand miles northwest of Hawaii.

There, on June 3 to 6, 1942, the Japanese suffered a significant defeat. The American fleet under Admirals Raymond A. Spruance and Frank J. Fletcher lost the carrier *Yorktown* to the excellent Japanese fighter planes, the "Zeroes" (named for the Japanese insignia, a red sun), but the Americans destroyed four large Japanese carriers and held on to vital Midway.

It was more than a one-for-four trade. Unlike the United States, Japan lacked the wealth and industrial capacity to replace the fabulously expensive ships during wartime. After Midway, Japan's offensive capability was smashed. Much earlier than he planned to do, and somewhat closer to Japan than he hoped, Yamamoto had to shift to defending what had been won. The great commander did not live to see the disastrous end of the war. In 1943, having cracked the Japanese naval code, Americans learned that Yamamoto would be flying over Bougainville in the Solomon Islands. They shot down his plane, and Yamamoto was killed. Inasmuch as he was opposed to the war, the revenge for Pearl Harbor was a political mistake. On the other hand, Japan never produced another naval commander of his brilliance.

Concentration Camps at Home

Not even the megalomaniacs among the Japanese leadership seriously entertained the possibility of invading the United States or Hawaii. Japan's goal was to force a negotiated Asian settlement on favorable terms. Nevertheless, the Japanese victories of early 1942 and the success of a few submarines in torpedoing ships off the beaches of Oregon and California caused ripples of invasion hysteria to wash over the Hawaiian Islands and the Pacific states. Newspaper magnate William Randolph Hearst hurriedly moved out of San Simeon,

This girl was one of thousands of Japanese-Americans who were forced into concentration camps in 1942 without trial or substantial evidence of their danger to national security.

his fantastic castle on an isolated stretch of the central California coast. He had baited the Japanese with racial insults for 50 years and now deluded himself into believing that his person was a prime Japanese target. Humbler but equally nervous citizens organized patrols to keep an eye on the surf from the Canadian border to San Diego.

In California, Oregon, and Washington, anger over Pearl Harbor coalesced with a long-standing resentment of Japanese-American prosperity and clannishness to result in spontaneous outbreaks of violence and government action that may represent the single worst violation of civil rights in American history. Gangs of teenage toughs (and grown men) beat up Japanese and other Asians. (People of Chinese and Korean descent took to wearing buttons identifying their origins and patriotism in order to avoid such attacks.)

Justice Department officials resisted the demands of West Coast politicians to go further and imprison Japanese-born residents and their children—United States citizens—the Nisei. But Roosevelt bent under the pressure of even moderate Californians like Governor Earl Warren and, in Executive Order 9066, defined coastal areas as forbidden to "Japanese" residence. About 9,000 Nisei left the zone voluntarily. (Some were turned back at the Nevada line; others were unable to buy gasoline.) About 110,000 were forcibly removed from their homes, and interned in concentration camps in seven states, from interior California to Arkansas.

Because the criteria for relocation were ancestry and race, the government seemed clearly to be violating the Constitution. But feelings were high. "If the Japs are released," Earl Warren said in June 1943 when there was talk of closing the camps, "no one will be able to tell a saboteur from any other Jap." In *Korematsu* v. *the United States* (1944) the Supreme Court, by a vote of 6 to 3, upheld the action that cost Japanese-Americans their freedom for several years and about $350 million in property.

A Better Record

In Hawaii, where about one-third of the population was of Japanese ancestry, the Nisei were treated brus-

quely but not abused. A few thousand known sympathizers with Japan were arrested, but, as a vital part of the islands' work force, Hawaiian-Japanese had to cope with only informal prejudice and the inconvenience of martial law. After repeated requests for a chance to prove their loyalty, 17,000 Hawaiian Nisei and some from the mainland fought against the Germans in Italy and turned in one of the war's best unit records for bravery.

Treatment of conscientious objectors and the few people who opposed the war on political grounds was exemplary in comparison with the treatment of Japanese-Americans. Never did it approach the ugliness of the First World War. While some 1,700 known Nazis

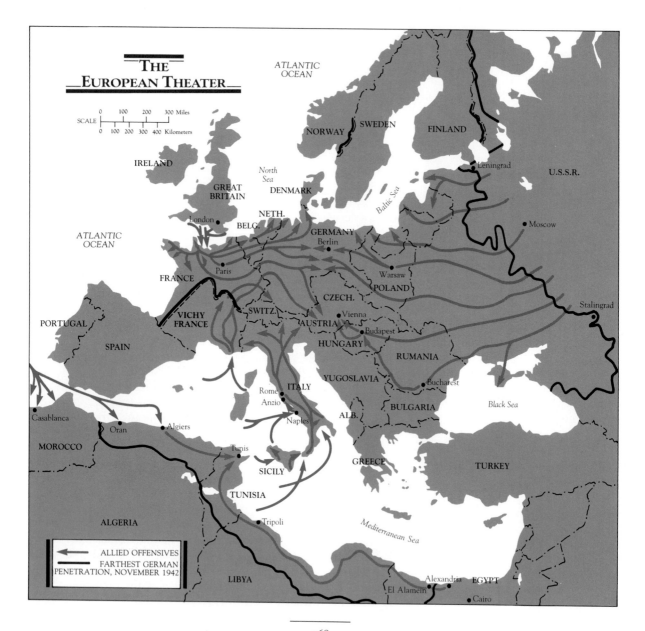

THE EUROPEAN THEATER

ALLIED OFFENSIVES
FARTHEST GERMAN PENETRATION, NOVEMBER 1942

and Fascists were arrested, German-Americans and Italian-Americans were not persecuted as a people. In retrospect, this might appear to be surprising since the war against Japan was essentially a war for economic domination of Asia, whereas Nazi Germany was palpably a criminal state that—it was clear by 1943—was practicing genocide against Europe's Jews.

But the Japanese were of a different race from most Americans and had a vastly different cultural attitude toward war. Surrender was always a disgrace to the Japanese soldier, and the Japanese army treated American prisoners of war with contempt and cruelty. Americans thus found it easier to hate the enemy in Asia.

SABOTEURS

The Germans attempted to put several teams of saboteurs in the United States from submarines, and there may have been some successful attempts at sabotage at defense plants. However, of 19,649 reported cases, the FBI was unable to trace a single one to enemy action. Between 1938 and 1945, the FBI arrested about 4,000 people, mostly German aliens, who were accused of espionage activities. Only 94 were convicted.

DEFEATING GERMANY FIRST

Nevertheless, President Roosevelt and his advisers were committed to defeating Germany first, and with good reason. Germany threatened the Western Hemisphere; Japan did not: the Nazis had good friends in several South American republics—and large German populations. If either Russia or England collapsed, or if Hitler were allowed too much time to entrench himself on the continent of Europe, it might be impossible to destroy Nazism. Strategists realized that Japan must eventually buckle under superior American power, particularly after Germany was defeated and the British and Russian allies were able to join the United States in the Pacific.

The first priority was to stop Hitler from increasing his control of the territory that Germany already occupied. To strike at German industry and the morale

The ruins of Dresden, Germany, following British and American bombing raids during February 1945.

of the people, the United States army air corps (only later the air force) joined the British in constant day and night bombing raids over Germany. Eventually, 2.7 million tons of bombs would level German cities.

The relentless aerial attacks pleased Soviet Premier Stalin, for Hitler was throwing the full force of the German *Wehrmacht* at the Russians. However, Soviet casualties were so horrendous (more than 6 million battle deaths eventually as opposed to just under 300,000 for the United States) that he demanded the British and Americans open a second front in Western Europe so that Germany would have to withdraw divisions from the Soviet Union.

The Second Front

Roosevelt and Churchill agreed that the beleaguered Red Army needed relief. However, they would not launch a slipshod campaign against Hitler's superb fortifications and insisted to Stalin that a successful second front required long, extensive preparation. F.D.R.'s impulsive promise to open up such a front in Europe in 1942 had to be cancelled.

In order to allay Stalin's suspicions that he and Churchill hoped to see Germany bleed Russia into impotence, Roosevelt dispatched huge shipments of war material to the Soviet Union. He also agreed to coordinate an attack on German and Italian forces in North Africa with the British and Anzacs (Australians and New Zealanders) who had fought a see-saw stalemate with German Field Marshal Erwin Rommel's seasoned *Afrika Korps*. With his front lines in Egypt in 1942, Rommel was threatening the Suez Canal, Britain's link with India.

The North African Campaign

In June 1942, his force beefed up by the arrival of Sherman tanks from the United States, British Marshal Bernard Montgomery began a counterattack against the *Afrika Korps* and Italian desert troops at El Alamein. In November, as he advanced from the east, Americans commanded by General Dwight D. Eisenhower landed far to the west in French North Africa. Making a deal with French forces, which had been under the thumb of the Germans, Eisenhower moved eastward and, at Kasserine Pass in February 1943, American tank forces fought the first major American battle in the European theater. It appeared to be a draw when Hitler recalled Rommel, "the desert fox," to Germany. The *Afrika Korps* collapsed.

About the same time, deep within the Soviet Union, the Russians had won a far more important victory, surrounding and capturing 250,000 seasoned German soldiers at Stalingrad. There seemed little doubt in any Allied capital that the course of the war

had been turned against the Germans. Stalin's Red Army began to drive slowly toward Germany. However, he stepped up his pleas and demands for a second front. Roosevelt joined him in arguing with Churchill: "Uncle Joe," as Roosevelt called Stalin, "is killing more Germans and destroying more equipment than you and I put together."

Catch-22

In July 1943, an American, British, and Anzac force invaded Sicily. After initial reverses, they conquered the island in six weeks. Americans got a new hero to crow about: the eccentric General George Patton, who rallied his troops in coarse "blood and guts" language and was a personally brave, even reckless commander of tanks, a cavalry officer from out of the past. (In fact, Patton believed in reincarnation and thought he had been any number of historical soldiers.)

The fall of Sicily knocked Italy out of the war. Mussolini's enemies among Socialists and Communists were joined by the conservative Field Marshal Pietro Badoglio, who, disturbed that his country had become Hitler's pawn, ousted *Il Duce* and made peace with the Allies.

Nevertheless, the victories in Italy were not decisive. Hitler rescued Mussolini from his captors and established him as the puppet head of the "Republic of Salo" in northern Italy. To take the place of the Italian troops who had gone over to the Allies, he withdrew German units to easily defended strongholds

CLEAN WAR

Desert warfare was "clean" compared to the other fighting in World War II. There was none of the hatred and viciousness that affected both sides in the Pacific. On the contrary, British and American troops admired, even liked, the opposing commander, Erwin Rommel. This was possible because desert warfare was a throwback to the time when professionals fought wars. Like naval battles, there were no civilians involved. The battles were fought in the wilderness; the bedouins who lived in the desert simply disappeared. There were none of the civilian casualties that aerial bombing and the sweep of armies across densely populated territory involved.

Nor were there massive numbers of troops involved in the fighting. It was a war of vehicles—armored cavalry—not masses of infantry. It was possible, in the midst of the colossal destruction and carnage of World War II, for a brief moment in 1942 and 1943, to think of war as "splendid." Most of the literature from the North African campaigns is romantic or good-humored, even comic.

south of Rome. It was mountainous country, and only after eight months of bloody, almost constant battle did the Americans reach the capital.

A generation later, novelist Joseph Heller wrote a black-comic novel about the war in Italy called *Catch-22*: a mentally disturbed soldier wants out of the army because of the horrors and senselessness of the fighting; this assessment, however, proves he is sane and therefore ineligible for discharge. Grotesque as it was, Heller's image was by no means absurd. Germany itself would fall before the Allies made much headway up the boot. Nevertheless, the American fighting man proved his mettle in the frustrating campaign. Cartoonist Bill Mauldin immortalized him in a strip that recounted the adventures of Willie and Joe, two GI's in Italy who wearily slogged on, no heroes, just ordinary men getting a job done.

Ike and D-Day

The Germans foiled the drive through Italy without withdrawing troops from the Soviet Union. Indeed,

> ## IKE'S CONTINGENCY PLAN
>
> Knowing that he would be busy on D-Day, General Eisenhower scribbled out the following note to be dispatched to Washington in the event that the invasion of Europe was a failure:
>
> *Our landings in the Cherbourg-Havre area have failed to gain a satisfactory foothold and I have withdrawn the troops. My decision to attack at this time and place was based upon the best information available. The troops, the air corps and the navy did all that bravery and devotion to duty could do. If any blame or fault attaches to the attempt it is mine alone.*

defeating "the Slav" came to obsess Hitler and the Red Army continued to suffer. Stalin stepped up his insistence on a second front and by the beginning of 1944, General Eisenhower, headquartered in London, had the operation under way. "Ike" had put in a solid

General Dwight D. Eisenhower briefs a group of paratroopers about to leave for the coast of France where they would be among 1 million Allied troops who began liberating that country from Nazi control, June 6, 1944.

but undramatic military career. He was not a colorful man. A plodding administrator rather than a glamorous figure like MacArthur or a daring combat commander like Patton, he was affable, even tempered, a diplomat. He was able to soothe sensitive egos and smooth over differences among headstrong associates.

They were these qualities that Army Chief of Staff George C. Marshall had in mind when he jumped Eisenhower over a number of senior officers to command the Allied forces in Europe. Marshall appreciated field officers. But he knew that modern warfare required the organizational and administrative talents of a corporation president.

Eisenhower was the perfect choice. He not only won the confidence of Churchill, a notoriously irascible character with whom to work, but usually could handle Montgomery, a prima donna who burned with envy of any superior. Ike dealt as well as could be expected with the proud leader of the Free French forces, Charles de Gaulle, and he made a fast personal friend of Soviet Marshal Georgi Zhukov. Eisenhower also was able to discipline Patton to the satisfaction of critics without losing his services in combat, after that erratic general slapped a shell-shocked soldier in Italy.

Most important, Eisenhower supervised Operation Overlord, the extremely complex and largest amphibious attack ever ventured in war. The task involved mobilizing 4,000 vessels, 11,000 aircraft, tens of thousands of motor vehicles of various sorts, and weapons, as well as billeting and training more than 2 million soldiers. Such a massive operation could not go unnoticed by the Germans, of course, but the British and Americans successfully kept secret the date and, more important, the place of the invasion.

The date was June 6, 1944, and the place was Normandy in northwestern France. Eisenhower's caution and meticulous planning of every detail paid off. The Allied troops—1 million men—marched across France and into Paris on August 25. Immediately thereafter they entered Belgium. By September, they were across the German border, farther than the Allies had penetrated during all of the First World War.

Politics and Strategy

The British and Americans disagreed about how to finish off Germany. Montgomery wanted to concentrate power in one thrust into the heart of Germany, a traditional strategy that had much to recommend it. Tactfully, Eisenhower overruled him. In part his decision was military, reflecting his innate cautiousness and perhaps his study of the American Civil War. He feared that extending supply lines too quickly would tempt the Germans into a massive counterattack that might lead to disaster, a much longer war, even the

General Anthony McAuliffe (left) and General George Patton inspect Bastogne during the Battle of the Bulge.

impulse to negotiate a peace. He preferred to exploit the overwhelming Allied superiority in arms and men by proceeding cautiously, advancing slowly on a broad front that extended from the North Sea to the border of Switzerland, strangling Germany as Grant had strangled the Confederacy.

Diplomatic considerations entered into Eisenhower's decision too. Still absorbing tremendous casualties as they slowly pushed the Germans westward, the Russians remained suspicious of American and British motives. Stalin jumped at every rumor that his allies were considering a separate peace. Some American diplomats feared that too rapid an American and British thrust would only arouse Stalin's suspicions. On an earthier level, Eisenhower worried about spontaneous trouble between his soldiers and the Red Army if an orderly rendezvous were not arranged in advance.

The Bulge

For a while in 1944, it appeared that Eisenhower's strategy of advancing slowly was a mistake. In the summer, V-2 rockets from sanctuaries inside Germany began to rain down on London, killing 8,000 people. The V-2's were not decisive weapons from a military point of view, but with the end of the war apparently in sight, their psychological effect was disheartening to civilians. There was no warning, as there was in conventional aerial attack—only a whine high in the air, a few seconds of silence, and an explosion.

Much more demoralizing was a German military counteroffensive in Belgium in a bitter cold and snowy December. In the Battle of the Bulge, German troops pushed the Americans back, forcing a "bulge" in the German front lines and threatening to split the Allied forces in two. But an isolated army under General Anthony McAuliffe at Bastogne refused to surrender ("Nuts!" McAuliffe replied to the German commander), creating a weak point in the German offensive, and a break in the weather allowed the Allies to exploit their air superiority. After two weeks, they advanced again and the Eisenhower plan resumed. One by one German defenses collapsed. Along with his oldest and closest Nazi party associates, a Hitler close to breakdown withdrew to a bunker under the streets of Berlin where he presided over the premature disintegration of his "Thousand-Year Empire." To the

end, he thought in terms of the perverted romanticism of his ideology. He was involved in Götterdämmerung, the mythical final battle of the gods. On April 30, 1945, he committed suicide after having named Admiral Karl Doenitz his successor as *Führer*. A few days later, Doenitz surrendered.

Wartime Diplomacy

Eisenhower's sensitivity to Russian suspicions reflected President Roosevelt's policy. At a personal meeting with Premier Stalin at Teheran in Iran late in 1943, and again at Yalta in the Crimea in February 1945, F.D.R. did his best to assuage the Russian's fears by agreeing to most of Stalin's proposals for the organization of postwar Europe.

In after years, when the Soviet Union was the Cold War enemy and Americans lamented Russian domination of Eastern Europe, *Yalta* became a byword for diplomatic blunder and even, to a few extremists, for treasonous "sellout" to "the Russkies." It was at Yalta

Winston Churchill, Franklin D. Roosevelt, and Joseph Stalin pose for photographers at Yalta, February 1945.

that Roosevelt and Churchill consented to Stalin's insistence that they recognize Soviet Russia's "special interests" in Eastern Europe, that is, governments friendly to the Soviet Union.

Right-wing extremists later said that F.D.R. sold out the Poles, Czechs, Hungarians, Rumanians, and Bulgarians because he was himself sympathetic to Communism. Other more rational analysts ridiculed such conspiracy theories, but suspected that the president's weariness and illness, obvious in the haggard face and sagging jaw of the official photographs, caused him to reason poorly in dealing with the calculating Stalin.

Whatever effect Roosevelt's failing health had on his mental processes, there was nothing irrational about his concessions to Russia. The recognition of special Soviet interests in Eastern Europe was an ancient Russian purpose, long preceding the Bolshevik Revolution. Moreover, Roosevelt and Churchill did not give Stalin anything that he did not already have. In February 1945, the Red Army was racing over and occupying the very countries that Stalin envisioned as buffer states against renewed German aggression or other threats from the West. No doubt Churchill and F.D.R. expected the postwar states of Eastern Europe to have greater independence than Stalin was eventually to allow. But historians disagree as to whether Stalin intended to enforce an iron grip in 1945 or altered his policy later, when the Cold War began.

THE TWILIGHT OF JAPAN, THE NUCLEAR DAWN

Also influencing Roosevelt at Yalta was his desire to enlist the Soviet Union in the war against Japan in order to save American lives in the final battles. While agreeing that the Red Army would attack Japanese forces in China, Stalin insisted on delaying action until the Soviet Union felt secure in Europe.

Pacific Strategy

After Midway in June 1942, American strategy in the war against Japan involved three distinct campaigns. First, just as the United States pumped material into Russia, supplies were flown into China from India, "over the hump" of the Himalayas, in order to keep the Chinese in the war. Unfortunately, Chiang Kai-shek was no Stalin, and his Kuomintang troops were no Red Army.

Chiang hated and feared his Chinese Communist allies as much as he hated the Japanese. He diverted thousands of troops to battling them, and never forced the kind of battle against Japan that the Americans

needed in order to tie down the Japanese army on the mainland. In addition, inefficiency and corruption in Chiang's government resulted in gross misuse of American supplies.

General Joseph W. "Vinegar Joe" Stilwell, the gritty American commander on the mainland, despised Chiang. He poured out an avalanche of warnings to Washington about "the monkey," as he called the general. But when Stilwell tried to get command of the Chinese army for himself, Roosevelt recalled him. Somewhat to Churchill's amazement, Roosevelt was convinced that Chiang was a valuable ally.

The second and third prongs of the attack on Japan were more successful, but extremely bloody. After driving the Japanese out of the Solomons in order to ensure Australia's security, one force under MacArthur began to push toward the Japanese homeland via New Guinea and the Philippines, while another commanded by Admiral Chester W. Nimitz struck through the central Pacific, capturing islands from which aircraft could reach and bomb Japan.

Island Warfare

To soldiers slogging through the mud and frigid cold of Italy and France, the troops in the Pacific were on a picnic, basking in a lovely climate and only periodically meeting the enemy in battle. Ernie Pyle, con-

An apprehensive Marine photographed during battle against the Japanese on Peleliu Island, Palau, May 1945.

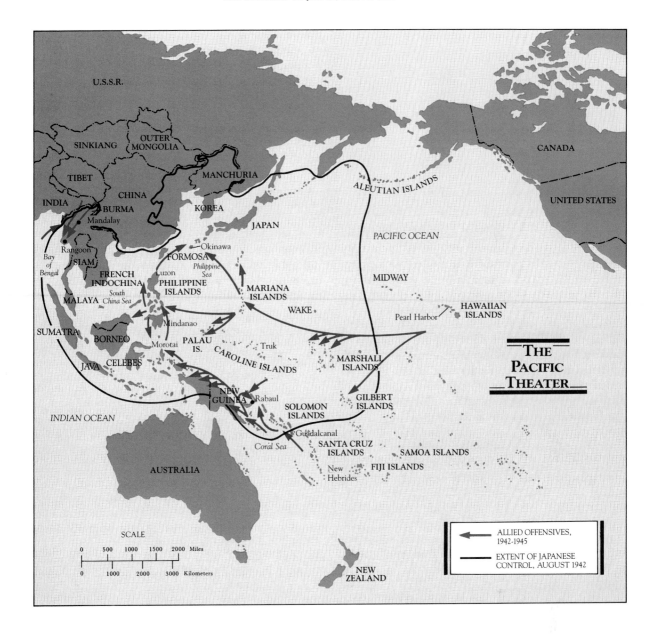

sidered the best Second World War correspondent, made this comparison in his celebration of the American fighting man in Europe. (Ironically, Pyle survived Europe and was killed by Japanese machine-gun fire on Ie Shima in the closing months of the war.)

Life behind the lines in the Pacific was pleasant, if not quite idyllic. But capturing islands that were specks on the map meant battles more vicious than those in Europe. The Japanese soldier was a formidable fighter. He was indoctrinated with a fanatical sense of duty and taught that it was a betrayal of national and personal honor to surrender, even when his army was obviously defeated. Japanese soldiers were expected to

fight to the death, taking down as many of the enemy as they could.

To an astonishing degree, this was how they fought. It took the Americans six months to win control of microscopic Guadalcanal in the Solomons after August 1942, even though the defenders had not had time to construct fortifications as strong as they had hoped to build.

In New Guinea and along the route through the Gilbert, Marshall, and Marianas islands that Nimitz was to follow, the concrete bunkers and gun emplacements were stronger than in the Solomons, and the resistance of the Japanese was chillingly effective. Ma-

WORLD WAR II CASUALTIES			
	Total mobilized	Killed or died	Wounded
United States	16,113,000	407,000	672,000
China	17,251,000	1,325,000	1,762,000
Germany	20,000,000	3,250,000	7,250,000
Italy	3,100,000	136,000	225,000
Japan	9,700,000	1,270,000	140,000
U.S.S.R.	—	6,115,000	14,012,000
United Kingdom	5,896,000	357,000	369,000
TOTAL	72,060,000	12,860,000	24,430,000

rines discovered at places like Tarawa in the Gilberts in November 1943 that when a battle was over, they had few prisoners. They had to kill almost every Japanese on the island at high cost to themselves.

As MacArthur and Nimitz moved closer to Japan, the fighting grew tougher. Attacking the Marianas and the Philippines in 1944, both American forces were hit hard. But MacArthur's dramatic return to Luzon boosted morale, and Nimitz's capture of the Marianas enabled larger land-based American planes to bomb the Japanese homeland at will. The wooden cities of Japan went up like tinder when hit by incendiary devices. A single raid on Tokyo on March 9, 1945, killed 85,000 people and destroyed 250,000 buildings.

By no means were all the Japanese-occupied islands retaken. Both MacArthur and Nimitz advocated "island hopping," leaving less-important Japanese holdings alone, to wither as they were cut off from supplies. When the war finally ended, there were still some Japanese units operating in New Guinea, the point of farthest Japanese advance.

Fighting to the Last Man

By the spring of 1945, Japan's situation was hopeless. Germany was defeated, thus freeing hundreds of thousands of battle-hardened soldiers for combat in the Pacific. Although Stalin was procrastinating, the Japanese leaders believed that the Soviet Union was on the verge of declaring war. After the huge Battle of Leyte Gulf in October 1944, the Japanese navy had ceased to exist as a fighting force, while the Americans cruised the seas with 4,000 ships. United States submarines, which were more effective than German U-boats ever had been, destroyed half of the island nation's vital merchant fleet within a few months.

And yet, the Japanese high command frustrated every attempt by civilians in the government to make peace. They were themselves victims of the extreme

nationalistic fervor they instilled in their men, and they had 5 million in uniform. There were 2 million in Japan itself, and about the same number in China, where Chiang's half-hearted warmaking had been just enough to make them first-rate soldiers without inflicting heavy casualties.

With so many soldiers fighting to the death, the taking of islands close to Japan resulted in hundreds of thousands of casualties. Iwo Jima, a desolate tiny volcano needed for a landing strip, cost 4,000 lives. Saipan was even bloodier and the invasion of Okinawa, considered part of Japan, killed or wounded 80,000 Americans. In the same fighting, more than 100,000 Japanese died, and only 8,000 surrendered. Planners said that the invasion of Japan itself, scheduled for November 1, 1945, would cost 1 million casualties, as many as the United States had suffered in over three years of fighting in both Europe and the Pacific.

A Birth and a Death

This chilling prediction helped to make the atomic bomb so appealing to policymakers. The Manhattan Project, code name of the group that built the bomb, dated from 1939, when the great physicist Albert Einstein wrote to President Roosevelt that it was possible to unleash inconceivable amounts of energy by nuclear fission, splitting an atom. Einstein hated war. But he was also a refugee from Nazism who knew that German science was capable of producing a nuclear bomb. Such a device in Hitler's hands was an appalling prospect.

Einstein was too prestigious a man to ignore and the government secretly allotted $2 billion to the Manhattan Project. Under the direction of J. Robert Oppenheimer, scientists working on Long Island, underneath a football stadium in Chicago, and at isolated Los Alamos in New Mexico progressed steadily and, by April 1945, told Washington that they were four months away from testing a bomb.

THE LETTER THAT LED TO THE BOMB

In his own hand, to emphasize the importance of his message, Albert Einstein wrote to President Roosevelt in 1939:

Some recent work by E. Fermi and L. Szilard, which has been communicated to me in manuscript, leads me to expect that the element uranium may be turned into a new and important source of energy in the immediate future. Certain aspects of the situation seem to call for watchfulness and, if necessary, quick action on the part of the Administration.

The decision whether or not to use it did not fall to President Roosevelt. Reelected to a fourth term in 1944 over Thomas E. Dewey, the unexciting governor of New York, Roosevelt died of a massive stroke on April 12, 1945. He was at Warm Springs, Georgia, sitting for a portrait painter when he said, "I have a terrific headache," slumped in his chair, and died.

The outpouring of grief that swept the nation at the loss of the man who had been in office longer than any other president was real and profound. Silent crowds lined the tracks to watch the train that brought F.D.R. back to Washington for the last time. People wept in the streets of every city. But in Washington, the sorrow was overshadowed by apprehensions that his successor, Harry S Truman, was not up to being president.

Truman, Little Boy, and Fat Man

Truman was an honest politician who had risen as a hard worker for the Kansas City machine of Boss Thomas J. Pendergast. He proved his abilities as chair-man of an important Senate committee during the war, but impressed few as the caliber of person to head a nation. Unprepossessing in appearance and manner, bespectacled, something of a midwestern dandy (he once operated a haberdashery), and given to salty language, Truman had been nominated as vice president in 1944 as a compromise candidate. Democratic conservatives wanted left-liberal Henry A. Wallace out of the number-two spot, but they could not force conservative James J. Byrnes on the liberals. The two wings of the party settled on Truman despite whispers about President Roosevelt's health.

Truman was as shocked by his accession as anyone else. "I don't know whether you fellows ever had a load of hay or a bull fall on you," he told reporters on his first full day in office, "but last night the moon, the stars, and all the planets fell on me." If he joined others in being unsure of his abilities, Truman knew how to make difficult decisions and never doubted his responsibility to lead. A plaque on his desk read "The Buck Stops Here"; as the president of the United States, he would not "pass the buck."

A view of Hiroshima after it was flattened by an atomic bomb, August 6, 1945.

STUDYING A NEW KIND OF WAR

"Tarawa was not a very big battle, as battles go," wrote G. D. Lillibridge, the historian who was a second lieutenant there in November 1943, "and it was all over in seventy-two hours." The casualties totaled only 3,300 U.S. Marines, about the same number of elite Japanese Special Naval Landing Forces, and 2,000 Japanese and Korean laborers who doubled as soldiers. A few months earlier, by comparison, half a world away in the Stalingrad campaign, the German *Wehrmacht* lost 500,000 men.

And yet, like Stalingrad, "Bloody Tarawa" was a landmark, even a turning point, of the Second World War. If the numbers were trivial, the incidence of the casualties was appalling, especially for a nation whose wartime leaders, since Lincoln and Grant, have thought of minimizing losses in battle as a major determinant of strategy. Lillibridge's 39-man platoon lost 26; 323 of 500 drivers of landing craft died; overall, more than one-third of the American attackers were killed or wounded. The figures stunned the admirals who planned the battle and the people at home who read about it.

So did the fanatacism of the Japanese defenders. Americans had heard that the Japanese fighting man considered surrender under any circumstances to be shameful. That was in the abstract. Few were prepared to learn that only 17 of 5,000 Japanese on the tiny atoll of Betio were captured, most of them because they were too seriously wounded to commit suicide.

This willingness to die for nothing but a code of honor incomprehensible to Americans was not something that could be taught in a training film. It was bred into Japan's young men from infancy. In his reflections on the battle, something of an attempt to exorcise demons that had haunted him for 25 years, Lillibridge remembered a Japanese man his platoon had trapped during the mopping-up operation. Another Japanese Marine was moaning in agony from his wounds. The defender would reassure his dying friend, then hurl challenges and insults at Lillibridge's platoon,

his voice raised against us in the raging pitch that comes from fear and anger and then lowered to a soothing tone as he sought to comfort his mortally wounded companion. . . . Doomed and knowing he was doomed, he never lost control of himself and remained in command of the situation until the end.

Betio, only two miles long and 800 yards wide—half the size of New York's Central Park—was the largest of the 25 islands of the Tarawa atoll, a coral formation in the sprawling Gilbert Islands. The Japanese airstrip there was the chief strategic objective of the American assault. Japanese planes based in Tarawa could worry American supply lines between Hawaii and Australia.

"Bloody Tarawa" the day after the battle, November 22, 1943.

In a way, by November 1943, Tarawa represented the final fragment of Japanese offensive capability.

It was a tiny fragment. Just as important as the airstrip to Admirals Chester W. Nimitz and Raymond Spruance was to use Tarawa to test their theories of amphibious assault before what was anticipated to be far more difficult fighting in the Marshall Islands early in 1944 and, after that, an island by island advance toward Japan.

"There had to be a Tarawa, a first assault on a strongly defended coral atoll," an American officer explained. An amphibious assault against an entrenched, waiting enemy was a new kind of war for the American military, or at least an untried technique. Ironically, the Americans thought that Tarawa would be easy, more training-exercise than battle. They had no illusions about the fierceness of Japanese troops. However, Betio was small; the Japanese had been digging in there a comparatively short time; the American assault force was huge, covering eight square miles of Pacific; and officers awed by the destructiveness of naval bombardment were sure they would "obliterate the defenses on Betio." Taking his cue from his superiors, Lieutenant Lillibridge told his platoon that "there was no need to worry, no necessity for anyone to get killed, although possibly someone might get slightly wounded."

In fact, the pre-dawn bombardment did destroy Rear Admiral Keiji Shibasaki's communications with most of his troops. However, the network of concrete blockhouses, coconut-log pillboxes, and underwater barricades he had built in just a few months, what one analyst called a "complete defensive system," was substantially untouched by the big guns and aerial bombs. The willingness of the Japanese marines and even common laborers to die more than compensated for their isolation from Shibasaki's bunker.

Nature more than compensated for the massiveness of the American attack. The tide was lower than hoped and the larger American landing crafts could not clear the reef that fringed Betio. This meant that all but the first wave of marines had to wade, breast deep, 800 yards to shore.

This was the element of amphibious attack in the Pacific that was really tested at Tarawa. Could men with no more armor than "a khaki shirt," no way to defend themselves, and in effect no support while they were slogging half a mile in water, even get to the beach, let alone establish enough of a base from which to displace enemies who, during this same critical time, were free to wreak havoc with them?

Getting to the beach was the first horror that would haunt the survivors of Tarawa and subsequent Pacific landings for the rest of their lives. Men remembered it as a "nightmarish turtle race," run in slow-motion. It was "like being completely suspended, like being under a strong anesthetic." "I could have sworn that I could have reached out and touched a hundred bullets." "The water never seemed clear of tiny men."

It was their tininess, perhaps, that enabled the Americans to reach the beach through a storm of machine-gun and cannon fire. They had to push through the floating corpses of their comrades, hundreds of thousands of fish killed by the bombardment, stepping on other dead marines. The lagoon was literally red with blood for hours.

The second nightmare waited on the beach. Shibasaki had constructed a sea wall of conconut logs, three to five feet high. At first it seemed to be a shelter. The exhausted marines threw themselves under it. In fact, Japanese mortars had been meticulously registered to batter the long thin line, while to peek above the palisade meant to draw the fire of 200 perfectly positioned Japanese machines guns. More than one marine remembered that he was capable of moving beyond the sea wall only because to remain there meant certain death. About half the American casualties were suffered in the water, most of the rest on the beach. The carnage was condensed in such a way as to leave lifelong psychological scars.

One by one, almost always at close quarters, the blockhouses and pillboxes were wiped out. Betio was taken in three days, only one more than called-for by commanders who thought it would be a "walkover." The aftermath was as morally devastating as the battle. Like at the Wilderness and the Marne, the vegetation that had covered the island was literally destroyed.

Hundreds of bodies floating in the surf and festering in the blockhouses bloated and rotted in the tropical heat. The triumphant marines looked like anything but victors. They sat staring, exhausted, just beginning to comprehend what they had been through, as if they had been captured by their enemies. "I passed boys who . . . looked older than their fathers," General Holland Smith said, "it had chilled their souls. They found it hard to believe they were actually alive."

Smith and the other commanders learned a great deal from the "training exercise" at Tarawa, not the least of which lessons was not to gamble on tides over coral reefs. Not until the last months of the Pacific War, when the close approach to the Japanese homeland made larger forces of Japanese defenders even fiercer in their resistance, would the extremity of Tarawa's terror be repeated.

The Pacific commanders also learned that while the vast American superiority of armament and firepower was essential and telling, taking the Pacific island was much more personal and human an effort than twentieth century military men had come to assume. With a grace rare in a modern officer, General Julian Smith frankly asserted,

There was one thing that won this battle . . . and that was the supreme courage of the Marines. The prisoners tell us that what broke their morale was not the bombing, not the naval gunfire, but the sight of Marines who kept coming ashore.

Soldiers in the European theater, Americans at home, and more than a few troops in the Pacific Campaign, looked on the Pacific war as a picnic. G. D. Lillibridge and others remembered the idyllic holiday quality, however involuntary the vacation was, of the long months between battles spent in Hawaii, Australia, or New Zealand. Correspondent Robert Sherrod, who lived through Tarawa, wrote of "the brilliant sunlight, the far-reaching, incredibly blue Pacific, the soft breezes at evening and the Southern Cross in the sky." The idyll became a part of American popular culture with the publication of James Michener's *Tales of the South Pacific*, and the musical comedy, *South Pacific*, that was based on it. Hawaii enjoyed a second great tourist boom (the first followed annexation) as a result of the Americans' rediscovery of the islands during the war.

But if life between battles was idyllic—and the whole Pacific war a pleasure to noncombat troops—the ferocity of battle was, as Lillibridge writes in another place, perhaps the greatest in the conflict.

It took the personal intervention of Emperor Hirohito to persuade the Japanese military to surrender to the United States. The official surrender took place aboard the battleship Missouri *on September 2, 1945.*

Was the Bomb Necessary?

At first there was only wonder at a weapon that could destroy a whole city, and joy that the war was over. Within a few years, however, many Americans began to debate the wisdom and morality of having used the atomic bomb. When novelist John Hersey's *Hiroshima* detailed the destruction of the ancient city in vivid, human terms, some of Truman's critics stated that he was guilty of a war crime worse than any the Japanese had perpetrated and exceeded only by the Nazi murder of 6 million European Jews. Truman and his defenders replied that the nuclear assaults on Hiroshima and Nagasaki were humane acts since millions of Japanese as well as Americans would have been killed had Japan been invaded.

When other critics said that the Japanese surrender could have been forced by a demonstration of the bomb on an uninhabited island, as Secretary of War Stimson had suggested in 1945, defenders pointed out that no one was positive that the device would actually work. An announced demonstration that fizzled would have encouraged the Japanese die-hards to fight all the harder. Less satisfactorily explained was the fact that neither Hiroshima nor Nagasaki were military targets of any consequence.

Much later, a group of historians who were called "revisionists" suggested that Little Boy and Fat Man were dropped not so much to end the war with Japan but to inaugurate the Cold War with the Soviet Union. Truman was showing the Russians that the United States held the trump card in any postwar dispute. Because history is not a science, capable of absolute proof, the debate over the use of the bomb will continue indefinitely. Only two things are certain: the atomic bomb did end the Second World War decisively and ahead of schedule, and it ushered in a new and dangerous epoch in world affairs, the nuclear age.

Truman met with Churchill and Stalin at Potsdam in July 1945, informing them of the existence of the bomb. When it was made clear to him that the alternative to using it was a conventional invasion of Japan and 1 million casualties, he opted as Roosevelt always had, to avoid massive carnage. On August 6, an atomic bomb nicknamed "Little Boy" was dropped on Hiroshima, killing 100,000 people in an instant and dooming another 100,000 to death from injury and radiation poisoning. Two days later, when the Japanese leadership showed no signs of buckling under, "Fat Man" was exploded over Nagasaki.

Incredibly, the Japanese high command still wanted to fight on. Had they known that the Americans had no more atomic bombs in their arsenal, they might have carried the debate. But Emperor Hirohito stepped in and agreed to surrender on August 15, 1945, if he were allowed to keep his throne. Because the Americans valued him as a symbol of social stability in Japan, they agreed. The war ended officially on the decks of the battleship *Missouri* on September 2.

THE COSTS OF WAR

The Second World War was the most expensive war that the United States ever fought:

Revolutionary War	$149	million
War of 1812	124	million
Mexican War	107	million
Civil War (Union only)	8	billion
Spanish-American War	2.5	billion
First World War	66	billion
Second World War	560	billion
Korean War	70	billion
Vietnam War	121.5	billion

For Further Reading

Overviews and Classics

Albert R. Buchanan, *The United States and World War II* (1962)

Winston Churchill, *The Second World War* (1948–53)

Robert Dallek, *Franklin D. Roosevelt and American Foreign Policy, 1932–1945* (1979)

Martha Hoyle, *A World in Flames: A History of World War II* (1970)

Fletcher Pratt, *War for the World* (1950)

Valuable Special Studies

Gar Alperovitz, *Atomic Diplomacy: Hiroshima and Potsdam* (1965)

Robert Beitzell, *The Uneasy Alliance: America, Britain, and Russia, 1941–1943* (1972)

John M. Blum, *V Was for Victory: Politics and American Culture During World War II* (1976)

Robert J. Burtow, *Tojo and the Coming of War* (1961)

Roger Daniels, *Concentration Camps USA* (1971)

Carl M. Degler, *At Odds: Women and the Family in America from the Revolution to the Present* (1980)

Robert A. Divine, *Roosevelt and World War II* (1969)

Herbert Feis, *The Atomic Bomb and World War II* (1966)

Jack Goodman, *While You Were Gone: A Report on Wartime Life in the United States* (1946)

Norman A. Graebner, *The Age of Global Power: The United States Since 1938* (1979)

Greg Herken, *The Winning Weapon* (1980)

Gabriel Kolko, *The Politics of War: The World and United States Foreign Policy, 1943–1945* (1968)

Richard Lingeman, *Don't You Know There's a War On* (1970)

Charles B. McDonald, *The Mighty Endeavor: American Armed Forces in the European Theater in World War II* (1969)

Samuel Eliot Morison, *The Two-Ocean War: A Short History of the United States Navy in the Second World War* (1963)

Richard Polenberg, *War and Society: The United States, 1941–1945* (1972)

E. E. Robinson, *The Roosevelt Leadership* (1955)

Cornelius Ryan, *The Longest Day* (1959)

Gaddis Smith, *American Diplomacy During the Second World War, 1940–1945* (1965)

John Toland, *The Last Hundred Days* (1966)

———. *The Rising Sun: The Decline and Fall of the Japanese Empire* (1970)

Michi Weglyn, *Years of Infamy: The Untold Story of America's Concentration Camps* (1976)

Russell F. Weigley, *The American Way of War: A History of United States Military Strategy and Policy* (1973)

William A. Williams, *The Tragedy of American Diplomacy* (1962)

Biographies and Autobiographies

Stephen Ambrose, *The Supreme Commander: The War Years of General Dwight D. Eisenhower* (1970)

James MacGregor Burns, *Roosevelt: The Soldier of Freedom* (1970)

Richard N. Current, *Secretary Stimson: A Study in Statecraft* (1954)

Dwight D. Eisenhower, *Crusade in Europe* (1948)

Frank Freidel, *Franklin D. Roosevelt* (1952–73)

Joseph P. Lash, *Roosevelt and Churchill* (1976)

William Manchester, *American Caesar: Douglas MacArthur, 1880–1960* (1978)

Elting E. Morison, *Turmoil and Tradition: A Study of the Life and Times of Henry L. Stimson* (1960)

J. W. Pratt, *Cordell Hull* (1964)

46

The United States in the Early Nuclear Age
A Time of Anxieties, 1946–1952

Rarely had a war ended so abruptly as the atomic bomb ended the Pacific theater of the Second World War. Never had a new historical era been so unmistakably proclaimed as by the fireballs over Hiroshima and Nagasaki. During the final months of 1945, people sensed that the world had undergone a vital change, that the old rules and guidelines would not necessarily help them to negotiate the future.

But they had not left the past behind. History is legacy. The consequences of past actions live on whether or not people study the past. Three great legacies of the Second World War were so profound that they fostered anxieties that loom menacingly over the United States and the world to this day.

A radioactive mushroom cloud covers Bikini Atoll following a test of the atomic bomb, July 25, 1946.

THE SHADOW OF COLD WAR

The first legacy of the Second World War was the atomic bomb that had ended it. Nuclear weapons made it technologically possible for humanity to destroy the civilization, perhaps even the world. It was a circumstance novel in history.

The second legacy of the war was the discovery in the spring of 1945 that reports of genocide in German

Europe had not been exaggerated. The Nazis had systematically exterminated 6 million Jews and probably 1 million other people in factories called "camps" that were in reality factories specifically designed for killing people and disposing of their bodies on a mass scale. The photographs and films of the walking skeletons of Dachau, Belsen, Auschwitz, and Buchenwald; the "shower baths" where the victims were gassed; the cremation ovens; the human garbage dumps, arms and legs protruding obscenely from heaps of corpses like discarded furniture: these shocking spectacles mocked human pretensions to enlightenment and decency such as not even the slaughter of the First World War had done. That, at least, had been mindless. Nazi genocide was deliberate, calculated, and methodical.

The capacity of the species for cruelty was nothing new. But the Hitler regime had gone beyond cruelty in coolly and deliberately applying modern technology and business methods to the destruction of human beings. The death camps were mass-production in reverse. Never again would it be possible to assume, as most of Western civilization had assumed for more than a century, that reason, science, technology, and efficiency were moving the human race toward an ever better future. If the atomic bomb showed that it was technologically feasible to destroy the world, the death camps proved that governments and peoples were morally capable of doing so.

The third legacy of the war was that only two genuine victors emerged from it, and that, once the Nazis were defeated, they had little in common. The United States and the Soviet Union faced each other across devastated Europe and East Asia, their other allies reeling almost as feebly as Germany and Japan. For about two years after the war, Russian and American leaders tried to preserve the wartime alliance or, at

Prisoners in a Nazi concentration camp await their release in this 1945 photo by Margaret Bourke-White.

least, to maintain the pretense of friendship and to come to an understanding that would govern postwar relations. By 1947, however, the two great powers were in a state of "cold war," belligerence without violent confrontation. At first, Americans were annoyed rather than frightened by what they believed was Soviet ingratitude and treachery. Their nation held the trump card, the atomic bomb. Then, in September 1949, the Soviets successfully tested a nuclear device. The total destruction of which humanity was capable seemed likely to be unleashed sooner or later.

Roots of Soviet-American Animosity

The origins of the Cold War lay in the nature of Soviet communism. The American commitment to liberal democratic principles was incompatible with the belief of the Bolsheviks of 1917 that they could overcome the "sluggishness of history" and achieve their revolution only by exercising dictatorial power at least temporarily. Just as important (for the United States often found it possible to come to terms with non-Communist dictators who were also ruthless), the American commitment to maintaining an "open door" for trade and investment everywhere in the world was incompatible with the Soviet determination to prevent capitalist economic penetration in the territory they controlled.

With such contradictory principles, the Soviet Union and the United States could form only a marriage of necessity. Both sides found themselves with a common enemy during the Second World War, and that was all that bound them together. At no time, despite cordial personal relations between Roosevelt and Stalin, did American or Russian policymakers believe that this conflict of interests had disappeared. People high in the American government continued to believe that Communism was a noxious ideology and that the lack of political democracy and individual freedom in the Soviet Union was an affront to common decency. The Russians, on the other side, remained suspicious of the intentions of the United States and Great Britain. Since 1917, the Western nations had isolated and threatened to destroy the revolution that the Bolsheviks had made.

During the war, personal friendships among the three leaders grew, but the old suspicions never died. Stalin seethed when Roosevelt and Churchill were slow to establish a second front in Europe. The Americans and the British worried that, after the war, Communist Russia would be a great power for the first time, in a position to dominate its neighbors. Indeed, the extraordinary shift in the apportionment of power that the Second World War worked may have been more important than ideology. Had previously weak Russia

not been a Communist state, but had nevertheless emerged from the war as powerful as it was, there would most likely have been a similar Cold War—a conflict between two superpowers with interests throughout the world.

An Insoluble Problem

Roosevelt believed that he could handle Stalin's frequently expressed determination that the nations bordering Russia be friendly to it. Although it is difficult to imagine what he had in mind, Roosevelt apparently thought that he could ensure that Poland, Czechoslovakia, and the Balkan countries would be democratic, open to American cooperation and trade while remaining friendly to the Soviet Union, not under Russian control as "satellites."

This was naïve at best. Political democracy, as it was defined in Roosevelt's and Churchill's Atlantic Charter, was alien to Eastern European history and culture. Moreover, some Eastern European countries, particularly Poland, were historically enemies of Russia. If the Western Allies suppressed the memory that the Soviet Union had joined Nazi Germany in invading Poland in 1939, the Poles did not. Indeed, Polish hatred for the Russians was given new life in 1943, when the Germans released evidence that the Red Army had secretly massacred 5,000 captured Polish officers at Katyn in 1939.

Late in the war, with Russian troops advancing rapidly toward Warsaw, the Polish government-in-exile in London called for an uprising behind the German lines. At this point, Stalin abruptly halted the Russian advance, and the relieved Germans were able to butcher the poorly armed rebels. Red Army soldiers were as brutal toward Polish civilians as they were toward Germans. A democratic Poland could not be subordinate to Russia in the sense that Stalin demanded Poland be. A Poland friendly to Russia could not be democratically governed.

Roosevelt's confidence that he could solve this riddle on the basis of personal friendship with Stalin also required that he defy his own mortality, to which he should have been very sensitive in early 1945 as his health rapidly deteriorated. Nevertheless, he continued to treat diplomacy as a personal monopoly. When he died before the war was over, he left an inexperienced and uninformed Harry S Truman to make a settlement with Stalin.

Truman Draws a Line

Truman was not the sly manipulator Roosevelt had been. His virtues as a man and as president were his frankness, bluntness, and willingness to make and stick by a decision. On the subject of the Soviet Union he had made a decision decades earlier. Like most Americans he did not like the Russian Communists. Even before he first met Stalin at Potsdam, he summoned Soviet Ambassador V. M. Molotov to the White House and scolded him so harshly for several apparent Russian policy turns that Molotov exclaimed, "I have never been talked to like that in my life!"

By March 1946, it was obvious that the Russians were not going to permit free elections in Poland. While Truman remained cautious in his official pronouncements on the subject, he gave full approval to Winston Churchill's speech that month in Fulton, Missouri. An "iron curtain" had descended across Europe, the former prime minister said, and it was time for the Western democracies to call a halt to the expansion of atheistic Communism.

In September 1946, Truman moved more directly. He fired Secretary of Commerce Henry A. Wallace, the one member of his cabinet who called openly for accommodating the anxieties of the Soviet Union.

Containment and the Truman Doctrine

By 1947, Truman had a policy that went beyond "getting tough with the Russians." First in a series of confidential memoranda, and then in an article signed by "Mister X" in the influential journal *Foreign Affairs,* a Soviet expert in the State Department, George F. Kennan, argued that because of the ancient Russian compulsion to expand to the west and the virtually pathological Soviet fear of the Western nations, it would be impossible to come to a quick, amicable settlement with Stalin. American policy must therefore be to contain Russian expansionism by drawing clear limits as to where the United States would tolerate Russian domination—namely, those parts of Europe that already were under Russian control, and no more.

In Kennan's view, the Soviets would test American resolve, but very carefully. The Soviet Union did not want war any more than did the United States; it did want as much control as it could exercise without war. In time, probably a long time, when the Russians felt secure, it would become possible to deal diplomatically with them and establish a true peace. In the meantime, Cold War was preferable to bloodletting and the possibility of world destruction.

At the same time "containment policy" was being "leaked" to the public, Truman was presented with an opportunity to put it into practice. In early 1947, the Soviets seemed to be stepping up their support of Communist guerrillas in Greece and Communist parties in Italy and France. On March 12, Truman asked Congress to appropriate $400 million in military assistance to the pro-Western governments of Greece and Turkey. This principle of supporting anti-Communist regimes with massive aid, even when they were less than democratic themselves, came to be known as the Truman Doctrine.

The Marshall Plan

On June 5, 1947, Secretary of State George C. Marshall proposed a much more ambitious program, which came to be called the Marshall Plan. The United States would invest vast sums of money in the economic reconstruction of Europe. Not only would the former Western European Allies be invited to apply for American assistance, but defeated Germany (now divided into two zones), the Soviet Union, and the nations behind Churchill's iron curtain were also welcome to participate.

Marshall and Truman calculated that Russia and its satellite states would reject the offer. By late 1947, Stalin's troops were firmly in control of the countries of Eastern Europe, including the one nation there with a strong democratic tradition, Czechoslovakia. Already in June 1946, Stalin had made it clear that he would brook no Western interference in these countries. He turned down a proposal by elder statesman Bernard Baruch to outlaw nuclear weapons because the plan involved enforcement on the scene by the United Nations, which had been formed in 1945 under a charter that had evolved from the agreements of the various wartime Allied conferences.

The Americans had calculated correctly: the Soviets condemned the Marshall Plan. Massive American aid was pumped only into those countries where a political

---

AN UNSORDID ACT

Winston Churchill called the Marshall Plan "the most unsordid act in history." In a speech at Harvard University in 1947, George Marshall explained his intentions:

The truth of the matter is that Europe's requirements for the next 3 or 4 years of foreign food and other essential products—principally from America—are so much greater than her present ability to pay that she must have substantial additional help, or face economic, social, and political deterioration of a very grave character.

The remedy lies in breaking the vicious circle and restoring the confidence of the European people in the economic future of their own countries and of Europe as a whole. The manufacturer and the farmer throughout wide areas must be able and willing to exchange their products for currencies the continuing value of which is not open to question.

purpose could be served by overcoming the economic and social chaos in which Communism flourished.

Containment policy worked. Neither Greece and Turkey nor Italy and France fell to pro-Russian guerrillas or Communist parties. The policy received its most severe test in June 1948, when Stalin blockaded West Berlin, deep within Communist East Germany. Unable to provision the city of 2 million by overland routes, the United States could have given up Berlin or invaded East Germany. Instead, a massive airlift was organized. For a year, huge C-47's and C-54's flew in the necessities and a few of the luxuries that the West Berliners needed in order to hold out. By this action, the Truman administration made it clear that the United States did not want war, but neither would it tolerate further Soviet expansion.

The Soviets responded as Kennan had predicted. Instead of invading West Berlin or shooting down the airlift planes, they watched. In May 1949, having determined that the United States would not give in, the Soviets lifted the blockade.

NATO and Warsaw

By that time, the Cold War had entered a new phase. In April 1949, with Canada and nine European nations, the United States signed a treaty that established the North Atlantic Treaty Organization (NATO), the first peacetime military alliance in

LEARNING FROM PAST MISTAKES

In a number of ways, F.D.R. and Harry S Truman pointedly departed from American policy toward Europe after the First World War. In sponsoring the United Nations, the United States departed radically from the American boycott of the League of Nations. Unlike Woodrow Wilson, who named no prominent Republican to his peace commission at Versailles, thus contributing to American opposition to the League, Roosevelt made Republican Senator Arthur H. Vandenberg, a former isolationist, a member of the American delegation that wrote the Charter of the United Nations.

With the Marshall Plan, President Truman recognized the folly of the Coolidge administration of the 1920s in refusing to help Europe economically by arranging for a significant modification of the flow of reparations from Germany and debt payments by Britain and France.

A plane carrying supplies flies into West Berlin following a move by Joseph Stalin in June 1948 to block overland routes to that city from West Germany.

American history. The NATO countries promised to consider an attack against any of them as grounds for going to war together. The Soviets responded by writing the Warsaw Pact, an alliance of the nations of Eastern Europe. In September 1949, the Soviet Union exploded its first atomic bomb, and soon thereafter the United States perfected the hydrogen bomb, a much more destructive weapon. The nuclear-arms race was under way.

DOMESTIC POLITICS UNDER TRUMAN

All the while Harry S Truman was designing and effecting a decisive foreign policy, he was struggling to cope with postwar domestic problems. These were considerable: rapid inflation, a serious shortage of housing, and a series of bitter industrial disputes. At first Truman seemed to founder. Professional politicians and ordinary voters alike began to suspect his competence. In his predecessor's regal shadow, Truman cut a second-rate figure. Compared with dynamic Eleanor Roosevelt, who was even more active in liberal causes after her husband's death, Bess Truman was a plain, frumpy homebody. The deadly serious nuclear age seemed to have caught the United States without a leader up to its challenges.

The Republican Comeback of 1946

Capitalizing on American anxieties about Truman, the Republicans ran their congressional election campaign of 1946 on a simple but effective two-word slogan, "Had Enough?" Apparently the voters had. They elected Republican majorities in both houses of Congress for the first time since 1930. One freshman Democratic senator who bucked the landslide, J. William Fulbright of Arkansas, suggested that Truman resign in favor of a Republican president. The Republicans did not take this proposal seriously, but, positive that they would elect their nominee in 1948, they set out to prepare that unknown person's way by dismantling as many New Deal reforms as they could.

In the Taft-Hartley Labor-Management Relations Act of 1947, the Republican Congress emphasized the rights of employees not to join a union. The law struck down several New Deal guarantees of labor union power, although it hardly crippled the movement. In fact, its chief effect was to arouse organized labor, now more than 10 million strong, to rally behind a president who had not previously been considered particularly distinguished as a friend.

Truman's veto of Taft-Hartley was overridden. Some of his 80 additional vetos of anti-New Deal laws were

sustained. In the meantime, the aggressive folly of the Republicans showed him the way to survive. He became a crusading liberal. If enemies mocked his homey manners and common appearance, he would turn the tables on them by becoming the common man, denouncing the Republicans as stooges of the rich and privileged. Behind his own slogan, Fair Deal, he sent to Capitol Hill proposal after proposal that expanded social services. Among his programs was a national health-insurance plan such as most European nations had adopted.

Civil Rights

The Truman health plan failed, as did the president's demand that Congress act to end discrimination against American blacks. In 1947, the Presidential Committee on Civil Rights reported to Truman on racial discrimination in the United States, particularly as it related to employment practices and the continued condoning of the lynching of blacks in the South. Truman sent its far-reaching recommendations to Congress, where an alliance of complacent Republicans and southern Democrats killed them. Truman responded with an executive order that banned racial discrimination in the army and navy, in the civil service, and in companies that did business with the federal government.

Truman's civil-rights program was moderate. He did not touch "Jim Crow," the system of strict social segregation that provided for separate public facilities for the white and black races in the southern and border states, including Truman's home state of Missouri. But he went further than Roosevelt had dared, and his program was politically very shrewd. Hundreds of thousands of blacks had moved out of the South, where they were politically powerless, into big cities in northern and midwestern states with large electoral votes. For a Democratic president to continue to support segregation was to risk throwing these big states to the Republicans, especially because the leading contenders for the Republican presidential nomination, Robert Taft and New York governor Thomas E. Dewey, had been friendly to black aspirations.

THE 52-20 CLUB

Members of the 52-20 Club of 1945 and 1946 were demobilized soldiers and sailors who were allowed $20 a week for 52 weeks or until such time as they found a job. Although many were accused of avoiding work because of this payment, the average length of membership in the club was only three months.

Give 'Em Hell, Harry

By the spring of 1948, Truman's popularity was on the upswing. Americans were getting accustomed to, even fond of, the president's hard-hitting style. Nevertheless, no political expert gave Truman a chance to survive the presidential election in November. The Democrats had been in power longer than any party since the Virginia Dynasty of Jefferson, Madison, and Monroe. The inefficiency of many government bureaucracies was undeniable, and the rumors of corruption were persistent. To make things worse, the party split three ways. Henry A. Wallace led left-wing liberals into the newly formed Progressive party. He claimed to be the true heir of New Deal liberalism and insisted that there was no reason to abandon the nation's wartime friendship with the Soviet Union.

Democrats from the Deep South, angry at Truman's civil-rights reforms and an even stronger plank in the party platform written by the young mayor of Minneapolis, Hubert H. Humphrey, formed the States' Rights, or "Dixiecrat," party. They named Strom Thurmond of South Carolina as their candidate. Thurmond had no more chance of winning than did Wallace. His purpose was to take credit for denying Truman the election and thus impress on the Democratic party the necessity of sticking with their traditional support of racial segregation in the South.

Presented with what looked like a gift victory, the Republicans chose the safe Dewey over the controversial anti-New Deal conservative Robert A. Taft, and Dewey did just as the rules of electioneering said he should. As F.D.R. had done in 1932, he ran a low-key, noncommittal campaign. He would not jeopardize a sure win by saying anything that would alienate any group of voters.

PLANNING AHEAD

So confident were the Republicans that they were going to win the election of 1948 that the Republican Congress made a record appropriation for the inauguration festivities on January 20. The benefactor of the lavish parade, of course, was the Democratic president whom the Republicans despised, Harry S Truman.

Following his narrow victory in 1948, Harry Truman gleefully displays a newspaper that relied on early returns to predict his defeat to Republican presidential candidate Thomas Dewey.

MARGARET'S DAD

Harry Truman believed that politicians, and presidents most of all, should be thick-skinned when it came to criticism. "If you can't stand the heat," he said, "get out of the kitchen." However, he did not think this principle applied to concert singers, particularly when the singer was his daughter, Margaret. When her recital was panned by the music critic of the *Washington Post* ("She is flat a good deal of the time."), Truman wrote to the critic: "You sound like a frustrated old man who never made a success, an eight-ulcer man on a four-ulcer job, and all four ulcers working. I never met you, but if I do you'll need a new nose and a supporter below."

Truman, faced with certain defeat, had nothing to lose by speaking out. "Give 'em hell, Harry," a supporter shouted at a rally, and Truman did. During the summer of 1948, he called Congress into special session and a corps of assistants led by Clark Clifford sent bill after bill to the Republican Congress. As Congress voted down his proposals, Truman toured the country, blaming the nation's problems on the "no-good, do-nothing" Congress. Did Americans want four more years of that sort of thing under a lackluster Thomas E. Dewey?

On election night, the editors of the Republican Chicago *Tribune* glanced at the early returns, which favored Dewey, and put out editions that declared the New Yorker to be the new president. The next day, Harry Truman took great pleasure in posing for photographs while pointing to their headlines—for Dewey had not won. Truman narrowly squeaked out victories in almost all the large industrial states and the majority of farm states. His popular vote was under 50 percent, and he lost a few Gulf states to Thurmond. But he was president and by a whopping 303 to 189 electoral-vote margin.

CONTAINMENT IN ASIA

The Fair Deal did not fare so well as its author did. Like many presidents who had other things in mind, Truman found himself preoccupied with such serious problems abroad that domestic reforms seemed insignificant by comparison. Also like other presidents who had to become diplomats, Truman discovered that he was not chief executive in world affairs, but only one player in a game in which the rules defied the power at his disposal and even his own understanding of them.

In Asia, only the Philippines and Japan developed as firm American allies. Given independence in 1946, the Philippines remained beholden to American financial aid and responded with friendship. In Japan, a prosperous capitalist democracy was emerging as a consequence of the massive Marshall Plan-type assistance and enlightened military occupation under Douglas MacArthur. Understanding Japanese traditions better than he understood American, MacArthur established himself as a *shogun,* or a dictator who ruled while the emperor reigned. The *shogun* was a familiar figure in Japanese history, and the Japanese were comfortable with a new one.

In China, the Truman administration failed because the president ignored the advice of his best advisers and tried to adapt to the Asian mainland the policy of containment that was working in Europe. The trouble was that the Soviet expansionism responsible in part for the Cold War in Europe did not lie at the bottom of Communist successes in China. Nor were, at least until after the Second World War, the Chinese Communists necessarily opposed to an understanding with the United States. Kennan understood the difference between Europe and China and tried to point it out. Truman, the State Department, and the American public did not listen.

The Choice in China Policy

During and after the Second World War, two "governments" claimed to represent the will of the Chinese people: the Kuomintang, or Nationalist, regime of Chiang Kai-shek, and the powerful Communist party and military force behind Mao Zedong. Some Amer-

Zhou Enlai, Mao Zedong, and Chu Teh in Yenan province during the final days of the civil war in 1946.

icans who were familiar with China urged Washington not to oppose Mao but to come to terms with him. During the war, General Joseph W. Stilwell repeatedly warned Roosevelt that the people around Chiang were hopelessly corrupt and unpopular, while Mao commanded the loyalty of China's largest social class, the peasantry.

After the war, acting as a special envoy to China, George C. Marshall suggested that the Chinese Communists were not necessarily tools of the Soviets but could be encouraged to chart an independent course through cooperation and friendship. Mao was bent on revolutionary change at home, particularly in regard to land, which was in the hands of an elite allied to Chiang. Marshall, like many others who were familiar with the Nationalists, did not find Mao's program unattractive since the Kuomintang party included butchers of peasants and thieves who misappropriated American material aid for their own profit.

The "China Lobby"

Supporting Chiang's case was a "China Lobby" headed by his brilliant wife, Madame Chiang, who spent much of her time in the United States. This group drew support from conservative congressmen; influential church leaders such as the Catholic archbishop of New York, Francis Cardinal Spellman; and much of the press, most importantly Henry L. Luce, the publisher of *Time* magazine, and Clare Boothe Luce, a Republican congresswoman and eloquent speaker.

Through 1949, the China Lobby bombarded Americans with false information: most Chinese supported Chiang; Chiang was defeating Mao's forces on the battlefield; Mao was a Soviet stooge like the puppet leaders of Eastern Europe. So effective was the campaign that Americans were shocked at the end of 1949 when Chiang suddenly fled the mainland for the island province of Taiwan (then better known by its Japanese name of Formosa). They thought that Chiang had been winning the war. Instead of admitting that they had been wrong, at least in regard to the power of the Nationalists, the China Lobby insisted that Chiang had not been repudiated but merely betrayed by inadequate American support. They urged that he be "unleashed" for an assault on the mainland.

Truman and his new Secretary of State, Dean Acheson, knew better than to "unleash" Chiang Kai-shek. To have done so would have meant either humiliation when he was defeated or involvement in a war on the mainland of Asia, which every military strategist, from Douglas MacArthur on down, warned against. Whether Truman and Acheson ever rued the fact that they had ignored Stilwell's and Marshall's advice is not known. Whether American friendship would have

significantly changed the course of Chinese history under Mao Zedong is also beyond certain knowledge. What is known is that China as a foe was dangerous and unpredictable precisely because China was not, as Americans continued to believe, a Soviet satellite.

Containment Policy Falters

Truman and Acheson were applying the principle of containment to East Asia when events left them behind. No one, including themselves, was quite certain about where the United States would accept Communist control and where the line of containment was to be drawn. Japan was off limits, of course, but what of Taiwan, Quemoy and Matsu, three tiny islands off the coast of China that were also occupied by Chiang's Nationalists? And what of the Republic of Korea, set up by the United States in the southern half of the former Japanese colony of Chosen? Was the little country, bordered on the north by the thirty-eighth parallel (38° north latitude), to be protected like the nations of Western Europe?

Feeling the sting of the Nationalist defeat in China and the pressure of the China Lobby, Truman's last and best Secretary of State, Dean Acheson, was vague, and the president was indecisive. In a similar situation in 1914, the mischievousness of two weak countries started a war and that was what happened in 1950. The Communist government of North Korea and the government of Syngman Rhee in South Korea exchanged ever more serious threats. In June, responding to South Korean troop movements, the North Korean army swept across the thirty-eighth parallel and quickly drove Rhee's ROK (Republic of Korea) troops to the toe of the peninsula.

The Korean War

Truman already had stationed an American fleet in Korean waters, and he responded immediately and forcibly. Thanks to the calculated absence of the Soviet delegation to the United Nations, he was able to win the minimal vote necessary to make the UN the sponsor of a "police action" on the peninsula. With the United States providing almost all the "police," General MacArthur took command of the expedition.

In a daring maneuver that might have served as the capstone of a brilliant military career, MacArthur engineered an amphibious landing at Inchon, deep behind North Korean lines, cutting off and capturing 100,000 enemy troops. The Americans and ROKs then surged rapidly northward, crossing the thirty-eighth parallel in September 1950. By October 26, they had occupied virtually the whole peninsula. At one point, American soldiers stood on the banks of the Yalu River, which divides Korea from Chinese Manchuria.

The headiness of winning so quickly prevented Truman and the UN from reflecting on MacArthur's assurances that the Chinese would not intervene in the war. He was wrong. With its coal and iron deposits, Manchuria was vital to Mao's plans to industrialize China. Furthermore, the northeastern province had, twice before, been the avenue through which the Middle Kingdom had been invaded. Mao threw 200,000 "volunteers" at the Americans. By the end of 1950, these veterans, still hardened by the wars with Chiang, drove MacArthur back to a line that zigzagged across the thirty-eighth parallel. There, whether because the Chinese were willing to settle for a "draw" or because American troops found their footing and dug in, stalemate ensued. For two years, the Americans, ROKs, and token delegations of troops from other United Nations countries slugged it out to little effect with the North Koreans and Chinese. Both sides sustained high casualties for the sake of capturing forlorn hills and ridges that did not even have names, only numbers. Even after armistice talks began, first at Kaesong and then in a truce zone at Panmunjom, the war dragged on. The Chinese had won their goal, which was to protect their borders, and the Americans had ensured the independence of the Republic of Korea.

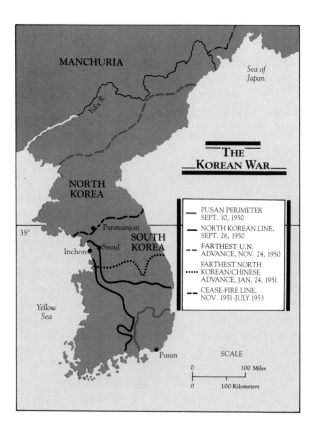

THE KOREAN WAR

—— PUSAN PERIMETER SEPT. 10, 1950
—— NORTH KOREAN LINE, SEPT. 26, 1950
---- FARTHEST U.N. ADVANCE, NOV. 24, 1950
•••• FARTHEST NORTH KOREAN/CHINESE ADVANCE, JAN. 24, 1951
---- CEASE-FIRE LINE, NOV. 1951-JULY 1953

In the days when the objects of war were clear and concrete, that was when wars were ended. But in the Cold War, with ideological rivalry taking on a religious significance on both sides, neither side knew quite what to do. Some days at Panmunjom, the negotiators simply sat at the table facing one another and saying nothing.

The Fall of MacArthur

With good reason, the American people were frustrated. Not five years after the Second World War, Korea put 5.7 million young men in uniform, killed 54,000, and wounded 100,000. Defense expenditures soared from $40 billion in 1950 to $71 billion in 1952. Truman and Acheson had said that the goal was containment, but having "contained," they were unable to conclude hostilities. What was wrong?

In the spring of 1951, General MacArthur offered an answer. Forgetting his own warning against a war with the Chinese in China, and perhaps bruised in the ego by the stalemate, he complained to reporters that the only reason he had not won the war was that Truman would not permit him to bomb the enemy's supply depots in Manchuria. In April, MacArthur went further; he sent a letter to Republican congressman Joseph W. Martin in which he wrote that "there is no substitute for victory" and directly assailed the commander-in-chief for accepting a stalemate.

This violation of civilian command of the army appalled Truman's military advisers, and on April 11, with their support, the president fired MacArthur. The American people, remembering the general's accomplishments in the Second World War and reckoning that he knew better how to fight than Truman did, cheered the old warrior upon his return to the United States. He was feted with ticker-tape parades in every city he visited, and addressed Congress in a broadcast speech that was listened to by more people than had tuned in to Truman's inaugural address in 1949.

MacArthur concluded his congressional appearance by quoting a line from an old barracks song, "old soldiers never die; they just fade away," but he had no intention of fading anywhere. Establishing residence and a kind of command headquarters at New York's Waldorf-Astoria Hotel, he continued to issue political proclamations. He wanted the Republican nomination for the presidency in 1952; then he would battle Truman's containment policy with his promises of victory in the Cold War.

But the good general was a poor politician. He had spent most of his life outside the country, and he was handicapped by a messianic vision of himself: the people would come to him. They did not. As the very clever politician Harry S Truman had calculated when

General Douglas MacArthur giving orders at the battle of Inchon, South Korea, in 1950.

he had dismissed the general, enthusiasm for Mac-Arthur faded within a few months. MacArthur was left to spend his final years in obscurity. In the meantime, the Korean War dragged on, chewing up lives like a machine.

THE ANXIETY YEARS

Historian Richard Hofstadter and others have pointed out that periodically in American history, during times of great stress, many people turn to "conspiracy theories" to account for their anxieties. The era of the Korean War was just such a time. Truman seemed to adopt a "no-win" policy; substantial numbers of Americans came to believe that the failure to achieve any security in the years following the Second World War was the result of widespread treason and subversion within the United States.

Twenty Years of Treason

The view that at Yalta, President Roosevelt had sold out Eastern Europe to Stalin was an early expression of this "paranoid streak," belief in a sinister conspiracy at work to destroy America from within. Then, in March 1947, President Truman inadvertently fueled

anxieties by ordering all government employees to sign loyalty oaths, statements that they did not belong to the Communist party or to other groups suspected of disloyalty. Eventually, 30 states followed this example, requiring an oath even of people who waxed the floors of state university basketball courts.

Truman also promoted the belief that there was treason in government by allowing his supporters to "Red bait" Henry Wallace in the 1948 presidential campaign. Wallace was an eccentric (he entertained all sorts of bizarre religious ideas), and he may well have been mistaken in his analysis of Soviet intentions. But he was no Communist party stooge, as many Democratic speechmakers accused him of being. Moreover, in exploiting fear of "the enemy within" in 1948, the Democrats created a political tactic that, in the end, could only work against them. If there were traitors in high places, the Democratic party was responsible, for, as of 1952, they had been running the country for twenty years.

Long before 1952, frustrated right-wing Republicans such as John Bricker of Ohio, William F. Knowland of California, and Karl Mundt of North Dakota raised the specter of "twenty years of treason." The two chief beneficiaries of the scare were Richard M. Nixon, a young first-term congressman from southern California, and Joseph McCarthy, the junior senator from Wisconsin.

The Case of Alger Hiss

Richard M. Nixon built the beginnings of his career on the ashes of the less illustrious but still distinguished career of a former New Dealer named Alger Hiss. A bright young Ivy Leaguer during the 1930s when he had gone to Washington to work in the New Deal Agriculture Department, Hiss had risen to be a middle-level aide to Roosevelt at the time of the Yalta Conference. He was aloof and fastidious in his manner, and was a militant liberal.

In 1948, a journalist named Whittaker Chambers, who confessed to having been a Communist during the 1930s, accused Hiss of having helped him funnel classified American documents to the Soviets. At first his testimony aroused little fuss. Chambers had a reputation for erratic behavior and making things up. From a legal point of view, there seemed scant reason to pursue the matter; all the acts of which Hiss was accused had transpired too long in the past to be prosecuted, and he was no longer in government service. It was Hiss who forced the issue to a reckoning. He indignantly swore under oath that everything Chambers said was false. Indeed, Hiss insisted, he did not even know Chambers.

To liberals, the well-spoken Hiss, with his exemplary record in public service, was obviously telling the truth. The seedy Chambers, with his background in Henry L. Luce's *Time* magazine, was a liar. But many ordinary Americans, especially working-class ethnics and citizens of western farming states, were not so sure. With his nasal aristocratic accent and expensive tailored clothing, Hiss represented the eastern Establishment, which they traditionally disliked, and the New Deal administrators, whom they were beginning to suspect.

Congressman Richard M. Nixon shared these feelings and, following a hunch, pursued the Hiss case when other Republicans lost interest. Nixon persuaded Chambers to produce microfilms that seemed to show that Hiss had indeed retyped classified documents for some reason, and, in cross-examination at congressional hearings, poked hole after hole in Hiss's defense.

Largely because of Nixon's efforts, Hiss was convicted of perjury. Additional thousands of Americans wondered how many other bright New Dealers were spies. More than one Republican pointed out that Hiss had been a friend of none other than the "no-win" Secretary of State Dean Acheson and that the men resembled each other in their manners and appearance. Indeed, Acheson's style grated even more harshly than Hiss's. He favored London-made tweeds and sported a bristling waxed moustache. Richard Nixon, whose social awkwardness and furtiveness at work might otherwise have obscured him for life, looked good by comparison.

Senator Joe McCarthy

Senator Joseph McCarthy of Wisconsin was another unlikely character to play a major role in the government of a nation. Not only awkward and furtive, he was a crude, bullying man who seems to have been less cruel than uncomprehending of what cruelty was. He was also facing an election in 1950 in which he seemed sure to be defeated, so lackluster had been his

Joseph McCarthy (right) and Joseph Welch at the Army-McCarthy hearings.

record in the Senate. Groping for an issue, he rejected friends' suggestions that he focus on the advantages the proposed St. Lawrence Seaway would bestow on Wisconsin, a Great Lakes state, and instead, almost by accident, discovered that anxiety about Communist subversion was his ticket to a kind of political stardom.

In 1950, McCarthy told a Republican audience at Wheeling, West Virginia, that he possessed a list of 205 Communists who were working in the State Department with the full knowledge of Secretary of State Acheson. In other words, Acheson himself, as well as other high-ranking government officials, actively abetted Communist subversion.

McCarthy had no such list, of course. Only two days later, he could not remember if he had said the names totaled 205 or 57. He never released a single name, and never fingered a single Communist in government. Because he was so reckless, interested in nothing but publicity, McCarthy probably was headed for a fall from the moment he stepped into the limelight. But the tumultuous response that met his use of the "big-lie" technique—making a complete falsehood so fabulous, and retelling it so often, that people believe that "it must be true"—was an alarming symptom of just how anxious American society had become.

When a few senators publicly denounced him, McCarthy showed just how sensitive was the nerve he had touched. Senator Millard Tydings of Maryland was a conservative whose family name gave him practically a proprietary interest in a Senate seat in that state. McCarthy threw his support behind Tydings's unknown opponent in 1950, forged a photograph showing Tydings shaking hands with American Communist party leader Earl Browder, and the senator went down to defeat.

McCarthyism

Following Tydings's defeat, civil libertarians outside politics worried because senators who opposed McCarthy's smear tactics were afraid to speak up lest they suffer the same fate. By 1952, McCarthy was so powerful that Republican presidential candidate Dwight D. Eisenhower, who worshiped his former commander George C. Marshall and detested the vulgar McCarthy, refrained from praising Marshall in Wisconsin because the former Secretary of State was one of McCarthy's "traitors."

In the meantime, liberal Democrats in Congress rushed to prove their loyalty by voting for dubious laws such as the McCarran Internal Security Act, which effectively outlawed the Communist party, by defining dozens of liberal lobby groups as "Communist fronts," and even by providing for the establishment of con-

centration camps in the event of a national emergency. The Supreme Court fell into line with its decision in *Dennis et al. v. United States* (1951).

By a vote of 6 to 2, the Court agreed that it was a crime to advocate the forcible overthrow of the government, a position that Communists were defined as holding by virtue of their membership in the party.

At the peak of McCarthy's power, only a very few opinion makers outside politics, such as cartoonist Herbert Block and television commentator Edward R. Murrow, and a few universities, including the University of Wisconsin in McCarthy's home state, refused to be intimidated by the senator's bullying. Not until 1954, however, did McCarthy's career come to an end. Failing to get preferential treatment for an intimate draftee friend of his chief aide, Roy Cohn, McCarthy accused the United States Army of being infiltrated by Communists. This recklessness emboldened the Senate to move against him. He was censured in December 1954 by a vote of 72 to 22. It was only the third time in American history that the nation's "most exclusive club" had turned on one of its own members, and McCarthy died in obscurity two years later.

Almost Everybody Likes Ike

Nixon and McCarthy built their careers on exploiting anxieties. To a certain extent, the personally dull leader of the congressional Republicans, Senator Robert A. Taft of Ohio, did the same. Taft encouraged his party's hell-raisers as a way of chipping at the Democrats. But the American people turned to no such political mover and shaker to take them through the 1950s. Instead, they chose a man with no political background, whose strength was a warm personality and whose talent was the ability to smooth over conflict.

The name of General Dwight David Eisenhower was mentioned as a presidential possibility as early as 1948,

FLYING SAUCER SCARE

In 1947, a commercial pilot over the state of Washington sighted a cluster of "saucer-like things" and reported them to the federal government. By 1950, 600 Americans a year were seeing flying saucers. No one ever proved if the sightings were frauds, the fruit of mass hysteria, evidence of visitors from outer space, or of some new top-secret air force plane. The movie industry, looking for a kind of film with which to combat television, had no trouble making a choice. The early 1950s were years of dozens of movies about creatures—usually, but not always, bent on destruction—who visited earth.

H O W   T H E Y   L I V E D

AWAKE!

*Jehovah's Witnesses from all over the world meet in
Yankee Stadium in 1953.*

During the Truman years, millions of Americans were introduced to the Jehovah's Witnesses for the first time. Rather than preaching from streetcorner soapboxes, as the sects they seemed to resemble did, the Witnesses showed up on the thresholds of grand homes, middle-class tract houses, and declining urban apartments and row houses alike. Always neatly dressed, always in pairs, often racially mixed, they clutched briefcases or handbags stuffed with their books, tracts, and copies of two monthly magazines, *The Watchtower* and *Awake!*. The Witnesses were never jolly nor backslapping in one well-known American evangelical tradition. Their manner was solemn, grim, thin-lipped. Their ice-breaking question was blunt and cheerless: did the householder (usually a housewife during the daytime hours) think that all was well with the world?

The Second World War left in its wake the lingering smell of the extermination camps and Hiroshima, the shock of the lowering of the Iron Curtain and the Communist triumph in China, news of cold war spies and the cries of subversion in Washington. In the vague but general sense that the war had created a more threatening world than it destroyed, the Jehovah's Witnesses won many invitations to come in and talk. The sect that was 70 years old in 1949, but still tiny, began to grow, and the numbers of its fulltime walkers of streets and ringers of doorbells (24,000 in 1984) became more conspicuous. In 1978, the Witnesses numbered more than 600,000 in the United States, two million worldwide. Their Watchtower Tract Society was one of the largest publishing houses in the world. *Awake!* alone had a circulation of eight million in 34 languages.

The Witnesses took shape during the 1870s in Allegheny City, Pennsylvania, in the midst of the iron and steel belt that epitomized industrial progress to some, a hell of soot, smoke, sparkling flame, and social insecurity to others. The founder, Charles Taze Russell, was a Presbyterian who, like many troubled believers before him, found grievous flaws in the traditional faiths, and styled himself "God's Mouthpiece."

At first, the Witnesses seemed like just another variant on the fundamentalist, millenarian, catastrophe-minded groups that have sprung up in times of trying social ferment. They taught that the Bible was "inspired and historically acccurate," a single, reassuring absolute in a world of whirling flux and instability. In 1987, the American Witnesses' street ministers were probably nimbler in finding the apt Biblical citation for an occasion than the deans and doyennes of America's most prestigious divinity schools.

Like the Millerites of the 1840s, the Witnesses said that "the end of the world" was nigh. In 1876, Russell predicted that Armageddon—the final battle between good and evil—would occur in 1914. When the First World War, with its unprecedented horrors, erupted in that year, Witness membership jumped. Russell's successor named 1918, the end of the Great War. Others have set the date at 1925, 1941, 1975, and 1984. In times of anxiety like the late 1940s and early 1950s, the perception that the state of the world incontrovertibly precludes an indefinite future is a common historical response, particularly by those whom society has rejected, despised, or merely left behind. Like other fundamentalist groups, the Witnesses were most successful among the poor, downtrodden, and ignorant.

However, the Witnesses were unique fundamentalists and millenarians in several ways. Hardly inclined to be "right-wingers" preaching antisemitism and antiblack racism, the Witnesses totally rejected racial discrimination of any kind. As a consequence, they have been immensely successful proselytizers among American blacks.

Hardly uncriticial super-patriots, the Witnesses considered all governments—America's included—as evil. Their meeting houses, called "Kingdom Halls," indicate that they consider themselves subjects of God's (Jehovah's) realm. They merely submit to those powers of the state that do not conflict with Jehovah's law. They do not participate in government or politics.

As a result of their refusal to serve in the armed forces, thousands of Witnesses were imprisoned during World War II. They puzzled authorities by their passivity and self-enforced order in prison, and also by their disdain for other political and conscientious objectors to military service. In fact, the Witnesses considered their fellow prisoners as misguided "instruments of satan," too. The Witnesses were not pacifists in any but the functional sense of the word. They looked forward with zest to Armageddon when they will themselves take up arms for Jehovah and exterminate those who have rejected their message and witness.

The Jehovah's Witnesses are also peculiar in that they do not believe in hell. When Jehovah's reign begins, the "instruments of satan" will simply cease to exist. A material universe will be ruled by 144,000 Witnesses who alone, with Jesus, will reside in heaven.

In their vision of the post-Armageddon earth, the importance of the Truman years in the development of the organization can be seen in a most curious way. Pictorial depictions of Jehovah's kingdom in *Awake!* and *Watchtower* show lions laying down with lambs (the ancient biblical image), but the restored Eden is a broad, weedless lawn mowed as closely as a golfing green surrounding a sprawling "ranch-type" house such as was the beau-ideal, the "good life," for millions of Americans in the late 1940s and early 1950s. Smiling, loving, neatly and conventionally dressed and barbered suburbanites (no wings and halos), albeit of all races, populate this paradise. Often, guests are arriving for a backyard barbecue.

The Witnesses' paradise bears a close resemblance to the consumer paradise that advertisers of automobiles, television sets, furniture, and carpets pictured during the postwar years; even the style of the artwork is similar. Such aspirations in a time of increasing affluance allowed most Americans to cope with the anxieties of the Truman Era. To the Witnesses, such things represented the post-millenial universe.

In the late 1980s, when much of society has questioned the suburban ideal of the 1950s, the Witnesses are still loyal to it, perhaps because so few of them have achieved it. The organization also shows signs of evolving into a large, wealthy, well-established, and increasingly bureaucratized body headquartered in Brooklyn, New York. Its chief official, William Van De Wall, said in 1984 that "we do not know the day or the hour, but we do feel that we are in the time of the end. We are living in the general time period." It was such an accommodation—a dodging of specific predictions that lead to crises—that in the nineteenth century transformed disreputable Millerites into acceptable Seventh Day Adventists.

when Truman told Ike that if he would accept the Democratic nomination, Truman would gladly step aside. Eisenhower was not interested. (He turned down the Republicans, too.) He was a career military man who, unlike MacArthur, believed that soldiers should stay out of politics. It is not certain that Eisenhower ever voted before 1948, and he identified with neither party. Instead, he accepted the presidency of Columbia University, found the job of shepherding academics intolerable, and took a leave of absence to command NATO troops in Europe.

After Truman's reelection and the Korean stalemate, Ike became increasingly distressed by the revelations of petty corruption among Truman aides, security problems, and the administration's apparent inability to end the Korean War. Moreover, Eisenhower naturally drifted into close professional and personal association with the wealthy eastern businessmen who dominated the moderate wing of the Republican party and placed no ideology above the goal of defeating the Democrats in a national election. They showered Ike with gifts and financial advice. As an administrator himself, something of a businessman in uniform, Eisenhower found it easy to absorb their political attitudes.

Unlike Taft and his conservative midwestern backers, Eisenhower and the moderate wing of the Repub-

lican party felt no compulsion to return government to its state in the days before F.D.R. They had come to terms with the America that Franklin D. Roosevelt had made. What disturbed them was corruption in government and particularly the excessive government expenditures and waste that led to high taxes. What impressed them most was that Eisenhower would almost certainly defeat any Democrat. His chief Republican rival, Senator Taft, might not.

Many conservative Republicans also supported Eisenhower over Taft. They were more interested in their party's victory than in honoring their veteran leader. Much as they admired Taft, they agreed with the Eisenhower moderates that the senator's uncompromising and frequently old-fashioned conservative statements would lose the votes of people who had benefited from the New Deal, but who were otherwise weary of the long Democratic era. Eisenhower's lack of a political record was an advantage. Even more attractive, he was immensely popular as a person. Almost everybody liked him ("I Like Ike" became his campaign slogan) because of his homey lack of pretension, his charming boyish smile, and his superb self-control that exuded both confidence and authority. He did not excite people; he reassured them. That was precisely what the nation craved in 1952, and the Republicans wanted to win an election.

Newly elected president Dwight D. Eisenhower and Vice President Richard Nixon wave to their supporters on election night, 1952.

The Election of 1952

Eisenhower's Democratic opponent was the governor of Illinois, Adlai E. Stevenson. He was a liberal, but had taken no part in the increasingly unpopular Truman government. For a few weeks in the summer of 1952, it appeared as though Stevenson were catching up to Eisenhower. He was a personable, witty, and eloquent speaker, while Eisenhower, who functioned best in small groups, was bumbling on the podium.

But Stevenson labored under too many handicaps, and Eisenhower's shrewd campaign managers made the most of them. Stevenson was, after all, a Democrat and had to defend the Truman record or lose the president's support. Moreover, the Eisenhower forces turned Stevenson's intelligence and speaking skills against him. Ike and his supporters pointed out that "eggheads," or intellectuals, were responsible for "the mess in Washington." Finally, in October, Eisenhower ensured his victory by promising a way out of the Korean mess: if he were elected, he would "go to Korea" and end the now aimless war.

Stevenson won nine southern states. Although a supporter of civil rights for blacks, he brought the Dixiecrats back into the Democratic party by naming an Alabama segregationist, John Sparkman, as his running mate. Otherwise, Eisenhower swept the nation, winning 55 percent of the popular vote and 442 electoral votes to Stevenson's 89. In December, he kept his promise. Eisenhower donned military gear, and was filmed talking and sipping coffee with soldiers in Korea. By recognizing that an all-out conventional offensive was foolish and by threatening to use the atomic bomb, he brought the hostilities to a close in July 1953. Eisenhower had not actually modified the concept of fighting a limited war that had been supported by Truman and Acheson. The Korean War ended with the acceptance of stalemate and satisfaction with containment rather than with the victory that MacArthur had demanded. With the termination of the war and the death in March 1953 of Soviet dictator Joseph Stalin, the 1950s promised to be a decade of normalcy.

For Further Reading

Overviews and Classics

James Gilbert, *Another Chance: America Since 1945* (1984)
Eric Goldman, *The Crucial Decade and After* (1961)
Godfrey Hodgson, *America in Our Time: From World War II to Nixon* (1976)
William E. Leuchtenburg, *A Troubled Feast: American Society Since 1945* (1979)

Valuable Special Studies

Carl Berger, *The Korea Knot: A Military-Political History* (1957)
William C. Berman, *The Politics of Civil Rights in the Truman Administration* (1970)
David Carter, *The Great Fear: The Anti-Communist Purge Under Truman and Eisenhower* (1978)
Bert Cochran, *Truman and the Crisis Presidency* (1973)
W. R. Deane, *The Strange Alliance* (1947)
Herbert Feis, *Between War and Peace: The Potsdam Conference* (1960)
———, *From Trust to Terror: The Onset of the Cold War, 1945–1950* (1970)
John L. Gaddis, *The United States and the Origins of the Cold War, 1941–1947* (1972)
Martin Gilbert, *Auschwitz and the Allies* (1981)
Norman A. Graebner, *The Age of Global Power: The United States Since 1938* (1979)
Susan Hartmann, *Truman and the Eightieth Congress* (1971)
John Hersey, *Hiroshima* (1946)
Gabriel Kolko, *The Limits of Power: The World and United States Foreign Policy, 1945–1954* (1972)
Walter LaFeber, *America, Russia, and the Cold War, 1945–1980* (1981)
Norman D. Markowitz, *Rise and Fall of the People's Century: Henry A. Wallace and American Liberalism, 1941–1948* (1974)
G. D. Paige, *The Korean Decision* (1968)
Thomas G. Paterson, *Cold War Critics: Alternatives to American Foreign Policy in the Truman Years* (1972)
David Rees, *Korea: The Limited War* (1964)
Walter and Miriam Schneir, *Invitation to an Inquest* (1972)
J. L. Snell, *Illusion and Necessity: The Diplomacy of Global War* (1963)
John W. Spanier, *The Truman-MacArthur Controversy* (1965)
Allen Weinstein, *Perjury! The Hiss-Chambers Conflict* (1978)
William A. Williams, *The Tragedy of American Diplomacy* (1962)
Allen Yarnell, *Democrats and Progressives: The 1948 Election as a Test of Postwar Liberalism* (1974)

Biographies and Autobiographies

R. F. Haynes, *The Awesome Power: Harry S Truman as Commander in Chief* (1973)
William Manchester, *American Caesar: Douglas MacArthur, 1880–1960* (1978)
Merle Miller, *Plain Speaking: An Oral Biography of Harry S Truman* (1974)
James T. Paterson, *Mr. Republican: A Biography of Robert A. Taft* (1975)
Thomas C. Reeves, *The Life and Times of Joe McCarthy* (1982)
Richard Rovere, *Senator Joe McCarthy* (1959)
Richard N. Smith, *Thomas Dewey and His Times* (1982)
Harry S Truman, *Memoirs* (1955–56)
Margaret Truman, *Harry S Truman* (1973)

47

Eisenhower Country
Life in the 1950s

The voters of 1952 wanted no upheaval. They wanted a change of pace. Almost all Americans accepted the necessity of the Cold War with Communism, but they wanted an end to the stalemate in Korea. Most Americans approved of the reforms that the Roosevelt and Truman administrations had carried out; they did not want to return to the days of Coolidge and Hoover. But after a generation of Democratic party government, they were ready for new faces in Washington.

Most of all, Americans wanted to cool off. They were weary of excitement, the intense moral demands of reform and war. There is a sense of 1920 about the election of 1952, people opting for a reassuring America in which they could enjoy the rewards of living in the world's richest nation.

The suburban communities that sprung up across the United States during the 1950s were characterized by rows of nearly identical single-family houses.

LEADERSHIP

Reassurance is what Dwight D. Eisenhower gave them. The grinning, amiable Ike was the perfect leader for the times. He ended the Korean War and kept the peace through two full terms in office. He replaced the jaded political pros, earnest intellectuals, and reform-minded liberals of the Democratic years with administrators like himself, and with the wealthy businessmen who had become his friends.

They were neither colorful nor exciting. "Eight millionaires and a plumber," a scornful Democrat sniffed about Eisenhower's cabinet, and Secretary of Labor Martin Durkin, the leader of the AFL plumbers union, resigned within a year of his appointment to be replaced by another rich businessman. When Congress created the cabinet-level Department of Health, Education, and Welfare, Eisenhower's choice to head it was not a social worker with a cause to serve, but Oveta Culp Hobby, head of the Women's Army Corps during the Second World War, a military bureaucrat like himself.

Ike's Style and Its Critics

Eisenhower's style was calculated to soothe. Rather than leaping into political cat fights with claws flashing, which had been Truman's way, Ike sidled away from disputes and left the shouting to subordinates. His special assistant, Sherman Adams of New Hampshire, screened every person who applied to see the president. Adams turned away anyone who might involve Ike in a controversy, or trick him into making an embarrassing statement, which Eisenhower was inclined to do. Adams also studied every document that crossed the president's desk, weeding out those he thought trivial and summarizing the rest. Eisenhower disliked reading more than a page or so on any subject, a "brief" such as he had dealt with in the army.

Dwight D. Eisenhower, "Ike," personified America in the 1950s.

Critics claimed that Adams was more powerful than an appointed official should be. They said that he made many presidential-level decisions himself, and he probably did. But there was never any doubt that the thin-lipped New Englander had Eisenhower's complete confidence. In 1958, when it was learned that Adams had rigged some government decisions in favor of a long-time friend, businessman Bernard Goldfine, and he was forced to resign his post, Eisenhower bitterly resented the loss of his right-hand man.

The president also delegated considerable power to the members of his cabinet. They were expected to study the details of issues, report to him, and, if they disagreed among themselves, debate the question. Ike, the commander with ultimate responsibility, listened and handed down the decision. Whenever possible, he preferred compromise to backing one adviser against another. That was how he had worked during the Second World War.

Liberal Democrats and intellectuals, outsiders in Washington during the 1950s, poked fun at Eisenhower's losing battle with the English language. Not a reflective man and never comfortable before a large audience, Eisenhower lapsed into gobbledygook under pressure or simply because he was preoccupied, yearning for the early retirement that high-ranking military officers assume they will enjoy. Eisenhower's apparent lethargy also aroused critics. The nation was drifting, they said, while Ike relaxed on his gentleman's farm on the battlefield at Gettysburg, and took too many vacations in climes where the golf courses were green and the clubhouses air-conditioned.

The majority of Americans did not object to a president who enjoyed himself. They were enjoying themselves too, and were delighted with the easygoing pace at the White House. In 1956, when Ike ran for reelection against Adlai Stevenson, a year after suffering a serious heart attack and just a few months after undergoing major abdominal surgery, the voters reelected him by an even larger margin than in 1952. Better Ike in questionable health than Stevenson, who was inculcated with New Deal ideas about reform and might unsettle a tranquil decade.

We're in the Money

For a majority of Americans, the 1950s were good times, an age of unprecedented prosperity. There had not been a shift in the distribution of wealth. The poor remained about as numerous as they had been. The lowest-paid and unpaid 20 percent of the population earned the same 3 to 4 percent of the national income that they had earned during the 1920s. The very rich held on to their big slice of the economic pie: the wealthiest 20 percent of the population continued to enjoy 44 to 45 percent of the national income. Proportionately, therefore, the middle 60 percent of the population were no better off than before.

What made the difference was the size of the pie from which all were taking their allotted slices. America was vastly richer as a result of the extraordinary economic growth of the Second World War decade. Thanks to New Deal tax reforms and the powerful labor unions that protected one worker in three and indirectly helping another third, Americans in the middle found themselves with a great deal of "discretionary income," money that was not needed to provide the immediate necessities of life. In 1950, discretionary income totaled $100 billion compared with $40 billion in 1940. This sum increased steadily throughout the decade.

Traditional values of thrift and frugality dictated that such extra money be saved or invested. However, with a generation of daily denial behind them—the hard times of the Great Depression and the sacrifices demanded by the Second World War—newly affluent Americans itched to spend their riches on goods and services that made life more comfortable, varied, and stimulating. A host of new consumer-oriented industries cropped up to urge them on.

Enjoy Yourself

"Enjoy yourself," a popular song went. "It's later than you think." Americans did. They lavished their extra money on a cornucopia of goods and services—some trivial, some momentous in their cultural consequences, and most designed to amuse and entertain people in their spare time. The middle classes upgraded their diets, eating more meat and vegetables and fewer of the bulk starchy foods (bread and potatoes) that had sustained their parents. Mass-produced convenience food such as frozen vegetables became staples of middle-class diet. They could be cooked in five or ten minutes, freeing people to enjoy additional leisure time.

Fashion in dress, buying clothes in order to be "in style," became a diversion in which tens of millions rather than just a handful of very rich people could indulge. Mass-producers of clothing imitated the creations of Paris couturiers with affordable department-store versions of "the latest," and the designers encouraged the impulse to be a step ahead of neighbors by changing styles annually. More people could identify Christian Dior (a French clothing designer) than the plumber in Eisenhower's cabinet.

The 1950s were a time of fads, frivolous behavior in which people participated for no better reason than they could afford to do so and others already were. In late 1954, a Walt Disney television program about the nineteenth-century frontiersman and politician Davy Crockett inspired a mania for coonskin caps (usually made from rabbit or synthetic fur), lunch boxes decorated with pictures of Davy shooting bears, and plastic "long rifles" and bowie knives reasonably safe for use in backyard Alamos. Virtually any homely object with the magic name printed on it became a best seller. Within six months, Americans spend more than $100 million in memory of the Tennessee adventurer and Whig who never quite made it big himself.

In 1958, a toy manufacturer brought out a plastic version of an Australian exercise device, a hoop that was twirled about the hips through hulalike gyrations. Almost overnight, 30 million "hula hoops" were sold for $1.98 (and, after the fad declined, for as little as 50 cents).

To some extent, the numerous manias of the 1950s were instigated and promoted by the advertising industry. For example, a chemical compound, chlorophyll, became the rage of the early 1950s when manufacturers of more than 90 products, ranging from chewing gum through soap and dog food, said that the organic green chemical improved the odor of the breath and body of those who ate or chewed it, shampooed or bathed in it. Americans responded by spending $135 million on chlorophyll products. The boom may have busted when the American Medical Association pointed out that goats, notoriously hard on the nose, consumed chlorophyll all day, every day. More likely, like all fads, chlorophyll simply ran its course.

Other fads profited no one but the newspapers and magazines that reported them. College students competed to see how many of them could squeeze into a telephone booth or a minuscule Volkswagen automobile, challenging others to top their record. Such behavior worried social critics. They concluded that inane faddism revealed the emptiness of lives based on material consumption: people defined themselves in terms of what they could buy. Others were distressed by the conformism of which fads were only the most bizarre example. The American people, it seemed, would do anything and think anything that they were told to do and think, or that others were doing and thinking. But they were afraid of the eccentric, the unpopular, and the adventurous.

The Tube

The most significant new consumer bauble of the 1950s, which became one of the greatest forces for conformism, was the home television receiver. Developed in workable form as early as 1927, "radio with a picture" remained a toy of electronics hobbyists and the very wealthy until after the Second World War.

Children born in the late 1940s and 1950s were the first generation of Americans to grow up with television.

In 1946, there were only 8,000 privately owned receivers in the United States, about one for every 18,000 people.

Then, gambling that Americans were ready to spend their extra money on a new kind of entertainment, the radio networks plunged into television, making more extensive programming available. By 1950, almost 4 million sets had been sold, one for every 32 people in the country. By 1960, the skeletons of obsolete small-screen receivers were conspicuous in dumps even in rural states. By 1970, more American households were equipped with a television set than had refrigerators, bathtubs, or indoor toilets. Never in history did a whole society fall so suddenly and hopelessly in love with a device.

The social and cultural consequences of America's marriage to "the tube" are still not fully appreciated. In the short run, television seemed to destroy other kinds of popular entertainment such as the movies, social dancing, and radio. Hollywood studios that specialized in churning out low-budget films for neighborhood theaters went bankrupt when empty neighborhood theaters closed their doors and decayed. However, prestigious movie companies such as Metro-Goldwyn-Mayer, Columbia Pictures, and Warner Brothers survived and prospered by concentrating on expensive, grandiose epics that could not be duplicated on the small black-and-white home screen; by experimenting with themes that were thought unsuitable for showing in homes; and, in the 1960s, by producing shows for home television.

The "big bands" that had toured the country playing for local dances since the 1930s broke up when deserted dance halls closed. But the recorded music industry survived in the age of television by emphasizing individual ballad singers, such as Perry Como, Jo Stafford, Patti Page, and Frankie Laine, who promoted sales of their recordings on television. Radio stations

TELEVISION AND THE MOVIES

In 1946, 82 million Americans went to the movies each week. Ten years later, only about half that many did. The others were at home watching television.

adapted to the big change by scrapping the dramatic and comedy shows that television could do with pictures and offering instead a format of music, news, and weather aimed at people who were driving their cars or working and could not, during those hours, watch television.

Curiously, the "one-eyed monster" did not much change the reading habits of older Americans. Americans were soon staring into the flickering blue light for three hours a day. However, the time they devoted to magazines and newspapers declined very little, and purchases of books, particularly the cheap paperback editions, rose 53 percent over what they had been during the 1940s.

Social Consequences of Television

What older Americans cut out in order to watch television was socializing with one another. Instead of chatting with neighbors or with other members of their families, Americans watched "Mr. Television," Milton Berle, a burlesque comic who became a national sensation; situation comedies about white middle-class families supposedly like themselves; and particularly Westerns. The networks tried out 40 dramas set in the Wild West as Americans liked to imagine it. One of the first, "Gunsmoke," ran through 635 half-hour episodes; it was estimated that one-quarter of the world's population saw at least one program in which Marshall Matt Dillon made Dodge City, Kansas, safe for decent law-abiding citizens. A less popular show, "Death Valley Days," revived the career of Ronald Reagan, and set him off on a trail that led to the White House.

Even movies and dances, social critics pointed out, had gotten people out of the house and talking to one another. Now they seemed to barricade themselves in, hushing up or resenting all interruptions. The frozen-food industry invented the "TV dinner," a complete meal that could be put in and taken out of the oven during commercials or station breaks and eaten in silence in front of the set on a "TV table," a metal tray on folding legs, one for each member of the nuclear family, perhaps an extra one or two for when grandparents, equally agog, paid a visit.

Fears for the Future

Early hopes for the educational potential of the new communications medium were dashed when people expressed a preference for frothy entertainment that demanded nothing but that a person "be there." More worrisome to educators, was the passive enthusiasm with which children born in the television age were enslaved to the tube. Networks and local stations filled late-afternoon hours and much of Saturday and Sunday mornings with programs that were aimed at children (sponsored by toymakers and manufacturers of breakfast cereals and sweets). If adults who had grown up before the advent of television continued to read, children did not. In 1955, a book by Rudolf Fleisch called *Why Johnny Can't Read* presented Americans with disturbing evidence that they were raising a generation of functional illiterates.

Nevertheless, and regardless of class, race, occupation, or region, Americans took television to their hearts. For good or ill, they were exposed at the same moment to the same entertainment, commercials, and even speech patterns. National businesses discovered that they could compete with local merchants thanks to the hypnotic influence of television advertising.

During the 1960s, American towns began to look alike with the growth of chain supermarkets and national franchise companies that drove family-owned businesses into bankruptcy.

Because the network and even local news programs preferred announcers who spoke "standard American English," regional variations in speech declined. City people and country people, who had been sharply divided by hostile world views in the previous generation, came to look, speak, and think alike. However, neither country folk nor city folk set the cultural tone of the age of Eisenhower. The people who did were pioneers of a new kind of American community, the middle-class suburb.

TELEVISION IN AMERICA

	Number of TV Households	Percentage of American Homes with TV
1945	5,000	—
1950	3,880,000	9.0
1955	30,700,000	64.5
1960	45,750,000	87.1
1970	59,550,000	95.2
1978	72,900,000	98.0

SUBURBIA AND ITS VALUES

The essence of the good life, to Americans of the 1950s, was to escape from the cities (and the country)

"MAD MAN" MUNTZ

Just as has happened when other completely new consumer goods attracted the fancy of Americans—automobiles, radio receivers, miniaturized calculators, computers—the early television industry was a competitive free-for-all, with dozens of manufacturers hoping to establish themselves as giants of the industry. One of the most intriguing companies was Muntz TV, which promoted its inexpensive sets as if the item were a dubious gadget being hawked at a county fair. "Mad Man" Muntz said that he got his name—he said it on TV as well as on billboards and in magazine advertisements—because he wanted to give his sets away but his wife wouldn't let him. "She says I'm crazy." Also, as in the cases of radios, calculators, computers, the era of all-out competition passed. After the "shakeout," a comparatively few TV set manufacturers remained, mostly old, large electronics makers. In their turn they were displaced by Japanese imports in the 1970s.

and set up housekeeping in single-home dwellings in the suburbs. In part, this massive movement of population in the late 1940s and 1950s was an expression of an antiurban bias that dates back to the nation's rural beginnings. As a people, Americans never have been quite comfortable with city life.

Flight from the Cities

In part, young couples of the postwar period had little choice as to where they would live. The Second World War had forced millions of them to delay marrying and starting a family for up to four years. In 1945 and 1946, they rushed into marriage, childbearing, and searching for a place to live. But because of the stagnation of domestic construction during the depression and the war, when young couples looked for housing in the cities, they found impossibly high rents and real-estate prices. To demolish old neighborhoods as a first step in construction meant temporarily worsening an already critical housing shortage. The solution was the rapid construction of whole new "tracts" or "developments" on the outskirts of cities, far enough from the centers that the price of land was reasonable, but close enough that breadwinners could get to their jobs. Of the 1 million housing starts in 1946 and the 2 million in 1950 (compared with 142,000 in 1944), the vast majority was in the suburbs.

The first of the great suburban developments was Levittown, New York, the brainchild of a family company that adapted the assembly line to home building. In order to keep selling prices low, the Levitt brothers used cheap materials and only a few different blue-

prints. The houses of suburbia were identical, constructed all at once and very quickly. Armies of workers swarmed over the tract, grading thousands of acres at a sweep, and laying out miles of gently curving streets within a few days. Practically before they were done, battalions of men laid down water, gas, sewer, and electrical lines, while teams of carpenters erected hundreds of simple, identical shells.

Then came waves of roofers, plumbers, electricians, carpet layers, painters, decorators, and other craftsmen, each finishing their specialized task on a given house within hours or even minutes. Buyers were so anxious to move in that they were happy to take care of the cleaning up and landscaping. Within four years, Levittown, New York, was transformed from a potato farm into a city of 17,000 homes. On the outskirts of most large cities, developers who imitated the Levitts worked similar miracles of construction. The population of suburbs, never more than a small fraction of the whole, soared. By 1960, as many Americans lived in suburbs as in large cities.

Conformists . . . ?

No sooner did suburbia take shape than it attracted social and cultural criticism. Novelists and sociologists pointed out that the population of the new communities was distressingly homogeneous: 95 percent white, young (20 to 35 years old), married couples with infant children who made roughly the same income from similar skilled and white-collar jobs.

Not only did the flight from the center cities leave urban centers to the elderly, the poor, and the racial minorities—an implausible tax base—but it segregated the suburbanites too, cutting them off from interaction with other ages, classes, and races of people. Homogeneous communities were narrow-minded communities, critics said; suburbia's values were timid, bland, and superficial.

In politics, people whose comforts and security were made possible by New Deal reforms were afraid to experiment. The suburbanites were staunch supporters of Eisenhower calm. They swelled the membership lists of churches and synagogues, but insisted on easy, undisturbing beliefs. Rabbi Joshua Liebman, Catholic Bishop Fulton J. Sheen, and the Reverend Norman Vincent Peale told the people of the three major faiths that the purpose of religion was to make them feel good: they, and no supreme being or eternal values, were at the center of the universe. The Reverend Billy Graham established himself as the country's leading revivalist by shunning the fire and brimstone of earlier evangelists and promoting his transparent blue eyes, wavy hair, and beautiful smile. A survey of Christians showed that while 80 percent believed that the Bible

With their move to suburbia, Americans needed automobiles to commute to their jobs in the city. Cars were also a means to display status.

was the revealed word of God, only 35 percent could name the authors of the four gospels and 50 percent could not name one. Among Jews, highly secular and social Reform Judaism displaced Conservative Judaism. Outside of the insular urban communities of Jews who clung to Polish and Russian pasts, Orthodox synagogues were hard to find.

Suburban life was isolated and fragmented, in part because of television, in part because the new communities were built with little thought for social services—schools, shops, parks, professional offices. When such traditional social centers were constructed, they were miles from residences; thus suburbanites had to drive some distance even to buy a quart of milk. As a result, the suburban single-family dwelling became a kind of fortress that residents left only to hop into a car and drive somewhere else and back again. The supermarkets encouraged weekly rather than daily shopping expeditions, thus eliminating another traditional occasion of social life.

. . . Or Social Pioneers?

Such criticisms made little impression on the people at whom they were aimed. Suburbanites wanted homes they could afford, and they found the physical roominess of life outside the cities well worth the social isolation and cultural blandness. If the houses were cheaply constructed and identical, they were far better than no houses. Moreover, the new suburbanites, thrown into brand new towns with no roots and traditions, were great creators of institutions. Lacking established social services and governments, they formed an intricate network of voluntary associations that were entirely supported by private funds and energies. There were the churches and synagogues built from scratch, thousands of new chapters of political parties, garden clubs, literary societies, and bowling leagues. Most important of all were programs that revolved around their children: dancing schools, Cub Scouts and Brownies, Little Leagues, community swimming pools.

Since everyone was a stranger in town, the informal cocktail party became an efficient means by which to

INTEGRATED NEIGHBORHOODS

Independent political organizer Saul Alinsky described the pattern of racial segregation in American cities in *Reveille for Radicals* in 1946: "A racially integrated community is a chronological term timed from the entrance of the first black family to the exit of the last white family."

introduce people to one another. Because guests milled around the stand-up parties at will, it was possible to invite the most casual supermarket or Little League grandstand acquaintances. Alcohol lubricated easy conversation among strangers, and statisticians noticed a change in American drinking habits toward the consumption of neutral spirits such as gin and vodka, which could be disguised in sweet soda pop or fruit juices. The conclusion was that people who did not like to drink were drinking to make themselves more comfortable and because it was the thing to do.

Insolent Chariots

The suburb could not have developed without the family automobile. In turn, the growth of suburbia made the automobile king, a necessity of life and in some ways a tyrant. Each family needed a car because suburbanites worked at some distance from their homes and public transportation to many of the new communities did not exist. Because it was necessary for a suburban housewife and mother to cover considerable distances each day, the two-car family became a common phenomenon: one suburban family in five owned two vehicles.

Sales of new cars rose from none during the Second World War to 6.7 million in 1950, and continued to maintain high levels throughout the 1950s. In 1945, there were 25.8 million automobiles registered in the United States. By 1960, with the population increased by 35 percent, car ownership more than doubled, to 61.7 million vehicles.

The automobile was the most important means by which people displayed their status. Unlike the size of paychecks and bank accounts, the family car *showed*; it sat in the driveway for all to see. Automobile manufacturers devised and encouraged finely graded images for their chariots. The family that was "moving up" was expected to "trade up" from a low-priced Ford, Plymouth, or "Chevy" to a Dodge, Pontiac, or Mercury, and aspire to eventual ownership of a Chrysler, Lincoln, or Cadillac. Indeed, the easy availability of credit made it possible for people to "keep up with the Joneses" by buying beyond their means, going deeply into debt for the sake of appearances. From 1946 through 1970, short-term loans—money borrowed in order to buy consumer goods—increased from $8 billion to $127 billion! Credit-card companies made easy spending even easier.

The Automobile Economy

Virtually universal car ownership among the middle classes fueled the growth of businesses that were devoted to cars or dependent on them. Service stations (gasoline consumption doubled during the 1950s),

parts stores, car washes, motels, drive-in restaurants, and drive-in movie theaters blossomed on the outskirts of residential suburbs. The suburban shopping mall displaced city and town centers as the middle-class American marketplace. In 1945, there were eight automobile-oriented shopping centers in the United States. In 1960, there were almost 4,000.

Automobiles demanded roads for use. In 1956, Washington responded with the Interstate Highway Act, under which the government began pumping a total of $1 billion a year into road construction. (By 1960, this expenditure rose to $2.9 billion a year.) Over 41,000 miles of new roads ran crosscountry, but 5,000 miles of freeway were urban, connecting suburbs to big cities.

Not only did this road network encourage further urban sprawl, but it made the cities less livable. Already sapped of their middle classes, once lively urban neighborhoods were carved into isolated residential islands that were walled off from one another by the massive concrete abutments of the freeways. Suburbanite cars roared in on them daily, clogging the streets, raising noise to unprecedented levels, and fouling the air for those who could not afford to move out. Progressively poorer without a middle-class tax base, cities deteriorated physically and suffered from neglected schools and hospitals and rising crime rates. During the 1960s, faced with these problems, the center-city department stores and light industries joined the suburban movement, relocating in shopping centers or on empty tracts near the residential suburbs. When they left, they took not only their tax contributions, but jobs previously available to city dwellers.

Baby Boom

During and immediately after the Second World War, the number of births in the United States took a gigantic leap. While about 2.5 million babies were born in each year of the 1930s, 3.4 million saw the light of day in 1946 and 3.8 million in 1947. Population experts expected this. The depression and war had forced young couples to put off starting families. After a few years of catching up, demographers said, the low birth rate typical of the first half of the century would reassert itself.

They were wrong. The annual number of births continued to increase until 1961 (4.2 million) and did not drop to low levels until the 1970s. The same young couples who were buying unprecedented numbers of new homes and automobiles were having larger families than their parents.

Although all social groups participated in the "baby boom," children were most noticeable in suburbia, where, because most adults were young, children were

Hip-swinging, guitar-strumming Elvis Presley popularized rock-'n'-roll during the 1950s.

proportionately more important. Beginning about 1952, when the first boom babies started school, massive efforts were required to provide educational and recreational facilities for them. Businesses oriented toward children, from toymakers to diaper services, sprouted and bloomed.

As the boom babies matured, they attracted attention to the needs and demands of each age group they swelled. By the end of the 1950s, economists observed that middle-class teenagers were a significant consumer group in their own right. They had $10 billion of their own to spend each year, and all of it was discretionary because their necessities were provided by their parents.

Magazines that appealed to young people prospered, including *Seventeen* (clothing and cosmetics for girls) and *Hot Rod* (automobiles for boys). Film studios made movies about adolescents and their problems.

Beginning in the early 1950s, a new kind of popular music swept the country. Rock-'n'-roll was based on the rhythms of black music as it had evolved in the twentieth century, but was usually performed by whites, often teenagers themselves. On the one hand, it was rebellious. Elvis Presley, a truck driver from Memphis, scandalized the country with an act that included suggestive hip movements which he said (probably truthfully) he was helpless to control. On the other hand, it was juvenile. Whereas popular songs had dealt with themes that were obviously adult, the new music's subjects were senior proms at high schools and double-dating. A new kind of record, the compact

and nearly unbreakable 45 rpm disk that sold for only 89 cents, became the medium of competition for teenage dollars.

What worried social critics was that older people, seemingly outnumbered by the young, often adopted adolescent ideals and role models. By the end of the decade, one of television's most popular programs was "American Bandstand," an afternoon show on which teenagers rock-'n'-rolled to recorded music and discussed adolescent problems. Adolescents watched it of course, but so did housewives at their irons. Adults discussed the relative merits of their favorite pubescent dancers. Never before had adult society taken much notice of teenage culture. Now, the baby-boom generation seemed to be proclaiming the society's cultural standards.

A New Role for Women

Middle-class America's twin obsessions with enjoying life and catering to its children caused a significant, if temporary, shift in the status of women. Since the beginning of the century, women of all social classes had been moving into occupations and professions that previously had been considered masculine monopolies. Throughout the 1940s, increasing numbers of women finished high school, attended college, studied medicine, the law, and other professions, and took jobs that would have been unthinkable for women before

Middle-class America's vision of the perfect woman of the 1950s was of a wife and mother with no interest in having a career outside the home.

1900. The Second World War seemed to hasten this blurring of the lines between what the two sexes could do as women took the place of men in heavy and dirty industrial jobs.

When the war ended, however, women willingly left those jobs and enthusiastically embraced the traditional roles of wife, homemaker, and mother. By the 1950s, middle America once more assumed that woman's place was in the home. However, the new woman was not the shrinking violet of the nineteenth century. If she was not employed, the woman of the 1950s was constantly out and about, the backbone of an active social whirl. Because the moral code that had required that women be sequestered had long since died, the modern American girl, wife, and mother were expected to be active and attractive. Wives were considered partners in furthering their husbands' careers as sociable hostesses and companions. Women's magazines such as *Cosmopolitan* and *Redbook* first hinted, then stated that wives should be "sexy."

AGAINST THE GRAIN

There would be no significant challenge to the new domesticity until 1963, when Betty Friedan published *The Feminine Mystique*. In her best seller, Friedan pointed out that American women had actually lost ground in their fight for emancipation since 1945. She considered the home to be a prison and said that women should move out into the world of jobs, politics, and other realms that she defined as productive. Criticism of other aspects of the culture of the 1950s, however, was widespread even during the age of Eisenhower.

Dissenters

As early as 1942, Philip Wylie's *Generation of Vipers* told the country that indulgence of children, particularly by their mothers ("Momism"), was creating tyrannical monsters. When juvenile-delinquency rates soared during the 1950s, even in the well-to-do suburbs, other writers elaborated on Wylie. John Keats attacked the sterility of suburban life, especially the social irresponsibility of the developers that left new developments without vital social centers. Later, in *Insolent Chariots*, he turned his attention to the automobile as an economic tyrant and a socially destructive force.

In *The Organization Man* (1956), William H. Whyte, Jr., fastened on the work place, arguing that jobs in the huge corporations and government bureaucracies that dominated the American economy placed

the highest premium on anonymity, lack of imagination and enterprise, and generally just fitting in. Sociologist David Riesman suggested in *The Lonely Crowd* (1950) that Americans were becoming "other-directed." They no longer took their values from their heritage or their parents, least of all from within themselves, but thought and acted according to what was acceptable to those around them.

Sloan Wilson fictionalized the conformism and cultural aridity of suburban life in *The Man in the Gray Flannel Suit* (1955), a novel about a suburban commuter who works in the advertising industry. In *The Hidden Persuaders* (1957), Vance Packard added to the attack on advertising by pointing out that all Americans were manipulated by advertisements that played not on the virtues of the product for sale but on people's feelings and insecurities.

Beatniks and Squares

The beat generation, or "beatniks" as people called its exemplars, offered a less articulate critique of Eisenhower tranquility. Originally a literary school centered around novelist Jack Kerouac and poet Allen Ginsberg, "beat" evolved into a bohemian lifestyle with capitals in New York's Greenwich Village, San Francisco's North Beach, and Venice, California, near Los Angeles.

Beatniks rebelled against what they considered to be the intellectually and socially stultifying aspects of 1950s America. They shunned regular employment. They took no interest in politics and public life. They mocked the American enchantment with consumer goods by dressing in T-shirts and rumpled khaki trousers, the women innocent of cosmetics and the intricate hairstyles of suburbia. They made a great deal of the lack of furniture in their cheap walk-up apartments, calling their homes "pads" after the mattress on the floor.

The beatniks were highly intellectual. They prided themselves on discovering and discussing obscure writers and philosophers, particularly exponents of an abstruse form of Buddhism called Zen. They rejected the ostensibly strict sexual morality of the "squares" and lived together without benefit of marriage; a few embraced homosexuality. Their music was jazz as played by blacks, whom they regarded as free of the corruptions of white America.

Beatniks simultaneously repelled, amused, and fascinated conventional American society. Traditional moralists demanded that police raid beatnik coffee houses in search of marijuana (which beatniks introduced to white America) and amateur poets reading sexually explicit verse. Preachers in the traditional churches inveighed against the moral decay that the beatniks represented.

But sexual mores were changing in suburbia, too. To be divorced was no longer to be shunned as a moral pariah, and in books published in 1948 and 1953, a researcher at Indiana University, Alfred Kinsey, revealed that the majority of Americans were sexually active before marriage and that the adultery rate was also high.

The high courts approved the publication of books formerly banned as obscene, with celebrated cases revolving around D. H. Lawrence's *Lady Chatterley's Lover* and Henry Miller's *Tropic of Cancer*. The furor over Ginsberg's long poem *Howl* (1955) made it a best seller. Suburbanites, the favorite targets of beat mockery, flocked to Greenwich Village and North Beach on weekends to dabble in beatnik fashions. Like most cultural rebels, the beatniks did not really challenge society's basic assumptions but merely provided another form of entertainment.

The Awakening of Black America

The protest against racial discrimination was an altogether different matter. Rather than sniping at trivialities such as lifestyle, America's blacks during the 1950s demonstrated to whites that their prosperous society was built in part on the systematic denial of civil rights to 15 million people.

For more than half a century, black leaders such as W. E. B. Du Bois, Mary McLeod Bethune, A. Philip Randolph, and Bayard Rustin had fought a frustrating battle against racial prejudice. Their most important organization, the National Association for the Advancement of Colored People, had won some significant victories in the courts. Lynching, formerly a weekly occurrence in the South and rarely punished, had become rare by the 1950s. Under Truman, the armed forces were desegregated (black recruits were no longer placed in all-black units), and the Supreme Court ordered a number of southern states to admit blacks to state-supported professional schools because the segregated medical and legal training they offered blacks was not equal in quality to that provided for whites.

Nevertheless, when Eisenhower moved into the White House, all the former slave states plus Oklahoma retained laws on the books that segregated parks, movie theaters, waiting rooms, trains, buses, and schools. Four more states legally permitted one form or another of racial segregation. (Fifteen states explicitly prohibited it.)

In the Deep South, public drinking fountains were labeled "white" and "colored," and some states actually

A self-service laundry for white patrons only in New Orleans.

provided different Bibles in court for the swearing in of witnesses. This strict color line had been legal since 1896, when, in the case of *Plessy v. Ferguson*, the Supreme Court had declared that racially separate public facilities were constitutional as long as they were equal in quality.

The Brown Case

In 1954, Thurgood Marshall, the NAACP's brilliant legal strategist, argued before the Supreme Court that racially separate educational facilities were intrinsically unequal and therefore unconstitutional because segregation burdened blacks with a constant reminder of their inequality. In *Brown v. Board of Education of Topeka* (1954), the Court unanimously agreed.

In some parts of the South, school administrators complied quickly and without incident. However, in Little Rock, Arkansas, in September 1957, an angry mob of white adults greeted the first black pupils to enroll in Central High School with shouts, curses, and rocks. Claiming that he was protecting the peace, but actually seeking to win the political approval of white racists, Governor Orval Faubus called out the Arkansas National Guard to prevent the black children from enrolling.

Eisenhower blamed the turmoil on both Earl Warren, the new Chief Justice, and Orval Faubus. Sharing

Throughout much of the United States, and particularly in the South, racial discrimination was evident in the segregation of schools, neighborhoods, bathroom facilities, and drinking fountains.

the belief of many Americans that there was no great harm done by segregation, Eisenhower regarded the *Brown* decision as a mistake. If nothing else, by arousing black Americans to protest, it disturbed the tranquility that Ike coveted, and he did not believe that laws could change people's feelings. He later said that his appointment of Earl Warren to the Supreme Court was the worst decision that he had ever made.

Nevertheless, the Supreme Court had spoken. The Court's ruling had the force of federal law, and Faubus was defying it. Eisenhower superseded the governor's command of the National Guard and ordered the troops to enforce the integration of Central High. Overnight, the mission of the Arkansas National Guard was reversed.

From the Courts to the Streets

The battle to integrate the schools continued for a decade. Beginning in 1955, however, the civil-rights movement ceased to be a protest of lawyers and lawsuits and became a peaceful revolution by hundreds of thousands of blacks who were no longer willing to be second-class citizens.

The leader of the upheaval was Martin Luther King, Jr., a young preacher in Montgomery, Alabama. In December 1955, Rosa Parks, a black secretary, refused to give up her seat on a bus to a white man, as city law required, and King became the spokesman for a black boycott of the Montgomery buses. When the city tried to defend the color line, the dispute attracted journalists and television reporters from all over the country.

King's house was bombed, and he explained his strategy for ending racial discrimination from the wreckage of his front porch. Nonviolent civil disobedience, King said, meant refusing to obey morally reprehensible laws such as those that sustained segregation, but without violence. When arrested, protestors should not resist. Not only was this the moral course of action—King hated violence of all kinds—but it was politically effective. When decent people were confronted with the sight of southern police officers brutalizing peaceful blacks and their white supporters simply because they demanded their rights as citizens, they would, King believed, force politicians to support civil rights.

Although it led to considerable suffering by demonstrators and to several deaths, King's strategy worked. A few important labor leaders such as Walter Reuther of the United Automobile Workers marched with the young minister and helped finance the Southern Christian Leadership Conference (SCLC), which King founded to spearhead the fight for equality. After 1960, when SCLC's youth organization, the Student Nonviolent Coordinating Committee (SNCC), peacefully violated laws that prohibited blacks from eating at lunch counters in the South, white university students in the North picketed branches of the offending chain stores in their hometowns. When white mobs burned a bus on which white and black "freedom riders" were defying segregation, the federal government sent marshals south to investigate and prosecute violent white racists.

Although King fell out of favor with some younger blacks in the late 1960s, he loomed over his times as did no other man or woman of either race. After his assassination in 1968, under circumstances that remain mysterious, several states made his birthday a holiday, and in 1986 it became an official federal holiday. But King and black Americans only began their fight for equality during the age of Eisenhower. It was the next decade, the troubled 1960s, which saw the end of civil discrimination on the basis of race.

A black airman contemplates the sign indicating the colored waiting room in a southern railroad station.

Black students, escorted and protected by the National Guard, enter the all-white Central High School in Little Rock, Arkansas, in 1957.

H O W   T H E Y   L I V E D

FASHION AND THE FIFTIES

In 1840, the British consul in Boston noted with distaste that Americans did not observe social propriety in the way they dressed. Instead of wearing clothes that were appropriate to their station in life, as an English gentleman thought should be done, Americans dressed more or less the same, and the democracy of dress did not mean a drabbest common denominator. On the contrary, servant girls were "strongly infected with the national bad taste for being over-dressed; they are, when walking the streets, scarcely to be distinguished from their employers." In other words, they were *fashionable*.

By the twentieth century, the democratization of fashion in the United States was complete. The wealthy had a monopoly of the latest from Paris for only as long as it took the American garment industry to copy designs and mass-produce cheap versions of expensive "originals." Indeed, the insistence of American women of almost every social class on their right to dress as the arbiters of fashion pleased accelerated the natural life cycle of a style. The only way the wealthy woman could conspicuously display her capability to spend freely was to move rapidly from one new look to another, always one frantic step ahead of the power shears and sewing machines of the New York garment district.

In 1940, very soon after the Great Depression, the American clothing industry was doing $3 billion in business annually. By the end of the 1950s, it was by some criteria the third largest industry in the United States. Also during those two decades, American dress designers established partial independence from Paris, the capital of fashion, but not from the social preoccupations and values that were neatly reflected in the garments they produced.

The fashions of the years of the Second World War were a product of four forces: the effective shutdown of the design business in occupied Paris; the rationing of materials; the unprecedented prominence of the military in daily life; and the entry of women into the professions and jobs previously held by men.

Because they had been so dependent on Paris for ideas, American fashion designers were disoriented by the fall of France and able on their own to come up with only a variant on 1930s styles. One of the factors that forced some change was the government's restrictions on the amount of fabric that might go into clothing. Skirts could be no larger than 72 inches around. Belts more than two inches wide, more than one patch pocket on blouses, and generous hems were forbidden, as were frills, fringes, and flounces. The result was a severe look in women's dress, accentuated by the fact that with so many uniforms on the streets, civilian clothing took on a military look. It also took on a "masculine look," according to fashion historians; the silhouette of women's clothing was straight and angular,

Full skirts and ponytails were a popular fashion during the 1950s for teenage girls and adult women alike.

with padded shoulders that emulated the male physique.

In 1947, Christian Dior, a Paris designer, reestablished French primacy in the fashion world. His "New Look" celebrated the end of wartime shortages with long, full, and flowing skirts. More interesting, Dior proclaimed a new femininity in fashion. "Your bosoms, your shoulders and hips are round, your waist is tiny, your skirt's bulk suggests fragile feminine legs," an American fashion editor wrote. Dior blouses were left unbuttoned at the top, and more formal bodices were cut in a deep V or cut low to expose shoulders.

The Frenchman either was very lucky or was a very shrewd psychologist. In the United States, the chief market for fashion in the postwar years, women were opting in droves for the home over the office, factory, and public life. As Betty Friedan would later explain, the new domesticity of the 1950s led to a halt and even a drop in the numbers of women entering the professions and other spheres that were traditionally the preserve of men.

But the domesticity of the 1950s was not the domesticity of a hundred years earlier. Thanks to labor-saving home appliances and the money to buy them, a yen for recreation after the austere years of rationing, and the steady relaxation of moral codes, the 1950s housewife was able to be "fashionable" to a degree previously open only to the doyennes of high society.

Another consequence of the new domesticity of the postwar years was the great baby boom, which in turn affected women's fashion. Just as the numerical dominance of young people led to the prominence of juvenile themes in films and popular music, the two-thirds of the female population that was under 30 years of age affected the way women dressed. "For the first time in fashion," wrote Jane Dormer, the British student of the subject, "clothes that had originally been intended for children climbed up the ladder into the adult wardrobe." While Dior and the Parisian couturiers continued to decree what was worn on formal occasions, American teenagers set the standards for casual wear, not only for themselves but for women of all but advanced age. The most conspicuous of these styles was that of the ingénue: "childlike circular skirts," crinolines, hoop skirts, frilled petticoats that were seen not only at junior high school dances but at cocktail parties on mothers of five. Girls and women began to wear their hair loose and flowing or in ponytails, both styles then closely associated with juveniles.

Hollywood both responded to and fed this kind of fashion by coming up with actresses such as Audrey Hepburn, Debbie Reynolds, and Sandra Dee, who specialized in innocent, naïve, little-girlish parts. Well into their thirties, these women clung to what clothing historian Anne Fogarty has called the "paper doll look." Not until the 1960s, when women adopted new values, would this fashion, like all fashions to a later age, look ridiculous.

Christian Dior's "New Look" offered a femininity to contrast with the "severe" fashions of the war years.

For Further Reading

Overviews and Classics

C. C. Alexander, *Holding the Line: The Eisenhower Era, 1952–1961* (1975)

James Gilbert, *Another Chance: America Since 1945* (1984)

Eric Goldman, *The Crucial Decade and After* (1961)

Godfrey Hodgson, *America in Our Time: From World War II to Nixon* (1976)

William E. Leuchtenburg, *A Troubled Feast: American Society Since 1945* (1979)

Valuable Special Studies

James Baldwin, *The Fire Next Time* (1963)

Bruce Cook, *The Beat Generation* (1971)

Archibald Cox, *The Warren Court: Constitutional Decision as an Instrument of Reform* (1968)

John Kenneth Galbraith, *The Affluent Society* (1958)

Paul Goodman, *Growing Up Absurd* (1960)

Richard Kluger, *Simple Justice: The History of Brown v. Board of Education and Black America's Struggle for Equality* (1975)

Philip B. Kurland, *Politics, the Constitution, and the Warren Court* (1970)

Louis E. Lomax, *The Negro Revolt* (1963)

Benjamin Muse, *Ten Years of Prelude: The Story of Integration Since the Supreme Court's 1954 Decision* (1964)

David Riesman et al., *The Lonely Crowd: A Study of the Changing American Character* (1950)

Sheila M. Rothman, *Woman's Proper Place: A History of Changing Ideas and Practices, 1870 to the Present* (1978)

F. M. Shattuck, *The 1956 Presidential Election* (1956)

C. E. Silberman, *Crisis in Black and White* (1964)

C. Taeuber, *The Changing Population of the United States* (1958)

William H. Whyte, *The Organization Man* (1956)

Robert C. Woods, *Suburbia* (1959)

Biographies and Autobiographies

Marquis Childs, *Eisenhower: Captive Hero* (1958)

Dwight D. Eisenhower, *The White House Years* (1965)

Martin Luther King, Jr., *Stride Toward Freedom* (1958)

Peter Lyon, *Eisenhower: Portrait of a Hero* (1974)

John Bartlow Martin, *The Life of Adlai E. Stevenson* (1976–77)

Stephen B. Oates, *Let the Trumpet Sound: The Life of Martin Luther King, Jr.* (1982)

James T. Paterson, *Mr. Republican: A Biography of Robert A. Taft* (1975)

Thomas C. Reeves, *The Life and Times of Joe McCarthy* (1982)

John D. Weaver, *Warren* (1967)

G. Edward White, *Earl Warren: A Public Life* (1982)

48

Consensus and Camelot
The Eisenhower and Kennedy Administrations, 1953–1963

More than a generation has elapsed since Dwight D. Eisenhower became president in 1953. Most of the leaders of that era are dead. Many of the issues over which they quarreled have long since been resolved. The events of the time seem remote to people who were, overwhelmingly, only children during the 1950s and early 1960s, or not yet born. In our age of sophisticated electronic communication, the electronic preservation of those events in grainy black-and-white film enhances the sense that this is the stuff of "ancient history."

And yet, the age of Eisenhower and Kennedy is in fact recent history. Its events are still vivid in the memories of a great many Americans. Historically, those times were—as a historian writing in 1931 called the 1920s—"Only Yesterday." The historian who tries to sift out the meaning of a time on which the long view—perspective—is lacking must sift very carefully, being content with a sieve that is less than precise. The many strands of continuity between those times and our own get in the way of objectivity. What was important? What was trivial? By comparison, understanding events that are truly ancient history is easy—or at least it seems that way.

Supreme Court Chief Justice Earl Warren swears in John F. Kennedy as president in 1961. Outgoing president Dwight Eisenhower stands solemnly on the far left, while a future president, Lyndon Johnson, stands on the far right.

One distinguishing mark of the decade of Eisenhower and Kennedy does stand out clearly. Both presidents enjoyed something that none of their successors did; the Americans of their times enjoyed a luxury that has grown rarer since: a consensus, the *general* accord of the people that almost all was well in the American corner of the world. There were dissidents and malcontents, as there must be in an open society. But most Americans of the 1950s and early 1960s felt that however serious the problems facing the nation, they were in the hands of leaders who were both capable and well intentioned.

Not that their victories in elections were so overwhelming. In 1960, Kennedy barely scraped through. In 1964, Lyndon B. Johnson won a bigger majority than Ike ever did, and so did Richard M. Nixon in 1972. But even the results of those elections, a great swooping swing of voters from the Democratic to the Republican party in only eight years, indicate the nature of the problem that has faced national leaders since 1963. Ameicans were divided about who was running the country, at least until 1980.

It would be an error to think of the age of Eisenhower and Kennedy as golden, the "Camelot" that Kennedy's devoted aides called his short administration. Many of the domestic tensions and foreign concerns that have unsettled and fragmented Americans since 1963 began to simmer when Eisenhower sat in the White House. Decisions that were taken by both his administration and Kennedy's contributed to their gravity. Nevertheless, because Americans grew conscious of most of them only since Kennedy's assassination in 1963, the preceding decade appears to have been an easier time in which to live.

IKE'S DOMESTIC COMPROMISE

In his heart and soul, Dwight D. Eisenhower was an old-fashioned conservative. As a career soldier, he was isolated from the mainstream of political development, and he thought of government in terms of his small-town childhood in Kansas and Texas at the turn of the century and the gruff platitudes about free enterprise spouted by the rich businessmen who befriended him after the Second World War.

The tremendous expansion of federal power since the New Deal disturbed him. He shuddered at the size of the government's budget and at the very notion of annual deficits piling up into a mountain of national debt. He believed that businessmen in the private sector were better qualified to manage the economy than were the bureaucratic agencies that had been created under Roosevelt and Truman. He publicly denounced the Tennessee Valley Authority, the liberals' model of regional economic and social planning, as "creeping socialism" and suggested that its facilities be sold off to private power companies.

Best-Laid Plans

Some of Ike's advisers, such as Secretary of Agriculture Erza Taft Benson of Utah, were downright reactionary in their hostility to government regulation, social-welfare programs, and the big bureaucracies that implemented them. Given his own way, Benson would have rampaged through the office buildings of Washington like an avenging angel.

Secretary of Defense Charles Wilson sounded like a ghost of the Coolidge era when he gave his opinion of the role that corporations should play in framing national policy. In what was only in part a slip of the tongue, Wilson told a Senate committee that "what was good for the country was good for General Motors and *vice versa.*" (Wilson came to government from the General Motors board of directors.)

When Jonas Salk, a research physician, perfected a vaccine that promised to wipe out polio, then a scourge of children, Secretary of Health, Education, and Welfare Oveta Culp Hobby warned that even though an immunization program might well eradicate the disease, for the government to sponsor the program would be socialistic.

Dynamic Conservatism

That was how some of Ike's advisers spoke and, no doubt, truly felt. When it came time to take action, however, the president was moderate, pragmatic, and realistic. He faced up to the facts that the America of his Kansas boyhood was gone forever and that the federal government had to take some responsibility for economic and social welfare in the complicated world of the mid-twentieth century. His administration did sponsor a polio immunization program.

Eisenhower also discovered the risks in trusting too closely to his businessmen friends when he supported a private company, Dixon-Yates, in a dispute with the TVA over which of them would construct a new generating facility for the Atomic Energy Commission (AEC). Rather than the contest between "free enterprise" and "creeping socialism" that had been described to him, Ike discovered that Dixon-Yates executives were mired deeply in collusion with friendly AEC officials in what amounted to a raid on the

Treasury—"socialism for the rich." He withdrew his support of Dixon-Yates and accepted a face-saving compromise in which the city of Memphis, in the public sector, built the plant.

Even Erza Taft Benson had to swallow his distaste for the agricultural-subsidy programs that he wanted to abolish. The 1950s were years of distress in the farm belt, and the application of free-market principles would have transformed them into years of catastrophe. As agricultural productivity continued to increase but neither domestic consumption nor foreign demand kept pace, grain piled up in volcano-shaped cones in the streets of farm towns throughout the Midwest. Agricultural income dipped, and farmers left the land for city and town jobs in numbers not seen since the 1920s. Actually, food production never lagged; agri-business corporations gobbled up and consolidated family farms, operating them like any other industry. One reason they were able to profit better was that the Eisenhower administration expanded the subsidy programs against which Benson had railed.

The Soil Bank Act of 1956 authorized the payment of money to landowners for every acre they took out of cultivation in order to reduce production. Within ten years, $1 of every $6 that farmers and agricultural corporations pocketed at havest time came not from sales but from the federal government—for crops that were never planted. Eisenhower also adopted New Deal-like policies when he introduced programs under which the federal government purchased surplus crops for school lunches and foreign-aid programs.

The clearest indication that "dynamic conservatism" (as Eisenhower called his political philosophy) included taking responsibility for the health of the economy came when the sharp reduction of military expenditures after the Korean War threatened to shove the country into a depression. Eisenhower responded by asking Congress to lower taxes, and he persuaded the Federal Reserve Board to loosen credit restrictions in order to put more money into the hands of consumers, that is, to make it easier for them to borrow and spend.

In 1957 and 1958, a worse recession threw 7 percent of the work force out of jobs. Ike launched several large public-works projects like the New Deal programs that he earlier had condemned. In the area of social welfare, over 10 million names were added to the lists of people who received Social Security payments during Eisenhower's presidency.

THE COLD WAR CONTINUES

The Cold War continued under Eisenhower. Indeed, every president after Harry S Truman had to design foreign policy around the overwhelming fact that the United States was locked into a competition with the Soviet Union that left very little room for maneuver.

The Nature of the Beast

Because the United States and the U.S.S.R. were nuclear superpowers, the contest could not rationally be resolved by the timeless test of decisive war. Already by the age of Eisenhower, it was obvious that armed conflict between the United States and the Soviet Union would lead to vast physical devastation in both countries and the death of tens of millions of people. By 1961, when Ike retired, nuclear technology was advanced to the point that a world war would lead to the destruction of civilization and, conceivably, the earth's capacity to support human life. Every president from Ike to Jimmy Carter has understood and clearly stated that there would be no winners in a nuclear war.

Therefore, until the United States and the Soviet Union trusted each other enough to agree on disarmament, policymakers had to live with the balance of

Although conservative, even Secretary of Agriculture Ezra Taft Benson reflected Ike's flexibility in his policies.

AMERICA UNDERGROUND

For a time in the early 1950s, fear of Soviet nuclear attack spawned a minor building boom in "fallout shelters," covered pits in backyards to which, upon hearing the sirens, families would repair and thus survive the atomic bomb. Although magazines such as *Popular Science* and *Popular Mechanics* suggested fairly cheap do-it-yourself models, a professionally built shelter, carpeted and painted beige, cost $3,000, the price of a decent house. Even if her family never used their shelter, a suburban Los Angeles woman said, it "will make a wonderful place for the children to play in." Other people pointed out that shelters were useful storage areas. In the theological journals, ministers and priests argued about a person's moral justification in shooting neighbors and relatives who had not built their own shelters and, in the moment of crisis, were trying to horn in.

terror and compete with their rivals under the threat of it. The history of American foreign relations after 1953 is the story of how a succession of presidents and Secretaries of State coped with these restraints.

More Bang for a Buck

Although Dwight D. Eisenhower spent much of his life in an army uniform, he wanted to be remembered as a man of peace. "I have seen enough war," he said, and as president he acted with moderation in crisis situations. By the time he left office, Eisenhower appeared to distrust the motives of his generals and the business leaders who supported him. In his farewell address of 1961, Ike told Americans to beware of the "military-industrial complex," the intimate and self-serving alliance of the Pentagon (the Defense Department), and the big corporations that made their money by selling weapons to the government. Along with like-minded intellectuals in the universities and "think tanks," with their ivory-tower theories of how to fight the Cold War, Ike said, the military establishment and arms industry were apt to be reckless in the use of armed force.

Eisenhower's fiscal conservatism also played a role in his defense policy. If he were to balance the federal budget—to spend no more money in a year than the Treasury collected in taxes—he had to cut military expenditures, the biggest single item in the budget. Because complete disarmament was out of the question, Eisenhower adopted a comparatively inexpensive plan for maintaining national security, the "more bang for a buck" policy. Encouraged by penny-pinching Secretary of the Treasury George Humphrey, the president cut spending on the conventional army and navy and

concentrated on building up America's nuclear deterrent: atomic and hydrogen bombs and the sophisticated ships, planes, and missiles capable of delivering them to Soviet targets. This purely defensive policy threatened no one, Ike told the world. The United States would never start a nuclear war, but the Soviet Union, unless it were deterred by the threat of "massive retaliation," might very well do so.

Critics claimed that the policy meant all or nothing. The United States could destroy the world, but could the nation respond in proportion to minor Soviet provocations? Secretary Humphrey was not impressed. With the frustrations of the limited war in Korea fresh in his mind, he growled that the United States had "no business getting into little wars. . . . Let's intervene decisively with all we have got or stay out."

Other Eisenhower supporters said that the reduced army and navy were more than adequate to act in minor crises. In 1958, when Eisenhower suspected that the Communists intended to take over Lebanon, he was able to send marines into the Middle Eastern nation to stabilize a government friendly to the United States. It was only a long, expensive, and demoralizing conventional war like Korea for which he did not choose to prepare.

Peaceful Coexistence

The United States was directly involved in no wars of any note during Eisenhower's eight years in office. In

U.S. Army Airborne troops occupy the Beirut, Lebanon, airport in 1958.

Vice President Richard Nixon debates with Russian premier Nikita Khrushchev in front of a mock-up of a typical American kitchen in Moscow, 1959.

part this may have been due to a significant change in Soviet leadership. Joseph Stalin, suspicious to the point of mental imbalance late in life, died in 1953. After a few years of figurehead leaders and murky maneuvering in the Kremlin, Stalin was succeeded by an altogether different kind of strong man, a rotund, homely, and clever Ukrainian named Nikita Khrushchev.

Khrushchev confused American Soviet watchers, which may have been his purpose. At times he seemed to be a coarse buffoon who habitually drank too much vodka and showed it. Visiting the United Nations, he stunned the assembly of dignitaries by taking off his shoe and banging it on the desk in front of him to protest a speaker whom he disliked. At other times he was witty and charming, almost slick.

The new premier could issue frightening warlike challenges to the United States. But he was also the man who denounced Stalinist totalitarianism at home

in 1956 and called for peaceful coexistence with American capitalism. Khrushchev claimed that the Cold War would be resolved by historical forces rather than by armed conflict. "We will bury you," he told American capitalists the world would peacefully choose the Soviet way of life.

A comparison of American and Soviet societies mocked Khrushchev's boast. Despite his reforms, Soviet citizens remained under tight political controls; the secret police was not dissolved. The Soviet economy was sluggish. Because a country inestimably poorer than the United States had to match American spending on armaments, daily life in Russia was drab. Long lines of people at shops waiting not only for modest luxuries but for basic foodstuffs was hardly preferable to the American consumer cornucopia. Vice President Richard Nixon understood the impact of the contrast on both Americans and people in other countries when he visited Moscow in 1959 and engaged

Khrushchev in a debate in front of a mock-up of an appliance-filled American kitchen. There was nothing like it in Russia, and Nixon was delighted to rest a comparison of the two societies on the contrast.

Khrushchev had one big edge in the salesmanship contest that he proposed. He was flexible and opportunistic, even cynical, while the chief foreign representative of the United States under Eisenhower, Secretary of State John Foster Dulles, was a man of antique principle, petrified mind, and the charm of the bullfrog he resembled.

Dull, Duller, Dulles

On the basis of his credentials, Dulles should have been a grand success. He was related to two previous secretaries of state, and he had begun his diplomatic career half a century earlier. During the years he was out of government, Dulles practiced international law with a firm that was considered the best in the business. At the top of that business in 1953, Dulles turned out to be handicapped by an impossible personality for a diplomat and a simplistic view of the world. He was a pious Presbyterian of the old school, as self-righteous, intolerant, and humorless as any Puritan of old New England. "Dull, Duller, Dulles," the Democrats intoned.

He believed that Communists were evil incarnate, veritable agents of Satan. He was unable to respond when Khrushchev hinted that he wanted to ease ten-

John Foster Dulles, secretary of state under Eisenhower, was a staunch supporter of the Cold War.

sions, and he found it difficult to deal with neutral nations that maintained friendly relations with the Soviets. Photographs of Dulles with neutral national leaders like Jawaharlal Nehru of India reveal a man who fears he will be defiled if he sits too closely.

This kind of behavior made him unpopular not only in the Third World (unaligned countries), but among the diplomats who represented America's allies. To make matters worse, Dulles insisted on carrying out his policies in person. He flew 500,000 miles on the job, demoralizing American ambassadors by converting them into mere ceremonial figures who greeted his plane and then disappeared.

In his conception of the emerging nations of the Third World and of revolutionary movements in the republics of Latin America, Dulles's limitations were even more damaging. The old colonial empires of the European nations were falling apart during the 1950s, and new Asian and African countries were founded almost annually. Often committed at least in word to social reform, including socialist institutions, the leaders of these countries were rarely pro-Soviet. They needed American friendship and aid. In Latin America, revolutionary movements rose against the exploitative and repressive dictatorships that were practically the rule there. The leaders of these movements were committed to reducing American economic power in their countries, but they also recognized the advantage of having good relations with the nation that had sponsored the Marshall Plan.

Picking the Wrong Friends

Instead of exploiting the widespread good will toward America and accommodating often oversensitive new leaders, Dulles divided the world into "us" and "them," with "us" defined as those nations that lined up behind the United States in every particular. He wrote off independently minded leaders and revolutionary movements as Communist inspired. Along with his brother, Allen Dulles, who headed the semisecret Central Intelligence Agency (CIA), he threw American influence behind compliant reactionary governments, including undemocratic and repressive dictatorships in Portugal, Nicaragua, the Dominican Republic, and Cuba.

In 1953, the United States helped the unpopular shah of Iran overthrow a reform-minded prime minister, Mohammed Mossadegh, despite the fact that because Iran borders on the Soviet Union, the country cannot afford to cozy up to Russia no matter who is in power. In 1954, the CIA took the lead in overthrowing a democratically chosen prime minister in Guatemala, Jacobo Arbenz, because he expropriated American-owned banana plantations.

THE COLD WAR CONTINUES

Also in 1954, Dulles refused to sign the Geneva Accords, which ended a long and tragic war in Vietnam between France and a Communist-led independence movement that was probably open to cooperation with the United States. Instead of courting the Vietnamese leader, Ho Chi Minh, the United States helped set up a petty dictator to oppose him in South Vietnam, Ngo Dinh Diem. In 1956, the CIA approved Diem's cancellation of democratic elections as required by the Geneva settlement.

In Dulles's hands, the Cold War with monolithic Communism took precedence over America's commitment to free institutions. What Dulles seemed to say was that the United States opposed social progress in those parts of the world where change was most sorely needed. This provided Khrushchev with the opportunity to play the friend of anticolonialism, freedom, and reform. The pretense ill-suited the imperialist, dictatorial, and hidebound Soviet Union, but Khrushchev and Dulles conspired to make it look plausible.

Brinksmanship

Dulles also demoralized America's allies by preaching a line that the prudent Eisenhower was unwilling to carry out. Instead of merely containing Communism, Dulles said, America would win the Cold War by going to the brink of hot war—"massive retaliation"—thus forcing the Communists to back down and, eventually, collapse. In 1953, Dulles hinted that he would support Chiang Kai-shek if the exiled Nationalist Chinese leader invaded the Communist People's Republic, and he led the peoples of Eastern Europe to believe that Americans would come to their aid if they rebelled against the Soviets.

However, when the Chinese Communists began to shell two tiny islands controlled by Chiang, Quemoy and Matsu, Ike and Dulles quickly backed off, stating that it was only Taiwan they would defend. The artillery exchanges between the two Chinas developed into a ludicrous ritual, a far more "limited war" than Korea. At one point, the Communists insisted only on the right to attack Quemoy and Matsu on alternate days of the month. The snafu was not untangled until after Eisenhower left office.

In Hungary in 1956, Dulles's talk of rolling back the iron curtain contributed to a more tragic event. Anti-Soviet Hungarians rebelled and took control of Budapest. The Soviets hesitated, as though waiting to see what the Americans would do. They regarded Hungary as vital to their security, but feared all-out war on the issue. When Eisenhower and Dulles did nothing, Soviet tanks and infantry rolled into Budapest, easily quashing the revolution. The net effect of

the episode was to undercut confidence in Dulles's bold words throughout the world.

Also in 1956, Eisenhower and Dulles angered three important allies by first appearing to encourage them to take action against increasingly pro-Soviet Egypt and then refusing to back them. Britain, France, and Israel invaded Egypt to prevent the government of President Gamal Abdel Nasser from taking control of the Suez Canal. When Khrushchev threatened to send Russian "volunteers" to Egypt's aid, Eisenhower announced his opposition to the allied assault. Humiliated, the British, French, and Israelis withdrew. They could not carry on without American support.

Summitry and the U-2

When Dulles resigned a month before he died in 1959 and Eisenhower took personal charge of foreign policy, American prospects brightened. Outdoing each other with statements of good will, Eisenhower and Khrushchev agreed to exchange friendly visits.

Khrushchev made his tour of the United States in 1959 and scored a rousing personal success. In the flesh he captivated many Americans with his unpretentious manner and interest in everyday things. Khrushchev made the nation laugh after having been refused admission to Disneyland for security reasons, when he explained that the real reason was that the amusement park was a disguise for rocket installations. (He seemed sincerely to have regretted missing his day there.) Eisenhower's visit to Russia was scheduled for May 1960. Because Eisenhower had been a hero in the Soviet Union during the Second World War, there was every reason to expect another amicable tour.

Then, on May 5, Khrushchev announced that the Russians had shot down an American plane in their air space. It was a U-2, a top-secret high-altitude craft designed for spying. Assuming that the pilot had been killed in the crash (or had committed suicide, as U-2 pilots were provided the means to do), Eisenhower said that it was a weather-monitoring plane that had flown off course.

Khrushchev pounced. He revealed that the U-2 pilot, Francis Gary Powers, was alive and had confessed to being a spy. Possibly because he hoped to salvage Eisenhower's forthcoming trip to Russia, Khrushchev hinted in the wording of his announcement that Ike should lay the blame on subordinates.

Ike refused to do so. Smarting under Democratic party attacks that he had never been in charge of foreign policy, he acknowledged his personal approval of all U-2 flights. Khrushchev attacked Eisenhower as a warmonger and canceled his invitation to tour Russia. The Cold War was suddenly chillier than at any time since the truce in Korea.

Khrushchev holds up evidence of spying found in an American U-2 plane shot down by the Russians on May 1, 1960.

1960: A CHANGING OF THE GUARD

This perfectly suited the strategy of the Democratic presidential nominee in 1960, John Fitzgerald Kennedy, the 42-year-old senator from Massachusetts. His chief criticism of the Eisenhower administration was his contention that Eisenhower had let American defenses and deterrent power slip dangerously low. The Soviet Union was winning the Cold War.

Kennedy had to be careful about his campaign tactics. Ike's personal popularity was still high. If the Twenty-second Amendment, adopted in 1951, had not made a third term unconstitutional, Ike undoubtedly could have beaten Kennedy or any other Democrat in the election of 1960. Americans still liked Ike.

Times Change

And yet the country was a little tired of the 1950s. The American population was young and restless un-der the cautious style of the dead decade. As prosperous as the age of Eisenhower was, it was a stale and boring time in the opinion of many Americans. The books of social critics such as Whyte and Packard had been best sellers, even in the suburbs. Although they were out of power, the Democratic liberals had loudly criticized Eisenhower lethargy in journals like *The Nation* and the *New Republic*. Liberal university professors were effective propagandists, spreading their views among young people. Although it was not a liberal majority, the Democrats had controlled both houses of Congress for six of Eisenhower's eight years in office.

As 1960 approached, the feeling that it was time "to get the country moving again" was in the air. In 1959, *Life,* the favorite magazine of the middle classes, published a series of articles by prominent Americans from Adlai Stevenson to Billy Graham on the subject of "the national purpose." Almost all the contributors conveyed the uneasy feeling that a sense of purpose was lacking.

John F. Kennedy

Kennedy was the politician who knew how to exploit this apprehension of drift. As Eisenhower was tailor-made for the 1950s, Kennedy seemed to fit the spirit of the new decade. He was rich and attractive, breezy and witty. He had distinguished himself for bravery during the Second World War, had an attractive young wife who could have modeled for a fashion magazine, and was ambitious.

Kennedy was unbeatable in Massachusetts politics. He had won election to the House and the Senate in years that had not been kind to Democrats, and in 1956, he had made a bid for the Democratic party's vice-presidential nomination. Tennessee Senator Estes Kefauver had beaten him, but that turned out to be a blessing. Kennedy had not shared in the humiliation of the party's defeat that year, but by putting up an exciting fight on national television (the only contest in a dull political year), he had made his name known in every corner of the country.

The avalanche of publicity in 1956 had done another favor for Kennedy by initiating discussion of his single political handicap, his religion. The senator was a Roman Catholic, and it was thought that too many people would vote against any Catholic for a member of that church to be elected to national office. The longer the question was examined, however, the less attractive the anti-Catholic position looked. When Martin Luther King, Jr.'s, father (a Baptist minister) expressed his anti-Catholic prejudices, the civil-rights leader so hastily dissociated himself from them that he became, in the process, virtually committed to the Democratic nominee.

Kennedy and his team of advisers, which he started to assemble in 1957, understood the importance of manipulating the mass media, especially television, in creating a favorable image of their candidate. The campaign that he launched was calculated to convince younger Americans that he was more flexible, more open to change, than any of his rivals.

The Campaign of 1960

Kennedy's competition for the nomination included Adlai Stevenson, badly shopworn in an age that craved novelty, but hoping to be drafted; Lyndon B. Johnson of Texas, the efficient leader of the Senate Democrats; Hubert H. Humphrey of Minnesota, a leading liberal; and several minor candidates who were praying for a deadlocked convention.

Humphrey was the only one to challenge Kennedy head-on in the primary elections, and he was quickly eliminated. By edging him in Wisconsin, which neighbors Minnesota, Kennedy established himself as a national figure. Kennedy then won in West Virginia, a heavily Protestant "Bible belt" state where, experts said, anti-Catholic feeling was strong. Humphrey dropped out, and Kennedy's forces talked old-time political bosses like Governor Mike Di Salle of Ohio and Mayor Richard E. Daley of Chicago into supporting him as the most likely to win in November. By the time of the convention, Lyndon Johnson had been outraced, and Kennedy won on the first ballot.

Kennedy chose Johnson as his vice-presidential running-mate, which turned out to be the shrewdest move of a brilliantly played game. Although Johnson's syrupy Texas drawl occasioned ridicule in the Northeast, he was popular in the southern states where Kennedy was weak. Single-handedly, Johnson won Texas for the Democrats, a key to a close election. In the North, Kennedy's religion actually helped him by winning

John F. Kennedy and Richard Nixon grimly face each other in a television studio during the presidential campaign debates of 1960.

back many upwardly mobile Catholics who had been drifting toward the Republicans as the party of respectability.

The Republican standard-bearer was Vice President Richard M. Nixon, who easily fought off a challenge by New York governor Nelson Rockefeller. Nixon had a difficult assignment. In order to keep the Republican organization behind him, he had to defend Eisenhower's policies. But he also had to appeal to the new spirit of youth and change.

A Modern Election

Nixon handled this juggling act remarkably well, but not without cost. Emphasizing his experience in the executive branch, he created an image of the responsible diplomat that did not mesh with his reputation for free-swinging smears and dirty tricks. Reporters revived the nickname "Tricky Dicky" and the line, "Would you buy a used car from this man?" Kennedy wisecracked that Nixon played so many parts that no one knew who the real Nixon was, including the vice president himself.

Mistrust would dog Richard Nixon to the end of his career. Nevertheless, in 1960 he almost won the election. The totals gave Kennedy a wafer-thin margin of 118,574 votes out of the almost 70 million cast. His 303 to 219 electoral vote margin, apparently more comfortable, concealed narrow scrapes in several large states. Some analysts believed that Illinois went Democratic only because of fraudulent vote counts in Richard E. Daley's Chicago.

Other commentators said that Kennedy won because his wife was more glamorous than Pat Nixon, who disliked public life, or because the Massachusetts senator looked better in the first of four nationally televised debates with Nixon. Kennedy was tan, healthy, confident, and assertive, while Nixon was visibly nervous, and an inept make-up job failed to cover his five-o'clock shadow.

It is impossible to know how much the appearances of the candidates affected the decisions of 70 million people. After 1960, however, many politicians and political scientists came to believe that in the age of television a candidate's image, rather than issues, was

Aided by a handsome family that included photogenic toddler John-John, John Kennedy increased his popularity among the public as his term in office progressed.

the key to winning elections. By 1984, few major political campaigns were run without the advice of high-priced advertising firms. Concerned observers wondered what it said for political democracy when a candidate's success depended on how skillfully a person was "packaged."

CAMELOT

As president, Kennedy remained a master at projecting an attractive image. Although no intellectual (his favorite writer was Ian Fleming, creator of the British superspy, James Bond), the new president won the hearts and talents of the intelligentsia to his cause; he invited the venerable poet Robert Frost to read his verses at the inauguration and cellist Pablo Casals to perform at the White House. Genuinely athletic and competitive, Kennedy appealed to young suburbanites by releasing photographs of his large family playing rough-and-tumble touch football at their Cape Cod vacation home.

There were plenty of Kennedy haters, but the vigor of his administration (*vigor* was a favorite Kennedy word) and his undeniable charm, wit, and self-deprecating humor captivated Americans. Inspired by the blockbuster musical of the early 1960s, *Camelot*, they spoke of the Kennedy White House as though it were an idyll, like King Arthur's reign in the mythical past.

Like Eisenhower, he seemed to be assembling a consensus. But just as in the Arthurian legend, Camelot was short lived.

The New Frontier

John F. Kennedy is more important as an inspiration for the reforms (and tragedies) of the 1960s than for what he actually accomplished. His inaugural address was eloquent and moving. "The torch has been passed to a new generation of Americans," he warned the

THE KENNEDY WIT

When we got into office, the thing that surprised me most was to find that things were just as bad as we'd been saying they were.

Washington is a city of southern efficiency and northern charm.

It has recently been observed that whether I serve one or two terms in the presidency, I will find myself at the end of that period at what might be called an awkward age—too old to begin a new career and too young to write my memoirs.

TO REACH THE MOON

In his address to Congress on May 25, 1961, President Kennedy said: "I believe that this nation should commit itself to achieving the goal, before this decade is out, of landing a man on the Moon and returning him safely to earth." Although Kennedy did not live to see it, his commitment—seemingly farfetched in 1961—was fulfilled. Astronaut Neil Armstrong set foot on the moon in 1969, more than a year ahead of schedule.

American astronaut Buzz Aldrin on the moon, July 1969.

world, and to Americans he said, "Ask not what your country can do for you; ask what you can do for your country." He sent Congress a pile of legislation that was more innovative than any presidential program between the time of F.D.R.'s Hundred Days and Ronald Reagan's conservative proposals of 1981.

The New Frontier, as Kennedy called his program, included federal aid to education (both to institutions and in the form of low-interest student loans), assistance to chronically depressed Appalachia and the nation's decaying center cities, and help for the poor, the ill, and the aged. In 1962, Kennedy proposed a massive space research and development program, which set the goal of overtaking the Soviet Union, which beat the United States in orbiting: the first artificial satellite in 1957 and the first human space traveler in 1961. Kennedy meant to send an American to the moon by 1970.

In Congress, however, despite comfortable Democratic majorities, the president found little but frustra-

A Peace Corps volunteer helps a girl learn to read in Chimbote, Peru.

tion. Not only did the Republicans oppose the New Frontier, but Kennedy was unable to swing the powerful bloc of southern Democrats behind his program. The southerners traditionally opposed big government spending on anything but defense and public-works projects located in the South, and were angered when the president and his brother, Attorney General Robert F. Kennedy, made friendly overtures to the growing civil-rights movement. As a result, Kennedy was able to push through only a few of his proposals, such as the Peace Corps (volunteers working in underdeveloped countries in Latin America, Asia, and Africa) and the space program (which brought money to the South). Kennedy's other plans were either defeated or bottled up in congressional committees.

We Shall Overcome

Sensitive to the power of the southern congressmen, Kennedy wanted to go slow on civil rights. But America's blacks and their white allies, foiled for so long, would not be put off. In addition to King's Southern Christian Leadership Conference, the Student Non-

violent Coordinating Committee (SNCC) and the Congress of Racial Equality (CORE) struck out at racial discrimination on a dozen fronts, sponsoring demonstrations, protests, and nonviolent civil disobedience throughout the South.

White mobs pummeled black and white demonstrators and law officers turned high-pressure fire hoses on them, unleashed vicious attack dogs, and tortured demonstrators with electric cattle prods. Black churches, the typical meeting place of civil-rights workers, were firebombed and several children were killed. A bus carrying CORE "freedom riders" was burned to the ground. In April 1963, Medgar Evers, the moderate leader of the NAACP in Mississippi, was shot to death in the driveway of his home.

The Kennedys could not ignore such violence or the defiance of two southern governors, Ross Barnett of Mississippi and George Wallace of Alabama, who said that they would personally prevent the integration of their state universities and tacitly encouraged mobs to riot. Most of all, the government was pushed into action by the March on Washington in August 1963, which was organized and led by Martin Luther King, Jr. Believing that the time had come for decisive federal action, King led 200,000 supporters to the Lincoln Memorial in Washington, where he delivered the greatest sermon of his life.

"I have a dream today," he began.

> I have a dream today that one day . . . little black boys and black girls will be able to join hands with little white boys and white girls and walk together as sisters and brothers. . . . When we let freedom ring, when we let it ring from every village and every hamlet, from every state and every city, we will be able to speed up that day when all of God's children, black men and white men, Jews and Gentiles, Protestants and Catholics, will be able to join hands and sing, in the words of that old Negro spiritual, "Free at last! Free at last! Thank God Almighty, we are free at last!"

Concluding that he had no choice but to choose between racist Democrats in the South (who were not

Police dogs attack a civil-rights demonstrator in Birmingham, Alabama, 1963.

supporting him on much of anything) and the large black vote in the North, which was strategically located in the cities of the states with the most electoral votes, Kennedy announced his support of a sweeping civil-rights bill to be debated in Congress in 1964.

The Assassination

How Kennedy would have fared in the contest is not known, for he was not the president who fought it. That president was Lyndon Baines Johnson, a very different kind of leader who had dramatically different strengths and limitations. Johnson became president just three months after Martin Luther King, Jr.'s, great march. Kennedy and Johnson were on a tour to shore up political support in Texas, when the president was assassinated by Lee Harvey Oswald, a ne'er-do-well ex-marine and worker in a textbook clearing house.

The murder unleashed a raft of pent-up anxieties and conspiracy theories. Because Dallas, where Kennedy was killed, was a hotbed of often paranoiac right-wing political organizations, including the John Birch Society, which believed that Dwight D. Eisenhower was a conscious agent of international Communism, liberals were inclined to blame Kennedy's loss on such unhealthy extremism. Stories circulated of Dallas schoolchildren cheering when they heard the news. But Lee Harvey Oswald had been associated with left-wing organizations and had lived for a time in the Soviet Union. Right-wingers were confirmed in their theories that Communist agents were everywhere. Oswald was not around to clear things up. Two days after the assassination, he was murdered in the basement of the Dallas police headquarters by a night-club operator named Jack Ruby, who was apparently distracted by the death of a president he idolized.

EARL WARREN (1891–1974)

Chief Justice Earl Warren, front and center, with members of the Warren Court.

For sixteen years, Earl Warren of California was Chief Justice of the Supreme Court. Appointed by Eisenhower in 1953, he served long enough to inaugurate another Republican Californian, whom he did not much like, Richard M. Nixon. In the meantime, he shaped a Court that did more to mold American historical development than any since the Marshall Court of the early nineteenth century, and Warren was the most controversial Chief Justice since Roger B. Taney and his divisive Dred Scott decisions of 1857.

Earl Warren was born in Los Angeles in 1891, attended the University of California at Berkeley, and, when he graduated from law school, remained in northern California. After service in the army during the First World War, he made his home in Oakland and, in 1925, was elected district attorney of Alameda County.

He appeared to be satisfied with a career in county politics, remaining district attorney for fourteen years and virtually unknown elsewhere. However, a tough policy toward organized rackets brought him to the attention of the state's Republican bosses, and Warren was elected California attorney general in 1938. The post traditionally was a stepping stone to the governorship in that state, and Warren's career took off. Fighting organized crime at the state level enabled him to win the Republican nomination for governor in 1942 and, quite easily, the election. Warren was so popular that, in 1946, because statewide nominations were made in a popular primary, he won both the Republican and Democratic nominations for governor and received 92 percent of the popular vote. Such a victory could not help but catch the eye of the national leadership of the Republican party, and in 1948, Warren was tapped to run for vice president with Thomas E. Dewey of New York. The Republicans believed that they were winners in 1948, so Warren, just 57 years old, seemed to be headed for the White House. Then Dewey was defeated in one of the most famous of presidential upsets.

As governor of California, Warren was aligned with neither the conservative nor the progressive wing of the Republican party. There was little in his career to anticipate what he would do after President Eisenhower named him Chief Justice in 1953.

What he did was to assume immediately the leadership of justices older and more distinguished than himself, most of whom had been appointed by Franklin D. Roosevelt. Giving voice to their liberalism, he spearheaded a rush of decisions that overturned long-entrenched policies and practices in racial segregation, apportionment of legislative districts, and police procedure.

Earl Warren's great monument was the unanimous decision he wrote forbidding racial segregation in the schools, *Brown v. Board of Education of Topeka* (1953). A series of similar decisions concerning segregation by race paved the way for congressional approval of the Civil Rights Acts of 1964 and 1965. They also made Warren the target of critics not only among segregationists but also among juridical conservatives who believed that the Warren Court had made its decision in the *Brown* case not on legal but on sociological grounds. (They had a point, but the Warren Court was not the first Supreme Court to do so.)

Warren won enemies among professional politicians as a result of a series of decisions on the issue of representation in elections to state legislatures. It was common in states that were both urban and rural for rural voters to be "over-represented"; because district lines had been drawn before cities had grown to house so many people, farm areas got to elect more legislators and congressmen than did city voters. In Virginia, for example, 84 rural voters had the same representation in the state legislature as 100 city voters. In 1946, the Supreme Court had refused to intervene in this practice on the grounds that it was a political matter, which indeed it was: rural state assemblymen did not want to give up their privileged position.

In *Baker v. Carr* (1962), however, the Warren Court ordered that states redraw the lines of legislative districts on the basis of "one man, one vote," all districts to contain approximately the same population. In *Westberry v. Sanders* (1964) and *Reynolds v. Sims* (1964), the Court went further. The justices ruled that "one man, one vote" applied to *both houses* of legislatures. Because the upper houses of many state legislatures were patterned on the United States Senate, with each member representing a county, these decisions revolutionized state government. Warren and a five to four majority of the Court said that whereas the Constitution provided for unequal representation of population in the U.S. Senate, the Constitution did not extend that mandate to the state legislatures. The decisions made it clear that the Warren Court intended to extend democracy whenever an opportunity presented itself.

But the series of decisions that cast a pall over Warren's career concerned extending the definition of individual rights and liberties beyond bounds thought quite reasonable by the Supreme Court for 170 years. Three landmark cases concerned police procedures in enforcing laws.

In *Mapp v. Ohio* (1961), the Court ruled that police could not use as a basis for criminal prosecution any evidence that had been seized without being specified, in a search warrant, as potential evidence. In the abstract, the decision was unexceptional, but in specific cases, it seemed to protect violators of the law. Mapp, for instance, was a woman whose house had been raided on suspicion that she dealt in drugs. No evidence to that effect was discovered, but police did discover obscene materials, which were used in court against her. There had been nothing in the warrant about pornography.

In *Escobedo v. Illinois* (1964), the Court overturned a conviction of a palpably guilty criminal. Because police had refused to allow Danny Escobedo the right to see his lawyer when they were questioning him, the Court ordered him freed.

Much more offensive to the growing anti-Warren forces was *Miranda v. Arizona* (1968), in which Warren himself wrote that a suspect in a crime must be informed immediately and in precise legal language of his constitutional rights (particularly under the Fifth Amendment, which protects against self-incrimination). To many police officers and a growing "law and order" movement, Escobedo and Miranda seemed to be putting procedural technicalities and the protection of "criminals' " rights above the public's right to be protected.

An "Impeach Earl Warren" movement sprang up during the 1960s, but never grew large enough to threaten the Chief Justice's job.

Immediately after President Kennedy's assassination in 1963, a reluctant Warren gave in to Lyndon Johnson's insistence that he head a commission to investigate the murder. He may have had a premonition that no possible findings would lay all anxieties to rest. He was right. Despite the voluminous report (26 volumes of testimony from 552 witnesses, with an 888-page summation of evidence and conclusions), the Warren Commission was criticized for slipshod work and even of a "cover-up" in its conclusions that Lee Harvey Oswald was the sole killer and that the murder of Oswald by Jack Ruby was also unconnected to any conspiracy. Nevertheless, no conclusive evidence to the contrary has since been presented.

Warren tried to resign his post when Johnson was still president so that his successor would also be a liberal. However, when Johnson tried to give the Chief Justiceship to an old friend, Associate Justice Abe Fortas, enemies in the Senate dug up some irregularities in Fortas's record and prevented the appointment. Warren remained in office until 1969, when Richard Nixon replaced him with Warren Burger, a more conservative jurist whose revisions of the Warren Court decisions did not turn them around as much as many of Warren critics had hoped. In 1986 however, when Burger retired, the Court drifted in a decidedly new direction.

John Kennedy, Jr., salutes his father's coffin on November 25, 1963. Behind him is his uncle,
Robert Kennedy, who was assassinated during his own presidential campaign in 1968.

A blue-ribbon investigating commission headed by Chief Justice Earl Warren found that Oswald had acted alone; he was neither associated with any political tendency nor assisted in his act. Simply put, he was a misfit. However, soft spots in one or another of the Warren Commission's conclusions continued to serve as grist for literally hundreds of articles and books that espoused theories about how the murder had taken place, the most common and plausible theme being that there was more than one gunman at the scene.

Beginning of an Era

The multifarious and contradictory theories about how Kennedy was killed were possible because of some dubious findings in the Warren Commission's report.

There was, as one theorist called it, a "rush to judgment." However, the conspiracy theories won large followings because the temper of Americans changed after November 22, 1963. If Kennedy had not been particularly successful in terms of the legislation passed during his "Thousand Days" in office, he seemed to have been building a basis of political support such as had allowed Dwight D. Eisenhower to govern with authority.

Lyndon Johnson's background as a political arm-twister and his southwestern background aroused distrust among many of the liberals who had been among Kennedy's chief supporters. But it was in the area of foreign policy that Johnson was undone.

As a grief-stricken America watched on television, Lyndon B. Johnson, his wife to his right and Jacqueline Kennedy to his left, take the oath of office aboard Air Force I, *November 22, 1963.*

For Further Reading

Overviews and Classics

C. C. Alexander, *Holding the Line: The Eisenhower Era, 1952–1961* (1975)

James Gilbert, *Another Chance: America Since 1945* (1984)

Eric Goldman, *The Crucial Decade and After* (1961)

Godfrey Hodgson, *America in Our Time: From World War II to Nixon* (1976)

William E. Leuchtenburg, *A Troubled Feast: American Society Since 1945* (1979)

James L. Sundquist, *Politics and Policy: The Eisenhower, Kennedy, and Johnson Years* (1968)

Valuable Special Studies

Ronald Berman, *America in the Sixties* (1968)

Chester Cooper, *The Lion's Last Roar: Suez 1956* (1978)

Archibald Cox, *The Warren Court: Constitutional Decision as an Instrument of Reform* (1968)

Michael Harrington, *Poverty in America* (1962)

Philip B. Kurland, *Politics, the Constitution, and the Warren Court* (1970)

William Manchester, *Death of a President* (1967)

Bruce Miroff, *Pragmatic Illusions: The Presidential Politics of John F. Kennedy* (1976)

William L. O'Neill, *Coming Apart: An Informal History of the 1960s* (1971)

L. G. Paper, *The Promise and the Performance: The Leadership of John F. Kennedy* (1975)

Arthur M. Schlesinger, Jr., *A Thousand Days* (1965)

Anthony Summer, *Conspiracy* (1980)

H. G. Vatter, *The U.S. Economy in the 1950s* (1963)

Theodore H. White, *The Making of the President 1960* (1961)

Biographies and Autobiographies

Ezra Taft Benson, *Crossfire: The Eight Years With Eisenhower* (1962)

Dwight D. Eisenhower, *The White House Years* (1965)

John K. Galbraith, *A Life in Our Times* (1981)

T. Hoopes, *The Devil and John Foster Dulles* (1973)

Peter Lyon, *Eisenhower: Portrait of a Hero* (1974)

Richard M. Nixon, *Six Crises* (1962)

Stephen B. Oates, *Let the Trumpet Sound: The Life of Martin Luther King, Jr.* (1982)

Herbert Parmet, *Jack: The Struggle of John Fitzgerald Kennedy* (1980)

———, *JFK: The Presidency of John Fitzgerald Kennedy* (1983)

49

Tragic Presidency
The Turbulent Johnson Years, 1963–1968

In classical drama, the tragic hero overcomes great obstacles to rise to lofty heights. Then, at the pinnacle of attainment and glory, he is destroyed, not so much by enemies (although they are present to pick up the pieces), as by flaws in the hero's own character.

Lyndon Baines Johnson and Richard M. Nixon were tragic figures. In the face of formidable personal and social handicaps, both rose to the presidency of the United States, and both were confirmed in their position by huge majorities at the polls. Both were able men; both enjoyed exercising power; both were successful in the spheres in which they preferred to work: Johnson as a domestic reformer in the footsteps of his idol, Franklin D. Roosevelt; Nixon as a diplomat, an arranger of relations among nations, which he regarded as the twentieth-century president's principal responsibility.

And both were cast out in disgrace, Johnson because he clung stubbornly to a cause both lost and discredited, and Nixon because of behavior that was not only unworthy of a great leader, but explicable only as a reflection of his character. Johnson's undoing came about in foreign policy, which had never particularly interested him, and Nixon's on the domestic front, which he believed could take care of itself.

Marchers protest the Vietnam War in Washington, D.C., 1965.

JOHNSON AND THE GREAT SOCIETY

Lyndon B. Johnson came out of what people call "the sticks," the Pedernales River country of rural Texas. His family's means were ordinary. Although it was nearby, Johnson did not attend the distinguished University of Texas, but a teacher's college. He taught school for a year, but the hubbub, machinations, and possibilities of politics fascinated him. In 1931, he went to Washington as a congressman's aide, became a devotee of the New Deal, and returned to Texas to win a special election to Congress for himself in 1937.

In 1948, Johnson won the Democratic nomination to the Senate in a controversial primary. Because his margin was a handful of dubious votes, Texans called him "Landslide Lyndon," but in the Lone Star State, the Democratic nomination was tantamount to election. Back in Washington in 1949, Johnson's rise was meteoric: he was party whip in 1951 and majority leader in 1955.

The Wheeler-Dealer

Johnson owed his speedy rise to the influence of his patron and fellow Texan, House Speaker Sam Rayburn, but he held on to it because he was good at what he did. He was the master assembler of Senate majorities. Johnson's method was a combination of folksy charm, bargaining with senators who were pursuing pet projects, arm-twisting, and, so it was said, a

---

L.B.J.: THREE OPINIONS

"Were there no outside world, . . . Lyndon Johnson might conceivably have gone down as the greatest of twentieth-century presidents."

Theodore H. White,
The Making of the President, 1968 (1969)

"I sleep each night a little better, a little more confidently because Lyndon Johnson is my President. For I know he lives and thinks and works to make sure that for all America and indeed, the growing body of the free world, the morning shall always come."

Jack Valenti,
Presidential Aide, 1964

"We've got a wild man in the White House, and we are going to have to treat him as such."

Eugene McCarthy announcing
his candidacy for the Democratic
nomination for president, 1967

---

little blackmail. Rumor was that Johnson "had something" on every Democrat and most of the Republicans in the Senate; he was not a man to be crossed when he was after something.

These political skills enabled President Johnson to push through a comprehensive program of national reform that he called the Great Society and to effect a revolution in race relations that was more important in the long run than the Fourteenth and Fifteenth Amendments because it was Johnson, a century after their enactment, who put civil equality to work for the first time in nearly a century.

A Southerner Ends Segregation

Between 1955 and 1965, when civil-rights activists were fighting to end racial segregation in the South, a few faint voices suggested that when the Jim Crow laws were gone, as they must go, white and black southerners would enjoy better, more human relations than black and white northerners would. These observers reasoned that while legal segregation was a southern institution, personal interaction between blacks and whites in the South was personal and even intimate, whereas in the North, while blacks suffered few legal disabilities, racism and comprehensive residential segregation isolated the two races as people. With southern police forces routinely beating blacks during those years, and high-ranking southern white politicians proclaiming that they would fight to the death for white supremacy, it was hard to take the suggestion seriously.

But it was a southerner, himself a nominal supporter of segregation as late as 1960, Lyndon B. Johnson, who pushed through the Civil Rights Act of 1964, effectively outlawing school segregation and the "white" and "colored" signs on public accommodations that had marked everyday life in the South for half a century. It was also Johnson who responded immediately to a challenge presented to him during the election campaign of 1964 that effectively rounded out the civil-rights revolution.

The Mississippi Freedom Democrats

Mississippi was the most stubborn of the segregated states. It took 400 marshals, 300 troops, $4 million, and a loss of two lives to enroll one black student at the state university at Oxford. Precisely because Mississippi was so tough, the Student Nonviolent Coordinating Committee chose the state as the scene of a campaign to register blacks to vote: if Mississippi could be cracked, the whole South would follow.

The campaign was not very successful at the grass roots. If anything, the arrival of hundreds of idealistic young black and white university students caused

A VISTA volunteer, one of thousands of recruits in the war on poverty, talks to a child in Alabama.

white extremists to step up harassment of outspoken local blacks. The SNCC workers were terrorized. Three were kidnapped near Philadelphia, Mississippi, and murdered, probably with the connivance of law-enforcement officials. Black people who could not hop in a car and leave such horrors behind often preferred to keep quiet and stay at home. Besides, as rural and provincial themselves, they were suspicious of outsiders, however friendly.

If it was a draw within Mississippi, national outrage encouraged activists in the state, led by the forceful and articulate Fannie Lou Hamer, to take a Mississippi Freedom Democratic party delegation to the 1964 Democratic party convention in Atlantic City, New Jersey. The Freedom Democrats, supported by most northern state delegates, demanded that they, and not the segregationists, be recognized by the party. (The symbol of the regular Mississippi Democrats was a white cock and the words "white supremacy.")

Working through longtime liberal Hubert Humphrey, whom he had selected to be his vice-presidential running mate, Johnson tried to work out a compromise, dividing Mississippi's convention votes between the rival groups. The Freedom Democrats were not happy with "half a loaf," but the segregationists were furious and walked out of the convention, announcing that they would vote Republican in November. It was a historic moment. Johnson and other Democratic policymakers concluded that it was futile and even undesirable to try to keep die-hard southern segregationists in the party. They opted to court black voters, southern and northern, and to leave the racists to their opponents.

The Election of 1964

The election of 1964 seemed to prove the political wisdom of Johnson's decision. The president's Republican challenger, Senator Barry Goldwater of Arizona,

"Ten, nine, eight, seven . . .

six, five, four, three . . .

two, one . . .

These are the stakes. To make a world in which all of God's children can live . . .

or to go into the dark. We must either love each other or we must die . . .

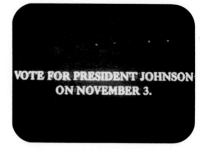

The stakes are too high for you to stay home."

One of the most powerful political messages ever seen on television, this commercial for Lyndon Johnson intimated that, if elected, Barry Goldwater would plunge the nation into nuclear war.

was no racist. Personally, he was a congenial and tolerant man. But racists and other extremists of the far right had made him their hero and their fanaticism helped transform his conservatism into a carping, vindictive campaign based on hatred, fear, and frighteningly simple solutions to problems that seemed to threaten democracy and the rights of the weak. Republican moderates cringed when Goldwater, accepting the party's nomination, said that "extremism in the pursuit of liberty is no vice." Worst of all in an age of nuclear terror, the grandson of a gun-toting frontier merchant sounded like a lover of war when he spoke on foreign policy. He seemed to say that the Cold War with the Soviet Union was a matter of which country was "tougher." Democratic strategists were able to depict him as a man who would rush for the red button in times of crisis. One Democratic television commercial depicted a little girl playing in a field of wildflowers and dissolved into a film of a nuclear blast.

The Democrat's victory was a landslide. Johnson won 61 percent of the popular vote and majorities in all but six states, five states of the Deep South plus Goldwater's native Arizona. As important as the prestige the victory meant, Johnson's coattails pulled in 70 first-term Democratic congressmen from normally Republican districts. The party's edge in the House was 295 to 140, in the Senate 68 to 32. Johnson legislated in great waves, not only rounding out his revolution in securing civil rights for blacks, but enacting his "Great Society," the creation of a government that assumed responsibility for the welfare of all.

The Voting Rights Act

The Voting Rights Act of 1965 put the federal power of enforcement behind the rights of blacks to vote. Secure in this right for the first time in almost a century, southern blacks rushed to register. In only ten years after Martin Luther King, Jr., had led his boycott against segregation on buses in Montgomery, the legal obstacles to black equality crumbled. Before long, southern white politicians who had built their careers on race baiting were showing up at black gatherings.

A former SNCC worker named Julian Bond elected to the Georgia state assembly was amused that businessmen who once called him a dangerous radical now wanted to take him out to lunch. By the early 1970s, all southern Democrats were courting black votes, however awkward it was for some. In Alabama's gubernatorial election of 1982, George Wallace, the onetime southern symbol of resistance to integration, not only courted black votes, but owed his election to them: Alabama blacks found his Republican opponent by far the worse choice. Even southern Republicans stopped expressing the sentiments that had originally taken them into the G.O.P. Strom Thurmond of South Carolina, whose career overlapped with the old generation of the open "nigger-baiting" school, and who became a Republican in part because of liberal Democratic policies on race, was addressing black audiences by 1982.

The Voting Rights Act of 1965 also prompted an increase in black voting in the northern and western states. Not only Atlanta and New Orleans, but Newark, Gary, and Detroit elected black mayors during the 1970s. By 1984, the nation's second and third largest cities, Chicago and Los Angeles, had black mayors and Tom Bradley of Los Angeles, a former policeman, just missed winning the governorship of California.

The Great Society

If Johnson's sponsorship of full civil rights for blacks was partly forced on him by political realities, his concern for the poor and disadvantaged of all races was sincere and deeply felt. He had had to struggle himself and, in Texas politics, had been regarded as a friend of mostly poor Mexican-Americans. Johnson worshiped Franklin D. Roosevelt and wanted to be remembered in history as the president who completed what the New Deal had started. He envisioned an America

> where no child will go unfed and no youngster will go unschooled; where every child has a good teacher and every teacher has good pay, and both have good classrooms; where every human being has dignity and every worker has a job; where education is blind to color and employment is unaware of race: where decency appeals and courage abounds.

His war on poverty program, which was directed by the new Office of Economic Opportunity, funded a Job Corps that retrained unemployed people for the new kinds of jobs available in high-technology industries. The OEO recruited boys and girls from impoverished families for catch-up education in special Head Start schools and young men and women for placement in universities. Other programs provided financial help and tutoring in order to compensate for the economic and cultural handicaps of growing up in poverty. Volunteers in Service to America (VISTA) was a domestic Peace Corps, sending social workers and teachers into decaying inner cities and poor rural areas. Medicare provided government-funded health insurance for the elderly, chronically ill, and very poor.

Nor did the Great Society neglect the middle and working classes. Generous funding of schools, colleges,

A young black man urges an elder to register to vote in Edwards, Mississippi.

and universities and extremely cheap student loans made it possible for hundreds of thousands of young people to secure an education otherwise closed to them.

Some of these acts were legislated before the lopsided election of 1964. But it was after his great victory, with the hordes of freshman Democratic congressmen beholden to his landslide for their seats, that the program was completed.

FOREIGN POLICY IN THE 1960s

Lyndon Johnson knew that the presidents whom history remembered were those who *acted*, and he wanted to be remembered. The reputation he hoped to earn was as a benefactor of America's poor and forgotten, and it may well be that future historians will center their attention on his Great Society.

During Johnson's five years in the White House, however, he involved, then mired, the United States in a war in a Southeast Asian country of which, before 1964, few Americans had even heard. The policy decisions that Johnson made in Vietnam owed in large part to his determination to be decisive and to have his way abroad as well as at home. However, in order to understand fully the morass that Vietnam became, it is necessary to understand the foreign policy shifts of Johnson's predecessor, John F. Kennedy.

Flexible Response

Both Kennedy and Johnson accepted the fact of the Cold War with the Soviet Union; indeed, they had little choice to do otherwise. "Freedom and communism are in deadly embrace," Kennedy said, "the world cannot exist half slave and half free." Johnson concurred in that opinion. Acting on the claim of 1960 that a missile gap between the Soviet Union and the United States threatened American security, both presidents lavished money on research programs designed to improve the rockets with which, in case of war with Russia, nuclear weapons would be delivered.

Advised by intellectuals from universities and "think tanks," such as Walt W. Rostow and McGeorge Bundy, Kennedy introduced the idea of "flexible response" to American foreign policy. Instead of threatening the use of nuclear weapons at every Soviet provocation, as Dulles had done, the United States would respond to foreign developments of which it disapproved in proportion to the threat. For example, if the Soviets were suspected of funding guerrilla movements in countries that were friendly to the United States, or of subverting elections, the United States would fund its own military forces to back and intervene clandestinely in the politics of other countries. Toward this end, Kennedy sponsored the development of elite antiguerrilla units in the army, such as the Green Berets, and increased funding of the spy network maintained by the Central Intelligence Agency.

Into the Third World

Unlike Eisenhower, who thought in traditional terms that wealthy Europe and Japan were the areas that counted in the Cold War competition, Kennedy stated that "the great battleground for the defense and expansion of freedom today is the whole southern half of the globe—Asia, Latin America, Africa, and the Middle East—the lands of the rising peoples."

He preferred to back democratic reform movements in the developing countries. Kennedy took the lead in organizing the Alliance for Progress in the Western Hemisphere, a program that offered economic aid to friendly Latin American nations in the hope that they would adopt free institutions.

However, the choice in the volatile Third World was rarely between liberal-minded reform movements and pro-Communist dictatorships. Envy of American riches, a legacy of American support for repressive and exploitative dictators, the easy flexibility and opportunism of the Soviets, and the romantic lack of realism common in revolutionary movements, particularly in Latin America, meant that the rebels were at best suspicious of American imperialism and willing to look to the Russians for assistance.

Often, instead of trying to woo these groups, Kennedy and Johnson took the advice of experts who saw the new leaders as pawns of "monolithic Communism."

The Bay of Pigs

At about the same time that Kennedy was inaugurated, Soviet leader Nikita Khrushchev reversed his movement toward détente with the United States. He may have been frightened by Kennedy's aggressive speeches (particularly the defiant inaugural address); he may have been under pressure by hard-line Cold Warriors within his own government; or he may have sensed that the youth and inexperience of the new president provided a rare opportunity for easy limited victories in the game of maneuver that Khrushchev loved so well. In any case, Kennedy's first year in office was a time of American setbacks in the international competition between the superpowers and increasing recklessness on the part of the Soviet Union.

The first humiliation was Kennedy's doing. He had inherited from Eisenhower a well-advanced plan to oust the anti-American dictator of Cuba, Fidel Castro, who had come to power on New Year's Day 1960. Under Eisenhower, the CIA had trained 2,000 anti-Castro Cubans and mercenary soldiers in Florida and Central America, and they were ready to invade Cuba when Kennedy took over. The Central Intelligence Agency assured the president that Castro was unpopular with the Cuban people. At the sound of the first shot, anti-Castro rebellions would break out all over the island. Cuba had been virtually an American fief; it was plausible to a president who had made no particular study of Latin American affairs. On April 17, 1961, the shot was fired. The anti-Castro forces waded ashore at a place called the Bay of Pigs.

It was a disaster. There was no uprising. Castro's crack troops, seasoned by a long revolution, made short work of the invaders. Castro's popularity soared at home for having resisted what he called imperialist aggression, and he moved closer to the Soviet Union. Kennedy was denounced all over Latin America, and, on national television, he assumed full responsibility for the fiasco.

Vienna and Berlin

At a summit meeting in Vienna in June, Kennedy was outwitted and upstaged by an arrogant Khrushchev.

John Kennedy peers over the Berlin Wall into East Berlin during a Cold War era visit to West Berlin, June 26, 1963.

The Russian tongue-tied him in private and, when they were before reporters, treated him like a nice boy who only needed teaching. A man of perhaps too much self-confidence, Kennedy returned home seething with anger, and Khrushchev was encouraged to act more recklessly. The Soviets resumed nuclear testing in the atmosphere and ordered the sealing of the border between East and West Berlin.

The Communist East Germans had been plagued by the defection of their citizens, particularly highly trained technologists who could double and triple their incomes in West Germany's booming economy. This "brain drain" threatened to cripple East German industry, and the Communists winced at each defection as a Western propaganda victory, people "voting with their feet." To put an end to it, Khrushchev built a wall the length of the city that was as ugly in reality as it was symbolically.

Kennedy allowed the Berlin Wall to stand, and he was immediately attacked by critics who said that he could have bulldozed it without interference from the Russians. Although that was an arguable proposition, Kennedy was determined not to allow Khrushchev to win another round.

Drawing the Line

The crunch came in October 1962. A U-2 flight over Cuba had revealed that the Soviets were constructing installations for nuclear missiles aimed at the United States. Kennedy rejected a proposal by Dean Acheson and others that bombers destroy them, preferring the caution counseled by his brother, Attorney General Robert F. Kennedy. He proclaimed a naval blockade of the island and demanded that the sites be dismantled and the nuclear weapons removed.

For four days, Khrushchev refused to budge. Work on the sites continued, and Soviet ships loaded with more missiles continued on their way to Cuba. Americans gathered solemnly around their television sets, apprehensive that the nuclear holocaust would begin any hour. Secretary of State Dean Rusk revealed that the White House was nervous too. "We're eyeball to eyeball," he said.

Rusk added, "I think the other fellow just blinked." The Cuba-bound freighters first stopped in mid-ocean and then turned around. On October 26, Khrushchev sent a long conciliatory letter to Kennedy in which he agreed to remove the missiles if the United States pledged never to invade Cuba. The next day, a second letter said that the Soviets would withdraw their nuclear weapons if the United States would remove its missiles from Turkey, which bordered the Soviet Union.

Before the Cuban missile crisis, Kennedy had considered dismantling the Turkish missile sites as a gesture of friendship. Calculating that the difference in the two Soviet offers indicated indecision in the Kremlin, he saw a chance for a prestigious victory. Kennedy ignored the second note and accepted the terms of the first. On October 28, Khrushchev accepted.

Relations Improve

The president thought that the Cuban missile crisis was the turning point of his presidency. He made commemorative gifts to everyone who had advised or merely stood by him during that tense October. In fact, both Kennedy and the Soviets were shaken by their flirtation with catastrophe and acted more responsibly after 1962. A "hot line" was installed in both the White House and the Kremlin so that, in future crises, Russian and American leaders could communicate instantly with one another. Then, following a Kennedy speech, the Soviet Union joined the United States and the United Kingdom in signing a treaty that banned nuclear testing in the atmosphere. (France and China, the only other nuclear powers, did not sign.)

While relations between the superpowers were periodically strained over the next two decades, the threat of a nuclear holocaust was not repeated. Kennedy's successors from Johnson to Carter learned the lesson of October 1962, and worked to avoid or nip conflicts that could become "eyeball to eyeball" nuclear confrontations before they did so.

If they shied away from the ultimate confrontation, neither the Soviets, headed by Leonid Brezhnev after 1964, nor the Americans ceased to maneuver for little victories in the Third World. Through diplomacy, economic aid and technological assistance to developing nations, and clandestine operations (by the CIA on the American side), both superpowers continued to act as though the globe were a game board with two players and a hundred pieces to be moved and taken. Between 1962 and 1976, the United States was openly involved in Cold War actions in the Dominican Republic, the Congo, Angola, the Middle East, and Latin America. It was, however, in Indochina where the United States saw international politicking turn into a monster.

Vietnam! Vietnam!

By the middle of 1963, Kennedy had given up on the pro-American dictator of South Vietnam whom he had inherited from Eisenhower and Dulles, Ngo Dinh Diem. Surrounded by corrupt relatives, Diem's repressive policies, high taxes, and favoritism toward Roman Catholic Vietnamese had made him an unpopular dictator. Capitalizing on Diem's failure, the National Liberation Front, then an alliance of many groups, including Communists, increased its power in the countryside. The NLF governed many villages, hit others in guerrilla raids, and selectively assassinated Diem's officials. Once the sun set, the Saigon government controlled little more than the capital, the major towns, and part of the fertile rice-growing Mekong River delta. Elsewhere, NLF guerrillas moved freely.

In 1963, Diem was assassinated in a military coup, possibly with CIA connivance. There followed a period of comic-opera political instability and steady gains by the National Liberation Front. Kennedy apparently gave up on the possibility of military victory and ordered a reduction in the 16,000-man American contingent in the country. When some advisers told him that an increase in troops might win the war, he said that to get involved more deeply in the war was like "taking a drink. The effect wears off, and you have to take another." Johnson, who was wary of the bottle, might have taken heed of this prophecy. But he was still thinking in terms of the loss of China and the McCarthyism that had flavored the Washington of the late 1940s and early 1950s, when he began his career in the Senate. He vowed that he was "not going

Buddhist monk Quang Duc immolates himself to protest the anti-Buddhist policies of South Vietnamese president Ngo Dinh Diem. The photo was taken by Malcolm Brown and was among the most shocking to come out of the Vietnam War.

to be the President who saw Southeast Asia go the way China went."

Johnson's vision, so broad on the home front, was blinded by past politics when he looked at the rest of the world. He did not see that "liberation" movements in the Third World, however unsavory their leaders often were, were nevertheless rooted in genuine grievances with which the United States might sympathize, and that they were inspired by outside powers, China or the Soviet Union or both. Thus misled, he believed that increased exertion of power by the United States on behalf of "our Vietnamese" could carry the day.

Escalation

In July 1964, in the Gulf of Tonkin, three North Vietnamese PT boats apparently attacked an American destroyer that was providing cover for a South Vietnamese commando raid in North Vietnam. In August, Johnson asked Congress to pass a resolution that would give him authority to respond to such threats to American forces. With only two dissenting votes, from maverick senators Wayne Morse of Oregon and Ernest Gruening of Alaska, Congress complied. The Gulf of Tonkin resolution was, in effect, a blank check to wage war.

During the election year, Johnson did little. Against Goldwater, he characterized himself as the peace candidate. Once Goldwater was defeated, however, Johnson began the process of "escalation" that became the catchword of his presidency. On election day 1964, there were 23,000 American troops in Vietnam. By September 1965, there were 130,000, and by December 1965, 184,000. When Johnson left office in 1969, the total was 541,000, a massive military force.

Johnson also ordered an air war in both North and South Vietnam in which more bombs were dropped than on all America's enemies during the Second World War. By the time the war was concluded in 1973, it had cost $140 billion, 200,000 American casualties, 800,000 South Vietnamese dead and wounded, and probably about the same number of North Vietnamese. During 1968, the most savage year of the war, 40 Americans were killed and 128 were wounded each day.

And yet, the American effort in Vietnam never came close to succeeding. Each escalation brought a counterescalation from Communist North Vietnam and increased aid from both China and the Soviet Union. What had begun as a civil war among South Vietnamese, with minimal outside interference, became a Cold War battlefield on which both superpowers and China participated, but only Americans were killed. The experience frustrated, mystified, and divided the United States.

A war protestor's sign hangs on the White House fence.

TROUBLED YEARS

No president ever craved consensus as did Lyndon B. Johnson. In making his plea for civil-rights legislation, he adopted the slogan of the movement, "We Shall Overcome." He meant that *all* Americans would overcome the blight of racial discrimination. Another favorite saying was a quotation from the biblical book of Isaiah, "Let us come together." Johnson did not want a majority, even a large one such as he won in 1964. He wanted an overwhelming unity of Americans behind him. What he got was a people divided.

The war in Vietnam was the chief source of Johnson's disappointment. Hundreds of thousands of Americans protested against it for a variety of reasons. Some believed that the enemy, which the administration called the Viet Cong, or Vietnamese Communists, more closely represented the will of the Vietnamese people than did the succession of governments that were set up in pro-American South Vietnam. In other words, the United States was on the wrong, undemocratic side.

Others believed that regardless of Vietnamese sentiments, the United States was betraying its ideals by unleashing a destructive modern technology on an already poor nation: the war in Vietnam was a particularly brutal and inhumane war. There were pacifists in the antiwar movement. And some high-placed

In response to the vocal demonstrations of antiwar activists, supporters of the Vietnam War organized rallies at which they displayed their sentiment with slogans such as "America, Love It or Leave It."

officials and even military men thought that the war was, simply, ill advised. The United States was draining its wealth and morale in a part of the world that did not matter in terms of American security.

If the antiwar movement was the protest that eventually toppled Johnson, it was not the only expression of discontent in the Great Society. What is remarkable about the troubles of the 1960s is that anti-Great Society protest came particularly from groups that most benefited from the Johnson reforms.

Black Separatism

Some of the fiercest anti-Johnson rhetoric came from the blacks, for whom the president believed he did so much. While the majority of black people supported the Great Society, many younger militants, particularly in the North, attacked the president's integrationist policies in the name of the "black-power" movement.

Black power meant many things. To sensible black leaders such as the Reverend Jesse Jackson, and to intellectuals such as sociologist Charles Hamilton, it meant pressure politics in the time honored tradition of American ethnic groups, blacks demanding concessions for people of their race on the basis of the votes they could either deliver to or withhold from a political candidate. To a tiny group of black nationalists, it meant demanding a part of the United States for the formation of a separate nation for blacks only. To the great majority of advocates of black power, the slogan reduced to nothing more than fashion, dressing up in dashikis, wearing hair styles called "Afros," and cutting off friendships and casual social relationships with whites.

Black power was not a political program, but a cry of anguish and anger against the discrimination of the past and the discovery that legal equality did little to remedy the social and psychological burdens from which American blacks suffered: poverty, high unemployment, inferior educational opportunities, severe health problems unknown to whites, high crime rates in black neighborhoods, a sense of inadequacy bred over three centuries of oppression.

Malcolm X and Violence

Malcolm Little, or Malcolm X as he called himself, stating that a slaveowner had stolen his real African name, was the spellbinding preacher who inspired the black-power movement. A member of the Nation of Islam, or Black Muslims, Malcolm said that black people should reject Martin Luther King, Jr.'s, call to integrate into American society and, instead, separate from whites and glory in their blackness. Many young blacks, particularly in the North, were captivated by this message of defiance. One important convert was a West Indian immigrant, Stokely Carmichael, who expelled all whites from SNCC in 1966, effectively taking that group out of the civil-rights movement.

Malcolm's admonition to meet white racist violence with black violence appealed to former civil-rights workers who had been beaten by police and to teenage blacks in the urban ghettos. Carmichael's successor as the head of SNCC, Hubert Geroid "H. Rap" Brown, proclaimed as his motto, "Burn, Baby, Burn." In Oakland, California, two college students, Huey P. Newton and Bobby Seale, formed the Black Panther Party

BLACK POWER

The most conspicuous individual in the emergence of the black-power movement was West Indian-born Stokely Carmichael. In 1966, he explained what he meant by black power: "If we are to proceed toward true liberation, we must cut ourselves off from white people. We must form our own institutions, credit unions, co-ops, political parties, write our own histories. . . ."

Malcolm X was a founder of the black-power movement of the 1960s.

worked in the civil-rights movement. In 1963, a new national youth organization, Students for a Democratic Society (SDS), issued the "Port Huron statement," a comprehensive critique of American society written by a graduate of the University of Michigan, Tom Hayden. The SDS called for young people to take the lead in drafting a program by which the United States could be made genuinely democratic and a force for peace and justice.

Like the advocates of black power, the New Left, as SDS and other organizations came to be called, was not so much a political movement as an explosion of anger and frustration. Hayden and a few other youth leaders tried to channel student energies to concrete concerns like civil rights for blacks, the problems of the poor, and the power of large corporations in American society; but most of the campus riots of the late 1960s were unfocused, aimed at local grievances such as student participation in setting university rules, or directed against the war in Vietnam, a matter beyond the competence of university presidents and local merchants (major targets of student rebellion) to solve.

Massive protest on campuses began at the University of California at Berkeley with the founding of the Free

for Self-Defense. They were immediately involved in violent confrontations with police because of their insistence that they be allowed to patrol black neighborhoods with firearms.

Violence haunted black America during the 1960s. Malcolm X fell out of favor with the Black Muslims and was gunned down by assassins in 1965. Also in 1965, a riot in the Watts district of Los Angeles resulted in 34 deaths and $35 million in property damages. In 1966 and 1967, black riots raged in the ghettos of many cities. When Martin Luther King, Jr., was killed by a white racist, James Earl Ray, in 1968, the smoke from burning set afire by rioters in Washington wafted into the White House itself.

The Student Movement

Just as troubling was discontent among another group that was favored by Johnson's Great Society reforms, university students. By 1963, it already was clear that the baby-boom generation was not so placid in its politics as the youth of the 1950s had been. Students demonstrated against capital punishment, protested against the violations of civil liberties by groups like the House Un-American Activities Committee, and

A mule-drawn cart carries the body of civil-rights leader Martin Luther King at his funeral in Atlanta, Georgia.

Speech Movement in 1964. By 1968, protest took a violent turn with students at Columbia University seizing several buildings and refusing to budge until they were forcibly removed by police.

The Counterculture

By 1966, many young people, high school as well as college students, were dropping out of politics to pursue a personal rebellion. In the Haight-Ashbury district of San Francisco and in the East Village of New York, thousands of teenagers gathered to establish what they called a "counterculture," a new way of living based on promiscuous sex, drugs (particularly marijuana and a synthetic hallucinogen, LSD), and extravagant colorful clothing. They called themselves "flower children," free of the pressures and preoccupations of American materialism. Other Americans called them "hippies" and alternately condemned them as lazy, immoral "long-haired kids" and were amused by them. In both New York and San Francisco, tour buses took curiosity seekers through hippie neighborhoods as though they were exotic foreign countries. When tourists from small towns snapped shots of counterculture fauna, some hippies whipped out cameras and took pictures of them.

When commercialization seemed to be destroying the vitality of the counterculture, numerous flower children retreated to communes in the California mountains and New Mexico desert. But because the self-fulfillment of individuals was the principal goal of the phenomenon, and because drugs played a large part in the culture, the communes were doomed from the start. The most fundamental matters of procuring the necessities of health and sanitation were neglected.

The Antiwar Movement

Black-power militants, student activists, and ostensibly political rebels called "yippies" joined with pacifists and hundreds of thousands of troubled Americans in

DEMONSTRATION DECADE

Between 1963 and 1968, according to the National Commission on the Causes and Prevention of Violence, there were

369 civil-rights demonstrations
239 black riots and disturbances
213 white terrorist attacks against civil-rights workers
104 antiwar demonstrations
91 student protests on campus
54 segregationist clashes with counter-demonstrators
24 anti-integration demonstrations

the single most important protest movement of the 1960s, the opposition to Lyndon Johnson's war in Vietnam. Each time the president escalated the American war effort, more and more people joined the angry opposition to it.

In the spring of 1965, organizers of a rally against the war in Washington made plans for 2,000 protesters, and 25,000 actually came. In October 1965, 100,000 people demonstrated in 90 cities. In April 1967, 300,000 people marched to protest the Vietnam War in New York and San Francisco. In Washington, in the autumn of 1969, after Johnson had left office

PROTEST IN AMERICA

Saul Alinsky, a well-known radical organizer, had little but contempt for the "New Left" of the 1960s. He regarded university student rebels as dilettantes and chided them for their claims that the United States was a repressive nation: "True, there is government harassment, but there still is that relative freedom to fight. I can attack my government, try to organize to change it. That's more than I can do in Moscow, Peking, or Havana."

After Eugene McCarthy's moral victory in the New Hampshire primary in March 1968, President Johnson announced his retirement.

*Police confront antiwar demonstrators during the Democratic national convention in Chicago,
August 28, 1968.*

and the war continued, almost 800,000 Americans rallied against the bloodletting.

By the time Johnson left office, a minority of the antiwar protesters turned to confrontation politics and even violence. A group called the Resistance urged those who opposed the war not to pay their taxes or, if they were young men, to refuse to serve in the armed forces. Some 40,000 young men did go into exile, usually to Canada or Sweden. Over 500,000 desertions and 250,000 "bad discharges" had been recorded. Protesters attempted to obstruct the induction process in Oakland, California. The greatest confrontation came in Chicago during the Democratic national convention in 1968, when several thousand young antiwar activists battled with Chicago police in the streets of the city.

Although Lyndon Johnson had heard the shouts of many demonstrators, he was not in Chicago to hear the battle. If he had run again, in 1968, won, and served a full term, he would have been in office longer than any other president except F.D.R. But Johnson had dropped out of the race early in the year. He said it was because he did not expect to have a long life; indeed, he died at his Texas home in 1973 at the age of 65. But Johnson was so quintessentially a political animal that almost every political analyst agreed that he had quit because he thought the voters of 1968 would repudiate him.

N O T A B L E   P E O P L E

BOB DYLAN (b. 1941)

Minstrel of the 1960s, Bob Dylan.

Bob Dylan is the stage name of Robert Zimmerman, who was born on May 24, 1941, in Duluth, Minnesota, and grew up in Hibbings, a drab hard-working industrial town in the Mesabi Range, America's principal source of iron ore. Hibbings was a working-class town; the majority of its people were immigrants or the children or grandchildren of immigrants, particularly from Finland and the Slavic nations of Eastern Europe. This made Bob Zimmerman twice alienated, not quite at home. His family was Jewish, albeit not religious, and was middle class; the proprietors of a furniture store.

The Zimmermans' fortunes were closely tied to employment in the iron mines. Later, as Bob Dylan, Zimmerman said that his least favorite job at the store was repossessing furniture on which the purchasers could not make payments. It is possible that he was assigned that unpleasant task, although the repossession of sofas and chairs from frustrated, burly miners was not the kind of job on which one sent a skinny teenager. Indeed, much of what Bob Dylan said about himself as one of the most successful entertainers of the troubled 1960s was romantic contrivance. He told of living a vagabond's life and of struggling to make his voice heard. But his story was much more that of an instant sensation. He enjoyed an ordinary middle-class youth, and it was perhaps for that reason that he was so important to the discontented middle-class youth of the 1960s who demonstrated their anger by protesting noisily and buying his recordings.

By 1965, half the American population was under the age of 25 and, as marketing experts had calculated before the decade began, they were extremely affluent. Because they could spend their money on things that amused them, teenagers were responsible for 75 percent of the phonograph records sold in the United States.

Bob Dylan was one of the major beneficiaries of this phenomenon. Already as a teenager in Hibbings, he was rebelling. He adopted the styles of 1950s beatniks and took an interest in both past and contemporary critics of comfortable, materialistic, security-conscious, and conformist middle-class America.

He expressed his own criticisms through a guitar and harmonica bought for him when he was a teenager, learning to play both instruments simultaneously in the manner of the old "one-man band" comedy acts.

The songs that he wrote were far from comic. On the contrary, they were serious, if maudlin, romanticizations of the "common people" and sarcastic assaults on the America of the corporations, racial prejudice, war, and the timid middle classes. He disdained the slick, professional groups that were recording folk songs in the late 1950s, such as the Weavers, the Kingston Trio, and the Limeliters, and searched in the past for their predecessors. His hero was the Oklahoma balladeer Woody Guthrie, who had been a genuine vagabond and the author of perhaps hundreds of songs that celebrated the common people and condemned wealth and power.

Not only did Bob Dylan visit Guthrie, who was dying in a New Jersey hospital of a rare hereditary disease, but he updated the flavor of Guthrie's protest and imitated his rough-edged, grating singing style. Dylan could not sing very well; there must have been many better guitarists in the country; and the lyrics he wrote were trite. But he struck a chord in young people. He arrived in New York at the beginning of 1961, was a sensation in the coffeehouses of Greenwich Village within months, and had a contract with Columbia Records by fall.

His first album, released in February 1962, was an immediate hit. The curly-headed kid from Minnesota was the heir to such singing sensations of the 1950s as Bill Haley and the Comets, the first white musical group to record rock-'n'-roll, and Elvis Presley, the entertainment king of the decade. During the first half of the 1960s, only the Beatles, a quartet from England, made more money than Dylan in the recorded-music business.

With the exception of the Beach Boys, who marketed a cheery romanticization of Southern California teenage indolence, there was something new about the entertainers of the 1960s. Bill Haley and Elvis Presley had been content to be show people, and troubadors such as Woody Guthrie and Pete Seeger, who sang about social issues, had only small followings. But songs of protest were at the center of the popular culture marketplace in the 1960s, and the stars of the decade were considered teachers and moral leaders by their fans.

They reacted in different ways to this beatification. John Lennon, the most articulate of the Beatles, commented on the absurd implications of the mass worship of his group that the Beatles were better known than Jesus. (Instead of recognizing Lennon's barbed criticism of Beatlemania, religious leaders attacked *him* for being blasphemous.) Joan Baez, the leading woman protest singer, took her messianic role very seriously, solemnly divulging intimate details of her life to "good friends" gathered in groups of 10,000 and 20,000. Dylan, however, was overwhelmed and angered by it.

He refused to play the moral spokesman and, after a near-fatal automobile accident, retired to his country home in Woodstock, New York. Even when the central event of the counterculture of the 1960s was held within a few miles of his farm, Dylan refused to appear. He was, however, still taken very seriously. Professors of psychology, sociology, history, and political science wrote serious studies of his songs. In 1970, Princeton University awarded Dylan an honorary doctorate, which he accepted.

For Further Reading

Overviews and Classics

Jim F. Heath, *Decade of Disillusion: The Kennedy-Johnson Years* (1975)
Godfrey Hodgson, *America in Our Time* (1976)
William L. O'Neill, *Coming Apart: An Informal History of the 1960s* (1971)

Valuable Special Studies

Ronald Berman, *America in the Sixties* (1968)
Joseph R. Conlin, *The Troubles: A Jaundiced Glance Back at the Movement of the 1960s* (1982)
Morris Dickstein, *Gates of Eden: American Culture in the Sixties* (1977)
Theodore Draper, *Abuse of Power* (1967)
Frances Fitzgerald, *Fire in the Lake* (1972)
Todd Gitlin, *The Whole World is Watching* (1981)
David Halberstam, *The Making of a Quagmire* (1956)
Kenneth Keniston, *Young Radicals* (1968)
Sar A. Levitan, William B. Johnson, and Robert Taggart, *Still a Dream: The Changing Status of Blacks Since 1960* (1975)
James T. Patterson, *America's Struggle Against Poverty, 1900–1980* (1981)
Marcus G. Raskin and Bernard Fall, *The Vietnam Reader* (1965)
Theodore Roszak, *The Making of a Counter-Culture* (1969)
Kirkpatrick Sale, *SDS* (1973)
Arthur M. Schlesinger, Jr., *Bitter Heritage: Vietnam and American Democracy* (1967)
Irwin Unger, *The Movement* (1974)
Richard Walton, *The Foreign Policy of John F. Kennedy* (1972)
Theodore H. White, *The Making of the President, 1964* (1965)
Howard Zinn, *SNCC* (1965)

Biographies and Autobiographies

Robert Caro, *The Years of Lyndon Johnson* (1982)
Alex Haley, *The Autobiography of Malcolm X* (1965)
Doris Kearns, *Lyndon Johnson and the American Dream* (1976)
David Lewis, *King: A Critical Biography* (1970)
Merle Miller, *Lyndon: An Oral Biography* (1980)
Stephen B. Oates, *Let the Trumpet Sound* (1982)

50

Repudiation and Resignation
Presidential Crisis, Cultural Disarray, 1968–1975

In 1967, Eugene McCarthy was in his second term as senator from Minnesota. He was a tall man with a gray solemnity, even a glumness about him. His record as a liberal workhorse was solid, but no one thought of him as a mover and shaker. Minnesota already had its walking earthquake of energy and exuberance in Hubert Humphrey, vice president under Johnson. McCarthy seemed just right to stay at home, anchoring Minnesota's long liberal tradition in bedrock.

But McCarthy was anguished by the issue that the vice president had to dodge, the war in Vietnam. Late in 1967, he announced that he would stand as a candidate for the Democratic presidential nomination, challenging Lyndon B. Johnson on that issue.

Richard M. Nixon with transcripts of the Watergate tapes that implicated him in the criminal cover-up of a break-in at the Democratic party headquarters.

THE ELECTION OF *1968*

Political experts admired McCarthy's principle and pluck. A few were enchanted by his diffidence: with plenty of mediocrities lusting unashamedly after public office, he seemed genuinely to believe that a public servant should serve a cause. But the experts gave him little chance. Mc-

Carthy's only base of support was within the largely middle-class antiwar movement. The labor unions, vital to Democratic party success at the polls, begrudged him several votes against their legislative programs; he struck no chord among either black or ethnic minorities (despite his somewhat mystical Roman Catholic religion); and he positively disdained big city mayors like Chicago's Richard E. Daley. A portion of the educated, cultured, affluent liberal middle class was not, the professionals said, a foundation on which to build an electoral majority.

McCarthy Ends Johnson's Career

Time was to prove them right. But in 1968, antiwar activists were so aroused that, like Goldwater's right-wingers among the Republicans in 1964, they were able to turn the Democratic party upside down (and, in 1972, to capture it). At McCarthy's call, thousands of university students dropped their studies and rushed to New Hampshire, scene of the first presidential primary. They agreed to get "clean for Gene," shearing their long "hippie" hair, shaving their beards, and donning neckties, brassieres, and proper dresses so as not to alienate the people of the conservative state from the issue at hand—the war. Sleeping on the floors of McCarthy storefront headquarters, they rang door-

Eugene McCarthy campaigns during the 1968 primaries.

bells, handed out pamphlets at supermarkets, and stuffed envelopes.

President Johnson knew enough of the country's anxiety over the war to be concerned. He kept his name off the ballot. Instead, the governor of New Hampshire ran as his proxy. The vote was evenly split, but such a rebuke of an incumbent president in a traditionally cautious and conservative state promised bigger McCarthy victories elsewhere. Johnson knew it. On national television, he announced that he would retire when his term expired.

The Democrats: Who Will End the War?

Johnson's announcement caught everyone by surprise. Vice President Humphrey, in Mexico on a good-will tour, rushed back to Washington to throw his hat in the ring. He had an immediate edge on McCarthy because of long-standing ties with labor, blacks, big city Democratic machines, the party's professionals, and contributors generous with a dollar.

The McCarthy backers expected Humphrey to run and welcomed the contest. What they could not foresee was that in the wake of Johnson's withdrawal, Robert F. Kennedy also rushed to enter the race. Kennedy was a real threat to both McCarthy and Humphrey. Johnson had eased him out of his cabinet as soon after John Kennedy's death as it was seemly to do so. L.B.J. did not like "Bobby," whose presence kept him in the Kennedy shadow. In fact, R.F.K. looked on Johnson almost as a usurper of a Kennedy birthright. After methodical public opinion polls typical of the Kennedy clan showed that he could win a Senate seat in New York despite his lack of association with the state, Robert Kennedy ran, won, and became a critic of the war and a leading liberal spokesman.

His connections with minorities were as strong as Humphrey's. He was a close personal friend of Cesar Chavez, leader of the mostly Hispanic farmworkers' union in California and the Southwest. Even with blacks, on whose behalf Humphrey had labored since the 1940s, Kennedy was popular. When Martin Luther King, Jr., was assassinated on April 4, 1968, Bobby's response seemed more sincere and was better received than the respects of any other Democrat. He had maintained his connections with the old-line party professionals and the labor movement. Indeed, within the Democratic party, his cynical political realism and opportunism made him anathema only to the group that continued to support McCarthy. They attacked him as avidly as they attacked Johnson and Humphrey.

Kennedy ran strong although not without setbacks. For example, McCarthy won the next-to-last primary, in Oregon. Then, on the very night he won the last

Minutes before he was assassinated, Senator Robert F. Kennedy celebrates his victory in the California Democratic primary.

1964. After 1964, Nixon attended every local Republican function to which he was invited, no matter how small the town, insignificant the occasion, or tawdry the candidate he was to endorse. By making himself so available to the party's grass-roots workers, Nixon built up energetic, active cadres of supporters.

The Democrats were badly split; many in the antiwar wing announced that they would vote for the pacifist pediatrician Benjamin Spock. This enabled Nixon to waffle on the war issue. He espoused a hawkish military policy at the same time that he reminded voters that a Republican president, Dwight D. Eisenhower, had ended the war in Korea.

The threat to Nixon's candidacy came not from within his party but from outside. This was the American Independent party, founded by Governor George Wallace when he calculated that he had no chance to win the Democratic nomination. A diminutive, combative man—reporters called him a bantam fighting cock—Wallace barnstormed the country and attempted to forge an odd alliance of Republican right-wing extremists and blue-collar workingpeople who felt that the Democratic party had forgotten them in its anxiety to appeal to the blacks. This "white backlash" vote appeared to grow after Robert Kennedy was killed. Already indifferent to the aloof McCarthy,

of the primaries in California, Robert Kennedy was assassinated, shot point-blank in the head by Sirhan B. Sirhan, a Jordanian who disliked Kennedy's support for the Jewish state of Israel.

The tragedy demoralized the antiwar Democrats and undoubtedly contributed to the week-long riots in Chicago that made a mockery of the Democratic national convention. Many Kennedy supporters found it impossible to swing behind McCarthy and backed Senator George McGovern of South Dakota instead. Humphrey won the Democratic nomination on the first ballot. As a gesture toward blue-collar ethnics whose aspirations had been aroused by John F. Kennedy, and who seemed to be supporting Bobby, Humphrey chose a Roman Catholic running mate, Senator Edmund B. Muskie of Maine.

Nixon and Wallace

Richard M. Nixon easily won the Republican nomination at a placid convention in Miami Beach. Although the former vice president had retired from politics in 1962, after failing in an attempt to become governor of California, he had doggedly rebuilt his position in the G.O.P. He firmed up his support among eastern moderate Republicans and won over Republican conservatives by working hard for Goldwater in

Hubert Humphrey with running mate Edmund B. Muskie.

many workingpeople who had liked Kennedy found Wallace much more to their taste than civil-rights pioneer Hubert Humphrey.

A Close Call

It was obvious that Wallace could not win the election. His purpose was to take just enough electoral votes from both Humphrey and Nixon to throw the election into the House of Representatives. Because each state had one vote in selecting the president in the House, anti-integration southern congressmen under his leadership could make a deal with Nixon: a reversal of Democratic party policies in return for their support.

Fearing this possibility, Humphrey called on Nixon to pledge with him that neither of them would deal with Wallace and his thinly veiled racism. Instead, Humphrey proposed, each would direct his supporters to vote for whoever of the two finished with the most votes.

Nixon evaded the challenge, and in the end it did not matter. Although Wallace did better than any third-party candidate since 1924, winning 13.5 percent of the popular vote and 46 electoral votes, Nixon eked out a plurality of 500,000 votes and an absolute majority in the electoral college. It was close. A rush of blue-collar workers back to Humphrey during the final week of the campaign indicated to some pollsters that he would have won had the election been held a week or two later. Indeed, the Democrats continued to hold a comfortable edge in both houses of Congress. The key to Nixon's victory may well have been those antiwar Democrats who could not bring themselves to vote for Humphrey.

THE NIXON PRESIDENCY

Richard M. Nixon is one of the most compelling and puzzling figures in twentieth-century politics. He lacked the qualities that are thought to be indispensable to political success in the late twentieth century: good looks, slick charm, social graces, wit, a camera presence. On the contrary, he was furtive in manner; even after careful rehearsing, he looked grotesquely insincere in front of a crowd. Liberals hated him from his days as a young congressman when his political methods were, in their opinion, totally unscrupulous. And yet, right-wing Republicans did not love him for the enemies he had made. The only political passion Richard M. Nixon aroused was negative. The best he could hope for—and he got it throughout his remarkable career—was acceptance because he was preferable to his opponents.

Richard Nixon in the Oval Office with aides Robert Haldeman (left) and John Erlichman (center, seated).

Through hard work and boundless tenacity he rose from a modest childhood in the sleepy citrus town of Whittier, California, to the highest office in the land. He was a real-life Horatio Alger hero. Whatever else may be said of Nixon, he earned everything he ever got.

Domestic Policy

Nixon was not interested in domestic policy. He confessed to intimates that the issues bored him. He was able to gratify his conservative supporters by replacing liberal Supreme Court justices, including Earl Warren, with conservatives, but even that exercise was a nuisance. In filling one vacancy, Nixon had to withdraw the names of two nominees, one because he had a segregationist past, the other because he was clearly incompetent. In both cases, the Senate withheld its usually free consent.

The president left dialogue with the nation on domestic issues to Vice President Spiro T. Agnew, a former governor of Maryland who delighted conservatives by baiting student protesters, "permissive" educators who tolerated their disruptive activities, liberal Supreme Court justices, defeatists, and the national news media. Agnew was best known for his fondness for alliteration in his speeches. His finest effort was "the nattering nabobs of negativism," which had been written out of a thesaurus.

The most troubling domestic problem of the Nixon years was inflation. The huge government expenditures of the Johnson years—financing the Great Society and the Vietnam War at the same time—caused prices to rise at an alarming rate, resulting in demands by workers for higher wages and, consequently, a renewal of the spiral. In 1970, the Democratic Congress voted the president authority to freeze wages and prices, but Nixon refused to do so until the summer of 1971. By freezing wages and prices and by abandoning a promise to balance the budget, Nixon joined his liberal predecessors in saying that the federal government, particularly the president, was responsible for vigilant adjustment of the economy. Conservative Republicans such as Goldwater and Governor Ronald Reagan of California were disappointed, but Nixon's shift helped him politically. While the economy was by no means robust in the election year of 1972, it was healthier than any other year of Nixon's first term and contributed to his reelection.

Nixon's Vietnam Policy

Nixon knew well that Johnson's political career had been snuffed out by the war in Vietnam. He was persuaded by his special assistant for national security, Henry A. Kissinger, that the war could not be won in the sense that Johnson, with his policy of escalation, had believed could be done. However, Nixon was beholden to the country's "hawks," those who advocated a "tough" war policy, and he was just as determined as Johnson not to be the first American president to be chased off a battlefield. He wanted some kind of favorable settlement with the North Vietnamese, who by this time completely dominated the National Liberation Front.

This meant bludgeoning them to the negotiations table, but first, Nixon had to quiet the antiwar movement at home. Agnew baited the protestors, placating the super-patriotic hawks with often irresponsible rhetoric. Calculating that the largely white middle-class protest was in large part self-interested, Nixon moved toward ending the draft. (The war was fought disproportionately by the poor and the black.) And he reduced the sickeningly long casualty lists that were featured on the television news each evening through his policy of "Vietnamization," replacing American units at the front with South Vietnamese troops.

In Vietnam itself, Nixon stepped up programs to train the never efficient and often corrupt South Vietnamese army. Winding down the American part in the ground war, he increased the bombing of North Vietnam. Air war casualties were comparatively low,

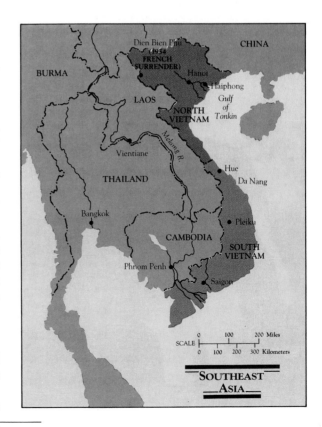

borne exclusively by military professionals and, he and Kissinger believed, Air Force and Navy planes would devastate North Vietnam—blasting it "back into the Stone Age" in the words of Air Force General Curtis LeMay—thus forcing the enemy to the conference table.

The Defeat of the Antiwar Movement

From a high of 541,000 men in 1969, American troops in Vietnam were reduced to 239,000 in 1970, and 48,000 in 1972, the year Nixon ran for reelection. By that time, the president had successfully flanked the antiwar movement on every front. With each withdrawal of troops, Nixon, with temperate tone, and Agnew, with shrill sarcasm, depicted the antiwar protestors as reckless radicals who were encouraging the North Vietnamese to hold out, and thus impeding a conscientious president's efforts to make peace.

In fact, Nixon's political advisers were happy for the violent protests. They believed that each incident worked to the president's benefit because a majority of Americans disapproved of the turmoil. Antiwar protestors who called for peaceful demonstrations suspected that shouting and throwing incidents were ac-

tually engineered by the White House. In any case, the final spasm of 1960s-style protest was quite spontaneous. In May 1970, after Richard Nixon ordered troops into Cambodia, ostensibly to root out enemy sanctuaries, students on more than 400 campuses shut down their universities, demonstrated noisily, and in many cases rioted.

At Kent State University in Ohio, National Guardsmen opened fire on demonstrating students, killing four. The incident was later condemned as avoidable and attributed by some critics to Agnew's inflammatory rhetoric. In any case, as if this were the first bloodshed during the decade of protest, the turmoil came to a halt. By the autumn of 1970, a hush had fallen over American universities.

Two years later, a more broadly based antiwar movement would capture the Democratic presidential nomination for Senator George McGovern of South Dakota, and he too was beaten. It was a momentous popular movement and worthy in its announced goals. But the antiwar activists never convinced a decisive number of Americans to join them.

In January 1973, the month of Nixon's second inauguration, America's Vietnam War ended, too. With the American antiwar movement dead, North Viet-

Children hit by napalm flee in agony in Trangbang, South Vietnam, June 8, 1972.

namese Le Duc Tho made some face-saving concessions and Henry Kissinger signed an armistice in Paris. Ostensibly, South Vietnam would remain independent. But few informed people believed that the tragic war would end in any other way than it actually did in April 1975, after Nixon had left office. North and South Vietnamese never really stopped fighting one another, and in that month South Vietnam disintegrated. The army of a now militaristic North Vietnam occupied Saigon, and renamed the capital Ho Chi Minh City.

The Limits of Superpower

The most striking lesson of America's defeat in Vietnam was the curious limitations it revealed as being intrinsic to the possession of great military power. Short of destroying Vietnam, which the United States had the capacity to do, massive force and modern military technology were of little avail against guerrillas employing hit-and-run tactics and refusing to be drawn into a battle in which sophisticated weaponry made the difference. Whereas massive aerial bombardment could have devastating effect against a highly industrialized country because it was dependent on modern transportation and communications systems, the very primitiveness of the North Vietnamese economy rendered massive air attacks ineffective.

Vietnamese industry was decentralized, and the enemy moved its men and supplies by foot and bicycle along dirt tracks and across bamboo bridges that could be rebuilt almost overnight after a bombing. Walter Lippmann compared the United States to an elephant in a war against mosquitoes. There was no doubt which was the greater beast, but there was no way that the elephant could win. In the meantime, civilians inevitably suffered from massive bombing, and the reputation of the United States sank all over the world.

NIXON TRIUMPHANT, NIXON DESTROYED

Even while the war in Vietnam continued, a diplomatic revolution was under way. While the Soviet Union and the People's Republic of China continued to aid North Vietnam in the fight against the United States, both countries signaled Nixon that they were prepared to establish détente, a recognition that in the nuclear age, regular diplomatic relations were preferable to sustained hostility and bickering that easily could lead to all-out war.

The first secret and then dramatically public invitations to détente were a result of the increasing hostility and, possibly, military engagements on the long

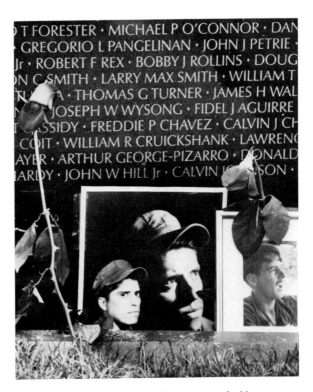

Photos and roses left behind by visitors to the Vietnam War Memorial. Though the war ended in 1975, a memorial was not erected in Washington, D.C., until November 1982, an indication, perhaps, of the nation's unwillingness to confront the tragedy of Vietnam.

Soviet-Chinese border. Both great powers were sufficiently afraid of a major war with one another to wish to assure the neutrality of the United States. However, a constructive American response to the signals was possible only because Henry A. Kissinger, Nixon's chief foreign-policy adviser, was a man of imagination who wanted to be remembered in history as a great diplomat, and the president himself craved a lasting monument for his presidency.

The Diplomatic Revolution

In 1971, an American table-tennis team on a tour of Japan was startled to receive an invitation from China to play a series of exhibition games in the People's Republic before they returned home. Diplomats noted wryly that the Chinese had picked an area of competition in which they would shine (the Americans were soundly trounced), but Henry Kissinger recognized the implications of the trivial event. After negotiations that remain shrouded in mystery, he flew secretly to Peking in the wake of the table-tennis tournaments and arranged for a good-will tour by Nixon himself in February 1972.

The visit was a grand success. Nixon toasted world peace with Chairman Mao Zedong and, more important, for Mao was senile and fading, with the Chairman's oldest surviving comrade, Zhou Enlai, long an advocate of better relations with the West, and Zhou's rising (but hardly young) protegé, Deng Xiaoping, who had spent some time in jail for his "counter-revolutionary" ideas.

Few sights could have astounded Americans more than the photographs of Richard M. Nixon tossing back fiery Chinese liquors with revolutionaries in baggy trousers, and picking his way ably with chopsticks through dozens of courses of exquisite Mandarin food in the Great Hall of the Emperors. For 25 years American anti-Communists, Nixon prominent among them, had described the People's Republic as an outlaw nation, and China had vilified the United States as the fount of all the world's exploitation and injustice. Now, gradually but inexorably, the United States dropped its opposition to China's application for a seat in the United Nations, allowed the unseating of Taiwan (formerly recognized by the United States as the legitimate government of China), and exchanged ambassadors and consuls with the People's Republic. Indeed, American industrialists involved in everything from oil exploration to the bottling of soft drinks flew to China by the thousands, anxious to sell American technology and consumer goods in the market that always had symbolized the ultimate sales opportunity.

Consequences of the New China Policy

China did not turn out to be much of an importer of American know-how and products. The Chinese population was huge, but the country was not rich; there was neither money nor goods with which to pay for the expensive high-technology exports in which alone, American industry was still supreme. Nor were the new leaders of China interested in resuming the status of a colonial market or in embracing free political institutions. Their principal motive in courting Amer-

Nixon and Chinese leader Zhou Enlai toast each other during Nixon's visit to China in 1972.

ican amity was diplomatic, to win some edge of security in their conflict with the Soviet Union by forestalling a joint Soviet-American opposition.

From the American point of view, the rapprochement with China opened the way for détente with the Soviets. In June 1972, just months after his China trip, Nixon flew to the Soviet Union and signed the preliminary agreement in the opening series of Strategic Arms Limitation Talks (SALT), the first significant step toward a slowdown of the arms race since the Kennedy administration.

At home, the photos of Nixon clinking champagne glasses with the Chinese and Russians bewildered his conservative supporters. They knew the president as one of the most vociferous Cold Warriors for more than 20 years. Now he was cozying up to the two great Communist powers as no Democratic liberal would have dared to do. Indeed, as Nixon and Kissinger understood, only a Republican with a Cold-Warrior past could afford to do what Nixon had done. Along with this and his New Deal-type price controls, however, Nixon appeared to betray everything that the conservatives stood for.

Henry A. Kissinger

The right-wing Republicans increasingly blamed Henry A. Kissinger for the Nixon policies. Kissinger's political background was liberal Republican—as foreign-policy adviser to Nelson A. Rockefeller—and he was from Harvard University, which conservatives

KISSINGER ON DÉTENTE

"The superpowers often behave like two heavily armed blind men feeling their way around a room, each believing himself in mortal peril from the other whom he assumes to have perfect vision. . . . Each tends to ascribe to the other side a consistency, foresight and coherence that its own experience belies. Of course, over time even two blind men can do enormous damage to each other, not to speak of the room."

Henry A. Kissinger,
The White House Years (1979)

considered to be a hothouse of un-American ideas. Kissinger's urbane charm, simultaneously arrogant and self-mocking, also infuriated the right-wingers. He was also a Jew, a refugee as a boy from Nazi Germany. Although the right-wingers had apparently left anti-Semitism behind when they had backed Barry Goldwater for president, hints of the old prejudice seemed to revive in the suspicion of Kissinger.

They were right about one thing. Nixon became progressively more impressed with and dependent on Kissinger's brilliance, eloquence, and diplomatic skills. The president wanted a niche in history, and Kissinger was the man most likely to win it for him. In 1973, Nixon accepted the resignation of Secretary of State William P. Rogers, who already was just a figurehead, and gave the job to Kissinger.

Shuttle Diplomacy

Well into 1974, the diplomatic successes piled up. Kissinger's greatest triumph came in the Middle East. During Yom Kippur in 1973, the Jewish high holy days devoted to atonement for sins and therefore a time of preoccupation, Egypt and Syria attacked Israel. After initial setbacks, Israeli troops held; the war was a draw; but it was the only time since the establishment of the Jewish state in 1948 that Israel had not decisively defeated its Arab neighbors.

Knowing that the Israelis were not inclined to accept less than victory—that would only encourage future Arab aggression—and fearing what a prolonged war in the oil-rich Middle East would mean for the United States, Kissinger shuttled seemingly without sleep among Damascus, Cairo, and Tel Aviv, carrying proposal and counterproposal for a settlement. Unlike John Foster Dulles, who also had tried to represent American interests in person, Kissinger was a genius at the negotiating table. The terms he prevailed on all the warring powers to sign actually increased American influence in the area by winning the gratitude and friendship of Egyptian President Anwar el-Sadat, while not alienating Israel.

After 1974, however, Kissinger lost his magic touch and reputation for infallibility. It became clear that he was less interested in ending the Cold War than in setting up spheres of influence dominated by the great powers while continuing the old rivalry in marginal areas. All the while right-wing Republicans stepped up their attacks on him, Kissinger practiced precisely the same kind of policy in the former Portuguese colony of Angola in Africa that had led to the Vietnam tragedy: fairly openly backing one faction in that land, while the Soviets backed another.

The most damaging mark on Kissinger's record as chief diplomat of a democratic country came with the discovery that, in September 1973, he had been aware of activities in Chile that had led to a coup against democratically elected President Salvador Allende, Allende's subsequent murder, and the establishment of a brutally repressive but pro-American regime in one of South America's few nations with a democratic tradition. Democratic liberals were almost comforted to see a Republican Secretary of State acting as they expected, but Kissinger's more congenial policies were not enough to win over the conservative Republicans who had already written him off.

By 1975, Kissinger was no longer serving Richard Nixon. The crisis of the presidency that had begun when Lyndon Johnson was repudiated took on a new dimension of gravity when Richard M. Nixon was forced to resign in disgrace.

The Election of 1972

Between 1968 and 1972, the activist middle-class liberal contingent of the Democratic party won control of several key party committees and remade party machinery according to its ideals. New methods of selecting convention delegates penalized old party stal-

warts—the unions, the big city organizations, those southern "good old boys" who had not gone Republican, the political pros—and guaranteed minimum representation of women and minority groups on the basis of their sex and ethnic origins. This shift was one of the first policy expressions of the principle of "affirmative action," by which members of previously disadvantaged groups were to be given preference in employment and educational opportunities. It marked a sharp break with the liberal tradition opposing any preferential, discriminatory policies. However, with the exception of the B'nai Br'ith Anti-Defamation League, a Jewish organization that had long fought racial, ethnic, or religious quotas of any kind, virtually every liberal group favored affirmative action. Democratic party liberalism was in the midst of a profound redefinition of goals.

As an immediate result of the changes, the delegates who gathered in Miami in the summer of 1972 formed the youngest convention in political history and reflected the antiwar politics of their generation. They nominated war critic Senator George McGovern of South Dakota to head their ticket.

Senator Sam Ervin (center) headed the special committee to inquire into charges of corruption in the 1972 election. The televised hearings reached an enraptured nation.

A sincere and decent man who was deeply grieved by the ongoing war in Vietnam, McGovern ran a two-issue campaign: peace and his integrity compared with Nixon's longstanding reputation for deviousness and dirty tricks. The Republicans countered by depicting McGovern as a bumbling and indecisive radical. When McGovern first defended his running mate, Senator Thomas Eagleton, who had undergone psychiatric treatment several years earlier, and then forced him to drop out, selecting Kennedy's brother-in-law, Sargent Shriver, his race was doomed. Nixon won 60.8 percent of the popular vote and carried every state but Massachusetts and the District of Columbia. In only eight years, he had reversed the overwhelming Republican defeat of 1964.

There was one significant difference between 1964 and 1972, however. Even though Nixon trounced McGovern, the Democrats held on to their comfortable majorities in Congress, sometimes by runaway margins. The American people did not want George McGovern as president. But they did not want as lawmakers those Republicans who spoke of dismantling the reforms of the New Deal and the Great Society. Soon, they learned, they did not want Richard M. Nixon as president either.

Watergate

On June 17, 1972, early in the presidential campaign, Washington police arrested five men who were trying to plant electronic listening devices in Democratic party headquarters in a Washington apartment and office complex called the Watergate. It was quickly learned that three of the suspects had White House contacts and were on the payroll of the Committee to Re-elect the President, which soon became unattractively abbreviated as CREEP.

McGovern tried to exploit this discovery, but the issue fizzled when Nixon and his campaign manager, Attorney General John Mitchell, denied any knowledge of the incident and condemned the burglary.

Nixon did not know about the burglary in advance, but he soon learned that the men had acted on orders from his aides. He instructed his staff to find money to hush up the burglars.

Unfortunately for the president, two of the burglars, James E. McCord and Howard Hunt, implicated government officials higher up. Robert Woodward and Carl Bernstein, two inquisitive reporters on the staff of the *Washington Post,* and a special Senate investigating committee headed by Sam Ervin of North Carolina picked away at the tangle from different directions and traced the Watergate break-in and other illegal actions to the White House. Judge John Sirica handed down several orders that crippled the cover-

Nixon announcing on television on August 8, 1974, that he is resigning from the presidency.

up, and Leon Jaworski, a Texas lawyer whom Nixon was forced to appoint as special prosecutor, proved to be an honest and relentless investigator.

A President Resigns

Highly placed Nixon advisers abandoned ship one by one, each convinced that he was being set up as a scapegoat and naming others in the cover-up. A snarl of half-truths and lies descended on the president. Nixon already was reeling when it was revealed that Vice President Spiro Agnew had accepted bribes when he was governor of Maryland. Agnew was forced to plead no contest to charges of income-tax evasion and resign from the vice presidency in October 1973; he was replaced under the Twenty-Fifth Amendment of 1967, by Congressman Gerald Ford of Michigan.

Nixon might have survived except that he had kept tape recordings of numerous conversations in his Oval Office that clearly implicated him in the cover-up. Why he did not destroy them early in the Watergate investigation remains a mystery. Some historians have suggested that greed—the money that the electronic documents would bring after Nixon left the presidency—was responsible for his fatal error. As it turned out, the House Judiciary Committee was considering the impeachment of the president when an obviously shattered Nixon resigned. Like Lyndon Johnson, he went from a landslide election victory to discredit within a few years.

A Ford, Not a Lincoln

Television news commentator Eric Sevareid began his nightly message: "A funny thing happened to Gerald

Gerald R. Ford appointed Nelson Rockefeller as his Vice President.

Ford on the way to becoming Speaker of the House of Representatives, his greatest ambition." Ford put his ordinariness in another way. He told Americans that they had "a Ford, not a Lincoln" in the White House.

Gerald Ford lacked high intelligence as well as high ambition. He had accomplished little in Congress beyond party regularity. He was best known for having led an abortive attempt to remove William O. Douglas from the Supreme Court in large part because the aged Douglas had married a twenty-year-old lawyer. Lyndon Johnson once told reporters that Ford's trouble was that he had played center on the University of Michigan football team without a helmet. Others quipped that he could not walk and chew gum at the same time.

And yet his simplicity and forthrightness were a relief after Nixon's squirming and deception. There was an uproar and cries of "deal" when the first unelected president pardoned Nixon of all crimes, but by 1976, Ford's popularity was on the upswing.

THE MOOD OF THE 1970s

Within a year of the Kent State massacre, social pulse takers noticed a significant turnaround in the general attitudes of those people who had become society's cultural style setters by virtue of their numbers: the children of the baby boom. Whereas the young people of the 1960s had seemed to be socially conscious,

concerned with pressing problems like racial injustice, poverty, dehumanization, and war, the young people of the 1970s turned inward, obsessed with themselves as individuals. Writer Tom Wolfe called the 1970s the "Me decade."

Us

Part of the reason for the retreat into self was age. The movement of the 1960s had a motto, "You can't trust anyone over thirty." In the 1970s, the first cadres of baby-boom babies celebrated their thirtieth birthdays. Their styles changed. It was not so much that the carefree life was in the past, but that the style setters of the era abandoned the mass demonstration as a means of self-gratification and turned to more personal outlets.

Because the 1970s generation was affluent, self-fulfillment took on commercial shape. One boom in consumer goods followed another, with the biggest profits made by companies that sold products that simultaneously provided fun and physical exercise. Successively, Americans spent billions of dollars on ski equipment, tennis paraphernalia, ten-speed bicycles, and backpacking gear. Research-and-development departments of sporting-goods companies worked overtime to devise new kinds of recreation that might have popular appeal, including hang gliders and parachutes for skydiving. Virtually no activity failed to gain some following, and some became national manias. For example, by 1980, one adult in five was jogging regularly. That most ancient and primitive form of exercise also became the subject of portentous analysis and the basis

---

CONSTITUTIONAL CONTRADICTION?

Gerald Ford was appointed to the vice presidency under the provisions of the Twenty-Fifth Amendment, ratified in 1967, which stipulates that "whenever there is a vacancy in the office of the Vice President, the President shall nominate a Vice President. . . ." When he succeeded to the presidency, he appointed Nelson A. Rockefeller to the vice presidency. Neither the president nor the vice president held office by virtue of election. However, as some constitutional experts were quick to point out, Article II, Section 1 of the Constitution provides that the president and vice president are to "be elected."

In fact, the contradiction was always there, if never put to the test. The U.S. Constitution and laws hold that the secretary of state and the Speaker of the House were next in line to the presidency after the vice president. A case could be made that the Speaker was elected, but not the secretary of state.

A woman works out with weight equipment, a popular form of exercise during the 1970s.

of a multimillion dollar business in the paraphernalia essential to running properly and, more important, attractively.

Self-Fulfillment

The affluent young of the 1970s became preoccupied with psychological as well as physical self-fulfillment. While Indian gurus had made their appearance in the 1960s, attracting acolytes from show business and the counterculture, they survived the end of the activist decade and multiplied. The Maharishi Mahesh Yogi, who became rich when the Beatles briefly adopted him in the mid-1960s, began to preach his transcendental meditation no longer as a way to reach spiritual fulfillment but as a means to make more money. Another guru took over a town in Oregon, encouraged free sexual expression, denounced material values, and accepted two dozen gifts of Rolls Royce automobiles from his happy followers.

Any number of other paths to complete self-fulfillment flourished; most of them involved some form of immediate pleasure, but others, such as a school of massage called "rolfing," were downright painful. For the most part these serial fads were ridiculous, but some attracted hostile criticism. The Hare Krishnas and the followers of Sun Myung Moon, a Korean preacher who claimed to be divine, seemed to be easily manipulated children who were, in effect, hypnotized to work for no wages in a variety of profitable enterprises. To critics it was a neat way to get around the Thirteenth Amendment, which forbids involuntary servitude, by appealing to the First, which guarantees freedom of religion.

Sources of the Sexual Revolution

The revolution in sexual morality that reached its apogee in the 1970s had its roots in the late nineteenth century and was accelerated in the 1960s from four different quarters. The sexual revolution owed first of all to the development of a reliable birth-control device—popularly called "the pill"—which eliminated the dread of pregnancy by single women. The control of venereal disease, which was made possible by antibiotics, eliminated yet another fear.

The third source of liberalized sexual attitudes was the decision by the Supreme Court in a number of cases that graphic discussion and depiction of sexual acts were protected by the constitutional right of free speech. While standards of enforcement varied radically from state to state and city to city, sexually explicit books and films became freely available. Finally, the bohemian streak among style-setting young people of the 1960s insisted that repressive sexual codes as well as traditional social strictures be defied.

The Natural History of Swinging

In the 1970s, acceptance of liberated sexuality, then open preoccupation and obsession with sex, became general among the "trendy" middle classes and even the culturally more cautious working class. "Singles bars," places where one went frankly rather than coyly to pick up a sexual partner for a "one night stand" (a phrase borrowed from musicians), became fixtures in every big city and many towns. "Adult motels" suspended mirrors on ceilings and pumped pornographic movies to TV sets in perfumed rooms. Landlords converted or constructed apartment complexes to accommodate "swinging singles" with party rooms, saunas, whirlpool "Jacuzzi" baths, and hot tubs.

Married people could hardly have been unaffected, and the divorce rate soared, reaching 50 percent of all marriages in California and higher percentages in fashionable, affluent communities like Marin, north of San Francisco, which became a by-word for the latest trends as Peoria was a by-word for conventional midwestern morality.

Homosexuals, previously quietly tolerated in large cities like New York, San Francisco, and New Orleans, "came out of the closet," renamed themselves "gays," won wide acceptance of the positive tag, and publicly demanded that their "sexual preference" and "alternate lifestyle" be recognized as equal to Peoria's. Many middle-class liberals, by the late 1970s almost totally preoccupied with questions of individual liberty, quickly obliged, but the loud howling of "the sin that dare not speak its name" alienated former liberal voters among the working class.

Just as the control of venereal disease played a part in initiating the sexual revolution, a disease was a key element in its leveling off about 1980. A penicillin-resistant strain of gonorrhea made its appearance, and herpes, an old and minor venereal infection, reached epidemic proportions among sexually active people who began to have second thoughts about Wednesdays and Fridays at the singles' bar. Worst of all was Acquired Immunity Deficiency Syndrome—AIDS—which, slowly and agonizingly, killed its victims. Apparently transmitted only by intimate sexual contact or direct introduction of the organism into the bloodstream, as late as 1985 AIDS mostly afflicted a few easily identified groups: Haitian immigrants, intravenous drug users, hemophiliacs, and male homosexuals. Horrible as it was, with cases increasing geometrically each year, the liberal obsession with sexual freedom helped retard the fight against the disease. While homosexual and some of the new liberal groups demanded increased AIDS research, they resisted large-scale testing for AIDS such as had been done in the past to fight other serious contagious diseases like tuberculosis. By 1986, AIDS was spreading among heterosexual people who did not fit into any of the vulnerable categories.

Even before the shocks of venereal disease slowed sexual liberation, one branch of the most significant political movement of the 1970s, the women's liberation movement, had condemned casual sexual relations as just one more way in which a male-dominated society exploited women.

Betty Friedan, feminist author and founder of the National Organization for Women.

Women's Liberation

After her book *The Feminine Mystique* (1963) received a rousing response, Betty Friedan was encouraged to form, in 1966, the National Organization for Women (NOW), a pressure group designed to secure legal and social equality for women.

At first, "women's lib" was widely ridiculed because of the activities of fringe "libbers," such as those who sponsored bonfires at which brassieres were burned. But the essence of the new feminism was too serious to be ignored. By the 1970s, NOW had established its leadership over the fringe groups and rapidly succeeded in striking down most state and federal laws and policies that explicitly discriminated against women.

Victories of the New Feminism

The early victories were deceptively easy. State laws that prevented married women from borrowing money without the approval of their husbands were easily repealed. Only a little more difficult was NOW's campaign to win for women entrance to jobs that were restricted to men, particularly in manual and dangerous work such as construction and firefighting. The organization was also successful in de-sexing words like *fireman*. Almost instantaneously, businesses and government took to speaking of "mailcarriers" and "chairpersons" and addressing women as "Ms." rather than "Miss" or "Mrs." which, to the feminists, represented demeaning patronization.

Other gains were made in the matters of equal pay for women who did the same jobs as men and the adoption in government and business of affirmative-action policies. Universities and employers were obligated to admit or to hire women (and members of ethnic minority groups) in preference to white males if the applicants were as qualified as the males. Because, in practice, less qualified women, blacks, Hispanics, and others were often given preferential treatment, resulting in a quota system such as liberals had fought against when it had been used to discriminate against minorities, the Supreme Court dealt a major blow to affirmative action. In the *Bakke* case (1978), the Court forced the University of California medical school to admit a white male applicant whose qualifications were better than those of several affirmative-action applicants whom the school had accepted. Gov-

No longer confined to traditional female occupations, women became everything from lawyers to telephone line workers following the women's liberation movement of the late 1960s and early 1970s.

ernment, business, and universities entered the 1980s searching for ways to evade the charge of "reverse discrimination," but early in the decade, the feminists suffered a defeat that NOW regarded as much more important—the rejection of the Equal Rights Amendment (ERA).

ERA

Sent to the states from Congress in 1972, the ERA was a Fourteenth Amendment for women, forbidding any kind of legal or social discrimination on the basis of sex. Debate of the amendment seemed to reveal that it would do little more than guarantee rights that women were winning by statute and policy directive, but the symbolic gesture seemed important. Within a few years the amendment was ratified by all but a handful of the 38 states needed to make it a part of the Constitution.

Then, seemingly from nowhere, emerged a ground swell of opposition to the ERA led by a longtime right-wing Republican writer, Phyllis Schlafly. Cautioning that ratification of the ERA would lead to the loss of certain privileges that women enjoyed, for example, exemption from military conscription, Schlafly encouraged hundreds of state legislators to oppose ratification. When the 1979 deadline for ratification was reached, the ERA was still three states short of approval.

Congress quickly extended the deadline to 1982, a dubious changing of the rules to which three states responded by withdrawing their votes for ratification, a clear indication that the momentum was with Schlafly. NOW contested the right to revoke ratification, but the case was never tested because the ERA won ratification in no more states.

Changing Times

Why did the ERA fail? In part the failure was due to the efficient campaign mounted by Schlafly and the increasingly powerful Republican conservatives. More fundamentally, however, the ERA was not ratified because the 1970s were not political years. As a novelty early in the decade, the new feminism was popular among the middle classes. When the feminists did not win quick, decisive victories, however, their project was doomed.

NOW and women's liberation never did spark much enthusiasm among lower-class women. Equal pay for equal work was important to them, but once that goal had been fairly well achieved, they turned to other economic problems that they shared with their fathers, husbands, and sons.

The failure of ERA was most important as an indication of the decay of the liberal majority that had

MEXICAN-AMERICANS:
CHANGING TIMES, CHANGING VALUES

In 1971, a Chicano teaching fellow at Harvard Law School told a reporter for the *Boston Sunday Globe* that "my parents pushed me very hard in an Anglo direction. I rejected every Chicano value. For 29 years I have lived a life of total pretension. It has led to horrible complications in myself. I am just now learning who I am." Having expressed a deep-felt wish to be reconciled to Chicano culture, he referred to the handful of Mexican-American students at Harvard and observed, "None of us would be here if we hadn't tried to be Anglo." The implication was that Harvard Law School should also bestow its appointments and generous salaries on people who had clung to Chicano culture.

Agonizing about "identity" was a favorite activity of the "Me Decade" among privileged members of minority groups as well as among affluent members of the majority culture. It was, among other things, a way to get ahead by playing on the sensitivity of the government, business, and academic establishments to their heritage of discrimination against minorities. It was difficult to sympathize with such identity crises when the vast majority of the members of minority groups such as Mexican-Americans struggled daily just to get by.

But such posing helped anthropologists and sociologists to focus on genuine clashes between traditional group values and the values that lead to success in the mainstream society. With Chicanos in the 1970s, as with immigrant groups of the early twentieth century, there was a wrenching cultural adjustment to be made in order to win a decent share of the benefits of American society. Old ways had to be abandoned, new ones adopted, and the process was more difficult for Chicanos because of the closeness of the mother country and the well-meaning but damaging policies of the Anglo establishment. (*Chicano* is a slang contraction of *Mexicano* and connotes political activism; in Chicano usage, *Anglo* refers to all white Americans, not just those of English descent.)

Mexican-Americans were the second largest minority in the United States in the 1970s; only blacks were more numerous. They made up the single largest ethnic group in the southwestern states of California, Arizona, New Mexico, Texas, and Colorado. As recently as the 1950s, they had been a majority in New Mexico.

A word of caution is in order. Sociologically, no other American ethnic group has such a variety of backgrounds as the 7 million people who are lumped together by the Census Bureau as "Spanish surname." Setting aside Puerto Ricans, Cubans, and immigrants from other Spanish-speaking countries, seven categories of Mexican-Americans can be identified, of which four are not immigrants at all: (1) descendants of the *californios*, inhabitants of California before it was seized by the United States, most of whom were Indians or of mixed race; (2) the more quickly assimilated descendants of the upper-class Caucasian *californios*; (3) *tejanos*, descendants of the inhabitants of Texas before it became independent; (4) *nuevo mexicanos*, descendants of pre-Anglo New Mexicans, who were self-consciously more Spanish than Mexican because they were never much under the control of or particularly fond of the government of the Mexican Republic; (5) descendants of the refugees from the Mexican Revolution during the 1910s and 1920s, many of them well educated and affluent; (6) descendants of the *braceros*, imported farm laborers, of the 1930s and 1940s; and (7) immigrants of the 1960s and 1970s, who entered the United States (many illegally) in search of work.

A people of so many origins may be spoken of as an ethnic group only because of the development of the Chicano consciousness movement in the mid-1960s, which led to the first successful expressions of Mexican-American wishes through Cesar Chavez's United Farm Workers; *La Raza Unida*, a political party formed in Texas and similar to the blacks' Mississippi Freedom Democrats; and any number of university campus organizations. It is ironic that, as with those who spoke for other minorities, it was possible to represent Chicano interests effectively only to the extent that spokesmen had transcended the values of Mexican-American subculture.

Sociologist Fernando Peñalosa found examples of Mexican-Americans whose forebears had lived in Texas for 200 years and yet "largely retained the language and culture." Such a phenomenon was possible only as long as Anglo prejudice shut such people out of the mainstream society and forced them to cling to traditional ways as solace. Despite their numbers in Texas, California, and New Mexico, communities of the sort Peñalosa discovered could not produce effective leaders so long as they were despised for being Mexican-Americans.

As a by-product of the black struggle for civil equality in the 1960s, the external, legal obstacles that had prevented Chicanos from winning a place in American society were also struck down. However, long-established cultural habits could not be abolished with the signing of a law, and they continued to impede Mexican-American progress. Studies of Mexican-American social mobility in Albuquerque, Los Angeles, and San Antonio in the 1970s revealed a direct correlation between income and social station, and the degree to which the more successful had broken with old ways and adopted those of Anglo society. For example, in all three cities, Chicanos and Chicanas who had married Anglos already had moved out of the *barrio* and up the economic ladder.

In a 1972 study, B. S. Bradshaw and F. D. Bean divided a sample of 348 Mexican-American couples in Austin, Texas, into two groups according to their socioeconomic status. They found that 74 percent of those in the higher group lived outside the Austin *barrio*, but only 27 percent of the lower group did. The women in the higher group were more likely to work outside the home and to demand of their husbands an equal voice in household decisions. The higher group was more likely to have close Anglo friends, to speak English exclusively or more than they spoke Spanish, and generally to have middle-class values.

"Making good" in the United States by adopting American ways had been the experience of almost all immigrant groups, from the Irish and Germans of the mid-nineteenth century to the Jews, Greeks, Italians, Slavs, and other New Immigrants of the early twentieth century. However, the Mexican-Americans of the 1970s labored under two burdens that these groups had not.

First, the closeness of Mexico and the steady influx of new immigrants from Mexico constantly reinvigorated the traditional values, including some that stood squarely in the way of social and economic advancement: valuing interpersonal relationships over competitiveness and acquisition of material wealth; emphasizing family welfare over individual advancement; recognizing male dominance *(machismo)* and female submissiveness; and producing extremely large families. In 1970, the Mexican-American annual fertility rate was higher than that of any other major ethnic group: 42.32 children per 1,000 women compared with 28.91 for Anglos and 34.89 for blacks.

Other ethnic groups had brought similar cultural baggage from Europe. But far from sentimentalizing the old ways and lamenting their loss, the leaders of Jews, Italians, Poles, and others browbeat their communities into recognizing that the United States was not Russia, Italy, or Poland and adjusting to that reality, however painful it might be to do so. Although the southern and Eastern European ethnic groups hardly approved of them, the immigration quota laws of 1921 and 1924 worked to their benefit by preventing the reinforcement of old-country ways by new arrivals.

Second, well-meaning state and federal policymakers in the 1970s did a disservice to Chicanos when they encouraged them to cling to traditional ways and particularly to the Spanish language by making it easy to do so. In California, for example, all state documents were published in Spanish (and Chinese) as well as in English. In many schools, catch-up classes in English for Spanish-speaking children were neglected and even abolished in favor of classes in which the regular curriculum was taught in Spanish.

Unlike the children of other ethnic groups, who were forced to learn English in public schools and therefore were given access to the world beyond their neighborhoods, Mexican-American children were chained to the *barrios*, in other words, to chronic poverty. While it was easy at the end of the 1970s to get along in the *barrios* speaking only Spanish, and to read every California state publication in that language, Harvard Law School, which is in Massachusetts, had not instituted a program for the training of attorneys who remained loyal to this aspect of "Chicano consciousness." Richard Rodriguez, a Chicano writer from Sacramento, California, who is ambivalent about the choices facing Mexican-Americans, summed it up: "Those who have the most to lose in a bi-lingual America are the foreign-speaking poor, who are being lured into a linguistic nursery."

Young Chicanos face a difficult choice between preserving their native language and traditional culture and adopting values that lead to success in American society.

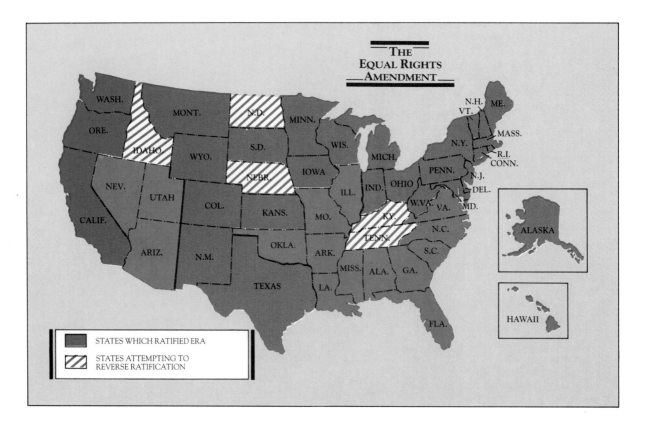

THE
EQUAL RIGHTS
AMENDMENT

■ STATES WHICH RATIFIED ERA

▨ STATES ATTEMPTING TO
REVERSE RATIFICATION

effectively governed the United States since 1932—the decay of New Deal liberalism itself. In effect, Lyndon B. Johnson had rounded out Roosevelt's New Deal and Truman's Fair Deal with his Great Society of 1964–65. Having accomplished for their traditional constituencies just about all they could accomplish within the American system, liberals turned to ways to favor some of them, as in affirmative-action preference for blacks and other racial minorities, and went fishing for others, like the affluent young people of the "Me Decade" and homosexuals, with official endorsement of maximum personal freedom to "do your own thing."

The trouble was that there was no way to effect the new liberal programs without alienating important constituents of the old New Deal coalition: southern whites, northern blue-collar ethnic workers who valued traditional morality, the labor unions.

Sensing an opportunity, first individuals like Phyllis Schlafly, and quickly the conservative wing of the Republican party, traditionally a group insensitive to modestly fixed people, made "morality" and "lifestyle" issues their chief appeal. Not until 1980 would their strategy bear fruit. The third American century, commencing in 1976, began with the apparent resurgence of the Democratic party.

An anti-ERA family advocates the "traditional" role of women.

868

For Further Reading

Overviews and Classics

Godfrey Hodgson, *America in Our Time* (1976)

William L. O'Neill, *Coming Apart: An Informal History of the 1960s* (1971)

Valuable Special Studies

Carl Bernstein and Robert Woodward, *All the President's Men* (1974)

Joseph R. Conlin, *The Troubles: A Jaundiced Glance Back at the Movement of the 1960s* (1982)

T. E. Cronin, *The State of the Presidency* (1975)

Frances Fitzgerald, *Fire in the Lake* (1972)

Jo Freeman, *The Politics of Women's Liberation* (1975)

Todd Gitlin, *The Whole World is Watching* (1981)

A. E. Goodman, *The Lost Peace: America's Search for a Negotiated Settlement of the Vietnam War* (1978)

Landon Y. Jones, *Great Expectations: America and the Baby Boom Generation* (1980)

Christopher Lasch, *The Culture of Narcissism* (1979)

Sar A. Levitan, William B. Johnson, and Robert Taggart, *Still a Dream: The Changing Status of Blacks Since 1960* (1975)

Richard Morris, *Uncertain Greatness: Henry Kissinger and American Foreign Policy* (1977)

Henry Parmet, *The Democrats: The Years After FDR* (1976)

James T. Patterson, *America's Struggle Against Poverty, 1900–1980* (1981)

Kirkpatrick Sale, *SDS* (1973)

Jonathan Schell, *The Time of Illusion* (1976)

Arthur M. Schlesinger, Jr., *The Imperial Presidency* (1973)

William Shawcross, *Sideshow: Kissinger, Nixon, and the Destruction of Cambodia* (1978)

Irwin Unger, *The Movement* (1974)

Theodore H. White, *Breach of Faith* (1975)

———, *The Making of the President, 1968* (1969)

———, *The Making of the President, 1972* (1973)

Biographies and Autobiographies

Fawn Brodie, *Richard Nixon* (1980)

Henry A. Kissinger, *White House Years* (1979)

Richard M. Nixon, *RN: The Memoirs of Richard Nixon* (1978)

Garry Wills, *Nixon Agonists* (1970)

Jules Witcover, *The Resurrection of Richard Nixon* (1970)

51

The Third Century
America
Since 1976

"Break out the flag, strike up the band, light up the sky!" With that disarming old-fashioned call, President Gerald R. Ford proclaimed America's bicentennial on July 4, 1976, and ushered in the nation's third century. The highlight of the festival was the arrival in New York harbor of a flotilla of sailing vessels from all over the world, a thrilling vision of the past.

The first decade of the third century drew to a close on July 4, 1986, with another international celebration in New York harbor. Again, the "tall ships" arrived, this time to celebrate the hundredth anniversary of the Statue of Liberty, as much a symbol of the United States as the Liberty Bell or the Stars and Stripes. At night, the sky was illuminated with a fireworks display said to be the greatest in history.

For those who looked for portents in the parties, there were plenty. The sailing ships were a nostalgic look backward, whereas, in 1876, the centerpiece of the centennial exposition in Philadelphia had been the giant Corliss steam engine, a symbol of the future. Were Americans uneasy with the world of the late twentieth century? Others noted that the mammoth exposition scheduled for 1976 had to be called off because the people who lived near the selected site in Philadelphia protested the proposal angrily, even violently. They did not want millions of their countrymen as guests. Have the party somewhere else—anywhere else—they said. But no one else wanted to be hosts either and the promoters, mourning the profits they would not pocket, gave up. Money seemed to be the mo-

Tall ships sailed in New York harbor as part of America's bicentennial celebration, July 4, 1976.

tive force behind the Statue of Liberty celebration, too. Exclusive rights to televise it were auctioned to the highest bidder, as if it were a prizefight.

Less pessimistic oracles had a reply. Unlike Americans of 1876, who celebrated the centennial by going to a fair, Americans of 1976 *participated* in their party. In practically every community, people restored historic buildings, planted trees, marched in parades, mixed in huge picnics on the Fourth, and recreated historic events or retraced the trails over which the American people had gone west. To prepare for Liberty's anniversary, the statue was rebuilt and refurbished largely by private contributions, raised by voluntary efforts. Americans might have been uneasy, but their vitality as a people had hardly been sapped.

THE FORD INTERREGNUM

The period after a monarch dies, but before the new monarch is crowned, is called an interregnum, a time of waiting between reigns. Gerald Ford did not intend his presidency to be an interregnum, but it was his fate to preside over two years of inconclusive grappling with inherited

President Gerald Ford and Secretary of State Henry Kissinger.

ANCESTORS

In 1982, the Census Bureau reported that 51.6 million Americans traced their ancestry to Germany compared with 43.7 million who claimed an Irish background and 40 million who had English forebears. But if Scots-Americans and Welsh-Americans were added to the English as being of British origin, that would have been the largest group. About 16 million claimed African ancestors; and 2.8 million, Asian.

problems. It was as if the country was waiting for the election of 1976, when the people would either give Ford a chance as president in his own right or replace him.

The first of the problems that faced Ford struck at one of the most firmly held assumptions of twentieth-century American life: the unlimited availability of cheap energy as a basis of both the economy and the freewheeling American lifestyle of the late twentieth century.

Running on Half-Empty

By the mid-1970s, 90 percent of the American economy was generated by the burning of fossil fuels: coal, natural gas, and petroleum. Fossil fuels are nonrenewable sources of energy. Unlike food crops, lumber, and water—or, for that matter, a horse and a pair of sturdy legs—they cannot be called on again once they have been used. There is only a limited amount of them in the earth. While experts disagreed about the extent of the world's reserves of coal, gas, and oil, no one challenged the obvious fact that one day they would be no more.

The United States was by far the biggest user of nonrenewable sources of energy. In 1973, while making up about 6 percent of the world's population, Americans consumed fully 33 percent of the world's annual production of oil. In the opinion of many, much of it was frivolously burned: overheating and overcooling offices and houses; fueling a wide variety of purely recreational vehicles, some of which brought the roar of the freeway to the wilderness and devastated fragile land; encouraging the wasteful private automobile instead of public mass transit systems; packaging consumer goods in throwaway containers of glass, metal, paper, and petroleum-based plastics: supermarkets wrapped lemons individually in transparent plastic and fast-food cheeseburgers were cradled in styrofoam plastics that were discarded within seconds of being handed over the counter. Resisting criticism and satire alike, American consumption increased.

The lines at a Los Angeles gas station stretched for blocks during a gasoline shortage in 1979.

OPEC and the Energy Crisis

About 61 percent of the oil that Americans consumed in 1973 was produced at home, and large reserves remained under native ground. Partly in order to conserve that oil, the nation imported huge quantities of crude, and in October 1973, Americans discovered just how little control they exercised over the 39 percent of their oil that was imported from abroad.

In that month, the Organization of Petroleum Exporting Countries (OPEC) temporarily halted oil shipments and announced the first of a series of big jumps in the price of their product. Their justification was that the irresponsible consumption habits of the advanced Western nations, particularly the United States, jeopardized their future. OPEC reasoned that if the oil-exporting nations continued to supply oil cheaply, consuming nations would continue to burn it promiscuously, thus hastening the day the wells ran dry. On that day, if the oil-exporting nations had not laid the basis for another kind of economy, they would be destitute. Particularly in the oil-rich Middle East, there were few other resources to support fast-growing populations. Therefore, by raising prices even higher,

the OPEC nations would earn capital with which to build for a future without oil while simultaneously encouraging the consuming nations to conserve, thus lengthening the period when oil would be available.

Americans were stunned. Motorists had to wait in long lines in order to pay unprecedented prices for gasoline. In some big cities and Hawaii, gasoline for private cars was not to be had for weeks.

The price of gasoline never climbed to European levels (as much as $5 a gallon), but it was shock enough for people who were accustomed to buying "two dollars' worth" to discover that $2 bought a little more than a gallon. Moreover, the prices of goods that require oil in their production climbed too. Inflation, already a problem, worsened.

For a decade, OPEC determined world oil prices and the cost of a Sunday drive in Iowa. However, like the pools American railroaders formed in the nineteenth century, the OPEC arrangement fell apart because its members went deeply into debt in the interests of the present, often the enrichment of corrupt elites. Individual OPEC members cut prices in order to gain an edge on their partners. By 1986, the "cartel" was in tatters and the price of crude oil declined to a third of its peak price.

Whip Inflation Now!

That was much too late to save Gerald Ford's career. By 1986 he had retired to a life of golf, skiing, and endorsing products for sale. As president in 1974, he seemed impotent as an inherited inflation rate of 9 percent a year rose to 12 percent.

Opposed to wage and price controls, Ford launched a campaign called WIN!, for "Whip Inflation Now," a great voluntary effort by Americans to slow down inflation by refusing to buy exorbitantly priced goods and by ceasing to demand higher wages from their employers. The campaign was ridiculed from the start, and within a few weeks Ford quietly retired the WIN! button that he had been wearing on his lapel. He had seen few others in his travels about the country and began to feel like a man in a funny hat.

Instead, Ford tightened the money supply in order to slow down the economy, which resulted in the most serious recession since the Second World War, with unemployment climbing to 9 percent. Ford was stymied by the same vicious circle that caught up his predecessor and successors: slowing inflation meant throwing people out of work; fighting unemployment meant inflation; trying to steer a middle course meant "stagflation," mild recession plus inflation.

Ford's Image Problems

As a congressman, Ford had been a hawk on Vietnam. When the North Vietnamese launched a major attack on South Vietnam early in 1975, Ford's first impulse was to intervene with American troops. Congress refused to respond and Henry Kissinger, who had stayed on as Secretary of State, talked him out of presidential action. However, Ford displayed his determination to exercise American armed might in May 1975, when Cambodian Communists seized an American ship, the *Mayagüez.* Ford ordered in the marines, who successfully rescued the captives. Many people were so pleased at the novelty of a successful American military action that they tended to forget that in order to rescue 39 seamen, 38 marines died.

Kissinger savored the reports that the president hung breathlessly on his every word. These stories not only angered the anti-Kissinger conservative wing of the Republican party, previously Ford's political home, but made it easier for the Democrats to mock the president as being not bright enough to handle his job.

Polls showed Ford losing to most of the likely Democratic candidates, and Ronald Reagan, the sweetheart of the right-wing Republicans, launched a well-financed campaign to replace him as the party's can-

didate in 1976. Ford beat Reagan at the convention but he could not overcome the image that he was the most accidental of presidents, never elected to national office. His full pardon of Richard M. Nixon for any crimes Nixon may have committed haunted Ford. In November, he lost narrowly to a most unlikely Democratic candidate. James Earl Carter of Georgia, who called himself Jimmy. The Democrats were back.

AN UNSUCCESSFUL PRESIDENT

Whether the perspective of time will attribute the failure of Jimmy Carter's presidency to his own unsuitability for the office or to the massiveness of the problems he faced, it is difficult to imagine future historians looking at the Carter years other than dolefully.

An Unlikely Candidate

Since Eisenhower, every president had been identified primarily with Congress, the arena of national politics. The day of the governor candidate seemed to be in the past. Then James Earl Carter, Jr., came out of nowhere to win the Democratic nomination in 1976. His political career consisted of one term in the Georgia assembly and one term as governor. Indeed, it was his lack of a past in the federal government that helped him win the nomination and, by a slim margin, the presidency. Without a real animus for Gerald Ford, Americans wanted an "outsider," which is how Carter presented himself. "Hello, my name is Jimmy Carter and I'm running for president," he told thousands of people face to face in a lilting Georgia accent. Once he started winning primaries, the media did the rest. When television commentators said that there was a bandwagon effect favoring Carter, people responded by jumping on the bandwagon.

Drift in Domestic Policy

"Carter believes fifty things," one of his advisers said, "but no one thing. He holds explicit, thorough posi-

JIMMY CARTER AND THE SEGREGATIONISTS

Future president Jimmy Carter had an unusual record for a white southerner of his age on the segregation issue. In the 1950s, as a successful businessman in Plains, Georgia, he had been asked to join the anti-black White Citizens' Councils, whose membership fee was only $5. Carter replied, "I've got $5 but I'd flush it down the toilet before I'd give it to you."

Jimmy Carter walks with his family from the capitol to the White House following his inauguration as president.

tions on every issue under the sun, but he has no large view of relations between them." In this, Carter was not unlike most Americans. He had an "engineer" mentality, which is often described as the American way of thinking: as it arises, face each specific problem and work out a specific solution.

Pragmatism had worked for Franklin D. Roosevelt. It did not work for Jimmy Carter. With him at the helm, pragmatic government resembled a ship without a rudder, drifting aimlessly. When Carter tried to fasten a grip on what he called the national malaise by picking the minds of 130 prominent men and women from every sector of American life, he was able to conclude only that there was "a crisis of the American spirit."

Inflation reached new heights under Carter, almost 20 percent during 1980. By the end of the year, $1 was worth only 15 cents in 1940 values. That is, on the average, it took $1 in 1980 to purchase what in 1940 cost 15 cents. The dollar had lost half of this value during the 1970s.

Carter could not be faulted for the energy crisis. After the crunch of 1974, Americans had become energy conscious, replacing their huge "gas guzzlers" with more efficient smaller cars and forming car pools for commuting to work. Even this sensible turn contributed to the economic malaise, however. American automobile manufacturers had repeatedly refused to develop small energy-efficient cars. For a while in the 1960s, after the success of the Germans' Volkswagen "Beetle," Ford, General Motors, and Chrysler had made compact cars. But within a few years, "compacts" had grown to be nearly as big as the traditional "full-sized car." Now, in the crunch of the 1970s, American auto makers had nothing with which to compete with a flood of Japanese imports: Toyotas, Datsuns, Hondas, and others.

Even then, by 1979, oil consumption was higher than ever, and an even higher proportion of it was being imported than in 1976! The oil refiners actually cut back on domestic production, which led many people to wonder if the crisis was genuine or was just a cover while the industry reaped windfall profits—which it did. As prices soared, all the refiners reported dividends of unprecedented size.

The price of electricity also rose, by 200 percent

MINORITY PRESIDENTS

When Jimmy Carter won the forty-eighth presidential election by just a hair under 50 percent of the popular vote, it was the sixteenth time the victor had the support of less than half the voters:

President	Year	Percent
John Quincy Adams	1824	30.5
James K. Polk	1844	49.6
Zachary Taylor	1848	47.4
James Buchanan	1856	45.3
Abraham Lincoln	1860	39.8
Rutherford B. Hayes	1876	48.0
James A. Garfield	1880	48.5
Grover Cleveland	1884	48.5
Benjamin Harrison	1888	47.9
Grover Cleveland	1892	46.1
Woodrow Wilson	1912	41.9
Woodrow Wilson	1916	49.4
Harry S Truman	1948	49.5
John F. Kennedy	1960	49.9
Richard M. Nixon	1968	43.4
Jimmy Carter	1976	50.0

Lincoln would surely not have won the election of 1864 by an absolute majority (or at all) had the southern states not been in rebellion. Three victorious candidates had fewer popular votes than their opponents who lost: John Quincy Adams in 1824, Rutherford B. Hayes in 1876, and Benjamin Harrison in 1888.

and more, because so much of it was generated by burning fossil fuels. The utility companies called for the construction of more nuclear power plants in anticipation of even higher rate increases. But Americans became apprehensive about nuclear energy as an alternative to fossil fuels following an accident and near catastrophe at the Three Mile Island nuclear plant near Harrisburg, Pennsylvania; the release, at about the same time, of *The China Syndrome,* a film that portrayed a similar accident; the discovery that a California reactor that was about to open was crisscrossed

URBAN DECAY

In New York City, every day between 1977 and 1980, 600 to 2,100 subway cars were out of service because of breakdowns due to age or mistreatment and vandalism. Between 80 and 300 trips had to be canceled each day. There were 2,200 to 5,000 fires in the New York subway system each year. In 1980 it took 40 minutes to take a trip that took only 10 minutes in 1910.

with flaws, and built astride a major earthquake fault; and the tremendous costs needed to build safe nuclear power plants. The nuclear power issue outlived the Carter presidency. In 1986, at Chernobyl in the Soviet Union, a nuclear power station malfunctioned and burned. The consequences of this catastrophe for the millions of people living around nearby Kiev will not be known until the twenty-first century.

Uncertain Foreign Policy

Carter named Cyrus Vance to be his Secretary of State. Then, however, just as Nixon had done with Kissinger, Carter installed in the White House a special assistant for national security, a Polish refugee from Communism, Zbigniew Brzezinski. Also like Nixon, he appeared to regard the Secretary of State as a figurehead and the special assistant as his adviser.

This policy had paid dividends to Nixon, but it did not help Carter. Whereas Kissinger had been flexible, Brzezinski's distrust of the Soviet Union blinded him to opportunities to improve relations between the nuclear superpowers. It was probably on Brzezinski's counsel that in March 1977 Carter interrupted and set back the Strategic Arms Limitation Talks with completely new proposals. (The SALT-II treaty was signed, but Carter withdrew it from Senate consideration when the Soviet Union invaded Afghanistan to prop up a friendly government in December 1979.)

Moreover, whereas Kissinger was a charmer, Brzezinski was tactless and crude in a world in which protocol and manners can be as important as substance. The foreign ministers of several of America's allies discreetly informed the State Department that they would not deal with him under any circumstances. By the end of Carter's term of office, détente was dead.

For a time, Carter's ambassador to the United Nations, former civil-rights activist and Georgia crony, Andrew Young, seemed to be improving relations with black Africa. Himself black, Young sympathized with the aspirations of the developing nations of sub-Saharan Africa. Then, however, Young met secretly, and without authorization, with leaders of the Palestine Liberation Organization (PLO), an anti-Israel terrorist organization that the United States did not recognize. It was an amateurish and irresponsible action and it cost Young his job: he had to resign. Carter's image did not improve.

A Triumph of Peacemaking

Nevertheless, Carter scored his greatest triumph in the snarl of Middle East politics. He saved the rapprochement between Israel and Egypt that began to take shape in November 1977, when Egyptian President

AN UNSUCCESSFUL PRESIDENT

CARTER'S BONERS

Jimmy Carter left himself wide open to unnecessary criticism when, running for president, he vowed somewhat sanctimoniously that he would never tell a lie. Again, by claiming that a nation's recognition of human rights would determine how the United States responded to it, and then supporting regimes like that of the Shah in Iran, his moralization caused him serious embarrassment. Perhaps his biggest mistake in this vein was confessing to an interviewer from *Playboy* magazine that he had many times lusted in his heart after women.

Anwar Sadat addressed the Israeli Knesset, or parliament, but showed signs of foundering because of Israeli prime minister Menachem Begin's reluctance to make concessions commensurate with Sadat's high-stakes gamble. Sadat had earned the enmity of the Arab world; Begin would not help him prove that détente with Israel was wise.

In 1978, Carter brought Sadat and Begin to meet with him at Camp David, the presidential retreat outside Washington. There, as was revealed only later in Carter's memoirs, Sadat grew so angry with Begin's refusal to compromise that he actually packed his suitcases. Although Carter was unable to persuade Begin to agree that the West Bank of the Jordan River, which Israel had occupied in 1967, must eventually be returned to Arab rule, he did bring the two men together. In March 1979, Israel and Egypt signed a treaty.

In the United States, the political effect of this dramatic diplomatic turn was to swing American sympathies in the dispute in the direction of Sadat, who appeared to be more sincerely committed to making peace than was Begin. Begin was unpopular even among American Jews, who traditionally were staunch supporters of Israel. Jewish contributions to Israeli causes dropped sharply while Begin held power. Carter himself betrayed impatience and annoyance with the Begin government and sympathy for the Palestinian refugees. In any case, the Nobel Committee did not award Carter the peace prize he deserved far more than most of its laureates.

Anwar Sadat, Jimmy Carter, and Menachem Begin share a toast following the signing of the Camp David Accords in 1978.

NO OLYMPICS

The 1980 Olympic Games were scheduled to be held in Moscow. After the invasion of Afghanistan, President Carter announced that in protest the United States would not send its athletes. Carter apparently assumed that because the Olympics were of great importance to the Soviets as a public-relations gesture, the Soviet Afghan policy might be revised. Although a few other nations followed Carter's example, the Soviet Union did not budge, and the games went on.

The Panama Treaty

President Carter also took price in responding to Panamanian protests over continued American sovereignty over the Panama Canal Zone. The narrow strip of U.S. territory bisected the small republic and was an insult in an age when nationalist sensibilities in small countries were touchy.

Beginning in 1964, Panamanians had protested the fact that American flags flew in the very heart of their country; they were foreigners on their own land. There were a few deaths in the rioting. After several false starts at working out a treaty under Johnson and Nixon, in 1978 the Senate narrowly ratified an agreement with Panama to guarantee the permanent neutrality of the canal itself while gradually transfering sovereignty over it to Panama, culminating on December 31, 1999.

It was clear that the United States would never brook political misuse of the canal and, in turning it over to Panama, Carter muted Latin American denunciations of *"yanqui imperialismo."* Nevertheless, right-wing politicians, including Ronald Reagan, denounced the treaty as yet another retreat from national greatness by a weak president. The rhetoric took on the assonance of banana republic tub-thumping and never really aroused the American people. By 1980, however, they had decisively soured on President Carter as the result of a genuine humiliation abroad, and turned to Reagan to lead them.

The Iranian Tragedy

Like Nixon and Ford, Carter was misinformed that Reza Pahlavi, the pro-Western shah of Iran, was popular in his homeland. The president described Iran as an "island of stability" in the Middle East.

This was a delusion. The shah had alienated every social group in the country save the military and the westernized middle and upper classes. Liberal and leftist Iranians suffered brutal tortures at the hands of SAVAK, the shah's secret police. And the deeply re-

ligious peasantry was under the thumb of reactionary Muslim religious teachers (mullahs and ayatollahs) who taught that the shah was blasphemous.

In January 1979, after months of rebellion, the shah left the country for a "vacation," never to return, and the right wing of the broadly based revolution, led by the fanatical Ayatollah Ruholla Khomeini, seized power. In October, despite warnings from the embassy in Teheran that his action could lead to reprisals against Americans in Iran, Carter admitted the dying shah to the United States for medical treatment.

A few days later, with the ayatollah's consent, if not at his instigation, a group of Iranian students seized the American embassy compound and took 50 Americans hostage. For more than a year, they languished in confinement. A raid by commandos in 1980 failed to rescue the hostages, but cost Carter his Secretary of State, who had opposed the adventure. When Vance resigned, Carter appointed Senator Edmund Muskie to the post.

Muskie proved to be an able diplomat, and even succeeded in whittling away at Brzezinski's influence over the president. But he was no more successful at freeing the hostages than Vance. Not until January 20, 1981, the day Jimmy Carter left the White House, were they released.

Consequences of the Hostage Crisis

Some leftist American student groups joined Iranian students in the United States in celebrating the ayatollah's rise to power, and the seizure of the hostages did not greatly affect these sympathies. Only when the Khomeini regime began to institute wholesale executions of opponents on a scale that the shah never had dared did support for it evaporate. Many Iranian students in the United States continued to back the ayatollah, but as the hostage crisis wore on, their demonstrations grew quieter. Remarkably, and to the credit of an emotionally tried American population, there were no incidents of anti-Iranian violence worth noticing.

The crisis won Jimmy Carter renomination. Late in 1979, Senator Edward Kennedy announced that he would lead a liberal campaign against Carter, and all polls showed him easily defeating the president. Almost immediately, however, support for the president welled up, and Kennedy found himself soundly defeated by the time of the Democratic national convention. Sympathy for Carter's plight and a sense that, during so serious a crisis, the people should stand behind the president, frustrated every one of Kennedy's attempts to rally the party behind him. Even the disastrous commando raid helped Carter in the public opinion polls.

Blindfolded American hostages at the United States embassy in Iran.

Such support could not last as month after month Carter failed to make progress. Hardly was the Democratic convention adjourned than popular sympathy for the president evaporated. For a time, Congressman John Anderson of Illinois, running as an independent, appeared to be a genuine contender for the presidency. In the end, however, it was to the Republican candidate that voters fled. He was Ronald Reagan, one-time movie star, commercial representative of General Electric, and leader of the conservative Republicans. With 50.8 percent of the popular vote, Reagan won an electoral college landslide.

RONALD REAGAN: A POPULAR PRESIDENT

When movie mogul Jack Warner heard that his former employee, Ronald Reagan, was going to run for governor of California in 1966, he joked, "No, no. Jimmy Stewart for governor, Ronald Reagan for best friend." He meant that, on the screen, Reagan played likeable fellows—supporting roles—tolerably well, but he did not project the image of a man of substance who could be trusted to wield power responsibly.

America's Best Supporting Actor?

Very few people who were acquainted with Reagan disliked him. He was cheerful, even-tempered, personally tolerant, and optimistic. He was also the life of every party, full of amusing stories from his long career in Hollywood, a walking *People* magazine.

But some of the same people who liked him believed that Reagan lacked the knowledge or even the interest in government that seemed necessary for making informed and responsible decisions. Reagan's critics maintained that he never ceased to be an actor. Others, particularly the Southern California businessmen who sponsored his political career, wrote the lines. He memorized them, smiled, and luxuriated with his devoted wife in the ceremonial adulation that goes with being chief executive. In a culture that had made show business personalities its royalty, he was a superb head of state.

But, critics said, having him as head of government was at best to sacrifice the common good to profits for

Newly inaugurated president Ronald Reagan and his wife Nancy greet a crowd during the inaugural parade.

business, at worst to risk catastrophe. Sometimes at press conferences Reagan stared dumbly at questioners. On one occasion in 1985, television news showed his wife whispering an answer of "We're working on that" when the president faltered. His own advisers admitted to being delighted when Reagan emerged from an unrehearsed confrontation with the press without saying something foolish.

By 1985, concerns over the president's health compounded anxieties over his capacities. He had shown himself to be in superb physical condition as an equestrian and, in 1981, he snapped back like a teenaged athlete after being shot in the chest by John Hinckley, the ne'er-do-well son of a Colorado oilman. But when Reagan celebrated his seventy-second birthday in 1983, he became the oldest man ever to be president. Already notorious for long Coolidge-like naps (he restored Silent Cal's portrait to the White House) and for nodding off during public appearances, in 1985 he underwent two operations for cancer, one quite minor, one worrisome.

Or America's Best Friend?

For all the criticisms and anxieties, Reagan remained an immensely popular president. In part this was due to his brilliance as the "Great Communicator." For a long time the host of a television series, he was more adept at using the medium than any president except, possibly, John F. Kennedy. Reagan projected confidence, an ingratiating charm, and the authority his critics said he lacked.

Reagan was also very lucky. Some of the problems that had injured Ford and destroyed Carter resolved themselves during his presidency. The OPEC nations broke ranks and oil prices collapsed. Iran was prevented from vexing the United States when it was attacked by neighboring Iraq and embroiled in a hideous war marked by the use of gas and human-wave attacks carried out by boys. The Soviet Union was preoccupied during Reagan's first term by a quiet power struggle within the Kremlin. After a long illness that precluded decisive action, Leonid Brezhnev died in November 1982 to be succeeded by Yuri Andropov, who lived only until 1984. His successor, Konstantin Chernenko, doddered from the start and passed away in 1985. Only then did a younger and apparently decisive Russian leader emerge in the person of Mikhail Gorbachev who was, tellingly, an outgoing public charmer like the American president.

The Teflon President

Rather more remarkable than good luck was Ronald Reagan's immunity from blame for his administration's blunders and revelations that many of his aides and advisors were less than selfless public servants. He was "the Teflon president," a columnist wrote. As with pots and pans coated with the substance, nothing stuck to him. He rebuffed apparent peace initiatives by Andropov, Cuba's Fidel Castro, and Gorbechev on the grounds they were "just propaganda." A public that otherwise expressed grave concern over the threat of war remained loyal to him. His first term was marred by revelations of wrongdoing and collusion by two dozen of his appointees, of whom several went to jail. But Reagan was not held responsible for the corruption. While he called for a constitutional amendment that would obligate Congress to balance the government's budget each year, he annually sponsored budgets that sent the deficit and the national debt soaring to record heights. Democratic attacks upon the grotesque anomaly found next to no audience.

In the summer of 1985, the president told a national audience that the racist regime in South Africa had dismantled its policy of apartheid, strict separation of the races. Gerald Ford had been ridiculed for a similar blunder in regard to the status of the nations of Eastern Europe. The American people shrugged off Reagan's gaffe.

In 1983, the president sent U.S. Marines to Lebanon, vowing they would withdraw only when that strife-torn country was stabilized. Instead, vicious fighting among Israelis, Syrians, Palestinians, and a bewildering array of mutually hostile Lebanese sects grew worse. In October 1983, a suicide bomber drove a truck loaded with explosives into an American barracks in Beirut, killing 241 marines. Reagan's critics lambasted him for wasting lives to no good end, but polls showed that the public supported him, even after he admitted failure by withdrawing the troops.

Two American embassies in the Middle East were also devastated by terrorists and it was revealed that the Reagan administration, while talking a hard line against terrorists, had been lax about defending against them, even refusing money for security precautions in terrorist hotbeds. After each incident the president said that his patience was exhausted: he would retaliate

swiftly and harshly after the next attack. In the summer of 1985, Shi'ite terrorists hijacked an American airliner, murdered a marine in cold blood, and brutalized many of the other passengers.

Finally, in the spring of 1986, the president acted. When the government of Libya was incontrovertibly implicated in a bombing of a nightclub in West Berlin, American ships and planes attacked several Libyan cities. Among allied governments, only the British openly backed Reagan. At home, however, (and in most Western European nations), public opinion applauded the president's action. Momentarily, at least, the bombing raid seemed to have worked. Terrorist attacks on Americans almost ceased in the months after the Reagan retaliation. At the end of the summer of 1986, his popularity rating in the public opinion polls stood higher than that of Franklin D. Roosevelt ever had.

The "Sleaze Factor"

The questionable integrity of many of President Reagan's appointees also failed to dent his popularity. Among his controversial aides were CIA director, William Casey, Secretary of Labor Raymond Donovan, Secretary of the Interior James Watt, director of the Environmental Protection Agency (EPA) Anne Burford, and Edwin Meese, who was finally confirmed as Attorney General only in 1985. Casey, considered the shrewdest of the president's political advisers, was accused of financial irregularities in his past; but with Reagan's full support, he fought off a powerful drive to force his resignation.

Raymond Donovan also survived attacks by his critics. Soon after taking office, he was accused of being a crony of labor racketeers in his home state of New Jersey. Twice he had to appear before congressional investigating committees. Both times the hard evidence against him was found to be so negligible that even some liberals concluded that congressional Democrats were out to "get" him. In February 1983, Burford was attacked because during an investigation of her allegedly anti-environmental actions, several paper shredders were installed in EPA offices. After a month, she resigned to be replaced by William Ruckelshaus, a conservative with a reputation for fair dealing, even among liberals.

Conservationists and environmentalists did not disguise the fact that they were out to get Secretary of the Interior James Watt of Colorado. Watt was a leader of the "Sagebrush Rebels," a loose consortium of western businessmen who wanted what remained of the federally owned lands "returned" to the states in which they were located so that they might be exploited to their full economic worth by cattlemen, lumbermen, and mining companies.

Return was not the proper word, as was quickly pointed out by lobbies such as the Sierra Club and the Wilderness Society, which are pledged to protect the public lands. The lands in question had been owned by the federal government and therefore the people long before the states in question had come into existence. Therefore, with James Watt at the head of the Interior Department, which administered the national parks and the lands under the Bureau of Land Management, these groups were worried and stepped up their recruiting and lobbying efforts.

They fought all of Watt's attempts to open federal lands to private exploitation, and by 1983, the secretary and the protective societies were locked in a bitter draw. Watt's personality did not help his cause. His hatred of "posy-sniffers" was so unguarded that tens of thousands of people who never had belonged to environmental societies joined such groups.

Edwin Meese, a long-time adviser of the president, worked most of Reagan's first term as a political strategist. His name cropped up in connection with several dubious appointments and apparent kickbacks—low-interest loans, a remarkably generous purchase price for Meese's southern California home by a Reagan beneficiary—but such shenanigans were common at the political end of any administration. Meese became an object of controversy only in 1984 when Reagan nominated him to succeed William French Smith as Attorney General. Democrats and some Republicans obstructed the appointment through intensive investigation of Meese's financial affairs and Democratic presidential candidate Walter Mondale had Meese in mind in the campaign of 1984 when he referred to the "sleaze factor" in the Reagan White House. After Reagan's resounding reelection, however, the Senate had no choice but to confirm Meese.

The Election of 1984

Walter Mondale of Minnesota was an old-line New Deal liberal who had been Jimmy Carter's vice president. With strong support from the labor movement and the Democratic party establishment, he was easily able to kill challenges in the party primaries from every other hopeful except young Senator Gary Hart of Colorado. Hart nearly derailed Mondale's campaign by appealing to affluent young Democratic voters with a call for new approaches to problems, the vagueness of which Mondale panned in a television debate by quoting a line from a popular commercial for a hamburger franchise company, "Where's the beef?" Where was the substance of Hart's appeal?

As the party's candidate, Mondale lacked personal flair. He tried to overcome his handicap by choosing as his running mate the first woman to stand as a major party candidate, New York Congresswoman Geraldine Ferraro.

To no avail: Reagan captured 59 percent of the popular vote and carried 49 states. Most astonishing was the extent of his popularity among groups that had been the mainstay of Mondale's Democratic party or beneficiaries of its liberalism and welfare policies for half a century. The Irish vote was for Reagan. Italian-Americans voted for Reagan. Slavic-Americans voted for him in all but three states. Some 56 percent of the Roman Catholic vote went Republican. Jews, who had been 80 to 90 percent Democratic, gave Mondale a bare majority as did union members. The blue collar vote as a whole went for Reagan. The president also won six of ten voters over 65 and two-thirds of the voters between the ages of 18 and 24.

And yet, except for a brief honeymoon at the beginning of his first term, President Reagan was unable to translate his monumental popularity into the "conservative revolution" of which his supporters spoke. There was a scant Republican majority in the Senate through 1987 thanks to a well-planned and well-funded campaign against specially targeted liberal senators in 1980 by fundamentalist, right-wing Political Action Committees (PACs), self-styled "the Moral Majority." But the House of Representatives remained Democratic throughout the Reagan era. Voters who endorsed the president personally also voted for representatives who opposed his policies.

THE REAGAN PRESIDENCY

On national economic and social issues, Reagan sounded moderate during the campaign of 1980. However, the president was long on record as calling for the dissolution of New Deal reforms. He stated that his administration would not act as a big brother to the American people but would reduce governmental responsibility for the economic and social welfare of individuals. Indeed, he blamed the troubled economy of the 1970s on liberal spending and the "national malaise" on what the welfare state had done to American morale.

Reaganomics

Just six days after his inauguration, Reagan abolished all price and allocation controls on oil, and on March 6, he cut the federal payroll by 37,000 jobs. His tax-reform bill reduced the levy in every income bracket, but frankly favored the rich. Reagan, Secretary of the Treasury Donald Regan, and budget director David Stockman argued that whereas the poor would simply spend any tax savings, thus fueling the inflation that the Reagan administration was determined to slow down, the wealthy would invest their windfalls in new factories and industries, thus creating jobs. This thinking was based on the "supply-side economics" of Arthur Laffer, although they reminded Democrats of the "trickle-down" policies of Andrew Mellon and Calvin Coolidge.

Having reduced government revenues and federal control of the economy, however, Reagan did not follow Coolidge's example and cut gross government expenditures. Social services were slashed, but defense spending increased. Congress had to double the debt ceiling (the amount that the government can legally borrow) from $506 billion to $985 billion. In 1982, the ceiling was raised to more than $1 trillion.

Reagan's Critics

The Democrats denounced the morality of cutting social benefits for the poor and the elderly in difficult

Bread lines, unknown since the 1930s, were prominent during the recession winter of 1983/84.

> ### DISPOSABLE AMERICA
>
> Each year, Americans throw out of their homes (not their places of work) some 160 to 180 million tons of what they variously call trash, garbage, or rubbish. This amounts to a half ton per person per year.
>
> Much of the total is made up of products designed to be disposable. Every day, on average, each American discards almost five pounds of "disposables." On a given day, Americans throw away 123 million paper and plastic cups, 44 million paper and plastic diapers, 5.5 million razor blades and disposable razors, 4.4 million disposable pens, and nearly a million disposable cigarette lighters.

times while, in an age of nuclear overkill, spending billions on weapons. Critics such as Senator Hart fastened on the apparent waste in the Reagan defense program, an intercontinental ballistic missile staging system called "densepack" (which Reagan allowed to die), and the refitting and recommissioning of several battleships that had been in mothballs for more than a decade. Experts in naval warfare pointed out that during the Falkland Islands conflict of 1982 between Great Britain and Argentina, one Argentine plane carrying a comparatively cheap missile was able to sink an extremely expensive and sophisticated British ship. The same could be done to an American aircraft carrier at the cost of $1 billion and thousands of lives.

Still, because the Republicans controlled the Senate and enough conservative, mostly southern Democrats supported Reaganomics, the president got what he wanted until the congressional election of 1982. While the Republicans maintained their slim majority in the Senate, the Democrats increased their edge in the House to a comfortable margin.

Reagan appeared to be responsive to the discovery by Republican party election strategists that he had fared very poorly among women voters, that if all eligible voters had voted in the proportions that women had, he might have lost the election. While he did not support the ERA, he appointed more women to high-level positions than had any previous president, including the first woman justice of the Supreme Court, Sandra Day O'Connor. By March 1983, two members of Reagan's cabinet were women.

Yet "Reaganomics" were not vindicated throughout 1983. Inflation slowed but unemployment remained higher than at any time since before the Second World War. Homeless people were camping permanently in state and national parks, and several hundred were said to be living under freeway viaducts in Los Angeles and in other cities with warm climates. In January

CRISIS IN AMERICAN MANAGEMENT

The steady loss of the domestic market in electronics and automobiles to Japanese companies was commonly blamed on American workers during the 1970s; they were paid too much, and their productivity was too low. By 1980, however, evidence indicated that management was at fault: too many executives who were making too much money were afraid to take chances. Thus, when workers purchased several factories in the Midwest from owners whose profits were failing and hired their own managers, the companies reversed their downward spiral. When Japan's Sanyo Corporation bought Warwick Television from Sears Roebuck, 300 middle-management jobs were eliminated, and the company turned in a profit within two years. (Workers were not fired, and wages were not lowered.)

The same thing happened in the Quasar Company, when Motorola sold it to Matsushita. Akio Morita, the chairman of Sony, a very successful manufacturer of electronics devices, said bluntly that "the problem in the United States is management"; he added that American workers were "excellent." American inventors repeatedly have expressed their disgust with American management. They have been forced to sell their patents to Japanese corporations because American business executives were afraid to make risky decisions.

1983, an auto-frame manufacturer in Milwaukee advertised 200 jobs, and 15,000 applicants showed up. A few days later, 3,000 people stood in line to apply for 35 jobs at the Sun Oil refinery in Marcus Hook, Pennsylvania.

The president expected this, and urged Americans to "stay the course." With time, he said, investment would create jobs without inflating the currency. Except for the very poor, who are not inclined to vote, Americans were enjoying better times by 1984, which contributed to Reagan's landslide victory.

After the election, Democratic critics (and an increasing number of Republicans) began to focus on the long-term effects of the president's grotesquely imbalanced budgets. Would his admiration of Calvin Coolidge also translate into a similar legacy: his happy personal retirement from the presidency with catastrophic after-effects for the economy? By the summer of 1986, economic growth had stalled, and, late in July, President Reagan issued an optimistic prognostication that smacked uneasily of Coolidge's assertion, during the Bull Market of 1928, that the price of stocks was cheap.

Foreign Policy

Because day-to-day diplomacy is in the hands of the executive branch, President Reagan found it easier to

Sandra Day O'Connor, the first woman to serve on the United States Supreme Court, poses with her new colleagues shortly after her appointment.

put his stamp on foreign policy than on domestic. He had criticized his predecessors for a lack of "toughness" in dealing with enemies and rivals abroad, particularly the Soviet Union. Attempting to cajole the Russians into peace with concessions like the SALT treaties, Reagan argued, was an illusion. It was necessary to take the hard-line with a country he called "the evil empire."

His first secretary of state was apparently of a mind with him. Alexander Haig had been a general and a top aide to Nixon who claimed to have run the country during Nixon's last days. Nevertheless, he resigned under pressure in 1982. While Reagan was recovering from the attempt to assassinate him, Haig had announced that no one should worry; he was in charge again. This preposterous claim (the vice president stands in for a disabled president) soured both Reagan and his personal advisors.

New Secretary of State George Schultz was a former executive with an internationally powerful corporation. Sometimes called the "dove" in the Reagan administration, Schultz hinted at a more accommodating approach to the arms race than most Reagan advisors. However, he also urged more militant responses to terrorists and anti-American "liberation movements" in the Third World than Secretary of Defense Caspar Weinberger.

The Arms Race

Weinberger, a compact, grim man, was the chief administration spokesman for accelerating the arms race with the Soviet Union. He argued that if the United States built up its arsenal, both nuclear and conventional, and developed new weapons systems such as "Star Wars," a highly speculative satellite-laser network based in space, the Soviets would be forced into a conciliatory policy. With profound domestic problems, the Russians were far less able to afford a runaway arms race than the United States.

The huge military expenditures were criticized at home for raising the deficit to dangerous levels. At home and abroad the United States was castigated as the chief threat to world peace. In 1985 and 1986, the Soviet premier, Mikhail Gorbachev, shrewdly exploited anxieties among American allies by plying a conciliatory line. When even British Prime Minister Margaret Thatcher, Reagan's firmest friend among the major powers, was charmed by the Soviet leader and the British Labour Party announced that it would demand the removal of American nuclear missiles from British soil if Labour won power, Reagan eased his rhetoric and agreed to resume arms control talks and to meet personally with Gorbachev.

Then, however, he appointed a truculent cold war-

Alexander Haig drifted from presidential timber to obscurity during the early Reagan years.

rior to head a vital American team at the talks and, through the summer of 1986, diplomatic wrangling prevented scheduling the proposed "summit" meeting. The president's critics accused him (and sometimes Gorbachev) of playing to the popular demand for disarmament while resisting substantive moves. In the spring of 1986, Reagan had announced that the United States would not even be bound by the terms of the signed and ratified SALT I treaty.

Central America

Reagan's "Third World" policy was flexible. Although his ambassador to the United Nations, Jeanne Kirkpatrick, stated that the United States would support "authoritarian" pro-American governments in poor countries and oppose "totalitarian communist" regimes, in 1986 the Reagan administration collaborated actively in deposing two anti-communist dictators, Jean-Paul Duvalier of Haiti and Ferdinand Marcos of the Philippines.

In El Salvador, the United States supported the democratically elected government of José Napoleon Duarte, a moderate who was assailed both by extreme

THE TYPICAL AMERICAN OF THE 1980s: A STATISTICAL PORTRAIT

The statistical American of the 1980s was a mother who very likely had a job. However, because of economic depression, her employment was precarious.

The statistical American of the year 1980 was a Caucasian female, a little more than 30 years old, married to her first husband, with one child and about to have another. She was a shade over 5 feet 4 inches tall, and weighed 134 pounds. Statisticians are not sure of the color of her hair and eyes, but they were probably on the brownish side. Statisticians are sure that she had tried marijuana when she was younger, but no longer used it in the 1980s (although some of her friends still did). She did not smoke cigarettes, but at least had tried them in the past; she still drank, just this side of moderately.

The statistical American adult female of the 1980s considered herself middle class, and had attended college but had not necessarily graduated. She was likely to work outside the home, but economic conditions during the first half of the decade made her opportunities uncertain. Her household income was about

$20,000 a year; she and her husband were watching their budget closely, which they were not accustomed to doing. It is a toss-up whether or not she voted in 1984 (or at all during the 1970s). She was decreasingly interested in feminism as the 1980s progressed and the failure of the ERA faded into memory. She was marginally more likely to be registered as a Democrat than as a Republican, but she was more likely to have voted for Ronald Reagan in 1984 than in 1980.

More than half of the statistical American's female friends were married. Most of her friends who have been divorced have married again within three years. The statistical American of the 1980s attached no stigma to divorce, and experienced only a slight sense of unease with people who lived with members of the opposite sex without benefit of marriage. But she found it difficult to agree that homosexuality is nothing more than an "alternate lifestyle" on a moral parity with heterosexuality. She was both amused and repelled by the culture of the "gay" communities about which she read, but by 1985 was not so indulgent as she had been because of the quantum leap in the spread of deadly AIDS.

She almost certainly had sex with her husband before they married, and almost as likely with at least one other man. There is a fair chance that she had a brief fling since marriage, probably during a "trial separation."

The statistical American was more likely to be Protestant than Catholic. However, she was more likely to be Catholic than a member of any other *individual* denomination. If a Catholic, she practiced birth control, most likely using the pill, in defiance of Church directives. Moreover, Catholic or Protestant, she attended church services far less frequently than had her mother.

The statistical American was in excellent health; she saw a dentist and a doctor more than once a year, and paid a little less than half of the cost of health care (state and federal government picked up about the same, private industry and philanthropy the rest). She had a life expectancy of almost 78 years, and would outlive her husband by eight years, with the prospects that her dotage would be economically trying.

The statistical American lived in a state with a population of about 3 million people—Colorado, Iowa, Oklahoma, Connecticut—and in a city of about 100,000 people—Roanoke, Virginia; Reno, Nevada; Durham, North Carolina.

Or perhaps, she lived at the population center of the United States, which in 1980 was west of the Mississippi River for the first time in American history. It was located "one mile west of the De Soto City Hall, Jefferson County, Missouri." An equal number of people in the continental United States lived east of that point as west, as many north of it as south.

As the question about her state and city of residence indicates, the statistical American is a somewhat absurd contrivance, distilled out of the majorities, means, and medians of the United States Census Bureau; the responses to surveys taken by a number of public-opinion experts; and, simply, the probabilities of the educated guess.

The virtue of the United States remains rooted in its diversity of people as well as of resources and in the survival of those people's right to change their minds as many times as they wish. And, as far as matters of public policy are concerned, to form majorities and effect their wishes. For a nation that has reached its third century, that is not so bad an accomplishment. In the star-crossed history of the human race, it has not been done in many other places.

right-wing elements within his government and a leftist guerrilla movement in the jungles.

Toward Nicaragua, where the leftist Sandinista movement had come to power in 1979, Reagan refused to talk cooperation. American policy was clearly to destroy the anti-American ruling group. After an attempt to mine Managua harbor aroused worldwide protest, the president turned to economic pressures and funding a rebel group known as the Contras. In June 1986, despite evidence that the Contra movement was shot-through with corruption, the president persuaded Congress to appropriate $100 million in aid. Much more threatening to the Sandinistas than the Contras, however, was the collapse of Nicaragua's economy. Between 1979 and 1986, Nicaraguan exports declined from $660 million to $249 million and its gross national product by 50 percent. To what extent the disaster was due to American sanctions and to what extent to Sandinista venality and incompetence cannot be determined.

The president's Nicaragua policy was not popular in the United States. Some critics romanticized the Sandinistas. Others called merely for responsible noninterventionist American policy and warned against repeating the Vietnam disaster in Central America.

Through the summer of 1986, the Reagan administration seemed oblivious to a far more ominous crisis brewing "south of the border." Mexico's debt, principally in the United States, reached fantastic heights that threatened to engulf that important country and neighbor in anarchy. The future of Mexico loomed as one of the greatest diplomatic challenges of the twentieth century's final decade.

South Africa

By the summer of 1986, the "Apartheid" system that governed race relations in South Africa was falling apart. Assailed by white liberals and black leaders at home, execrated by virtually every country in the world, the strict segregation and inferior social status forced on the black majority of the country resulted in a spate of riots and the proclamation of a state of emergency, with broad arbitrary powers accorded to prime minister Pieter Willem Botha. Although more amenable to change than his predecessors, Botha was unable to accommodate black aspirations (and foreign demands for reform) while maintaining the support of the Afrikaaner voters whose high standard of living depended largely on their racial privileges.

Along with British Prime Minister Margaret Thatcher, President Reagan maintained that the South African government could be better persuaded

Walter Mondale and the first woman vice-presidential candidate Geraldine Ferraro on the campaign trail, 1984.

to change its policies by quiet diplomacy than by imposing economic sanctions. The Afrikaaners were prepared for a siege economy—their culture was rooted in the idea of siege—and the blacks of the country would suffer first and most grievously from an economic collapse. Better slow, stable progress in Africa's richest country than the horrors of repression during a siege or the chaos that might result from too sudden a social and political upheaval. Reagan's critics answered that to tolerate the gross injustice of Apartheid mocked American ideals.

Assessing the Reagan Revolution

Ronald Reagan worked fewer changes in American life than his conservative supporters hoped for and his liberal opponents feared. He was unable to translate his fabulous personal popularity into an electoral repudiation of the social, economic, and political structure formulated during the New Deal of the 1930s. Even the Republican control of the Senate through 1987 was something of a fluke, the result of an intensive campaign in 1980 by right-wing PACs against only six liberal senators. There was no "conservative

revolution," only a monumental groundswell of personal affection for Ronald W. Reagan.

Nevertheless, Reagan's retirement in 1989, which the Constitution required, by no means assured the return to power of the party that had authored the system the president assailed but could not topple. The voters' refusal to support President Reagan's policies while they warmly endorsed his leadership and told pollsters that he had lifted the nation's morale from malaise to patriotic pride, seemed to indicate that the Democratic party had erred not in clinging to its "hard" social and economic program, but by its emphasis during the 1970s of its "soft" sentiments, what conservatives mocked as "New Age Liberalism."

By making central to the party's image such campaigns as school busing, endorsement of unpopular Supreme Court rulings on the rights of accused lawbreakers, abortion on demand, definition of pornography as a form of free speech, and aggressive support of the "Gay Liberation" movement, the "New Age Liberals" pleased affluent middle-class voters, particularly intellectuals. However, they affronted the traditional moral values of ordinary people, farmers and

On July 4, 1986, the Independence Day celebration centered on the unveiling and relighting of the Statue of Liberty, in time for its hundredth anniversary.

workers and their families, the mainstay of their party since the New Deal. Ordinary People are still America's "bone and sinew." In their hands—and not with noisy pressure groups, no matter how chic, nor with well-funded extremist PACs—the fate of the democratic republic will lie, as always, in the end, it has.

For Further Reading

To the extent that a writer's detachment is vital to the writing of history, recent history is not history at all. There are plenty of books in print dealing with the last decade of the American experience. There are plenty of books dealing with current events among every month's new titles! But there are as yet no authoritative historical *overviews* nor, surely, *classics* dealing with years which are, to historians, the present.

Nor is it possible to list with confidence the *special studies* that will withstand the test of time, such as is easy to do in connection with, say, the Civil War or the Progressive Era. The book about the foreign policy of the Carter or Reagan years that is compelling today may prove in another decade to be ill-informed or hogwash. The same applies to works on politics and such subjects as the energy crisis or national economic policy. Consider the differences of analysis (and sometimes the facts reported) of the same incident in the conservative *National Review* and the liberal *New York Review of Books.* The prudent student will do well to read widely in such journals of opinion and to rely on library files of periodicals that strive to be factual—*Time, Newsweek,* the *New York Times,* the Los Angeles *Times*—for basic information.

Gerald Ford has written his memoirs, *A Time to Heal: The Autobiography of Gerald R. Ford* (1979), and Jimmy Carter his, *Keeping Faith: Memories of a President* (1982). As of this writing there is no detached analysis of Ronald Reagan's place in American history.

Appendixes

The Declaration of Independence*

The Unanimous Declaration of the Thirteen United States of America,

When in the Course of human events it becomes necessary for one people to dissolve the political bands which have connected them with another, and to assume among the Powers of the earth, the separate and equal station to which the Laws of Nature and of Nature's God entitle them, a decent respect to the opinions of mankind requires that they should declare the causes which impel them to the separation.

We hold these truths to be self-evident, that all men are created equal, that they are endowed by their Creator with certain unalienable Rights, that among these are Life, Liberty and the pursuit of Happiness. That to secure these rights, Governments are instituted among Men, deriving their just Powers from the consent of the governed. That whenever any Form of Government becomes destructive of these ends, it is the Right of the People to alter or to abolish it, and to institute new Government, laying its foundation on such principles and organizing its Powers in such form, as to them shall seem most likely to effect their Safety and Happiness. Prudence, indeed, will dictate that Governments long established should not be changed for light and transient causes; and accordingly all experience hath shewn, that mankind are more disposed to suffer, while evils are sufferable, than to right themselves by abolishing the forms to which they are accustomed. But when a long train of abuses and usurpations, pursuing invariably the same Object evinces a design to reduce them under absolute Despotism, it is their right, it is their duty to throw off such Government, and to provide new Guards for their future security. Such has been the patient sufferance of these Colonies; and such is now the necessity which constrains them to alter their former Systems of Government. The history of the present King of Great Britain is a history of repeated injuries and usurpations, all having in direct object the establishment of an absolute Tyranny over these States. To prove this, let Facts be submitted to a candid world.

He has refused his Assent to Laws, the most wholesome and necessary for the public good.

He has forbidden his Governors to pass Laws of immediate and pressing importance, unless suspended in their operation till his Assent should be obtained; and when so suspended, he has utterly neglected to attend to them.

He has refused to pass other Laws for the accommodation of large districts of people, unless those people would relinquish the right of Representation in the Legislature, a right inestimable to them and formidable to tyrants only.

He has called together legislative bodies at places unusual, uncomfortable, and distant from the depository of their Public Records, for the sole Purpose of fatiguing them into compliance with his measures.

He has dissolved Representative Houses repeatedly, for opposing with manly firmness his invasions on the rights of the People.

He has refused for a long time, after such dissolutions, to cause others to be elected; whereby the Legislative Powers, incapable of Annihilation, have returned to the People at large for their exercise; the State remaining in the mean time exposed to all the dangers of invasion from without, and convulsions within.

He has endeavoured to prevent the Population of these States; for that purpose obstructing the Laws for Naturalization of Foreigners; refusing to pass others to encourage their migrations hither, and raising the conditions of new Appropriations of Lands.

He has obstructed the Administration of Justice, by refusing his Assent to Laws for establishing Judiciary Powers.

He has made Judges dependent on his Will alone, for the tenure of their offices, and the amount and payment of their salaries.

He has erected a multitude of New Offices, and sent hither swarms of Officers to harass our People, and eat out their substance.

He has kept among us, in times of peace, Standing Armies without the consent of our legislatures.

He has affected to render the Military independent of and superior to the Civil Power.

He has combined with others to subject us to a jurisdiction foreign to our constitution, and unacknowledged by our laws; giving his Assent to their Acts of pretended Legislation:

---

*Reprinted from the facsimile of the engrossed copy in the National Archives. The original spelling, capitalization, and punctuation have been retained. Paragraphing has been added.

For Quartering large bodies of armed troops among us:

For protecting them, by a mock Trial, from Punishment for any Murders which they should commit on the Inhabitants of these States:

For cutting off our Trade with all parts of the world:

For imposing Taxes on us without our Consent:

For depriving us in many cases, of the benefits of Trial by Jury:

For transporting us beyond Seas to be tried for pretended offences:

For abolishing the free System of English Laws in a neighbouring Province, establishing therein an Arbitrary government, and enlarging its Boundaries so as to render it at once an example and fit instrument for introducing the same absolute rule into these Colonies:

For taking away our Charters, abolishing our most valuable Laws, and altering fundamentally the Forms of our Governments:

For suspending our own Legislatures, and declaring themselves invested with Power to legislate for us in all cases whatsoever.

He has abdicated Government here, by declaring us out of his Protection, and waging War against us.

He has plundered our seas, ravaged our Coasts, burnt our towns, and destroyed the lives of our people.

He is at this time transporting large Armies of foreign Mercenaries to compleat the works of death, desolation and tyranny, already begun with circumstances of Cruelty and perfidy scarcely paralleled in the most barbarous ages, and totally unworthy the Head of a civilized nation.

He has constrained our fellow Citizens taken Captive on the high Seas to bear Arms against their Country, to become the executioners of their friends and Brethren, or to fall themselves by their Hands.

He has excited domestic insurrections amongst us, and has endeavoured to bring on the inhabitants of our frontiers, the merciless Indian Savages, whose known rule of warfare, is an undistinguished destruction of all ages, sexes and conditions.

In every stage of these Oppressions We have Petitioned for Redress in the most humble terms: Our repeated Petitions have been answered only by repeated injury. A Prince, whose character is thus marked by every act which may define a Tyrant, is unfit to be the ruler of a free People.

Nor have We been wanting in attentions to our British brethren. We have warned them from time to time of attempts by their legislature to extend an unwarrantable jurisdiction over us. We have reminded them of the circumstances of our emigration and settlement here. We have appealed to their native justice and magnanimity, and we have conjured them by the ties of our common kindred to disavow these usurpations, which, would inevitably interrupt our connections and correspondence. They too have been deaf to the voice of justice and of consanguinity. We must, therefore, acquiesce in the necessity, which denounces our Separation, and hold them, as we hold the rest of mankind, Enemies in War, in Peace Friends.

We, therefore, the Representatives of the United States of America, in General Congress, Assembled, appealing to the Supreme Judge of the world for the rectitude of our intentions, do, in the Name, and by Authority of the good People of these Colonies, solemnly publish and declare, That these United Colonies are, and of Right ought to be FREE AND INDEPENDENT STATES; that they are Absolved from all Allegiance to the British Crown, and that all political connection between them and the State of Great Britain, is and ought to be totally dissolved; and that, as Free and Independent States, they have full Power to levy War, conclude Peace, contract Alliances, establish Commerce, and to do all other Acts and Things which Independent States may of right do. And for the support of this Declaration, with a firm reliance on the protection of divine Providence, we mutually pledge to each other our Lives, our Fortunes and our sacred Honor.

The Constitution of the United States of America*

We the People of the United States, in Order to form a more perfect Union, establish Justice, insure domestic Tranquility, provide for the common defence, promote the general Welfare, and secure the Blessings of Liberty to ourselves and our Posterity, do ordain and establish this Constitution for the United States of America.

Article. I.

Section. 1. All legislative Powers herein granted shall be vested in a Congress of the United States, which shall consist of a Senate and House of Representatives.

Section. 2. The House of Representatives shall be composed of Members chosen every second Year by the People of the several States, and the Electors in each State shall have the Qualifications requisite for Electors of the most numerous Branch of the State Legislature.

No Person shall be a Representative who shall not have attained to the Age of twenty five Years, and been seven Years a Citizen of the United States, and who shall not, when elected, be an Inhabitant of that State in which he shall be chosen.

Representatives and direct Taxes† shall be apportioned among the several States which may be included within this Union, according to their respective Numbers, which shall be determined by adding to the whole Number of free Persons, including those bound to Service for a Term of Years, and excluding Indians not taxed, three fifths of all other Persons.‡ The actual Enumeration shall be made within three Years after the first Meeting of the Congress of the United States, and within every subsequent Term of ten Years, in such Manner as they shall by Law direct. The Number of Representatives shall not exceed one for every thirty Thousand, but each State shall have at least one Representative; and until such enumeration shall be made, the State of New Hampshire shall be entitled to chuse three; Massachusetts eight; Rhode Island and Providence Plantations one; Connecticut five; New York six; New Jersey four; Pennsylvania eight; Delaware one; Maryland six; Virginia ten; North Carolina five; South Carolina five; and Georgia three.

When vacancies happen in the Representation from any State, the Executive Authority thereof shall issue Writs of Election to fill such Vacancies.

The House of Representatives shall chuse their Speaker and other Officers; and shall have the sole Power of Impeachment.

Section. 3. The Senate of the United States shall be composed of two Senators from each State, chosen by the Legislature thereof, for six Years; and each Senator shall have one Vote.*

Immediately after they shall be assembled in Consequence of the first Election, they shall be divided as equally as may be into three Classes. The Seats of the Senators of the first Class shall be vacated at the Expiration of the second Year, of the second Class at the Expiration of the fourth Year, and of the third Class at the Expiration of the sixth Year, so that one third may be chosen every second Year; and if Vacancies happen by Resignation, or otherwise, during the Recess of the Legislature of any State, the Executive thereof may make temporary Appointments until the next Meeting of the Legislature, which shall then fill such Vacancies.†

No Person shall be a Senator who shall not have attained to the Age of thirty Years, and been nine Years a Citizen of the United States, and who shall not, when elected, be an Inhabitant of that State for which he shall be chosen.

The Vice President of the United States shall be President of the Senate, but shall have no Vote, unless they be equally divided.

The Senate shall chuse their other Officers, and also a President pro tempore, in the Absence of the Vice President, or when he shall exercise the Office of President of the United States.

The Senate shall have the sole Power to try all Impeachments. When sitting for that Purpose, they shall be on Oath or Affirmation. When the President of the United States is tried, the Chief Justice shall preside: And no Person shall be convicted without the Concurrence of two thirds of the Members present.

Judgment in Cases of Impeachment shall not extend further than to removal from Office, and disqualification to hold and enjoy any Office of honor, Trust or Profit under the

---

*From the engrossed copy in the National Archives. Original spelling, capitalization, and punctuation have been retained.
†Modified by the Sixteenth Amendment.
‡Replaced by the Fourteenth Amendment.

*Superseded by the Seventeenth Amendment.
†Modified by the Seventeenth Amendment.

United States: but the Party convicted shall nevertheless be liable and subject to Indictment, Trial, Judgment and Punishment, according to Law.

Section. 4. The Times, Places and Manner of holding Elections for Senators and Representatives, shall be prescribed in each State by the Legislature thereof, but the Congress may at any time by Law make or alter such Regulation, except as to the Places of chusing Senators.

The Congress shall assemble at least once in every Year, and such Meeting shall be on the first Monday in December, unless they shall by Law appoint a different Day. *

Section. 5. Each House shall be the Judge of the Elections, Returns and Qualifications of its own Members, and a Majority of each shall constitute a Quorum to do Business; but a smaller Number may adjourn from day to day, and may be authorized to compel the Attendance of absent Members, in such manner, and under such Penalties as each House may provide.

Each House may determine the Rules of its Proceedings, punish its Members for disorderly Behaviour, and, with the Concurrence of two thirds, expel a Member.

Each House shall keep a Journal of its Proceedings, and from time to time publish the same, excepting such Parts as may in their Judgment require Secrecy; and the Yeas and Nays of the Members of either House on any question shall, at the Desire of one fifth of those Present, be entered on the Journal.

Neither House, during the Session of Congress, shall, without the Consent of the other, adjourn for more than three days, nor to any other Place than that in which the two Houses shall be sitting.

Section. 6. The Senators and Representatives shall receive a Compensation for their Services, to be ascertained by Law, and paid out of the Treasury of the United States. They shall in all Cases, except Treason, Felony and Breach of the Peace, be privileged from Arrest during their Attendance at the Session of their respective Houses, and in going to and returning from the same; and for any Speech or Debate in either House, they shall not be questioned in any other Place.

No Senator or Representative shall, during the Time for which he was elected, be appointed to any civil Office under the Authority of the United States, which shall have been created, or the Emoluments whereof shall have been encreased during such time; and no Person holding any Office under the United States, shall be a Member of either House during his Continuance in Office.

Section. 7. All Bills for raising Revenue shall originate in the House of Representatives; but the Senate may propose or concur with Amendments as on other bills.

Every Bill which shall have passed the House of Representatives and the Senate shall, before it become a Law, be presented to the President of the United States; If he approve he shall sign it, but if not he shall return it, with his Objections to that House in which it shall have originated, who shall enter the Objections at large on their Journal, and proceed to reconsider it. If after such Reconsideration two thirds of that House shall agree to pass the Bill, it shall be sent, together with the Objections, to the other House, by which it shall likewise be reconsidered, and if approved by two thirds of that House, it shall become a Law. But in all such Cases the Votes of both Houses shall be determined by yeas and Nays, and the Names of the Persons voting for and against the Bill shall be entered on the Journal of each House respectively. If any Bill shall not be returned by the President within ten Days (Sundays excepted) after it shall have been presented to him, the Same shall be a Law, in Manner as if he had signed it, unless the Congress by their Adjournment prevent its Return, in which Case it shall not be a Law.

Every Order, Resolution, or Vote to which the Concurrence of the Senate and House of Representatives may be necessary (except on a question of Adjournment) shall be presented to the President of the United States; and before the Same shall take Effect, shall be approved by him, or being disapproved by him shall be repassed by two thirds of the Senate and House of Representatives, according to the rules and Limitations prescribed in the Case of a Bill.

Section. 8. The Congress shall have Power To lay and collect Taxes, Duties, Imposts and Excises, to pay the Debts and provide for the common Defence and general Welfare of the United States; but all Duties, Imposts and Excises shall be uniform throughout the United States;

To borrow Money on the credit of the United States;

To regulate Commerce with foreign Nations, and among the several States, and with the Indian Tribes;

To establish an uniform Rule of Naturalization, and uniform Laws on the subject of Bankruptcies throughout the United States;

To coin Money, regulate the Value thereof, and of foreign Coin, and fix the Standard of Weights and Measures;

To provide for the Punishment of counterfeiting the Securities and current Coin of the United States;

To establish Post Offices and post Roads;

To promote the Progress of Science and useful Arts, by securing for limited Times to Authors and Inventors the exclusive Right to their respective Writings and Discoveries;

To constitute Tribunals inferior to the supreme Court;

To define and punish Piracies and Felonies committed on the high Seas, and Offences against the Law of Nations;

To declare War, grant Letters of Marque and Reprisal, and make Rules concerning Captures on Land and Water;

To raise and support Armies, but no Appropriation of

*Superseded by the Twentieth Amendment.

Money to that Use shall be for a longer Term than two Years;

To provide and maintain a Navy;

To make Rules for the government and Regulation of the land and naval Forces;

To provide for calling forth the Militia to execute the Laws of the Union, suppress Insurrections and repel Invasions;

To provide for organizing, arming, and disciplining, the Militia, and for governing such Part of them as may be employed in the Service of the United States, reserving to the States respectively, the Appointment of the Officers, and the Authority of training the Militia according to the discipline prescribed by Congress;

To exercise exclusive Legislation in all Cases whatsoever, over such District (not exceeding ten Miles square) as may, by Cession of particular States, and the Acceptance of Congress, become the Seat of the Government of the United States, and to exercise like Authority over all Places purchased by the consent of the Legislature of the State in which the Same shall be, for the Erection of Forts, Magazines, Arsenals, dock-Yards, and other needful Buildings;—And

To make all Laws which shall be necessary and proper for carrying into Execution the foregoing Powers, and all other Powers vested by this Constitution in the Government of the United States, or in any Department or Officer thereof.

Section. 9. The Migration or Importation of such Persons as any of the States now existing shall think proper to admit, shall not be prohibited by the Congress prior to the Year one thousand eight hundred and eight, but a Tax or Duty may be imposed on such Importation, not exceeding ten dollars for each Person.

The Privilege of the Writ of Habeas Corpus shall not be suspended, unless when in Cases of Rebellion or Invasion the public Safety may require it.

No Bill of Attainder or ex post facto Law shall be passed.

No Capitation, or other direct, Tax shall be laid, unless in Proportion to the Census or Enumeration herein before directed to be taken.

No Tax or Duty shall be laid on Articles exported from any State.

No Preference shall be given by any Regulation of Commerce or Revenue to the Ports of one State over those of another: nor shall Vessels bound to, or from, one State, be obliged to enter, clear, or pay Duties in another.

No Money shall be drawn from the Treasury, but in Consequence of Appropriations made by Law, and a regular Statement and Account of the Receipts and Expenditures of all public Money shall be published from time to time.

No Title of Nobility shall be granted by the United States: And no Person holding any Office of Profit or Trust under them, shall, without the Consent of the Congress, accept of any present, Emolument, Office, or Title, of any kind whatever, from any King, Prince, or foreign State.

Section. 10. No State shall enter into any Treaty, Alliance, or Confederation; grant Letters of Marque and Reprisal; coin Money; emit bills of Credit; make any Thing but gold and silver Coin a Tender in Payment of Debts; pass any Bill of Attainder, ex post facto Law, or Law impairing the Obligation of Contracts, or grant any Title of Nobility.

No State shall, without the Consent of the Congress, lay any Imposts or Duties on Imports or Exports, except what may be absolutely necessary for executing its inspection Laws: and the net Produce of all Duties and Imposts, laid by any State on Imports or Exports, shall be for the Use of the Treasury of the United States; and all such Laws shall be subject to the Revision and Controul of the Congress.

No State shall, without the Consent of Congress, lay any Duty of Tonnage, keep Troops or Ships of War in time of peace, enter into any Agreement or Compact with another State, or with a foreign Power, or engage in War, unless actually invaded, or in such imminent Danger as will not admit of delay.

Article. II.

Section. 1. The executive Power shall be vested in a President of the United States of America. He shall hold his Office during the Term of four Years, and, together with the Vice President, chosen for the same Term, be elected, as follows:

Each State shall appoint, in such Manner as the Legislature thereof may direct, a Number of Electors, equal to the whole Number of Senators and Representatives to which the State may be entitled in the Congress: but no Senator or Representative, or Person holding an Office of Trust or Profit under the United States, shall be appointed an Elector.

The Electors shall meet in their respective States, and vote by Ballot for two Persons, of whom one at least shall not be an Inhabitant of the same State with themselves. And they shall make a List of all the Persons voted for, and of the Number of Votes for each; which List they shall sign and certify, and transmit sealed to the Seat of the Government of the United States, directed to the President of the Senate. The President of the Senate shall, in the Presence of the Senate and House of Representatives, open all the Certificates, and the Votes shall then be counted. The Person having the greatest Number of Votes shall be the President, if such Number be a Majority of the whole Number of Electors appointed; and if there be more than one who have such Majority, and have an equal Number of Votes, then the House of Representatives shall immediately chuse by Ballot one of them for President; and if no Person have a Majority, then from the five highest on the List the said House shall in like Manner chuse the President. But in chusing the President, the Votes shall be taken by States, the Representation from each State having one Vote; A quorum for this Purpose shall consist of a Member or Members from two thirds of the States, and a Majority of all the States shall be necessary to a Choice. In every Case, after the Choice of the President, the Person having the greatest Number of Votes of the Electors shall be the Vice President. But if there should remain two or more who have equal Votes, the Senate shall chuse from them by Ballot the Vice President.*

The Congress may determine the Time of chusing the Electors, and the Day on which they shall give their Votes; which Day·shall be the same throughout the United States.

No Person except a natural born Citizen, or a Citizen of the United States, at the time of the Adoption of this Constitution, shall be eligible to the Office of President, neither shall any Person be eligible to that Office who shall not have attained to the Age of thirty five Years, and been fourteen Years a Resident within the United States.

In Case of the Removal of the President from Office, or of his Death, Resignation, or Inability to discharge the Powers and Duties of the said Office, the Same shall devolve on the Vice President, and the Congress may by Law provide for the Case of Removal, Death, Resignation or Inability, both of the President and Vice President, declaring what Officer shall then act as President, and such Officer shall act accordingly, until the Disability be removed, or a President shall be elected.†

The President shall, at stated Times, receive for his Services, a Compensation, which shall neither be encreased nor diminished during the Period for which he shall have been elected, and he shall not receive within that Period any other Emolument from the United States, or any of them.

Before he enter on the Execution of his Office, he shall take the following Oath or Affirmation:—"I do solemnly swear (or affirm) that I will faithfully execute the Office of President of the United States, and will to the best of my Ability, preserve, protect and defend the Constitution of the United States."

Section. 2. The President shall be Commander in Chief of the Army and Navy of the United States, and of the Militia of the several States, when called into the actual Service of the United States; he may require the Opinion, in writing, of the principal Officer in each of the executive Departments, upon any Subject relating to the Duties of their respective Offices, and he shall have Power to grant Reprieves and Pardons for Offences against the United States, except in cases of Impeachment.

He shall have Power, by and with the Advice and Consent of the Senate, to make Treaties, provided two thirds of the

Senators present concur; and he shall nominate, and by and with the Advice and Consent of the Senate, shall appoint Ambassadors, other public Ministers and Consuls, Judges of the supreme Court, and all other Officers of the United States, whose Appointments are not herein otherwise provided for, and which shall be established by Law; but the Congress may by Law vest the Appointment of such inferior Officers, as they think proper, in the President alone, in the Courts of Law, or in the Heads of Departments.

The President shall have Power to fill up all Vacancies that may happen during the Recess of the Senate, by granting Commissions which shall expire at the End of their next Session.

Section. 3. He shall from time to time give to the Congress Information of the State of the Union, and recommend to their Consideration such Measures as he shall judge necessary and expedient; he may, on extraordinary Occasions, convene both Houses, or either of them, and in Case of Disagreement between them, with Respect to the Time of Adjournment, he may adjourn them to such Time as he shall think proper; he shall receive Ambassadors and other public Ministers; he shall take Care that the Laws be faithfully executed, and shall Commission all the Officers of the United States.

Section. 4. the President, Vice President and all civil Officers of the United States, shall be removed from Office on Impeachment for, and Conviction of, Treason, Bribery, or other high Crimes and Misdemeanors.

Article. III.

Section. 1. The judicial Power of the United States, shall be vested in one supreme Court, and in such inferior Courts as the Congress may from time to time ordain and establish. The Judges, both of the supreme and inferior Courts, shall hold their Offices during good Behaviour, and shall, at stated Times, receive for their Services, a Compensation, which shall not be diminished during their Continuance in Office.

Section. 2. The judicial Power shall extend to all Cases, in Law and Equity, arising under this Constitution, the Laws of the United States, and Treaties made, or which shall be made, under their Authority;—to all Cases affecting Ambassadors, other public Ministers and Consuls;—to all Cases of admiralty and maritime Jurisdiction;—to Controversies to which the United States shall be a Party;—to Controversies between two or more States;—between a State and Citizens of another State;*—between Citizens of different States,—between Citizens of the same State claiming Lands under Grants of different States, and between a State, or the Citizens thereof, and foreign States, Citizens or Subjects.

*Superseded by the Twelfth Amendment.
†Modified by the Twenty-fifth Amendment.

*Modified by the Eleventh Amendment.

In all Cases affecting Ambassadors, other public Ministers and Consuls, and those in which a State shall be Party, the supreme Court shall have original Jurisdiction. In all the other Cases before mentioned, the supreme Court shall have appellate Jurisdiction, both as to Law and Fact, with such Exceptions, and under such Regulations as the Congress shall make.

The Trial of all Crimes, except in Cases of Impeachment, shall be by Jury; and such Trial shall be held in the State where the said Crimes shall have been committed; but when not committed within any State, the trial shall be at such Place or Places as the Congress may by Law have directed. Section. 3. Treason against the United States, shall consist only in levying War against them, or in adhering to their Enemies, giving them Aid and Comfort. No Person shall be convicted of Treason unless on the Testimony of two Witnesses to the same overt Act, or on Confession in open Court.

The Congress shall have Power to declare the Punishment of Treason, but no Attainder of Treason shall work Corruption of Blood, or Forfeiture except during the Life of the Person attainted.

Article. IV.

Section. 1. Full Faith and Credit shall be given in each State to the public Acts, Records, and judicial Proceedings of every other State. And the Congress may by general Laws prescribe the Manner in which such Acts, Records and Proceedings shall be proved, and the Effect thereof.
Section. 2. The Citizens of each State shall be entitled to all Privileges and Immunities of Citizens in the several States.

A Person charged in any State with Treason, Felony, or other Crime, who shall flee from Justice, and be found in another State, shall on Demand of the executive Authority of the State from which he fled, be delivered up, to be removed to the State having Jurisdiction of the Crime.

No Person held to Service or Labour in one State, under the Laws thereof, escaping into another, shall, in Consequence of any Law or Regulation therein, be discharged from such Service or Labour, but shall be delivered up on Claim of the Party to whom such Service or Labour may be due.
Section. 3. New States may be admitted by the Congress into this Union; but no new State shall be formed or erected within the Jurisdiction of any other State, nor any State be formed by the Junction of two or more States, or Parts of States, without the Consent of the Legislatures of the States concerned as well as of the Congress.

The Congress shall have Power to dispose of and make all needful Rules and Regulations respecting the Territory or other Property belonging to the United States; and nothing in this Constitution shall be so construed as to Prejudice any Claims of the Untied States, or of any particular State.
Section. 4. The United States shall guarantee to every State in this Union a Republican Form of Government, and shall protect each of them against Invasion; and on Application of the Legislature, or of the Executive (when the Legislature cannot be convened) against domestic Violence.

Article. V.

The Congress, whenever two thirds of both Houses shall deem it necessary, shall propose Amendments to this Constitution, or, on the Application of the Legislatures of two thirds of the several States, shall call a Convention for proposing Amendments, which, in either Case, shall be valid to all Intents and Purposes, as Part of this Constitution, when ratified by the Legislatures of three fourths of the several States, or by Conventions in three fourths thereof, as the one or the other Mode of Ratification may be proposed by the Congress; Provided that no Amendment which may be made prior to the Year One thousand eight hundred and eight shall in any Manner affect the first and fourth Clauses in the Ninth Section of the first Article; and that no State, without its Consent, shall be deprived of its equal Suffrage in the Senate.

Article. VI.

All Debts contracted and Engagements entered into, before the Adoption of this Constitution, shall be as valid against the United States under this Constitution, as under the Confederation.

This Constitution, and the Laws of the United States which shall be made in Pursuance thereof; and all Treaties made, or which shall be made, under the Authority of the United States, shall be the supreme Law of the Land; and the Judges in every State shall be bound thereby, any Thing in the Constitution or Laws of any State to the Contrary notwithstanding.

The Senators and Representatives before mentioned, and the Members of the several State Legislatures, and all executive and judicial Officers, both of the United States and of the several States, shall be bound by Oath or Affirmation, to support this Constitution; but no religious Test shall ever be required as a Qualification to any Office or public Trust under the United States.

Article. VII.

The Ratification of the Conventions of nine States, shall be sufficient for the Establishment of this Constitution between the States so ratifying the Same.

done in Convention by the Unanimous Consent of the States present the Seventeenth Day of September in the Year of our Lord one thousand seven hundred and Eighty seven and of the Independence of the United States of America the Twelfth. *In witness* whereof We have hereunto subscribed our Names,

Articles in Addition to, and Amendment of, the Constitution of the United States of America, Proposed by Congress, and Ratified by the Legislatures of the Several States, Pursuant to the Fifth Article of the Original Constitution.

Amendment I*

Congress shall make no law respecting an establishment of religion, or prohibiting the free exercise thereof; or abridging the freedom of speech, or of the press; or the right of the people peaceably to assemble, and to petition the Government for a redress of grievances.

Amendment II

A well regulated Militia, being necessary to the security of a free State, the right of the people to keep and bear Arms shall not be infringed.

Amendment III

No Soldier shall, in time of peace, be quartered in any house, without the consent of the Owner, nor in time of war, but in a manner to be prescribed by law.

Amendment IV

The right of the people to be secure in their persons, houses, papers, and effects, against unreasonable searches and seizures, shall not be violated, and no Warrants shall

*The first ten amendments were passed by Congress September 25, 1789. They were ratified by three-fourths of the states December 15, 1791.

issue, but upon probable cause, supported by Oath or affirmation, and particularly describing the place to be searched, and the persons or things to be seized.

Amendment V

No person shall be held to answer for a capital or otherwise infamous crime, unless on a presentment or indictment of a Grand Jury, except in cases arising in the land or naval forces, or in the Militia, when in actual service in time of War or public danger; nor shall any person be subject for the same offence to be twice put in jeopardy of life or limb; nor shall be compelled in any criminal case to be a witness against himself, nor be deprived of life, liberty, or property, without due process of law; nor shall private property be taken for public use, without just compensation.

Amendment VI

In all criminal prosecutions, the accused shall enjoy the right to a speedy and public trial, by an impartial jury of the State and district wherein the crime shall have been committed, which district shall have been previously ascertained by law, and to be informed of the nature and cause of the accusation; to be confronted with the witnesses against him; to have compulsory process for obtaining witnesses in his favor, and to have the Assistance of Counsel for his defence.

Amendment VII

In suits at common law, where the value in controversy shall exceed twenty dollars, the right of trial by jury shall be preserved, and no fact tried by a jury, shall be otherwise reexamined in any Court of the United States, than according to the rules of the common law.

Amendment VIII

Excessive bail shall not be required, nor excessive fines imposed, nor cruel and unusual punishments inflicted.

Amendment IX

The enumeration in the Constitution, of certain rights, shall not be construed to deny or disparage others retained by the people.

Amendment X

The powers not delegated to the United States by the Constitution; nor prohibited by it to the States, are reserved to the States respectively, or to the people.

Amendment XI*

The Judicial power of the United States shall not be construed to extend to any suit in law or equity, commenced or prosecuted against one of the United States by Citizens of another State, or by Citizens or Subjects of any Foreign State.

Amendment XII†

The Electors shall meet in their respective States and vote by ballot for President and Vice-President, one of whom, at least, shall not be an inhabitant of the same State with themselves; they shall name in their ballots the person voted for as President, and in distinct ballots the person voted for as Vice-President, and they shall make distinct lists of all persons voted for as President, and of all persons voted for as Vice-President, and of the number of votes for each, which lists they shall sign and certify, and transmit sealed to the seat of the government of the United States, directed to the President of the Senate;—The President of the Senate shall, in the presence of the Senate and House of Representatives, open all the certificates and the votes shall then be counted;—The person having the greatest number of votes for President, shall be the President, if such number be a majority of the whole number of Electors appointed; and if no person have such majority, then from the persons having the highest numbers not exceeding three on the list of those voted for as President, the House of Representatives shall choose immediately, by ballot, the President. But in choosing the President, the votes shall be taken by states, the representation from each state having one vote; a quorum for this purpose shall consist of a member or members from two-thirds of the states, and a majority of all the states shall be necessary to a choice. And if the House of Representatives shall not choose a President whenever the right of choice shall devolve upon them, before the fourth day of March next following, then the Vice-President shall act as President, as in the case of the death or other constitutional disability of the President.—The person having the greatest number of

votes as Vice-President, shall be the Vice-President, if such number be a majority of the whole number of Electors appointed, and if no person have a majority, then from the two highest numbers on the list, the Senate shall choose the Vice-President; a quorum for the purpose shall consist of two-thirds of the whole number of Senators, and a majority of the whole number shall be necessary to a choice. But no person constitutionally ineligible to the office of President shall be eligible to that of Vice-President of the United States.

Amendment XIII*

Section. 1. Neither slavery nor involuntary servitude, except as a punishment for crime whereof the party shall have been duly convicted, shall exist within the United States, or any place subject to their jurisdiction.
Section. 2. Congress shall have power to enforce this article by appropriate legislation.

Amendment XIV†

Section. 1. All persons born or naturalized in the United States, and subject to the jurisdiction thereof, are citizens of the United States and of the State wherein they reside. No State shall make or enforce any law which shall abridge the privileges or immunities of citizens of the United States; nor shall any State deprive any person of life, liberty, or property, without due process of law; nor deny to any person within its jurisdiction the equal protection of the laws.
Section. 2. Representatives shall be apportioned among the several States according to their respective numbers, counting the whole number of persons in each State, excluding Indians not taxed. But when the right to vote at any election for the choice of electors for President and Vice-President of the United States, Representatives in Congress, the Executive and Judicial officers of a State, or the members of the Legislature thereof, is denied to any of the male inhabitants of such State, being twenty-one years of age, and citizens of the United States, or in any way abridged, except for participation in rebellion, or other crime, the basis of representation therein shall be reduced in the proportion which the number of such male citizens shall bear to the whole number of male citizens twenty-one years of age in such State.
Section. 3. No person shall be a Senator or Representative in Congress, or elector of President and Vice-President, or hold

---

*Passed March 4, 1794. Ratified January 23, 1795.
†Passed December 9, 1803. Ratified June 15, 1804.

*Passed January 31, 1865. Ratified December 6, 1865.
†Passed June 13, 1866. Ratified July 9, 1868.

any office, civil or military, under the United States, or under any State, who, having previously taken an oath, as a member of Congress, or as an officer of the United States, or as a member of any State legislature, or as an executive or judicial officer of any State, to support the Constitution of the United States, shall have engaged in insurrection or rebellion against the same, or given aid or comfort to the enemies thereof. But Congress may by a vote of two-thirds of each House, remove such disability.

Section. 4. The validity of the public debt of the United States, authorized by law, including debts incurred for payment of pensions and bounties for services in suppressing insurrection or rebellion, shall not be questioned. But neither the United States nor any State shall assume or pay any debt or obligation incurred in aid of insurrection or rebellion against the United States, or any claim for the loss or emancipation of any slave; but all such debts, obligations, and claims shall be held illegal and void.

Section. 5. The Congress shall have the power to enforce, by appropriate legislation, the provisions of this article.

Amendment XV*

Section. 1. The right of citizens of the United States to vote shall not be denied or abridged by the United States or by any State on account of race, color, or previous condition of servitude—

Section. 2. The Congress shall have power to enforce this article by appropriate legislation.

Amendment XVI†

The Congress shall have power to lay and collect taxes on incomes, from whatever source derived, without apportionment among the several States, and without regard to any census or enumeration.

Amendment XVII‡

The Senate of the United States shall be composed of two Senators from each State, elected by the people thereof, for six years; and each Senator shall have one vote. The electors in each State shall have the qualifications requisite for electors of the most numerous branch of the State legislatures.

When vacancies happen in the representation of any State in the Senate, the executive authority of such State shall issue writs of election to fill such vacancies: *Provided,* That the legislature of any State may empower the executive thereof to make temporary appointments until the people fill the vacancies by election as the legislature may direct.

This amendment shall not be so construed as to affect the election or term of any Senator chosen before it becomes valid as part of the Constitution.

Amendment XVIII*

Section. 1. After one year from the ratification of this article the manufacture, sale, or transportation of intoxicating liquors within, the importation thereof into, or the exportation thereof from the United States and all territory subject to the jurisdiction thereof for beverage purposes is hereby prohibited.

Section. 2. The Congress and the several States shall have concurrent power to enforce this article by appropriate legislation.

Section. 3. This article shall be inoperative unless it shall have been ratified as an amendment to the Constitution by the legislatures of the several States, as provided in the Constitution, within seven years from the date of the submission hereof to the States by the Congress.

Amendment XIX†

The right of citizens of the United States to vote shall not be denied or abridged by the United States or by any State on account of sex.

Congress shall have power to enforce this article by appropriate legislation.

Amendment XX‡

Section. 1. The terms of the President and Vice-President shall end at noon on the 20th day of January, and the terms of Senators and Representatives at noon on the 3d day of January, of the years in which such terms would have ended if this article had not been ratified; and the terms of their successors shall then begin.

Section. 2. The Congress shall assemble at least once in every year, and such meeting shall begin at noon on the 3d day of January, unless they shall by law appoint a different day.

*Passed February 26, 1869. Ratified February 2, 1870.
†Passed July 12, 1909. Ratified February 3, 1913.
‡Passed May 13, 1912. Ratified April 8, 1913.

*Passed December 18, 1917. Ratified January 16, 1919.
†Passed June 4, 1919. Ratified August 18, 1920.
‡Passed March 2, 1932. Ratified January 23, 1933.

Section. 3. If, at the time fixed for the beginning of the term of the President, the President elect shall have died, the Vice-President elect shall become President. If a President shall not have been chosen before the time fixed for the beginning of his term, or if the President elect shall have failed to qualify, then the Vice-President elect shall act as President until a President shall have qualified; and the Congress may by law provide for the case wherein neither a President elect nor a Vice-President elect shall have qualified, declaring who shall then act as President, or the manner in which one who is to act shall be selected, and such person shall act accordingly until a President or Vice-President shall have qualified.

Section. 4. The Congress may by law provide for the case of the death of any of the persons from whom the House of Representatives may choose a President whenever the right of choice shall have devolved upon them, and for the case of the death of any of the persons from whom the Senate may choose a Vice-President whenever the right of choice shall have devolved upon them.

Section. 5. Sections 1 and 2 shall take effect on the 15th day of October following the ratification of this article.

Section. 6. This article shall be inoperative unless it shall have been ratified as an amendment to the Constitution by the legislatures of three-fourths of the several States within seven years from the date of its submission.

Amendment XXI*

Section. 1. The eighteenth article of amendment to the Constitution of the United States is hereby repealed.

Section. 2. The transportation or importation into any State, Territory, or possession of the United States for delivery or use therein of intoxicating liquors, in violation of the laws thereof, is hereby prohibited.

Section. 3. This article shall be inoperative unless it shall have been ratified as an amendment of the Constitution by conventions in the several States, as provided in the Constitution, within seven years from the date of the submission hereof to the States by the Congress.

Amendment XXII†

No person shall be elected to the office of the President more than twice, and no person who has held the office of President, or acted as President, for more than two years of a term to which some other person was elected President shall be elected to the office of the President more than once.

But this Article shall not apply to any person holding the office of President when this Article was proposed by the Congress, and shall not prevent any person who may be holding the office of President, or acting as President, during the term within which this Article becomes operative from holding the office of President or acting as President during the remainder of such term.

Amendment XXIII*

Section. 1. The district constituting the seat of Government of the United States shall appoint in such manner as the Congress may direct:

A number of electors of President and Vice President equal to the whole number of Senators and Representatives in Congress to which the District would be entitled if it were a State, but in no event more than the least populous State; they shall be in addition to those appointed by the States, but they shall be considered, for the purposes of the election of President and Vice President, to be electors appointed by the State; and they shall meet in the District and perform such duties as provided by the twelfth article of amendment.

Section. 2. The Congress shall have power to enforce this article by appropriate legislation.

Amendment XXIV†

Section. 1. The right of citizens of the United States to vote in any primary or other election for President or Vice President, or for Senator or Representative in Congress, shall not be denied or abridged by the United States or any State by reason of failure to pay any poll tax or other tax.

Section. 2. The Congress shall have power to enforce this article by appropriate legislation.

Amendment XXV‡

Section. 1. In case of the removal of the President from office or of his death or resignation, the Vice President shall become President.

Section. 2. Whenever there is a vacancy in the office of the Vice President, the President shall nominate a Vice President who shall take office upon confirmation by a majority vote of both Houses of Congress.

Section. 3. Whenever the President transmits to the Presi-

*Passed February 20, 1933. Ratified December 5, 1933.
†Passed March 12, 1947. Ratified March 1, 1951.

*Passed June 16, 1960. Ratified April 3, 1961.
†Passed August 27, 1962. Ratified January 23, 1964.
‡Passed July 6, 1965. Ratified February 11, 1967.

dent pro tempore of the Senate and the Speaker of the House of Representatives his written declaration that he is unable to discharge the powers and duties of his office, and until he transmits to them a written declaration to the contrary, such powers and duties shall be discharged by the Vice President as Acting President.

Section. 4. Whenever the Vice President and a majority of either the principal officers of the executive department or of such other body as Congress may by law provide, transmit to the President pro tempore of the Senate and the Speaker of the House of Representatives their written declaration that the President is unable to discharge the powers and duties of his office, the Vice President shall immediately assume the powers and duties of the office of Acting President.

Thereafter, when the President transmits to the President pro tempore of the Senate and the Speaker of the House of Representatives his written declaration that no inability exists, he shall resume the powers and duties of his office unless the Vice President and a majority of either the principal officers of the executive department or of such other body as Congress may by law provide, transmit within four days to the President pro tempore of the Senate and the Speaker of the House of Representatives their written declaration that the President is unable to discharge the powers and duties of his office. Thereupon Congress shall decide the issue, assembling within forty-eight hours for that purpose if not in session. If the Congress, within twenty-one days after receipt of the latter written declaration, or, if Congress is not in session, within twenty-one days after Congress is required to assemble, determines by two-thirds vote of both Houses that the President is unable to discharge the powers and duties of his office, the Vice President shall continue to discharge the same as Acting President; otherwise, the President shall resume the powers and duties of his office.

Amendment XXVI*

Section. 1. The right of citizens of the United States, who are eighteen years of age or older, to vote shall not be denied or abridged by the United States or by any State on account of age.

Section. 2. The Congress shall have power to enforce this article by appropriate legislation.

*Passed March 23, 1971. Ratified July 5, 1971.

Admission of States

Order of Admission	State	Date of Admission	Order of Admission	State	Date of Admission
1	Delaware	December 7, 1787	26	Michigan	January 26, 1837
2	Pennsylvania	December 12, 1787	27	Florida	March 3, 1845
3	New Jersey	December 18, 1787	28	Texas	December 29, 1845
4	Georgia	January 2, 1788	29	Iowa	December 28, 1846
5	Connecticut	January 9, 1788	30	Wisconsin	May 29, 1848
6	Massachusetts	February 7, 1788	31	California	September 9, 1850
7	Maryland	April 28, 1788	32	Minnesota	May 11, 1858
8	South Carolina	May 23, 1788	33	Oregon	February 14, 1859
9	New Hampshire	June 21, 1788	34	Kansas	January 29, 1861
10	Virginia	June 25, 1788	35	West Virginia	June 20, 1863
11	New York	July 26, 1788	36	Nevada	October 31, 1864
12	North Carolina	November 21, 1789	37	Nebraska	March 1, 1867
13	Rhode Island	May 29, 1790	38	Colorado	August 1, 1876
14	Vermont	March 4, 1791	39	North Dakota	November 2, 1889
15	Kentucky	June 1, 1792	40	South Dakota	November 2, 1889
16	Tennessee	June 1, 1796	41	Montana	November 8, 1889
17	Ohio	March 1, 1803	42	Washington	November 11, 1889
18	Louisiana	April 30, 1812	43	Idaho	July 3, 1890
19	Indiana	December 11, 1816	44	Wyoming	July 10, 1890
20	Mississippi	December 10, 1817	45	Utah	January 4, 1896
21	Illinois	December 3, 1818	46	Oklahoma	November 16, 1907
22	Alabama	December 14, 1819	47	New Mexico	January 6, 1912
23	Maine	March 15, 1820	48	Arizona	February 14, 1912
24	Missouri	August 10, 1821	49	Alaska	January 3, 1959
25	Arkansas	June 15, 1836	50	Hawaii	August 21, 1959

Growth of U.S. Population and Area

Census	Population of United States	Increase over the Preceding Census — Number	Increase over the Preceding Census — Percent	Land Area (Sq. Mi.)	Pop. per Sq. Mi.
1790	3,929,214			867,980	4.5
1800	5,308,483	1,379,269	35.1	867,980	6.1
1810	7,239,881	1,931,398	36.4	1,685,865	4.3
1820	9,638,453	2,398,572	33.1	1,753,588	5.5
1830	12,866,020	3,227,567	33.5	1,753,588	7.3
1840	17,069,453	4,203,433	32.7	1,753,588	9.7
1850	23,191,876	6,122,423	35.9	2,944,337	7.9
1860	31,433,321	8,251,445	35.6	2,973,965	10.6
1870	39,818,449	8,375,128	26.6	2,973,965	13.4
1880	50,155,783	10,337,334	26.0	2,973,965	16.9
1890	62,947,714	12,791,931	25.5	2,973,965	21.2
1900	75,994,575	13,046,861	20.7	2,974,159	25.6
1910	91,972,266	15,997,691	21.0	2,973,890	30.9
1920	105,710,620	13,738,354	14.9	2,973,776	35.5
1930	122,775,046	17,064,426	16.1	2,977,128	41.2
1940	131,669,275	8,894,229	7.2	2,977,128	44.2
1950	150,697,361	19,028,086	14.5	2,974,726 *	50.7
1960 †	179,323,175	28,625,814	19.0	3,540,911	50.6
1970	203,235,298	23,912,123	13.3	3,536,855	57.5
1980	226,504,825	23,269,527	11.4	3,536,855	64.0

*As measured in 1940; shrinkage offset by increase in water area.
†First year for which figures include Alaska and Hawaii.

Political Party Affiliations in Congress and the Presidency, 1789–1987*

		House			Senate			
Congress	Year	Majority Party	Principal Minority Party	Other except Vacancies	Majority Party	Principal Minority Party	Other except Vacancies	President and Party
1st	1789–1791	Ad-38	Op-26	—	Ad-17	Op-9	—	F (Washington)
2d	1791–1793	F-37	DR-33	—	F-16	DR-13	—	F (Washington)
3d	1793–1795	DR-57	F-48	—	F-17	DR-13	—	F (Washington)
4th	1795–1797	F-54	DR-52	—	F-19	DR-13	—	F (Washington)
5th	1797–1799	F-58	DR-48	—	F-20	DR-12	—	F (John Adams)
6th	1799–1801	F-64	DR-42	—	F-19	DR-13	—	F (John Adams)
7th	1801–1803	DR-69	F-36	—	DR-18	F-13	—	DR (Jefferson)
8th	1803–1805	DR-102	F-39	—	DR-25	F-9	—	DR (Jefferson)
9th	1805–1807	DR-116	F-25	—	DR-27	F-7	—	DR (Jefferson)
10th	1807–1809	DR-118	F-24	—	DR-28	F-6	—	DR (Jefferson)
11th	1809–1811	DR-94	F-48	—	DR-28	F-6	—	DR (Madison)
12th	1811–1813	DR-108	F-36	—	DR-30	F-6	—	DR (Madison)
13th	1813–1815	DR-112	F-68	—	DR-27	F-9	—	DR (Madison)
14th	1815–1817	DR-117	F-65	—	DR-25	F-11	—	DR (Madison)
15th	1817–1819	DR-141	F-42	—	DR-34	F-10	—	DR (Monroe)
16th	1819–1821	DR-156	F-27	—	DR-35	F-7	—	DR (Monroe)
17th	1821–1823	DR-158	F-25	—	DR-44	F-4	—	DR (Monroe)
18th	1823–1825	DR-187	F-26	—	DR-44	F-4	—	DR (Monroe)
19th	1825–1827	Ad-105	J-97	—	Ad-26	J-20	—	C (J. Q. Adams)
20th	1827–1829	J-119	Ad-94	—	J-28	Ad-20	—	C (J. Q. Adams)
21st	1829–1831	D-139	NR-74	—	D-26	NR-22	—	D (Jackson)
22nd	1831–1833	D-141	NR-58	14	D-25	NR-21	2	D (Jackson)
23rd	1833–1835	D-147	AM-53	60	D-20	NR-20	8	D (Jackson)
24th	1835–1837	D-145	W-98	—	D-27	W-25	—	D (Jackson)
25th	1837–1839	D-108	W-107	24	D-30	W-18	4	D (Van Buren)
26th	1839–1841	D-124	W-118	—	D-28	W-22	—	D (Van Buren)
27th	1841–1843	W-133	D-102	6	W-28	D-22	2	W (Harrison) W (Tyler)
28th	1843–1845	D-142	W-79	1	W-28	D-25	1	W (Tyler)
29th	1845–1847	D-143	W-77	6	D-31	W-25	—	D (Polk)
30th	1847–1849	W-115	D-108	4	D-36	W-21	1	D (Polk)
31st	1849–1851	D-112	W-109	9	D-35	W-25	2	W (Taylor) W (Fillmore)
32d	1851–1853	D-140	W-88	5	D-35	W-24	3	W (Fillmore)
33d	1853–1855	D-159	W-71	4	D-38	W-22	2	D (Pierce)
34th	1855–1857	R-108	D-83	43	D-40	R-15	5	D (Pierce)
35th	1857–1859	D-118	R-92	26	D-36	R-20	8	D (Buchanan)
36th	1859–1861	R-114	D-92	31	D-36	R-26	4	D (Buchanan)
37th	1861–1863	R-105	D-43	30	R-31	D-10	8	R (Lincoln)
38th	1863–1865	R-102	D-75	9	R-36	D-9	5	R (Lincoln)
39th	1865–1867	U-149	D-42	—	U-42	D-10	—	R (Lincoln) R (Johnson)
40th	1867–1869	R-143	D-49	—	R-42	D-11	—	R (Johnson)
41st	1869–1871	R-149	D-63	—	R-56	D-11	—	R (Grant)
42d	1871–1873	R-134	D-104	5	R-52	D-17	5	R (Grant)
43d	1873–1875	R-194	D-92	14	R-49	D-19	5	R (Grant)
44th	1875–1877	D-169	R-109	14	R-45	D-29	2	R (Grant)
45th	1877–1879	D-153	R-140	—	R-39	D-36	1	R (Hayes)
46th	1879–1881	D-149	R-130	14	D-42	R-33	1	R (Hayes)

*Letter symbols for political parties. Ad—Administration; AM—Anti-Masonic; C—Coalition; D—Democratic; DR—Democratic-Republican; F—Federalist; J—Jacksonian; NR—National-Republican; Op—Opposition; R—Republican; U—Unionist; W—Whig.

Political Party Affiliations in Congress and the Presidency, 1789–1987* *(continued)*

Congress	Year	House			Senate			President and Party
		Majority Party	Principal Minority Party	Other except Vacancies	Majority Party	Principal Minority Party	Other except Vacancies	
47th	1881–1883	R-147	D-135	11	R-37	D-37	1	R (Garfield)
								R (Arthur)
48th	1883–1885	D-197	R-118	10	R-38	D-36	2	R (Arthur)
49th	1885–1887	D-183	R-140	2	R-43	D-34	—	D (Cleveland)
50th	1887–1889	D-169	R-152	4	R-39	D-37	—	D (Cleveland)
51st	1889–1891	R-166	D-159	—	R-39	D-37	—	R (B. Harrison)
52d	1891–1893	D-235	R-88	9	R-47	D-39	2	R (B. Harrison)
53d	1893–1895	D-218	R-127	11	D-44	R-38	3	D (Cleveland)
54th	1895–1897	R-244	D-105	7	R-43	D-39	6	D (Cleveland)
55th	1897–1899	R-204	D-113	40	R-47	D-34	7	R (McKinley)
56th	1899–1901	R-185	D-163	9	R-53	D-26	8	R (McKinley)
57th	1901–1903	R-197	D-151	9	R-55	D-31	4	R (McKinley)
								R (T. Roosevelt)
58th	1903–1905	R-208	D-178	—	R-57	D-33	—	R (T. Roosevelt)
59th	1905–1907	R-250	D-136	—	R-57	D-33	—	R (T. Roosevelt)
60th	1907–1909	R-222	D-164	—	R-61	D-31	—	R (T. Roosevelt)
61st	1909–1911	R-219	D-172	—	R-61	D-32	—	R (Taft)
62d	1911–1913	D-228	R-161	1	R-51	D-41	—	R (Taft)
63d	1913–1915	D-291	R-127	17	D-51	R-44	1	D (Wilson)
64th	1915–1917	D-230	R-196	9	D-56	R-40	—	D (Wilson)
65th	1917–1919	D-216	R-210	6	D-53	R-42	—	D (Wilson)
66th	1919–1921	R-240	D-190	3	R-49	D-47	—	D (Wilson)
67th	1921–1923	R-301	D-131	1	R-59	D-37	—	R (Harding)
68th	1923–1925	R-225	D-205	5	R-51	D-43	2	R (Coolidge)
69th	1925–1927	R-247	D-183	4	R-56	D-39	1	R (Coolidge)
70th	1927–1929	R-237	D-195	3	R-49	D-46	1	R (Coolidge)
71st	1929–1931	R-267	D-167	1	R-56	D-39	1	R (Hoover)
72d	1931–1933	D-220	R-214	1	R-48	D-47	1	R (Hoover)
73d	1933–1935	D-310	R-117	5	D-60	R-35	1	D (F. Roosevelt)
74th	1935–1937	D-319	R-103	10	D-69	R-25	2	D (F. Roosevelt)
75th	1937–1939	D-331	R-89	13	D-76	R-16	4	D (F. Roosevelt)
76th	1939–1941	D-261	R-164	4	D-69	R-23	4	D (F. Roosevelt)
77th	1941–1943	D-268	R-162	5	D-66	R-28	2	D (F. Roosevelt)
78th	1943–1945	D-218	R-208	4	D-58	R-37	1	D (F. Roosevelt)
79th	1945–1947	D-242	R-190	2	D-56	R-38	1	D (Truman)
80th	1947–1949	R-245	D-188	1	R-51	D-45	—	D (Truman)
81st	1949–1951	D-263	R-171	1	D-54	R-42	—	D (Truman)
82d	1951–1953	D-243	R-199	1	D-49	R-47	—	D (Truman)
83d	1953–1955	R-221	D-211	1	R-48	D-47	1	R (Eisenhower)
84th	1955–1957	D-232	R-203	—	D-48	R-47	1	R (Eisenhower)
85th	1957–1959	D-233	R-200	—	D-49	R-47	—	R (Eisenhower)
86th	1959–1961	D-283	R-153	—	D-64	R-34	—	R (Eisenhower)
87th	1961–1963	D-263	R-174	—	D-65	R-35	—	D (Kennedy)
88th	1963–1965	D-258	R-177	—	D-67	R-33	—	D (Kennedy)
								D (Johnson)
89th	1965–1967	D-295	R-140	—	D-68	R-32	—	D (Johnson)
90th	1967–1969	D-247	R-187	1	D-64	R-36	—	D (Johnson)
91st	1969–1971	D-243	R-192	—	D-58	R-42	—	R (Nixon)
92nd	1971–1973	D-255	R-180	—	D-54	R-44	2	R (Nixon)
93rd	1973–1975	D-242	R-192	1	D-56	R-42	2	R (Nixon, Ford)
94th	1975–1977	D-291	R-144	—	D-61	R-37	2	R (Ford)
95th	1977–1979	D-292	R-143	—	D-61	R-38	1	D (Carter)
96th	1979–1981	D-277	R-158	—	D-58	R-41	1	D (Carter)
97th	1981–1983	D-242	R-192	—	R-54	D-45	1	R (Reagan)
98th	1983–1985	D-266	R-167	2	R-55	D-45	—	R (Reagan)
99th	1985–1987	D-252	R-183	—	R-53	D-47	—	R (Reagan)

Source: U. S. Bureau of the Census, *Historical Statistics of the United States: Colonial Times to the Present*, Department of Commerce, Washington, D.C., 1957.

Presidential Elections, 1789–1984

Year	Voter Participation (Percentage)	Candidates	Parties	Popular Vote	Electoral Vote	Percentage of Popular Vote
1789		GEORGE WASHINGTON	No party designations		69	
		John Adams			34	
		Minor Candidates			35	
1792		GEORGE WASHINGTON	No party designations		132	
		John Adams			77	
		George Clinton			50	
		Minor Candidates			5	
1796		JOHN ADAMS	Federalist		71	
		Thomas Jefferson	Democratic-Republican		68	
		Thomas Pinckney	Federalist		59	
		Aaron Burr	Democratic-Republican		30	
		Minor Candidates			48	
1800		THOMAS JEFFERSON	Democratic-Republican		73	
		Aaron Burr	Democratic-Republican		73	
		John Adams	Federalist		65	
		Charles C. Pinckney	Federalist		64	
		John Jay	Federalist		1	
1804		THOMAS JEFFERSON	Democratic-Republican		162	
		Charles C. Pinckney	Federalist		14	
1808		JAMES MADISON	Democratic-Republican		122	
		Charles C. Pinckney	Federalist		47	
		George Clinton	Democratic-Republican		6	
1812		JAMES MADISON	Democratic Republican		128	
		DeWitt Clinton	Federalist		89	
1816		JAMES MONROE	Democratic-Republican		183	
		Rufus King	Federalist		34	
1820		JAMES MONROE	Democratic-Republican		231	
		John Quincy Adams	Independent Republican		1	
1824	26.9	JOHN QUINCY ADAMS	Democratic-Republican	108,740	84	30.5
		Andrew Jackson	Democratic-Republican	153,544	99	43.1
		William H. Crawford	Democratic-Republican	46,618	41	13.1
		Henry Clay	Democratic-Republican	47,136	37	13.2
1828	57.6	ANDREW JACKSON	Democratic	647,286	178	56.0
		John Quincy Adams	National Republican	508,064	83	44.0
1832	55.4	ANDREW JACKSON	Democratic	687,502	219	55.0
		Henry Clay	National Republican	530,189	49	42.4
		William Wirt	Anti-Masonic	33,108	7	2.6
		John Floyd	National Republican		11	
1836	57.8	MARTIN VAN BUREN	Democratic	765,483	170	50.9
		William H. Harrison	Whig		73	
		Hugh L. White	Whig	739,795	26	49.1
		Daniel Webster	Whig		14	
		W. P. Mangum	Whig		11	
1840	80.2	WILLIAM H. HARRISON	Whig	1,274,624	234	53.1
		Martin Van Buren	Democratic	1,127,781	60	46.9
1844	78.9	JAMES K. POLK	Democratic	1,338,464	170	49.6
		Henry Clay	Whig	1,300,097	105	48.1
		James G. Birney	Liberty	62,300		2.3
1848	72.7	ZACHARY TAYLOR	Whig	1,360,967	163	47.4
		Lewis Cass	Democratic	1,222,342	127	42.5
		Martin Van Buren	Free Soil	291,263		10.1
1852	69.6	FRANKLIN PIERCE	Democratic	1,601,117	254	50.9
		Winfield Scott	Whig	1,385,453	42	44.1
		John P. Hale	Free Soil	155,825		5.0

Candidates receiving less than 1 percent of the popular vote have been omitted. For that reason the percentage of popular vote given for any election year may not total 100 percent.

Before the passage of the Twelfth Amendment in 1804, the Electoral College voted for two presidential candidates; the runner-up became Vice President. Figures are from *Historical Statistics of the United States, Colonial Times to 1957* (1961), pp. 682–83; the U. S. Department of Justice.

Presidential Elections, 1789–1984 (continued)

Year	Voter Participation (Percentage)	Candidates	Parties	Popular Vote	Electoral Vote	Percentage of Popular Vote
1856	78.9	JAMES BUCHANAN	Democratic	1,832,955	174	45.3
		John C. Frémont	Republican	1,339,932	114	33.1
		Millard Fillmore	American	871,731	8	21.6
1860	81.2	ABRAHAM LINCOLN	Republican	1,865,593	180	39.8
		Stephen A. Douglas	Democratic	1,382,713	12	29.5
		John C. Breckinridge	Democratic	848,356	72	18.1
		John Bell	Constitutional Union	592,906	39	12.6
1864	73.8	ABRAHAM LINCOLN	Republican	2,206,938	212	55.0
		George B. McClellan	Democratic	1,803,787	21	45.0
1868	78.1	ULYSSES S. GRANT	Republican	3,013,421	214	52.7
		Horatio Seymour	Democratic	2,706,829	80	47.3
1872	71.3	ULYSSES S. GRANT	Republican	3,596,745	286	55.6
		Horace Greeley	Democratic	2,843,446	*	43.9
1876	81.8	RUTHERFORD B. HAYES	Republican	4,036,572	185	48.0
		Samuel J. Tilden	Democratic	4,284,020	184	51.0
1880	79.4	JAMES A. GARFIELD	Republican	4,453,295	214	48.5
		Winfield S. Hancock	Democratic	4,414,082	155	48.1
		James B. Weaver	Greenback-Labor	308,578		3.4
1884	77.5	GROVER CLEVELAND	Democratic	4,879,507	219	48.5
		James G. Blaine	Republican	4,850,293	182	48.2
		Benjamin F. Butler	Greenback-Labor	175,370		1.8
		John P. St. John	Prohibition	150,369		1.5
1888	79.3	BENJAMIN HARRISON	Republican	5,477,129	233	47.9
		Grover Cleveland	Democratic	5,537,857	168	48.6
		Clinton B. Fisk	Prohibition	249,506		2.2
		Anson J. Streeter	Union Labor	146,935		1.3
1892	74.7	GROVER CLEVELAND	Democratic	5,555,426	277	46.1
		Benjamin Harrison	Republican	5,182,690	145	43.0
		James B. Weaver	People's	1,029,846	22	8.5
		John Bidwell	Prohibition	264,133		2.2
1896	79.3	WILLIAM McKINLEY	Republican	7,102,246	271	51.1
		William J. Bryan	Democratic	6,492,559	176	47.7
1900	73.2	WILLIAM McKINLEY	Republican	7,218,491	292	51.7
		William J. Bryan	Democratic; Populist	6,356,734	155	45.5
		John C. Wooley	Prohibition	208,914		1.5
1904	65.2	THEODORE ROOSEVELT	Republican	7,628,461	336	57.4
		Alton B. Parker	Democratic	5,084,223	140	37.6
		Eugene V. Debs	Socialist	402,283		3.0
		Silas C. Swallow	Prohibition	258,536		1.9
1908	65.4	WILLIAM H. TAFT	Republican	7,675,320	321	51.6
		William J. Bryan	Democratic	6,412,294	162	43.1
		Eugene V. Debs	Socialist	420,793		2.8
		Eugene W. Chafin	Prohibition	253,840		1.7
1912	58.8	WOODROW WILSON	Democratic	6,296,547	435	41.9
		Theodore Roosevelt	Progressive	4,118,571	88	27.4
		William H. Taft	Republican	3,486,720	8	23.2
		Eugene V. Debs	Socialist	900,672		6.0
		Eugene W. Chafin	Prohibition	206,275		1.4

*Greeley died shortly after the election; the electors supporting him then divided their votes among minor candidates.

Candidates receiving less than 1 percent of the popular vote have been omitted. For that reason the percentage of popular vote given for any election year may not total 100 percent.

Presidential Elections, 1789–1984 (continued)

Year	Voter Participation (Percentage)	Candidates	Parties	Popular Vote	Electoral Vote	Percentage of Popular Vote
1916	61.6	WOODROW WILSON	Democratic	9,127,695	277	49.4
		Charles E. Hughes	Republican	8,533,507	254	46.2
		A. L. Benson	Socialist	585,113		3.2
		J. Frank Hanly	Prohibition	220,506		1.2
1920	49.2	WARREN G. HARDING	Republican	16,143,407	404	60.4
		James N. Cox	Democratic	9,130,328	127	34.2
		Eugene V. Debs	Socialist	919,799		3.4
		P. P. Christensen	Farmer-Labor	265,411		1.0
1924	48.9	CALVIN COOLIDGE	Republican	15,718,211	382	54.0
		John W. Davis	Democratic	8,385,283	136	28.8
		Robert M. La Follette	Progressive	4,831,289	13	16.6
1928	56.9	HERBERT C. HOOVER	Republican	21,391,993	444	58.2
		Alfred E. Smith	Democratic	15,016,169	87	40.9
1932	56.9	FRANKLIN D. ROOSEVELT	Democratic	22,809,638	472	57.4
		Herbert C. Hoover	Republican	15,758,901	59	39.7
		Norman Thomas	Socialist	881,951		2.2
1936	61.0	FRANKLIN D. ROOSEVELT	Democratic	27,752,869	523	60.8
		Alfred M. Landon	Republican	16,674,665	8	36.5
		William Lemke	Union	882,479		1.9
1940	62.5	FRANKLIN D. ROOSEVELT	Democratic	27,307,819	449	54.8
		Wendell L. Willkie	Republican	22,321,018	82	44.8
1944	55.9	FRANKLIN D. ROOSEVELT	Democratic	25,606,585	432	53.5
		Thomas E. Dewey	Republican	22,014,745	99	46.0
1948	53.0	HARRY S. TRUMAN	Democratic	24,105,812	303	49.5
		Thomas E. Dewey	Republican	21,970,065	189	45.1
		J. Strom Thurmond	States' Rights	1,169,063	39	2.4
		Henry A. Wallace	Progressive	1,157,172		2.4
1952	63.3	DWIGHT D. EISENHOWER	Republican	33,936,234	442	55.1
		Adlai E. Stevenson	Democratic	27,314,992	89	44.4
1956	60.6	DWIGHT D. EISENHOWER	Republican	35,590,472	457	57.6
		Adlai E. Stevenson	Democratic	26,022,752	73	42.1
1960	64.0	JOHN F. KENNEDY	Democratic	34,227,096	303	49.9
		Richard M. Nixon	Republican	34,108,546	219	49.6
1964	61.7	LYNDON B. JOHNSON	Democratic	43,126,506	486	61.1
		Barry M. Goldwater	Republican	27,176,799	52	38.5
1968	60.6	RICHARD M. NIXON	Republican	31,785,480	301	43.4
		Hubert H. Humphrey	Democratic	31,275,165	191	42.7
		George C. Wallace	American Independent	9,906,473	46	13.5
1972	55.5	RICHARD M. NIXON	Republican	47,169,911	520	60.7
		George S. McGovern	Democratic	29,170,383	17	37.5
1976	54.3	JIMMY CARTER	Democratic	40,827,394	297	50.0
		Gerald R. Ford	Republican	39,145,977	240	47.9
1980	53.2	RONALD W. REAGAN	Republican	43,899,248	489	50.8
		Jimmy Carter	Democratic	35,481,435	49	41.0
		John B. Anderson	Independent	5,719,437		6.6
		Ed Clark	Libertarian	920,859		1.0
1984	53.3	RONALD W. REAGAN	Republican	54,281,858	525	59.0
		Walter Mondale	Democratic	37,457,215	13	41.0

Candidates receiving less than 1 percent of the popular vote have been omitted. For that reason the percentage of popular vote given for any election year may not total 100 percent.

Picture Credits

134 Library of Congress
135 Maryland Historical Society, Baltimore
136 *The Declaration of Independence* (*detail*) by John Trumbull (American, 1755–1843). © Yale University Art Gallery

Chapter 9
138–139 *Washington Crossing the Delaware* by Emmanuel Leutze, 1851. All rights reserved, Metropolitan Museum of Art
140 The British Museum
141 Library of Congress
144 Princeton University Library
145 The Bettmann Archive
146 *Washington at Verplanck's Point* by John Trumbull, 1790. (*Detail.* Oil on canvas 30″ × 20⅛″, rectangular) Courtesy, Henry Francis de Pont Winterthur Museum
147 The Granger Collection
148 Free Library of Philadelphia
149 Anne S. K. Brown Military Collection, Brown University
151 Washington University Gallery of Art, St. Louis

Chapter 10
154–155 Eastern National Park and Monument Association
157 Abigail S. Adams by Benjamin Blythe, c. 1766. Courtesy the Massachusetts Historical Society
164 The Bettmann Archive
165 New York Public Library, Rare Books Room
166 New York Public Library Picture Collection
167 Alexander Hamilton by John Trumbull. © Yale University Art Gallery
168 Library of Congress
169 *John Jay* by John Trumbull. © Yale University Art Gallery
170 New-York Historical Society

Chapter 11
174–175 *Election Day at Independence Hall* by John Lewis Krimmel, 1787. Courtesy IBM Corporation
176 All rights reserved, The Metropolitan Museum of Art
177 Continental Insurance Company, Historical Paintings Collection
180 HBJ Collection
182 *Edmond Charles Genêt* by Ezra Ames. Collection Albany Institute of History and Art
183 Library of Congress
185 Indiana Historical Society Library
186 The Bettmann Archive
188 Brown Brothers
190 *John Adams* by John Singleton Copley. Gift of Mrs. Charles Francis Adams. Courtesy, Museum of Fine Arts, Boston
191 The Granger Collection

Chapter 12
194–195 Library of Congress
196 Thomas Jefferson by Rembrandt Peale. New-York Historical Society
198 Maryland Historical Society
200 Chicago Historical Society
202 (*both*) Missouri Historical Society
203 New-York Historical Society
205 Rhode Island Historical Society
207 (*left*) New York Public Library; (*right*) New-York Historical Society
208 The Bettmann Archive
210 (*left*) Courtesy, Field Museum of Natural History, Chicago; (*right*) *The Open Door, Known as The Prophet, Brother of Tecumseh* by George Catlin, 1830. National

Museum of American Art, Smithsonian Institution, gift of Mrs. Joseph Harrison, Jr.
212 New-York Historical Society

Chapter 13
214–215 *Fairview Inn* by Thomas Ruckle. Maryland Historical Society
217 North Carolina Department of Archives and History
218–219 Smithsonian Institution
223 (*left*) The Granger collection; (*right*) Bureau of Public Roads, Department of the Interior
224 All rights reserved, Metropolitan Museum of Art, gift of I. N. Phelps Stokes, Edward S. Hawes, Alice Mary Hawes, Marion Augusta Hawes, 1937
226 The Bettmann Archive
228 Library of Congress
231 *Flax Scutching Bee* by Linton Park. National Gallery of Art, Washington, D.C., gift of Edgar William and Bernice Chrysler Garbisch
232 Daguerreotype by Fontayne and Porter of Packet Brooklyn. Cincinnati Public Library

Chapter 14
234–235 (*Detail*) *Fourth of July Celebration* by John Lewis Krimmel, 1819. Historical Society of Pennsylvania
237 Art Commission of the City of New York
239 Courtesy, The Shelburne Museum, Shelburne, Vermont
240 *Winter Scene in Brooklyn* by Francis Guy. 1817–1820. Oil on canvas, 58¾″ × 75″. The Brooklyn Museum, gift of the Brooklyn Institute of Arts and Sciences
241 Culver Pictures
242 The Rhode Island Historical Society
244 Courtesy, Massachusetts Historical Society
245 *The Morning Bell* by Winslow Homer, 1866. Yale University Art Gallery, Bequest of Stephen Carlton Clark, B. A. 1903
246 The Bettmann Archive
247 New-York Historical Society

Chapter 15
252–253 Robert Cruikshank's lithograph, *The President's Levee, or All Creation Going to the White House.* White House Collection
255 University of Hartford, J Doyle DeWitt Collection
256 Daguerreotype by Southworth and Hawes. All rights reserved, Metropolitan Museum of Art, gift of I. N. Phelps Stokes, Edward S. Hawes, Alice Mary Hawes, Marion Augusta Hawes, 1937
257 Brown Brothers
258 Library of Congress
260 New-York Historical Society
261 *Andrew Jackson* by Thomas Scully. In the collection of The Corcoran Gallery of Art, gift of William Wilson Corcoran
264 Courtesy of the Edward E. Ayer Collection, The Newberry Library, Chicago
265 The Cherokee Phoenix, June 4, 1828. The New York Public Library, Rare Books Room
266 Culver Pictures

Chapter 16
268–269 *The County Election* (*detail*) 1851 by George Caleb Bingham. The St. Louis Art Museum
270 Photo by Mathew Brady, Library of Congress
271 New-York Historical Society
273 Library of Congress
275 Photo by Mathew Brady. Library of Congress
276 The Bettmann Archive

277 Chicago Historical Society
279 (top) New-York Historical Society; (bottom) Library of Congress
281 Library of Congress
283 Mt. Holyoke College Library/Archives

Chapter 17
284–285 HBJ Collection
287 Child's Gallery, Boston, MA
290 Utah State Historical Society
291 Utah State Historical Society
292 New York Public Library
294 The Bettmann Archive
295 (left) Daguerreotype by J. J. Hawes. International Museum of Photography at George Eastman House; (right) The Bettmann Archive
296 Beinecke Rare Book and Manuscript Library, Yale University
297 Beinecke Rare Book and Manuscript Library, Yale University
298 (left) Museum of fine Arts, Boston; (right) The Bettmann Archive

Chapter 18
300–301 Museum of the City of New York
302 Sophia Smith Collection, (Women's History Archive), Smith College, Northampton, MA.
303 (left) State Department of Archives and History, Raleigh, North Carolina; (right) The Bettmann Archive
305 The Bettmann Archive
306 Library of Congress
308 Library of Congress
309 (top) The Bettmann Archive; (bottom) Sophia Smith Collection, (Women's History Archive), Smith College, Northampton, MA.
310 The Granger Collection
311 The Bettmann Archive

Chapter 19
312–312 Portraits in an Office by Edgar Degas, 1873. Musee des Beaux-Arts de Paul/Photographie Giraudon, Paris
316 National Archives
317 Sophia Smith Collection (Women's History Archive) Smith College, Northampton, MA.
318 Library of Congress
319 (top) U.S. Army Military History Institute; (bottom) Old Court House Museum, Vicksburg, Mississippi
320 Abby Aldrich Rockefeller Folk Art Center
322 Kansas State Historical Society/Kennedy Galleries, NY
323 The Last Moments of John Brown by Thomas Hovenden, 1884. All rights reserved, Metropolitan Museum of Art
324 Brown Brothers

Chapter 20
326–327 New-York Historical Society
328 New-York Historical Society
329 National Portrait Gallery, Smithsonian Institution
330 (top) Daguerreotype by Southworth and Hawes. All rights reserved, Metropolitan Museum of Art, gift of I. N. Phelps Stokes, Edward S. Hawes, Alice Mary Hawes, and Marion Augusta Hawes, 1937; (bottom) New-York Historical Society
331 Library of Congress
332 National Archives
333 U.S. Army Military History Institute
334 U.S. Army Military History Institute
337 Culver Pictures
338 Photo by Timothy O'Sullivan, Library of Congress

Chapter 21
340–341 Albert Bierstadt, Emigrants Crossing the Plains (detail). The National Cowboy Hall of Fame and Western Heritage Center, Oklahoma City
343 The Bancroft Library, University of California, Berkeley
345 Library of Congress
346 The Bettmann Archive
349 Association of American Railroads
350 The Granger Collection
351 (left) Western Americana Collection, Beinecke Rare Book and Manuscript Library, Yale University; (right) All rights reserved, Metropolitan Museum of Art, gift of I. N. Phelps Stokes and the Hawes Family, 1937
352 Kansas State Historical Society

Chapter 22
356–357 Kansas State Historical Society
360 San Diego Historical Society, Ticor Collection
362 U.S. Army Military History Institute
363 Library of Congress
364 Photo by Mathew Brady, Culver Pictures
366 Library of Congress
367 Print Collection, New York Public Library. Astor, Lenox and Tilden Foundation.
368 California State Library

Chapter 23
370–371 U.S. Army Military History Institute
372 Franklin Pierce, by George Peter Alexander Healy. National Portrait Gallery, Smithsonian Institution, Washington, D.C. Transfer from National Gallery of Art; gift of Andrew W. Mellon
373 New-York Historical Society
376 Sophia Smith Collection (Women's History Archive), Smith College, Northampton, MA.
378 Photo by Mathew Brady, February 27, 1860. The Bettmann Archive
380 Library of Congress
381 National Archives
382 Library of Congress
383 (left) Meserve Collection, Library of Congress; (right) Kentucky Historical Society
384 The Bettmann Archive
385 Chicago Historical Society
386 New-York Historical Society

Chapter 24
388–389 Photo by James F. Gibson, Library of Congress
391 Photo by Timothy O'Sullivan, National Archives
392 Library of Congress
393 (both) U.S. Army Military History Institute
394 Photo by Mathew Brady, National Archives
395 Panic on the Road Between Bull Run and Centreville, probably July 21, 1861. Pencil sketch, Anonymous. Museum of Fine Arts, Boston. M. and M. Karolik collection.
399 Library of Congress
400 The Bettmann Archive
401 Photo by Alexander Gardner, U.S. Army Military History Institute
402 Devil's Den at Gettysburg. Photo by Timothy O'Sullivan, Library of Congress
404 U.S. Army Military History Institute

Chapter 25
406–407 Photo by Alexander Gardner, Library of Congress
408 Photo by Mathew Brady, Library of Congress
409 Old Court House Museum, Vicksburg, Mississippi
410 Library of Congress

541 New-York Historical Society
542 Bureau of American Ethnology, Smithsonian Institution
543 Library of Congress
545 Library of Congress
546 Library of Congress
547 Illustration by Charles Graham from Harper's Weekly, 1886
548 Denver Public Library
549 National Archives
551 Keystone-Mast Collection, California Museum of Photography, University of California, Riverside
552 Keystone-Mast Collection, California Museum of Photography, University of California, Riverside

Chapter 33
554–555 National Archives
557 (both) Photo by Solomon D. Butcher. Solomon D. Butcher Collection, Nebraska State Historical Society
558 Library of Congress
559 Brown Brothers
560 New York Public Library Picture Collection
561 Kansas State Historical Society
563 Brown Brothers
566 Keystone-Mast Collection. California Museum of Photography, University of California, Riverside
567 Library of Congress
568 Brown Brothers
569 Duke University Archives

Chapter 34
570–571 Photo by P. F. Rockett, c. 1899. Library of Congress
572 Library of Congress
573 (top) The Bettmann Archive; (bottom) Granger Collection
574 Library of Congress
576 Library of Congress
579 New-York Historical Society
580 Theodore Roosevelt Association
582 Hawaii State Archives
583 National Archives
584 Keystone-Mast Collection, California Museum of Photography, University of California, Riverside
587 Keystone Stereograph by B. L. Singley, 1898. Library of Congress
588 Library of Congress

Chapter 35
590–591 Brown Brothers
592 Library of Congress
593 Photo by Byron, 1896. Byron Collection, Museum of the City of New York
594 Library of Congress
595 Stanford University Archives
597 (left) The Gross Clinic by Thomas Eakins, 1875. From the Jefferson Medical College of Thomas Jefferson University, Philadelphia; (right) Culver Pictures
598 Brown Brothers
599 Culver Pictures
601 San Diego Historical Society Title Insurance and Trust Collection
602 Photo by Byron, 1896. Byron Collection, Museum of the City of New York
603 U.S. Department of Labor
604 The Bettmann Archive
606 Wide World

Chapter 36
608–609 Brown Brothers
610 Museum of the City of New York

613 Library of Congress
614 Library of Congress
616 State Historical Society of Wisconsin
618 Tamiment Institute Library, New York University
619 Brown Brothers
620 Library of Congress
621 Sophia Smith Collection (Women's History Archive) Smith College, Northampton, MA
623 Brown Brothers
624 Providence Public Library

Chapter 37
626–627 Library of Congress
628 Culver Pictures
629 Brown Brothers
631 Culver Pictures
633 Ralph E. Becker Collection of Political Americana, Smithsonian Institution
634 Culver Pictures
636 Culver Pictures
637 Brown Brothers
639 Library of Congress
641 Culver Pictures
642 Culver Pictures

Chapter 38
644–645 HBJ Collection
646 Library of Congress
648 Culver Pictures
649 The Bettmann Archive
652 UPI/Bettmann Archive
653 © 1915 by the New York Times Company. Reprinted by permission
655 Brown Brothers
656 New York Public Library
657 National Archives
658 Brown Brothers
659 National Archives
660 Photoworld/FPG

Chapter 39
662–663 National Archives
664 HBJ Collection
666 Library of Congress
667 National Archives
669 UPI/The Bettmann Archive
671 Library of Congress
672 National Archives
674 United States Army Signal Corps photo
677 Culver Pictures
678 Library of Congress

Chapter 40
680–681 Culver Pictures
682 The Bettmann Archive
684 The Granger Collection
686 UPI/Bettmann Newsphotos
688 Chicago Historical Society
689 UPI/Bettmann Newsphotos
690 UPI/Bettmann Newsphotos
691 Brown Brothers
692 UPI/Bettmann Newsphotos
693 Culver Pictures
694 Culver Pictures
695 Brown Brothers
696 The Bettmann Archive

Index

B 7
C 8
D 9
E 0
F 1
G 2
H 3
I 4
J 5